USING
FINANCIAL
ACCOUNTING:
AN
INTRODUCTION

USING FINANCIAL ACCOUNTING: AN INTRODUCTION

DENNIS MURRAY
University of Colorado at Denver

BRUCE R. NEUMANN
University of Colorado at Denver

PIETER ELGERS
University of Massachusetts at Amherst

SOUTH-WESTERN College Publishing

An International Thomson Publishing Company

Production Credits

Composition
Parkwood Composition Service

Copyediting
Lorretta Palagi

Cover Image
David Bishop/San Francisco, CA

Illustrations
Randy Miyake, Miyake Illustrations

Index
Bernice Eisen

Interior Design
Diane Beasley

West's Commitment to the Environment

In 1906, West Publishing Company began recycling materials left over from the production of books. This began a tradition of efficient and responsible use of resources. Today, 100% of our legal bound volumes are printed on acid-free, recycled paper consisting of 50% new fibers. West recycles nearly 27,700,000 pounds of scrap paper annually—the equivalent of 229,300 trees. Since the 1960s, West has devised ways to capture and recycle waste inks, solvents, oils, and vapors created in the printing process. We also recycle plastics of all kinds, wood, glass, corrugated cardboard, and batteries, and have eliminated the use of polystyrene book packaging. We at West are proud of the longevity and the scope of our commitment to the environment.

West pocket parts and advance sheets are printed on recyclable paper and can be collected and recycled with newspapers. Staples do not have to be removed. Bound volumes can be recycled after removing the cover.

Production, Prepress, Printing and Binding by West Publishing Company.

Photo Credits

Page 2 Ralph Mercer Photography   Page 30 © 1996, Comstock, Inc.   Page 74 © Todd Davidson/The Image Bank   Page 114 © Michel Tcherevkoff/The Image Bank   Page 166 Cameron Davidson   Page 218 © 1996, Comstock, Inc.   Page 280 © Copyright 1996 C. O'Rear/Westlight   Page 324 Katvan—New York City   Page 370 © The Stock Market/Myron J. Dorf, 1993   Page 418 © 1996, Comstock, Inc.   Page 464 Rhoda Sidney/PhotoEdit   Page 504 Susan Van Etten Lawson/PhotoEdit   Page 544 © Steven Greenberg Photography, 1996   Page 588 SuperStock   Page 604, Exhibit 14–4 FASB Concepts Statement No. 2, *Qualitative Characteristics of Accounting Information,* is copyrighted by the Financial Accounting Standards Board, 401 Merritt 7, P.O. Box 5116, Norwalk, Connecticut, 06856-5116, U.S.A. Portions are reprinted with permission. Copies of the complete document are available from the FASB. Page 626 © 1996, Comstock, Inc.   Page 652 © Elle Schuster/The Image Bank   Page 664 OshKosh B'Gosh   Page 681 Courtesy Wendy's International, Inc., 1994 Shareholder Report   Page 699 Courtesy Bristol-Myers Squibb Company, 1994 Annual Report   Page 715 Courtesy Reebok International Ltd., 1994 Annual Report   Page 730 © Michel Tcherevkoff/The Image Bank

BRITISH LIBRARY CATALOGUING-IN-PUBLICATION DATA. A CATALOGUE RECORD FOR THIS BOOK IS AVAILABLE FROM THE BRITISH LIBRARY.

COPYRIGHT © 1997   by South-Western College Publishing
Cincinnati, Ohio

I(T)P®

International Thomson Publishing
South-Western College Publishing is an ITP Company.
The ITP trademark is used under license.

Library of Congress Cataloging-in-Publication Data

Murray, Dennis.
    Using financial accounting: an introduction/Dennis Francis Murray, Bruce Richard Neumann, Pieter Thomas Elgers.
        p. cm.
    Includes index.
    ISBN 0-314-06125-8 (alk. paper)
    1. Accounting.   I. Neumann, Bruce R.   II. Elgers, Pieter T.   III. Title.
HF5635.M9679 1997   96-38399
657—dc20   CIP

DENNIS MURRAY, Ph.D., CPA, is Professor of Accounting at the University of Colorado–Denver. He received his doctoral degree from the University of Massachusetts–Amherst and his undergraduate and masters degrees from the State University of New York at Albany. Professor Murray has published articles in a number of journals including *The Accounting Review, Journal of Accounting and Economics, Journal of Accounting Research,* and *Accounting Organizations and Society.* He serves on the editorial boards of *Advances in Accounting* and *The Journal of Managerial Issues.* Professor Murray has public accounting experience with KPMG Peat Marwick and is a member of the American Accounting Association and the Colorado Society of CPAs. He has received several awards recognizing his academic accomplishments.

BRUCE R. NEUMANN is Professor of Accounting and Health Administration at the University of Colorado–Denver. He received his doctoral degree from the University of Illinois and his undergraduate and masters degrees from the University of Minnesota. Dr. Neumann's primary research interests focus on analyses of costs in public and private organizations and on behavioral issues related to the interpretation and use of financial reports. His work has appeared in the *Journal of Accounting Research, Journal of Accountancy, Management Accounting,* and *Accounting and Business Research.* He has held visiting professorships at Bond University (Australia) and the University of Auckland. He has also served as a research fellow at the National Center for Health Services Research (Washington, DC) and at the Health Services Management Unit at the University of Manchester (U.K.).

PIETER ELGERS is Professor of Accounting at the University of Massachusetts at Amherst, and has previously served on the faculties of the College of William and Mary and Boston University, and visited at Yale University and the University of Auckland. His research has appeared in the *Journal of Accounting Research, The Accounting Review, Journal of Accounting and Economics, Journal of Finance, Management Science,* and various other academic and professional journals in accounting and finance. He has co–authored and edited books in the areas of financial management, accounting theory, lease–buy analysis, and financial accounting.

DEDICATION

To Lucy and
In memory of Mary, Francis, and Anastasia
D. M.

This text is dedicated in honor of my children:
    Elizabeth and Del Shannon
    Rebecca Neumann
    Susan Neumann
    David Neumann
to whom it may be said, as it was said of the Rector of Albermalia at St. John's
Church, England, 1741:
    "was exerted with uncommon penetration and judgment upon their proper
    object without noise or ostentation."
B. R. N.

To May and Dorian Elgers-Lo
P. E.

CONTENTS IN BRIEF

TABLE OF CONTENTS

CHAPTER **3**

THE BALANCE
SHEET 74

CHAPTER **5**

STATEMENT OF CASH
FLOWS   166

CHAPTER **7**

NONCURRENT
ASSETS 280

CHAPTER **8**

CURRENT
LIABILITIES 324

CHAPTER **10**

SHAREHOLDERS'
EQUITY 418

CHAPTER **11**

A FRAMEWORK FOR
FINANCIAL STATEMENT
ANALYSIS 464

CHAPTER **14**

ADDITIONAL
DIMENSIONS OF
FINANCIAL
REPORTING 588

Preface

This is an exciting time in accounting education. Various constituencies have emphasized the need for change and accounting educators have been quick to respond. Colleges and universities have developed innovations in their curricula, methods of instructional delivery, and course materials. We believe this book will assist those students and faculty members seeking an innovative approach to introductory financial accounting.

For several years now, nearly all introductory texts have offered new and various pedagogical features that proclaim to follow a "user" approach. We have attempted to advance this trend. *Using Financial Accounting* is truly written from the user's perspective. We emphasize (1) the effects of transactions on financial statements, (2) the interrelationships among the financial statements, and (3) the interpretation of financial statement information.

The mechanical aspects of the accounting process, such as journals, ledgers, debits/credits, trial balances, etc., are virtually eliminated from the text. Beginning students too frequently become immersed in detailed bookkeeping procedures and lose sight of the underlying objective of accounting: to assist in making business and economic decisions.

By taking an analytical and interpretative approach, students are able to understand and use financial statements. They will retain this ability longer than the knowledge of detailed accounting procedures. This approach "adds value" to students' potential contributions as business professionals.

Target Audience

This text is intended to serve both accounting majors and nonmajors. Nonmajors view a rules-based presentation as procedural rather than conceptual. Majors are also limited by a mechanical approach in that they do not really understand the goals and purposes of financial accounting until much later in their academic or professional careers. The target audience for this text includes:

1. Undergraduate accounting majors
2. Students other than accounting majors who want to interpret financial statements and interact with accounting professionals (this student group includes business majors and students in nonbusiness disciplines, such as engineering, health services, and law)
3. MBA students, who are particularly well served by an interpretative approach.

Features

This text's distinctive combination of features enhances value to students. These features include (1) the use of transaction analysis, rather than journal entries, to describe business events; (2) incorporation of "Reality Checks" that relate the text material to current real-world companies; (3) attention to international issues and accounting conventions for non-U.S. firms; (4) discussions and problem materials dealing with ethical issues facing managers and accountants; (5) evaluations of economic consequences associated with accounting policy decisions; (6) inclusion of an unusually large, diverse, and flexible set of end-of-chapter assignment material; and (7) a host of Internet-based problems in each chapter and an appendix showing students how to access financial accounting information on the Internet.

Transaction Analysis

To understand and interpret financial statements, students must gain an understanding of how transactions affect financial statements. This is accomplished by using the basic accounting equation:

$$\text{ASSETS} \quad = \quad \text{LIABILITIES} \quad + \quad \text{SHAREHOLDERS' EQUITY}$$

Transaction analysis, using the accounting equation, provides students with the background and tools to analyze financial statements. In addition to showing how business events affect the accounting equation, significant parts of each chapter are devoted to analysis and interpretation. Ratio analysis is introduced as early as Chapter 3 (The Balance Sheet) and appears in every subsequent chapter.

Reality Checks

Because we focus on the uses of financial accounting information, each chapter includes numerous real-world illustrations. These illustrations show how financial statements provide insights into a firm's performance. As part of this real-world orientation, Reality Checks are interspersed throughout the text. Reality Checks are self-contained, limited-scope problems based on actual financial statements and other disclosures. They help students see how financial statements can be used to answer important questions. Solutions to Reality Checks are included at the end of each chapter.

International Coverage

Many chapters also address international issues. These topics are interwoven into the discussion of financial statement analysis. The reader is shown how international differences in accounting standards can affect the inferences drawn from financial statements. For example, the discussion of noncurrent assets indicates that firms in some countries (e.g., Australia) report the market value of property, plant, and equipment. Moreover, case problems involving non-U.S. firms are included at the ends of several chapters. International accounting issues are summarized in Chapter 13.

Ethics

Ethical issues are considered throughout the text. Ethical dilemmas are presented in each chapter and the reader is asked to identify the proper course of action. We use a flag called "What Would You Do?" to alert readers to these ethical issues as they arise.

Economic Consequences

During the past 20 years, we have become more aware of the economic consequences and managerial motivations related to accounting policy decisions. Sophisticated users of financial statements should know that motivations stemming from compensation plans and debt covenants can affect the relevance and reliability of financial accounting information. These discussions are relatively self-contained so that they can be included at the instructor's option.

End-of-Chapter Material

Each chapter ends with (1) questions, (2) exercises, (3) problems, and (4) cases and extensions. The questions and exercises are relatively short, straightforward applications of the text material. Problems are straightforward, yet longer and more involved than the exercises.

Most chapters also contain sets of alternative problems or exercises. It is the authors' intent that students only complete one of the alternatives available. While most such sets contain two alternatives, noted as Problem A or B, some contain three alternatives (noted as A, B, or C). Please see Problem 2–29 for the first such example of how these alternatives are listed. In addition, some problems and cases are presented in a multi-part format noted as a "continuation." Please see Problem 2–25 through 2–28 for the first example of multi-part problems. The authors would suggest that these multi-part problems might be used profitably for class discussion or examination purposes. If so, the instructor might assign the first part as homework and the second or later parts can then be used for discussion or examination purposes.

Cases and other extended discussion questions have been included to challenge students' understanding of how financial statements can be used. They often require qualitative, narrative responses; some require research and writing. Our focus on the user orientation, real-world information, international issues, and ethics is carried through to the end-of-chapter material. Much of this material is based on actual financial statements from companies from around the world. The end-of-chapter material also contains situations requiring the application of ethics and Internet exercises.

ORGANIZATION

This book is arranged into four major components that make it readily adaptable for use in quarter, semester, or modular-type programs.

Part 1 consists of Chapters 1 through 5. This part is an introduction to financial accounting and the three primary financial statements: the balance sheet, the income statement, and the statement of cash flows.

Part 2 is comprised of Chapters 6 through 10. These chapters examine in more detail current and noncurrent assets, current and noncurrent liabilities, and share-holders' equity.

Part 3 consists of Chapter 11. This chapter is a synthesis of financial statement analysis. Although all chapters focus on the analysis and interpretation of financial statements, Chapter 11 provides an overall framework for financial statement analysis. Most instructors will use this chapter to unify the topics covered earlier in the text.

Part 4 consists of Chapters 12 through 14. These chapters consist of several self-contained modules that explore relatively complex topics such as leases, pensions, consolidated reporting, and international reporting. Many instructors will choose to cover only a subset of these topics.

Finally, *Using Financial Accounting* has seven appendixes. Appendix A contains an overview of the accounting process. Journal entries, adjusting entries, closing entries, and other procedural aspects of accounting are discussed. This appendix is intended primarily for those students (e.g., accounting majors) who wish to engage in further study of financial accounting. Most instructors who elect to utilize this appendix would likely use it in an end-of-course module to prepare students for intermediate financial accounting.

Appendix B examines various career options in accounting. This material would be of interest to a wide array of readers.

In keeping with our real-world approach, Appendixes C through F contain the annual reports of OshKosh B'Gosh, Inc., Wendy's International, Inc., Bristol-Myers Squibb Company, and Reebok International Limited, respectively. These reports serve as the basis for a number of exercises and problems.

Appendix G, prepared by W. David Albrecht of Bowling Green State University and Niranjan Chipalkatti of Ohio Northern University, shows students how to access information on the Internet. The Securities and Exchange Commission database and corporate home pages contain volumes of extremely up-to-date financial information. Each chapter also includes several problems based on accessing the Internet.

The following supplements are available for use with this text.

Instructor's Manual. Prepared by Linda Kidwell of Niagara University, this ancillary provides chapter overviews, learning objectives, and material designed to encourage group work.

Test Bank. Prepared by Lola F. Rhodes of Southern Methodist University, this text bank provides a variety of true/false, multiple-choice, matching, fill-in, and essay problems, 80 to 100 per chapter. Each chapter includes a page linking the problems to the learning objectives and providing a difficulty level for each problem.

Study Guide. Cecelia M. Fewox, CPA, of Trident Technical College, provides an overview for each chapter, a review of each specific chapter objective, and self-test material that utilizes matching, completion, and multiple-choice formats, as well as demonstration problems.

Solutions Manual. Prepared by Elizabeth C. Conner, of the University of Colorado at Denver, provides solutions to the text's extensive end-of-chapter review material.

Acetates. Approximately 80 four-color teaching acetates are available.

WESTEST 3.1. This computerized testing software provides the entire written test bank in a computerized format to facilitate test preparation in a DOS or Macintosh environment.

ACKNOWLEDGMENTS

We are grateful to a number of individuals who have contributed to the completion of this book. We are especially indebted to four individuals who had major roles in revising and formatting various draft versions during manuscript development and review: Kathleen Godek, Matt Moore, Jay Moore, and Mark Sandvik. We are also grateful to Robert Horan of West Educational Publishing for his advice and support.

Thanks are also due to former students Deborah Cabel, Tevis Morrow, Debbie Van Heusen, and Lesley Dmytrenko. Feedback from faculty colleagues Connie Boyer, Gary Colbert, Betty Connor, and John Jacob, who helped class-test these materials, was very valuable. We are especially indebted to the more than 1,000 University of Colorado at Denver students who participated in class testing.

We also thank our colleagues who took the time to provide us with helpful comments on the three drafts of this text. The reviewers include:

D'Arcy Becker
The University of New Mexico

Connie R. Boyer
University of Colorado at Denver

Sarah R. Brown
University of North Alabama

Jane E. Campbell
Kennesaw State College

Janice Carr
California Polytechnic State University, San Luis Obispo

Alan Cherry
Loyola Marymount University

Gary J. Colbert
University of Colorado at Denver

Elizabeth C. Conner
University of Colorado at Denver

Paul R. Graul
Eastern Washington University

Paul A. Griffin
University of California, Davis

Leon J. Hanouille
Syracuse University

Michael Haselkorn
Bentley College

Carol Olson Houston
San Diego State University

Sara York Kenny
The University of Utah

Linda A. Kidwell
Louisiana State University in Shreveport

Janet I. Kimbrell
Oklahoma State University

Raymond D. King
University of Oregon

Jerry Kreuze
Western Michigan University

Wayne A. Label
University of Nevada, Las Vegas

James A. Largay, III
Lehigh University

Linda Lessing
State University of New York College of Technology at Farmingdale

David Malone
University of Idaho

Ann Martin
University of Colorado at Denver

Aniello Massa
Ithica College

Theodore D. Morrison, III
Valparaiso University

Mary Nisbet
University of California, Santa Barbara

Mary Ann Prater
Clemson University

Mary Ann Reynolds
The University of Puget Sound

George N. Sanderson
Moorhead State University

Christine Schalow
California State University, San Bernardino

Douglas Sharp
Wichita State University

Ross E. Stewart
Seattle Pacific University

Tom Tolleson
University of North Texas

Michael Trubnick
California State University, San Bernardino

Karen Schuele Walton
John Carroll University

Charles D. Webb
Marshall University

Gerald P. Weinstein
John Carroll University

Linda K. Whitten
San Francisco State University

DENNIS MURRAY
BRUCE R. NEUMANN
PIETER ELGERS

CHAPTER 1

STUDYING THIS CHAPTER
WILL ENABLE YOU TO

1. Identify the objectives of accounting.
2. Distinguish among the three major types of accounting.
3. List the three primary financial statements and briefly summarize the information contained in each.
4. Identify financial statement users and the decisions they make.
5. Explain how generally accepted accounting principles are determined.
6. Describe the role of auditing.
7. List the economic consequences of the choice of accounting principles.
8. Assess the importance of ethics in accounting.

FINANCIAL ACCOUNTING AND ITS ENVIRONMENT

INTRODUCTION

Jane Johnson is considering selling T-shirts in the parking lot during her university's football games. Jane, of course, will only do this if she expects to make a profit. To estimate her profits, Jane needs certain pieces of information, such as the cost of a shirt, the university's charge for the right to conduct business on its property, the expected selling price, and the expected sales volume. Suppose Jane has developed the following estimates:

Sales price per shirt	$ 12
Cost per shirt	$ 7
Number of shirts sold per game day	50
University fee per game day	$100

Although developing estimates is tricky, let's take these estimates as given. Based on the estimates, Jane would earn a profit of $150 per game day.

Sales ($12 × 50)		$600
Less expenses:		
Cost of merchandise ($7 × 50)	$350	
University fee	100	
Total expenses		450
Net income		$150

Since this looks like a reasonable profit, Jane puts her plan into action. After her first game day, Jane needs to assess her success (or failure). Based on her actual results, Jane prepares the following information:

Sales ($12 × 40)		$480
Less expenses:		
Cost of merchandise ($7 × 40)	$280	
University fee	100	
Total expenses		380
Net income		$100

Jane's business was profitable, but not as profitable as she planned. This is because Jane sold fewer shirts than she hoped; but Jane is confident that she can sell any remaining shirts on the next game day.

The preceding illustration shows two ways in which accounting can be used. First, Jane used accounting to help plan her business. That is, she used accounting to project her expected profit. Second, after Jane operated her business for a day, she used accounting to determine if, in fact, she had made a profit. In general, accounting is used during all phases of planning and operating a business.

The Primary Objective of Accounting

The purpose of **accounting** is to provide useful information to those who make business and economic decisions. Accounting information is used in many different situations. The illustration in the introductory section shows how a business owner (Jane) can use accounting information. Bankers use accounting information when deciding whether or not to make a loan. Stockbrokers and other financial advisers base investment recommendations on accounting information. Government regulators use accounting information to determine if firms are complying with various laws and regulations.

Types of Accounting

The examples mentioned in the last section show that accounting information can be helpful in a number of situations. In fact, the field of accounting consists of a number of specialty areas that are based on the nature of the decision. The following sections describe the three major types of accounting that are summarized in Exhibit 1–1.

EXHIBIT 1–1
The Three Major Types of Accounting

Accounting Specialty	Decision Maker	Examples of Decisions
Financial accounting	Shareholders	Buy shares Hold shares Sell shares
	Creditors	Lend money Determine interest rates
Managerial accounting	Managers	Set product prices Buy or lease equipment
Tax	Managers	Comply with tax laws Minimize tax payments Assess the tax effects of future transactions

Financial Accounting

Financial accounting provides information to decision makers who are external to the business. To understand the role of financial accounting, consider a large corporation such as IBM. The owners of corporations are called shareholders, and IBM has more than 760,000 shareholders. Obviously, each shareholder cannot participate directly in the running of IBM. Also, because IBM needs to maintain various trade secrets, its many thousands of shareholders are not permitted access to much of the firm's information. Because of this, shareholders delegate most of their decision-making power to the corporation's board of directors and officers. Exhibit 1–2 contains an organizational chart for a typical corporation. Shareholders, however, need information to evaluate (1) the performance of IBM and (2) the advisability of retaining their investment in IBM. Financial accounting provides some of the information for this purpose. Financial accounting information is also used by *potential* shareholders who are considering an investment in IBM.

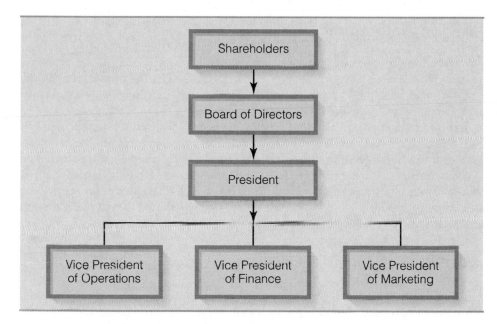

EXHIBIT 1–2
ORGANIZATIONAL CHART OF A
TYPICAL CORPORATION

Creditors and potential creditors are also served by financial accounting. Firms often seek loans from banks, insurance companies, and other lenders. Although creditors are not internal parties of those firms, they need information about them so that funds will be loaned only to credit-worthy organizations. Financial accounting will usually provide at least some of the information needed by these decision makers.

Managerial Accounting

Managers make numerous decisions. These include (1) whether to build a new plant, (2) how much to spend for advertising and research and development, (3) whether to lease or buy equipment and facilities, (4) whether to manufacture or buy component parts for inventory production, and (5) whether to sell a certain product. **Managerial accounting** provides information for these decisions. This information is usually more detailed and more tailor-made to the decision than is financial accounting information. It is also proprietary; that is, the information is not disclosed to parties outside the firm.

Wal-Mart provides a good illustration of managerial accounting at work. In response to the North American Free Trade Agreement of 1994, Wal-Mart significantly expanded its operations in Canada and Mexico. Wal-Mart undertook the expansion because it expected property and transportation to cost less in those countries. Managerial accountants played a major role in estimating these cost reductions and justifying Wal-Mart's international expansion.

Although distinguishing between financial and managerial accounting is convenient, the distinction is somewhat blurred. For example, financial accounting provides information about the performance of a firm to outsiders. Because this information is essentially a performance report on management, managers are appropriately interested in and influenced by financial accounting information. Accordingly, the distinction between financial and managerial accounting depends on who is the *primary* user of the information.

Tax Accounting

Tax accounting encompasses two related functions: tax compliance and tax planning. Tax compliance refers to the calculation of a firm's tax liability. This process entails the completion of sometimes lengthy and complex tax forms. Tax compliance takes place after the transactions for a year have been completed.

In contrast, tax planning takes place before the fact. Many business transactions can be structured in a variety of ways. For example, a car can be purchased by securing a loan, or it can be leased from the dealer. The structure of a transaction determines its tax consequences. A major responsibility of tax accountants is to provide advice about the tax effects of a transaction's various forms. Although this activity may seem to be an element of managerial accounting, it is separately classified due to the necessary specialized tax knowledge.

Other Types of Accounting

A few additional types of accounting exist. **Accounting information systems** are the processes and procedures required to generate accounting information. These include

1. identifying the information desired by the ultimate user,
2. developing the documents (e.g., sales invoices) to record the necessary data,
3. assigning responsibilities to specific positions in the firm, and
4. applying computer technology to summarize the recorded data.

Another type of accounting deals with **nonbusiness organizations.** These organizations do not attempt to earn a profit. They exist to fulfill the needs of certain groups of individuals. Nonbusiness organizations include

1. hospitals,
2. colleges and universities,
3. churches,
4. the federal, state, and local governments, and
5. many other organizations such as museums, volunteer fire departments, and disaster relief agencies.

Nonbusiness organizations have a need for all of the types of accounting we have just reviewed. For example, a volunteer fire department might need to borrow money to purchase a new fire truck. Its banker will need financial accounting information to make the lending decision.

Nonbusiness organizations are fundamentally different from profit-oriented firms: They have no owners and they do not attempt to earn a profit. Because of this, the analysis of the financial performance of business and nonbusiness organizations is considerably different. This text addresses only business organizations. Most colleges and universities offer an entire course devoted to the accounting requirements of nonbusiness organizations.

A CLOSER LOOK AT FINANCIAL ACCOUNTING

This text is primarily concerned with financial accounting, which summarizes the past performance and current condition of a firm. An overview of financial accounting is presented in Exhibit 1–3. Each element of the exhibit is discussed in the following sections.

EXHIBIT 1–3
OVERVIEW OF FINANCIAL ACCOUNTING

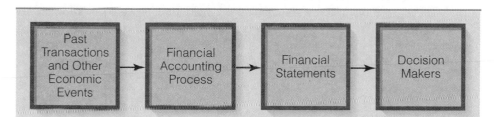

Past Transactions and Other Economic Events

Past transactions and events are the raw material for the financial accounting process. **Transactions** typically involve an *exchange* of resources between the firm and other parties. For example, purchasing equipment by paying cash is a transaction that would be incorporated in the firm's financial accounting records. Purchasing equipment on credit is also a transaction; equipment is obtained in *exchange* for a promise to pay for it in the future.

Financial accounting also incorporates significant economic events that do not involve exchanges with other parties. For example, assume a firm owns an uninsured automobile that is completely destroyed in an accident. Financial accounting would reflect the effect of this event.

Keep in mind that financial accounting deals with *past* transactions and events. It provides information about the past performance and current financial standing of a firm. Financial accounting itself does not usually make predictions about the future. Although financial statement users need to assess a firm's future prospects, financial accounting does not make these predictions, but it does provide information about the past and present that is useful in making predictions about the future.

The Financial Accounting Process

The financial accounting process consists of

1. *categorizing* past transactions and events,
2. *measuring* selected attributes of those transactions and events, and
3. *recording* and *summarizing* those measurements.

The first step places transactions and events into categories that reflect their type or nature. Some of the categories used in financial accounting include (1) purchases of inventory (merchandise acquired for resale), (2) sales of inventory, and (3) wage payments to workers.

The next step assigns values to the transactions and events. The attribute measured is the fair value of the transaction on the exchange date. This is usually indicated by the amount of cash that changes hands. For example, if equipment is purchased for a $1,000 cash payment, the equipment would be valued at $1,000. The initial valuation is not subsequently changed (some exceptions are discussed in later chapters). This original measurement is called **historical cost.**

The final step in the process is to record and meaningfully summarize these measurements. Summarizing is necessary because, otherwise, decision makers would be overwhelmed with an extremely large array of information. Imagine, for example, that an analyst is interested in Ford Motor Company's sales for 1997. Providing a list of every sales transaction and its amount would yield unduly detailed information. Instead, the financial accounting process summarizes the dollar value of all sales during a given time period. This single sales revenue number is included in the financial statements.

Financial Statements

Financial statements are the end result of the financial accounting process. Firms prepare three major financial statements: the balance sheet, the income statement, and the statement of cash flows. The following sections briefly describe these statements.

The Balance Sheet. The **balance sheet** shows a firm's assets, liabilities, and owners' equity. **Assets** are valuable resources that a firm owns. The simplified balance sheet shown in Exhibit 1–4 includes four assets. Cash obviously has value. Accounts receivable are amounts owed to Newton Company by its customers. Accounts receivable have value because they represent future cash inflows. Inventory is merchandise acquired that is to be sold to customers. Newton expects its inventory to be converted into accounts receivable and ultimately into cash. Finally, equipment (perhaps delivery vehicles or showroom furniture) enables Newton to operate its business.

Liabilities are obligations of the business to convey something of value in the future. Newton's balance sheet shows two liabilities. Accounts payable are unwritten promises that arise in the ordinary course of business. For example, Newton purchases inventory on credit, and has promised to make payment within a short period of time. Notes payable are more formal, written obligations. Notes payable often arise from borrowing money.

The final item on the balance sheet is **owners' equity,** which refers to the owners' interest in the business. It is a residual amount that equals assets minus liabilities. The owners have a positive financial interest in the business only if the firm's assets exceed its obligations.

The Income Statement. Just as each of us is concerned about our income, investors and creditors are interested in the ability of an organization to produce income (sometimes called earnings or profits). The **income statement** summarizes the earnings

The Newton Company
Balance Sheet
December 31, 1997

Assets		Liabilities and Owners' Equity	
Cash	$ 5,000	Liabilities	
Accounts receivable	7,000	Accounts payable	$ 8,000
Inventory	10,000	Notes payable	2,000
Equipment	7,000	Total liabilities	10,000
		Owners' equity	19,000
Total assets	$29,000	Total liabilities	
		and owners' equity	$29,000

EXHIBIT 1–4
A BALANCE SHEET

generated by a firm during a specified period of time. Exhibit 1–5 contains Newton Company's income statement for 1997.

Income statements contain at least two major sections: revenues and expenses. **Revenues** are inflows of assets from providing goods and services to customers. Newton's income statement contains one type of revenue: sales to customers. This includes sales made for cash and sales made on credit.

Expenses are the costs incurred to generate revenues. Newton's income statement includes three types of expenses. Cost of goods sold is the cost to Newton of the merchandise that was sold to its customers. General and administrative expenses include salaries, rent, and other items. Tax expense reflects the payments that Newton must make to the Internal Revenue Service and other taxing authorities. The difference between revenues and expenses is **net income** (or **net loss** if expenses are greater than revenues).

The Statement of Cash Flows. From a financial accounting perspective, income is not the same as cash. For example, suppose that a sale is made on credit. Will this sale be recorded on the income statement? Yes. It meets the definition of a revenue

The Newton Company
Income Statement
For the Year Ended December 31, 1997

Revenues		
Sales		$63,000
Expenses		
Cost of goods sold	$35,000	
General and administrative	20,000	
Tax	3,000	
Total expenses		58,000
Net income		$ 5,000

EXHIBIT 1–5
AN INCOME STATEMENT

transaction: an inflow of assets (the right to receive cash in the future) in exchange for goods or services. Moreover, including this transaction in the income statement provides financial statement readers with useful information about the firm's accomplishments. However, no cash has been received. Thus, the income statement does not provide information about cash flows.

Financial statement users, though, are also interested in a firm's ability to generate cash. After all, cash is necessary to buy inventory, pay workers, purchase equipment, etc. The **statement of cash flows** summarizes a firm's inflows and outflows of cash. Exhibit 1–6 illustrates Newton Company's statement of cash flows. It has three sections. One section deals with cash flows from **operating activities,** such as the buying and selling of inventory. The second section contains information about **investing activities,** such as the acquisition and disposal of equipment. The final section reflects cash flows from **financing activities.** These activities include obtaining and repaying loans, as well as obtaining financing from owners.

EXHIBIT 1–6
A STATEMENT OF CASH FLOWS

The Newton Company Statement of Cash Flows For the Year Ended December 31, 1997	
Cash flows from operating activities:	
Cash received from customers	$61,000
Cash paid to suppliers	(37,000)
Cash paid for general and administrative functions	(19,900)
Taxes paid	(3,000)
Net cash provided by operating activities	1,100
Cash flows from investing activities:	
Purchase of equipment	(2,000)
Cash flows from financing activities:	
Net borrowings	1,000
Net increase in cash	100
Cash at beginning of year	4,900
Cash at end of year	$ 5,000

Notes to Financial Statements. A full set of financial statements includes a number of **notes** that clarify and expand on the material presented in the body of the financial statements. The notes indicate the accounting principles (rules) that were used to prepare the statements, provide detailed information about some of the items in the financial statements, and, in some cases, provide alternative measures of the firm's assets and liabilities.

Notes to financial statements are not illustrated in this chapter because they are highly technical and apply to specific accounting topics covered in subsequent chapters. Notes are, however, emphasized throughout much of this book.

Annual Reports. All large firms, and many smaller ones, issue their financial statements as part of a larger document referred to as an **annual report.** In addition to the financial statements and its accompanying notes, the annual report includes descriptions of significant events that occurred during the year, commentary on future plans and strategies, and a discussion and analysis by management of the year's results. Appendices C through F of this text contain substantial portions of several annual reports.

Decision Makers

Recall that the primary goal of financial accounting is to provide decision makers with useful information. This section identifies the major users of financial statements and describes the decisions they make.

Owners. Present and potential owners (investors) are prime users of financial statements. They continually assess and compare the prospects of alternative investments. The assessment of each investment is often based on two variables: expected return and risk.

Expected return refers to the increase in the investor's wealth that is expected over the investment's time horizon. This wealth increase is comprised of two parts: (1) increases in the market value of the investment and (2) dividends (periodic cash distributions from the firm to its owners). Both of these sources of wealth depend on the firm's ability to generate cash. Accordingly, financial statements can improve decision making by providing information that helps present and potential investors estimate a firm's future cash flows.

Risk refers to the uncertainty surrounding estimates of expected return. The term *expected* implies that the return is not guaranteed. For most investments, numerous alternative future returns are possible. For example, an investor may project that a firm's mostly likely return for the upcoming year is $100,000. However, the investor recognizes that this is not the only possibility. There is some chance that the firm might generate returns of $90,000 or $110,000. Still other possibilities might be $80,000 and $120,000. The greater the difference among these estimates, the greater the risk. Financial statements help investors assess risk by providing information about the historical pattern of past income and cash flows.

Investment selection involves a trade-off between expected return and risk. Investments with high expected returns generally have high risk. Each investor must assess whether investments with greater risk offer sufficiently higher expected returns.

To illustrate the trade-off between risk and expected return, assume an investor has two choices: investment A and investment B. Each investment costs $100. The return provided by the investments during the next year depends on whether the economy experiences an expansion or recession. The following chart summarizes the possibilities:

	Expected Return	
	Investment A	Investment B
Expansion	$10	$4
Recession	$ 0	$2

Assuming that expansion and recession are equally as likely, the expected return of the two investments can be calculated as follows:

$$\text{Investment A} \quad (\$10 \times .5) + (\$0 \times .5) = \$5$$
$$\text{Investment B} \quad (\$4 \times .5) + (\$2 \times .5) = \$3$$

Although investment A has the higher expected return, it also has the higher risk. Its return next year can vary by $10 while investment B's return can vary by only $2. Investors must decide for themselves whether investment A's higher expected return is worthwhile, given its greater risk.

Creditors. The lending decision involves two issues: whether or not credit should be extended, and specification of a loan's terms. For example, consider a bank loan officer evaluating a loan application. The officer must make decisions about the amount of the loan (if any), interest rate, payment schedule, and collateral. Because repayment of the loan and interest will rest on the applicant's ability to generate cash, lenders need to estimate a firm's future cash flows and the uncertainty surrounding those flows. Although investors generally take a long-term view of a firm's cash generating ability, creditors are concerned about this ability only during the loan period.

Lenders are not the only creditors who find financial statements useful. Suppliers often sell on credit, and they must decide which customers will or will not honor their obligations.

Other Users. A variety of other decision makers find financial statements helpful. Some of these decision makers and their decisions include the following:

1. *Financial analysts and advisors.* Many investors and creditors seek expert advice when making their investment and lending decisions. These experts use financial statements as a basis for their recommendations.
2. *Customers.* The customers of a business are interested in a stable source of supply. They can use financial statements to identify suppliers that are financially sound.
3. *Employees and labor unions.* These groups have an interest in the viability and profitability of firms that employ them or their members. As described in Reality Check 1–1, unions in the airline industry have recently made several important decisions based, in part, on financial statements.
4. *Regulatory authorities.* Federal and state governments regulate a large array of business activities. The Securities and Exchange Commission (SEC) is a prominent example. Its responsibility is to ensure that capital markets, such as the New York Stock Exchange, operate smoothly. To help achieve this, corporations are required to make full and fair financial disclosures. The SEC regularly reviews firms' financial statements to evaluate the adequacy of their disclosures. Reality Check 1–2 describes another regulatory use of accounting information.

The accounting profession views financial statements as being *general purpose.* They are intended to meet the common information needs of a wide variety of users, such as those in the preceding list.

GENERALLY ACCEPTED ACCOUNTING PRINCIPLES

Decision makers often wish to compare the financial statements of several firms. To permit valid comparisons, the firms' statements need to be based on the same set of accounting principles. Accounting principles are the rules and procedures used to produce the financial statements.

To illustrate how one event might be accounted for in more than one way, consider a movie production company that has just produced a new film costing $25,000,000.

EMPLOYEES MAKE USE OF FINANCIAL ACCOUNTING

United Airlines: In 1994, employees of United Airlines gained control of United's parent, UAL Corporation. In exchange for control of UAL, United's employees gave up billions of dollars of wages and benefits. The employees needed to estimate the value of UAL so that they could determine the extent of the wages and benefits to sacrifice. Financial statements are frequently used in valuing businesses.

Delta Airlines: In 1994, Delta asked its pilots to forgo a scheduled wage increase. Delta asserted that its financial position did not permit payment of this increase. The pilots agreed to Delta's request. Delta's financial statements, showing consistent losses, probably helped the employees determine if Delta's assertion was reasonable.

Assume that a balance sheet is to be prepared before the film is marketed. Does the firm have a $25,000,000 asset? The real value of the film rests on its ability to generate future revenues. A successful film will generate revenue that is many times greater than its cost; an unsuccessful film may not even cover its cost. At the balance sheet date, the future revenue is unknown.

As a potential investor or creditor, how would you prefer that this film be reflected on the balance sheet? Two obvious alternatives are $25,000,000 and $0. The latter is clearly more conservative; it results in a lower asset value. Some financial statement readers would prefer the conservative approach. Others would maintain that management expects to reap at least $25,000,000 in revenue; otherwise, they would not have undertaken the project. Thus, they feel that $25,000,000 is the most reasonable figure. There is no obvious answer to this issue. However, to permit comparisons of various firms' balance sheets, the same accounting principle should be used. Current accounting practice is to record assets at historical cost; in this case, the movie would be recorded at $25,000,000.

 The Financial Accounting Standards Board

The most widely used set of accounting principles is referred to as **generally accepted accounting principles (GAAP).** GAAP is currently set by the **Financial Accounting**

GOVERNMENT REGULATORS MAKE USE OF FINANCIAL ACCOUNTING

California has perhaps the country's toughest standards for vehicle emissions. One aspect of its program requires the major automakers to generate 2% of their California sales from electric vehicles by 1998. Compliance with this regulation will be assessed from financial accounting information.

Standards Board (FASB). The FASB is a private organization located in Norwalk, Connecticut. The board is comprised of seven voting members who are supported by a large staff. As of June 30, 1995, the FASB had issued 121 **Statements of Financial Accounting Standards (SFASs).** These standards are the primary source of GAAP.

The FASB's predecessor was the **Accounting Principles Board (APB).** The APB issued 31 *Opinions,* which are still part of GAAP, unless they have been superseded by an SFAS.

The FASB faces a difficult task in setting GAAP. Financial accounting is not a natural science. There are no fundamental accounting laws that have been proven to be correct. Accounting exists to provide information useful for decision making. The FASB's responsibility is to specify the accounting principles that will result in highly useful information. However, given that financial statement users are rather diverse, this is not a simple task.

The FASB employs an elaborate due process procedure prior to the issuance of an SFAS. Exhibit 1–7 summarizes the FASB's procedures. This process is designed to

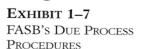

EXHIBIT 1–7
FASB's DUE PROCESS
PROCEDURES

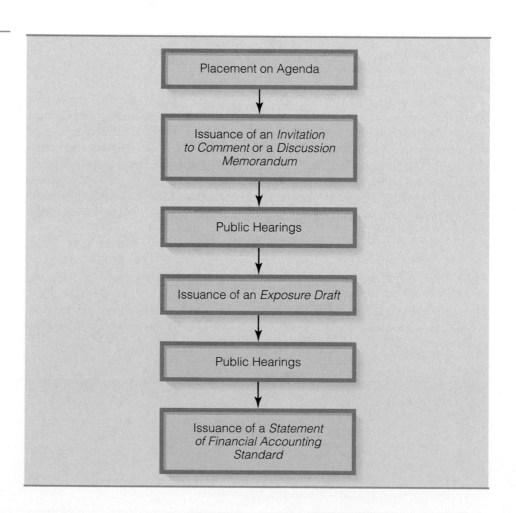

Placement on Agenda

Issuance of an *Invitation to Comment* or a *Discussion Memorandum*

Public Hearings

Issuance of an *Exposure Draft*

Public Hearings

Issuance of a *Statement of Financial Accounting Standard*

ensure that all those who wish to participate in the setting of accounting standards have an opportunity to do so.

The FASB publishes several preliminary documents during its deliberations on each SFAS. The documents include an *Invitation to Comment* or a *Discussion Memorandum,* which identify the fundamental accounting issues to be addressed. An *Exposure Draft* is the FASB's initial attempt at resolving those issues. These documents are widely disseminated, and interested parties are invited to communicate with the Board, both in writing and by making presentations at public hearings. An affirmative vote of five of the seven FASB members is needed to issue a new SFAS.

An interesting aspect of GAAP is that more than one accounting method (or principle) is acceptable for some transactions. For example, there are several acceptable inventory accounting methods. This provides managers with considerable discretion in preparing their financial statements.

Several accountants, judges, and legislators have criticized this situation. They believe that only a single method should be allowed for a given transaction. In general, the FASB is attempting to narrow the availability of multiple acceptable accounting procedures.

THE SECURITIES AND EXCHANGE COMMISSION

The **Securities and Exchange Commission (SEC)** was created by the Securities Exchange Act of 1934. That act empowered the SEC to set accounting principles and financial disclosure requirements for the corporations that it regulates. These corporations are quite large and have ownership interests that are widely dispersed among the public. Such corporations are referred to as *publicly held.* Thus, for at least publicly held corporations, the SEC has legislative authority to set GAAP. This raises a question about the relationship between the SEC and the FASB.

The FASB is a private (i.e., nongovernment) organization whose authority to set GAAP derives from two sources. First, the business community and the accounting profession, by accepting FASB rulings, provide one source of support. In the United States, accounting principles have traditionally been set in the private sector, and the FASB's standards have received a reasonable amount of support. At the same time, not everyone is entirely happy with the FASB's pronouncements. For example, some businesspeople and accountants criticize the FASB for issuing standards that are too complex and too costly to implement. Part of the FASB's responsibility is to balance financial statement users' demands for better information with the costs incurred by those who must provide that information.

The second source of the FASB's standard-setting authority is the SEC. Although the SEC has legislative authority to set GAAP for publicly held corporations, it prefers to rely on the accounting profession's private rule-making bodies to do this. In fact, the SEC has formally indicated that it will recognize GAAP as prescribed by the FASB. The SEC does, however, retain the right to overrule FASB pronouncements, and it occasionally exercises this right. Exhibit 1–8 shows the relationships among the different organizations involved in setting accounting standards.

EXHIBIT 1–8
GROUPS INVOLVED IN SETTING
ACCOUNTING STANDARDS

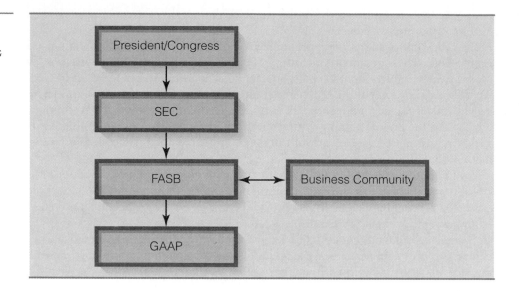

THE ROLE OF AUDITING

A firm's management is primarily responsible for preparing its financial statements. Yet, the financial statements can be viewed as a report on the performance of management. The conflict of interest in this situation is apparent. As a result, the financial statements of all corporations reporting to the SEC must be audited by a firm of independent certified public accountants (CPAs). **Audits** are required because they enhance the credibility of the financial statements. Exhibit 1–9 depicts the relationships among the parties involved in an audit.

The financial statements of many privately held businesses are also subjected to an audit. For example, banks require many loan applicants to submit audited financial statements.

EXHIBIT 1–9
AUDITING RELATIONSHIPS

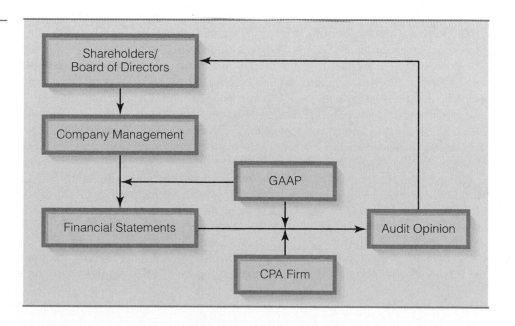

Exhibit 1–10 contains an auditor's report. The wording has been carefully chosen by the accounting profession to communicate precisely what an audit does and does not do. The first paragraph identifies the company, the specific financial statements that were audited, and the years of the audit. Management's responsibility for the financial statements is also acknowledged.

The second paragraph states that the audit has been conducted in accordance with **generally accepted auditing standards (GAAS).** These standards have been developed by the accounting profession to provide guidance in the performance of an audit. The audit consists of an examination of evidence supporting the financial statements. Because audits are costly, auditors cannot retrace the accounting for every transaction. Accordingly, only a sample of a corporation's many transactions are reviewed. Based on the results of these tests, the auditor draws an inference about the reasonableness of the financial statements.

The second paragraph also notes that audits provide reasonable (not absolute) assurance that financial statements are free of material error. The lesser standard of reasonable assurance is employed for two reasons. First, auditors do not examine every transaction and thus they are unable to state conclusions in too strong a fashion. Second, even if auditors were to examine every transaction, collusion between two parties could make the detection of an error virtually impossible.

The third paragraph contains the auditor's **opinion.** The opinion reflects the auditor's professional judgment regarding whether the financial statements are fairly presented in accordance with GAAP. Some readers mistakenly assume that auditors "certify" the financial statements. Auditors do not provide financial statement readers with that level of assurance. Auditors do not guarantee the correctness of the financial statements. Auditors merely express an educated professional judgment based on audit tests conducted according to acceptable professional standards.

An analogy can be drawn to a medical doctor diagnosing a patient. Based on a series of appropriate tests, the doctor develops a diagnosis. In many cases, the doctor cannot be absolutely certain of the diagnosis. This is why, for example, exploratory surgery is sometimes necessary. Doctors do not issue guarantees, and neither do auditors.

The report that appears in Exhibit 1–10 is an unqualified opinion, indicating that Ernst & Young has no reservations about the reasonableness of OshKosh B'Gosh's financial statements. However, a variety of concerns may arise that would cause the auditor to qualify the opinion, or to include additional explanatory material. For example, we know that there are several acceptable methods of accounting for inventory. If a company were to change its inventory method from one year to the next, the comparability of the financial statements for those years would be impaired. Financial statement readers would certainly want to be aware of such a situation. Because of this, changes in accounting methods are noted in the auditor's report. Observe that Ernst & Young's audit report in Exhibit 1–10 mentions that OshKosh B'Gosh changed its methods of accounting for income taxes and nonpension postretirement benefits in 1992. These changes were required by new accounting standards issued by the FASB, and similar mention is included in the auditor's reports for most companies' financial statements issued in 1992.

CPAs are licensed by the individual states. To be licensed, an individual must meet specified educational and experience requirements and must pass the uniform CPA exam, which takes two days to complete. CPAs are required to attend continuing professional education classes, and participate in a peer review process, whereby one CPA firm reviews and critiques the work of another firm. All of these requirements are intended to promote high-quality audits. More detailed descriptions of the accounting profession are provided in Appendix B.

ECONOMIC CONSEQUENCES AND MANAGERIAL PREFERENCES FOR ACCOUNTING PRINCIPLES

The selection of accounting principles occurs at two levels. First, the FASB determines which principles constitute GAAP. However, in a number of instances the FASB allows the use of more than one method. Thus, corporate managers also make accounting policy decisions. What criteria are used by the FASB and corporate managers to select accounting principles?

The FASB's primary objective is to select accounting principles that provide useful information to financial statement readers. However, businesses incur costs to generate the information required by the FASB. Thus, the FASB attempts to balance the costs and benefits of its rulings.

EXHIBIT 1–10
AN AUDITOR'S REPORT

The Board of Directors
OshKosh B'Gosh, Inc.
and subsidiaries (the Company)

We have audited the accompanying consolidated balance sheets of OshKosh B'Gosh, Inc. and subsidiaries (the Company) as of December 31, 1994 and 1993, and the related consolidated statements of income, changes in shareholders' equity, and cash flows for years then ended. These financial statements are the responsibility of the Company's management. Our responsibility is to express an opinion on these financial statements based on our audits. The financial statements of the Company for the year ended December 31, 1992 were audited by other auditors whose report, dated February 15, 1993, expressed an unqualified opinion on those statements.

We conducted our audits in accordance with generally accepted auditing standards. Those standards require that we plan and perform the audit to obtain reasonable assurance about whether the financial statements are free of material misstatement. An audit includes examining, on a test basis, evidence supporting the amounts and disclosures in the financial statements. An audit also includes assessing the accounting principles used and significant estimates made by management, as well as evaluating the overall financial statement presentation. We believe that our audits provide a reasonable basis for our opinion.

In our opinion, the 1994 and 1993 financial statements referred to above present fairly, in all material respects, the consolidated financial position of the Company at December 31, 1994 and 1993, and the consolidated results of its operations and its cash flows for the years then ended in conformity with generally accepted accounting principles.

As discussed in Notes 1 and 10 to the consolidated financial statements, effective January 1, 1992, the Company changed its method of accounting for income taxes and nonpension post-retirement benefits.

Ernst & Young
Milwaukee, Wisconsin
February 6, 1995

Some members of the financial community suggest that corporate managers act in the same way. For example, in choosing an inventory method, managers balance the costs of implementing each method with the quality of the information that each method yields. A more sophisticated view recognizes that accounting principles have economic consequences to managers and their firms, and that these consequences are considered by managers when choosing accounting principles. Beyond implementation costs, accounting principles can affect the wealth of managers and firms via (1) compensation plans, (2) debt contracts, and (3) political costs.

Compensation Plans

Many corporations pay their top managers a fixed salary plus an annual bonus. The bonus is often a percentage of reported net income. A number of bonus agreements include a floor and a ceiling on the bonus. The floor requires that net income must exceed a predetermined amount before the bonus is activated. The ceiling places a limit on the size of the bonus; once the annual bonus reaches the ceiling, additional increases in net income no longer increase the bonus.

Bonus plans are intended to align the interests of managers and shareholders. Managers frequently face alternative courses of action, where one course is in their best interest, and another course is in the shareholders' best interest. For example, managers' careers might be aided by expanding the business (empire building), even when such expansion is not particularly profitable and is not in the shareholders' best interest. Expansion may result in more prestige and visibility for the firm and its managers, thus enhancing the managers' employment opportunities. Since (1) bonus plans motivate managers to make decisions that increase net income and (2) increased net income is usually in the shareholders' best interest, the goals of these two groups come more in line when managers' compensation depends on reported net income.

Given that managers' compensation is tied to reported accounting earnings, how would we expect managers to select accounting principles? Most managers probably consider the effect different accounting principles have on net income, and consequently on their compensation. In particular, bonuses clearly motivate managers to select accounting methods that increase reported net income.

Debt Contracts

Lenders are concerned about limiting their risk and maximizing the probability that principal and interest will be paid. **Debt contracts** between borrowers and lenders can help accomplish this. Many of these contracts impose constraints on the behavior of borrowers. For example, some contracts limit the total amount of debt a borrower can incur. In such cases, measurement of the borrower's debt is based on the liabilities reported in the balance sheet. As another example, some contracts limit the cash dividends a borrower can distribute. This limitation is defined in terms of retained earnings, a component of owners' equity that appears on the balance sheet. Penalties exist for violating debt contracts. These include

1. an interest rate increase,
2. an increase in collateral (assets pledged to secure the debt),
3. a one-time renegotiation fee, and
4. an acceleration in the maturity date.

Since these contracts are defined in terms of financial statement numbers, the use of accounting principles that increase reported net income can reduce the chances of contract violation. Accordingly, the likelihood of violating debt contracts is another influence on managers' accounting policy choices.

Political Costs

Federal and state governments have the power to regulate many aspects of the operations of a business. Pollutant emissions and employment practices are just two of these activities. Governments also have the power to tax corporations. Because regulation and taxation are costly to firms, managers can be expected to take actions that minimize these costs. Since these costs are imposed via the political process, they are referred to as **political costs.**

Some accountants suggest that highly profitable firms are more exposed to political costs than less profitable ones. Relatively profitable firms are more likely to be the target of antitrust investigations or special tax assessments. For example, in the mid-1970s firms in the oil industry earned unusually high profits due to a steep rise in oil prices. As a result Congress enacted the Windfall Profits Tax, which subjected these companies to an additional tax on their earnings.

Some accountants also argue that larger firms are more susceptible to regulation and taxation because their size attracts more attention. Accordingly, the managers of larger firms are particularly motivated to undertake actions that minimize these costs. One of these actions is the selection of accounting principles that reduce reported net income. Note that compensation plans and debt contracts motivate managers to select accounting principles that increase reported income, whereas political costs have the opposite effect.

The Two Roles of Financial Accounting

At the beginning of this chapter, the informational role of financial accounting was emphasized. From this perspective, both the FASB and corporate managers select accounting principles that yield the most useful information. However, accounting principles also have economic consequences. These consequences arise in several ways. First, accounting serves as a basis for contracting. That is, some contracts (compensation plans and debt contracts) are based on accounting numbers. Since different accounting principles result in different accounting numbers, the choice of accounting principles can modify the terms of these contracts. Second, accounting principles may affect a firm's exposure to political costs, such as taxes and regulation. Finally, the costs to implement different accounting principles vary. Some accounting principles are quite complex and costly, whereas others are rather simple.

For all these reasons, accounting principles can affect the wealth of a firm and its managers. The managers have an obvious incentive to select those principles that increase their wealth. Such an incentive may conflict with the notion that managers select accounting principles to provide useful information. This implies that financial statement readers must carefully evaluate the accounting principles used by a firm. The selection may not result in the most useful financial statement information. In subsequent chapters, managers' selection of accounting principles will be examined from both informational and economic incentive perspectives.

The Political Nature of Accounting Standard Setting

Economic incentives associated with accounting principles might motivate an additional element of managerial behavior. As mentioned in an earlier section, the FASB conducts an elaborate due process procedure prior to issuing an accounting standard. This process provides corporate managers an opportunity to lobby the FASB. What underlies their comments to the board? Again, two possibilities exist. The comments may reflect managers' assessments of which principles generate the most useful financial statement information. Alternatively, their comments may also reflect, perhaps in a disguised way, how the various accounting principles will affect their wealth.

Some observers believe that the FASB has been overly responsive to the latter arguments. Of course, others believe that the FASB is not sufficiently sensitive to the effects its pronouncements have on individual managers or firms. Thus, accounting standard setting is now widely recognized as a political process in which various parties argue for the selection of those accounting principles that further their own self-interest. Some accountants believe that self-interest arguments have had a negative effect on the usefulness of the information required by some FASB rulings.

Accountants have a significant responsibility to the public. This responsibility exists because outside shareholders, creditors, employees, and others rely on financial statements in making various business decisions. Business organizations employ internal accountants to prepare financial statements. These statements are then audited by a firm of independent CPAs. Both the internal accountants and the external auditors have a responsibility to perform their tasks with integrity and due care.

Various accounting organizations promote high standards of ethical behavior. One example is the American Institute of Certified Public Accountants (AICPA), which is a professional organization that serves CPAs who work for public accounting firms or other organizations (e.g., corporations). Its *Code of Professional Conduct* emphasizes the obligation of CPAs to serve the public interest, and their responsibility to act with integrity, objectivity, independence, and due professional care.

In a given situation, formalized codes of ethics can often help in deciding the proper course of action. However, some situations are sufficiently complex that the codes do not provide clear guidance. Fortunately, ethicists have developed frameworks for examining ambiguous ethical situations. Two of these frameworks, utilitarianism and deontology, are briefly described next.

Utilitarianism judges the moral correctness of an act based solely on its consequences. The act that should be taken is the one that maximizes overall favorable consequences (net of unfavorable ones). Consequences to all parties should be considered, not only consequences to the actor.

The proponents of **deontology** assert that the consequences of an act do not exclusively dictate moral correctness. They believe that the underlying nature of the act itself influences its correctness. There are two types of deontologists. Some deontologists feel

ETHICS AND
ACCOUNTING

that the nature of an act is the *only* thing to be considered in assessing its moral correctness. For example, they believe that killing and lying are morally wrong under any circumstances. Other deontologists assert that the nature of the act and its consequences in a particular situation should both be considered.

To illustrate these approaches, imagine you are in the process of filling out an expense report after having just completed a business trip. Your employer does not reimburse child-care costs while away from home. However, most of your colleagues (including your immediate supervisor) feel that child care is a legitimate expense. They recoup this expenditure by overstating the cost of meals (most restaurants provide you with a blank receipt). Is it ethically correct for you to overstate your meal cost?

Many deontologists would assert that the act of lying is ethically wrong, and that falsifying an expense report is the equivalent of lying. Utilitarians, on the other hand, would examine the consequences of the action, and it is not clear that their analysis would reach the same conclusion. An assessment would need to be made of how you versus the shareholders would be affected by the falsification.

To develop a strong personal code of ethics, each of us must understand how we think about ethical situations. We suggest that you consider how utilitarianism and deontology can be used to analyze ethical situations, and that you assess which of those approaches, if either, is consistent with your own moral framework.

WHAT WOULD YOU DO?

Lifetime Products, Inc., sold part of its business to its chief executive and to the wife of its board of directors' chairman. Some of Lifetime's shareholders subsequently filed a lawsuit seeking to rescind the sale.

Why might Lifetime's shareholders be upset? Would you have authorized the sale?

SUMMARY OF LEARNING OBJECTIVES

1. **Identify the objectives of accounting.**

   The primary objective of accounting is to provide useful information to those who make business and economic decisions. Users of accounting information include present and potential investors and creditors, investment advisers, corporate managers, employees, unions, and government regulators. A secondary objective of accounting is to help develop and enforce contracts. That is, in certain instances people and organizations find the use of accounting numbers in contracts to be quite helpful.

2. **Distinguish among the three major types of accounting.**

   The three major types of accounting are determined based on the identity of the user of the information. Financial accounting provides information to outsiders who do not have access to the firm's confidential records. This includes shareholders, creditors, employees, unions, and government regulators. Managerial accounting provides information to corporate managers to help them with their decisions. Tax accounting has two elements. Tax compliance involves the periodic preparation of tax forms as required by various taxing authorities. The purpose of this is to calculate a firm's tax liability. Tax compliance takes place after transactions have been completed. Tax planning takes place before transactions have been undertaken. Its purpose is to structure transactions so as to minimize their tax effect.

3. **List the three primary financial statements and briefly summarize the information contained in each.**

The balance sheet, income statement, and statement of cash flows are the three primary financial statements. The balance sheet shows a firm's assets, liabilities, and owners' equity at a point in time. The income statement summarizes a firm's revenues and expenses for a period of time. The difference between revenues and expenses is net income (or loss). The statement of cash flows shows a firm's inflows and outflows of cash for a period of time. The three categories of this statement are cash flows from (1) operating activities, (2) investing activities, and (3) financing activities.

4. **Identify financial statement users and the decisions they make.**

The main users of financial statements are shareholders, creditors, management, and government regulators. Shareholders decide whether to buy, hold, or sell shares in the firm. Creditors must determine whether to extend credit and on what terms. Since financial statements are a performance report on corporate management, managers are concerned about the effect of their decisions on the financial statements. Government regulators use financial statements to determine if firms are complying with various laws and regulations.

5. **Explain how generally accepted accounting principles are determined.**

Currently, the FASB sets GAAP. The FASB's authority rests on (1) the acceptance of its rulings by the financial community and (2) the delegation by the SEC of its legislative authority to determine GAAP for large, publicly held corporations. Prior to issuing a new ruling, the FASB conducts an elaborate process to permit all interested parties to participate.

6. **Describe the role of auditing.**

A firm's management is responsible for preparing financial statements. Yet, those same statements are a performance report on management. Because of this conflict of interest, the financial statements of many organizations are audited by a firm of independent CPAs. Auditors examine a sample of an organization's transactions to provide a reasonable basis for expressing an opinion on the fairness of the financial statements. CPAs do not certify financial statements. They merely express a professional opinion regarding their fairness in conformity with GAAP.

7. **List the economic consequences of the choice of accounting principles.**

Accounting principles not only affect the quality of the information contained in financial statements, but they also affect the wealth of various parties. Accounting principles have economic consequences because of implementation costs, compensation plans, debt contracts, and political costs. Managers, therefore, have certain preferences for accounting principles that are not necessarily related to the inherent quality of the resulting information. Accordingly, care must be taken in interpreting both financial statements and managers' recommendations about accounting standards.

8. **Assess the importance of ethics in accounting.**

Accountants have an important responsibility to the public. This responsibility arises because financial statements are used by large numbers of people for a variety of purposes. It is essential that accountants adhere to the highest levels of ethical conduct.

KEY TERMS

Accounting
Accounting information systems
Accounting Principles Board (APB)
Annual report
Assets
Audit
Auditor's opinion
Balance sheet
Compensation plans
Debt contracts
Deontology
Expected return
Expenses
Financial accounting
Financial Accounting Standards Board (FASB)
Financing activities
Generally accepted accounting principles (GAAP)
Generally accepted auditing standards (GAAS)
Historical cost

Income statement
Investing activities
Liabilities
Managerial accounting
Net income
Net loss
Nonbusiness organizations
Notes
Operating activities
Owners' equity
Political costs
Revenues
Risk
Securities and Exchange Commission (SEC)
Statement of cash flows
Statements of Financial Accounting Standards (SFASs)
Tax accounting
Transactions
Utilitarianism

QUESTIONS

1–1   The chapter discussed two general functions of financial accounting. Briefly describe them.

1–2   List the three types (specialty areas) of accounting. Who are the users of each type of accounting? How do the needs of these users differ?

1–3   Compare the cash flows of a business to its profitability.

1–4   Describe the accounting process.

1–5   List the three major financial statements. What information do they contain?

1–6   Write a short essay describing four different users of accounting reports, and indicate their particular interests.

1–7   What decisions do present and future owners of a business need to make? How are financial statements helpful?

1–8   What information do present and potential creditors need to make decisions? How are financial statements helpful?

1–9   The selection of accounting principles can affect the wealth of a firm's managers in several ways. Describe how this can occur.

1–10 An old joke goes as follows:

• Questioner: What is 2 + 2?
• Accountant: Whatever you want it to be.

What do you think this joke is designed to communicate?

1–11 Accounting principle selection has economic effects. How might this affect managers' behavior?

1–12 Is accounting standard setting an art or a science? Why?

1–13 What considerations are used by the FASB in setting GAAP?

1–14 What is the relationship between the FASB and the SEC? What role does Congress play in accounting standard setting?

1–15 Why do many businesses that are not regulated by the SEC elect to have their financial statements audited?

CASES AND EXTENSIONS

Conceptual Distinctions: Maps Versus Financial Statements

1–16 Some accountants draw an analogy between developing financial statements and cartography (map making). They maintain that just as maps reflect the geographical reality of the area under study, so should financial statements reflect the economic reality of the organization. Critique this position by discussing the differences between a map and a financial statement.

Critical Essay: Measurement Criteria

1–17 Write a short essay identifying three measurement criteria that you believe should be followed by accountants. Indicate why each criterion is important to you.

Identification of Accounting Transactions

1–18 Which of the following transactions or events should be recorded in the firm's accounting records? Explain your answer.

    a. Cash is received from a sale previously made on credit.

    b. A year after obtaining a bank loan, a business owes the bank interest charges. These charges remain unpaid at the end of the year.

    c. A professional baseball player, hitting .425, expects a bonus under his incentive contract for leading the league in hitting for the season. The bonus was "pegged" at $1,000 for every point that he exceeded the batting target of .375. How much should the baseball player record in his checkbook at the end of the season?

    d. An employer and a labor union sign a new collective bargaining agreement.

    e. An item of factory equipment is removed from service. The item has a net book value of $10,000. It is determined that the equipment is worthless.

Conceptual Discussion: Audits and Loan Applications

1–19 Refer to the T-shirt business described at the beginning of this chapter. The owner has decided to expand her business by trying to secure a bank loan. After meeting with the bank loan officer, she asked for your help in answering several questions before proceeding with the loan application.

    a. An audit may be required in order to obtain the bank loan. What is an audit, and why would a bank require an audit?

    b. Do you think audits are expensive? Will an audit delay her application? Why?

    c. Identify several alternative types of loans that the owner might consider.

d. The owner is considering whether to purchase and install a computer-based accounting system to replace the checkbook that she has been using. How would you advise her?

Conceptual Discussion: Multiple Accounting Principles

1–20 A number of situations exists where more than one accounting principle is acceptable. Is this advisable? Why?

WHAT WOULD YOU DO?

Company Perquisites and Cash Transactions

1–21 Assume you are employed by a law firm as a staff accountant. The firm has purchased four season tickets for the Colorado Rockies (a baseball franchise!). Your boss, one of the partners in the firm, has offered individual game tickets to you, but also asked you to pay $10 for each ticket. Since they are $14 tickets, you are happy to get a bargain. You are even happier to get a chance to go to the game because tickets are in short supply.

Next month, while reviewing the financial statements for your department, you are unable to find the $40 of cash receipts for these tickets. Since you know that the firm has purchased these tickets, you wonder what happened to your $40 payment. After discussing this matter with several other junior staff members who had also paid the partner for tickets to Rockies' games, you guess that the partner has pocketed the money and not reported the revenue to the other partners.

REQUIRED

a. What should/would you do? Why?
b. Would it make any difference if the firm was a single proprietorship, and not a partnership? Why?
c. Would it make any difference if all the partners followed the same procedure and pocketed the ticket money? Why?
d. Is this an issue that should be reported to any other parties, e.g., the Internal Revenue Service, the State Auditor, the Attorney General, etc.? Why?

Conceptual Discussion: Choosing Accounting Principles

1–22 The Homestead Furniture Store has just begun selling a new line of inventory. Management must now decide on an inventory method to use. Method A results in higher net income and higher assets than method B. Method A is more costly to implement. What advice would you give to the chief executive officer?

Critical Essay: Users of Accounting Information

1–23 Write a short essay describing how information requirements might differ between internal and external users of accounting.

Conceptual Discussion: Historical Information Versus Forecasts

1–24 Some members of the financial community believe that annual reports should not only contain historical financial statements, but should also contain forecasts by management of future results. Evaluate this proposal.

Reporting Errors in Wages

1–25 At the end of every year, all employers send W–2 forms to their employees. These forms report the employees' wages and the amount of tax withheld by the employer. These forms are the government's only record of earned wages. Assume that an employee receives a W–2 form that understates the wages but correctly states the withholding amount. Ethically, how should the employee handle this situation?

WHAT WOULD
YOU DO?

Critical Essay or Discussion: Identifying Useful Information

1–26 The auditor's report, e.g., Exhibit 1–10, contains much useful information. Write a short essay, or form small groups in your class, discussing the kinds of information you think that auditors should provide. You may identify specific kinds of information that you think would be helpful to an investor or creditor. Indicate why you think such information would be helpful.

Personal Experience: Uses of Accounting Information

1–27 Describe two ways that you have already used accounting information in your personal decisions.

Critical Essay: Expectations and Uses of Accounting Information

1–28 Write a short essay indicating how you might use accounting in a professional capacity after you graduate.

Critical Essay: Changes in Accounting Disclosure Requirements

1–29 The accounting profession is considering increasing its required disclosures and the type of information that is required from public companies. The following paragraphs appeared in *The Wall Street Journal* (August 26, 1993, p. A4):

> A key accounting group calls for a sharp increase in the amount of information companies must disclose in their annual reports. The prospect alarms corporate financial officers.
>
> If adopted, the recommendations could force companies to change the way they figure profits. It could make them disclose more data about the competitive pressures they face. They could transform the auditor's report from the current boiler-plate message to a longer and much more revealing statement about the company's health. Information about changes in the firm's product prices in response to competitive price shifts would be required.
>
> The new requirements would favor more segmenting of data so that sales and profits for each company unit would be shown. More meaningful breakdowns of company data would be required. Much more data would be required from larger companies, than from small companies.

REQUIRED

a. Write a short memo from a company president in response to the proposed changes in accounting disclosures.

Critical Essay: Changing How Profits Are Measured

1–30 An accounting group has called for new definitions of earnings or profits. These changes might include the following:

- Reporting core and comprehensive earnings, along with net income for the company. This could result in three separate profit numbers for most companies.
- Core profits would include only continuing operations and would eliminate revenues from the sale of part of the company.
- Comprehensive earnings would include external market effects of changes in the value of foreign currency and changes in the prices of investments (shares) in other companies.

REQUIRED

a. Write a short essay supporting or criticizing these proposed changes in the definitions of income or profit.

USING FINANCIAL ACCOUNTING ON THE INTERNET

1–31 Bowling Green State University maintains a "Directory of CPA Firms" with World Wide Web pages at these two sites:

www.cba.bgsu.edu/amis/cpafirms
www.cba.bgsu.edu/amis/cpafirms.html

Access this page and locate the site for Ernst & Young, a Big Six accounting firm.

REQUIRED

a. List six countries (other than the United States, Canada, and the United Kingdom) where Ernst and Young (E&Y) has a presence.
b. On a worldwide basis, list the services that E&Y member firms can provide to their clients, and list the industries on which E&Y focuses.
c. In the United States, list the services that E&Y member firms can provide to their clients, and list the industries on which E&Y focuses.
d. Within the United States, name the career paths available at E&Y.
e. The E&Y office nearest to your university is located in which city?

1–32 Go to the home page of the United States Securities and Exchange Commission (SEC) located at:

www.sec.gov/

REQUIRED

a. Briefly describe the role of the SEC. Which laws does it enforce?
b. How many commissioners sit on the board of the SEC? Who is the current chairperson of the SEC? Who has the authority to appoint the chairperson?
c. List three cities where regional or district offices of the SEC are located. (*Hint:* Washington, D.C., is not a regional or district office.)
d. Name the principal divisions of the SEC.

1–33 Find out more about a career in accounting by pointing to Ohio State University's home page containing information on "Careers in Finance, Accounting and Consulting," one of the pages located at:

www.cob.ohio-state.edu/dept/acctmis/students/careers.html

REQUIRED

a. List the key job functions in accounting.
b. List the key job skills required for a career in accounting.
c. List the key job contexts in accounting.

1–34 Certifications in accounting include the Certificate of Public Accounting (CPA), Certificate of Internal Auditing (CIA), and Certificate of Management Accounting (CMA). Certification examinations must be passed before gaining these professional qualifications. Identify the subject areas covered in each exam.

Exam	Site
CPA	**www.ais-cpa.com**
CIA	**www.rutgers.edu/Accounting/raw/iia**
CMA	**www.rutgers.edu/Accounting/raw/ima/ima.htm**

CHAPTER 2

BASIC CONCEPTS OF FINANCIAL ACCOUNTING

INTRODUCTION

This chapter describes the financial accounting process. It shows how information about transactions and events is accumulated to produce the balance sheet and the income statement. This early presentation is quite basic; subsequent chapters will present more complex issues. Also, although the cash flow effects of various transactions are addressed in this chapter, the statement of cash flows is actually covered in detail in Chapter 5.

THE BASIC ACCOUNTING EQUATION

Refer to Exhibit 2–1, which illustrates the balance sheet. Balance sheets contain three sections: assets, liabilities, and owners' equity. The total of the left side (assets) equals the total of the right side (liabilities and owners' equity).

Financial accounting is based on one simple, three-element equation, referred to as the **basic accounting equation:**

$$\text{ASSETS} = \text{LIABILITIES} + \text{OWNERS' EQUITY}$$

The basic accounting equation is simply an algebraic form of the balance sheet. The following sections elaborate on the definitions of the equation's elements.

Assets

Assets are valuable resources that are owned by a firm. They represent probable future economic benefits and arise as the result of past transactions or events. Examples of assets include cash, accounts receivable (the right to receive cash in the future), inventory (merchandise manufactured or acquired for resale to customers), equipment, land, and investments.

EXHIBIT 2–1
A BALANCE SHEET

Newton Company
Balance Sheet
December 31, 1997

Assets		Liabilities and Owners' Equity	
Cash	$ 5,000	Liabilities	
Accounts receivable	7,000	Accounts payable	$ 8,000
Inventory	10,000	Notes payable	2,000
Equipment	7,000	Total liabilities	10,000
		Owners' equity	19,000
Total assets	$29,000	Total liabilities and owners' equity	$29,000

Two aspects of the definition deserve emphasis. First, the term *probable* suggests that in some situations accountants are not certain that future economic benefits exist. For example, many business owners feel that a loyal customer base and a highly skilled workforce enhance a firm's competitive advantage. While few would argue with this position, the link in any particular situation between customer loyalty or workforce skill and future benefits is sufficiently uncertain that these factors are not recognized as assets.

Second, assets must be owned by the firm. This component of the definition is designed to exclude public goods from balance sheets. For example, although many firms benefit from roadways, sewers, national defense, and the public education system, these items are not owned by individual firms. Because of this, they do not appear on balance sheets of individual firms.

Liabilities

Liabilities are present obligations of the firm. They are probable future sacrifices of economic benefits (usually cash) that arise as the result of past transactions or events. Common examples of liabilities are notes payable (written obligations), accounts payable (obligations to suppliers arising in the normal course of business), and taxes payable.

Two aspects of the definition of liabilities need elaboration. First, as with assets, the term *probable* is used. This is an important part of the definition. While in some instances the existence of a liability is virtually certain (as when one arises from obtaining a bank loan), other situations are less clear. For example, consider a firm that has been sued. At the inception of the suit, the outcome may be highly uncertain. However, as the litigation proceeds, it may seem more likely (but not certain) that the firm will be forced to pay some amount. Accountants need to exercise judgment in determining the existence of a liability. They do so by assessing whether a potential future sacrifice is probable.

Second, the definition requires that liabilities arise from past transactions or events. Consider a definition that did not include this criterion. Most firms expect to be in existence for a considerable period of time. They anticipate employing workers, buying inventory, and so on. These planned activities may well result in probable future sacrifices of economic benefits. However, the organization is not obliged to make those payments until a transaction has occurred.

Because of the "past transaction" criterion, financial accounting does not reflect **executory contracts.** These are contracts that initially involve merely an exchange of promises. For example, in 1993, David Letterman signed a three-year contract to host a late night show for the Columbia Broadcasting System (CBS). The contract stipulated that Letterman's compensation for each year was to be $14 million. At the time of contract signing, a substantive exchange had not taken place. Neither side had actually done anything. Letterman had not yet hosted the shows, and CBS had not provided payment. This type of contract is not incorporated in the financial accounting process. Subsequently, when one or both parties have performed, a substantive exchange has occurred, and then it is appropriate to reflect the transaction in the financial statements.

Owners' Equity

Owners' equity represents the owners' interest in the assets of the business. Owners can obtain an interest in their business either by making direct investments or by operating the business at a profit and retaining the profits in the firm.

Owners' equity is also referred to as the **residual interest,** a term that implies the owners' interest is what remains after creditors' claims have been honored. This can most easily be seen by rearranging the basic accounting equation:

$$\text{OWNERS' EQUITY} = \text{ASSETS} - \text{LIABILITIES}$$

This version of the equation suggests that at a given point in time, the accountant measures a firm's assets and liabilities. If assets exceed liabilities, the excess (residual) amount is attributed to the owners. Other terms used to refer to assets minus liabilities are **net assets** and **net worth.**

The balance sheet and the original form of the basic accounting equation can be interpreted as providing two views of the business. The left side details the composition of the firm's assets: cash, inventory, and the like. It shows "what the firm has." The right side indicates the amount of financing supplied by the creditors and the amount supplied by the owners. It shows how assets were acquired. It also shows the extent to which the creditors and the owners have a claim against the assets. This will become clearer after you study the next section on transaction analysis.

Transaction analysis is the central component of the financial accounting process. During this phase, the accountant identifies transactions (exchanges with other organizations), assigns monetary values (usually an exchange amount), and records the

TRANSACTION ANALYSIS

effects of the transactions on the three elements of the basic accounting equation. The remainder of this section analyzes a number of transactions.

Owners' Original Investment

Harry Jacobs has decided to open a golf and tennis store. The business is organized as a sole proprietorship. Sole proprietorships are businesses owned and operated by one individual. Keep in mind that we are concerned about the records of Harry's business; we are not interested in Harry's personal affairs. The **entity assumption** indicates that accounting records are kept for business units (entities), distinct from their owners.

Harry opens a bank account in the name of the business, Jacobs Golf and Tennis (JG&T), and deposits $50,000 of his own money. From the firm's perspective, the $50,000 deposit is a transaction (an exchange between the business and its owner), and it would be analyzed by increasing cash and owners' equity by $50,000 each. Increasing owners' equity indicates that the owner has invested $50,000 and that he has an interest in or claim against the assets to the extent of $50,000. The word **capital** is conventional terminology in sole proprietorships. It simply denotes the owners' interest in (or claim on) the assets of the business.

	ASSETS	=	LIABILITIES	+	OWNERS' EQUITY
	Cash				H. Jacobs, capital
(1)	+$50,000				+$50,000

Notice that the equation balances for this transaction, as it does for all transactions.

Exhibit 2–2, shown later, contains a summary of all the transactions to be reviewed in this section. For simplicity, assume all transactions occur on January 1, 1998.

Bank Loan

Harry realizes that his new business needs more cash than the $50,000 he invested. The firm applies for and is granted a $20,000 bank loan. The loan carries an interest rate of 8%, and both principal and interest are due on January 1, 1999.

This transaction increases cash and liabilities by $20,000. Liabilities increase because JG&T is obligated to repay the loan in the future; this constitutes a virtually certain sacrifice of future economic benefits. Additionally, the obligation has arisen as the result of a past transaction (i.e., having obtained the cash on January 1, 1998). The liability item that increases is notes payable. Banks usually require borrowers to sign written promises to repay loans, and the word **notes** indicates that JG&T has a written obligation to repay the loan.

	ASSETS	=	LIABILITIES	+	OWNERS' EQUITY
	Cash		Notes payable		
(2)	+$20,000		+$20,000		

The equation balances for this transaction, too. Since the equality holds for all transactions, it holds for the sum of all transactions. After the first two transactions, JG&T has cash of $70,000, which equals liabilities of $20,000 plus owners' equity of $50,000.

You might be wondering about the interest on the loan. Interest is a charge for borrowing money during a specified period of time. Since this time period has just begun, no interest is immediately recorded. As you will see, interest is recorded periodically throughout the life of the loan.

Rent

JG&T enters into an agreement to lease retail space from another company. The lease is for one year, and the entire $12,000 rent is paid on January 1, 1998, the date the lease is signed. Cash obviously declines by $12,000. However, what other equation item is affected? JG&T has acquired another asset, the right to occupy the retail space for a year. This will enable JG&T to carry on its normal business operations. The asset is referred to as **prepaid rent,** and is assigned a value equal to its **historical cost** (exchange price on the date of acquisition). *Assets are usually recorded at their historical cost.*

	ASSETS		=	LIABILITIES	+	OWNERS' EQUITY
	Cash	Prepaid rent				
(3)	−$12,000	+$12,000				

Inventory

Inventory is merchandise acquired for resale to customers. It is an asset because firms expect to receive cash from selling it to customers.

JG&T is in the business of buying and selling sporting goods. Assume JG&T purchases goods for $30,000. The purchase is **on account** (on credit). This transaction increases inventory, and since payment is not made immediately, liabilities increase. Because notes are not used for ongoing purchases from suppliers, another liability item, **accounts payable,** is increased. Accounts payable are unwritten obligations that arise in the normal course of business.

	ASSETS	=	LIABILITIES	+	OWNERS' EQUITY
	Inventory		Accounts payable		
(4)	+$30,000		+$30,000		

Equipment

Because the retail space that JG&T leased contains no equipment (cash registers, display cases, etc.), equipment must be purchased. JG&T makes a purchase for $25,000. Cash decreases, equipment increases, and total assets are unchanged.

	ASSETS	=	LIABILITIES	+	OWNERS' EQUITY
	Cash	Equipment			
(5)	−$25,000	+$25,000			

Preparation of the Balance Sheet

The last two lines in Exhibit 2–2 reflect the cumulative effect of JG&T's transactions. This summary is equivalent to the balance sheet. To prepare a balance sheet, simply summarize the various equation elements into the appropriate balance sheet format. The balance sheet for JG&T as of January 1, 1998, is shown in Exhibit 2–3, but the important information used in preparing the balance sheet is contained in the last two lines of Exhibit 2–2.

EXHIBIT 2–2 TRANSACTION ANALYSIS

	ASSETS				LIABILITIES		OWNERS' EQUITY
	Cash	Prepaid Rent	Inventory	Equipment	Accounts Payable	Notes Payable	H. Jacobs, Capital
(1)	+50,000						+50,000
(2)	+20,000					+20,000	
(3)	−12,000	+12,000					
(4)			+30,000		+30,000		
(5)	−25,000			+25,000			
Totals	33,000	12,000	30,000	25,000	30,000	20,000	50,000
		100,000				100,000	

Evaluation of Historical Cost

An asset's historical cost is a very good indication of its economic value to the firm at the time of acquisition. As times goes on, however, the historical cost becomes outdated. That is, it no longer reflects the asset's economic value.

Instead of valuing assets at historical cost, accountants could use other measures. For example, current replacement cost could be used. Current replacement cost is the cost of replacing the asset on the balance sheet date. Many analysts feel that this amount better reflects the value of an asset to the firm. They feel that current replacement cost is more *relevant* to financial statement readers.

Why, then, does financial accounting use historical cost? Primarily because it is *reliable*. Historical cost is the result of an actual bargained transaction between two independent parties. Moreover, supporting documents, such as canceled checks, contracts,

**Jacobs Golf and Tennis
Balance Sheet
January 1, 1998**

Assets		Liabilities and Owners' Equity	
Cash	$ 33,000	Liabilities	
Prepaid rent	12,000	Accounts payable	$ 30,000
Inventory	30,000	Notes payable	20,000
Equipment	25,000	Total liabilities	50,000
Total assets	$100,000	H. Jacobs, capital	50,000
		Total liabilities and	
		owners' equity	$100,000

EXHIBIT 2–3
JG&T BALANCE SHEET

or invoices, exist to verify the amount. In contrast, current replacement cost is based on appraisals and estimates, which accountants view as "soft" numbers. In general, the accounting profession believes that use of historical cost provides the best trade-off between relevance and reliability.

REVENUES AND EXPENSES

The transactions examined thus far are related to start-up activities. Businesses are organized to earn a profit, and this section discusses revenue and expense transactions. All transactions reviewed in this section are summarized in Exhibit 2–4.

 ### Revenues

Revenues are inflows of assets (or reductions in liabilities) in exchange for providing goods and services to customers. Suppose during January JG&T provides services (golf lessons) to customers and charges them $600. The customers pay $200 immediately and agree to pay the remaining $400 in February. This transaction meets both aspects of the preceding definition. First, JG&T has received assets of $600. The receipt of the $200 is obviously an asset inflow. The $400 to be received next month is also an asset and is called an **account receivable.** Second, the services were provided by the end of January. That is, they have been earned; JG&T has done everything it has promised to do. Accordingly, revenue of $600 is recorded in January.

This transaction increases cash by $200, accounts receivable by $400, and owners' equity by $600. Why has owners' equity increased by $600? The assets of the business have expanded, and it must be decided who has a claim against or an interest in those assets. Since this transaction has not increased the creditors' claims, the owners' interests must have increased. This conclusion makes sense. Owners are the primary risk-takers, and they do so with the hope of expanding their wealth. If the firm enters into a profitable transaction, the owners' wealth (their interest in the business) should expand.

EXHIBIT 2–4 REVENUE AND EXPENSE TRANSACTIONS

	ASSETS					LIABILITIES				OWNERS' EQUITY	
	Cash	Accts. Receivable	Prepaid Rent	Inventory	Equipment	Accts. Payable	Notes Payable	Unearned Revenue	Util. Payable	H. Jacobs, Capital	
Bal	33,000	0	12,000	30,000	25,000	30,000	20,000	0	0	50,000	
(6)	+200	+400								+600	(service revenue)
(7)	+100							+100			
(8)	−700									−700	(salary expense)
(9)									+120	−120	(utility expense)
(10)		+4,000		−2,200						+4,000	(sales revenue)
										−2,200	(cost of goods sold)
Totals	32,600	4,400	12,000	27,800	25,000	30,000	20,000	100	120	51,580	

101,800   101,800   101,800

	ASSETS		=	LIABILITIES	+	OWNERS' EQUITY
	Cash	Accounts receivable				H. Jacobs, capital
(6)	+$200	+$400				+$600 (service revenue)

Of course, we cannot be absolutely certain that the customers will eventually pay the additional $400. This concern will be addressed in a subsequent chapter. For now, assume we are quite confident about this future receipt.

This transaction holds an important lesson. Although revenue equals $600, only $200 of cash has been received. Thus, from an accounting perspective, revenue does *not* necessarily equal cash inflow. Although revenue is recorded when assets are received in exchange for goods and services, the asset received need not be cash. This underscores the need for both an income statement to summarize earnings and a statement of cash flows to identify the sources and uses of cash.

As another illustration, assume that on January 10 a customer pays $100, in advance, for golf lessons. The lessons are to be rendered during the last week in January and the first week in February. Has a revenue transaction occurred on January 10? No. A requirement for revenue recognition is that the services must be rendered. As of January 10, this has not yet occurred. The transaction increases cash, but the owners' claim on assets has not increased. Instead, the *customer* now has a claim on the assets. If JG&T does not provide the lessons, the customer has the right to expect a refund. JG&T has a liability. It is obligated to either provide the lessons, which have a $100 value, or return the $100 payment. In either case, a $100 liability exists on January 10. **Unearned revenue** is the liability that has increased. Another appropriate name is **advances from customers.**

	ASSETS	=	LIABILITIES	+	OWNERS' EQUITY
	Cash		Unearned revenue		
(7)	+$100		+$100		

Reality Check 2–1 illustrates a revenue situation in the franchising industry.

Expenses

Expenses occur when resources are consumed in order to generate revenue. For example, during January JG&T employed salespersons and golf instructors. Assume these employees earned total wages of $700, which were paid in cash by JG&T. Since JG&T used the employees' services during January, this is an expense transaction for that month.

The transaction decreases cash and owners' equity by $700. The decrease in cash is obvious. Why does owners' equity decrease? An analogy can be drawn to revenue. When assets increase because of profitable operations, the owners' interest in the firm's assets expands. With expenses, when assets decrease in order to generate revenue, the owners' interest in the firm's assets declines.

FRANCHISING

Franchisors are firms that sell the right to market their products. McDonald's Corporation, for example, sells the right to operate its restaurants to other businesses and individuals. These franchisees usually pay a fee at the time of signing the contract, plus ongoing fees based on the amount of their sales.

In exchange for the initial fee at the time of contract signing, a franchisor is required to help the franchisee select an appropriate site, supervise construction, train employees, and install the franchisee's accounting system.

REQUIRED

When should the franchisor recognize the revenue associated with the initial fee?

	ASSETS	=	LIABILITIES	+	OWNERS' EQUITY
	Cash				H. Jacobs, capital
(8)	−$700				−$700 (salary expense)

Exhibit 2–5 graphically depicts this analysis. The first rectangle reflects JG&T's assets, liabilities, and owners' equity before the salary expense transaction. The second rectangle reflects the situation after the expense transaction. Assets and the owners' claim have both decreased.

Consider another example. Assume JG&T receives its utility bill on January 31 for electricity used during January. The bill is for $120. JG&T elects not to pay immediately. Even though cash has not been paid, an expense transaction has occurred in January. JG&T has consumed resources (electricity) in order to generate revenue.

Since JG&T is now obligated to the utility company, liabilities increase by $120, and owners' equity decreases by $120. Owners' equity decreases because assets have not changed, yet the creditors' claims have increased by $120. There is no alternative but to recognize that owners' equity has decreased by $120.

EXHIBIT 2–5
EXPENSE TRANSACTION
ANALYSIS

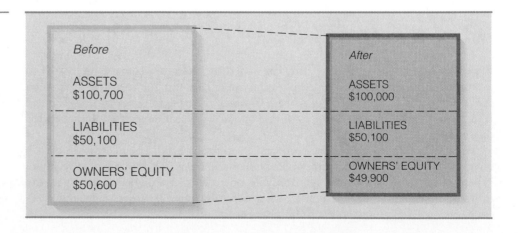

	ASSETS	=	LIABILITIES	+	OWNERS' EQUITY
			Utilities payable		H. Jacobs, capital
(9)			+$120		−$120 (utility expense)

Exhibit 2–6 displays the analysis graphically. It shows the assets remaining fixed while (1) the creditors' claims increase and (2) the owners' claims decrease. Also note that expenses do not necessarily equal cash outflows. Goods and services can be consumed to generate revenue without a cash outflow.

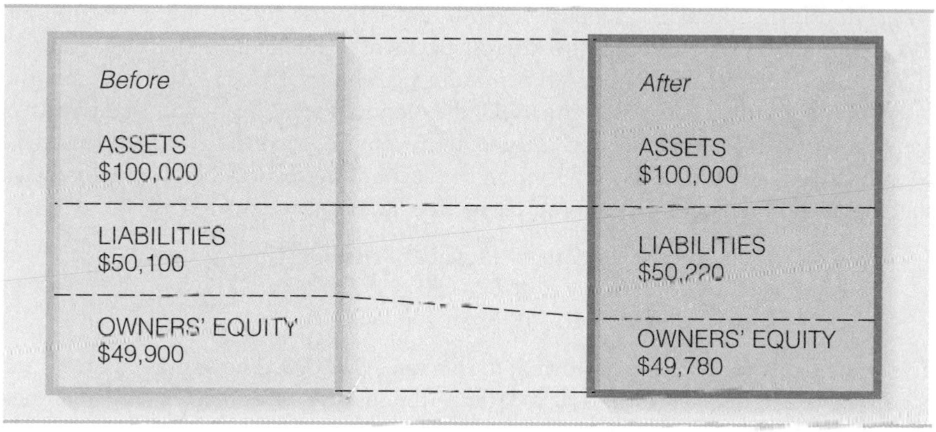

EXHIBIT 2–6
EXPENSE TRANSACTION ANALYSIS

Before

ASSETS
$100,000

LIABILITIES
$50,100

OWNERS' EQUITY
$49,900

After

ASSETS
$100,000

LIABILITIES
$50,220

OWNERS' EQUITY
$49,780

Sales of Inventory

Sales of inventory contain both revenue and expense components. Assume JG&T makes sales on account (credit) during the month totaling $4,000. The cost of the inventory to JG&T was $2,200.

A revenue transaction exists because an asset (accounts receivable) has been obtained, and the goods have been provided to customers. An expense transaction exists because the asset inventory has been consumed to generate the revenue. That is, JG&T has fewer assets because the inventory has been transferred to its customers. This expense is called **cost of goods sold (CGS)**. The net increase in assets and owners' equity is $1,800.

	ASSETS		=	LIABILITIES	+	OWNERS' EQUITY
	Accounts receivable	Inventory				H. Jacobs, capital
(10)	+$4,000					+$4,000 (sales revenue)
		−$2,200				−$2,200 (cost of goods sold)

ADJUSTMENTS

At the end of January, Harry Jacobs wishes to prepare a balance sheet and an income statement. Before doing so, several adjustments must be made to the accounting records. These adjustments are necessary because certain events do not have normally occurring source documents, such as sales tickets or checks, to trigger their accounting recognition. At the end of each period (usually each month or year), the accountant undertakes a deliberate search to identify and record these items. All adjustments reviewed in this section are summarized in Exhibit 2–7.

Interest

As previously mentioned, on January 1, 1998, JG&T borrowed $20,000 at 8% interest (on an annual basis). Although the interest payment is not required until January 1, 1999, JG&T has incurred interest expense during January 1998. During that month, JG&T has consumed a resource: the use of the money. The utilization of that resource has enabled JG&T to operate and to generate revenues. Accordingly, an expense has been incurred, and it must be reflected in the accounting records before the financial statements are prepared. The interest charge for January is calculated as

$$\begin{aligned}
\text{Interest expense} &= \text{Principal} \times \text{Rate} \times \text{Time} \\
&= \$20,000 \times .08 \times \tfrac{1}{12} \\
&= \$133 \text{ (rounded)}
\end{aligned}$$

The principal is the amount borrowed, in this case, $20,000. The annual interest rate is 8%. Stated in decimal form, it is .08. Since the interest rate is stated on an annual basis, the time period must be expressed similarly. Given that one month has elapsed, the time period is $\tfrac{1}{12}$ of a year.

The general form of the analysis is similar to the earlier utility bill situation. Because the bank's services (use of the bank's money) have been consumed, JG&T has an additional obligation (interest payable) in the amount of $133. Further, since assets have remained constant and liabilities have increased, owners' equity must decrease.

	ASSETS	=	LIABILITIES	+	OWNERS' EQUITY
			Interest payable		H. Jacobs, capital
(11)			+$133		−$133 (interest expense)

WHAT WOULD YOU DO?

In 1993, Woolworth Corporation experienced some accounting irregularities. Although its yearly results were accurate, Woolworth initially reported quarterly figures that subsequently needed to be restated. An investigation into this matter determined that senior management created an environment that prompted the inaccurate reporting. Senior management placed great emphasis on never reporting a quarterly loss.

One way in which reporting a quarterly loss might be avoided is by delaying expense recognition. At the end of any quarter, a corporation will have consumed resources (say, utilities or interest) for which it has not made payment. By overlooking these expenses during the adjustment process, reported quarterly net income can be increased. Of course, when these payments are made, the next quarter's net income will be decreased.

Imagine that you work for a large corporation whose senior managers are quite intent on never reporting a quarterly loss. Assume you supervise the quarterly adjustment process. What would you do if the chief executive officer and the chief financial officer instructed you to delay recognizing some expenses for the most recent quarter?

Rent

On January 1, JG&T paid a year's rent in advance. The amount was $12,000, and an asset (prepaid rent) was appropriately recorded. By January 31, one month of the payment has been consumed; thus, an expense should be reflected in the accounting records. The analysis is

	ASSETS	=	LIABILITIES	+	OWNERS' EQUITY
	Prepaid rent				H. Jacobs, capital
(12)	−$1,000				$1,000 (rent expense)

Depreciation

On January 1, JG&T purchased equipment for $25,000. As you recall, this transaction increased the asset equipment. Assume the estimated life of the equipment is 10 years, at which time it will be worthless. Since the service potential of the equipment will be consumed over the course of its 10-year life, the cost of the equipment should be charged as an expense over that period. This expense is referred to as **depreciation.** Monthly depreciation expense is calculated as:

$$\text{Depreciation expense} = \frac{\text{Historical cost (less anticipated salvage value)}}{\text{Number of months in the useful life}}$$

$$= \frac{\$25,000}{120}$$

$$= \$208 \text{ (rounded)}$$

Note that the estimated salvage amount, at the end of an estimated useful life, is included in this depreciation calculation.

Because the service potential of the equipment has declined, the asset's recorded value is decreased; and because an expense has been incurred, owners' equity declines.

EXHIBIT 2–7 ADJUSTMENTS AND OWNER WITHDRAWAL

	ASSETS					LIABILITIES					OWNERS' EQUITY	
	Cash	Accts. Rec.	Prepaid Rent	Inventory	Equip.	Accts. Pay.	Notes Pay.	Unearned Revenue	Util. Pay.	Interest Pay.	H. Jacobs, Capital	
Bal	32,600	4,400	12,000	27,800	25,000	30,000	20,000	100	120		51,580	
(11)										+133	–133	(interest expense)
(12)			–1,000								–1,000	(rent expense)
(13)					–208						–208	(depreciation expense)
(14)								–50			+50	(service revenue)
(15)	–100										–100	(withdrawal)
Totals	32,500	4,400	11,000	27,800	24,792	30,000	20,000	50	120	133	50,189	
			100,492								100,492	

ASSETS	=	LIABILITIES	+	OWNERS' EQUITY
Equipment				H. Jacobs, capital
(13) −$208				−$208 (depreciation expense)

⬒ Unearned Revenue

On January 10, JG&T received a $100 advance payment from a customer for golf lessons to be delivered during the last week of January and the first week in February. At that time, cash increased, as did a liability, unearned revenue. Assume one-half of the lessons were given in January. An adjustment to the accounting records is now required because (1) JG&T's obligation to its customer has declined by $50, and (2) $50 of revenue has been earned. Revenue is now recognized because assets have already increased and the services have now been provided. Since $50 of revenue has been earned, owners' equity increases.

ASSETS	=	LIABILITIES	+	OWNERS' EQUITY
		Unearned revenue		H. Jacobs, capital
(14)		−$50		+$50 (service revenue)

Assume Harry withdraws $100 from JG&T's bank account on January 31 so that he can pay some personal living expenses. Since Harry worked in the shop during the month, the withdrawal could be viewed as an expense to the business (i.e., Harry's salary). However, because the owner of a sole proprietorship cannot really establish an independent relationship with the business, the "salary" amount does not have a great deal of reliability. For example, Harry could simply withdraw amounts based on his personal needs, rather than on the value of the services he contributed to the business. Because of this, owner withdrawals are not viewed as salary expense. Instead, they are considered to be capital transactions, which involve investments or disinvestments by the owner. Thus, the analysis is exactly the opposite of a contribution by the owner.

WITHDRAWAL BY OWNER

ASSETS	=	LIABILITIES	+	OWNERS' EQUITY
Cash				H. Jacobs, capital
(15) −$100				−$100 (withdrawal)

Note that four types of transactions affect owners' equity:

1. owner contributions,
2. owner withdrawals,
3. revenues, and
4. expenses.

FINANCIAL STATEMENTS

All transactions and events for JG&T have now been properly recorded. The accounting records are correct and up to date, so they can be used to prepare the financial statements.

The Balance Sheet

The cumulative effect of all transactions and events on the various equation items is shown in the last two lines of Exhibit 2–7. The **balance sheet** is prepared by simply rearranging the numbers so that they appear in the proper format. The balance sheet as of January 31 appears in Exhibit 2–8. Each item on the balance sheet is often referred to as an **account.**

Note the date on the balance sheet: January 31. All balance sheets summarize a firm's assets, liabilities, and owners' equity at a discrete point in time.

EXHIBIT 2–8
JG&T BALANCE SHEET

Jacobs Golf and Tennis
Balance Sheet
January 31, 1998

Assets		Liabilities and Owners' Equity	
Cash	$ 32,500	Liabilities	
Accounts receivable	4,400	Accounts payable	$ 30,000
Prepaid rent	11,000	Unearned revenue	50
Inventory	27,800	Utilities payable	120
Equipment	24,792	Interest payable	133
Total assets	$100,492	Notes payable	20,000
		Total liabilities	50,303
		H. Jacobs, capital	50,189
		Total liabilities and owners' equity	$100,492

The Income Statement

The **income statement** summarizes a firm's revenues and expenses for a period of time. The income statement for JG&T for the month of January appears in Exhibit 2–9.

The income statement is prepared by compiling information from the owners' equity account. Recall that all revenue transactions increase owners' equity and that all expense transactions reduce owners' equity. This makes owners' equity a convenient place to look for information about revenues and expenses. To help you see that JG&T's income statement summarizes its revenue and expense transactions for the month of January, Exhibit 2–10 summarizes all of JG&T's transactions for that month.

Jacobs Golf and Tennis
Income Statement
For the Month Ended January 31, 1998

Revenue		
Sales	$4,000	
Service	650	
Total revenue		$4,650
Expenses		
Cost of goods sold	2,200	
Rent	1,000	
Salary	700	
Depreciation	208	
Interest	133	
Utilities	120	
Total expenses		4,361
Net income		$ 289

EXHIBIT 2–9
JG&T INCOME STATEMENT

An alternative method that can be used to prepare the income statement would be to examine asset and liability accounts. However, such an approach would be much more cumbersome. For example, some revenue transactions affect cash, other revenue transactions affect accounts receivable, and still others affect unearned revenue. Thus, the information about revenue transactions appears in a variety of asset and liability accounts. Moreover, many nonrevenue transactions affect assets and liabilities, complicating the identification of revenue transactions. An easier approach is simply to examine owners' equity. A similar argument can be made for expenses.

Care must be taken, however, not to include in the income statement all transactions that affect owners' equity. Direct contributions by owners increase owners' equity, but they do not constitute revenue. Similarly, withdrawals by owners reduce owners' equity, but they are not viewed as expenses.

The income statement provides financial statement readers with information about the profitability of the organization for a past period of time. It indicates how successful the organization was in generating revenues and controlling costs. During January, JG&T earned a net income of $289. While this amount might not seem very impressive in light of total revenues of $4,650 and an investment of $50,000 by Harry, January was JG&T's first month of operation. Simply operating above breakeven (a zero profit or loss) is an accomplishment.

Within the context of a large corporation, an income statement can also be thought of as a report on management's performance. One of management's major responsibilities is to enhance shareholder wealth. Managers serve as agents of the shareholders, and they must be held accountable for their performance. Since profitable operations are essential to adding value to the firm, the income statement can be used to assess how well managers have performed.

Reported net income is an extremely useful figure to investors and plays a major role in their decisions. To illustrate, when the Aluminum Company of America reported healthy first quarter earnings in 1992, the value of the company's stock on the New York Stock Exchange surged $5.75 per share (8.5%). On the other hand, Digital

EXHIBIT 2–10 TRANSACTION ANALYSIS SUMMARY

	ASSETS					LIABILITIES					OWNERS' EQUITY	
	Cash	Accts. Rec.	Prepaid Rent	Inventory	Equip.	Accts. Pay.	Notes Pay.	Unearned Revenue	Util. Pay.	Interest Pay.	H. Jacobs, Capital	
(1)	+50,000										+50,000	
(2)	+20,000						+20,000					
(3)	−12,000		+12,000									
(4)				+30,000		+30,000						
(5)	−25,000				+25,000							
(6)	+200	+400									+600	(service revenue)
(7)	+100							+100				
(8)	−700										−700	(salary expense)
(9)									+120		−120	(utility expense)
(10)		+4,000		−2,200							+4,000	(sales revenue)
											−2,200	(cost of goods sold)
(11)										+133	−133	(interest expense)
(12)			−1,000								−1,000	(rent expense)
(13)					−208						−208	(depreciation expense)
(14)								−50			+50	(service revenue)
(15)	−100										−100	(withdrawal)
Totals	32,500	4,400	11,000	27,800	24,792	30,000	20,000	50	120	133	50,189	
	100,492					100,492						

Equipment Corporation's stock plunged $5.25 per share (9.8%) on the day it reported a $294,100,000 loss for the quarter ended March 28, 1992.

Note that income statements are prepared for periods of time, usually a month, quarter, or year. Income must be related to a specific period of time to be interpretable. For example, assume you apply for a job and are told the job pays $5,000. An evaluation of the job's desirability would be impossible without knowing if you would earn $5,000 per week, month, year, or some other time period. For this reason, the income statement in Exhibit 2–9 contains the caption "For the Month Ended January 31, 1998."

Many firms prepare income statements for calendar years, that is, for the period January 1 through December 31. Other firms use 12-month periods that do not end on December 31. These firms usually select an ending date that corresponds to a low point in their activity. For example, many clothing stores, such as The GAP, have **fiscal years** that run from February 1 through January 31. January 31 is selected as the end of the fiscal year because it shortly follows the busy holiday period and provides time for refunds and exchanges to take place.

Statement of Owners' Equity

In addition to the balance sheet and the income statement, firms also prepare a **statement of owners' equity.** This statement summarizes the changes that took place in owners' equity during the period under review. Since investments and withdrawals by the owners affect owners' equity, they appear on this statement. Revenue and expense transactions also affect owners' equity. Instead of listing each revenue and expense transaction separately, their difference, net income, is included on the statement of owners' equity.

Exhibit 2–11 contains JG&T's statement of owners' equity for the month of January. Now refer back to Exhibit 2–10. As you can see, the statement of owners' equity reflects all of JG&T's transactions that affected owners' equity.

Jacobs Golf and Tennis Statement of Owners' Equity For the Month Ended January 31, 1998	
Balance, January 1	$ 0
Investment by owner	50,000
Net income	289
Withdrawal by owner	(100)
Balance, January 31	$50,189

EXHIBIT 2–11
STATEMENT OF OWNERS' EQUITY

Relationship Between the Balance Sheet and the Income Statement

As you know, the balance sheet reports assets, liabilities, and owners' equity at a moment in time. The income statement summarizes revenue and expense transactions that occur during a period of time. Since revenue and expense transactions affect owners' equity, net income explains most of the change that takes place in owners' equity during a period. Contributions and withdrawals by owners also affect owners' equity. Thus, the change in owners' equity is explained by net income, owner contributions, and owner withdrawals. Since owners' equity must equal assets minus liabilities (i.e., net assets), the changes in one side of the equation must equal the changes in the other side. Therefore, changes in net income, owner contributions, and owner withdrawals also explain changes in net assets.

THE ACCRUAL BASIS OF ACCOUNTING

An important aspect of a financial accounting system is the timing of recording revenue and expense transactions. Recording a transaction in the accounting records is referred to as **recognition.** Consider JG&T's first revenue transaction in January. Customers were given golf lessons and charged $600. The customers paid $200 in January and promised to pay the remainder in February. (Keep in mind our assumption that the customers will honor this pledge.) There is little argument that at least $200 of revenue should be recorded in January. But when should the other $400 be recorded: in January when the services were provided or in February when the cash is ultimately collected?

The **accrual basis of accounting** records revenues when goods or services have been earned, regardless of when cash is received. At the time of rendering the service, JG&T has earned the revenue; the entire $600 is recognized as revenue at that time under the accrual basis. All of JG&T's previous transactions have used the accrual basis.

The **cash basis of accounting** records revenue when cash is received. Under that approach, JG&T would recognize $200 of revenue in January and $400 of revenue in February.

Let's evaluate these two approaches. Which provides the most useful information to financial statement readers? If the income statement is viewed as providing information about increases in a firm's wealth, the accrual basis seems to be the preferable approach. In January, JG&T received not only $200 in cash, but also the right to receive $400 in the future. Recording $600 of revenue in January is appropriate.

Income statements can also be viewed as reports on a firm's performance. Which number, $600 or $200, is a better indicator of JG&T's accomplishments in January? Since $600 of golf lessons were provided in January, $600 seems a better measure of accomplishment (or performance).

Now consider one of JG&T's expense transactions. During January, $120 of utility services were consumed. This amount will be paid in February. Should a $120 expense be recorded in January or February? The accrual basis records expenses when resources are consumed (regardless of when payment is made) while the cash basis records expenses when the cash is actually paid. The utility's services were used in January, and the accrual basis would record the $120 as an expense in that month. The cash basis would defer recognition until JG&T pays the utility company in the following month.

Again, let's evaluate the usefulness of the information produced by the two approaches. Consumption of the utility services took place in January. At that time, the firm's liabilities increased, and its net worth decreased. This reduction in the firm's value should be reflected in January's income statement. The accrual basis would do this. Moreover, in measuring a firm's performance, all resources consumed in generating revenue should be shown on the same income statement as that revenue. Accountants refer to this as the **matching principle.** The utility services were consumed in January to help generate the revenue reported on January's income statement. Accordingly, the accrual basis provides a better portrayal of a firm's performance.

GAAP requires the use of the accrual basis. However, as previously discussed, cash flow information is also important to financial statement readers. Accordingly, GAAP also requires the statement of cash flows, which is discussed in Chapter 5. Also note that some small businesses, which do not need audited financial statements, use the cash basis.

FORMS OF BUSINESS ORGANIZATION

Financial accounting is used by a wide variety of organizations, including businesses organized to earn a profit, not-for-profit organizations, and governmental entities. This book focuses on profit-oriented enterprises, which can be organized in one of the three ways described next.

Sole Proprietorships

Sole proprietorships are businesses that are owned by one individual and usually operated by that individual. They are not separate legal entities apart from the owner, and no special legal steps are required to launch or operate this form of business. Jane's T-shirt business, discussed in Chapter 1, would probably be organized as a sole proprietorship. As another example, if you decided to earn money by mowing lawns during the summer, your business would probably be organized as a sole proprietorship.

Since no legal procedures are needed to begin operating sole proprietorships, their primary advantage is ease of formation. The major disadvantage is unlimited legal liability. Since owners are not legally distinct from their businesses, any claims against sole proprietorships are also claims against the owners' personal assets.

Although sole proprietorships are not separate legal entities, they are accounting (or economic) entities. The **entity assumption** indicates that the actions of the owner, serving as an agent of the business, can be (and should be) separated from the personal affairs of the owner. Based on this distinction, information about the transactions of the business can be accumulated via the financial accounting process. This enables the owner to assess the status and performance of the business on a stand-alone basis.

 Partnerships

Partnerships are very similar to sole proprietorships, except that partnerships have more than one owner. Partnerships are not separate legal entities apart from their owners, but they are accounting entities. They are almost as easy to form as sole proprietorships. However, since there are multiple owners, care must be taken to specify the rights and responsibilities of each owner. This is usually done in a partnership agreement, which is a legal contract among the partners.

Corporations

Corporations differ substantially from sole proprietorships and partnerships. Corporations are separate legal entities. They are granted their right to exist by the individual states. A corporation must develop bylaws governing its operation, issue stock to its owners (i.e., shareholders) to represent their ownership interests, elect a board of directors who are responsible for the management of the corporation, pay taxes, and adhere to a variety of laws and regulations. Most large and many smaller businesses are organized as corporations.

As might be expected, forming a corporation is a relatively cumbersome and expensive process. Costs include filing fees paid to the state of incorporation, legal fees, and amounts paid for corporate records, such as stock certificates, bylaws, and so on. Corporations, unlike sole proprietorships and partnerships, must pay income taxes. Moreover, shareholders are also taxed on any dividends paid to them. Thus, corporations are subject to **double taxation.** Since sole proprietorships and partnerships are not separate legal entities, they do not pay income taxes; sole proprietors and partners include the income of their businesses on their individual income tax returns.

The corporate form of organization has certain advantages that can outweigh the costs. Perhaps the primary benefit is the limited liability offered to shareholders. Since the corporation is a legal entity, the corporation itself is responsible for its actions. While shareholders risk losing their investment, their personal assets are protected from claims against the corporation. Such is not the case for sole proprietorships and partnerships.

Hybrid Forms of Organization

Many states are now offering forms of organization that combine certain characteristics of partnerships and corporations. These forms include professional corporations, limited liability companies, and limited liability partnerships. Although an evaluation of the advantages and disadvantages of these forms of organization is beyond our scope, keep in mind that careful consideration must be given to this issue when starting a new business.

Accounting Implications

The accounting differences among these three organizational forms lie mainly in the owners' equity section of the balance sheet. The accounting for partnerships is very similar to that for sole proprietorships. Since each partner is an owner, each partner has a capital account where his or her interest in the firm is shown. The accounting for corporations is slightly more complex and is described in the following section.

ACCOUNTING FOR CORPORATIONS

Two differences exist in the accounting for owners' equity in corporations. First, since shareholders are the owners of the corporation, this section is called shareholders' equity. Second, the shareholders' equity section is divided into two subcategories.

One category is **invested capital.** It reflects the shareholders' interest in the firm that arises from direct contributions by the shareholders. For example, if Harry Jacobs had formed a corporation when he started his golf and tennis shop, his initial investment would be recorded by increasing cash and increasing the invested capital part of shareholders' equity.

ASSETS	=	LIABILITIES	+	SHAREHOLDERS' EQUITY
Cash				Invested capital
+$50,000				+$50,000

The other category of shareholders' equity is **retained earnings.** This section contains the effect of revenue and expense transactions on shareholders' equity. That is, it reflects the increase (or decrease) in the shareholders' interest in the firm that arose from operations since the firm's inception.

Consider again transaction (10) from earlier in this chapter. Inventory that was previously purchased for $2,200 was sold, on account, for $4,000. The only change in the analysis for a corporation is that the retained earnings component of shareholders' equity reflects the effect of this transaction on the shareholders' interest in the firm.

ASSETS		=	LIABILITIES	+	SHAREHOLDERS' EQUITY
Accounts receivable	Inventory				Retained earnings
+$4,000					+$4,000 (revenue)
	−$2,200				−$2,200 (cost of goods sold)

SUMMARY OF LEARNING OBJECTIVES

1. **Define the terms** *assets, liabilities,* **and** *owners' equity.*
   Assets are valuable resources owned by a firm. They represent probable future economic benefits. Liabilities are present obligations of a firm. They are probable future sacrifices of economic benefits. Owners' equity reflects the owners' interest in the firm.

2. **Explain why the balance sheet must balance.**
   The balance sheet shows two views of the same thing: the resources of the firm. The left side of the balance sheet shows the composition of a firm's resources (cash, inventory, etc.). The right side shows the amount of resources supplied by creditors and the amount supplied by owners. Since resources must be supplied by either creditors or owners, the total of the left side of the balance sheet must equal the total of the right side.

3. **Describe revenues and expenses.**
   Revenues are inflows of assets (or reductions in liabilities) in exchange for providing goods and services to customers. Expenses occur when resources are consumed in order to generate revenue.

4. Use the basic accounting equation to analyze transactions.

The basic accounting equation is

$$\text{ASSETS} = \text{LIABILITIES} + \text{OWNERS' EQUITY}$$

The financial accounting process consists of analyzing a transaction's effect on the elements of this equation. The equation balances for each transaction and for the summation of all transactions.

5. Prepare simple balance sheets and income statements.

Balance sheets are prepared by cumulating the effect of all transactions on the elements of the basic accounting equation. Income statements summarize all revenue and expense transactions that took place during a period of time. The difference between revenues and expenses is net income.

6. Describe the relationship between the balance sheet and the income statement.

Revenue and expense transactions affect owners' equity. Therefore, the income statement summarizes the impact these transactions have on the balance sheet item owners' equity.

7. Distinguish between the accrual basis and the cash basis of accounting.

The accrual basis recognizes revenues when they are earned, that is, when the goods are delivered or the service is rendered. The cash basis recognizes revenues when cash is received from the customer. The accrual basis recognizes expenses when resources are consumed. The cash basis recognizes expenses when cash is paid. The accrual basis provides a better measure of performance. GAAP requires use of the accrual basis.

8. Explain the differences between the balance sheets of sole proprietorships and those of corporations.

The primary difference involves owners' equity. In sole proprietorships, only one component of owners' equity is used; it is referred to as capital, and it reflects the owners' interests that arise from both direct contributions and profitable operations. Corporations use two components: invested capital, which reflects owners' direct contributions, and retained earnings, which show the owners' interest that arose from profits.

KEY TERMS

Account	Cash basis of accounting
Accounts payable	Corporation
Accounts receivable	Cost of goods sold (CGS)
Accrual basis of accounting	Depreciation
Advances from customers	Double taxation
Assets	Entity assumption
Balance sheet	Executory contracts
Basic accounting equation	Expenses
Capital	Fiscal year

Historical cost
Income statement
Inventory
Invested capital
Liabilities
Matching principle
Net assets
Net worth
On account
Owners' equity

Partnership
Prepaid rent
Recognition
Retained earnings
Residual interest
Revenues
Sole proprietorship
Statement of owners' equity
Unearned revenue

SOLUTION TO REALITY CHECK 2–1

Many franchisors prefer to recognize the revenue when the cash is received at the time of contract signing. This enables them to show improved performance. However, are the revenue recognition rules met at that point in time? In particular, has the franchisor performed the promised services? No, it has not. Because of this, the FASB has ruled that the revenue from the initial franchise fee cannot be recognized as revenue until all the initial services have been performed. In general, this occurs when the franchisee begins operations.

2–1 Describe each part of the basic accounting equation. Identify one example of each item or term in this equation and describe why it fits in that particular category.

2–2 Using the definition of assets in this chapter, describe why each of the following items should not be listed as an asset on the firm's balance sheet:

a. Favorable location.
b. Skilled employees.
c. Reputation for honesty and fairness.
d. Brand recognition in the market.
e. Steady customers.
f. Customers' names, addresses, and product preferences.

2–3 Discuss the concept of an executory contract.

a. Why might a firm sign such a contract?
b. How should such a contract be recorded in the firm's financial statements?

2–4 Identify two forms of business organizations, and list the major advantage and disadvantage of each.

2–5 Indicate whether each of the following statements concerning possible organization structures is true or false. If a statement is false, indicate why it is false.

a. A sole proprietorship and its owner are legally the same entity.
b. The partners in a partnership are not liable for the debts of the partnership.
c. All partners in a partnership must agree on all decisions.

d. A sole proprietorship and its owner are the same entity for financial reporting.
e. A partnership is less risky (for its owners) than a sole proprietorship.
f. Two people can form a sole proprietorship.
g. Twenty people cannot form a partnership.
h. It is more expensive to form a partnership than a sole proprietorship.
i. Any five people can, by oral agreement, form a partnership.

2–6 Indicate whether each of the following statements concerning possible organization structures, is true or false. If a statement is false, indicate why it is false.

a. A corporation and its investors are legally the same entity.
b. The shareholders of a corporation are not liable for the debts of the corporation.
c. A publicly held corporation usually sends its financial statements to all of its owners (investors).
d. A corporation is less risky (for its owners) than a partnership or sole proprietorship.
e. It is more expensive to form a corporation than a sole proprietorship.
f. Shareholders are taxed on the corporation's net income.

2–7 Define accrual accounting. Contrast accrual accounting with cash basis accounting.

2–8 Define an asset. Define a liability. When can one firm's asset be another firm's liability?

2–9 Define owners' equity. How does this differ from retained earnings? How can one firm's asset be another firm's equity?

2–10 Indicate the effects [(+) increase, (−) decrease, (0) no effect] on the accounting equation from the following transactions:

a. Owner invested cash in the business.
b. Performed services for cash.
c. Purchased equipment by signing a note payable.
d. Customers paid in advance for services to be performed.
e. Purchased a two-year insurance policy.
f. Paid employees for the period's work.
g. Purchased supplies on account.
h. Performed services referred to in part d.
i. Paid note from part c in full plus interest.
j. Recorded depreciation adjustment.

EXERCISES

Transaction Analysis

2–11 The Western Fittings Corporation began business on July 1, 1997. The following transactions occurred during its first six months:

1. Three individuals each invested $30,000 in exchange for capital stock.
2. One year's rent was paid for $12,000 on July 1.
3. On August 1, several pieces of property, plant, and equipment were purchased for $75,000 on account.

4. During the six months, clothing, boots, and accessories were purchased for $60,000 cash.
5. The corporation had sales revenue of $85,000 of which $35,000 has not yet been collected in cash.
6. The cost of the clothing, boots, and accessories sold in item 5 was $55,250.
7. Employees were paid $24,000 in wages.
8. The corporation paid utilities and telephone expenses of $5,000.

REQUIRED

a. Analyze and record the above transactions in the basic accounting equation.
b. Record the following adjustments for the six months ended December 31, 1997: rent expense and depreciation expense (assume a 10-year life and zero residual value).
c. What is the net income (loss) for the six months ended December 31, 1997?

Transaction Analysis

2–12 John Hasty opened his bakery on March 1, 1997, as a sole proprietor. The following transactions took place at the beginning of March:

1. Deposited $10,000 into a checking account in the name of the Hasty Bakery.
2. Leased a small kitchen and paid the first month's rent of $500.
3. Purchased kitchen equipment for $3,000 cash.
4. Purchased baking ingredients for $6,000 on account.
5. Obtained a $2,000, 9%, one-year loan.
6. Obtained a one-year insurance policy on the kitchen equipment. Paid the entire premium of $500.

REQUIRED

a. Analyze the above transactions for March, using the basic accounting equation.
b. Record necessary adjustments: interest expense, insurance expense, and depreciation expense (assume a 60-month life and zero residual value).
c. What additional information is needed to fully analyze Hasty Bakery results for March?

Fill in the Blanks

2–13 Find the missing elements in the following (independent) cases:

	ASSETS	=	LIABILITIES	+ SHAREHOLDERS' EQUITY
a.	$100,000		$ 30,000	?
b.	?		$450,000	$200,000
c.	$350,000		$450,000	?
d.	$675,000		?	$310,000

Fill in the Blanks

2–14 Ascertain the missing items (A, B, and C) in the following situation:

Assets, January 1	$10,000
Assets, December 31	$14,000
Liabilities, January 1	A
Liabilities, December 31	$ 7,000
Owners' equity, January 1	$ 8,000
Owners' equity, December 31	B
Owners' contributions	0
Owners' withdrawals	C
Net income	$ 2,000

Transaction Analysis

2–15 Record the following business transactions in the basic accounting equation. Use headings for Cash, Accounts Receivable, Land, Accounts Payable, Unearned revenue, Notes Payable, Invested Capital, and Retained Earnings.

   a. Three individuals each invested $70,000 in a newly formed corporation in exchange for capital stock.
   b. Paid $12,500 for land.
   c. Performed services for customers, all on account, for $24,300.
   d. Received a utility bill for $850 and immediately paid it.
   e. Received $11,200 for services not yet performed.
   f. Received a telephone bill for $650, but did not pay it yet.
   g. Borrowed $34,000 cash from a bank and signed the loan papers.
   h. Received $10,000 from customers on account.
   i. Performed the services described in part e.

Transaction Analysis: Income Statement and Balance Sheet Effects

2–16 Identify the effects of the following events on the first year's income statement and balance sheet:

   a. A company paid a $2,000 bill for a fire insurance policy that covers the current year and the next year.
   b. A company purchased for $200 a trash compactor that has an expected life of five years. What are the balance sheet effects of treating the $200 as an expense this year versus the effects of depreciating the trash compactor over five years? What are the effects on net income?
   c. Two attorneys, associated in a (limited liability) corporation, decide that a ski chalet at Vail is necessary to entertain current and prospective clients. At the same time, they are considering the addition of a third attorney. This new attorney has a ski chalet that she purchased five years ago for $120,000. Its current market value is $200,000. How should the ski chalet be reflected on the financial statements, assuming the new attorney is hired and the ski chalet is transferred to the corporation?

Transaction Analysis

2–17 You have just formed a sole proprietorship to sell and service personal computers. Use the balance sheet equation to analyze the effects of the following transactions:

   a. Invest $50,000 in the business.
   b. Purchase a four-wheel drive pickup truck for $22,000 (on account) that will be used in the business.

c. Record the truck's fuel and repair costs of $1,750 (paid in cash) for the year.

d. Shortly after buying the truck, it proves to be a "lemon" and it is "junked" (sold to a used car dealer) for $1000. If you think the $21,000 loss should appear on the income statement, indicate why this might be appropriate.

Identifying Accounting Transactions

2–18 R & R Travel entered into the following transactions. Which of these transactions or events should be recorded in R & R's accounting process? Explain your answer.

a. Obtained a bank loan.

b. Repaid a bank loan.

c. Signed a one-year agreement to rent office space. The first month's rent is paid at this time.

d. Signed a one-year agreement to rent office space. No cash is transferred at this time.

e. Purchased office equipment on credit.

f. Agreed with the local newspaper to place advertising in next month's special travel section. No cash yet paid.

Transaction Analysis: Accrual Adjustments

2–19 Seaver & Co., CPAs, prepares its own financial statements at the end of each year. Based on the following information, prepare, in terms of the basic accounting equation, any adjustments that are needed to the accounting records as of December 31, 1997.

a. As of December 31, Seaver & Co. has rendered $2,500 worth of services to clients for which they have not yet billed the client and for which they have not made any accounting entry.

b. Seaver & Co. owns equipment (computers, etc.) having an original cost of $12,000. The equipment has an expected life of six years.

c. On January 1, 1997, Scaver borrowed $15,000. Both principal and interest are due on January 1, 1998. The interest rate is 11%.

d. On January 1, 1997, Seaver rented storage space for three years. The entire three year charge of $1,500 was paid at this time. Seaver correctly created a prepaid rent account in the amount of $1,500.

e. As of December 31, workers have earned $1,200 in wages that are unpaid and unrecorded.

Transaction Analysis: Preparing Financial Statements

2–20 The following account balances are shown on November 30, 1997, for the Clever Bookstore:

Cash	$ 8,000	Accounts payable	$ 4,000
Accounts receivable	9,000	Salaries payable	2,000
Inventory	60,000	Notes payable	35,000
Supplies	3,000	J. Clever, capital	39,000
Total	$80,000	Total	$80,000

The following transactions occurred during December.

1. Paid workers the $2,000 owed them on November 30.
2. Made sales totaling $40,000. One-half of the sales were for cash. The other half were on account. The cost of goods sold was $25,000.
3. Purchased inventory on account, $15,000.
4. Collected in cash $22,000 of receivables.
5. Used supplies totaling $800.
6. Paid accounts payable of $12,000.
7. Paid all December's interest on the note payable in the amount of $300.

REQUIRED

a. Analyze all transactions using the basic accounting equation. Begin your analysis with the November 30 account balances.
b. Prepare a balance sheet as of December 31, 1997.
c. Prepare an income statement for the month ended December 31, 1997.

PROBLEMS

Transaction Analysis: Preparing Financial Statements

2–21 Susan's Sweets, a candy shop, opened on January 1, 1997, with the following transactions:

1. Susan invested $100,000 in cash on January 1, 1997 (sole proprietorship).
2. Susan also owned a lease on commercial space, suitable for the candy shop. She personally had paid $20,000 for the lease on December 26 of the prior year, and now transferred all rights under the six-month lease to her new business. The lease is renewable for another six months on July 1. (*Note:* Increase owners' equity capital account.)
3. Susan purchased candy and other "sweetments" at a cost of $40,000 in cash.
4. Susan purchased store fixtures at a cost of $15,000, paying $5,000 in cash and the balance on account. These store fixtures have a useful life of five years, with no expected salvage value.
5. The six-month lease expired. She renewed the lease for another six months and paid $20,000.
6. During the first year of operations, Susan's sales totaled $132,000 on account.
7. Collections from receivable customers totaled $130,500.
8. During the first year, her other operating expenses were $37,300 on account. In addition she also paid herself a "salary" of $10,000, which was really a withdrawal.
9. At the end of the first year, Susan's Sweets had $2,000 of inventory.
10. Record depreciation for the first year.
11. Record the adjustment to prepaid rent.

REQUIRED

a. Use the basic accounting equation to show the effects of the following transactions, and any necessary accruals, during Susan's first year of business.
b. Based on that analysis, prepare a balance sheet and an income statement for the first year. (*Hint:* Record the transactions in the balance sheet equation first.)

Transaction Analysis: Preparing Financial Statements

2–22 Susan's Shoe Shop opened on January 1. The following transactions took place during the first month:

1. Deposited $30,000 in the firm's checking account.
2. Purchased shoes, boots, socks, and other inventory for $45,000 on account.
3. Purchased display shelving, chairs, and other fixtures for $10,000 cash and $40,000 on account. Assume a useful life of five years.
4. Obtained $20,000 and signed a three-year, $20,000 bank loan at 8% annual interest.
5. Had sales revenue during January of $75,000. Of this amount, $25,000 was received in cash and the balance was on account.
6. The cost of the merchandise sold in item 5 was $32,000.
7. Paid $10,000 to two different creditors.
8. Signed an application for a one-year insurance policy and paid the year's premium of $2,400.
9. Paid three employees a monthly salary of $2,000 each.
10. Collected $35,000 from (accounts receivable) customers.

REQUIRED

a. Analyze these transactions, including any appropriate adjustments, using the basic accounting equation.
b. Prepare a simple income statement for the firm.
c. Identify any significant missing elements in your income statement.
d. Prepare a simple balance sheet for Susan's Shoe Shop.

Fill in the Blanks

2–23 Ascertain the missing items (A–L) in the following *independent* situations. (*Note:* You do *not* have to find the answers in any particular sequence.)

	1	2	3
Assets, January 1	$ 5,000	E	I
Assets, December 31	$ 8,000	F	$ 9,000
Liabilities, January 1	A	$ 2,000	$ 3,000
Liabilities, December 31	$ 3,000	$ 2,200	J
Owners' equity, January 1	$ 3,000	$ 4,000	K
Owners' equity, December 31	B	$ 4,800	$ 7,000
Revenues	$20,000	$15,000	L
Expenses	$18,500	G	$20,000
Contributions by owners	$ 1,000	H	$ 1,000
Withdrawals by owners	C	1,200	$ 3,000
Net income	D	2,000	$ 5,000

Note: Situation 1 is shown below:

January 1:   Assets − Liabilities = Owners' equity
$5000 − (A) = $3,000
$2,000 = Liabilities (A)
December 31: Assets − Liabilities = Owners' equity
$8,000 − $3,000 = (B)

$$\$5,000 = \text{Owners' equity (B)}$$
$$\text{Revenues} - \text{Expenses} = \text{Net Income}$$
$$\$20,000 - \$18,500 = \text{Net income}$$
$$\$1,500 = \text{Net income (D)}$$

Beginning owners' equity + contributions by owners − Withdrawals by owners + Net Income = Ending owners' equity

$$\$3,000 \text{ (A)} + \$1,000 - \text{(C)} + \$1,500 \text{ (D)} = \$,5000 \text{ (B)}$$
$$\$5,500 - \text{(C)} = \$5,000$$
$$\$500 = \text{Withdrawals by owners (C)}$$

Fill in the Blanks

2–24 Ascertain the missing items (*A–L*) in the following *independent* situations. (*Note:* You do *not* have to find the answers in any particular sequence.)

	1	2	3
Assets, January 1	$ 2,000	*E*	*I*
Assets, December 31	$ 9,000	*F*	$ 9,500
Liabilities, January 1	*A*	$ 5,000	$ 3,200
Liabilities, December 31	$ 7,500	$ 5,200	*J*
Owners' equity, January 1	$ 7,500	$ 3,200	*K*
Owners' equity, December 31	*B*	$ 5,300	$ 8,000
Revenues	$25,000	$12,000	*L*
Expenses	$16,200	*G*	$22,000
Contributions by owners	$ 2,000	*H*	$ 2,000
Withdrawals by owners	*C*	$ 1,200	$ 3,500
Net income	*D*	$ 3,000	$ 4,000

Analyzing Investment Alternatives

2–25 Assume that you inherit $10,000, which according to the terms of the will must be invested in a single company. After much research, you find two attractive alternatives: The Salt Company and The Pepper Company. On the basis of the following limited information, which of the following would you prefer (M = million)?

	Salt Co.	Pepper Co.
Total assets	$40M	$25M
Net income	$4M	$4M

Analyzing Investment Alternatives (continuation of Problem 2–25)

2–26 With regard to the preceding exercise, which company would you prefer after uncovering the following information about each company's liabilities?

	Salt Co.	Pepper Co.
Total liabilities	$20M	$23M

Analyzing Investment Alternatives (continuation of Problems 2–25 and 2–26)

2–27 With regard to the two preceding exercises, which company would you prefer after learning about each firm's future prospects from various investment advisors?

	Salt Co.	Pepper Co.
Next year's predicted net income	$1M	$10M

Analyzing Investment Alternatives (continuation of Problems 2– 25 thru 2–27)

2–28 With regard to the preceding three exercises, write a short memo describing any additional information that you might find helpful in choosing between the two companies.

2–29 Identifying Transactions: Cash Versus Accrual—Alternate Problems (A) or (B)

Problem (A)

Identify which of the following events should be reported on financial statements under

1. the cash basis of accounting,
2. the accrual basis of accounting,
3. both methods, or
4. neither method.

Explain each choice.

a. Verbally agreed to purchase a used car from Slee-Z-Auto.
b. Paid $300 for a warranty on the used car.
c. Took the car on a test drive, found it faulty and told the salesperson you wanted a different car.
d. The sales manager agreed to let you choose another car.
e. The sales manager kindly agreed to let you transfer the warranty to the second vehicle.
f. Paid $6,500 for the vehicle.
g. Paid license and taxes of $275.
h. Bought new tires for $450.
i. On a cold winter morning, the car failed to start.
j. Purchased a new battery for $65.
k. Filed a warranty claim for the new battery.
l. Received $45 payment under the warranty.

Problem (B)

Identify which of the following events should be reported on financial statements under

1. the cash basis of accounting,
2. the accrual basis of accounting,
3. both methods, or
4. neither method.

Explain each choice.

a. Signing a contract for the purchase of land.
b. Paying a deposit on the land purchase.
c. Receiving money in advance from a customer.
d. Listing land for sale with a local realtor.
e. Using equipment, such as a computer, daily in your business.
f. Having your computer repaired; the repair person just leaves a bill, but cannot accept any money for the repair.
g. Paying the repair bill.
h. Providing services to customers who will not pay you until next month.

i. Getting compliments from customers about your fine store.

j. Hiring a well-trained accountant to prepare your financial statements and advise you on financial matters (assume no payments have been made).

k. Collecting money from customers who have already been billed.

l. Having employees work for you this month, but delaying the payroll (payments) until the following month.

m. Failing to pay suppliers for three months because you do not have enough money in your bank account.

n. Receiving supplies from a vendor, along with a bill.

o. Selling the land under a contract for 10 future payments.

p. Collecting one of the contract payments for the land sale.

Identifying Transactions: Cash Versus Accrual

2–30 Identify which of the following events should be reported on financial statements under

1. the cash basis of accounting,
2. the accrual basis of accounting,
3. both methods, or
4. neither method.

Explain each choice.

a. Ordered airline tickets, hotel accommodations, and tour guidance from Hugo's U-Go Travel.

b. Changed the airline reservation.

c. Paid a $35 fee to change the reservation.

d. Paid $2,000 for the airline tickets, room, and tour.

e. Arrived at the hotel and checked in.

f. Found your room to be next to the hotel laundry, and facing the noisy loading zone. Furthermore, the room only had two cheap radios, no television!

g. Asked the hotel manager for a more suitable room.

h. Tipped the bellhop $5 after your luggage was moved.

i. Charged $257 for meals and telephone calls during the week.

j. Upon checking out of the hotel at the end of the week, found a $40 per day (for five days) upgrade charge on your hotel bill.

k. Paid for the meals and phone charges on your hotel bill, but denied liability and responsibility for the upgrade charges.

l. The hotel manager insisted that the upgrade charges were your responsibility, and would be added to your credit card balance.

m. Filed a complaint with Hugo's U-Go Travel and with the credit card issuer.

n. Received a credit for the upgrade charges from the credit card issuer.

o. Took films from your vacation to a photo shop for developing. Charges for developing and printing these films were expected to be $45, not yet paid.

p. Paid the $45 two weeks later.

Transaction Analysis

2–31 Identify the effects of the following events on the income statement and the balance sheet:

a. Sugar Loaf Enterprises bought inventory for resale at a cost of $350,000 on account.
b. Half of the inventory was sold to customers for $525,000, all on account.
c. Customers paid $200,000 on account.
d. A particularly interested customer paid $10,000 in advance to reserve an especially desirable item.
e. The item was shipped at an invoiced charge of $2,500 more than the deposit. The inventory cost was $6,000.
f. The customer paid the $2,500 invoice, after reducing the invoice by the $55 freight cost, which, in the customer's opinion, should have been waived because of the $10,000 advance payment.

Transaction Analysis

2–32 Identify the effects of the following events on the income statement and the balance sheet for each year:

a. Sunshine House borrowed $20,000 at 5% interest per annum.
b. Interest for the first year was accrued, but not paid.
c. Two months into the next year, the interest was paid for the first year.
d. At the end of the second year, the loan was repaid, plus the second year's interest.

2–33 Transaction Analysis–Alternate Problems (A) or (B)

Problem (A)

Heidi's Golf and Swim Club borrowed $500,000 at 12% per annum.

REQUIRED

a. Calculate Heidi's expected annual interest expense.
b. Calculate Heidi's expected monthly interest expense.
c. Show the effect of Heidi's $500,000 loan on her accounting equation.
d. Show the effect of the first month's interest accrual.
e. Show the effect of the second month's interest accrual.
f. Show the effect of Heidi's payment of two months' interest.
g. Show the effect of the interest accrual for the remainder of the first year.

Problem (B)

Bob's Swim and Tennis Club borrowed $200,000 at 8% per annum.

REQUIRED

a. Calculate Bob's expected annual interest expense.
b. Calculate Bob's expected monthly interest expense.
c. Show the effect of Bob's $200,000 loan on his accounting equation.
d. Show the effect of the first month's interest accrual.
e. Show the effect of the second month's interest accrual.
f. Show the effect of Bob's payment of two months' interest.
g. Show the effect of the interest accrual for the remainder of the first year.

2–34 Transaction Analysis–Alternate Problems (A) or (B)

Problem (A)

John's Anti-Mediation League (JAML), a sole proprietorship, engaged in the following transactions in 1997:

1. On January 1, JAML borrowed $100,000 at 6% per year with interest due quarterly.
2. JAML paid a $1,000 kickback to a good friend who helped obtain the loan.
3. JAML had not yet paid any interest after the loan had been in effect for three months.
4. On June 30, JAML paid the interest due.
5. On July 1, JAML renegotiated the terms of the loan, which increased the interest rate to 9% per year.
6. At the end of September, John paid the interest on the loan from his personal account.
7. At the end of December, JAML accrued the interest due.
8. On January 1, 1998, JAML paid the interest due to the lender and to John's personal account.

REQUIRED

a. Show the effects of these transactions on the accounting equation:

ASSETS = LIABILITIES + OWNERS' EQUITY

Problem (B)

Sue's Mediation League (SML), a sole proprietorship, engaged in the following transactions in 1997:

1. On January 1, SML borrowed $250,000 at 9% per year with interest due quarterly.
2. SML paid $1,000 to a bank consultant who assisted in obtaining the loan.
3. SML had not yet paid any interest after the loan had been in effect for three months.
4. On June 30, SML paid the interest due.
5. On July 1, SML renegotiated the terms of the loan, which decreased the interest rate to 6% per year.
6. At the end of September, Sue paid the interest on the loan from her personal account. (*Note:* Set up an accounts payable to Sue.)
7. At the end of December, SML accrued the interest due.
8. On January 1, 1998, SML paid the interest due to the lender and to Sue's personal account.

REQUIRED

a. Show the effects of these transactions on the accounting equation:

ASSETS = LIABILITIES + OWNERS' EQUITY

2–35 Transaction Analysis–Alternate Problems (A) or (B)

Problem (A)

Sharon's Affairs and Parties (SAAP), a sole proprietorship, engaged in the following transactions in 1997:

1. SAAP borrowed $150,000 at 10% per year to begin operations.
2. SAAP accrued the first month's interest on the loan.
3. SAAP accrued the second month's interest.
4. SAAP paid the interest due.
5. Sharon loaned SAAP $10,000 at 24% interest per year.
6. SAAP accrued interest for the next month on both loans.
7. SAAP paid the accrued interest.
8. SAAP repaid Sharon's loan, along with a loan "cancellation" fee of $2,500.
9. SAAP accrued interest for the next month.
10. SAAP repaid the original loan, along with the accrued interest.

REQUIRED

a. Show the effects of these transactions on the accounting equation:

ASSETS = LIABILITIES + OWNERS' EQUITY

Problem (B)

Hilger's Intimate Promises (HIP), a sole proprietorship, engaged in the following transactions in 1997:

1. HIP borrowed $50,000 at 8% per year to begin operations.
2. HIP accrued the first month's interest on the loan.
3. HIP accrued the second month's interest.
4. HIP paid the interest due.
5. Hilger loaned HIP $10,000 at 24% interest per year.
6. HIP accrued interest for the next month on both loans.
7. HIP paid the accrued interest.
8. HIP repaid Hilger's loan, along with a loan "cancellation" fee of $1,500.
9. HIP accrued interest for the remaining months of 1997.
10. HIP repaid the original loan, along with accrued interest, at the end of 1997.

REQUIRED

a. Show the effects of these transactions on the accounting equation:

ASSETS = LIABILITIES + OWNERS' EQUITY

2–36 Transaction Analysis: Describing Underlying Events—Alternate Problems (A) or (B)

Problem (A)

Shown here are several transactions recorded by Beth's coffee shop, The Bitter Bean (TBB):

	ASSETS	=	LIABILITIES	+	OWNERS' EQUITY
a.	Cash, +$30,000				Capital, +$30,000
b.	Inventory, +$12,000		Accounts payable, +$12,000		
c.	Cash, −$3,000		Loans, −$3,000		
d.			Loans, −$27,000		Capital, +$27,000
e.	Accounts receivable +$10,000				Revenue, +$10,000
f.	Inventory, −$3,000				Cost of goods sold, −$3,000
g.	Cash, +$8,000 Accounts receivable −$8,000				
h.			Accounts payable, +$30,000		Operating expenses −$30,000

REQUIRED

a. For each transaction, describe the event or activity that occurred. For example:

	ASSETS	=	LIABILITIES	+	OWNERS' EQUITY
	Cash, +$20,000		Loans, +$20,000		

Answer: The firm borrowed $20,000.

Problem (B)

Shown next are several transactions recorded by Bruce's tea shop, The Better Leaf (TBL):

	ASSETS	=	LIABILITIES	+	OWNERS' EQUITY
a.	Cash, +$50,000				Capital, +$50,000
b.	Inventory, +$22,000		Accounts payable, +$22,000		
c.	Cash, +$3,000		Loans, +$3,000		
d.			Loans, −$23,000		Capital, +$23,000
e.	Accounts receivable +$32,000				Revenue, +$32,000
f.	Inventory, −$13,000				Cost of goods sold, −$13,000
g.	Cash, +$28,000 Accounts receivable −$28,000				
h.	Inventory, +$30,000		Loans, +$30,000		

REQUIRED

a. For each transaction, describe the event or activity that occurred. For example:

ASSETS	=	LIABILITIES	+	OWNERS' EQUITY
Cash +$20,000		Loans +$20,000		

Answer: The firm borrowed $20,000.

CASES AND EXTENSIONS

WHAT WOULD YOU DO?

Cash Versus Accrual Accounting

2–37 Suppose that Tina's Frame Shop is anticipating applying for a bank loan in the near future. While Tina's has been using accrual accounting, the bookkeeper suggests that the firm switch to a cash basis in order to improve its financial picture.

REQUIRED

a. Assuming the bank requires financial statements on a cash basis, what actions could the bookkeeper and the firm take to report more favorable results under the cash basis?

b. How do you think the bank may react when it compares any of Tina's earlier statements under the accrual method with statements that are much more favorable under the cash basis?

c. Do you think that Tina's auditor is obligated to provide both sets of statements to the bank and explain any differences? Why?

d. Now assume the bank permits either cash or accrual accounting. Do you think that it is ethical for Tina's to try to "fool" the bank with statements prepared using the most favorable accounting procedures? Why?

e. If you were Tina's bookkeeper, would you expect to be fired if you gave the bank both sets of financial statements? How would this possibility change your views?

Valuing Contract Terms

2–38 A professional baseball player signs a contract for next season to play for the Colorado Rockies. The contract includes payment terms of $7,000,000 over the next two years. The player receives an extra "signing bonus" of $1,000,000. How should each of these two amounts be recorded by the Rockies? Note that the $7,000,000 is contingent on the player "making" the team.

Analyzing Effects of Cash and Accrual Accounting

2–39 Assume you are auditing a small bank that uses the cash basis of accounting to record interest on its customers' accounts. On the other hand, the bank uses the accrual basis of accounting for interest earned on its investments.

a. If most of the bank's investments were earning daily interest, while most of the bank's customers had their money invested in five-year certificates of deposit, do you think that the income reported by the bank represents a fair or useful measure of accomplishment? Why?

b. Reconsider your prior answer. What if you find out that most of the five-year certificates of deposit had just been issued? What if you find out that the bank issued and redeemed the same number of five-year certificates every month? How do the issues of timing or renewal cycles affect your view of this situation?

Analyzing Transactions: Effects of Missing Information

2–40 Answer each of the following *independent* questions:

a. The Dennis Company has assets of $125,000 and owners' equity of $40,000. What are its liabilities? If these liabilities include an outstanding mortgage of $60,000, identify some of the other liabilities that Dennis Company might have.

b. The Bruce Company has assets of $300,000 and liabilities of $110,000. Suppose that the original owners invested $200,000 in this business. What might account for the difference between the original investment and the current balance in owners' equity?

c. The Pieter Company has liabilities of $400,000 and owners' equity of $155,000. What are its assets? Suppose that Pieter has conducted an appraisal and has found that its assets are valued at $1,000,000. How can such a difference occur?

d. The Elizabeth Company has assets of $500,000 and liabilities of $600,000. What conclusions can you draw about this firm?

Identifying Accounting Transactions

2–41 Refer to the T-shirt business first described in Chapter 1. The firm now has a small store near the football stadium to display and sell various sporting goods. During the first week that the shop is open, the following events occur. Should they be recorded in the financial statements of the firm? Why or why not?

a. A famous football player donates a signed football to the store, where it will be displayed in a trophy case.

b. The firm received a bill from the Public Service Co. for gas and electricity used by the prior tenants in the store.

c. The owner bought three lottery tickets for $6.

d. One of the three lottery tickets won $150. (In this case, assume that you did not originally record the purchase of the tickets and that the owner did not want to record the winnings.)

e. The owner learned that the Super Bowl will be held at the nearby stadium in three years.

WHAT WOULD
YOU DO?

Identifying Unusual Transactions and Events

2–42 Assume you are the staff accountant for Gil's Plumbing. You notice that a $1,000 check is drawn (payable to "Cash") on the third Monday of each month and is charged to miscellaneous expenses. You also notice that a sleazy character with a canvas bag comes into the office on the third Tuesday of each month for a 30-second meeting with Gil. After inquiring about what the $1,000 check is for and to which account it might more properly be charged, Gil suggests that you should "mind your own business" and just record the expenses where you are told.

REQUIRED

a. What would you guess is really happening in this situation?
b. Is the $1,000 properly recorded in Gil's accounts? Why?
c. Is this a personal transaction or a business transaction?
d. If Gil is the sole owner of the plumbing business, can he do whatever he wants with his money? How would this situation differ if Gil were merely the manager who was making these payments without the owner's knowledge? What should/would you do in this case? Why?

Conceptual Discussion: Objectivity

2–43 Financial statements, and the underlying accounting processes, rely on many subjective estimates. Review the 15 sample transactions described in this chapter and indicate which of them are absolutely objective. Which would you prefer to be more objective? Why?

Critical Essay: Measuring Liabilities

2–44 Write a one- to two-paragraph essay assessing the following statement:

Liabilities must be precisely measured because the firm needs to know how much is owed to its creditors. If such amounts are not precisely known, the firm risks bankruptcy or other liquidity crises whenever the actual liabilities may have been underestimated.

Critical Essay: Asset Valuation

2–45 Write a one- to two-paragraph essay defending the following statement:

Assets need not be objectively measured and valued because they can be sold at any time. If the firm feels that asset values are going to decline, it can avoid any potential losses merely by selling the assets before they decline.

Conceptual Discussion: Effects of Overstating Expenses

2–46 Consider a situation in which you learn that your employer's accounting staff has consistently overestimated the firm's expenses (e.g., depreciation, bad debts). As a department manager in the firm, what actions could/would you take in response to this knowledge? Why?

Conceptual Discussion: Contracts

2–47 When Charles Barkley joined the Phoenix Suns, his contract was "booked" or recorded at a value in excess of $5,000,000.

a. Since a person cannot be owned, how can a basketball franchise record a player's contract in its financial statements?

b. What measurement rules might apply to the valuation of such athletic contracts? When should this contract be recorded by the Suns? When has either party actually performed (executed) its part of the contract?

c. How do you think accountants might handle the uncertainties associated with the length of a player's career, possible injuries, trades, etc.?

d. How would the existence of guarantees in the contract affect your view of these uncertainties?

USING FINANCIAL ACCOUNTING ON THE INTERNET

2–48 Select two of the following companies (your instructor might specify which two) and locate the most recent set of financial statements. You may use either the 10-K available at EDGAR (**www.sec.gov/edgarhp.htm**) or the annual report available at the company page on the WWW. The annual report is usually located in the Investor Information section.

Corporation	WWW Page Location
Xerox	**www.xerox.com**
Ben & Jerrys	**www.benjerry.com**
Lewis Galoob Toys	**www.galoob.com**
Microsoft	**www.microsoft.com** (go to index)
Compaq	**www.compaq.com** (go to overview)
Eli Lilly	**www.lilly.com**

REQUIRED

a. Obtain the following information for each corporation: Total Assets, Total Liabilities, Total Shareholders' Equity, Net Income.

b. Verify the accounting equation for each corporation.

2–49 A major asset for most companies is facilities. Use the SEC's EDGAR corporate database (**www.sec.gov/edgarhp.htm**) to locate the 10-K for Rockwell International dated September 30, 1995, and filed on December 21, 1995.

REQUIRED

a. Locate and read Item 2, properties (pp. 7–8). For the United States, Europe, South America, and Canada, identify the types of operations for which facilities are maintained.

b. Scroll down to the Balance Sheet. Net Property, Plant and Equipment forms what percentage of total assets on September 30, 1995?

Cases and Extensions

2–50 This question is based on Question 1–30 (page 28) which refers to the report made by the Jenkins Committee. The Jenkins Committee was formed to analyze users' needs in financial reporting and to suggest improvements in financial reporting keeping in mind these needs.

REQUIRED

a. Locate Chapter Six of the Jenkins Committee report (located at **www.rutgers.edu/Accounting/raw/aicpa/business/chap6.htm**), and scroll down to Recommendation 4. How does the Committee define the core activities of a firm?

b. List the core activities for the following corporations:

Corporation	Home-page Location
Kodak	www.kodak.com
Ryder	ryder.inter.net/ryder/
Rockwell International	www.rockwell.com
Rohm and Haas Company	www.rohmhaas.com

CHAPTER 3

STUDYING THIS CHAPTER
WILL ENABLE YOU TO

1. Identify the basic elements of the balance sheet.
2. Recognize the types of assets, liabilities, and owners' equity that are found on the balance sheets of most business firms.
3. Comprehend the ordering and classification of items on the balance sheet.
4. Appreciate why balance sheets differ for firms in different industries.
5. Use balance sheet relationships to obtain information useful to investors and lenders.
6. Be alert to the limitations as well as the usefulness of balance sheet information.

THE BALANCE SHEET

INTRODUCTION

This chapter focuses solely on the balance sheet, which is often called the statement of financial position. Beginning with formal definitions of the basic elements of the balance sheet, the discussion describes the types of assets, liabilities and owners' equity that are found on the balance sheets of most business firms. The variety of balance sheet ratios are presented to show how managers and investors use balance sheet information in making decisions.

ELEMENTS OF THE BALANCE SHEET

The previous two chapters introduced you to the three basic financial statements. They showed how transactions and other events affecting business firms cause changes in the elements reported in the financial statements. This chapter focuses solely on the balance sheet, which is often called the **statement of financial position.** At any given date, the balance sheet shows the sources from which the firm has obtained its resources and the ways in which those resources are currently employed. Recall the basic accounting equation:

$$ASSETS = LIABILITIES + OWNERS' \ EQUITY$$

Another way to state this relationship is

$$Uses \ of \ resources = Sources \ of \ resources$$

In other words, liabilities and owners' equity are the sources from which the firm has obtained its funds, and the listing of assets shows the way in which the firm's managers have put those funds to work. To illustrate this relationship, refer to the balance sheet for Sample Company at the end of 1998, which is presented in Exhibit 3–1.

Uses of resources	=	Sources of resources
Assets	=	Liabilities + Owners' Equity
$2,057,000	=	$1,199,000 + 858,000
$2,057,000	=	$2,057,000

Viewed in this manner, there is no mystery to the fact that both sides of the balance sheet have the same total. They are merely two sides of a single coin, or two ways of describing the total wealth of the firm. The firm's wealth can be viewed in terms of sources of financing (from creditors and owners) and in terms of uses of resources (owning or controlling assets).

Another useful way to view the balance sheet is as the cumulative result of the firm's past activities. Liabilities represent the total amount the firm has borrowed during its existence, minus the amounts that have been repaid to date. The owners' equity items show the total amount invested by owners, plus the total profits earned by the firm during previous periods, minus any amounts that have been distributed to owners. Similarly, the assets of the firm represent the total resources obtained by the firm from

EXHIBIT 3–1
A BALANCE SHEET

Sample Company Balance Sheet at December 31, 1998

Assets		Liabilities and Owners' Equity	
Current assets		Current liabilities	
Cash	$ 110,000	Accounts payable	$ 260,000
Accounts receivable	466,000	Notes payable	225,000
Inventories	812,000	Warrantee obligations	112,000
Prepaid expenses	32,000	Accrued expenses	75,000
Total current assets	1,420,000	Taxes payable	27,000
Property, plant, and equipment		Total current liabilities	699,000
		Noncurrent liabilities	
Land	85,000	Bonds payable	350,000
Buildings and equipment	865,000	Mortgage payable	150,000
Less: Accumulated depreciation	−313,000	Total noncurrent liabilities	500,000
Net book value	552,000	Total liabilities	1,199,000
Total property, plant, and equipment assets	637,000	Shareholders' equity	
		Invested capital	600,000
		Retained earnings	258,000
Total assets	$2,057,000	Total shareholders' equity	858,000
		Total liabilities and shareholders' equity	$2,057,000

lenders and owners, minus those that have been consumed in the firm's operations, repaid to lenders, or distributed to owners.

⬥ Definitions of Assets, Liabilities, and Owners' Equity

The Financial Accounting Standards Board (FASB) has identified the essential characteristics of assets, liabilities, and owners' equity. The FASB definitions, which were introduced in Chapter 2 and are summarized in Exhibit 3–2, provide a frame of reference that helps accountants identify the items to be included in the balance sheet. They will be referred to frequently during the remaining discussions in this chapter. For now, note that according to the FASB's definitions, *assets* represent future benefits; *liabilities* represent future sacrifices; and *owners' equity* is the residual amount, or difference, between assets and liabilities.

The following pages introduce you to the types of individual assets, liabilities, and owners' equity to be found on the balance sheets of most business firms. In studying these individual balance sheet items, keep in mind the FASB's definitions shown in Exhibit 3–2.

ASSETS

As noted in Exhibit 3–2, assets represent ". . . probable future economic benefits obtained or controlled by a particular entity as a result of past transactions or events." Future economic benefits come in many forms. For example, cash is an asset because it represents purchasing power; the firm can use cash to acquire goods and services, to repay debts, or to make distributions to owners. Inventories are assets because they are merchandise intended for sale to customers for cash and other assets. The firm's buildings and equipment are assets because they enable the firm to perform its operations and to earn profits in the future.

Assets typically represent tangible economic resources, e.g., cash, buildings, and trucks. On the other hand, some economic resources are intangible, such as patent rights and copyrights to a text or musical score. Assets may also be represented by promises of future payments from customers who bought goods or services on credit. Assets can be created by contract or acquisition of property rights, and yet they may

EXHIBIT 3–2
FASB DEFINITIONS OF ASSETS, LIABILITIES, AND OWNERS' EQUITY

Assets are probable future economic benefits obtained or controlled by a particular entity as a result of past transactions or events.

Liabilities are probable future sacrifices of economic benefits arising from present obligations of a particular entity to transfer assets or provide services to other entities in the future as a result of past transactions or events.

Equity is the residual interest in the assets of an entity that remains after deducting liabilities. In a business enterprise, the equity is the ownership interest.

SOURCE: Statement of Financial Accounting Concepts No. 6, "Elements of Financial Statements" (Stamford, CT: FASB, 1980).

not be visible to the human eye. All assets, however, have a common characteristic in that they represent probable future economic benefits to the firm.

Asset Classifications

Assets are classified into two overall categories: current assets and noncurrent assets. This distinction is based on the length of time before the asset is expected to be consumed or converted to cash. **Current assets** include cash and other assets that will typically become cash or be consumed in one year or one operating cycle, whichever is greater. Current assets are used quickly and repeatedly during a firm's normal operations. This notion of using assets on a cyclical basis corresponds to a concept called *turnover.* Current assets turn over quickly—anywhere from daily to annually. Current assets are usually generated in the normal course of business operations. The notion of turnover is used to differentiate current assets from other asset categories that are used (turn over) much more slowly over a number of years.

To illustrate, Sample Company's balance sheet in Exhibit 3–1 shows that the firm's total assets of $2,057,000 are comprised of $1,420,000 in current assets and $637,000 in property, plant, and equipment assets. The balance sheet equation is easily expanded to show this additional detail:

ASSETS		=	LIABILITIES	+	OWNERS' EQUITY
Current	Noncurrent				
$1,420,000	+ $637,000	=	$1,199,000	+	$858,000
$2,057,000		=	$2,057,000		

This classification of assets is useful to the analyst concerned with the liquidity of the firm. **Liquidity** reflects the ability of the firm to generate sufficient cash to meet its operating cash needs and to pay its obligations as they become due. This focus on liquidity will become clear as we discuss the ordering and valuation of individual current assets, in the next section.

Current Assets

Current assets are listed in the order in which they are expected to be consumed or converted to cash. For example, Sample Company's current assets are listed (in Exhibit 3–1) in the following typical order of maturity or collectibility:

- cash and cash equivalents,
- accounts receivable,
- inventories, and
- prepaid expenses.

Cash and cash equivalents includes currency, bank deposits, and various marketable securities that can be turned into cash on short notice merely by contacting a bank or broker. These amounts are presently available to meet the firm's cash payment requirements. Note that only securities that are purchased within 90 days of their maturity dates, or are scheduled to be converted to cash within the next 90 days, may be classified as cash equivalents.

Accounts receivable represent credit sales that have not been collected yet. Accounts receivable are converted into cash as soon as the customers or clients pay their bills (their accounts). Accounts receivable should "turn over," or be collected, within the firm's normal collection period, which is usually 30 or 60 days. A slower accounts receivable turnover embodies more risk to the organization because the probability of nonpayment usually increases as turnover decreases. Overdue accounts may imply that the customer is either unable to pay or is unwilling to pay because of disagreement over the amounts billed. Both cases imply that the amount of cash that will ultimately be collected is less than the amount originally billed to the customer.

Managers are interested less in the total amount of accounts receivable than in the estimated cash to be generated from collections of the accounts. For this reason, accounts receivable are listed on the balance sheet at the amounts estimated to be actually collectible. This amount is termed the **net realizable value** of the receivables. For example, if management estimates that some portion of the amounts billed to customers will ultimately be uncollectible, then the estimated uncollectible portion will be deducted in valuing the accounts receivable on the balance sheet. The uncollectible portion of the receivables is termed an *allowance account* and is discussed in Chapter 6.

Inventory represents items that have been purchased or manufactured for resale to customers. That is, inventory can either be created through the manufacturing and assembly efforts of the organization or be acquired from others and held for resale. Inventory is the "stuff of commerce" dating back to merchants on camels and pirates raiding the high seas looking for bounty. Inventory can be as prosaic as black tea or salt, or it can be as glamorous as gold bullion or silver coins. In modern times, inventory is often "high tech," such as silicon wafers, memory chips, or disk drives. Should the company discover that some of its inventory is unsalable, or marketable only at a greatly reduced price, the reported value of the inventory should be reduced accordingly.

Prepaid expenses, the final category of current assets shown in Exhibit 3–1, represent unexpired assets such as insurance premiums. For example, insurance policies frequently are paid ahead on an annual basis. The unexpired portion, the portion of the policy paid for but not yet used, is shown as part of prepaid expenses. Prepaid expenses are interpreted as current assets. Prepaids are usually minor elements of the balance sheet, and, in the usual course of events, prepaids will not be converted or turned into cash. Instead, the rights to future benefits will be used up in future periods.

The Operating Cycle and Liquidity

Manufacturing and merchandising firms' **operating cycles** include turning inventory into cash. Using three of the current assets discussed earlier, the operating cycle evolves from the purchase of inventory, to the exchange of inventory for a promised payment by a customer (an account receivable), and, finally, to the conversion of the receivable into cash. Operating cycles may vary in length from just a few days (e.g., food retailers) to months (e.g., consumer appliance sellers) or even years (e.g., defense contractors). Exhibit 3–3 illustrates the operating cycle.

Exhibit 3–3
The Operating Cycle

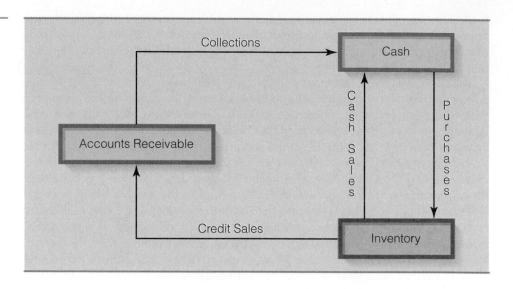

The more quickly this cycle is completed, the more quickly the inventory is turned into cash, and liquidity is higher. When the operating cycle becomes longer, the firm's liquidity usually is lower. Should the operating cycle become too long, the firm will be forced to incur debt in order to pay its suppliers of inventory. To some extent, the length of the operating cycle is outside management's control. For example, the length of time permitted customers to pay their accounts may be governed by industry practice. To attract and retain customers, the firm may need to offer credit terms as liberal as those offered by its competitors. Likewise, the amount of inventory that the firm keeps on hand may be related to the length of its "production pipeline": Some products require a lengthy production process, which entails a substantial investment in inventory at various stages of completion.

On the other hand, the turnover of accounts receivable and inventory may be influenced by management. For instance, managers may have considerable leeway in offering credit terms to customers or in deciding how much inventory to keep on hand. The analyst, in attempting to assess the firm's liquidity, needs to understand these underlying factors that cause differences in the amounts of accounts receivable and inventories across firms and industries. Reality Check 3–1 illustrates how the composition of current assets differs for two firms engaged in different industries.

Noncurrent Assets

Noncurrent assets are long-term assets that are used in the conduct of the business. Whereas current assets are liquid and turn over in relatively short time periods, noncurrent assets usually turn over very slowly—on the order of once in several years. However, in a high-tech organization, some noncurrent assets may be replaced more frequently. In other words, while the operating cycle for current assets is usually less than a year, the replacement cycle for noncurrent assets is longer than a year.

All noncurrent assets are recorded on the balance sheet at their historical acquisition costs. With the passage of time, the historical costs of many noncurrent assets become

COMPOSITION OF CURRENT ASSETS: ABBOTT LABORATORIES AND DELTA AIR LINES

The following schedule summarizes the current assets reported in the end of 1993 balance sheets of Abbott Laboratories, a company that develops, manufactures, and markets health care products, and Delta Air Lines, a major provider of passenger freight and mail air transportation.

	Abbott Laboratories	Delta Air Lines
	(dollars in thousands)	
Current Assets		
Cash and equivalents	$ 300,676	$1,180,364
Investment securities	78,149	—
Accounts receivable, net of allowance	1,336,222	1,024,869
Supplies	—	90,593
Inventories	940,533	—
Prepaids and other	929,955	526,094
Total current assets	3,585,535	2,821,920
Noncurrent, total	4,103,034	9,049,103
Total assets	$7,688,569	$11,871,023

REQUIRED

a. Identify the major differences between these two firms in the composition of current assets. Try to explain these differences in terms of the types of goods and services that each company produces.
b. Based solely on the information provided here, which company appears to be more liquid?

---

out of date relative to their current market values. Consequently, they indicate little about the market value of the organization and about the future resources necessary to replace the assets. However, the historical costs listed on the balance sheet do represent the costs of these assets that will eventually be consumed by future operations.

Property, Plant, and Equipment. For most firms, noncurrent assets consist mainly of property, plant, and equipment. These assets are widely referred to as **fixed assets.** **Property** usually represents the land on which the firm's offices, factories, and other facilities are located. In most cases, property is a relatively minor portion of the total noncurrent assets. In some cases, however, such as for firms engaged in mining, logging, or oil and gas exploration, property may constitute a major operating asset. Property is valued on the balance sheet at its historical acquisition cost. Because property is usually one of the oldest assets held by an organization, its recorded historical cost is often the most out of date in terms of current market values.

Buildings and equipment represent the largest category of noncurrent assets, as shown in Exhibit 3–1. **Buildings** or **plant** may be office, retail, or factory buildings;

warehouses or supply depots; or hospitals or health clinics. **Equipment** includes office desks and chairs, tools, drill presses, robots, computers, x-ray and other scanners, podiums, and so on. In other words, buildings and equipment are the primary productive assets of any organization. Whether widgets or rings are produced, whether knowledge or health is improved, buildings and equipment are necessary to produce most goods and services.

Because buildings and equipment are long lived, it would not make sense to treat their entire cost as expenses in the year they are acquired. On the other hand, because buildings and equipment will gradually lose their economic value over time, it does not make sense to wait until the end of their service lives to recognize their declining usefulness to the firm. As a consequence, accountants gradually and systematically reduce the reported values of buildings and equipment on successive balance sheets in order to allocate expenses to individual years of asset use. The reduction in the reported value of buildings and equipment during a period is called **depreciation expense.**

On the balance sheet, the total amount of depreciation expense recognized to that date is called **accumulated depreciation.** It is subtracted from the initial cost of the asset. The resulting carrying value is referred to as the **net book value** of the asset. In Exhibit 3–1, the net book value of $552,000 for buildings and equipment is calculated by subtracting the $313,000 of accumulated depreciation from the original cost of $865,000:

Buildings and equipment	$ 865,000
Less: Accumulated depreciation	−313,000
Net book value	$ 552,000

In other words, of the original cost of $865,000, a total of $313,000 has been expensed, or written off, in previous periods. The net book value of these assets is unlikely to reflect their current resale value because of changes in technology, price inflation, and many other factors. Accumulated depreciation is not an attempt to adjust carrying values to current resale values. Also, accumulated depreciation does not represent any cash or other investments that the company has set aside for replacing the buildings and equipment. Rather, depreciating an asset is an attempt to apportion or allocate its original cost as an expense to the periods that benefit from the asset's use.

The net book value of buildings and equipment may be used to estimate the remaining productive capacity of the organization. For example, Sample Company's buildings and equipment are about 36% depreciated ($313,000 accumulated depreciation divided by $865,000 initial cost). If Sample Company does not purchase additional buildings and equipment, then each successive balance sheet will show a lower net book value for these assets. Such a declining net book value will signal to analysts that Sample Company is not replenishing its productive capacity on a regular basis.

As a practical matter, most firms regularly invest in new plant and equipment and, as a result, the net book value of these assets usually increases over time. The percentage relationships between the initial cost and the accumulated depreciation of these assets may give analysts a rough gauge of the overall age of the firm's productive capacity. However, the analyst must usually refer to other disclosures in the financial statements to evaluate the firm's productive capacity.

Other Noncurrent Assets. In addition to property, plant, and equipment, many firms possess other noncurrent assets such as intangibles. **Intangibles** are noncurrent assets that lack physical substance and yet are important resources in the regular operations of a business. Intangibles often consist of legal rights, such as patents or copyrights. Such legal rights are vital to the operations of many firms and, in some cases, may be the most valuable resources owned by the organization.

Consider, for example, the importance of copyrights to computer software developers or to book publishers. The value of such firms depends almost entirely on the value of the copyrights that protect their legal rights to the products that they have developed. Accounting for intangible assets is similar to that for buildings and equipment because the initial costs are systematically recognized as expenses over the years that benefit from the use of the assets. Intangible assets are valued on the balance sheet at their historical costs, minus any amounts subsequently recognized as expenses. The term **amortization** is used in place of depreciation when referring to the consumption of intangible assets.

Another important type of intangible asset is goodwill. **Goodwill** is a general label used by accountants to denote the economic value of an acquired firm in excess of the value of its identifiable net assets (assets minus liabilities). Goodwill reflects the adage that "the value of the whole differs from the sum of its parts." This economic value is due largely to factors such as customer loyalty, employee competence and morale, management expertise, and so on. For example, the value of a successful business firm is usually much greater than the total values of its individual assets.

The balance sheet recognition of goodwill depends on whether the firm's goodwill was internally generated or externally acquired. **Internally generated goodwill** evolves gradually as the firm develops a good reputation and customer base. It also evolves as the firm cultivates successful relationships with its suppliers, trains and retains a skilled labor force, and conducts other value-enhancing activities. The costs incurred in generating this goodwill are generally not recorded as assets by the firm, and instead are recognized as expenses when incurred. The argument used to support the immediate expensing of these costs is the uncertainty and subjectivity involved in identifying future benefits. **Externally acquired goodwill,** on the other hand, usually arises when one business firm acquires another. In this case, the amount that the purchaser is paying for the goodwill of the seller can be more objectively determined by appraisers. Externally acquired goodwill is discussed more extensively in Chapter 13, which deals with various business combinations.

The composition of noncurrent assets, and the relative amounts of current to noncurrent assets, varies across industries. Reality Check 3–2 shows how noncurrent assets differ between two firms in different industries.

Assets: Summary and Evaluation

Before leaving the asset side of the balance sheet, it is helpful to summarize the conventions used by accountants to define and value the firm's assets. We also identify here some of the limitations faced by analysts who must use asset values shown in the balance sheet to evaluate the firm's liquidity and productive capacity.

As we have seen, accountants classify assets into two broad groups: current and noncurrent. In reporting current assets, the focus is on liquidity. For this reason, current assets are generally valued at the lower of their acquisition costs or present resale values. An exception to this rule is made for investments in the securities of other firms, as is discussed in Chapter 6. These practices are useful to the analyst concerned with the ability of the firm to meet its short-term cash needs.

COMPOSITION OF NONCURRENT ASSETS:
HEWLETT-PACKARD AND BETHLEHEM STEEL

The following schedule summarizes the noncurrent assets reported in the end of 1993 balance sheets of Hewlett-Packard, a company that designs, manufactures, and services electronic data and communications systems, and Bethlehem Steel, a major steel fabricator.

	Hewlett-Packard	Bethlehem Steel
	(dollars in millions)	
Current assets (total)	$10,236	$1,591
Noncurrent assets		
Property, plant, and equipment (at cost)	7,527	6,741
Less: Accumulated depreciation	(3,347)	(4,107)
Net	4,180	2,634
Other long-term receivables and other	2,320	1,652
Total noncurrent assets	6,500	4,286
Total assets	$16,736	$5,877

REQUIRED

a. Identify the major differences between these two firms in the composition of noncurrent assets. Try to explain these differences based on the types of products that each company produces.
b. Based solely on the information provided here, which company appears to have the older assets?

Noncurrent assets, on the other hand, are generally valued at their acquisition costs, minus amounts that have been recognized as expenses in previous periods. These previously recognized expenses will have been shown as depreciation of buildings and equipment or as amortization of intangibles such as patents or goodwill. In reporting noncurrent assets the focus is on the **operating capacity** of the firm; that is, the firm must focus on the structure of its long-lived assets, both tangible and intangible, which are necessary in order for the firm to produce goods or services. The carrying values of these noncurrent assets represent the portion of their original acquisition costs that will be recognized as expenses in future periods. The carrying values of noncurrent assets rarely reflect their market values because inflation has usually caused asset replacement costs to increase beyond their reported values.

The experienced financial statement analyst is alert to two central issues in examining a firm's asset structure as reported on the balance sheet:

1. Different valuation methods are used for various types of assets (e.g., cost, market values, lower of cost or market value).
2. Many assets that are critical to the firm's successful operations are not shown on the balance sheet.

With respect to these "missing" assets, chief executive officers (CEOs) are fond of proclaiming:

- "Our employees are our most important resource."
- "Research today provides profits tomorrow."
- "Our reputation for quality ensures our success."

Regardless of these lofty statements, resources such as employee morale and productivity, research and development expertise, and a loyal and satisfied network of customers and suppliers are absent from the balance sheet. Accountants justify these omissions either because these valuable resources do not meet the conditions stated in the FASB's definition of assets (see Exhibit 3–2) or because there is no reliable method for measuring or valuing such resources.

LIABILITIES

As noted in Exhibit 3–2, liabilities represent ". . . probable future sacrifices of economic benefits" that are the result of past transactions or events. Many times they entail cash payments to other entities, e.g., repayment to lenders of amounts that had been previously borrowed. The concept of a liability is somewhat broader than this. Liabilities include any probable obligation that the firm has incurred as a consequence of its past activities. For example, many firms warranty their products and consequently are obliged to perform repairs or pay refunds when defects are later uncovered, so, as you can see, not all liabilities require that the firm repay specific dollar amounts on specified dates. Moreover, some liabilities require estimation and judgment in order to determine their amounts. All liabilities, however, have a common characteristic: They represent probable future economic sacrifices by the firm.

Liability Classifications

Just as with assets, liabilities are classified into two overall categories: current liabilities and noncurrent liabilities. The distinction is based on the length of time before the liability is expected to be repaid or otherwise satisfied by the firm and on whether payment will require the use of assets that are classified as current. **Current liabilities** are short-term obligations that are expected to utilize cash or other current assets within a year or an operating cycle, whichever is longer. **Noncurrent liabilities** represent obligations that generally require payment over periods longer than a year.

To illustrate, Sample Company's balance sheet in Exhibit 3–1 shows that the firm's total liabilities of $1,199,000 are comprised of $699,000 in current liabilities and $500,000 in noncurrent liabilities. The following balance sheet equation shows this additional detail:

ASSETS		=	LIABILITIES		+	OWNERS' EQUITY
Current	Noncurrent		Current	Noncurrent		
$1,420,000	+ $637,000	=	$699,000	+$500,000	+	$858,000
$2,057,000		=	$2,057,000			

Current Liabilities

The current liabilities of Sample Company, shown in Exhibit 3–1, consist of accounts payable, notes payable, warranty obligations, accrued expenses, and taxes payable. These liabilities represent various claims against the firm's economic resources.

Accounts payable usually represent debts that the firm incurs in purchasing inventories and supplies for manufacturing or resale purposes. Accounts payable also include amounts that the firm owes for other services used in its operations, such as rentals, insurance, utilities, and so on. Accounts payable are often called *trade debt* because they represent debt that occurs in the normal course of any trade or business.

Notes payable, the next current liability shown in Exhibit 3–1, are more formal current liabilities than the accounts payable. A note may be signed on the borrowing of cash from a local bank. The note represents a legal document that a court can force the firm to satisfy.

Warranty obligations represent the firm's estimated future costs to fulfill its obligations for repair or refund guarantees. These obligations refer to any products sold or services provided prior to the balance sheet date. Unlike the cases of accounts and notes payable, the exact amount of the firm's obligations for warranties cannot be determined by referring to purchase documents, formal contracts, or similar evidence. Instead, the amount reported for the warranty obligation is based on management's judgment about future claims for repairs and refunds that may arise from past sales. The amount reported is an estimate, based in part on the past experience of the firm and its competitors. Recall that the FASB defines liabilities in terms of "probable future economic sacrifices" (see Exhibit 3–2). If Sample Company's products have required warranty repairs in the past, then it is probable that items sold recently will also require warranty repairs in the future. Because the sales have already occurred, the obligation exists at the balance sheet date, and these estimated amounts must be reported as liabilities.

The next item listed among Sample Company's current liabilities is **accrued expenses,** which represent liabilities for services already consumed, but not yet paid for or included elsewhere in liabilities. These accrued liabilities usually constitute only a minor part of current liabilities.

Taxes payable comprise the final account listed among the current liabilities of Sample Company. **Taxes payable** represent unpaid taxes that are owed to a governmental unit and will be paid within a year. Taxes payable may include employee withholding taxes, unemployment taxes, employer income taxes, or any number of other taxes that are incurred in the normal course of operations. Taxes payable are typically a relatively minor portion of current liabilities because governmental units require that taxes be paid on a timely basis. Taxes payable should not be increasing at a faster rate of growth than that enjoyed by the entire firm. If so, those increases may indicate that tax payments are not being made on a timely basis.

The current liabilities of Sample Company are a representative sample of many short-term liabilities. Businesses engage in many credit-based transactions; e.g., most sales to businesses involve accounts receivable, and most purchases by businesses correspondingly involve accounts payable. As a result, the largest of the current liabilities usually consists of trade accounts payable. The other liability items, although less significant in dollar amount, also represent common business transactions and circumstances.

Noncurrent Liabilities

Noncurrent liabilities generally have longer maturities than the current liabilities discussed in the preceding section. Their maturity date is more than one year. Most noncurrent liabilities represent contracts to repay debt at specified future dates. In addition, these borrowing agreements often place some restrictions on the activities of the firm until the debt is fully repaid. In Chapter 9, we discuss a variety of different borrowing arrangements that are widely used.

Exhibit 3–1 shows that Sample Company has two types of noncurrent liabilities: bonds payable and mortgage payable. These liabilities are similar because they require Sample Company to make future payments of interest and principal. Yet they differ in terms of the **collateral** that Sample Company used to obtain the loan.

Bonds payable are a major source of funds for larger business firms. They represent liabilities that the firm incurs by selling a contract called a bond. A **bond** contains the firm's promise to pay interest periodically (usually every six months) and to repay the money originally borrowed **(principal)** when the bond matures. The amount of money that the firm receives from investors for its bonds depends on investors' views about the riskiness of the firm and the prevailing rate of interest. Investors rely on the ability of the firm to generate sufficient cash flows from its operations to meet the payments as they become due.

Mortgage payable is similar to bonds payable because firms must also make principal and interest payments as they come due. Unlike most bonds, a mortgage represents a pledge of certain assets that will revert to the lender if the debt is not paid. The simplest example of a mortgage is that of a bank holding title to your house until your loan is fully paid. If the loan is not paid, the bank can sell the house and use the proceeds to pay off the debt. Mortgages on factories and hospitals are very similar. The problem in such cases is that there are often very few buyers for specialized assets such as factory buildings and equipment. In such cases, possible mortgage default represents more risk and higher costs to lenders. It also indicates that most lenders will cooperate with borrowers to find alternative solutions to avoid defaults. From an analytical perspective, the analyst or manager must make sure that mortgage terms are being satisfied and that payments have been promptly remitted. For both bonds and mortgages, analysts will try to discern whether cash flows from operations are sufficient to pay the interest and principal.

Liabilities: Summary and Evaluation

Before leaving the liabilities or "borrowed resources" part of the balance sheet, it is useful to summarize various liabilities and to point out some limitations faced by analysts in assessing the firm's liabilities.

Liabilities are classified as either current or noncurrent, based on their maturity dates. The current liabilities of the firm are closely related to its operations. As examples, trade accounts payable arise as a direct consequence of purchasing inventory; accrued expenses and taxes payable result from the firm's operating and tax expenses; and product warranty obligations occur because the firm has sold products covered by warranties. For this reason, analysts often refer to these types of obligations as *spontaneous* or *operating liabilities*.

In contrast, noncurrent liabilities consist mainly of long-term borrowing contracts that managers have negotiated with investors, banks, and other parties. This type of borrowing reflects a deliberate decision by managers to obtain funds from lenders, rather than to obtain additional investments from owners. The decision about how much of the firm's resources should be provided by long-term borrowing and how much should be invested by owners is a fundamental issue faced by all firms.

Financial statement users are concerned with the firm's ability to pay both its short-term and long-term obligations as they mature. Later in this chapter, we discuss some ratios that are useful for making these assessments. The analyst is aware of two important features of liability reporting. First, not all liabilities result from promises by the firm to repay specific amounts at determinable future dates. Instead, many liabilities require estimates of future events, e.g., the warranty obligations reported in Sample Company's balance sheet. Many other obligations reported by business firms entail similar liability estimates, as we discuss later in Chapters 8 and 9.

Second, the analyst is aware that some potential obligations of business firms either are not reported on the balance sheet or are reported at amounts that do not adequately reflect their potential future claims against the assets of the firm. Consider, for example, lawsuits against the firm. At present, tobacco firms are disputing a lengthy list of ailments allegedly associated with cigarette smoking. Similarly, large chemical and nuclear industry firms are being sued over toxic wastes. In these cases, the potential damages awarded to plaintiffs could result in awards of billions of dollars. Although these potentially ruinous lawsuits are based on business activities prior to the current balance sheet date, none of these firms reports significant contingent liabilities because the loss cannot be reliably estimated at this time. Contingent liabilities are discussed further in Chapter 9.

OWNERS' EQUITY

This final element of the balance sheet represents the equity of the firm's owners. As shown in Exhibit 3–2, the FASB defines **owners' equity** simply as the ". . . residual interest in the assets of an entity that remains after deducting liabilities." This definition makes it clear that the balance sheet valuation of owners' equity is determined by the balance sheet valuations of assets and liabilities. This view of owners' equity as a *residual amount* is apparent when we rearrange the balance sheet equation in the following way:

$$\text{OWNERS' EQUITY} = \text{ASSETS} - \text{LIABILITIES}$$

Sample Company's balance sheet in Exhibit 3–1 shows a firm that has been organized as a **corporation,** which is an entity that is owned by a group of shareholders. While a corporation's owners' equity may be called shareholders' equity, in Sample Company it comprises both **paid-in capital,** which represents direct investments by the owners of the firm, and **retained earnings,** which represents the earnings of the firm that have been reinvested in the business. Sample Company's balance sheet in Exhibit 3–1 shows that owners have paid $600,000 for shares of stock of the company. Sample Company has received this invested capital (probably in cash from investors) in exchange for its shares of stock. In addition, the firm has been profitable in the past, and Sample Company has reinvested $258,000 of those profits in the business. This $258,000 represents Sample's retained earnings.

If in the next year Sample Company reports profits of $200,000 and pays dividends to shareholders of $75,000, then retained earnings will increase by $125,000 ($200,000 − $75,000). Bear in mind, however, that retained earnings do not represent cash available for the payment of dividends. Rather, retained earnings reflect the amount of resources that a firm has obtained as a result of operations. The firm has retained this increase for use in its operations rather than returning it immediately to the investors as dividends. Those resources are presently invested as shown on the asset side of the balance sheet. For this reason, it is possible that a firm may have a large retained earnings balance, but have insufficient cash available for dividends.

Reality Check 3–3 illustrates the reporting of shareholders' equity for two firms, one of which reports a negative (deficit) balance in retained earnings.

REALITY CHECK 3–3

COMPOSITION OF SHAREHOLDERS' EQUITY: NUCLEAR METALS AND KOLLMORGEN

The following schedule summarizes the components of shareholders' equity reported in the end of 1993 balance sheets of Nuclear Metals and Kollmorgen.

	Nuclear Metals	Kollmorgen
	(dollars in thousands)	
Shareholders' equity:		
Paid-in capital	$13,905	$ 50,322
Retained earnings (deficit)	29,132	(30,166)
Other		(12,571)
Total shareholders' equity	$43,037	$ 7,585

REQUIRED

a. Which firm has obtained the larger amount of capital through sale of stock to investors?

b. Which firm has obtained the larger amount of capital through reinvestment of earnings?

c. Explain why Kollmorgen reports a negative (deficit) balance in retained earnings at the end of 1993.

d. Suppose Nuclear Metals earns $15,000 and pays dividends of $9,000 during 1994. What would be the firm's ending balance in retained earnings? (All dollars are in thousands.)

This discussion of owners' equity completes our tour of Sample Company's balance sheet, and, at this point, you are aware of the typical components of the balance sheets of most business firms. In future chapters, we will generally use the term shareholders' equity, rather than the more generic term, owners' equity. The following section illustrates a variety of balance sheet relationships that are of interest to analysts.

BALANCE SHEET ANALYSIS

Various ratios are used to help interpret and understand financial statements. These ratios are guides to understanding changes in financial performance for one company from year to year and differences in financial performance between two or more companies. Ratios are most useful when comparisons are made, either between time periods or among different companies. Ratios are useful shortcuts that permit the analyst to collapse the myriad details in financial statements into a few simple numbers. But remember that the ratio calculations are not the answers—they just show relationships. The analyst or manager must understand those relationships and make decisions on the basis of a host of information.

Ratios are just one input to those decisions. In other words, ratios are one indicator of financial health and viability, but they do not tell the whole story. Users of financial statements must be careful not to become too enamored of the ratios themselves and should not forget to look for other indicators that will permit better decision making. Also, ratios are historical. Judgment is needed to use them for decision making because future conditions may change. Bear in mind that ratios are only as good as the data that comprise them. The discussions in later chapters will help you to be aware of differences in accounting policies that can cause differences in ratios.

Balance sheet ratios aid the analyst in assessing a firm's liquidity, asset management, and debt management policies. Each of these uses is discussed in this section.

Vertical Analysis

Analysts usually begin with a review of the composition of the firm's assets, as well as the composition of its liabilities and owners' equity. This review begins with the preparation of a common-size balance sheet, which shows the percentage component of each major section to the grand totals on each side of the balance sheet. This analysis is called **vertical analysis**, or **vertical percentage analysis**, because it is based on the percentage relationship of each line in the balance sheet to the total. Exhibit 3–1 has been revised as Exhibit 3–4 showing the vertical percentages for each account on the balance sheet. These percentages were calculated by dividing each line by the total assets ($2,057,000). Note that either total assets or total liabilities plus owners' equity could be used as the denominator for this calculation because the number is the same ($2,057,000).

Liquidity Ratios

Liquidity represents the ability of a company to convert its assets to cash. **Liquidity ratios** are often calculated from balance sheet data. Although there are many types of liquidity ratios, we focus here on a few of the more basic ones.

Current Ratio. The most popular liquidity ratio is the current ratio. The **current ratio** is calculated by dividing all current assets by all current liabilities:

$$\text{Current ratio} = \frac{\text{Current assets}}{\text{Current liabilities}}$$

For the data in Exhibit 3–1,

$$\text{Current ratio} = \frac{\$1,420,000}{\$699,000} = 2.03$$

Current ratios that represent good liquidity and financial health vary widely across firms and industries. Currently, many companies have a current ratio between 1.3 and 1.5. Many companies have short-term lines of credit and other borrowing capacity that permit them to operate with a nearly balanced amount of current assets and current liabilities. In any event, the analyst would be worried to find current liabilities substantially in excess of current assets (i.e., when the current ratio is considerably less than 1). Declining trends in the current ratio would also cause concern, especially in conjunction with declining trends in other ratios.

Quick Ratio. Another major liquidity ratio is the quick ratio, which is often called the *acid test.* In this context, "quick" means close to cash. To calculate this ratio, cash and cash equivalents and receivables are added and then divided by all current liabilities. In computing the quick ratio, the net realizable value of the accounts receivable should be used.

The purpose of the **quick ratio** is to indicate the resources that may be available quickly, in the short term, for repaying the current liabilities. For this reason, inventory and prepaid expenses are left out. In other words, the quick ratio is a type of

EXHIBIT 3–4
A BALANCE SHEET

Sample Company Balance Sheet: Vertical Analysis at December 31, 1998

Assets		Liabilities and Owners' Equity	
Current assets		Current liabilities	
Cash	5.3%	Accounts payable	12.6%
Accounts receivable	22.6	Notes payable	10.9
Inventories	39.5	Warranty obligations	5.4
Prepaid expenses	1.6	Accrued expenses	3.6
Total current assets	69.0%	Taxes payable	1.3
Property, plant and equipment		Total current liabilities	33.8%
Land	4.1%	Noncurrent liabilities	
		Bonds payable	17.1
Buildings and equipment	42.0	Mortgage payable	7.3%
Less: Accumulated		Total noncurrent liabilities	24.4%
depreciation	−15.1	Total liabilities	58.2%
Net book value	26.9%	Shareholders' equity	
Total property, plant, and		Invested capital	29.3%
equipment assets	31.0%	Retained earnings	12.5
Total assets	100.0%	Total shareholders' equity	41.8%
		Total liabilities and	
		shareholders' equity	100.0%

NOTE: All percentage amounts in this exhibit were obtained by dividing the dollar amounts reported in Exhibit 3–1 by $2,057,000, Sample Company's total assets (which also equal total liabilities plus shareholders' equity) at December 31, 1998.

"disaster" ratio that is used to indicate a worst case scenario that might apply if no other resources were available to pay the current liabilities that are due within the next year.

$$\text{Quick ratio} = \frac{\text{(Cash and cash equivalents + Receivables)}}{\text{Current liabilities}}$$

For the data in Exhibit 3–1,

$$\text{Quick ratio} = \frac{(\$110,000 + \$466,000)}{\$699,000}$$

$$= .82$$

Values for the quick ratio are often less than 1.0, and a rule of thumb used by some analysts is that the quick ratio should not be less than .30. Again, declining trends should cause the most concern. When comparing two companies, a lower quick ratio and a lower current ratio do not, in and of themselves, indicate that the company with the lower values is in worse financial condition. Lower liquidity may be offset by a variety of other financial indicators such that the company with lower liquidity ratios could still rank higher on its overall financial stability and financial health.

Information useful for calculating the current and quick ratios for two firms in dissimilar industries is shown in Reality Check 3–4.

Asset Management Ratios

Asset management ratios focus on the composition of the firm's assets and on changes in the composition of assets over time (e.g., changes between successive balance

CURRENT RATIO AND QUICK RATIO COMPARISONS: DELTA AIR LINES AND BETHLEHEM STEEL

REALITY CHECK 3–4

The following schedule summarizes the composition of current assets and current liabilities reported in the end of 1993 balance sheets of Delta Air Lines and Bethlehem Steel.

	Delta Air Lines	Bethlehem Steel
	(dollars in thousands)	
Total current assets	$2,821,920	$1,591,100
Inventories included in current assets	0	852,500
Prepayment and supplies included in current assets	586,751	6,500
Total current liabilities	$2,972,831	$914,200

REQUIRED

a. Based on the information given here, determine each firm's current ratio and quick ratio at the end of 1993.
b. Which firm do you consider to be in better financial condition? Explain.

sheets). A vertical analysis of the left side of the balance sheet allows the analyst to examine the percentages of the total assets devoted to each category. This examination gives some indication of the resources used for current assets relative to those used to provide operating capacity.

In reviewing the **percentage composition** of a firm's assets, the analyst keeps several factors in mind. First, to a large extent the composition of assets depends on the industry in which the firm operates. In some cases, comparisons between industries may be meaningless. For example, "smokestack" industries such as metal fabrication require large investments in factory buildings and heavy equipment such that a major portion of these firms' assets are noncurrent. Merchandising industries such as department stores, on the other hand, require large amounts of accounts receivable and also substantial investments in inventories available for resale, but relatively minor investment in buildings and equipment. Financial firms such as banks and insurance companies have relatively little in the way of inventories, factory buildings, and equipment. Instead, the assets of financial firms consist mainly of loans receivable and investments in securities (stocks and bonds) of other firms. A first step for the analyst in assessing a firm's asset composition is to be aware of any peculiar industry norms or special circumstances.

In addition to industry characteristics, the analyst knows that managers may have sound business reasons for structuring a firm's assets differently than those of its competitors. For example, some managers may extend liberal credit terms to customers as a way of improving sales and, as a result, may have a large accounts receivable balance. Other managers may carry large inventories for customer convenience or may stockpile inventories in anticipation of price rises or supply bottlenecks. On the other hand, large amounts of accounts receivable may indicate that a firm has difficulty collecting its accounts. Similarly, large inventories may reflect obsolete items or declining product sales. In short, increases or decreases in specific components of a firm's total assets may be either good news or bad news. Any ratio computations are only the first step for the analyst. The creative art in ratio analysis is understanding the reasons for ratio differences among firms and over time.

Debt Management Ratios

The most inclusive and most useful **debt management ratios** are the composition ratios drawn from a vertical analysis of the right side of the balance sheet. Note the liability and equity composition ratios in the right-hand column of Exhibit 3–4. These percentage composition ratios indicate the relative proportions of various forms of debt and owners' equity used to finance the organization.

The vertical analysis of Sample Company's sources of funds shows that 33.8% of all financing came from current liabilities. A smaller amount (24.4%) came from long-term liabilities, and the largest portion (41.8%) came from owners. Of the 41.8% portion that came from owners, 29.3% was in the form of direct investment, and 12.5% was in the form of profits reinvested in the business.

The ratio of total debt to total assets, also called the **debt-to-assets ratio,** is often used as a primary indicator of the firm's debt management. Exhibit 3–4 shows that Sample Company's total liabilities are equal to 58.2% of total assets. As this key ratio increases or decreases, it indicates the firm's changing reliance on borrowed resources. The lower the ratio, the lower the firm's risk because the organization will usually be better able to meet its obligations for interest and debt payments. A lower debt-to-assets ratio also suggests a lower risk of default. Default on a firm's liabilities is a costly event from both a lender's and a borrower's perspective and should be avoided if at all possible.

The fact that Sample Company's owners' equity provides 41.8% of the firm's resources suggests that the owners' equity of this firm offers substantial protection to lenders. For example, suppose Sample Company were unable to continue its operations and had to **liquidate** its assets, i.e., convert its assets to cash. In such a situation Sample Company could incur losses of 41.8% of the assets' carrying value, and the cash received would still be sufficient to pay off all the firm's debts. Of course, nothing would then be left for the owners.

≋ Limitations of Balance Sheet Analysis

Although the ratios reviewed in this section provide a useful starting point for assessing a firm's financial management policies, several limitations must be considered. First, ratio calculations are only the initial step in analyzing a firm's condition. They merely provide the analyst with a point of departure for asking further questions. Second, individual financial statements such as the balance sheet are seldom analyzed separately from other statements described in the next two chapters. In fact, many of the most useful ratios used by analysts measure relationships among financial statements, rather than relationships within a single financial statement. For this reason, we will expand and enrich our study of ratio analysis after first describing the other primary financial statements. Third, information useful for analyzing and clarifying financial statements is contained in other parts of a company's financial reports.

An important limitation in comparing financial ratios across firms is the fact that their accounting methods may differ. Later chapters discuss the varieties of different methods that firms may use in measuring assets, liabilities, shareholders' equity, revenues, and expenses. For now, be aware that financial ratios may be significantly affected by alternative accounting methods. The analyst attempts to adjust for differences caused by accounting methods in order to make valid ratio comparisons among different firms. The notes to the financial statements alert the analyst to the principal methods being used.

SUMMARY OF LEARNING OBJECTIVES

1. **Identify the basic elements of the balance sheet.**

   The basic elements of the balance sheet are assets, liabilities, and owners' equity. Liabilities and owners' equity are the sources from which a firm has obtained its funds, and assets show the way that the firm's managers have invested those funds.

2. **Recognize the types of assets, liabilities, and owners' equity that are found on the balance sheets of most business firms.**

   Assets are resources that are expected to benefit the firm in future periods, including cash, accounts receivable, inventories held for production and sale, prepayments of expenses, and property, plant, and equipment. Liabilities are obligations to provide future services or to make future payments, and include trade accounts payable, short- and long-term borrowings, and other debts. Owners' equity is the difference between assets and liabilities. For a corporation, owners' equity consists of invested capital, which has been paid by investors to obtain ownership shares, and retained earnings, which represent earnings that have been reinvested in the business.

3. **Comprehend the ordering and classification of items on the balance sheet.**
Both assets and liabilities are listed in order of liquidity or maturity on the balance sheet. They are further classified into current and noncurrent portions. Current assets will become cash or be consumed in a year or an operating cycle, whichever is longer. Current liabilities require payment from current assets.

4. **Appreciate why balance sheets differ for firms in different industries.**
"Smokestack" industries require large investments in factory buildings and heavy equipment, and a major portion of their assets are noncurrent. Merchandising industries, however, require large investments in accounts receivable and inventories and relatively minor investments in buildings and equipment. Financial firms such as banks have relatively little investment in inventories, factory buildings, and equipment. Instead, their assets consist mainly of loans receivable and investments in securities (stocks and bonds) of other firms.

5. **Use balance sheet relationships to obtain information useful to investors and lenders.**
Various ratios help assess a firm's liquidity, asset management, and debt management policies. Liquidity ratios aid in assessing how the firm may pay its debts and meet its other short-term cash requirements. Asset management ratios show how the funds invested in the firm are being used. Debt management ratios show the firm's reliance on borrowed capital and the buffer or "safety zone" provided by owners' equity.

6. **Be alert to the limitations as well as the usefulness of balance sheet information.**
Balance sheet relationships do not provide direct answers to the analyst in assessing the firm's potential risks and returns. They merely provide a base for further questions. Also, the balance sheet is seldom analyzed separately from the other financial statements to be discussed in subsequent chapters. Moreover, an important limitation in comparing financial relationships across firms is the fact that their accounting methods may differ.

KEY TERMS

Accounts payable
Accounts receivable
Accrued expenses
Accumulated depreciation
Amortization
Asset management ratios
Bond
Bonds payable
Buildings
Cash and cash equivalents
Collateral
Corporation
Current assets
Current liabilities
Current ratio

Debt management ratios
Debt-to-assets ratio
Depreciation expense
Externally generated goodwill
Fixed assets
Goodwill
Intangibles
Internally generated goodwill
Inventory
Liquidate
Liquidity
Liquidity ratio
Mortgage payable
Net book value
Net realizable value

Noncurrent assets	Principal
Noncurrent liabilities	Property, plant and equipment
Notes payable	Quick ratio
Operating capacity	Retained earnings
Operating cycles	Statement of financial position
Owners' equity	Taxes payable
Paid-in capital	Vertical percentage analysis
Percentage composition	Warranty obligations
Prepaid expenses	

REALITY CHECK SOLUTIONS

SOLUTION TO REALITY CHECK 3–1

a. The major differences in the composition of current assets are the amounts invested in inventories and accounts receivables.

- *Inventories:* Abbott Laboratories is a manufacturer, and maintains inventories of raw materials, work-in process, and finished products. Delta is a service firm and, hence, does not require inventories. The supplies account reported on Delta's balance sheet represents mainly fuel oil and repair parts.
- *Accounts receivable:* Abbott Laboratories invests about 17.4% of its total assets in customer accounts receivable ($1,336,222/$7,688,569 = 17.4%), and the corresponding percentage for Delta is 8.6% ($1,024,869/$11,871,023 = 8.6%). Manufacturers such as Abbott Laboratories sell primarily on credit and have relatively large accounts receivable balances. Service firms such as Delta derive much of their revenues from cash and credit card sales, and require smaller accounts receivable balances.

b. Abbott Laboratories has a larger amount of current assets than does Delta Air Lines. On the other hand, Delta's current assets appear to be more liquid. As a result, most analysts would consider Delta to be more liquid based solely on the information provided.

SOLUTION TO REALITY CHECK 3–2

a. Bethlehem Steel invests 72.9% of its resources in noncurrent assets ($4,286/$5,877 = 72.9%), and the corresponding amount for Hewlett-Packard is just 38.8% ($6,500/$16,736 = 38.8%). Bethlehem Steel is a highly capital-intensive firm because the technology of steel production requires large investments in plant and equipment. Also, steel firms usually invest in properties containing natural resources (e.g., coal, iron ore) used in steel fabrication. In comparison, Hewlett-Packard is moderately capital intensive because of the property, plant, and equipment required by its product development and manufacturing activities.

b. Bethlehem Steel appears to have the older assets. Bethlehem's assets are about 60.9% depreciated ($4,107/$6,741 = 60.9%), while Hewlett-Packard's are about 44.5% depreciated ($3,347/$7,527 = 44.5%). These percentages are only approximations, however, because these amounts include property (land) that is not being depreciated.

SOLUTION TO REALITY CHECK 3–3

a. Paid-in capital represents the amount that each firm has received through sale of stock to investors. Kollmorgen has obtained $50.3 million, and Nuclear Metals has obtained just $13.9 million from this source.

b. Nuclear Metals has obtained $29.1 million of its investment in net assets through retention of earnings. Kollmorgen, on the other hand, has a negative balance in its retained earnings. For this reason, Kollmorgen has not obtained any of its capital through reinvestment of earnings.

c. Retained earnings are increased when a firm is profitable and decreased when a firm pays dividends to shareholders or incurs losses. The negative (deficit) balance in Kollmorgen's retained earnings indicates that since the firm began operations, its total dividends and losses have exceeded its total income.

d. Nuclear Metals would report a balance in retained earnings at the end of 1994 of $35,132 (in thousands), computed as follows:

Retained earnings, end of 1993	$29,132
Add: Net income for 1994	15,000
Less: Dividends in 1994	(9,000)
Retained earnings, end of 1994	$35,132

SOLUTION TO REALITY CHECK 3–4

a. Calculation of current ratio and quick ratio:

		Delta Air Lines	Bethlehem Steel
Current ratio	= $\dfrac{\text{Current assets}}{\text{Current liabilities}}$	$\dfrac{\$2,821,920}{\$2,972,831}$ = .95	$\dfrac{\$1,591,100}{\$914,200}$ = 1.74
Quick ratio	= $\dfrac{\text{Quick assets}^*}{\text{Current liabilities}}$	$\dfrac{\$2,235,169}{\$2,972,831}$ = .75	$\dfrac{\$732,100}{\$914,200}$ = .80

*Quick assets are estimated as current assets, minus the amounts in inventories, prepayments, and supplies.

b. Bethlehem Steel has a current ratio substantially larger than that of Delta Air Lines (1.74 versus .95). Bethlehem Steel's quick ratio, however, is just slightly above Delta's (.80 versus .75). Although Bethlehem Steel appears to be more liquid using either of these widely used measures, the analyst would seek additional information from the financial statements, and elsewhere, before making a final judgment.

QUESTIONS

3–1 Rearrange the balance sheet equation into several alternative versions or formats. Why are these differences helpful? Should an analyst always use the simplest version possible? Why or why not?

3–2 Discuss the role of the balance sheet. Discuss how the balance sheet achieves this role or purpose.

3–3 Explain why both sides of the balance sheet must have the same total dollar amount. Does this equality imply that the balance sheet is "correct" as a measure of financial position? Discuss.

3–4   The chapter states that the balance sheet may be viewed as "the cumulative result of the firm's past activities." Explain how the assets, liabilities, and owners' equity amounts may be interpreted in this way.

3–5   All assets represent probable future economic benefits to the firm. Identify the probable future benefit associated with each of the following: (a) inventories, (b) accounts receivable, and (c) building and equipment.

3–6   Compare and contrast current assets and current liabilities. How and why are they different? In what ways are they similar?

3–7   Compare and contrast prepaid expenses and accrued expenses. How and why are they different? Could they be easily confused? How could they be kept separate?

3–8   Differentiate between current and noncurrent assets, and explain why this distinction may be useful to readers of financial reports.

3–9   Compare and contrast noncurrent assets and long-term liabilities. How and why are they different? In what ways are they similar?

3–10 Suppose that your employer asks you to reclassify a short-term note payable as a long-term liability.

   a. What effect will this have on the current ratio?
   b. Could such an effect be viewed beneficially by a current or prospective lender?
   c. How would your answer change if the lender agreed to extend the due date on the loan by 18 months?
   d. How would your answer in part b change if a prospective lender also held other long-term liabilities? Why?

WHAT WOULD YOU DO?

3–11 Refer to Question 3–10 and consider the ethical implications of reclassifying the note, assuming that you know the note's maturity is at the end of the current fiscal year. You may also assume that the size of the note is significant (or material). As an accountant within the firm, what should/would you do? As the firm's auditor, how would you view this reclassification?

3–12 Describe the concept of an operating cycle. Identify reasons why operating cycles may differ for firms in different industries, and also for firms in the same industry.

3–13 What is meant by the term *net book value* of a firm's building and equipment? Explain why net book value differs from the initial cost of these assets and is also likely to differ from current market (i.e., resale) values.

3–14 Differentiate between tangible and intangible assets. Do you believe that both types of assets are equally important in measuring a firm's financial position? Discuss.

3–15 Distinguish between internally generated and externally acquired goodwill. Which of these is reported on the balance sheet? State and defend your agreement or disagreement with this accounting convention.

3–16 Analysts often attempt to estimate the values of assets that are "missing" from the balance sheet. Identify at least two types of missing assets, and discuss reasons for this omission from the balance sheet.

3–17 Provide several examples of liabilities that do not require payments of specific dollar amounts to lenders.

3–18 Identify the essential difference between bonds payable and mortgages payable. As a potential lender, which type of debt would you prefer to hold?

3–19 Discuss the concept of owners' equity on the balance sheet. In what ways does owners' equity represent a residual concept? Why could you call owners' equity the "leftover" amounts?

3–20 Is it possible for a firm to report a substantial amount of retained earnings on its balance sheet and still be unable to pay its shareholders a cash dividend? Explain.

3–21 Compare and contrast the current ratio and the quick ratio.

    a. When might these two ratios be similar in amount?

    b. When will they be different in amount?

    c. If the current ratio is at an acceptable level, but the quick ratio is weak, what factors might cause this?

3–22 How much flexibility should the analyst or manager accept in constructing ratio definitions for use within the same company or organization? For example, why might the analyst be more flexible in defining the quick ratio, but not the current ratio?

3–23 Discuss and evaluate the construction and use of balance sheet vertical (composition) ratios. Why are these ratios important?

EXERCISES

Classifying Accounts

3–24 Classify each account listed below into one of the following categories:

    1. current assets,

    2. noncurrent assets,

    3. current liabilities,

    4. noncurrent liabilities, and

    5. owners' equity.

      a. cash

      b. retained earnings

      c. land

      d. invested capital

      e. accounts payable

      f. accounts receivable

      g. mortgage payable

      h. marketable securities

      i. prepaid expenses

      j. wages payable

      k. unemployment taxes payable

      l. accumulated depreciation

      m. inventory

Arranging Accounts in Balance Sheet Order

3–25 Rearrange the following accounts in the order in which you would expect to find them in a typical balance sheet:

a. Mortgage payable.
b. Accounts payable.
c. Taxes payable.
d. Long-term notes payable.
e. Accrued expenses.

Preparing a Balance Sheet

3–26 Given the following data, set up a balance sheet equation and a balance sheet.

Cash	$100,000
Accounts payable	55,000
Retained earnings	?
Invested capital	150,000
Buildings and equipment	600,000
Mortgage payable	400,000

What other accounts might usually be found in such a balance sheet? Why are they likely not in this balance sheet?

Preparing a Balance Sheet

3–27 Prepare a balance sheet and a balance sheet equation for Tom's Track Shoe Store at the end of 1998, given the following information. What conclusions can be drawn regarding this business? Why?

Accounts receivable	$ 6,500
Accounts payable	106,500
Accumulated depreciation, equipment	21,500
Bonds payable	180,000
Invested capital	300,000
Cash	14,500
Equipment	88,000
Income taxes payable	11,500
Inventory	497,500
Other long-term assets	110,000
Notes payable	50,000
Prepaid rent	54,000
Retained earnings, 12-31-97	94,500

Note: The balance sheet does not balance. What could have caused the imbalance?

Preparing a Balance Sheet

3–28 The following balances appear in the records of May Co. at the end of its first month of operations:

Cash	$ 12,000	Land	$100,000
Equipment	6,500	Accounts payable	3,400
Supplies	2,700	Accounts receivable	7,500
Taxes payable	2,110	Truck	22,500
Mortgage	80,000	Owners' equity	?

REQUIRED

a. Determine the missing quantity by preparing a balance sheet or a balance sheet equation.

b. Identify two other typical accounts that might appear on May's balance sheet, but are not shown at this time.

Effects of Transactions on Balance Sheet

3–29 Indicate the positive and/or negative effects of the transactions given below on the balance sheet equation:

ASSETS = LIABILITIES + OWNERS' EQUITY

For example, if the company issues capital stock for cash,

ASSETS	=	LIABILITIES	+	OWNERS' EQUITY
+				+

a. A corporation issues common stock in exchange for cash.

b. The firm buys land with part of the cash.

c. It issues common stock in exchange for a building and equipment.

d. The firm purchases inventory by issuing notes payable.

e. It collects cash from a customer for merchandise sold several months previously.

f. A corporation exchanges some of its common stock to pay off its mortgage from the bank.

g. The firm returns defective merchandise to the supplier on account.

h. The firm sells its equipment to a friend of the owner at its original cost.

Preparing a Balance Sheet

3–30 The account balances given below were shown on the balance sheet of a corporation. Arrange three columns corresponding to the balance sheet equation:

ASSETS = LIABILITIES + OWNERS' EQUITY

REQUIRED

Put each account into the proper column and total each column to see that the equation is in balance.

Marketable securities	$ 20,000
Invested capital	200,000
Buildings and equipment	400,000
Accounts receivable	80,000
Prepaid rent	17,000
Bonds payable	230,000
Inventories	85,000
Taxes payable	30,000
Accounts payable	16,000
Advance payments from customers	3,000
Interest payable	9,000
Land	19,000
Retained earnings	133,000

3–31 Transaction Analysis—Alternate Exercises (A) or (B)

Exercise (A)

Indicate the positive or negative effects of the transactions given below on the balance sheet equation:

$$\text{ASSETS} \quad = \quad \text{LIABILITIES} \quad + \quad \text{OWNERS' EQUITY}$$

For example, if the company issues capital stock for $100 cash,

ASSETS	=	LIABILITIES	+	OWNERS' EQUITY
+100				+100

Add your column totals after including all appropriate transactions, and prepare a simple balance sheet.

a. A corporation issued capital stock in exchange for land valued at $300,000.
b. A corporation issued capital stock in exchange for $200,000.
c. The corporation hired a chief executive officer (CEO) at $180,000 per year.
d. The firm agreed to rent office space at $2,000 per month.
e. It paid the first month's rent.
f. It paid the last month's rent as a security deposit.
g. The firm bought supplies for $2,500.
h. The firm ordered office equipment costing $15,000 (assume no obligation has occurred yet).
i. The CEO finished her first month's work.
j. The firm paid the CEO her first month's salary.
k. It received the office equipment and the bill. The equipment is expected to last for five years.
l. It recorded depreciation for the first month.

Exercise (B)

Indicate the positive or negative effects of the transactions given below on the balance sheet equation:

ASSETS = LIABILITIES + OWNERS' EQUITY

For example, if the company issues capital stock for $100 cash,

ASSETS	=	LIABILITIES	+	OWNERS' EQUITY
+100				+100

Add your column totals after including all appropriate transactions, and prepare a simple balance sheet.

a. A law firm was formed by 10 lawyers, each investing $200,000.
b. The firm charged its clients $1,200,000 for services rendered in May.
c. The law firm collected $900,000 from its clients.
d. One disgruntled client sued the law firm for malfeasance in the amount of $5,000,000. The firm believes the lawsuit is frivolous.
e. The law firm paid its lawyers $333,000 for work performed in May.
f. The law firm ordered and received supplies costing $33,000 on account. However, 10% of the order was damaged, so the firm returned the damaged supplies for credit.
g. The law firm paid $155,000 for rent and other administrative costs.
h. The law firm settled the suit with the disgruntled client by paying $10,000 for court costs.

PROBLEMS

Evaluating Loans: Memo to Loan Manager

3–32 Assume a businessperson applies for a loan from a bank. What questions and additional information might the banker request after reviewing the following representations from the business person? Should the banker grant the loan on the basis of this information?

1. Cash has increased by $100,000 this year.
2. Property has increased by $300,000 this year.
3. Withdrawals of owners' equity were $200,000.
4. The business is stronger than it has ever been.
5. The business grew by $600,000 this year.

REQUIRED

a. Write your answer in the form of a memo to the manager of the commercial loan department.

Transaction Analysis: Expanded Accounting Equation

3–33 Arrange columns corresponding to the following expanded balance sheet equation (assume zero beginning balances):

> CASH + PREPAID INSURANCE + INVENTORY + BUILDING AND EQUIPMENT + ACCUMULATED DEPRECIATION = ACCOUNTS PAYABLE + UNEARNED REVENUE + MORTGAGE PAYABLE + INVESTED CAPITAL + RETAINED EARNINGS

Given these transactions:

1. Owners invest $500,000 into this business in exchange for stock.
2. Buildings and equipment are purchased for $200,000 cash and a mortgage of $600,000.
3. Inventory is purchased on account for $100,000.
4. Insurance of $8,000 for two years is paid in advance.
5. Interest of $60,000 is paid on the mortgage.
6. Defective merchandise costing $5,000 is returned for credit.
7. Customers pay $10,000 in advance as a deposit.
8. Depreciation of $80,000 is recorded.
9. One year of insurance that has expired is recorded.

REQUIRED

a. Enter transactions 1 through 9 into the columns. Total each column and verify that the balance sheet equation does balance. Prepare a classified balance sheet from the totals of your spreadsheet.

Interpretation (continuation of Problem 3–33)

3–34 Given your answers to Problem 3–33, assume the company had cash sales of $200,000 during the year and inventory balances at year-end were $40,000. Record these transactions. What conclusions can be drawn about the success of this firm?

Using Ratios to Evaluate Liquidity

3–35 Use the following balance sheet accounts to evaluate the company's liquidity and its management of assets and liabilities. Compute using the balance sheet ratios described in this chapter.

	1997	1996
Cash	$ 45,000	$ 35,000
Fixed assets	330,000	270,000
Current liabilities	95,000	45,000
Long-term liabilities	300,000	320,000
Accounts receivable	115,000	95,000
Invested capital	100,000	100,000
Inventories	100,000	80,000
Retained earnings	95,000	15,000

3–36 Fill in the Blanks: Preparing a Balance Sheet, Analyzing Liquidity— Alternate Problems (A) or (B)

Problem (A)

Given the following data:

	1996	1997
Cash	$ 30,000	$ 40,000
Retained earnings	175,000	225,000
Current liabilities	17,000	16,000
Invested capital	600,000	600,000
Accounts receivable	27,500	38,000
Inventories	45,000	47,000
Fixed assets, net	?	?

REQUIRED

a. Rearrange these data into a classified balance sheet format, for each year.
b. Find the missing quantity of Fixed Assets (necessary to balance the balance sheet).
c. Evaluate the firm's liquidity and management of its assets and liabilities, using the balance sheet ratios described in this chapter.

Problem (B)

Given the following data:

	1996	1997
Cash	$300,000	$340,000
Retained earnings	165,000	325,000
Accounts payable	20,000	11,000
Wages payable	7,000	5,000
Interest payable	10,000	30,000
Bonds payable	40,000	100,000
Mortgage payable	60,000	300,000
Invested capital	500,000	600,000
Accounts receivable	37,500	118,000
Inventories	55,000	87,000
Fixed assets, net	?	?

REQUIRED

a. Rearrange these data into a classified balance sheet format, for each year.
b. Find the missing quantity of Fixed Assets (necessary to balance the balance sheet).
c. Evaluate the firm's liquidity and management of its assets and liabilities, using the balance sheet ratios described in this chapter.

Fill in the Blanks: Preparing a Balance Sheet, Analyzing Liquidity

3–37 Given the following data:

	1996	1997
Cash	$350,000	$240,000
Retained earnings	145,000	225,000
Current liabilities	77,000	66,000
Long-term liabilities	0	500,000
Invested capital	650,000	600,000
Accounts receivable	45,700	88,000
Inventories	66,000	78,000
Fixed assets, net	?	?

REQUIRED

a. Rearrange these data into a classified balance sheet format, for each year.
b. Find the missing quantity of Fixed Assets (necessary to balance the balance sheet).
c. Evaluate the firm's liquidity and management of its assets and liabilities, using the balance sheet ratios described in this chapter.

Transaction Analysis: Expanded Accounting Equation

3–38 Arrange columns in a spreadsheet, corresponding to the balance sheet equation using these balance sheet accounts: Cash, Accounts Receivable, Prepaid Rent, Supplies, Property Plant and Equipment, Accumulated Depreciation, Accounts Payable, Interest Payable, Mortgage Payable, Common Stock, Retained Earnings. Consider these transactions:

1. Investors purchase $900,000 of common stock from the firm.
2. The firm purchases land, buildings, and equipment valued at $1,300,000, paying $300,000 in cash, and signing a mortgage for the balance due.
3. The firm pays rent of $10,000 for five automobiles.
4. The firm realizes that the auto rental covers two months, one of which is the current month.
5. The firm purchases supplies on account for $55,000.
6. The firm provides services on account to customers at a retail value of $3,200,000.
7. The firm receives payments of $3,000,000 from customers on account.
8. The firm pays for its supplies.
9. The firm records its monthly depreciation of $22,000.
10. The firm accrues one month's interest on its mortgage at 12% per annum.

REQUIRED

a. Enter transactions 1 through 10 into the columns. Total each column and verify that the balance sheet equation does, indeed, balance. Prepare a classified balance sheet, using the column totals from your spreadsheet.

Performance Evaluation (continuation of Problem 3–38)

3–39 With regard to Problem 3–38, evaluate the firm's performance. What important information is missing? Even though the firm's performance seems spectacularly good, could the missing information change your opinion? Why?

Transaction Analysis: Expanded Accounting Equation

3–40 Arrange five columns in a spreadsheet, corresponding to the following expanded balance sheet equation (assume zero beginning balances):

CURRENT ASSETS + FIXED ASSETS = CURRENT LIABILITIES + LONG-TERM LIABILITIES + OWNERS' EQUITY

Given these transactions:

1. An engineering firm is formed with three engineers each investing $50,000 in the firm.
2. Each founder also has pick-up trucks, inclinometers, and other specialty equipment, valued at $10,000 (each) that is invested in the firm.
3. The firm borrows $50,000 on account to provide additional operating funds.
4. The firm rents office space at $1,000 per month.
5. It pays the first month's rent.
6. It pays a security deposit of $2,000.
7. The firm finds a wealthy individual who wants to invest in the firm, but this individual does not want to become an owner. So, the firm borrows $500,000 from this individual at 18% per year.
8. Additional staff are hired at $6,000 per month.
9. These staff earn their first month's salaries, but the firm has not yet paid them.
10. Supplies costing $45,000 are purchased.
11. Record depreciation for the first month. Assume the equipment items in transaction 2 have useful lives of five years.
12. Accrue interest for the first month on the loan.

REQUIRED

a. Enter transactions 1 through 12 into the five columns. Total each column and verify that the balance sheet does, indeed, balance. Prepare a classified balance sheet, using the column totals from your spreadsheet.

Performance Evaluation (continuation of Problem 3–40)

3–41 With regard to Problem 3–40, evaluate the firm's performance. What important information is missing? Even though the firm's performance seems somewhat questionable, could the missing information change your opinion? Why?

CASES AND EXTENSIONS

Transaction Analysis: Expanded Equation Including Fund Balances

3–42 Arrange five columns corresponding to the following expanded balance sheet equation for a nonprofit hospital (assume zero beginning balances), where FUND BALANCES is used instead of OWNERS' EQUITY:

CURRENT ASSETS + FIXED ASSETS = CURRENT LIABILITIES + LONG-TERM LIABILITIES + FUND BALANCES

Given these transactions:

1. Community donations of $150,000 are received.
2. A mortgage of $1.5M is secured and a hospital is constructed.
3. Donated land worth $1M is received.
4. Short-term lines of credit are used to acquire supplies of $50,000.
5. Obstetrics clients pay $20,000 in advance as a deposit.

6. Operating lease payments of $30,000 on x-ray equipment are made.
7. Donations of $1,000 by the hospital to the American Cancer Society are recorded.
8. Half of the land is sold for $2M.
9. Depreciation expense of $6,250 on the hospital building is recorded.

REQUIRED

a. Enter transactions 1 through 9 into the five columns. Total each column and verify that the balance sheet does balance. Note that FUND BALANCES can be used in the same manner as OWNERS' EQUITY for a commercial firm. Prepare a simple balance sheet from the totals of your spreadsheet.

Performance Evaluation (continuation of Case 3–42)

3–43 What conclusions can be drawn about the financial status of the hospital described in Case 3–42?

Interpreting Financial Statements

3–44 CSX Corporation's 1994 and 1993 balance sheets are summarized below (dollars in millions):

Current Assets	**12-31-94**	**12-31-93**
Cash and temporary investments	$ 535	$ 499
Receivables, less allowances	706	668
Materials and supplies	211	199
Prepaid and other	213	215
Total current assets	1,665	1,581
Property, plant, and equipment		
Net property, plant and equipment	11,044	10,778
Investment in affiliates and other companies	302	268
Other assets and deferred charges	713	793
Total assets	$13,724	$13,420
Current Liabilities		
Debt maturing within one year	312	146
Accounts payable and other current liabilities	1,992	1,965
Short-term debt	201	164
Total current liabilities	2,505	2,275
Long-term debt	2,618	3,133
Deferred income taxes	2,570	2,341
Long-term liabilities and deferred gains	2,300	2,491
Shareowners' equity		
Common stock and retained earnings	3,731	3,180
Total liabilities and shareowners' equity	$13,724	$13,420

REQUIRED

a. With regard to CSX's balance sheet, identify any unusual or unfamiliar terms. Describe how you interpret each new or unfamiliar term.

Ratio Analysis (continuation of Case 3–44)

3–45 Refer to the CSX balance sheets in Case 3–44.

a. Calculate the current ratio for each year.
b. Using the balance sheet data, analyze CSX's liquidity in each year.
c. What recommendations might you make about its future strategies concerning liquidity?
d. Calculate and evaluate CSX's debt-to-asset ratios for each year.

Interpreting Financial Statements

3–46 Pioneer Resource's comparative balance sheets are summarized below (dollars in millions):

Current Assets	12-31-97	12-31-96
Cash and equivalents	$ 121.5	$ 722.3
Receivables, less allowances	1,742.3	1,607.9
Supplies	310.4	306.2
Prepaids	284.2	171.8
Subtotal	2,458.4	2,808.2
Property, plant, and equipment; other long-term assets		
In use	34,742.3	32,655.2
Under construction	844.4	631.5
Less: Accumulated depreciation	(11,318.7)	(10,562.7)
Net property, plant, and equipment	24,268.0	22,724.0
Investment in Olivier Corp. of Belgium	2,173.4	—
Other assets	742.8	225.4
Total assets	$ 29,642.6	$ 25,757.6
Current Liabilities		
Current portion of long-term debt	1,795.5	615.3
Accounts payable	1,546.7	1,505.2
Other current liabilities	1,625.9	1,489.7
Subtotal	4,968.1	3,610.2
Long-term debt	7,215.1	7,159.8
Other long-term deferred credits	8,061.8	7,795.4
Shareowners' Equity		
Common stock and retained earnings	9,397.6	7,192.2
Total liabilities and shareowners' equity	$ 29,642.6	$ 25,757.6

REQUIRED

a. With regard to Pioneer Resource's balance sheet, identify any unusual or unfamiliar terms. Describe how you interpret each new or unfamiliar term.

b. Identify and discuss the acquisition of an interest in Olivier Corp. of Belgium. How may this acquisition reflect a change in Pioneer Resource in 1997 (vs. 1996)?

c. Why might the corporation's cash decline so dramatically in a single year? Does this decline seem significant? Why?

Ratio Analysis (continuation of Case 3–46)

3–47 Refer to Pioneer Resource's balance sheet in Case 3–46.

a. Calculate the current ratio for each year.

b. Using the balance sheet data, analyze Pioneer Resource's liquidity in each year.

c. What recommendations might you make about its future strategies concerning liquidity?

d. Calculate and evaluate Pioneer Resource's debt-to-asset ratios for each year.

Interpreting Financial Statements: Ratio Analysis

3–48 Consider Sigma Designs' balance sheets for 1993 and 1992 (dollars in thousands). Sigma Designs is a high-tech software development company specializing in imaging and multimedia computer applications.

Assets	1993	1992
Current Assets		
Cash and equivalents	$ 5,086	$ 9,283
Marketable securities	14,326	19,537
Accounts receivable, net of allowances	6,471	2,987
Inventories	12,275	10,066
Prepaid expenses and other	435	753
Income taxes receivable	1,582	2,428
Total current assets	40,175	45,054
Equipment, net	1,626	1,607
Other assets	2,466	2,388
Total assets	$44,267	$49,049
Liabilities and Shareholders' Equity		
Current liabilities		
Accounts payable	$ 4,933	$ 1,826
Accrued salary and benefits	809	594
Other accrued liabilities	737	1,119
Total current liabilities	6,479	3,539
Other long-term liabilities	—	755
Shareholders' Equity		
Common stock	19,287	19,088
Retained earnings	18,501	25,667
Shareholders' equity	37,788	44,755
Total liabilities and shareholders' equity	$44,267	$49,049

REQUIRED

a. Conduct a vertical analysis of Sigma Designs' balance sheets. What conclusions can be drawn from these ratios?

b. Calculate the current and quick ratios for each year.

c. Does it seem that Sigma Designs has any liquidity problems? What major changes in current assets and current liabilities may contribute to these liquidity comparisons?

d. Calculate and evaluate the debt-to-assets ratio for Sigma Designs.

e. Concentrate on the equity section of the balance sheet. What may have caused the changes shown, i.e., the decrease in Retained Earnings and in Shareholders' Equity?

f. Examine the Income Taxes Receivable section. How can a company have income taxes that are receivable, and not payable? How are such receivables usually satisfied? Will the government just issue a refund check to Sigma Designs?

Interpreting Financial Statements: Ratio Analysis

3–49 Comparative balance sheets for Creative Cabinetry, Inc., for the past two years are as follows:

Assets	12-31-97	12-31-96
Cash	$ 95,000	$ 33,000
Accounts receivable	23,160	22,500
Inventory	30,000	123,650
Prepaid rent	3,840	5,850
Total current assets	152,000	185,000
Land	83,000	72,000
Equipment	800,000	600,000
Accumulated depreciation	(140,000)	(90,000)
Total long-term assets	743,000	582,000
Total assets	$895,000	$767,000

Liabilities and Shareholders' Equity		
Current Liabilities		
Accounts payable	$ 83,300	$ 48,100
Accrued liabilities	23,500	24,200
Short-term notes payable	62,000	51,000
Total current liabilities	168,800	123,300
Mortgage payable	547,200	383,500
Shareholders' Equity		
Common stock	150,000	150,000
Retained earnings	29,000	110,200
Total stockholders' equity	179,000	260,200
Total liabilities and shareholders' equity	$895,000	$767,000

REQUIRED

a. Using the format in Exhibit 3–4, prepare common-size comparative balance sheets for the two years.

b. Calculate the liquidity and debt ratios for each year.

c. What comments can you make about the changes in the relative composition of the corporation's accounts and the changes in their liquidity and debt? List at least five observations.

USING
FINANCIAL
ACCOUNTING°
ON THE
INTERNET

3–50 Locate the most recent set of financial statements for the companies listed below. You may use either the 10-K available at EDGAR (**www.sec.gov/edgarhp.htm**) or the annual report available at the company page on the WWW. The annual report is usually located in the Investor Information section.

Corporation	WWW Page Location
Xerox (office products)	**www.xerox.com**
Ben & Jerrys (food)	**www.benjerry.com**
Lewis Galoob Toys (toys)	**www.galoob.com**
Eli Lilly (pharmaceutical)	**www.lilly.com**

REQUIRED

a. For each company, perform a vertical analysis for the four major categories of assets (Current Assets, Investments, Property, Plant and Equipment, Other).

b. Discuss the impact that different types of business have on the composition of total assets.

3–51 Locate the most recent set of financial statements for the corporations listed below. You may use either the 10-K available at EDGAR (**www.sec.gov/edgarhp.htm**) or the annual report available at the company page on the WWW. The annual report is usually located in the Investor Information section.

Corporation	Home Page Location
Ameritech	**www.ameritech.com**
U S West	**www.uswest.com**
Bell Atlantic	**www.bell-atl.com**
BellSouth	**www.bst.bls.com**

REQUIRED

For each company compute the:

a. current ratio
b. quick ratio
c. Property, Plant, and Equipment as a percent of total assets
d. debt-to-assets ratio

3–52 Locate the balance sheet for IBM and Banc One. You may use either the 10-K available at EDGAR (**www.sec.gov/edgarhp.htm**) or the annual report available at the company page on the WWW. The annual report is usually located in the Investor Information section.

Corporation	WWW Page Location
IBM	**www.ibm.com**
Banc One	**www.bankone.com**

REQUIRED

a. Discuss the similarities and differences between the two balance sheets.

b. Property, Plant, and Equipment are used directly by companies such as IBM to generate earnings. However, Property, Plant, and Equipment are classified by banks as Other Assets. Why?

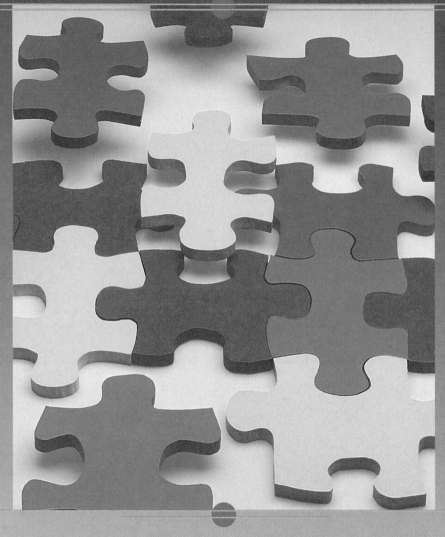

The Income
Statement

INTRODUCTION

The **income statement** summarizes the results of a firm's operations for a period of time: Four major types of items appear on income statements: revenues, expenses, gains, and losses.

Revenues are inflows of assets (or reductions in liabilities) that result from providing goods and services to customers; they arise from a firm's ongoing operations. Sales of inventory to customers, for example, generate assets (cash or accounts receivable) and constitute revenues. **Expenses** arise from consuming resources in order to generate revenues. The cost of inventory sold to customers illustrates an expense.

Gains, as with revenues, increase assets or decrease liabilities. However, they arise from activities that are not central to a firm's major operations. For example, a gain would result from selling land for more than its carrying (book) value. **Losses** are similar to expenses in that they decrease assets or increase liabilities. However, they are not central to a firm's major activities. The sale of land at an amount less than its carrying value would result in a loss.

AN ILLUSTRATED INCOME STATEMENT

Exhibit 4–1 contains the 1992 income statement for Jostens, Inc. which sells products such as yearbooks and class rings. The income statement is for the year ended June 30, 1992. The choice of a June 30 fiscal year-end is a good one for Jostens. The selling season for its products is during the spring, before the end of the school year. By the end of June, Jostens has completed its busy season, it has made any exchanges or refunds, and its inventory levels are probably rather low. This is a good time to tally results.

Jostens' income statement, similar to the income statements of many corporations, is highly condensed. It contains one revenue item, four expense items, and no gains or losses. However, Jostens almost certainly did experience gains and losses, but their relative sizes were probably so small that they were combined with other items on the income statement. This is an application of the **materiality principle,** which states that

EXHIBIT 4–1
MULTIPLE-STEP INCOME
STATEMENT

Jostens, Inc.
Income Statement
For the Year Ended June 30, 1992
(dollars in thousands)

Net Sales	$924,167
Cost of products sold	486,200
Gross profit	437,967
Selling and administrative expenses	331,251
Operating income	106,716
Interest expense	8,449
	98,267
Income taxes	36,293
Net income	$ 61,974

separate disclosure is not required if an item is so small that knowledge of it would not affect the decision of a reasonable financial statement reader. This principle can actually improve the usefulness of financial statements by eliminating the disclosure of inconsequential items, which helps analysts concentrate on items of importance.

The sole revenue line on Jostens' income statement is labeled **Net sales.** The terms *sales* and *revenue* are used interchangeably for firms that sell products to customers. The term **net** implies that certain items have been deducted from the gross (or full) sales price. For example, most firms allow their customers to return merchandise within a specified period. Customers are usually offered a full refund upon returning the merchandise. The original sales amount is included in gross sales. The refund amount is termed a **sales return,** and it is subtracted from gross sales in calculating net sales. Even if the term *net* is omitted, reported sales on the income statement are usually net sales.

Cost of products (or merchandise) sold is often referred to as **cost of goods sold.** It reflects the cost to Jostens of the goods sold to its customers. The difference between sales and cost of goods sold is called **gross profit** or **gross margin.**

Jostens has elected to combine selling and administrative expenses, although some companies report separate figures. **Selling expenses** include advertising costs, commissions to salespersons, depreciation of equipment used in the selling function, and a number of other items. **Administrative expenses** consist of senior managers' salaries, accounting and auditing costs, insurance, depreciation of administrative offices, and so on.

Operating income equals sales minus all costs and expenses incurred by normal operations. Operating income is a primary indicator of how well a firm has managed its operations and, as you will see, serves as a basis for comparing firms within the same industry.

Interest expense reflects the firm's cost of borrowing money from creditors. **Income taxes** are imposed by the federal government, state and local governments, and foreign jurisdictions. Neither interest nor income taxes directly relate to a firm's operations. For example, interest expense is largely a function of how much the firm has borrowed to *finance* its operations. Differences in interest expense between firms are determined primarily by choices the firms have made in financing their businesses. Some firms elect to borrow heavily; this results in large interest charges. Other firms rely on investments by owners. Interest charges are not paid on these funds. Because of this, interest expense is deducted after operating income is calculated.

The **bottom line** of the income statement is called **net income, earnings,** or **profit.** Although interest and income tax expenses do not affect operating income, they are appropriate deductions in the calculation of overall profitability. Because net income reflects the increase in net assets from all profit-oriented activities, it is the focus of much scrutiny by analysts, investors, and other financial statement readers.

Keep in mind the difference between *revenue* and *profit*. Revenue refers to the total inflow of assets (or reduction in liabilities) from customers. Profit is the net increase in a firm's recorded wealth after deducting expenses.

Jostens' income statement presented in Exhibit 4–1 is in the **multiple-step format.** Multiple-step income statements calculate certain subtotals for the reader. Jostens' statement contains subtotals for gross profit and operating income. In contrast, income statements using the **single-step format** summarize all revenues in one section and all expenses in another. Exhibit 4–2 illustrates a single-step income statement. Whereas the single-step approach is simpler, the multiple-step approach provides more information.

EXHIBIT 4–2
SINGLE-STEP INCOME
STATEMENT

Jostens, Inc.
Income Statement
For the Year Ended June 30, 1992
(dollars in thousands)

Revenues

Net sales		$924,167
Expenses		
Cost of products sold	$486,200	
Selling and administrative expenses	331,251	
Interest expense	8,449	
Income taxes	36,293	
Total expenses		862,193
Net income		$ 61,974

USES OF THE INCOME STATEMENT

A major purpose of the income statement is to show a firm's profitability. However, the income statement provides a number of additional performance measures. For example, revenue is a key measure of growth that reflects a firm's success in expanding its market. Additionally, comparisons of expense numbers from year to year indicate a firm's success in controlling costs. As previously mentioned, operating income measures managers' performance in conducting a firm's operations.

Decisions

Income statement information provides the basis for a variety of decisions. Because earnings underlie a firm's ability to generate cash flows for dividends and growth, equity investors are interested in the income statement. Lenders are also interested in the income statement because a firm's ability to pay principal and interest in a timely manner ultimately depends on its profitability.

A firm's management can use income statement information to make a variety of decisions. For example, managers must constantly evaluate the prices they set for the firm's products and services. Pricing affects both profitability and growth. The income statement tells managers and investors how well the firm's pricing strategy has accomplished stated objectives.

Many corporations have recently restructured their operations to reduce costs. The income satement also measures the success of cost-cutting initiatives. For example, a recent *Wall Street Journal* article stated that "Companies . . . have benefitted from determined cost-cutting and somewhat improved volume to post better-than-expected first-quarter earnings."

As a final illustration, managers often use the income statement when setting dividends. Net income is a primary measure of a firm's ability to pay dividends. In fact, some firms set a dividend target equal to a certain percentage of net income.

REVENUE RECOGNITION

A firm's earnings process often takes place over an extended period of time. A manufacturer's typical earning process, which is depicted in Exhibit 4–3, entails purchasing raw materials, manufacturing, storing and selling the finished product, and collecting cash from the customer. The manufacturer creates value through all these steps. However, for accounting purposes, a discrete point in time is usually selected at which to recognize (record) revenue.

EXHIBIT 4–3

TIME LINE OF A MANUFACTURER'S EARNINGS PROCESS

| Purchase Raw Material | Manufacture Product | Store Product | Sell Product | Collect Cash |

General Rule

The **revenue recognition principle** states that revenue should be recognized in the accounting records when

1. the earnings process is substantially complete, and
2. the amount to be collected is reasonably determinable.

The first criterion prevents the recognition of revenue before a firm has fulfilled its obligation to the customer. The second criterion indicates that the sales price has been set and that the customer will probably pay the amount due. Both criteria ensure that revenue is not recognized prematurely. If revenue is recognized too soon, the income statement will indicate that the firm has accomplished activities that it has not. This would mislead financial statement users.

In most situations, these criteria are met at the point of sale: that is, when a product is delivered or a service is rendered to a customer. Even if payment is not immediately received, a claim to cash (an account receivable) has been obtained, and revenue recognition is proper.

Two additional points need to be made about revenue recognition at the point of sale. First, many sellers guarantee their products' performance for a period of time. If a product malfunctions, the seller is obligated to incur the cost of correcting the problem. Does the existence of such a warranty indicate that the earnings process is not substantially complete at the time of sale? No, it does not. For most sellers, the warranty cost is relatively minor. Thus the earnings process is *substantially* complete at the time of sale. Chapter 8 discusses warranty costs in more depth.

Second, when accounts receivable are obtained at the point of sale, can we be certain that cash will ultimately be collected? In most cases, absolute assurance cannot be obtained. However, if the seller has done a good job of checking customers' credit histories, a reasonable estimate of worthless accounts receivable can be made. This estimate is used to adjust both the income statement and the balance sheet. Chapter 6 discusses this issue in more detail.

Exceptions

A number of exceptions exist to the general rule of thumb that revenue is recognized at the point of sale. One exception deals with the collectibility of receivables. If the seller is highly uncertain about the collectibility of a receivable, revenue recognition should be delayed beyond the point of sale to the point when cash is actually collected. This approach is sometimes used in the real estate industry.

Another exception deals with long-term construction contracts (for bridges, highways, etc.). These projects can take several years to complete. If revenue recognition is delayed until the earnings process is substantially complete, no revenue is recognized in any contract year except the final one, at which point, all of the revenue would be recognized.

Such an uneven pattern of revenue recognition would contrast with the actual earnings process, which took place throughout the life of the contract. Accordingly, if (1) a binding contract exists between the buyer and the seller and (2) the seller can reasonably estimate its costs to complete the project, then revenue, the related costs, and the resultant profit should be estimated and recognized each year by the **percentage-of-completion method.** This method recognizes a portion of the revenue, cost, and profit each year according to the percentage of the job completed.

A similar situation exists with some service contracts. For example, consider a health club that sells one-year memberships for an immediate payment of $600. Revenue recognition at the point of sale is inappropriate, since the earnings process has barely begun. However, delaying revenue recognition until the twelfth month, when the earnings process is substantially complete, is also inadvisable. GAAP permits proportional revenue recognition each month over the contract's life.

Most firms describe their revenue recognition policies in a note to the financial statements. Reality Check 4–1 contains an excerpt from the financial statements of

READER'S DIGEST REVENUE RECOGNITION POLICY

Sales of subscriptions to magazines are recorded as unearned revenue at the gross subscription price at the time the order is received. Proportionate shares of the gross subscription price are credited to revenues as the subscription is fulfilled.

REQUIRED

a. Assume Reader's Digest receives $48 from a customer for a two-year subscription. Analyze this transaction in terms of the basic accounting equation.
b. Assume that the subscription is for 24 monthly issues. In terms of the basic accounting equation, what analysis would Reader's Digest undertake when each issue is mailed?

Reader's Digest, which frequently receives payments for subscriptions at the inception of a contract. Because the earnings process has just begun at that point, Reader's Digest records a liability, instead of revenue. Recording a liability recognizes that Reader's Digest has an obligation to provide its customers something of value: either the magazine or a refund. Revenue is recognized as the magazines are mailed to the customers.

EXPENSE RECOGNITION

The **matching principle** governs expense recognition. It states that all costs that were incurred to generate the revenue appearing on a given period's income statement should appear as an expense on the same income statement. In other words, we should match expenses against revenues. Revenues are first recognized, and expenses are then matched with those revenues. By doing this, the income statement contains measures of both accomplishment (revenue) and effort (expenses), thereby enabling an assessment of firm performance. The matching principle is implemented in one of three ways.

Associating Cause and Effect

One method is referred to as **associating cause and effect.** This implies that a clear and direct relationship exists between the expense and the associated revenue. Cost of goods sold is a good example; a retail store certainly cannot generate sales revenue without consuming inventory. Salespersons' commissions are another example. Because commissions are usually paid as a percentage of sales revenue, commission expense is tied directly to revenue.

Systematic and Rational Allocation

Another method used to implement the matching principle is **systematic and rational allocation.** Many costs cannot be directly linked to specific revenue transactions. They can, however, be tied to a span of years and allocated as an expense to each of those years. For example, sales equipment is essential to generate revenue. However, linking the cost of each display case, piece of furniture, and the like to specific sales transactions is difficult. Instead, the equipment's cost is systematically allocated as depreciation expense to the years during which the equipment helps generate revenue.

Immediate Recognition

The final method of applying the matching principle is **immediate recognition.** Some expenditures have no discernable *future* benefit. In these cases, the expenditure is expensed immediately. Officers' salaries, utilities, and interest are treated in this manner.

WHAT WOULD YOU DO?

Software Programs International (SPI) designs and markets several software packages. SPI's word processing program has not generated as many sales as management had forecast. Because of this, SPI is evaluating two alternative strategies. One strategy is to discontinue the product. The other strategy involves a renewed effort to improve the product and make it more attractive to potential customers. SPI's consideration of these strategies began in October 1997. A final decision will be made around July 1998.

SPI is a calendar year-end firm. SPI realizes that its financial statement readers would find information about these plans useful. On the other hand, disclosing that the word processing product might be discontinued would probably make customers hesitant to purchase the product; customers would be reluctant to buy and learn a system that will never be upgraded or improved. The decline in sales would, of course, negatively affect SPI's shareholders.

Should SPI disclose its strategy evaluation in its 1997 financial statements?

A CLOSER LOOK AT THE INCOME STATEMENT

Income statements summarize *past* transactions and events. Many users of income statements are interested in the past only to the extent that it can help predict the future. Financial statement users are concerned about earnings **sustainability,** which refers to the likelihood that earnings will persist in the future.

Historical income statements will be less useful for predicting the future if the results of ongoing operations are combined with the effects of events that are unusual or are not expected to recur in the future. Consequently, GAAP requires that income statements separately report certain items. This section describes these items and shows how they are displayed on the income statement.

Discontinued Operations

If a firm ceases to operate (or plans to cease operating) a major segment of its business, separate disclosure is required of its (1) continuing operations and (2) **discontinued operations.** Exhibit 4–4 contains CPI Corporation's income statement, which reflects the discontinuation of its Tender Sender venture.

EXHIBIT 4–4
INCOME STATEMENT

**CPI Corporation
Statement of Earnings
For the Year Ended February 3, 1990**

Net sales	$350,501,956
Costs and expenses	307,786,819
Income from operations	42,715,137
Net interest income	4,837,656
Other income	742,273
Earnings before income taxes	48,295,066
Income tax expense	17,379,000
Net earnings from continuing operations	30,916,066
Discontinued operations:	
Loss from operations, net of income tax	
benefit of $1,196,000	**(331,922)**
Loss on disposal, net of tax benefit	
of $1,133,000	**(1,913,665)**
Net loss from discontinued operations	**(2,245,587)**
Net earnings	$ 28,670,479

The first eight lines of the income statement reflects the results of continuing operations. The discontinued operations section contains two line items. The first reports the results of operating the segment, and the second indicates the loss realized on the disposal. In making predictions about future earnings, most analysts would remove the effects of these items from CPI's reported net earnings. Since these items have reduced CPI's reported earnings, they would be added back:

Reported net earnings	$28,670,479
Plus loss from operating discontinued segment	331,922
Plus loss on disposal of discontinued segment	1,913,665
Adjusted net earnings	$30,916,066

To qualify for separate reporting, the discontinued operation must represent an *entire* major line of business. Many divestitures do not qualify as an entire line of business and do not necessitate separate reporting.

For example, a *Wall Street Journal* article stated: "HCA-Hospital Corp. of America, bowing to weakness in the psychiatric hospital industry, said it will sell 22 hospitals and take an after-tax charge of as much as $300 million in the third quarter." The charge reflects operating losses and anticipated losses on the sale. Since HCA retained ownership of 26 psychiatric hospitals and 73 general hospitals, it did not dispose of an entire line of business. Treatment as a discontinued operation would be inappropriate. The $300 million charge would be included in continuing operations. Thus, financial statement readers must be aware that continuing operations might contain revenues, expenses, gains, and losses that will not persist in the future. Some analysts would prefer to remove the $300 million charge from the current quarter's earnings when making projections about the future.

On the other hand, some analysts might view HCA's sale of hospitals as a normally recurring modification of the firm's strategy. Since these modifications are expected to occur periodically, these analysts would not remove the $300 million from reported earnings.

Reality Check 4–2 describes a disposal by Ford Motor Company.

REALITY CHECK 4–2

FORD MOTOR COMPANY

Ford Motor Company reported a 1994 first quarter profit of $904 million. However, that profit included a $440 million loss from the sale of First Nationwide, a financial institution. Since Ford did not dispose of its entire financial services unit, this disposal does not qualify as a discontinued operation. However, some analysts might prefer to exclude the disposal loss from Ford's earnings when making projections about future earnings.

REQUIRED

a. Eliminate the First Nationwide loss from Ford's reported net income.

 Extraordinary Items

Extraordinary items are events and transactions that are unusual in nature and infrequent in occurrence. Unusual in nature implies that the event or transaction is, at most, incidentally related to a firm's typical operations. Infrequent in occurrence suggests that the item is not expected to recur in the foreseeable future. Extraordinary items usually include natural disasters and actions by foreign governments, such as expropriation of assets. Separate disclosure of extraordinary items enables analysts to make better projections of a firm's future operations.

Exhibit 4–5 shows an American Building Maintenance Industries, Inc. (ABM), partial income statement for the year ended October 31, 1990, and an accompanying note.

American Building Maintenance Industries, Inc.
Partial Income Statement
For the Year Ended October 31, 1990
(dollars in thousands)

Income before extraordinary gain	$ 9,846
Extraordinary gain (net of income taxes of $1,047)	1,387
Net income	$11,233

Note:
The Company's former headquarters building in San Francisco was severely damaged by the earthquake of October 17, 1989. After the settlement with the insurers in November 1989, the Company retired the building and recognized an extraordinary gain of $1,387,000, net of income taxes of $1,047,000.

EXHIBIT 4–5
PARTIAL INCOME STATEMENT

It discloses that ABM lost a building in the 1989 San Francisco earthquake. Earthquakes meet the criterion of being unusual in nature. A question arises as to whether they are expected to recur in the foreseeable future. In California, earthquakes continue to occur with some regularity. In the end, this is another accounting situation that requires judgment. Evidently, ABM and its auditors feel that earthquakes in San Francisco occur with sufficient irregularity that they are not expected to recur in the foreseeable future. Based on the footnote disclosures, analysts can exercise their own judgment about reported extraordinary items.

Note that ABM recognized a gain. A gain arose because the proceeds from the insurance settlement exceeded the carrying value of the building. Recall that buildings are carried in the accounting records at depreciated historical cost, which does not reflect current market values.

When making predictions about ABM's future income levels, most analysts would remove the extraordinary gain from ABM's reported net income:

Reported net income	$11,233,000
Less extraordinary gain	1,387,000
Adjusted net income	$ 9,846,000

Income Taxes

Given that many income statements have several major sections (continuing operations, discontinued operations, and extraordinary items), a decision must be made about where to report income tax expense. GAAP takes the reasonable position that taxes should be allocated to each major section. Consider again Exhibit 4–4. One item listed is income tax expense. This is not CPI's total income tax expense, however. It is the income tax associated with continuing operations. The tax effect associated with discontinued operations is shown parenthetically in that section. This format shows discontinued operations **net of tax.**

Note that discontinued operations generated a loss and that the tax effect is labeled a **tax benefit.** Losses yield tax benefits because they lower the taxes a firm must pay. Consider a simple example. In 1998, Crimp Corporation earned, before taxes, a profit of $10,000 on continuing operations. It also incurred a $2,000 loss on discontinued operations. Assume a tax rate of 30%.

Had the $2,000 loss not been incurred, Crimp's total tax expense would have been $3,000:

$$\text{Total tax expense} = \$10,000 \times .3 = \$3,000$$

However, given that Crimp did incur the $2,000 loss, its total tax expense is $2,400:

$$\text{Total tax expense} = (\$10,000 - \$2,000) \times .3 = \$2,400$$

Thus, the loss from discontinued operations reduced income tax expense by $600. The tax expense allocated to continuing operations is $3,000, and the tax benefit allocated to discontinued operations is $600. A partial income statement would appear as follows:

Crimp Corporation
Partial Income Statement
For the Year Ended December 31, 1998

Earnings before taxes	$10,000
Income tax expense	3,000
Net earnings from continuing operations	7,000
Loss from discontinued operations (less income tax benefit of $600)	1,400
Net income	$ 5,600

Earnings per Share

Many financial numbers are stated on a per-share basis. Price per share and dividends per share are widely quoted in the financial press. Because a share of stock is the basic ownership unit in corporations, this mode of expression is quite useful. Consequently, GAAP requires that publicly held companies state net income on a per-share basis. In general terms, this requires dividing net income by the average number of shares of stock outstanding. The result is **earnings per share (EPS):**

$$EPS = \frac{\text{Net income}}{\text{Shares outstanding}}$$

Per-share amounts make it easier to relate the dividends, prices, and earnings of a given firm.

ANALYZING THE INCOME STATEMENT

The income statement contains a great deal of useful information about a firm. This section shows how to extract and interpret that information. The income statements of OshKosh B'Gosh, Inc. (OB), for the years 1994 and 1993, which are summarized in Exhibit 4–6, serve as the basis for the illustrations.

One item on OB's income statement deserves special mention. In 1993, OB incurred a $10,836,000 restructuring charge. This charge reflects OB's decision to consolidate its retail operations. The charge includes costs to close facilities, write down assets, and lay off employees (see the Note in Exhibit 4–6). Because OB did not discontinue an entire line of business, the restructuring does not qualify as a discontinued operation. However, this charge might not recur in the near future. Consequently, some analysts would delete this $10,836,000 loss in calculating ratios and evaluating trends. Such adjustments are demonstrated later in the chapter.

Vertical Analysis

Vertical analysis examines relationships within a given year. To do this with the income statement, divide each line by the first item, net sales. Net sales are a summary measure of a firm's total activities, so evaluating each income statement item relative to net sales makes sense. The result yields **common-size income statements** in percentage terms. OB's common size statements appear in Exhibit 4–7.

The first line of a common-size income statement is always 100% because the net sales figure is divided by itself. The second line of the common-size income statement, cost of products sold divided by net sales, is referred to as the **cost of goods sold percentage.** For a firm that is a **merchandiser,** one that simply buys and resells goods

EXHIBIT 4–6
INCOME STATEMENTS FOR
1994 AND 1993

OshKosh B'Gosh, Inc.
Income Statements
(dollars in thousands)

	Year Ended December 31, 1994	1993
Net sales	$363,363	$340,186
Cost of products sold	259,416	244,926
Gross profit	103,947	95,260
Selling, general, and administrative expenses	94,988	78,492
Restructuring (note)	—	10,836
Operating income	8,959	5,932
Interest expense	(1,034)	(626)
Other income	5,033	3,986
Income before taxes	12,958	9,292
Income taxes	5,919	4,769
Net income	$ 7,039	$ 4,523

Note 3:
During 1993, the Company recorded a pre-tax restructuring change of $10.836 million, including approximately $3.3 million for facility closings, write-down of the related assets and severance costs pertaining to workforce reductions, and approximately $7.5 million for write-off of unamortized trademark rights and expenses related to consolidating the Company's retail operations. Restructuring costs (net of income tax benefit) reduced net income by $7.1 million ($.49 per share) in 1993.

without changing their shape or form, this percentage reflects the relationship between the price the firm pays for the goods and the price it charges customers. For a **manufacturer,** a firm that buys raw materials and component parts and reshapes them into

EXHIBIT 4–7
COMMON-SIZE INCOME
STATEMENTS

OshKosh B'Gosh
Common-Size Income Statements

	Year Ended December 31, 1994	1993
Net sales	100.0%	100.0%
Cost of products sold	71.4	72.0
Gross profit	28.6	28.0
Selling, general, and administrative expenses	26.1	23.1
Restructuring costs	—	3.2
Operating income	2.5	1.7
Interest expense	(.3)	(.2)
Other income	1.4	1.2
Income before taxes	3.6	2.7
Income taxes	1.6	1.4
Net income	2.0%	1.3%

a finished product, the cost of goods sold percentage could also indicate the efficiency of the manufacturing process.

In assessing a firm's ability to generate cash flows, lower costs and consequently lower cost of goods sold percentages are desirable. This provides a larger profit per item sold. For every dollar of revenue in 1994, OB paid more than $0.71 to manufacture the associated clothing.

The third line, **gross profit** (or **gross margin**) **percentage,** is calculated either by dividing gross profit by net sales or by subtracting the cost of goods sold percentage from 100%. It reflects the percentage of the sales price that exceeds cost of goods sold. It measures the percentage of revenue that is available to cover expenses other than cost of goods sold and to contribute toward profits. In 1994, nearly $0.29 of every OB sales dollar was available for these purposes. Given that a lower cost of goods sold percentage is desirable, a higher gross profit percentage is preferable.

Two basic strategies exist to increase the gross profit percentage (or, in other words, to decrease the cost of goods sold percentage). First, unit selling prices could be increased. This option is limited because of competition from other companies in the firm's industry. Second, efforts can be made to reduce the cost of goods sold. This can be done through more astute purchasing (such as buying in bulk to obtain a discount) or a more efficient manufacturing process.

The fourth line of OB's common-size income statement reflects the relationship between marketing and administrative expenses and net sales. Managers have substantial control over these costs, and percentages that increase over time are usually viewed with disfavor.

Of the remaining items in Exhibit 4–7, the two most important are the **operating income percentage** and the **net income percentage.** The operating income percentage is an indicator of management's success in operating the firm. The numerator, operating income, excludes both interest expense and taxes. Since these expenses are not directly affected by operating (e.g., buying and selling) decisions, the operating income percentage is a better reflection of how management handled the day-to-day affairs of the firm. The net income percentage reflects the firm's overall profitability, after interest and taxes, relative to its level of activity (net sales). Both ratios are indicators of a firm's financial success.

Exhibit 4–8 graphically depicts the information contained in Exhibit 4–7.

Trend Analysis

Trend analysis involves comparing financial statement numbers across time. One way to implement this is to compare the common-size income statement items over time. The trends in OB's cost of goods sold percentage and its gross profit percentage are favorable. For example, the cost of goods sold percentage decreased from 72.0% in 1993 to 71.4% in 1994. This decrease could reflect decreases in the prices of raw materials, increased demand for its products (allowing an increase in selling prices), or efficiencies in the manufacturing process.

The trend in marketing and administrative costs as a percentage of net sales is not favorable. It has increased from 23.1% to 26.1% of sales. This increase, partly offset by the decrease in the cost of goods sold percentage, helps to explain the changes in the operating income percentage and the net income percentage.

EXHIBIT 4–8

OSHKOSH B'GOSH GRAPHIC
DEPICTION OF COMMON-SIZE
INCOME STATEMENTS

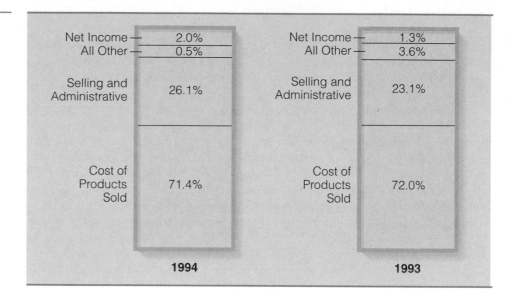

If OB's restructuring costs are not expected to recur, the operating income percentage and net income percentage should be adjusted for purposes of forecasting future results. To adjust the 1993 operating income percentage, the restructuring charge should be added to operating income, since it has already been subtracted in arriving at that number.

$$\text{Adjusted operating income percentage} = \frac{\text{Operating income} + \text{Restructuring loss}}{\text{Net sales}}$$

$$= \frac{\$5,932 + 10,836}{\$340,186} = 4.9\%$$

Since net income is an after-tax figure, the adjusted net income percentage must be modified on an after-tax basis. Exhibit 4–6 indicates that the after-tax effect of the restructuring was $7,100,000. The after-tax cost is smaller than the pre-tax cost of $10,836,000 becuase it reflects the benefit of a reduction in taxes due to the loss. The adjustment is accomplished by adding the $7,100,000 after-tax loss to net income.

$$\text{Adjusted net income percentage} = \frac{\text{Net income} + \text{After-tax restructuring loss}}{\text{Net sales}}$$

$$= \frac{\$4,523 + 7,100}{\$340,186} = 3.4\%$$

Horizontal Analysis

Horizontal analysis is another form of trend analysis. It uses the figures from a prior year's income statement as the basis for calculating percentage increases over time. Exhibit 4–9 contains a horizontal analysis of OB's income statement. The figures in the exhibit are obtained by dividing the items in the 1994 income statement by their corresponding amounts in the 1993 income statement.

OshKosh B'Gosh Income Statements—Horizontal Analysis	Year Ended December 31, 1994	1993
Net sales	106.8%	100%
Cost of products sold	105.9	100
Gross profit	109.1	100
Selling, general and administrative expenses	121.0	100
Operating income	151.0	100
Interest expense	165.2	100
Other income	126.3	100
Income before taxes	139.5	100
Income taxes	124.1	100
Net income	155.6	100

EXHIBIT 4–9
HORIZONTAL ANALYSIS OF INCOME STATEMENTS

Exhibit 4–9 shows that net sales increased 6.8% between 1993 and 1994. This increase could reflect an increase in sales activity (number of units sold), or it could merely reflect increases in unit selling prices. The income statement itself cannot answer this question.

The increases in cost of products sold (5.9%) is less than the increase in net sales (6.8%). This is consistent with the results of the common-size income statements that showed cost of products sold had decreased as a percentage of sales.

Operating income and net income increased over the two-year period. Such an increase will occur whenever net sales increases faster than expenses. Recall, however, that OB's 1993 income statement includes substantial restructuring charges. Some analysts may prefer to eliminate these charges before measuring trends in income. If such adjustments are made to OB's 1993 reported expense, then operating income and net income will show decreases from 1993 to 1994.

 ## Other Ratios

Several ratios link the income statement and the balance sheet. **Return on shareholders' equity (ROE)** is of utmost importance to shareholders. To calculate ROE, divide net income by average shareholders' equity:

$$\text{ROE} = \frac{\text{Net income}}{\text{Average shareholders' equity}}$$

ROE relates the earnings generated by a firm to the assets invested by its shareholders. It is obviously in the shareholders' best interest to have larger earnings generated on their investments. A potential investor, faced with competing investment choices, will use ROE to help identify the preferred investment.

The denominator of ROE is *average* shareholders' equity. Because net income is earned over the course of a year, it makes sense to use the firm's average shareholders' equity during the year. As a practical matter, average shareholders' equity is usually calculated by averaging beginning and end-of-year shareholders' equity amounts, which are found on the balance sheet.

Exhibit 4–10 summarizes the OB ratios discussed in this section. OB's 1994 ROE is:

$$\text{ROE} = \frac{\$7,039}{(\$158,814 + \$171,998)/2} = 4.3\%$$

Another important ratio is **return on assets (ROA).** This ratio relates a firm's earnings to *all* the assets the firm has available to generate those earnings. ROA differs from ROE in that ROE utilizes only the assets that the shareholders supplied. ROE measures management's success in using the assets invested by shareholders, whereas ROA measures how successfully management utilized all the assets entrusted to it. To calculate ROA, divide net income, adjusted for interest expense, by average total assets.

$$\text{ROA} = \frac{\text{Net income} + \text{Interest expense } (1 - \text{tax rate})}{\text{Average total assets}}$$

Why is interest expense added to net income in the numerator? Recall that a firm can acquire assets from two sources: owners and creditors. Interest expense is a cost incurred to acquire assets from creditors (e.g., interest expense on bank borrowings). It arises from a financing decision (obtaining funds from creditors rather than owners), not an operating decision (utilizing assets). Because ROA is designed to measure managers' success in utilizing assets, interest expense is irrelevant. Its effect on net income should be eliminated when calculating ROA.

Interest expense has direct and indirect effects on net income, and both effects should be eliminated. Regarding the direct effect, since interest expense has already been subtracted in calculating net income, it is now added back. The indirect effect relates to taxes. Because interest expense is a deduction for tax purposes, tax expense is lower, and net income is higher, by an amount equal to (interest expense × tax rate). Therefore, to adjust fully for the elimination of interest expense, net income must be increased by interest expense and decreased by (interest expense × tax rate). The difference between these two amounts is [interest expense × (1 − tax rate)]:

$$\begin{array}{l} + \text{ Interest expense} \\ - \underline{\text{ Interest expense} \times \text{tax rate}} \\ \text{ Interest expense} \times (1 - \text{tax rate}) \end{array}$$

EXHIBIT 4–10
SUMMARY OF RATIOS

	OshKosh B'Gosh Selected Information and Ratios (dollars in thousands, except ratios)	
	1994	**1993**
Total shareholders' equity	$158,814	$171,998
Total assets	$217,211	$229,131
Return on shareholders' equity (ROE)	4.3%	*
Return on assets (ROA)	3.4%	*
Times interest earned	13.5	15.8

*Cannot be calculated based on the information provided in the exhibits.

Eliminating the effects of interest expense facilitates the comparison of asset utilization across firms that have different amounts of debt.

Financial statements disclose, in the notes, firms' tax rates. OB's effective rate in 1994 was 45.7%. Its ROA for 1994 is

$$\text{ROA} = \frac{\$7,039 + \$1034\,(1 - .457)}{(\$217,211 + \$229,131)/2} = 3.4\%$$

The final ratio discussed in this section is **times interest earned.** Because profits ultimately are a source of cash, and because cash is necessary for the payment of interest charges, creditors are concerned about the relationship between profits and interest expense. The times interest earned ratio shows how many times interest expense is covered by resources generated from operations. It is calculated by dividing earnings before interest and taxes by interest expense:

$$\text{Times interest earned} = \frac{\text{Earnings before interest and taxes}}{\text{Interest expense}}$$

Creditors prefer higher times interest earned ratios.

Earnings before interest and taxes, not net income, is used in the numerator. Because interest expense is already deducted in calculating net income, net income understates the resources available to cover interest expense. Tax expense is not deducted in the numerator because in a worst case scenario, as income declines, taxes would be eliminated.

OB's income statement, presented in Exhibit 4–6, does not contain a line item for income before interest and taxes. The easiest way to calculate this figure, given OB's income statement format, is to add interest expense to income before taxes. In 1994 and 1993, income before interest and taxes would be determined as follows:

	1994	1993
Income before taxes	$12,958,000	$9,292,000
Interest expense	1,034,000	626,000
Income before interest and taxes	$13,992,000	$9,918,000

OB's 1994 times interest earned ratio is 13.5, which indicates that interest expense is covered 13.5 times at present income levels. In 1993, OB's interest expense was covered 15.8 times.

$$\text{Times interest earned} = \underset{\textbf{1994}}{\frac{\$13,992}{\$\ 1,034} = 13.5} \qquad \underset{\textbf{1993}}{\frac{\$9,918}{\$\ 626} = 15.8}$$

LIMITATIONS OF ACCOUNTING INCOME

Although financial statement readers find reported accounting income very useful, it does have several limitations. Conceptually, we often think of income as an increase in wealth. If our bank account grows by $100 because of interest, we feel as though our income is $100. For many assets, however, accounting does not recognize an increase in value when it occurs. Instead, the value increase, and the associated income, is recognized at the time of the asset's disposal.

Sometimes the difference between historical cost and current value can be quite large. Consider Hiroshi Fujishige, who owns a 58-acre farm across the street from

Disneyland. The farm was purchased in 1953 for $2,500. Southern California real estate experts estimate its value to be $55,000,000. In spite of this estimate, the Fujishige Farm balance sheet reflects the land at $2,500, and the increase in value has not appeared on any of Fujishige's income statements. In general, to recognize a value increase, accounting rules require the occurrence of a transaction for verification purposes.

Financial statements do not reflect still other accomplishments of a firm. For example, the *Wall Street Journal* reported that Connaught Laboratories Inc. was awarded a multimillion-dollar contract to supply the federal government with its DTP children's vaccine. This was extremely good news for Connaught Labs; however, this event was not included in its accounting records when the contract was signed. At that time, Connaught had merely entered into an executory contract, which is not immediately recorded. The sales to the government will be recognized in the accounting records as they occur throughout the life of the contract.

Accounting's **conservatism principle** may also limit the extent to which accounting income reflects changes in wealth. This principle states that when doubt exists about the accounting treatment for a given transaction, a conservative alternative should be selected. In other words, select the alternative that reports lower asset values and lower net income. For example, expenditures for research and development are immediately expensed, even when they result in valuable products or patents. Spending on employee training is expensed immediately, even though its objective is to create a more highly skilled workforce. These examples suggest that the balance sheets of some companies may have undervalued or unrecorded assets; this, of course, implies that the net income figure on the income statement does not necessarily reflect changes in wealth. On the other hand, most accountants support the conservatism principle, since it helps avoid overly optimistic financial statements.

In summary, to ensure that reliable and verifiable financial statements emerge from the accounting process, GAAP precludes the recognition of certain potential value changes. Because of this, accounting income does not strictly measure changes in wealth. However, it is a very useful performance measure on which the business community relies heavily.

ACCOUNTING INCOME AND ECONOMIC CONSEQUENCES

Recall from Chapter 2 that the managers of many publicly held corporations receive bonuses that are based on reported accounting net income. These bonus plans typically include a floor and a ceiling. The floor requires that net income must reach a certain level before the bonus is activated. The ceiling places a limit on the size of the bonus. That is, the bonus is not increased as net income increases above the ceiling. Thus, managers prefer that net income fall at the high end of the range between the floor and the ceiling.

Bonuses can motivate managers to undertake actions that will improve the operations of the firm, thereby increasing profits. Unfortunately, bonuses can also motivate managers to make accounting-related decisions that do not affect the underlying profitability of the firm, but that do affect *reported* accounting income.

For example, firms occasionally engage in **big baths.** These are accounting decisions that result in large losses in a single year. If reported earnings would otherwise have been below a bonus plan's floor, such losses have no effect on the current year's bonus. Moreover, by taking the losses all at one time, subsequent periods are relieved of those charges, and the chances of higher reported profits and bonuses in the future will be maximized. Reality Check 4–3 describes a big bath taken by General Motors.

GENERAL MOTORS' BIG BATH

GM recently took several large charges. One charge amounting to $744 million was from GM's National Car Rental Systems Corporation. This charge was more than double GM's original estimate. GM also took a $20.8 billion charge for retiree health benefits. In general, GM said it was taking a more conservative approach to accounting issues. Perhaps more than coincidentally, GM had recently selected a new chairman. Some analysts suggest that new corporate administrations are inclined to take big baths.

REQUIRED

a. List two reasons why recently installed corporate managers might want to take a big bath.

The actions taken by General Motors are well within the bounds of allowable managerial discretion. Other corporations, however, have been accused of much more questionable actions. Miniscribe, a bankrupt disk-drive manufacturer, is alleged to have recognized revenue prematurely on shipments that customers had not ordered, improperly estimated uncollectible accounts receivable, and falsified inventory.

The application of GAAP requires the exercise of judgment. At the same time, manager's self-interest is affected by reported accounting income. Accordingly,. financial statement users should not be surprised that managers' self-interests influence their accounting policy judgments. As a result, financial statements may not be unbiased reflections about the underlying economic activities of firms.

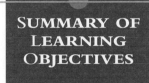

SUMMARY OF LEARNING OBJECTIVES

1. **Explain when to recognize revenues.**
   Revenue should be recognized when the earnings process is substantially complete and the amount to be collected is reasonably determinable. These criteria ensure that revenue is not recognized before the firm has honored its obligation to the customer and is reasonably assured of collecting cash from the customer. Revenue is usually recognized at the point of sale.

2. **Explain when to recognize expenses.**
   The matching principle states that expenses should be recognized when resources have been consumed to help generate revenue. Showing revenues and the related expenses on the same income statement results in a net income figure that best reflects a firm's performance for the period. The matching principle is implemented in one of three ways: associating cause and effect, systematic allocation, and immediate recognition.

3. Interpret the components of the income statement.

Income statements may contain several major sections: income from continuing operations, income from discontinued operations, and extraordinary items. This format helps financial statement users assess the past performance of a firm and predict the results of future operations. When making forecasts based on historical information, the effect of transactions and events that are not expected to recur in the future should be eliminated from net income. Because of the way accounting definitions have been developed, even income from continuing operations may include nonrecurring items.

4. Analyze income statement information using various ratios.

The income statement contains a number of measures related to a firm's ability to generate earnings. This helps analysts assess a firm's expected return. Vertical analysis examines relationships within the income statement of one period; each line of the income statement is expressed as a percentage of sales. Horizontal analysis shows the trend over time in income statement numbers. Return on shareholders' equity and return on assets are good summary measures of a firm's performance. Finally, the times interest earned ratio provides creditors with an indication of the firm's ability to pay interest charges.

5. Describe the effects that reported earnings have on managers' wealth and, consequently, on their accounting policy decisions.

Many corporations tie the compensation of their top officers to reported accounting earnings. These bonus plans often contain a floor and a ceiling. The floor is the level of net income that must be exceeded before the bonus is activated. The ceiling limits the amount of the bonus, regardless of how large net income is. This situation motivates managers to report a net income figure that is at the high end of the floor–ceiling range. Managers are also motivated to undertake "big baths." Taking large charges in one year relieves future years' income of those expenses, and paves the way for higher reported earnings and higher bonuses for management.

KEY TERMS

Administrative expenses	Gross profit percentage
Associating cause and effect	Horizontal analysis
Big bath	Immediate recognition
Bottom line	Income statement
Common-size income statements	Income taxes
Conservatism principle	Interest expense
Cost of goods sold	Losses
Cost of goods sold percentage	Matching principle
Discontinued operations	Materiality principle
Earnings	Manufacturer
Earnings per share (EPS)	Merchandiser
Expenses	Multiple-step format
Extraordinary items	Net
Gains	Net income
Gross margin	Net income percentage
Gross margin percentage	Net of tax
Gross profit	Net sales

Operating income
Operating income percentage
Percentage-of-completion method
Profit
Return on assets (ROA)
Return on shareholders' equity (ROE)
Revenue recognition principle
Revenues
Sales return

Selling expenses
Single-step format
Sustainability
Systematic and rational allocation
Tax benefit
Times interest earned
Trend analysis
Vertical analysis

REALITY CHECK SOLUTIONS

SOLUTION TO REALITY CHECK 4–1

a.

ASSETS	=	LIABILITIES	+	SHAREHOLDERS' EQUITY
Cash		Unearned revenue		
+$48		+$48		

b.

ASSETS	=	LIABILITIES	+	SHAREHOLDERS' EQUITY
		Unearned Revenue		Retained earnings
		– $2		+$2 (subscription revenue)

SOLUTION TO REALITY CHECK 4–2

Reported net income	$ 904,000,000
Plus loss on disposal	440,000,000
Adjusted income	$1,344,000,000

SOLUTION TO REALITY CHECK 4–3

First, these charges can easily be blamed on the former management. Second, they help the company report favorable earnings in the future, which reflects well on the new management team. Moreover, the higher reported net income might increase the bonuses paid to the new managers.

QUESTIONS

4–1 Distinguish between revenues and gains. Also distinguish between expenses and losses. Explain why these items are usually presented separately on income statements.

4–2 Explain why a firm might elect to report its annual income using a noncalendar (i.e., other than December 31) fiscal year-end.

4–3 In deciding the number of items to be disclosed on the income statement, managers are guided by the materiality principle. Explain how this principle would affect a decision about whether to disclose a firm's research expenses separately.

4–4 Often the first item on a firm's income statement is labeled "Net sales." Discuss the measuring of this term. Do you agree with this reporting convention? Explain.

4–5 Why do manufacturing and merchandising firms usually disclose the cost of merchandise sold as a separate item on the income statement?

4–6 Explain why interest expense is not considered to be an operating expense by most firms. Can you suggest industries where interest expense might be reported as an operating expense?

4–7 Distinguish between a single-step and a multiple-step income statement. Do you agree that a multiple-step format is usually more informative to the reader? Discuss.

4–8 Identify and dicuss several ways in which managers may base decisions on what type of information will be contained in the income statement.

4–9 Identify and discuss several types of information that investors in a firm's debt and equity securities may seek when reading the income statement.

4–10 Explain the two criteria that must be met for a firm to report revenue in its income statement, and discuss how these criteria might be applied to revenue recognition by (a) a fast-food restaurant and (b) a home appliance merchandiser.

4–11 Contact local firms with which you are familiar, or review several annual reports from firms in the same industry, and examine their revenue recognition principles and procedures. Review the notes to their financial statements to see how they describe their revenue recognition principles. Write a short description and critique their revenue recognition policies.

4–12 Discuss the purpose of the matching principle, and explain the three ways in which this principle is implemented.

4–13 Determine how the matching principle would affect recognition of the following items: (a) cost of inventory sold, (b) depreciation expense of production equipment, and (c) expenditures for new product development.

4–14 Income statements are often used in order to provide a historical measure of a firm's performance, and also are used as a basis for predicting future profitability. Do you believe that the same income statement is useful for both purposes? Discuss.

4–15 Discuss the differences between an operating loss and a nonoperating loss.

4–16 Critique the following:

> An owner of a firm with negative income (losses) would prefer that these losses be the result of nonoperating (e.g. loss from discontinued operations) activities, as compared to losses on operating activities.

4–17 Why are extraordinary items reported separately in the income statement? Can you identify an event that would be classified by one firm as an ordinary operating item and by another firm as an extraordinary item? Discuss.

4–18 Explain why GAAP requires that income taxes be allocated to each major section of the income statement.

4–19 Under what circumstances might an income statement report a tax *benefit?*

4–20 Discuss the measuring of a "restructuring charge" and explain why you believe that such charges should (or should not) be reported as extraordinary items in the income statement.

4–21 Describe the construction of a common-size income statement, and discuss how such a statement is used in a vertical analysis of the income statement.

4–22 Identify three reasons why a firm's gross profit (gross margin) percentage might change over time.

4–23 Discuss several reasons why a firm's net income percentage might change over time. Do you believe that the financial statements contain sufficient information to allow the reader to evaluate the reasons for a change in the net income percentage over time?

4–24 Distinguish between vertical analysis and trend analysis of the income statement, and describe two ways of implementing a trend analysis.

4–25 Provide two examples of ratios that link the income statement and the balance sheet. In each case, explain why it is useful to relate the items that appear in the numerator and the denominator of the ratio.

4–26 The ratios discussed in this chapter include return on assets, return on shareholders' equity, and times interest earned. In each case, a different measure of income is used. Explain why income is measured differently in each of these ratio calculations.

4–27 The chapter states that "accounting income does not strictly measure changes in wealth." Provide two examples of changes in wealth that would not be reported currently in the income statement. In each case, evaluate whether reporting these changes would improve the usefulness of the income measure.

4–28 Describe the nature of a "big bath" reported in the income statement. How would you expect a big bath to affect reported income in later years? How would you expect a big bath to affect a firm's stock price in the year that the losses are reported?

4–29 Explain the role of the floor and ceiling provisions in a bonus plan. How might these provisions influence the amount of income (or loss) that a manager might wish to report in a given year?

EXERCISES

4–30 For each numbered item, indicate the letter of the classification that describes where it belongs.

a. Revenues
b. Cost of Goods Sold
c. Selling Expenses
d. General and Administrative Expenses

e. Other Income and Expenses
f. Separate line item, net of tax, after Income from Continuing Operations
g. Not on the income statement

____ 1. Commissions expense
____ 2. Gain on sale of land
____ 3. Dividends declared and paid
____ 4. Prepaid rent
____ 5. Depreciation expense for office equipment
____ 6. Interest expense
____ 7. Tornado loss (business located in Kansas)
____ 8. Merchandise inventory
____ 9. Income tax payable
____ 10. Loss on discontinued operations

Preparing an Income Statement

4–31 On the basis of the following data from the Woodway Company's 1997 annual report (dollars in million's), prepare an income statement using a multiple-step format similar to Exhibit 4–6.

Interest expense	$ 2,489
Investment income	11,218
Other income	9,033
Depreciation	1,257
Revenues	591,762
Other expenses	8,482
Cost of sales	482,355
Operating expenses	98,576
Income taxes	522

Revising an Income Statement (continuation of Exercise 4–3)

4–32 Revise your income statement from Exercise 4–31 to include the following two additional items from Woodway's 1997 annual report (dollars in million's):

Loss on discontinued operations, net of tax	$1,025
Extraordinary loss, net of tax	314

Interpreting Financial Statements

4–33 The Woodway Company included the following note in its 1997 annual report:

> In June 1997, Woodway Company and its principal subsidiaries filed for protection under Chapter 11 of the United States Bankruptcy Code. Woodway recorded a provision for possible impairment of $24 million at December 31, 1996, and recorded an additional provision of $19 million in the second quarter of 1997.

REQUIRED

a. Do you think this $19 million loss should be reported on Woodway's 1997 income statement? Why or why not?

b. Based on the data in Exercises 4–31 and 4–32, what estimate would you make regarding Woodway's sustainable operating profit?

Sorting Accounts: Income Statement Versus Balance Sheet

4–34 Sort the following accounts according to whether they would appear on the income statement or the balance sheet:

Supplies expense	Salaries payable
Accounts payable	Cost of goods sold
Land	Trucks
Capital stock	Sales revenue
Interest earned	Interest expense
Accrued taxes payable	Tax expense
Interest payable	Retained earnings
Rent expense	Rent revenue
Cash sales	Cash
Depreciation expense	Accumulated depreciation

Financial Ratios

4-35 Answer each of the following *independent* questions:

a. The return on equity for the Hammond Corporation for the year ended December 31, 1997, is 9%. The owners' equity balances on December 31, 1996 and 1997, were $180,000 and $200,000, respectively. What is the net income for 1997?

b. The Beachfront Resort Company had the following income statement information:

Sales revenue	$500,000
Gross profit percentage	30%
Net income percentage	5%

What is their cost of goods sold? What is the total of their operating and other expenses?

c. The return on assets for the Wicker Chair Company is 12%. The average total assets is $230,000 and net income is $20,100. What is interest expense, net of tax? What is gross interest expense if the income tax rate is 25%?

Income Statement

4-36 You have obtained the following data for the Bluebird Company for calendar year 1997:

Sales	$350,000
Gross margin percentage	45%
Net income percentage	8%
Income tax percentage	25%

REQUIRED

a. Based on the above data, determine the following:

1. Cost of goods sold
2. Net income
3. Income taxes
4. Operating expenses (assume no "other expenses and revenues")

b. Prepare a multiple-step income statement for the year ended December 31, 1997.

Recording Transactions and Preparing an Income Statement

4-37 Spinner Sewing Corporation was incorporated on January 1, 1997. Three investors *each* invested $150,000 in exchange for $150,000 of common stock of the corporation. The following transactions took place during 1997:

1. Purchased merchandise inventory on account, $200,000.
2. Rent paid on January 2 for a two-year period, $48,000.
3. Borrowed $100,000 on March 31; 10% annual interest rate loan for one year.
4. Sold goods at retail $300,000, half for cash, half on account. (Cost of goods sold was $170,000.)
5. Paid $120,000 on outstanding bills owed to inventory suppliers.

6. Received $80,000 from receivable customers.
7. Incurred operating expenses of $36,000 of which $14,000 was paid in cash and the balance on account.

REQUIRED

a. Record the above transactions, including the initial investment, in the accounting equation. Set up separate account columns for assets, liabilities, and stockholders' equity.
b. Record the following year-end adjustments:

1. expired portion of prepaid rent
2. accrued interest expense
3. accrued income tax, assume 20% tax rate

c. Prepare a single-step income statement for the year ended December 31, 1997.

Ratio Analysis (continuation of Exercise 4–37)

4–38 Refer to the previous exercise. Answer each of the following questions:

a. Calculate:

1. gross profit percentage
2. operating income percentage
3. net income percentage

b. Calculate:

1. return on assets
2. return on equity

c. Evaluate the performance of the corporation. What other transactions would you expect to see that are missing?
d. What if the corporation discontinued part of its operations during the year and incurred a loss of $45,000 on the disposal? What impact would this have on the income statement?

Recording and Analyzing Transactions

4–39 Assume Boomingdales, Inc., had the following transactions:

1. Purchased $150 of equipment on account. The corporation has over $1 million in assets.
2. Sold merchandise at retail $150,000 during the year on account. Customers returned $10,000 of merchandise at retail for credit on their accounts. (Ignore cost of goods sold.)
3. Received $40,000 *in advance* from customers.
4. Recorded annual depreciation of $280,000.

REQUIRED

a. Record the above transactions in the accounting equation. Set up separate account columns as needed.
b. Discuss the generally accepted accounting principle that guides accountants on recording each of these transactions properly.

Interpreting Income Statements: Ratio Analysis

4–40 The following comparative income statements can be used to evaluate Clarkson Brewery's performance for the year ended December 31, 1998 and 1997.

	1998	1997
Net sales	$405,000	$378,000
Operating expenses		
Cost of goods sold	163,250	154,400
Selling expense	81,000	48,360
General and administrative expense	121,500	102,650
Total operating expenses	365,750	305,410
Operating income	39,250	72,590
Other income:		
Gain on sale of property	34,000	—
Income before tax	73,250	72,590
Income tax expense	21,975	21,777
Income before extraordinary item	51,275	50,813
Extraordinary loss net of tax	—	(25,000)
	$ 51,275	$ 25,813

REQUIRED

a. Calculate horizontal and vertical analyses.

b. In which year was the company more successful?

c. Why did the company report its gains and losses differently in 1998?

Profit Recognition: Multiyear Operating Cycle

4–41 Evergreen Structures, Inc., specializes in the construction of storage facilities, and has just entered into a contract with the following features:

Contract signed	December 31, 1997
Total contract price	$12,000,000
Total estimated costs of construction	$ 8,000,000
Total estimated costs to perform subsequent warranty repairs	$ 1,000,000

Construction costs will be incurred evenly during 1998 and 1999. Warranty repairs will be performed during the year 2000. The contract price will be paid in equal installments of $4,000,000 at the ends of 1998, 1999, and 2000.

REQUIRED

a. Determine the firm's total profit in the contract described above.

b. Propose and justify a method of recognizing the amounts of profit (if any) to be reported in 1997, 1998, 1999, and 2000.

Income Tax Expense and Income Statement Classifications

4–42 Amherst Trucking Co. has the following pre-tax amounts of revenues, expenses, gains, and losses during 1998. All items are subject to an income tax rate of 40%.

Revenues	$1,500,000
Operating expenses	$ 900,000
Extraordinary loss	$ 400,000

REQUIRED

a. Determine the firm's total income tax expense during 1998.
b. What amount would be reported as operating income after tax?
c. What is the amount of tax benefit (tax reduction) associated with the extraordinary loss?
d. What is the net of tax amount of the extraordinary loss?
e. What amount would the firm report as net income of 1998?

Trend Analysis: Net Income and EPS

4–43 Equity Cushion Co. reports the following items in its financial statements:

	1997	1998
Net income	$16,000,000	$24,000,000
Common shares outstanding	1,000,000 shares	1,200,000 shares

REQUIRED

a. Determine the firm's earnings per share (EPS) in both 1997 and 1998.
b. Determine the percentage change in net income and EPS from 1997 to 1998.
c. Based on your answers to part b, what would you expect Equity Cushion's net income and EPS to be in 1999? Clearly state any assumptions made in developing your answers.

Vertical Analysis of the Income Statement

4–44 P-Town O'Malley's 1998 income statement reports net income of $6 million. A vertical analysis of the income statement shows the following:

Net sales percentage	?%
Cost of products sold percentage	?%
Gross profit percentage	48%
Selling and administrative expense percentage	?
Operating income percentage	?
Income tax* percentage	?
Net income percentage	6%

*Income tax rate: 40% of operating income.

REQUIRED

a. Determine the missing percentages and the dollar amounts that are reported in P-Town's income statement for each of the above items.

Horizontal and Vertical Analysis of the Income Statement

4–45 The Miami Rockies, a recently transplanted baseball franchise, reports the following income statement and horizontal percentages:

	1997 Amount (000's of $)	Percentage Changes During 1998
Revenues	$ 6,500	+10%
Operating expenses	(4,800)	+ 8%
Operating income	$ 1,700	?
Income tax (40%)	(680)	?
Net income	$ 1,020	?

REQUIRED

a. Complete the "Percentage Changes during 1998" column, and determine the dollar amounts reported in the Rockies' 1998 income statement.
b. Prepare a vertical analysis of the income statements for both 1997 and 1998.
c. Comment on any apparently favorable or unfavorable changes between 1997 and 1998, revealed by your analyses in parts a and b.

Gross Margin Changes: Two-Product Firm

4–46 Ben-Shien's Wonton Works produces two grades of dumpling wrappers, standard and deluxe. Sales and cost of sales for both products are provided below for 1997 and 1998:

	1997		1998	
	(dollars in thousands)			
	Standard	Deluxe	Standard	Deluxe
Sales	$600	$900	$900	$600
Cost of sales	$500	$600	$750	$400

REQUIRED

a. Determine Ben-Shien's total sales, gross profit, and gross profit percentage in each year.
b. Provide a horizontal (percentage change) analysis of the sales, cost of sales, and gross margin amounts.
c. Explain why Ben-Shien's overall gross profit declined during 1998.

Gross Margin Changes: Two-Product Firm

4–47 Hadley Hot Tubs produces two models, the Sierra and the Madres. Partial revenue and cost information for 1997 is provided below:

	1997	
	(dollars in thousands)	
	Sierra	Madres
Sales	$1,200	$1,600
Cost of sales	(500)	(1,000)
Gross profit	$ 700	$ 600

Additional information relating to 1998:

1. The firm had total sales of $3 million, and sales revenues were equal for both models.
2. The sales price of the Sierra model remained constant, but the sales price of the Madres declined by 25%.
3. The cost of producing the Sierra increased by 10% and the cost of producing the Madres declined by 5% per unit.

REQUIRED

a. Determine the percentage change in the number of units sold for each product.
b. Determine Hadley's gross profit for 1998, in total and for each model.

c. Compare Hadley's total gross margin percentage in 1997 and 1998, and briefly summarize the reasons for the change in gross margin over the two years.

Bonus Payments: Floor and Ceiling Amounts

4–48 Timing Adjusters, Inc., pays annual bonuses to managers based on reported pre-tax operating profits. Total bonus payments are determined by the following formula:

> 10% of (pre-tax operating profit, less $20 million);
> Maximum total bonus: $5 million.

The formula implies that no bonuses are paid for profits below $20 million (the "floor"), or for profits above $70 million (the "ceiling").*

---

*The maximum total bonus in $5 million. This amount corresponds to profits of $70 million: [10% × ($70 million − $20 million) = $5 million].

REQUIRED

Determine the total bonus payments that would result given the following amounts of pre-tax income:

a. $10 million
b. $25 million
c. $65 million
d. $90 million

Bonus Payments: Motives for Managing Earning (continuation of Exercise 4–48)

4–49 Consider the bonus plan of Timing Adjusters, Inc. described in the preceding exercise. Assume that management expects the following amount of pre-tax income over the next four years.

Year	Pre-Tax Income (Before Bonus) (dollars in millions)
1997	$ 18
1998	$ 45
1999	$ 95
2000	$ 60
Total	$218

REQUIRED

a. Determine the total bonus payments to management over the four-year period (1997–2000).
b. Assume that managers have some discretion in the timing of accounting recognition of revenues and expenses. In which years would managers attempt to postpone profits (i.e., defer revenues or accelerate expense recognition)? In which year would managers attempt to increase the amount of reported income? Assume that total income over the four-year period will be $218 million, in any event.

Vertical and Horizontal Analysis of the Income Statement

4–50 Denny's CPA School provides the following vertical analysis of its income statements for 1997 and 1998:

| | Percentage of Revenues | |
	1997	1998
Revenues	100%	100%
Salaries expense	40%	45%
Rentals expense	20%	25%
Books and supplies	10%	10%
Advertising	10%	15%
Operating income	20%	5%
Income tax	8%	2%
Net income	12%	3%

In addition, you are informed that Denny's earned tuition revenues of $500,000 in 1997, and $400,000 in 1998.

REQUIRED

a. Based on the above information, prepare the firm's income statements for 1997 and 1998. Provide a horizontal analysis of the changes in each item in the income statement. Based on your analysis, comment about the expected future performance of Denny's CPA School.

Transaction Analysis: Preparing an Income Statement, Cash Versus Accrual

4–51 Jill Zimmer wants to know how successful her restaurant, Planet Broadway, was in 1998. She has assembled the following 1998 data:

1. Wages were $270,000, paid in cash.
2. Collection from customers were $675,000 (assume all customers paid their bills by year-end.)
3. A $5,000 deposit for a future wedding reception is included in these collections.
4. Insurance expense was $3,500, paid in cash.
5. Rental expense was $120,000, paid in cash.
6. Food costs were $85,000, paid in cash.
7. Advertising bills totaled $13,000; however, Jill had only agreed to pay $1,000 each month under her contract with the advertising firm. The extra $1,000 pertained to 1997.
8. Interest revenues were $350, collected in cash.
9. Cab fares (for inebriated customers) were $875.
10. The income tax rate is 28% of income before taxes.
11. Jill's salary was $10,000 per month.

REQUIRED

a. Prepare a single-step income statement using the accrual basis of accounting.
b. Prepare another income statement using the cash basis of accounting.
c. Discuss the differences between these two statements.

Performance Evaluation (continuation of Problem 4–51)

4–52 Refer to Jill's restaurant in Problem 4–51.

    a. What managerial concerns might Jill have upon seeing your income statement?

    b. What additional items usually appear in such an income statement for a small business?

    c. Which costs do you feel are high, relative to Jill's volume of business?

    d. On which costs should she concentrate most in order to improve her profitability?

    e. What else could she do to improve her net income?

4–53 **Revenue Recognition: Cash versus Accrual—Alternate Problems (A) or (B)**

Problem (A)

Consider the following transactions:

1. The firm sells merchandise for $1,000, but no cash is received.
2. The firm collects the $1,000 from transaction 1.
3. A medical clinic provides treatment for a patient and bills the patient's insurance company for $65. The patient is responsible for any deficiency not paid by insurance.
4. The insurance company pays the clinic only $49.
5. The physician bills the patient for the balance due.
6. The patient pays the physician $11.
7. Safeway Market sells three bags of groceries for $110, but the customer pays for the groceries with a credit card.
8. The State of Arkansas and Shannon Engineers sign a contract for $10,000,000 to design and build a bridge over the Arkansas River. It will take Shannon two years to complete this project, and no work will be started until next year.
9. The state of Arkansas pays Shannon a deposit of $1,000,000 after the contract is signed, but before any other work has commenced.
10. The state of Arkansas pays $4,000,000 to Shannon during the first year of work, even though two-thirds of the bridge has been completed—way ahead of schedule. How much revenue should Shannon now recognize?
11. The state of Arkansas pays the remaining $5,000,000 at the end of the second year, long after the bridge has been completed. Indicate how much revenue Shannon should recognize in the second year.

REQUIRED

    a. Determine the amount of revenue that would be recognized under accrual accounting.

    b. Determine the amount of revenue that would be recognized under cash basis accounting.

Problem (B)

Consider the following transactions:

1. Sarah Jones, R.N., provides home nursing services to her clients and bills them for 20 hours of service at $65 per hour.
2. Ms. Jones collects $60 per hour from her state's Medicaid program for the services in transaction 1. Patients are not required to make up any shortfall

for the 20 hours of service. Therefore, Sarah expenses the balance in the receivable account.

3. Quick-Shop Grocery sells food and other merchandise for $3,500, on account. (Ignore the cost of goods sold.)

4. Quick-Shop Grocery enters into a contract with Bob's Bakery to provide flour, sugar, and other ingredients at a standard fee of $100 per day.

5. Andy's Aerobic Aerie sells annual memberships to exercise fanatics at $30 per month. This entitles members to unlimited access to aerobics classes, workouts, and so on. On January 1, Andy signed 100 members, who pay the first month's fee.

6. Andy signs an agreement with Sarah Jones to provide discounted memberships to 10 of her impoverished clients at $20 per month. Half of them pay at the end of the first month.

7. Andy decides to prepare and distribute a monthly aerobics guide, in magazine form. This wonderful publication is available to members at $5 per issue. Only half of Andy's 110 members take advantage of this offer, and they pay the annual subscription.

8. Andy puts 30 copies of his aerobics guide on display in the Quick-Shop. These copies are "consigned" to the Quick-Shop, and payment is not due until the issues are sold.

9. All 30 copies of the guide are sold. Andy collects $4 per issue from Quick-Shop ($5 minus 20% consignment fee).

REQUIRED

a. Determine the revenue associated with each item that would be recognized during the first month under the accrual method.

b. Similarly, determine the revenue that would be recognized under the cash basis of accounting.

Transaction Analysis: Preparing an Income Statement, Accrual Basis

4–54 The Lick Skillet Bakery provides deli meals, bakery goods, and espresso to restaurant customers. It also sells take-out specialty foods, including bakery goods, hot and cold entrees, and so on. The owners of Lick Skillet want to know how successful the bakery was in 1998, based on the following information:

1. Lick Skillet sold goods and collected $400,500 (cash) from restaurant customers. (Ignore the cost of goods sold until transaction 8.)

2. Lick Skillet contracted with local firms to provide them with catering services totaling $560,000 during 1998.

3. Lick Skillet provided the contract catering services and collected $456,000 from its catering clients.

4. Lick Skillet purchased (with cash) restaurant equipment, expected to last three years, at a cost of $30,000.

5. Lick Skillet paid employees $475,000 during 1998.

6. Lick Skillet owed employees $55,000 for work performed during December 1998.

7. Lick Skillet owed employment taxes of $67,500 for the entire year of 1998, but had not obtained the appropriate forms from the state and federal governments.

8. Lick Skillet purchased food and other consumable supplies costing $236,700 and paid cash. While it had no inventory at the beginning of 1998, its inventory on December 31, 1998, was estimated at $6,500.
9. Items returned by disgruntled customers resulted in refunds totaling $3,550.
10. Lick Skillet purchased an insurance policy on January 1, 1998, that cost $4,400 and provided insurance for both 1998 and 1999.

REQUIRED

a. Record these business transactions, including any necessary adjustments, using the accrual basis of accounting in the basic accounting equation. Set up headings as follows: Cash, Accounts Receivable, Inventory, Prepaid Insurance, Equipment, Accumulated Depreciation, Accrued Liabilities, and Owners' Equity.
b. Prepare a multistep income statement.
c. How successful was Lick Skillet in 1998?
d. What important items might Lick Skillet be ignoring in its income statement?
e. If you now find that Mr. and Mrs. Lick have baked the entire year at no salary, how would that change the analysis?
f. If you then find that the bakery is located in the Lick personal residence, how does that affect your analysis? Assume that the Licks pay rent of $3,000 per month, and that the bakery covers about two-thirds of the unit's total floor space.

Transaction Analysis: Preparing an Income Statement, Cash Basis (continuation of Problem 4–54)

4–55 For the following items, refer to the information from Problem 4–54 regarding Lick Skillet Bakery.

REQUIRED

a. Record business transactions for Lick Skillet using the cash basis of accounting in the basic accounting equation. Set up the headings as follows: Cash, Accounts Receivable, Inventory, Prepaid Insurance, Equipment, Accumulated Depreciation, Accrued Liabilities, and Owners' Equity. *Note:* You will not need many of these accounts.
b. Prepare a multistep income statement.
c. Discuss the differences between the income statements presented on the cash versus accrual basis.
d. Which statement accurately portrays Lick Skillet's future cash flows?

Transaction Analysis

4–56 The Bichette Company had the following transactions during the year ended December 31, 1977:

1. Sales on account were $155,000. Cash sales were $38,000.
2. Cost of goods sold during the year was $42,000.
3. Wages earned by employees was $32,000. Three quarters of the amount was paid during the year as the wages were incurred. The remainder was accrued at year end.
4. A two-year insurance policy was purchased on January 1, 1997, for $4,800.

5. Equipment with a five-year life was acquired on June 30, 1997, for $10,000 with a note bearing interest at an annual rate of 9%. The interest and principal are not due until June 30, 1998.
6. Rent and other operating expenses paid in cash were $14,500.
7. The company sold a short-term investment and recorded a gain of $800.
8. Dividends declared and paid were $24,015.
9. The income tax rate was 30%.

REQUIRED

a. Prepare a multistep income statement similar to Exhibit 4–6 for the year ended December 31, 1997. *Note:* Make the necessary adjustments before preparing the income statement.
b. Assume stockholders' equity at the beginning of the year was $740,000. The only changes recorded in stockholders' equity during 1997 were net income and dividends. Calculate return on equity and evaluate your results.
c. Calculate earnings per share. Assume the number of shares outstanding was 140,000 shares.
d. Calculate times interest earned.

Income Statement Preparation, Calculate EPS

4–57 The following information shows the revenue, expense, and other accounts of the Stackwell Enterprises Company for the year ended December 31, 1997:

Cost of goods sold	$135,000	Utilities expense	$ 4,800
Depreciation expense	12,000	Income tax rate	30%
Dividends declared and paid	4,000	Earthquake loss (gross	
Advertising expense	1,600	amount; assume not in	
Office wages expense	28,000	an earthquake area)	$15,000
Insurance expense	2,400	Interest expense	10,000
Gain on sale of short-term		Repairs and maintenance	
investments	3,500	expense	1,700
Commission expense	15,000	Interest income	2,000
		Sales revenue	230,000

REQUIRED

a. Prepare a multistep income statement similar to Exhibit 4–6 for the year ended December 31, 1997. Selling expenses include advertising and commission expense.
b. Calculate earnings per share. Assume the number of shares outstanding is 100,000 shares.

Revenue Recognition: Percentage-of-completion method

4–58 For the following transactions, determine the amount of revenue that should be recognized under the percentage-of-completion method (assuming that the percentage of work actually completed corresponds to the amounts billed):

1. Woody's Engineering consultants contract to design and build a bridge. The contract calls for payments of $4 million per year for each of the next four years.
2. Woody's designs the bridge, starts construction, and bills the client at the end of the first year for the first year's amount of $4 million. Construction is approximately one-fourth complete.

3. Woody's collects $4 million on February 15 of the second year.
4. Woody's bills the client for $4 million at the end of the second year.
5. Woody's works very hard and completes the project at the end of the third year and bills the client for $8 million.
6. Woody's collects $4 million on February 15 of the third and fourth years.
7. Woody's provides a $500,000 bonus payment to the project manager.
8. At the end of the fourth year, Woody's collects the final payment of $4 million.

Performance Evaluation (continuation of Problem 4–58)

4–59 Consider Problem 4–58 and answer these questions:

a. In which year, or years, did Woody's perform exceptionally well, even beyond expectation?
b. In what year should the income statement reflect this exceptional performance?
c. Under the cash basis, which year would stand out?
d. If the client had paid the $16 million when the bridge was finished, which year would stand out under the cash basis?
e. Discuss the merits of the accrual basis of accounting versus the cash basis for a company such as Woody's.

Revenue Recognition

4–60 Consider the following for the publishers of *Mobile Home Improvement*. This magazine is produced monthly and sold on newsstands and to annual subscribers. Determine the amount of revenue that should be recorded on an accrual basis in each circumstance.

1. *Mobile Home Improvement* receives 100 two-year subscriptions ($48 each) and 3,000 one-year subscriptions ($36 each).
2. *Mobile Home Improvement* sells 30,000 copies of the January issue to newsstand vendors at $1.50 each, and receives payment.
3. In February, the same vendors order and receive 30,000 copies, but payment is not received until March.
4. In March, the same vendors order and receive 30,000 copies, but payment is not received until April.
5. In addition, in March, a new vendor places a standing order for 40,000 copies for each month for the rest of year. They provide a retainer, or advance payment, for one month's supply, which is to be kept on deposit to reflect their purchase commitment. In return, the publishers of *Mobile Home Improvement* reduce their purchase price by 10 cents each. The publishers ship March's 40,000 copies to the vendor on account.

4–61 Analyzing Financial Statements—Alternate Problems (A) or (B)

Problem (A)

Consider the following income statement:

	1998	1997
Net Revenues		
Software sales	$ 77,350,000	$ 66,450,000
Customer support and service	48,500,000	39,040,000
Total net revenues	125,850,000	105,490,000

Operating Expenses

Cost of goods sold	4,700,000	4,580,000
Sales and marketing	60,650,000	40,235,000
Research, development and support	31,990,000	25,102,000
General and administrative	19,036,000	19,438,000
Total operating expenses	116,376,000	89,355,000
Income from operations	$ 9,474,000	$ 16,135,000

REQUIRED

a. Conduct horizontal and vertical analyses of the firm's income statement.
b. Why do you suppose that the firm's income from operations declined in 1998?
c. In what areas was the firm successful in 1998?
d. Based on the approximate trends shown here, do you suppose that the firm's income from operations will increase or decrease in 1999? Why?

Problem (B)

Consider the following income statement:

	1998	1997
Net Revenues		
Computer sales	$ 75,250,000	$ 62,250,000
Customer support and service	45,400,000	38,600,000
Total net revenues	120,650,000	100,850,000
Operating Expenses		
Cost of goods sold	4,205,000	4,500,000
Sales and marketing	63,520,000	45,542,000
Research, development and support	30,100,000	21,587,000
General and administrative	20,026,000	19,000,000
Total operating expenses	117,851,000	90,629,000
Income from operations	$ 2,799,000	$ 10,221,000

REQUIRED

a. Conduct horizontal and vertical analyses of the firm's income statement.
b. Why do you suppose that the firm's income from operations declined in 1998?
c. In what areas was the firm successful in 1998?
d. Based on the approximate trends shown here, do you suppose that the firm's income from operations will increase or decrease in 1999? Why?

Revenue Recognition

4–62 Matching and revenue recognition are fundamental accrual accounting principles. Discuss how each of these principles would be used to determine the revenue or expense in each of the following transactions:

1. Rent for two months of $1,200 was paid in advance.
2. A customer's order was received for a bridal veil that will be billed at delivery for $120.
3. Supplies, purchased three months ago at a cost of $300, were used in the current month.
4. An etching by Picasso was purchased in 1960 for $400. A similar etching just sold at Sotheby's for $45,000.

5. Equipment purchased 10 years ago had monthly depreciation recorded of $900. The equipment had an original useful life of five years and is still in use.
6. An architect was paid a $2,000 retainer for preparing designs and plans for a new office.
7. Wages of $120 , earned by employees on New Year's Eve, will be paid on January 5.
8. A mortgage loan was issued last year, but the creditors are now three months delinquent in their monthly payments.

Preparing Financial Statements: Performance Evaluation

4–63 Susan's Drawing Studio has been very successful and 1997's sales and profits were at a record high. Susan wants to evaluate and better understand last year's performance based on the following year-end account balances:

Sales	$400,000	Supplies used	$ 25,600
Property tax expense	2,550	Cash	32,300
Supplies inventory	12,400	Building and equipment	110,000
Accounts payable	2,450	Wages payable	1,200
Wages expense	13,240	Shareholders' equity	?
Receivables	2,200	Advertising expense	2,400
Taxes payable	2,670	Miscellaneous expenses	120,000

REQUIRED

a. Prepare a balance sheet and a single-step income statement.
b. Evaluate Susan's net income relative to her sales volume.
c. What is Susan's net income as a percentage of sales? Why do you think most firms do not have net income ratios this high?
d. Would your conclusions about Susan's net income change if you learned that she had been withdrawing $10,000 every month and charging these payments to Miscellaneous Expenses? Why?
e. How would your conclusions change if you learned that Susan, who is a very gifted artist, could be earning $40,000 a month by working for her former employer, the Degas Drawing Corporation?
f. Given that Susan has a Building and Equipment account, what basic type of expense is missing from her income statement? Would calculation of that item change your conclusions about her relative profitability? How large would this item have to be to change your views about Susan's profitability? Why? What other information would you need before drawing firm conclusions about this issue?
g. Why do you think shareholders' equity has a lower balance than net income?
h. Are there any other major elements of information missing? If so, what are they, and why would you like more information about these items?

CASES AND EXTENSIONS

Determining Revenues and Expenses

4–64 McGucken's Software sold $1,354,000 of merchandise for cash and had credit sales totaling $2,658,000. It collected cash from customers in the amount of $3,396,000. McCucken's received merchandise from suppliers invoiced at $1,100,000 and paid suppliers $900,000.

REQUIRED

a. Determine the amount of revenue that should be recognized this year.
b. Determine the cost of goods sold (amount) that should be matched with this year's revenue, assuming no change in inventory (that is, beginning inventory = ending inventory).

WHAT WOULD YOU DO?

Revenue Recognition

4–65 Using the time line from Exhibit 4–3, identify when, and how much, revenue should be recognized in each of the following cases:

1. Banana Republic sells clothes for cash or on credit card vouchers, which are collected from banks within a few days after the sale.
2. Micropoint Computer Systems sells hardware and software on installment or time-payment plans. Micropoint runs a credit check on every customer and only extends credit to customers with high credit ratings.
3. Backdoor Appliances sells used and new household appliances on installment or time-payment plans. They sell on credit to anyone who signs a purchase agreement, even though many of their customers have dubious credit histories. Accordingly, Backdoor experiences many customer defaults, incurs substantial collection costs, and is rarely able to recover its merchandise.
4. Ball Aerospace manufactures satellites and satellite parts under contract to the NASA. NASA requires Ball to maintain certain inventories of spare parts, as well as the expertise to provide consultants and technical assistance as needed. Their contract obligates NASA to buy all parts, such as satellites, produced by Ball. Under the contract, Ball produced spare parts at a cost of $2 million and billed NASA for $3 million.
5. Assume that the correct accounting was conducted for part 4. Now assume that the sales manager at Ball is trying to boost her performance for 1998 and sells a complete weather satellite to Russia for $5 million in violation of the NASA contract. What revenue should be recognized and what should the firm's controller do when informed of this situation?

Determining Expected Revenues and Expenses and Preparing an Income Statement

4–66 Beth's Espresso Cart Inc. sells coffee, pastries, and mineral water on the Boulder Mall. Last year, Beth leased a coffee cart and opened her business. She initially felt that cash flows were a useful measure of her performance. The cart's owner is now running a competitive coffee cart on the next block. Beth has heard about accrual accounting and is hoping to develop a better measure of her performance this year.

1. Beth paid $5,200 for a coffee cart, which she expects to use for the next four years.
2. She purchased coffee pots, cups, and other supplies at a cost of $2,000 and paid cash. Half of these supplies will be replaced each year.
3. Electricity and propane costs have averaged $40 per month.
4. Beth started and ended the year with negligible amounts of coffee beans and mineral water.

5. Each month, Beth needs to earn a salary of $500 for personal living expenses.
6. Last year, Beth purchased a three-year insurance policy for liability and related incidents costing $1,200.
7. Beth expects to have six really good months of sales revenue during the summer and six slower months. Based on last year, her purchases of coffee, pastries, and mineral water during the good months averaged about $2,000 each month. During the slower months, these items cost about $1,400 each month.
8. During the peak months, Beth generally collected $4,500 each month and during the slower months collected $3,000 each month.

REQUIRED

a. Identify the amount of annual revenues and expenses that would be expected for each of the items above. Construct a single-step income statement for Beth's Espresso Cart for the next year.
b. What should Beth consider as she makes plans for next year? What other items should be considered for inclusion in her income statement? Why?
c. Why do you think this income statement will be more useful to Beth than the cash flow indicators used in the prior year?

Interpreting Financial Statements

4–67 Consider the following income statement:

Commission revenue	$120,000	
Rental revenue	9,900	
Interest income	4,100	
Total revenue		$134,000
Salaries expense	54,000	
Depreciation expense	23,000	
Interest expense	2,550	
Miscellaneous expense	10,400	(89,950)
Operating income		44,050
Income taxes		(16,825)
Extraordinary items, net of tax		12,000
Net income		$ 39,225

REQUIRED

a. Review and analyze this income statement, using vertical analysis.
b. What other items might usually be found in such an income statement (i.e., what is missing)?

Effects of Changing Depreciation Policies

4–68 Given the following balance sheet equations and income statement for the year, show how the balance sheet at the end of the year might change to reflect the proposed change in depreciation policies. Indicate how the key profitability ratios will also change.

Beginning of the Year:

ASSETS	=	LIABILITIES	+	OWNERS' EQUITY
$350,000		$125,000		$225,000

During the year:

Revenues	$650,000
−Expenses	(475,000)
Net income	$175,000

End of the Year:

ASSETS	=	LIABILITIES	+	OWNERS' EQUITY
$450,000		$50,000		$400,000

The firm is proposing to lengthen the useful life of its long-term assets because new technologies have been discovered that permit their useful lives to be doubled at a modest cost. This change in useful life will reduce the annual depreciation expense by $100,000. No other changes are contemplated at this time. (Assume this change will affect the current year, above, and each succeeding year.)

Effects of Changing Depreciation Policies (continuation of Case 4–68)

4–69 Using the same balance sheet equations and income statement in Case 4–68, conduct a similar analysis on the basis of the following scenario. (Assume depreciation will not change.) Analyze the effects of a change in revenues for the current year, assuming these new events *were noted during the audit before the final statements were prepared.*

1. The firm sold and delivered a computer system on the last day of the year for $125,000. It expected to be paid in January of the following year. The customer had an excellent credit rating and had always paid promptly under similar circumstances.
2. At the due date, the buyer of the merchandise sent a check for $25,000 and a note explaining that their company had laid off half its employees and was not able to make further payment for six months at which time it expected to pay an additional $25,000.

How would this new information change the income statement and ending balance sheet if the seller had anticipated full payment in January according to prior practices?

Interpreting Financial Statements

4–70 SILLA, Inc., is a producer and supplier of natural gas and petroleum-based products. Its condensed statements of operations for the first quarters of 1996 and 1997 are shown below ($ in thousands):

	1997	1996
Revenues:		
Natural gas, oil, and other liquids	$63,405	$59,088
Other	1,065	176
	64,470	59,264

Statement continued on page 156

Costs and expenses:

Operating, exploration, and taxes	19,099	18,844
General and administrative	5,780	5,819
Depreciation, etc.	29,450	25,650
	54,329	50,313
Operating income	$10,141	$ 8,951

REQUIRED

a. Based on this (partial) income statement, evaluate SILLA's first quarter performance for 1997. To accomplish this objective, conduct the following analyses:
   1. Calculate horizontal and vertical ratio analyses.
   2. Calculate any other appropriate ratios, using the income statement data.
b. Identify any other issues or information that would help you evaluate SILLA's profitability. (That is, what is missing?)

Interpreting Financial Statements (continuation of Case 4–70)

4–71 Refer to Case 4–70. Review the remainder of SILLA's income statement as follows:

	1997	1996
Operating income	$10,141	$8,951
Interest expense, net of interest income	(32,259)	(32,575)
Securities gains	5,509	3,280
Other	(370)	(1,851)
Net loss	$ (16,979)	$ (22,195)
Average total assets	$542,500	$553,000
Average total stockholders' equity	105,345	106,950
Interest expense, net of tax	42,400	43,200

REQUIRED

a. Based on the now-completed income statement (see the preceding case) evaluate SILLA's first quarter performance for 1997.
b. To accomplish this objective, extend the ratio calculations from the preceding case to include return on assets and return on equity for both years.
c. How has this new information changed your assessment of SILLA's performance? What do you think is the major topic of concern and focus for SILLA's board of directors? Why? What suggestions might you have that may be useful for SILLA's Board?

Interpreting Financial Statements

4–72 With respect to Microbyte Corporation's consolidated statement of operations shown below ($ in thousands), identify any unusual trends or categories of information. Identify any potential problems or questions based on this analysis. What other information would be helpful? Why? (Note that Microbyte is a computer company, specializing in data storage devices.)

	1997	1996
Sales	$184,355	$92,642
Cost of goods sold	102,453	53,344
Gross profit	81,902	39,298

Operating expenses:		
Selling, general, and administrative	20,188	12,272
Research and development	15,669	6,785
Income from operations	46,045	20,241
Other income	1,831	1,744
Income before income taxes and extraordinary item	47,876	21,985
Income taxes	(17,040)	(8,056)
Income before extraordinary item	30,836	13,929
Extraordinary item	—	1,049
Net income	$ 30,836	$14,978

Interpreting Financial Statements (continuation of Case 4–72)

4–73 With respect to Microbyte Corporation's consolidated statement of operations, shown in Case 4–72, conduct horizontal and vertical ratios analyses for each year, as shown in this chapter. Identify any potential problems or issues based on this analysis. What other information would be helpful? Why? Would you rate Microbyte as a very profitable company? Why or why not?

Interpreting Financial Statements (continuation of Case 4–72)

4–74 With respect to Microbyte Corporation (see Case 4–72), assume that its annual report contained the following footnote:

Because research is so important to the future of Microbyte, the corporation has budgeted $23,000,000 for research and development for 1998. These funds are presently committed to a new facility under construction and to 42 engineers and computer analysts who have been hired to begin work January 1, 1998.

On the basis of this footnote, estimate what would have happened to 1997 earnings if these charges had been incurred in 1997. Construct a simple balance sheet equation including these charges, as though they happened in 1997.

Interpreting Financial Statements (continuation of Case 4–72)

4–75 With respect to Microbyte Corporation (see Case 4–72), assume the annual report contained the following footnote:

Because interest rates are expected to be low during 1998, Microbyte Corporation has signed commitments and pledges to effectively refinance all of its short and long-term liabilities. Accordingly, Microbyte expects to recognize a $12 million gain (on debt refinancing) in 1998.

On the basis of this footnote, estimate what would have happened to 1997 earnings, assuming this gain had been recognized in 1997. Construct a simple balance sheet equation for 1997, as though the gain had been recognized in 1997.

Interpreting Financial Statements

4–76 Pioneer Resource Inc.'s 1997 income statement ($ in millions) is summarized below. Pioneer Resource is involved in telecommunications.

	1997	1996
Revenues	$13,932.3	$13,231.1
Costs and expenses		
Network operations	3,787.1	3,642.3
Selling, general, and administrative	4,219.7	4,007.5
Taxes, other than income taxes	661.0	570.2
Interest expense	481.9	410.6
Depreciation expense	1,951.7	1,818.9
Other income, net	(87.4)	(55.4)
Subtotal	11,014.0	10,394.1
Income before income taxes	2,918.3	2,837.0
Income taxes	897.3	855.6
Net income	$ 2,021.0	$ 1,981.4

REQUIRED

a. Conduct horizontal and vertical analyses of Pioneer Resource's income statement.

b. Would you conclude that Pioneer Resource's operating activities were stable or unstable across these two years? Why?

c. What types of costs do you suppose were included in "Network operations"? In "Selling, general, and administrative"? Why do you suppose that the latter costs were so much larger than the former?

d. Why is "Other income, net" shown in parentheses? Are these items significant? Would it have changed your opinion about Pioneer Resource's operations if these amounts had been included in "Revenues"? Why?

e. Consider depreciation expense. Your vertical analysis should have indicated that depreciation expenses are more than 13% of revenues. In this case, depreciation is the third largest expense category. Would you consider that unusual for many companies? Why? Why do you suppose that Pioneer Resource has such high depreciation expenses?

WHAT WOULD
YOU DO?

Interpreting Financial Statements (continuation of Case 4–76)

4–77 Consider Pioneer Resource's income statement in Case 4–76. Suppose you were Pioneer Resource's controller and suppose the board members had forecast, and widely publicized, their goal of increasing net income by 5% in 1997. Your horizontal analysis should have indicated that net income only increased by 2%, whereas revenues increased by almost 5% (actually 5.3%).

REQUIRED

a. What explanations might you offer as to why the 5% net income goal was not achieved?

b. Suppose Pioneer Resource's chairman of the board and the CEO met with you, the controller, prior to publishing this income statement. In this meeting, they strongly encouraged you to make some accounting adjustments in order to achieve the 5% goal. They suggested that interest expense be recalculated at a lower rate of interest, which would cut the "Interest expense" by 50%. Interest rates in the external market were declining rapidly. The chairman's and CEO's rationale was that Pioneer Resource was refinancing its debts and would soon enjoy the lower interest rates. They also suggested that some revenues from January 1998, which had already been realized, should be transferred to the 1997 income statement. Their rationale was that Pioneer Resource did the work to get the sales in 1997, therefore, the revenues should be properly matched with other revenues and expenses in 1997 and should be shown on the 1997 income statement. Write a short paragraph to the chairman and CEO indicating your response to their suggestions.

Research Project: Comparing Two Regional Communications Companies

4–78 Ameritech is the parent company of five Bell companies providing communication services to the Great Lakes states. Several U.S. companies are comparable to Ameritech.

REQUIRED

a. Using the resources of your library, obtain the income statements of one other regional communications company, e.g., U S West or Bell Atlantic, for similar fiscal periods.

b. Conduct horizontal and vertical analyses of Ameritech and your identified company. Use the results of your analysis to identify any unusual trends or patterns in the firms' operating costs. Note that even if the report dates are not identical, the relative cost comparisons may be instructive.

c. Write a short report examining the relative profitability of these companies. Identify the major similarities and differences in the cost structures of these two companies. For example, are the depreciation expenses relatively as high in each company? Are the operating costs in the same proportion to revenues across the two companies? Is the growth rate in revenues and net income the same? Why do you suppose that such similarities or differences exist?

Interpreting Financial Statements

4–79 Sigma Designs is a high-tech software development company specializing in imaging and multimedia computer applications. Sigma's balance sheets are reproduced below ($ in thousands):

Assets	1993	1992
Cash and equivalents	$ 5,086	$ 9,283
Marketable securities	14,326	19,537
Accounts receivable, net of allowances	6,471	2,987
Inventories	12,275	10,066
Prepaid expenses	435	753
Income taxes receivable	1,582	2,428
Total current assets	40,175	45,054
Equipment, net	1,626	1,607
Other assets	2,466	2,388
Total assets	$44,267	$49,049

Balance sheet continued on page 160

Liabilities and Shareholders' Equity

Current Liabilities

Accounts payable	$ 4,933	$ 1,826
Accrued salary and benefits	809	594
Other accrued liabilities	737	1,119
Total current liabilities	6,479	3,539
Other long-term liabilities	—	755

Shareholders' Equity

Common stock	19,287	19,088
Retained earnings	18,501	25,667
Total shareholders' equity	37,788	44,755
Total Liabilities and shareholders' equity	$44,267	$49,049

Sigma's 1991–1993 statements of operations are summarized below ($ in thousands):

	1993	1992	1991
Net sales	$27,058	$27,567	$35,968
Costs and expenses:			
Cost of sales	23,045	20,255	23,438
Sales and marketing	7,476	7,261	6,840
Research and development	5,043	5,105	3,323
General and administrative	1,951	1,788	1,722
Total cost and expenses	37,515	34,409	35,323
Income (loss) from operations	(10,457)	(6,842)	645
Interest income-net	1,207	1,742	1,964
Other, net	(67)	(6)	59
Income (loss) before income taxes	(9,317)	(5,106)	2,688
Provision for income taxes	(2,151)	(1,663)	880
Net income (loss)	$ (7,166)	$ (3,443)	$ 1,788

REQUIRED

a. Before making any calculations, state in your own words what each item in the income statement means. In particular, identify which items are positive or negative and why.

b. Using information from both statements, evaluate Sigma's profitability and operating performance. To accomplish this objective, conduct the following analyses:

  1. Calculate horizontal and vertical analyses.

  2. Calculate operating income ratios and net income ratios for each year.

  3. Calculate Sigma's return on assets ratio for 1992 and 1993. Assume average total assets for 1992 was $51,000 and assume interest expense included in the line item "Interest income, net" for 1993 and 1992 was $35 and $105. All numbers are in thousands.

  4. Calculate Sigma's return on equity ratio for 1992 and 1993. Assume average total equity for 1992 was $46,000. All numbers are in thousands.

c. Identify any unusual items or information that is typically found in an income statement, but not included in Sigma's. How would access to this information affect your analysis of Sigma's performance?

d. How does the information shown in the categories of "Interest income, net" and "Other, net" affect your conclusions about Sigma's performance? What else might you like to know about these items?

Critical Essay: Interpreting Expense Reclassifications

4–80 Borden, Inc., in response to pressure from the Securities and Exchange Commission, restated its 1993 and 1992 earnings. It restated the effects of a $642 million restructuring charge taken in 1992, which contributed significantly to Borden's reported 1992 loss of $439.6 million. It reclassified $145.5 million of the restructuring charge as operating expenses in 1992, and it reversed $119.3 million, for a total restatement of $264.8 million. Therefore, the entire restatement was more than 40% of the original restructuring charge, which is a very large change. The original restructuring charge must have included some very aggressive accounting procedures, which have now been, largely, restated.

The after-tax effects of these restatements on Borden's net income are:

	1992	1993
Net loss, as originally reported	$(439.6)	$(593.6)
1994 restatements, reported net of tax	75.2	(37.1)
Net loss, as adjusted	$(364.4)	$(630.7)

According to the *Wall Street Journal* (March 22, 1994, p. B8), Borden reported that these restatements would have no further effect on 1994 earnings. Borden further reported that the expenses included in the original 1992 charge of $642 million were "truly incremental and related to one-time advertising and promotion programs not occurring in the normal course of business."

REQUIRED

a. Write a short memo to your superior at Borden, Inc., justifying these restatements.
b. Write a short memo to an investor explaining why these restatements would affect the investor's decision to purchase (or sell) shares of Borden's common stock.
c. Explain, in your own words why you think Borden was so aggressive in taking the original $642 million restructuring charge. What will it accomplish by restating its 1992 and 1993 net losses?

Conceptual Analysis: Revenue Recognition

4–81 The following scenario presents some possible managerial issues concerning revenue recognition, particularly impacting sustainable operating profit.

A computer firm designs, builds and sells a microcomputer, called a PEAR, for $1,800. The design costs of the computer are well in excess of $30,000,000 and only 10,000,000 computers are expected to be sold before they are obsolete. A Korean company is currently selling identical computers for $1,500. A Japanese company has just invested a new cursor device to replace the mouse (they call it a RAT). This new RAT will only work with computers sold by the Japanese company. The Japanese computers perform very similar functions to each of the computers described earlier. It sells for $1,200. Discounters have been selling the PEAR for $1,100 via telephone and catalog sales. The PEAR and the Korean clone are essentially obsolete, but will still reach their original volume projections.

The primary developer of the PEAR has just resigned and formed a new company that is expected to design a competitive computer that will be superior to any of these other three models (PEAR, Korean clone, Japanese computer).

REQUIRED

a. Indicate how the PEAR managers might view each of these issues in forecasting their operating income for next year.

Interpreting Financial Statements: Effects of Asset Write-Downs

4–82 Byte City, Inc., is a leading independent provider of systems and network management software. Its 1996 and 1997 income statements are abbreviated as follows:

	1997	**1996**
Net Revenues		
Software products	$64,282,171	$52,392,108
Product support and enhancements	32,545,876	27,419,766
Total net revenues	96,828,047	79,811,874
Operating Expenses		
Cost of goods sold	3,614,919	3,215,778
Sales and marketing	45,782,349	38,372,418
Research, development, and support	23,582,478	27,652,020
General and administrative	14,622,594	14,887,923
Write-down of marketing rights and restructuring expenses	0	17,236,845
Total operating expenses	87,602,340	101,364,984
Income (loss) from operations	$ 9,225,707	($21,553,110)

REQUIRED

a. Prepare a horizontal and vertical analysis of Byte City's income statement.
b. Identify any major unusual items in either year. How might these items affect the future? How might they have been reflected in prior years? How might they have been caused by events in prior years?
c. Discuss why Byte City's cost of goods sold is so low relative to other expenses, and also with respect to revenues.
d. Restate 1996's income (loss) from operations by excluding the $17,236,845 write-down. What does this restated amount indicate about possible trends in Byte City's total operating expenses? How does this affect the trend in income from operations?
e. Based only on the information provided, would you predict that Byte City would have a positive income from operations in 1998? Why? By extending the trends in net revenues and in operating expenses to 1998, what amount of income from operations would you predict?

Interpreting Financial Statements: Horizontal Analysis

4–83 Consider the following horizontal analysis of a firm's income statement (assume that 1996 is the base year used for comparison, when all items equal 100%):

	1998	1997
Net Revenues		
Product sales	116.4%	118.2%
Product support and enhancement	124.2	177.9
Total net revenue	119.3	134.9
Operating Expenses		
Cost of goods sold	102.8	40.2
Sales and marketing	120.7	172.1
Research, development and support	91.1	181.8
General and administrative	97.9	161.3
Total operating expenses	103.5	132.2
Income (loss) from operations	114.3%	101.5%

REQUIRED

a. Evaluate the firm's performance.

b. In which year was it more successful? Why?

c. In which year did it control costs most effectively? Why?

d. In which year did the market respond best to the firm's products and services? Why?

e. In which area of expenses should management concentrate the most attention? Why?

f. Did this firm have a positive or a negative income from operations in 1997? Why? In 1998? Why?

Timing and Revenue Recognition

4–84 You are the chief accountant for the Seal Company, which produces candy bars. You like your job very much, and one reason is that your best friend, Stacy Monroe, is a salesperson for Seal.

Seal primarily markets its candy bars to grocery chains, which buy in large quantities. As December 31 (Seal's year-end) approaches, your friend Stacy worries that she will not achieve her sales quota. If the quota is not met, Stacy will not receive the rather large bonus she had been counting on.

With just one week to go before year-end, Stacy receives a big order; in fact, the order will enable her to meet her quota and receive her bonus. There's just one problem. Seal's sales terms are that the customer takes title to the candy when Seal transfers the candy to an independent trucker. At that point, Seal records the revenue and Stacy gets credit for the sale. You assure Stacy that one week is plenty of time to process the order. Stacy is so elated, that she celebrates by buying a $20,000 car.

On December 31, Stacy's order is ready to be shipped, and is awaiting the trucker. Although this particular trucker is usually reliable, he phones to say a blizzard will prevent him from arriving until January 2.

Stacy is understandably upset. She purchased a new car based on your assurance that she would receive her bonus, and it now appears that her bonus will not materialize.

REQUIRED

a. Describe how you decided to record the sale on December 31, thus enabling Stacy to receive or not receive the bonus.

WHAT WOULD
YOU DO?

Interpreting Financial Statements: Critical Essay

4–85 A computer company reported the following summary of operations in its annual report:

> Revenues are in a downward spiral and the company is reporting a loss of more than half a billion dollars for 1996. It has a negative net worth of $750 million. It will be in default if it cannot get new financing by the end of 1998. Its total debt is $1.4 billion.
>
> The company is struggling with all the issues facing the computer industry: vicious price cutting, weak markets (both in the United States and overseas) cautious customers worried about rapid technological change, and technological obsolescence.

REQUIRED

a. Write a one- to two-page conclusion to the above report from the perspective of the company's president, who believes that all of the problems have been solved and that the company will survive. You may "invent" additional numbers or circumstances to support the president's position.

Recognizing Revenues: Critical Analysis

4–86 With regard to Case 4–84, write a short news article, describing the computer company's situation from the perspective of a critical analyst who believes that the company must surely fail in the near future. Again, you may invent additional numbers or circumstances to support your position.

USING
FINANCIAL
ACCOUNTING
ON THE
INTERNET

4–87 Locate the most recent set of financial statements for the regional telecommunications companies listed below. You may use either the 10-K available at EDGAR (**www.sec.gov/edgarhp.htm**) or the annual report available at the company page on the WWW. The annual report is usually located in the Investor Information section.

Corporation	Home Page Location
Ameritech	**www.ameritech.com**
U S West	**www.uswest.com**
Bell Atlantic	**www.bell-atl.com**
BellSouth	**www.bst.bls.com**

REQUIRED

Calculate the following for each corporation:

a. cost of goods sold percentage
b. gross profit percentage
c. operating income percentage
d. net income percentage
e. return on equity
f. return on assets
g. times interest earned

4–88 Locate the most recent 10-K filing by Wal-Mart and by Kmart at the EDGAR archives **(www.sec.gov/edgarhp.htm).** Scroll down to the Summary of Financial Information (in the financial report section).

REQUIRED

a. Calculate the following for the last five years:

1. percentage change in net sales for each year
2. percentage change in net income for each year
3. net income percentage
4. return on equity (use the beginning of the year balance for the denominator)
5. return on assets (use the beginning of the year balance for the denominator)
6. times interest earned

b. Based on the above calculations, which company in your opinion has been more successful during the last five year?

4–89 Locate the most recent 10-K filing by Toys 'R' Us and by Gillette from the EDGAR archives **(www.sec.gov/edgarhp.htm).**

REQUIRED

a. What is each company's major product line? (This information should be near the start of the 10-K.) For each company, do you expect sales to be fairly constant throughout the year or to peak during a particular season?

b. Scroll down to the summaries of annual calculations that both companies included at the end of their Notes to Financial Statements. Based on the annual calculations data, calculate:

1. percentage change in net sales, cost of goods sold, gross profit, and net income for each quarter
2. the gross profit percentage for each quarter
3. the net income percentage for each quarter

c. Does your response in part a match the sales pattern you observed in part b? If it does not, why not?

STATEMENT OF
CASH FLOWS

INTRODUCTION

Thus far, our focus has been on the two long-standing, conventional financial statements: the balance sheet and the income statement. We now turn our attention to the **statement of cash flows.** This chapter describes the statement of cash flows, indicates how cash flow information can be used in analyzing the financial performance of a business, and explains the relationships among this statement, the balance sheet, and the income statement.

OVERVIEW

The statement of cash flows is designed to provide information about a firm's inflows and outflows of cash during a period of time. It explains the change in cash from the beginning of a period to the end of the period. Exhibit 5–1 contains an illustration of a statement of cash flows.

Objectives

According to SFAS No. 95, the statement of cash flows is intended to help financial statement readers assess

1. a firm's ability to generate positive future net cash flows;
2. a firm's ability to meet its obligations, its ability to pay dividends, and its need for external financing;
3. the reasons for differences between net income and associated cash receipts and payments; and
4. the effects on a firm's financial position of both its cash and its noncash investing and financing transactions.

Ultimately, a firm's cash generating ability affects its solvency, its capacity to pay dividends and interest, and the price of its securities. Accordingly, a firm's ability to generate cash is important to financial statement users.

EXHIBIT 5–1
STATEMENT OF CASH FLOWS—
DIRECT APPROACH

The Peak Company
Statement of Cash Flows
(Direct Approach)
For the Year Ended December 31, 1998

Cash flows from operating activities:		
Cash received from customers	$68,200	
Interest received	1,300	
Payments to employees	(17,100)	
Payments to suppliers	(40,500)	
Interest paid	(800)	
Taxes paid	(2,000)	
Net cash provided from operating activities		$ 9,100
Cash flows from investing activities:		
Purchase of equipment	(3,500)	
Purchase of IBM stock	(12,000)	
Net cash used in investing activities		(15,500)
Cash flows from financing activities:		
Proceeds from issuing long-term debt	25,000	
Proceeds from issuing common stock	5,000	
Payment of short-term debt	(12,000)	
Net cash provided by financing activities		18,000
Net increase in cash		11,600
Cash at beginning of year		22,000
Cash at end of year		$33,600

 Accrual Earnings versus Cash Flow
as a Performance Measure

Keep in mind that accrual earnings (net income from the income statement) do not necessarily reflect cash flows. Many revenue and expense transactions have no *immediate* cash flow effect. Nevertheless, net income is a very useful performance measure. It reflects accomplishments by the firm (such as credit sales that will subsequently result in cash inflows), as well as resources consumed by the firm in generating revenue (for example, employee salaries that remain unpaid at the end of a period).

If net income is a useful performance measure, why is cash flow information needed? An analogy to baseball can be drawn. Many aspects of a baseball player's performance are measured. For example, home runs measure power hitting, while on-base percentage reflects the ability to reach base safely. Similarly, earnings and cash flows are different performance measures of a business organization. They should be viewed as complements, rather than substitutes. Each measure contains information not necessarily reflected in the other. In particular, the statement of cash flows provides information about a firm's liquidity and financial flexibility (the ability to respond to unexpected events by altering the amounts and timing of its cash flows).

Cash and Cash Equivalents

Firms can elect to focus their statement of cash flows on either (1) cash or (2) cash and cash equivalents. The term *cash* includes cash on hand and cash in bank accounts that can be withdrawn on demand. **Cash equivalents** are short-term, highly liquid financial instruments with maturities of less than three months; they are quickly convertible into cash. Examples include money market funds, treasury bills, and certificates of deposit (CDs). Since cash equivalents are so similar to cash, many firms prefer to combine them with cash, rather than with other investments.

Firms must consistently apply a policy of using either cash or cash and cash equivalents. Additionally, the beginning and ending balances that appear on the statement of cash flows must correspond to similarly titled items on the balance sheet.

As illustrated in Exhibit 5–1, a firm's cash flows are placed in one of three categories: operating, investing, or financing. This section describes each of these categories. Examples of each activity are given in Exhibit 5–2.

CLASSIFICATION OF ACTIVITIES

 ## Operating Activities

Operating activities typically involve transactions related to providing goods and services to customers. They reflect the cash flow effects of the typical and recurring

---

Operating Activities

Cash Inflows	Cash Outflows
From customers	To employees
From interest	To suppliers
From dividends	For interest
All other cash inflows	For taxes
not defined as an	All other cash outflows not defined
investing or financing activity	as an investing or financing activity

Investing Activities

Cash Inflows	Cash Outflows
Sale of property, plant, and	Purchase of property, plant, and
equipment	equipment
Collections of loans	Making of loans
Sale of investments	Acquisition of investments

Financing Activities

Cash Inflows	Cash Outflows
Issuing common stock	Reacquiring common stock
Obtaining loans	Repaying loans
	Paying dividends

EXHIBIT 5–2
SUMMARY OF ACTIVITIES
GENERATING CASH FLOWS

transactions that appear on the income statement. Examples of operating cash inflows are receipts from customers and the receipt of interest and dividends from investments. Operating cash outflows include payments to employees and suppliers and payments for interest and taxes.

Investing Activities

Investing activities usually involve cash flows from the acquisition and disposal of noncurrent assets. Cash outflows arise from purchasing (investing in) property, plant, and equipment; making loans; and acquiring investments in other corporations. Cash inflows result from disposing of property, plant, and equipment; collecting loans (other than the interest); and selling investments.

Financing Activities

Financing activities include cash flows from obtaining and repaying financing. Cash inflows result from contributions by owners (e.g., issuing stock to shareholders in exchange for cash) and from loans. Cash outflows arise from payments to shareholders (as dividends or payments to repurchase their shares) and the repayment of loans (but not the associated interest).

Exhibit 5–1 shows that the net cash provided (or used) in each of the three classifications is summarized in the far right column of the statement. The sum of these amounts equals the change in the cash balance that occurred during the period. This change is added to the cash balance at the beginning of the year to compute the ending cash balance. These beginning and ending cash amounts must, of course, correspond to the cash figures appearing on the balance sheet.

The remainder of this section addresses two additional format issues: (1) the direct versus the indirect approach to preparing the operating activities section and (2) non-cash investing and financing activities.

Direct versus Indirect Approach

The operating activities section of Peak's statement of cash flows in Exhibit 5–1 is prepared based on the **direct approach.** Under the direct approach, a separate line item is provided for each type of operating cash inflow and outflow. These items usually correspond to categories on the income statement. For example, cash received from customers corresponds to sales revenue on the income statement. Keep in mind, however, that the income statement and the statement of cash flows provide different information. The income statement discloses sales made to customers during the year, regardless of whether cash has been collected during the year. The statement of cash flows indicates the amount of cash collected from customers during the year from the current year's sales, past years' sales, and even future sales if the firm has collected cash prior to the point of sale.

An acceptable alternative in preparing the operating activities section is the **indirect approach.** This method begins with net income and makes adjustments to it in order to arrive at cash generated by operating activities. The indirect approach is illustrated in Exhibit 5–3.

EXHIBIT 5–3

STATEMENT OF CASH FLOWS—
INDIRECT APPROACH

The Peak Company
Statement of Cash Flows
(Indirect Approach)
For the Year Ended December 31, 1998

Cash flows from operating activities:

Net income	$ 5,300	
Adjustments to net income		
Depreciation expense	2,000	
Increase in accounts receivable	(500)	
Decrease in interest receivable	200	
Increase in inventory	(1,000)	
Increase in accounts payable	3,000	
Decrease in salaries payable	(100)	
Increase in interest payable	200	
Net cash provided from operating activities		$ 9,100

Cash flows from investing activities:

Purchase of equipment	(3,500)	
Purchase of IBM stock	(12,000)	
Net cash used in investing activities		(15,500)

Cash flows from financing activities:

Proceeds from issuing long-term debt	25,000	
Proceeds from issuing common stock	5,000	
Payment of short-term debt	(12,000)	
Net cash provided by financing activities		18,000
Net increase in cash		11,600
Cash at beginning of year		22,000
Cash at end of year		$33,600

Although both the direct and indirect approaches produce the same figure for cash provided from operating activities, the internal compositions of the statements differ substantially. A major advantage of the direct method is that the primary sources and uses of cash are listed. As will be seen in a later section, this is highly useful information. A major advantage of the indirect method is that the reasons for the difference between net income and cash generated by operations are detailed. This can help reduce uncertainties or answer questions raised by financial statement readers.

As Exhibit 5–3 shows, under the indirect approach, depreciation expense is added to net income. Because of this, some financial statement readers erroneously believe that depreciation expense is a source of cash. It is not. Depreciation expense is added to net income in arriving at cash provided from operating activities because (1) it has already been subtracted in the computation of net income and (2) it does not involve any cash outflow. Adding depreciation expense to net income, therefore, eliminates the effect of this noncash expense.

The FASB has expressed a preference for the direct approach. In spite of that, the indirect approach is used more frequently. This is partly due to historical convention;

the indirect approach is similar to the statement that was required prior to SFAS No. 95. Additionally, a firm using the direct approach must provide a schedule that reconciles net income with cash provided by operating activities. This reconciliation essentially consists of the information contained in the indirect approach. Thus, a firm that opts for the direct approach must really provide both methods. Some firms are reluctant to do this, either because additional costs are involved or because they feel that the statement will become too cluttered and, therefore, less informative. (For brevity, the reconciliation has been omitted from Peak's statement of cash flow appearing in Exhibit 5–1.)

Noncash Investing and Financing Activities

A firm may engage in investing and financing activities that do not involve cash. For example, a firm might acquire property by issuing common stock. Although no cash is involved, this transaction is both an investing activity (the acquisition of a noncurrent asset) and a financing activity (the issuance of stock). Because these transactions do not involve cash, they do not appear in the major sections of the statement of cash flows. However, **noncash investing and financing activities** are summarized in a schedule that appears at the end of the statement. This provides readers of the cash flow statement with a complete picture of a firm's investing and financing activities.

USING CASH FLOW INFORMATION: OPERATING ACTIVITIES

Many financial statement users find the operating activities section to be quite informative. Creditors, for example, recognize that loans can only be repaid with cash and that a firm's operations are a likely source of cash for debt repayment.

Because the ability to generate cash determines dividends and share price increases, shareholders and their advisors are interested in cash provided by operating activities. Moreover, some analysts believe that because reported net income can be manipulated by accounting ploys, cash flow from operating activities is a more reliable performance measure than net income. We will subsequently discuss how managers can also manipulate cash flow figures.

Keep in mind, however, that not all healthy firms have a large positive cash flow from operations. Firms that experience growth in sales invariably need to expand their accounts receivable and inventory. These asset acquisitions must be financed, and cash generated by operations is a frequently used source.

For example, Best Buy Company increased its sales from $929,692,000 in 1992 to $1.6 billion in 1993. Best Buy's 72% increase in sales necessitated a $136,140,000 increase in accounts receivable and inventory. Some of this increased investment was funded from operations and by increasing accounts payable; but ultimately, operations generated a net cash outflow of $31,049,000 in 1993. The cash outflow was not due to poor operating performance. In fact, Best Buy doubled its income in 1993. Thus, a small (or even negative) net cash flow from operations may indicate growth, rather than poor operating performance. In general, however, a negative cash flow from operating activities should prompt further investigation.

Ratios

This section describes several ratios that can be computed from the statement of cash flows. Information from Wendy's International's financial statements, which appears in

Exhibit 5–4, is used for illustrative purposes. Because the statement of cash flows is a relatively recent addition to GAAP, the development of cash flow ratios is at an early stage, and there is no general consensus about which ratios are the most informative. Also note that some of these ratios require information disclosed only by the direct approach for preparing the operating activities section.

Cash Return on Assets. The **cash return on assets ratio** is calculated by adding cash flow from operating activities (CFOA), and interest payments, and then dividing by average total assets:

$$\text{Cash return on assets} = \frac{\text{CFOA} + \text{Interest paid}}{\text{Average total assets}}$$

Cash return on assets measures management's success, given the assets entrusted to it, in generating cash from operating activities. Since CFOA is available to pay dividends and to finance investing activities, a high ratio is desirable.

Interest payments are added to CFOA in the numerator for the same reason that interest expense was added to net income in the return on assets calculation discussed in Chapter 4. That is, cash return on assets is designed to measure management's success in making operating decisions. Since interest payments are determined by financing decisions, and since they have already been subtracted in calculating CFOA, they are added back. Also note that interest payments are not disclosed under the indirect approach. In those situations, analysts must be satisfied to use CFOA in the numerator or must obtain the interest payment information elsewhere in the notes.

Wendy's 1994 cash return on assets is 17.8%:

$$\text{Cash return on assets} = \frac{\text{CFOA} + \text{Interest paid}}{\text{Average total assets}}$$

$$= \frac{\$165,711 + 19,236}{(\$1,086,092 + \$996,486)/2}$$

$$= 17.8\%$$

EXHIBIT 5–4

SELECTED FINANCIAL INFORMATION USED TO ILLUSTRATE CASH FLOW RATIOS

Wendy's International, Inc.
Selected Financial Statement Information
(Dollars in Thousands)

	1994	1993
Total assets	$1,086,092	$996,486
Total owners' equity	681,498	660,795
Debt	144,860	200,633
Sales	1,256,192	1,198,777
Accounts receivable	28,015	27,381
Depreciation expense	73,726	68,978
Interest paid	19,236	21,874
Taxes paid	52,937	41,517
Purchases of property, plant, and equipment	141,507	116,573
Net cash outflow from investing activities	94,960	106,887
Cash flow from operating activities	165,711	146,676
Net income	97,156	79,267

Some analysts question the use of CFOA in cash return on assets and other ratios. Their reservation is that CFOA makes no provision for replacing worn-out equipment. These expenditures are necessary to maintain productive capacity and current operating levels. Since CFOA is not reduced for these expenditures, it overstates the amount of discretionary cash flow generated from operations.

Instead of using CFOA in ratio calculations, some analysts use **free cash flow.** Free cash flow is calculated by subtracting from CFOA the cash payment necessary to replace worn-out equipment. Unfortunately, firms rarely disclose this figure. Although the investing activities section of the statement of cash flows shows total payments for the acquisition of productive assets, the amounts spent to (1) replace assets and (2) expand productive capacity are not detailed. Because of this, depreciation expense is sometimes used as an imperfect estimate of the cash expenditure needed to maintain productive capacity. Because depreciation expense is based on historical cost, it probably understates the cash necessary to replace productive assets.

Quality of Sales. The **quality of sales ratio** is computed by dividing cash received from customers by sales (revenue):

$$\text{Quality of sales} = \frac{\text{Cash received from customers}}{\text{Sales}}$$

Wendy's quality of sales ratio cannot be computed from the information shown in Exhibit 5–4. Why not? The numerator, cash received from customers, is available only from the cash flow statement under the direct approach. It can also be approximated by looking at changes in accounts receivable, as shown later.

All other things being equal, a firm is in a more advantageous position if a large portion of its sales is collected in cash. Not only is final realization of the transaction assured, but also the investment in accounts receivable is minimized.

This ratio is particularly useful for analyzing firms that use liberal revenue recognition policies or firms that, of necessity, employ revenue recognition policies that require the use of judgment. In both of these situations, a deterioration of this ratio over time might indicate that a firm is inflating earnings by the use of questionable accounting judgments.

The quality of sales ratio can also reflect a firm's performance in making collections from customers. Suppose a firm increases sales by the questionable strategy of reducing the credit standards that customers must meet. These customers are likely to be relatively tardy in making payments. This situation will be revealed to financial statement readers by a declining quality of sales ratio.

Statements of cash flows prepared under the indirect approach do not disclose cash received from customers. However, this figure can be approximated by the following relationship:

$$\begin{array}{ccc} \text{Cash collected} \\ \text{from customers} \end{array} = \begin{array}{c} \text{Beginning balance in} \\ \text{Accounts Receivable} \end{array} + \text{Sales} - \begin{array}{c} \text{Ending balance in} \\ \text{Accounts Receivable} \end{array}$$

To understand this relationship, recognize that both the beginning balance in accounts receivable and sales might potentially be collected in cash during the current year. In fact, the sum of these two amounts is collected in cash, except for the balance that remains in accounts receivable at the end of the year.

Wendy's estimated cash collections from customers is $1,255,558 (in thousands).

$$
\begin{array}{ll}
\text{Cash received} & = \quad \text{Beginning balance} \quad + \text{Sales} \quad - \quad \text{Ending balance in} \\
\text{from customers} & \quad\quad \text{in Accounts Receivable} \quad\quad\quad\quad\quad\quad \text{Accounts Receivable}
\end{array}
$$

$$= \quad \$ \quad 27{,}381 \quad\quad + \ \$1{,}256{,}192 \ - \quad \$28{,}015$$

$$= \quad \$1{,}255{,}558$$

Wendy's quality of sales ratio for 1994 is 99.9%.

$$\text{Quality of sales} = \frac{\text{Cash received from customers}}{\text{Sales}}$$

$$= \frac{\$1{,}255{,}558}{\$1{,}256{,}192}$$

$$= \quad 99.9\%$$

This is a very high quality of sales ratio. It is high primarily because Wendy's is a cash-oriented business.

Reality Check 5–1 describes how the quality of sales ratio provides useful insights into the software industry.

QUALITY OF SALES RATIO

REALITY CHECK 5–1

Several firms in the software industry have been criticized for their revenue recognition policies. The allegations suggest that these firms have recognized revenue prematurely. Such a practice would not only overstate sales, but net income as well.

Revenue overstatements can be achieved in various ways. Some companies were said to double-bill customers. Other companies booked revenue when they shipped goods to their own warehouses in foreign countries. Ultimately, such practices catch up with companies. For example, Oracle Corporation recently paid $24,000,000 to settle shareholder lawsuits, and Cambridge Biotech Corporation was forced to file for bankruptcy.

The quality of sales ratio can help investors detect and avoid such situations. Consider the following information for two software companies.

	Cambridge Biotech	Kendall Square Research
	(dollars in thousands)	
Accounts receivable		
Beginning of year	$ 5,951	$ 804
End of year	10,520	2,785
Sales for year	28,981	10,066

REQUIRED

a. Estimate the cash collected from customers for each firm.

b. Compute the quality of sales ratio for each firm.

c. What do you conclude from these ratios?

Quality of Income. The **quality of income ratio** is computed by dividing CFOA by net income:

$$\text{Quality of income} = \frac{\text{CFOA}}{\text{Net income}}$$

This ratio indicates the proportion of income that has been realized in cash. As with quality of sales, high levels for this ratio are desirable. The quality of income ratio has a tendency to exceed 100% since (1) depreciation expense has reduced the denominator and (2) cash spent to replace productive assets has not been subtracted in calculating the numerator. Wendy's 1994 quality of income ratio is 170.6%.

$$\text{Quality of income} = \frac{\$165,711}{\$97,156} = 170.6\%$$

In 1994, Wendy's ratio substantially exceeded 100%, indicating high quality.

In the discussion of quality of sales, we indicated that revenue recognition may be judgmental. The same is true with expense recognition. A variety of alternatives for expense allocations are available to firms, and firms have considerable discretion in the selection of these alternatives. The quality of income ratio can provide an overall indication of how liberal a firm's accounting judgments have been. Reality Check 5–2 provides information about the software industry's quality of income ratio.

You should realize that cash flows can be manipulated by management. For example, customers can be induced to remit payments early if they are provided with a sufficiently large cash discount. Although the short-term consequences of this action may be to increase net cash flow, large discounts might not be in the shareholders' best long-term interest.

WHAT WOULD YOU DO?

As a successful college student, you feel that you can make money by sharing your secrets of success with others. Specifically, you decide to begin a Scholastic Aptitude Test (SAT) review course. The course will be taught by yourself and several of your friends. Classroom space can be rented at a local community college.

Because of the costs you will incur, a minimum of 20 students is necessary to make the course profitable. If fewer than 20 students enroll, you intend to cancel the course.

Marketing is, of course, a key to the success of any new business. Attracting new students is essential. This presents you with a dilemma. On the one hand, you cannot afford to run the course with less than 20 students. On the other hand, potential students always ask if you are certain that the course will be offered. Understandably, they prefer to enroll in a course that will not be canceled. You have many competitors; students can choose from among several review courses.

How would you respond to the students' questions about course cancellation? Keep in mind that being perfectly honest may result in the failure of your business.

Cash Interest Coverage. The **cash interest coverage ratio** is used by creditors to assess a firm's ability to pay interest. It is calculated by summing CFOA and interest and tax payments and then dividing by interest payments. Interest and tax payments are added to CFOA because they have been subtracted in the calculation of CFOA and because those payments are available to cover interest. In particular, tax payments are added because in the unfortunate case of zero profitability, those payments would not be made and would provide another measure of relief for the creditors.

REALITY CHECK 5–2

QUALITY OF INCOME RATIO

As with the quality of sales ratio, the quality of income ratio can help detect situations involving questionable accounting judgments. Reality Check 5–1 showed that the quality of sales ratios for Cambridge Biotech and Kendall Square Research were both below 85%. Consider the following information:

	Cambridge Biotech	Kendall Square Research
	(dollars in thousands)	
Cash provided by operating activities	($5,696)	($27,194)
Net income (loss)	$ 348	($21,619)

REQUIRED

a. Compute the quality of income ratio for each firm.
b. What inferences can you draw from these ratios?

$$\text{Cash interest coverage} = \frac{\text{CFOA} + \text{Interest paid} + \text{Taxes paid}}{\text{Interest paid}}$$

The cash interest coverage ratio reflects how many times greater cash provided by operations is than the interest payment itself. Creditors prefer high levels of this ratio. Wendy's 1994 cash interest coverage ratio is 1236% or 12.36 to 1:

$$\text{Cash interest coverage} = \frac{\$165,711 + \$19,236 + \$52,937}{\$19,236} = 1236\%$$

This ratio is quite high and should provide creditors with reasonable assurance that Wendy's is currently generating more than enough cash to meet its interest payments.

Although interest payments are not disclosed under the indirect approach, many firms report interest payments elsewhere in the notes. To calculate the cash interest coverage ratio, the interest paid must be obtained from the annual report.

USING CASH FLOW INFORMATION: INVESTING AND FINANCING ACTIVITIES

The investing and financing activities sections of the statement of cash flows summarize the inflows and outflows of cash generated by nonoperating activities. Because these sources of cash are not closely related to the performance of a firm, they are scrutinized less intensely than cash from operations. Moreover, the investing and financing sections reflect long-term strategies that are based on a variety of strategic decisions that draw upon many components of the organization (e.g., marketing and finance). These issues are addressed in many upper level business courses.

As an example, however, consider Wendy's investing activities. The amount of cash spent by Wendy's on purchases of property, plant, and equipment increased from $116,573,000 in 1993 to $141,507,000 in 1994, an increase of 21.4%. This suggests that Wendy's is expanding its productive capacity, thus paving the way for possible future improvements in market share and profitability.

1. **Describe the objectives of the statement of cash flows.**

The statement of cash flows explains the change in cash from the beginning to the end of a period. It provides financial statement users with information to assess a firm's ability to generate positive future net cash flows, to meet its obligations, to pay dividends, and to generate financing internally.

2. **Explain the complementary nature of accrual earnings and cash flows.**

Accrual earnings reflects a firm's success in providing goods and services to customers. Cash flow figures show a firm's solvency and its capacity to pay dividends and interest.

3. **Identify the three types of activities that generate and use cash.**

Operating activities include providing goods and services to customers (for example, collecting cash from customers and paying cash to suppliers). Investing activities involve acquiring or disposing of noncurrent assets (such as property, plant, and equipment and investments in other corporations). Financing activities include the obtaining of and returning of investments in the firm by shareholders and obtaining and repaying loans.

4. **Explain the difference between the direct and indirect methods of presenting a statement of cash flows.**

This distinction lies in the operating section. Under the direct method, a separate line item is provided for each major operating inflow and outflow of cash. In contrast, the indirect approach starts with net income and makes various adjustments to arrive at cash generated by operating activities. Although the direct method provides the most useful information, most firms use the indirect method.

5. **Draw inferences about the financial performance of a firm from the statement of cash flows.**

Much of the information included in the statement of cash flows can be extracted by the use of ratios. These ratios provide insights into a firm's ability to generate cash in light of the assets it has, the quality of the firm's sales and net income, the ability of the firm to generate cash to meet its interest and debt payments, the firm's capacity to finance its investments internally, and the ability of the firm to generate cash to meet its interest payments.

Cash
Cash equivalents
Cash interest coverage ratio
Cash return on assets ratio
Direct approach
Financing activities
Free cash flow
Indirect approach

Investing activities
Noncash investing and financing
  activities
Operating activities
Quality of income ratio
Quality of sales ratio
Statements of cash flows

REALITY
CHECK
SOLUTIONS

SOLUTION TO REALITY CHECK 5–1

a.

	Cambridge Biotech	Kendall Square Research
Sales	$28,981	$10,066
Plus: Beginning accounts receivable	5,951	804
Less: Ending accounts receivable	(10,520)	(2,785)
Cash collected from customers	$24,412	$ 8,085

b.

$$\text{Quality of sales} = \frac{\$24,412}{\$28,981} \qquad \frac{\$ 8,085}{\$10,066}$$

$$= \qquad 84\% \qquad 80\%$$

c. These ratios are considerably below 100%. This should certainly prompt financial statement readers to undertake further investigation.

SOLUTION TO REALITY CHECK 5–2

a.

	Cambridge Biotech	Kendall Square Research

$$\text{Quality of income} = \frac{(\$5,696)}{\$ 348} \qquad \frac{(\$27,194)}{(\$21,619)}$$

$$= \qquad -1637\% \qquad 126\%$$

b. Cambridge's negative quality of income ratio results from a negative numerator and a positive denominator. This indicates that while Cambridge generated a positive net income, its operations resulted in a net cash outflow. The ratio is quite large, which should be rather alarming to financial statement readers.

Regarding Kendall Square, interpreting ratios generated from negative numbers is often difficult. A ratio of 126% usually indicates that a firm generated more cash than income. However, when a 126% ratio is computed from two negative numbers, it indicates that the firm's cash outflow exceeded its reported loss. Both the loss and the cash outflow from operations should concern financial statement readers.

QUESTIONS

5–1 The income statement and the cash flow statement focus on profitability and liquidity, respectively. Distinguish between these concepts, and discuss their importance to users of financial statements.

5–2 Which of a firm's financial statements is useful primarily for each of the following purposes:

   a. To evaluate a firm's ability to generate future cash flows available to pay dividends to shareholders.

   b. To evaluate a firm's ability to meet its' short-term obligations, and its needs for external financing.

5–3 What are cash and cash equivalents? Why should both be used in preparing a statement of cash flows?

5–4 Why would cash and cash equivalents be of greater concern to managers, creditors, and investors than other assets?

5–5 Discuss three major business activities that usually produce cash inflows or outflows.

5–6 What information is provided in a statement of cash flows that is not found in a balance sheet or an income statement?

5–7 Identify three types of operating, financing, and investing activities. Identify several noncash investing or financing activities.

5–8 Could a firm report positive amounts of net income and negative cash flows from operating activities? How?

5–9 Define the following cash flow concepts in your own words as you would describe them to the owner of a small business:

  a. Cash flow from operating activities
  b. Cash used for investing activities
  c. Cash provided by financing activities
  d. Cash collected from clients
  e. Cash payments to vendors
  f. Cash payments to federal, state, and local governments
  g. Cash paid for interest

5–10 A firm's reported net income is related to changes in its operating cash flows and shareholders' equity. Explain the relation between net income and operating cash flows, and also the relation between net income and changes in shareholders' equity.

5–11 Identify each of the following activities as either operating, investing, or financing activities:

  a. Cash received from customers
  b. Cash paid to acquire operating equipment
  c. Cash paid as dividends to shareholders
  d. Cash received from issuing common stock
  e. Cash paid for income taxes

5–12 Under the indirect method of preparing the statement of cash flows, each of the following items would be added to net income in measuring cash flows from operating activities (CFOA). Which (if any) of these items may be considered to be a source of cash?

  a. Depreciation expense
  b. Loss on sale of plant and equipment
  c. Reductions in customer accounts receivable
  d. Increases in supplier accounts payable

5–13 Describe two investing and financing activities that do not involve cash receipts or payments. Discuss whether it is useful to include such noncash activities in a statement of cash flows.

5–14 Evaluate the following conventions in preparing a statement of cash flows:

  a. Dividend payments to shareholders are reported as a financing activity, and interest payments on debt are reported as an operating activity.
  b. Purchases of inventory are operating activities, but purchases of plant and equipment are investing activities.

c. Accounts payable transactions are operating activities, but most other liability transactions are treated as financing activities.

5–15 In each of the following cases, indicate whether the amount of cash inflow (or outflow) is greater or less than the related revenue (or expense):

    a. A firm's accounts receivable balance has increased during the period.

    b. A firm's salaries payable balance has increased during the period.

    c. A firm's accumulated depreciation balance has increased during the period.

    d. A firm's inventory balance has increased during the period, and the supplier accounts payable balance has also increased by a greater amount.

5–16 Evaluate the usefulness of cash return on assets (CROA) as a measure of managerial performance. Distinguish between CROA and "free cash flow."

5–17 A government agency once reported to one of the authors that it could not extend a job offer because it was "financially embarrassed." What do you suppose this term meant? Could a commercial company also be financially embarrassed? What mechanisms might a firm have that a government agency would not have to avoid financial embarrassment?

5–18 Consider the differences between owning and managing an apartment building and a retail store. Would the owner of one prefer a cash-based measure of performance? Would one prefer an accrual-based performance measure? Would either have an advantage if only the income statement, or only the statement of cash flows, were used to evaluate annual operations? Why?

EXERCISES

5–19 **Effects of Transactions: Cash versus Accrual—Alternate Exercises (A) or (B)**

Exercise (A)

Consider the following transactions or events:

    1. Sold merchandise on account.
    2. Sold a used computer for cash.
    3. Paid a supplier's overdue account.
    4. Recorded depreciation on a building.
    5. Signed a mortgage and received cash.
    6. Purchased inventory on account.
    7. Gave a refund after hearing a customer's complaint.
    8. Received a check from a customer.
    9. Sold shares of IBM stock for cash and recorded a gain.
   10. Recorded a loss after discarding obsolete inventory.
   11. Received a personal cash gift from a friend.
   12. Made an "even" swap of a used truck for another truck.
   13. Paid quarterly unemployment taxes.
   14. Received a tax refund after sending duplicate checks to the IRS.

REQUIRED

    a. Show the effects on cash of each transaction or event using the format below:

Effects on Cash

Increase	**Decrease**	**No Change**

b. Show the effects of each transaction or event on revenues or expenses using a similar format:

Effects on Net Income

Increase	Decrease	No Change

Exercise (B)

Consider the following events or transactions:

1. Delivered groceries and accepted payment by personal check.
2. Took a taxi ride, paid the metered fare, but no tip, and survived.
3. Gave a refund for defective merchandise.
4. Recorded the month's depreciation.
5. Sold a building, received a note receivable in exchange, and recorded a gain.
6. Made a donation to the Youth Services Community Foundation.
7. Received loan proceeds from a bank.
8. Received title to a classic Corvette in settlement of a customer's account.
9. Returned merchandise to a supplier for credit.
10. Traded in a 1965 Datsun truck and acquired a new truck with the balance owed on account.
11. Found securities in the bottom of an old trunk in the attic that are now worth $100,000.
12. Filed an insurance claim for water damage to inventory.
13. Recorded a loss due to water damages.
14. Received a refund from a supplier who had been overpaid.

REQUIRED

a. Show the effects on cash of each transaction or event using the format below:

Effects on Cash

Increase	Decrease	No Change

b. Show the effects of each transaction or event on revenues or expenses using a similar format:

Effects on Net Income

Increase	Decrease	No Change

5–20 Effects of Transactions on Cash Flows—Alternate Exercises (A) or (B)

Exercise (A)

The following transactions were reported by Colorado Company in its statement of cash flows. Indicate whether each transaction is an operating (O), a financing (F), an investing (I), or a noncash (NC) activity. Note that a noncash activity would have no effect on cash flows.

1. Office supplies were purchased and paid for.
2. Land was sold for cash.
3. Employees' salaries and wages were paid.
4. The firm made a short-term loan to its president.
5. A short-term loan from Western Bank was obtained.
6. Interest on this loan was paid.

7. The maturity date on this loan was extended.
8. Depreciation for the year was recorded.
9. The firm's tax return was filed with a request for a refund.
10. The firm paid its unemployment taxes to the state.

Exercise (B)

The following transactions were reported by Simpson Paraphernalia, Inc., in its statement of cash flows. Indicate whether each transaction is an operating (O), a financing (F), an investing (I), or a noncash (NC) activity. Note that a noncash activity would have no effect on cash flows.

1. Rent was paid in advance.
2. Goods were sold retail on account.
3. Purchased inventory and paid cash.
4. Sold a building and accepted a 20-year 10% note from the purchaser.
5. Recorded gain on the sales of the building.
6. Received cash from receivable customers.
7. Paid dividends to stockholders.
8. Paid interest on an outstanding loan.
9. Recorded rent expense for the portion of prepaid rent that has expired.
10. Received interest income on the note (from the sale of the building).

Transaction Analysis

5–21 Indicate where each of the following transactions would be reported on the statement of cash flows (operating section, investing section, financing section, or not a cash flow item).

1. Purchased inventory on account.
2. Issued common stock for cash.
3. Paid loan principal.
4. Paid interest on the loan.
5. Lent money to a customer.
6. Received cash from sales.
7. Paid inventory suppliers.
8. Sold a building for cash.
9. Recorded a gain on the sale of the building in transaction 8.
10. Received a dividend from short-term investments.
11. Recorded depreciation for the period.

Transaction Analysis: Expanded Accounting Equation

5–22 The following transactions were recorded by May G&M Retail Stores. Classify each transaction into the following balance sheet equation and, if an item affects cash, note next to the cash item where it would appear in the statement of cash flows (using the direct method).

Balance Sheet Equation

CASH + OTHER ASSETS = LIABILITIES + SHAREHOLDERS' EQUITY

1. Merchandise inventory was sold on account for $120,000.
2. The cost of merchandise sold in transaction 1 is $62,500.
3. Collections from customers were $125,000.
4. A $900,000 long-term note was paid by check.
5. A $10,000 loan to the company's president was repaid.
6. One hundred thousand dollars was invested in short-term certificates of deposit issued by a major bank.
7. Merchandise inventory was purchased on account for $65,000.
8. Payments of $62,500 were made to suppliers.
9. Interest of $9,000 is due on a long-term note.
10. Half of the interest from transaction 9 was paid.
11. A $45,000 refund from a supplier was received unexpectedly.
12. Land was purchased for $95,000 cash and a $300,000 note.
13. Salaries and wages due at the end of the fiscal period were accrued at $7,800.
14. Depreciation on equipment of $4,650 was recorded.

Interpreting Cash Flow Concepts

5–23 Discuss the differences in the following terms:

a. Cash received from customers and sales revenue
b. Cash paid to suppliers and cost of goods sold
c. Cash proceeds from the sale of equipment and gain on the sale of equipment
d. Cash paid to employees and wages expense
e. Cash paid for property and equipment and depreciation expense

Recording Transactions and Preparing a Simple Income Statement and Partial Cash Flow Statement

5–24 The following transactions were taken from Manning, Inc., for the year 1998:

1. Merchandise purchased for $180,000 cash.
2. Sales during the year (half received in cash) were $250,000.
3. Cost of goods sold in transaction 2 was $130,000.
4. Wages earned by employees was $42,000, of which $20,000 was still unpaid at year-end.
5. Rent prepaid at the beginning of the year was $36,000. This represented 18 months.
6. Utilities incurred during the year totaled $8,500. Three-fourths of this was paid by year-end.

REQUIRED

a. Record these transactions using the accounting equation. Set up separate accounts (columns) for assets, liabilities, and shareholders' equity.
b. Prepare an income statement for the year ended December 31, 1998.
c. Prepare the operating activities section of the statement of cash flows.
d. Comment on the differences in net income and cash flow from operating activities.

Interpreting Cash Flow Statement

5–25 The following cash flow statement was prepared by the Brainard Music Company for the year ended December 31, 1998:

Cash flow from operating activities		$(346,000)
Cash flow from investing activities:		
Purchase of Musicbox, Ltd.	$(280,000)	
Purchase of property and equipment	(120,000)	
Total from investing activities		(400,000)
Cash flow from financing activities:		
Proceeds from issuance of stock	130,000	
Proceeds from short-term bank loans	540,000	
Payment of dividends	(110,000)	
Total from financing activities		560,000
Net decrease in cash		$(186,000)

REQUIRED

a. Give three reasons why Brainard engaged in these investing and financing activities.

b. Assume Brainard received dividends from Musicbox, Ltd. Why aren't they reported as part of investing activities?

c. Discuss the concept of depreciation in terms of cash flow.

d. Do you think the future outlook for this company is optimistic?

Transaction Analysis

5–26 The following transactions were made by Macintosh Corporation. Record these transactions in terms of the balance sheet equation given below and indicate which transactions would be reported on the statement of cash flows by labeling the transaction as an operating, investing, or financing activity

Balance Sheet Equation

CASH + OTHER ASSETS = LIABILITIES + SHAREHOLDERS' EQUITY

1. Purchased a building and signed the mortgage for $150,000.
2. Purchased merchandise for $12,000 cash.
3. Collected an account receivable of $4,000.
4. Recorded depreciation of $20,000.
5. Paid dividends to shareholders of $8,000.
6. Received $15,000 cash from the sale of short-term investment, and recorded a loss of $2,000 on the sale.
7. Issued additional common stock and received $5,000.
8. Paid interest incurred on the loan of $11,000.

Converting from Cash Flows to Revenues and Expenses

5–27 Determine the amounts of revenue or expense associated with each of the following cash flows:

1. Cash received from customers is $8.5 million, and accounts receivable have increased by $1.6 million.
2. Salaries paid are $3 million, and salaries payable have decreased by $.6 million.
3. Cash paid to suppliers is $4.5 million, supplier accounts payable have increased by $.5 million, and inventories have decreased by $1 million.

Converting from Revenues and Expenses to Cash Flows

5–28 Determine the amounts of cash flows associated with each of the following:

1. Sales revenue is $20 million, and accounts receivable have decreased by $2 million.
2. Salary expense is $7.5 million, and salaries payable have decreased by $1 million.
3. Cost of goods sold is $9 million, inventories have decreased by $1.2 million, and supplier accounts payable have increased by $1.6 million.

Effects of Asset Disposals on Cash Flows

5–29 The Shifting Sands Company reported an increase in its property (land) account of $4 million during 1997. During 1997 the firm sold land with an initial cost of $12 million for cash proceeds of $9 million and purchased additional land for $16 million. Determine the effects of these transactions on the following elements of the firm's 1997 financial statements:

a. Net income (ignore income tax effects)
b. Adjustments to net income to compute cash flows from operations
c. Cash flows from investing activities

Preparing a Cash Flow Statement Using Comparative Balance Sheets

5–30 The Limpid Pool Company reports net income of $25 million for 1998. Balance sheets at the beginning and end of the year are shown below:

	December 31	
	1997	**1998**
	(dollars in millions)	
Cash	$ 50	$ 70
Other current assets	80	145
Property, plant, and equipment (net)	170	135
Total assets	$300	$350
Current liabilities	$ 20	$ 15
Noncurrent liabilities	180	195
Common stock	80	110
Retained earnings	20	30
Total liabilities and shareholders' equity	$300	$350

The firm did not acquire any noncurrent assets during 1998.

REQUIRED

Determine the following amounts for 1998:

a. Dividends paid
b. Cash flow from operating activities
c. Cash flow from investing activities
d. Cash flow from financing activities

Working from Operating Cash Flows to Net Income

5–31 The Blunt Instrument Company reports cash flow from operations of $65 million for 1997. You are provided the following additional information for the year:

1. Customer accounts receivable increased by $6 million.
2. Dividends paid to common shareholders were $20 million.
3. Depreciation expense was $24 million.
4. Noncurrent debt was increased by $35 million.
5. Supplier accounts payable decreased by $8 million.
6. Inventory balances increased by $18 million.
7. Income tax payable increased by $9 million.

REQUIRED

a. Based on the above information, determine the amount of net income reported by Blunt for 1997.

Preparing a Cash Flow Statement from a Listing of Transactions

5-32 Haywire Systems had the following cash receipts and payments during 1998 ($ in millions):

1. Cash received from customers	$130
2. Cash paid to inventory suppliers	42
3. Cash paid to employees	38
4. Cash paid as income taxes	31
5. Cash paid for other operating expenses	17
6. Cash dividends paid to shareholders	10
7. Cash paid to acquire long-lived operating assets	75
8. Cash paid to retire bank loans	25
9. Cash received upon sale of land	8
10. Cash paid upon issuance of common stock	85

REQUIRED

Based on the above information,

a. Determine cash flow from operations.
b. Determine cash flow from investments.
c. Determine cash flow from financing.
d. Can you determine Haywire's net income for 1998? If not, identify the additional information that you require in order to determine the net income amount.

PROBLEMS

Interpreting Financial Statements: Cash Flow Effects

5-33 The following statement of cash flows has been provided by Davo's Surf Company of Malibu, California:

Davo's Surf Company
Statement of Cash Flows
For the Year Ended December 31, 1997

Cash flows from operating activities		$ 225,000
Cash flows from investing activities		
Investment in Susie's Swim-Wear, Ltd.	$(215,000)	

Financial statement continued on page 188

Purchase of marketable securities	(550,000)	
Proceeds from sale of building	1,000,000	235,000
Cash flows from financing activities		
Proceeds from debt issuance	$ 600,000	
Gift from friends and family	400,000	
Payment of dividends	(200,000)	800,000
Net increase in cash		$1,260,000

REQUIRED

a. Explain and discuss each item that resulted in a change in cash for Davo's Surf Company.
b. Based on this limited information for only one year, what can you say about the company's future prospects?
c. What other information would you need to expand your answer to part b?

Interpreting Financial Statements: Cash Flow Effects

5–34 Byte City, Inc., provided the following cash flow information in the form of subtotals on its cash flow statements:

	1998	1997
Net cash provided by operating activities	$ 2,956,020	$ 587,249
Net cash used in investing activities	(8,123,648)	(33,942,808)
Net cash provided by financing activities	3,880,973	31,672,955
Net decrease in cash and cash equivalents	$(1,286,655)	$(1,682,604)

REQUIRED

a. Did Byte City's cash and cash equivalents increase or decrease in 1997? In 1998? Why?
b. How would you assess Byte City's cash flows from operating activities?
c. What financing and investing strategies was Byte City apparently following in 1997? How did this strategy change in 1998?
d. If you now learn that Byte City purchased other companies in 1997 for more than $47 million, and borrowed almost $37 million, what does this new information indicate about their financing and investing strategies?
e. If you later learn that Byte City made almost zero payments on long-term debt in 1997, but that its payments in 1998 totaled more than $26 million, what does this new information indicate about their financing strategies?
f. What other information would be helpful in answering these types of questions?

Calculate Cash Flow Ratios

5–35 Given the following information extracted from Byte City's financial statements, calculate and evaluate its cash flow ratios:

	1998	1997
Interest paid	$ 4,186,532	$ 3,695,431
Interest received	718,574	1,218,940
Income taxes paid	150,000	1,997,600
Total assets	107,219,075	103,542,717
Long-term debt	58,742,916	62,671,335
Shareholders' equity	42,827,531	35,912,651

Net income (loss)	7,459,828	(32,818,050)
Net revenues	129,485,952	109,948,716
Net cash provided by operations	2,956,020	587,249
Cash received from customers	118,158,941	101,879,383

REQUIRED

a. Discuss the differences between net cash provided by operations and cash received from customers.

b. Discuss the differences between net revenues and cash received from customers.

c. From the data above, can you draw any conclusions about Byte City's overall cash flows, or cash balances, at the end of 1997 or 1998? Why?

d. Refer to the data in the Problem 5–34. Can you now draw any better conclusions about Byte City's overall cash flows, or cash balances, at the end of either year? Why?

e. Calculate the following ratios, for each year:
   1. cash return on assets (1998 only)
   2. quality of sales
   3. quality of income
   4. cash interest coverage

f. Based on your ratios, evaluate Byte City's performance each year. In what areas do the cash flow ratios represent positive, or negative, performance?

g. What additional information would be useful in evaluating Byte City's performance?

**5 36 Interpreting Financial Statements: Cash Flow Effects—
Alternate Problems (A), (B), or (C)**

Problem (A)

The following summary information has been extracted from the financial statements of Hi-Tech Vaporware:

	1998	1997
Total net revenues	$126,000,000	$106,000,000
Operating expenses	(105,100,000)	(93,500,000)
Interest income	700,000	950,000
Interest expense	(3,560,000)	(3,815,000)
Provision for income taxes	(355,000)	(215,000)
Net income	$ 17,685,000	$ 9,420,000
Total assets	$131,900,000	$101,500,000
Total long-term debt	30,150,000	36,450,000
Total shareholders' equity	99,759,000	62,420,000
Cash received from customers	116,580,000	98,987,000
Cash paid to suppliers	(114,371,000)	(94,641,000)
Income taxes paid	(125,000)	(1,840,000)
Income tax refunds received	4,410,000	—
Interest received	680,000	1,138,000
Interest paid	(1,474,000)	(1,886,000)
Net cash provided by operating activities	5,700,000	1,758,000

Financial statement continued on page 190

Sale of marketable securities	716,000	3,873,000
Capital expenditures	(1,902,000)	(3,124,000)
Proceeds from sale of product line	2,838,000	1,571,000
Purchase of 2DVIEW and LINKMASTER	(10,544,000)	(46,464,000)
Net cash used in investing activities	(8,892,000)	(44,144,000)
Proceeds from bank loans	11,467,000	40,593,000
Payments on bank loans	(16,380,000)	—
Proceeds from issuing preferred stock	11,000,000	—
Proceeds from issuing common stock	2,794,000	1,875,000
Net cash provided by financing activities	8,881,000	42,468,000
Net increase in cash and cash equivalents	$ 5,689,000	$82,000

REQUIRED

a. Discuss the differences between net cash provided by operating activities and cash received from customers.

b. Discuss the differences between net revenues and cash received from customers.

c. From the data above, can you draw any conclusions about Hi-Tech Vaporware's overall cash flows, or cash balances, at the end of 1998 or 1997? Why?

d. What part of the balance sheet or cash flow statement, would help you draw any better conclusions about Hi-Tech Vaporware's overall cash flows, or cash balances, at the end of either year? Why?

e. Calculate the following ratios for each year:
   1. cash return on assets (1998 only)
   2. quality of sales
   3. quality of income
   4. cash interest coverage

f. Based on your ratios, evaluate Hi-Tech Vaporware's performance each year. In what areas do the cash flow ratios represent positive, or negative, performance?

g. What additional information would be useful in evaluating Hi-Tech Vaporware's performance?

Problem (B)

The following summary information has been extracted from Lo-Tech Software's financial statements:

	1998	1997
Total net revenues	$12,550,000	$16,005,000
Operating expenses	(5,040,000)	(3,485,000)
Interest income	10,000	35,000
Interest expense	(60,000)	(15,000)
Provision for income taxes	(35,000)	(15,000)
Net income	$ 7,425,000	$12,525,000
Total assets	170,000,000	155,000,000
Total long-term debt	51,500,000	24,500,000
Total shareholders' equity	108,800,000	88,420,000
Cash received from customers	11,580,000	9,987,000
Cash paid to suppliers	(5,961,000)	(5,741,000)

Income taxes paid	(125,000)	(840,000)
Interest received	680,000	138,000
Interest paid	(3,474,000)	(2,886,000)
Net cash provided by operating activities	2,700,000	658,000
Sale of marketable securities	617,000	13,783,000
Capital expenditures	(2,942,000)	(6,014,000)
Proceeds from sale of product line	838,000	5,571,000
Purchase of OCEANVIEW and SURFNET	(6,305,000)	(47,474,000)
Net cash used in investing activities	(7,792,000)	(34,134,000)
Proceeds from bank loans	18,106,000	30,828,000
Payments on bank loans	(26,290,000)	—
Proceeds from issuing preferred stock	12,000,000	—
Proceeds from issuing common stock	785,000	1,820,000
Net cash provided by financing activities	4,601,000	32,648,000
Net decrease in cash and cash equivalents	$ (491,000)	$ (828,000)

REQUIRED

a. Discuss the differences between net cash provided by operating activities and cash received from customers.
b. Discuss the differences between net revenues and cash received from customers.
c. From the data above, can you draw any conclusions about Lo-Tech Software's overall cash flows, or cash balances, at the end of 1998 or 1997? Why?
d. What part of the balance sheet or cash flow statement would help you draw any better conclusions about Lo-Tech Software's overall cash flows, or cash balances, at the end of either year? Why?
e. Calculate the following ratios, for each year:
  1. cash return on assets (1998 only)
  2. quality of sales
  3. quality of income
  4. cash interest coverage
f. Based on your ratios, evaluate Lo-Tech Software's performance each year. In what areas do the cash flow ratios represent positive, or negative, performance?
g. What additional information would be useful in evaluating Lo-Tech Software's performance?

Problem (C)

The following summary information has been extracted from Bostonware Inc.'s financial statements:

	1998	1997
Total net revenues	$ 75,538,000	$ 47,875,000
Operating expenses	(26,223,000)	(13,560,000)
Interest expense	456,000	(1,316,000)
Provision for income taxes	(5,435,000)	(2,315,000)
Net income	44,336,000	30,684,000

Financial statement continued on page 192

Total assets	270,650,000	252,120,000
Total long-term debt	33,150,000	41,200,000
Total shareholders' equity	228,600,000	180,920,000
Cash received from customers	71,580,000	39,987,000
Cash paid to suppliers	(30,673,000)	(12,011,000)
Income taxes paid	(5,125,000)	(1,840,000)
Interest received	567,000	318,000
Interest paid	(3,474,000)	(2,886,000)
Net cash provided by operating activities	32,875,000	23,568,000
Sale of marketable securities	876,000	3,873,000
Capital expenditures	(9,202,000)	(2,497,000)
Proceeds from sale of product line	2,383,000	1,171,000
Purchase of NOVIEW and		
WAVEMASTER	(2,849,000)	(30,970,000)
Net cash used in investing activities	(8,792,000)	(28,423,000)
Proceeds from bank loans	5,367,000	8,916,000
Payments on bank loans	(12,925,000)	—
Proceeds from issuing preferred stock	3,959,000	—
Proceeds from issuing common stock	10,000,000	—
Net cash provided by financing activities	6,401,000	8,916,000
Net increase in cash and cash equivalents	$ 30,484,000	$ 4,061,000

REQUIRED

a. Discuss the differences between net cash provided by operating activities and cash received from customers.

b. Discuss the differences between net revenues and cash received from customers.

c. From the data above, can you draw any conclusions about Bostonware's overall cash flows, or cash balances, at the end of 1998 or 1997? Why?

d. What part of the balance sheet or cash flow statement would help you draw any better conclusion about Bostonware's overall cash flows, or cash balances, at the end of either year? Why?

e. Calculate the following ratios, for each year:
  1. cash return on assets (1998 only)
  2. quality of sales
  3. quality of income
  4. cash interest coverage

f. Based on your ratios, evaluate Bostonware's performance each year. In what areas, do the cash flow ratios represent positive, or negative, performance?

g. What additional information would be useful in evaluating Bostonware's performance?

Interpreting Financial Statements: Cash Flow Effects

5–37 United States Surgical Corporation (USSC) provided the following consolidated statement of cash flows, as abbreviated:

	Year Ended December 31,	
	1993	1992
Cash flows from operating activities:		
Cash received from customers	$1,103,300	$1,087,700
Cash paid to suppliers and employees	(941,200)	(905,900)
Interest paid	(18,300)	(15,600)
Income taxes paid	(12,800)	(18,400)
Net cash provided by operating activities	131,000	147,800
Cash flows from investing activities:		
Property, plant, and equipment purchases	(216,400)	(270,700)
Other asset purchases	(31,100)	(31,100)
Net cash used in investing activities	(247,500)	(301,800)
Cash flows from financing activities:		
Long-term debt borrowings	2,614,400	1,840,800
Long-term debt repayments	(2,495,900)	(1,696,000)
Common stock issued	8,100	35,200
Dividends paid	(13,700)	(16,400)
Repurchases of common stock	—	(16,100)
Net cash provided by financing activities	112,900	147,500
Net decrease in cash	$ (3,600)	$ (6,500)

REQUIRED

a. Identify and discuss any unfamiliar terms, or unusual treatments, in USSC's cash flow statement.

b. Discuss the differences between net cash provided by operating activities and cash received from customers.

c. From the data above, can you draw any conclusions about USSC's overall cash flows, or cash balances, at the end of 1993 or 1992? Why?

d. What part of the balance sheet or cash flow statement would help you draw any better conclusions about USSC's overall cash flows, or cash balances, at the end of either year? Why?

e. Given the following additional balance sheet and income statement data:

	1993	1992
Net sales	$1,037,200	$1,197,200
Net income (loss)	(138,700)	138,900
Interest expense	18,500	14,700
Income taxes	1,300	54,000
Total assets	1,170,500	1,168,000
Long-term debt	137,500	110,700
Stockholders' equity	$ 443,900	$ 590,000

Calculate the following ratios, for each year:
1. cash return on assets (1993 only)
2. quality of sales
3. quality of income

4. cash interest coverage

f. Based on your ratios, evaluate USSC's performance each year. In what areas do the cash flow ratios represent positive, or negative, performance?

g. What additional information would be useful in evaluating USSC's performance?

Interpreting Financial Statements: Cash Flow Effects

5–38 StorageTek's consolidated statement of cash flows contained the following information, as abbreviated ($ in thousands):

	Year Ended	
	December 31, 1993	December 25, 1992
Operating Activities		
Cash received from customers	$1,532,183	$1,572,892
Cash paid to suppliers and employees	(1,446,321)	(1,456,835)
Interest received	54,251	67,136
Interest paid	(40,519)	(47,751)
Income taxes paid	(12,048)	(28,327)
Net cash from operating activities	87,546	107,115
Investing Activities		
Short-term investments, net	(15,377)	40,227
Purchase of property, plant, and equipment	(67,720)	(106,119)
Business acquisitions, net of cash	—	(51,761)
Other assets, net	(6,945)	(4,136)
Net cash used in investing activities	(90,042)	(121,789)
Financing Activities		
Proceeds from preferred stock offering	166,479	—
Proceeds from nonrecourse borrowings	87,508	114,935
Repayments of nonrecourse borrowings	(147,647)	(169,005)
Proceeds from other debt	79,740	21,320
Repayments of other debt	(44,144)	(27,538)
Other financing activities	2,009	61,050
Net cash from financing activities	143,945	762
Effect of exchange rate changes	(4,341)	(4,884)
Increase (decrease) in cash	$ 137,108	$ (18,796)

REQUIRED

a. Identify and discuss any unfamiliar terms, or unusual treatments, in StorageTek's cash flow statement.

b. Discuss the differences between net cash provided by operating activities and cash received from customers.

c. From the data above, can you draw any conclusions about StorageTek's overall cash flows, or cash balances, at the end of 1993 or 1992? Why?

d. What part of the balance sheet or cash flow statement would help you draw any better conclusions about StorageTek's overall cash flows, or cash balances, at the end of either year? Why?

e. Given the following additional balance sheet and income statement data, ($ in thousands):

	1993	1992
Net sales	$ 902,482	$1,079,130
Net income (loss)	(77,796)	9,334
Interest expense	43,670	48,706
Income taxes	5,000	17,700
Total assets	1,793,009	1,739,043
Long-term debt	361,718	369,988
Stockholders' equity	$1,017,303	$ 927,913

Calculate the following ratios, for each year:
1. cash return on assets (1993 only)
2. quality of sales
3. quality of income
4. cash interest coverage

f. Based on your ratios, evaluate StorageTek's performance each year. In what areas do the cash flow ratios represent positive, or negative, performance?

g. What additional information would be useful in evaluating StorageTek's performance?

h. If you now learn that StorageTek's 1991 fiscal year ended on December 27, would the difference in the number of days, or number of weeks, in each fiscal year, affect any of the above analyses? Why?

CASES AND EXTENSIONS

Performance Evaluation: Alternative Scenarios

5–39 Evaluate the following two scenarios and identify the possible sources of information that would be used by each union in asserting its demands.

a. Firm 1 reported record high earnings, but also told its union representatives that it could not afford even a small increase in wages.

b. In contrast, Firm 2 reported huge decreases in its earnings and, at the same time, was considering accepting its union's proposed 15% average increase in wages.

5–40 Interpreting Financial Statements: Cash Flow Effects— Alternate Cases (A) or (B)

Case (A)

The following (summary) statement of cash flows has been provided by Sigma Designs. Sigma Designs is a diversified graphic systems corporation, specializing in graphics, document imaging, and multimedia markets.

Sigma Designs, Inc.
Statement of Cash Flows (abbreviated)
For the Years Ended January 31, 1993 and 1992
(Dollars in Thousands)

	1993	1992
Cash flows from operating activities:		
Net loss	$(7,166)	$(3,443)
Summary of adjustments to net loss activities	(659)	4,731
Net cash provided by (used for) operating activities	(7,825)	1,288

Financial statement continued on page 196

Cash flows from investing activities:		
Purchases of marketable securities	(25,367)	(28,598)
Sales of marketable securities	30,518	23,189
Equipment additions	(801)	(702)
Software development costs (capitalized)	(551)	(1,070)
Other asset transactions	(339)	87
Net cash provided by (used for)		
investing activities	3,460	(7,094)
Cash flows from financing activities:		
Common stock sold	312	329
Repayment of long-term debt	(39)	(35)
Other financing transactions	(105)	24
Net cash provided by (used for)		
financing activities	168	318
Decrease in cash and equivalents	$ (4,197)	$ (5,488)

REQUIRED

a. Explain and discuss each item that resulted in a change in cash for Sigma Designs.

b. Based on this information, what can you say about the company's future prospects?

c. Is Sigma using the direct or indirect method to calculate its cash flows from operations? How do you know this?

Case (B)

The following (summary) statement of cash flows has been provided by Sigma Designs. Sigma Designs is a diversified graphic systems corporation, specializing in graphics, document imaging, and multimedia markets.

Sigma Designs, Inc.
Statement of Cash Flows (abbreviated)
For the Years Ended January 31, 1995 and 1994
(Dollars in Thousands)

	1995	**1994**
Cash flows from operating activities:		
Net loss	$(1,000)	$(2,145)
Summary of adjustments to net loss		
activities	2,997	2,731
Net cash provided by (used for)		
operating activities	1,997	586
Cash flows from investing activities:		
Purchases of marketable securities	(20,547)	(23,288)
Sales of marketable securities	35,245	32,155
Equipment additions	(625)	(502)
Software development costs (capitalized)	(300)	(1,200)
Other asset transactions	(273)	215
Net cash provided by (used for)		
investing activities	13,500	7,380

Cash flows from financing activities:

Common stock sold	594	450
Repayment of long-term debt	(47)	(40)
Other financing transactions	(252)	(75)
Net cash provided by (used for) financing activities	295	335
Decrease in Cash and Equivalents	$15,792	$ 8,301

REQUIRED

a. Explain and discuss each item that resulted in a change in cash for Sigma Designs.

b. Based on this information, what can you say about the company's future prospects?

c. Is Sigma using the direct or indirect method to calculate its cash flows from operations? How do you know this?

Critical Essay (continuation of Case 5–40)

5–41 Write a short memo to Sigma Designs' controller regarding the effect of net losses (see either of the 5–40 cases) on net cash outflows for 1992 and 1993, or 1994 and 1995.

Interpreting Financial Statements: Cash Flow Effects

5–42 A condensed version of Microbyte Corporation's consolidated statements of cash flows for 1996 and 1997 are shown below ($ in thousands):

	1997	1996
Cash flows from operating activities:		
Cash received from customers	$164,177	$82,152
Cash paid to suppliers and employees	(142,336)	(69,507)
Interest received	2,622	722
Interest paid	(87)	(224)
Income taxes paid	(16,121)	(5,187)
Net cash provided by operating activities	8,255	7,956
Cash flows from investing activities:		
Sale (purchase) of short-term investments	600	(16,200)
Capital expenditures	(9,740)	(1,932)
Net cash used for investing activities	(9,140)	(18,132)
Cash flows from financing activities:		
Proceeds from issuing common stock	496	22,114
Payments under capital leases	(472)	(347)
Other	(9)	31
Net cash provided by financing activities	15	21,798
Net increase (decrease) in cash	(870)	11,622
Cash balances at beginning of year	14,808	3,186
Cash balances at end of year	$13,938	$14,808

REQUIRED

a. Is Microbyte's statement of cash flows based on the direct or indirect method? Why?

b. By how much did Microbyte's Cash Flow from operations increase?

c. During these two years, how much did Microbyte spend to purchase marketable securities and other short-term investments? Did Microbyte buy or sell securities each year? On what basis can you answer these questions?

d. How much did Microbyte spend on capital expenditures during the two years? Did Microbyte purchase or sell capital assets each year? How do you know?

e. During these two years, how much money did Microbyte receive by issuing common stock? Given these proceeds, what do you suppose Microbyte did with it? Why do you suppose that Microbyte took these actions?

f. By how much did Microbyte's collections from customers increase between 1996 and 1997? Does this increase represent modest or significant growth? Is the increase in cash paid to suppliers and employees consistent with this growth? Why?

g. By how much did Microbyte's cash balances increase between the beginning of 1996 and the end of 1997? Is this increase significant? Does it represent a significant increase in Microbyte's liquidity? Why?

h. Why do you think the amounts shown for interest payments are so low? Why is interest received so much larger than interest payments? Under what circumstances is this a favorable relationship?

Graphical Analysis: Cash Flow Effects (continuation of Case 5–42)

5–43 Consider the following graph, included in Microbyte's annual report, showing Microbyte's cash from operations (see Case 5–42).

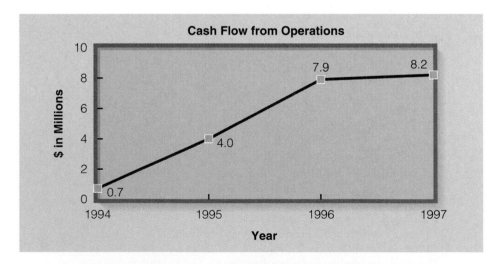

REQUIRED

a. Has Microbyte's cash flow from operations changed during the past four years? Why do you suppose these changes are so dramatic?

b. During which period was Microbyte more successful? During which periods do you think that Microbyte had higher net income? Why?

Interpreting Financial Statements (continuation of Case 5–42)

5–44 During 1996, Microbyte's cash increased by $11,622,000 (see Case 5–42). On the other hand, during 1997, its cash decreased by $870,000. Is this trend alarming? Does it indicate any problems for Microbyte?

Interpreting Financial Statements (continuation of Case 5–42)

5–45 How would an analyst evaluate the relationship between Microbyte's cash provided by operations of $8,255,000 and its cash used for investing activities of $9,140,000 (see Case 5–42)? Is this relationship affected by Microbyte's financing activities? Would you conclude that Microbyte has been a prudent manager of its cash during 1997? Why?

Interpreting Financial Statements: Ratio Calculations (continuation of Case 5–42)

5–46 Compute the following ratios or amounts for Microbyte Corporation for 1997, using the data from Case 5–42. Explain each ratio in the context of Microbyte's statement of cash flows.

   a. Cash flow from operating activities
   b. Cash return on assets, assuming average total assets are $81,613,000
   c. Cash return on stockholders' equity, assuming average stockholders' equity is $60,386,000
   d. Quality of sales, assuming sales revenues are $170,290,000
   e. Quality of income, assuming net income is $40,513,000
   f. Cash interest coverage

Interpreting Financial Statements: Ratio Calculations (continuation of Case 5–42)

5–47 a. Compute the following ratios or amounts for Microbyte Corporation for 1996, using the data from Case 5–42.
      1. Cash flow from operating activities
      2. Quality of sales, assuming sales revenues are $88,655,000
      3. Quality of income, assuming net income is $17,848,000
      4. Cash interest coverage
   b. Explain each ratio in the context of Microbyte's statement of cash flows.
   c. If you have also completed Case 5–46, compare and evaluate any trends in these ratios over the two years.
   d. If you have also completed Case 5–46, evaluate Microbyte's future prospects, using the cash flow ratios and its cash flow statement.

Interpreting Financial Statements: Cash Flow Effects

5–48 Consider the following (summary) consolidated statements of cash flows from Pioneer Resource, Inc., for 1996 and 1997:

Consolidated Statements of Cash Flows
Pioneer Resource, Inc.
For the years ending December 31, 1997 and 1996
(Dollars in Millions)

	1997	1996
Cash flows from operating activities:		
Net cash from operating activities	$ 2,989.5	$3,125.7

Financial statement continued on page 200

Cash flows from investing activities:		
Acquisitions of property, plant, and equipment	$(2,454.0)	(2,111.9)
Acquisitions of new companies	(796.3)	(65.4)
Other investing activities, net	125.8	(185.6)
Net cash from investing activities	(3,124.5)	(2,362.9)
Cash flows from financing activities:		
Net change in short-term debt	818.4	17.5
Issuance of long-term debt	97.5	32.9
Retirements of long-term debt	(102.3)	(89.2)
Dividend payments	(825.4)	(776.4)
Repurchase of common stock	(588.1)	(807.2)
Other financing activities, net	205.3	895.7
Net cash from financing activities	(394.6)	(726.7)
Net increase (decrease) in cash and temporary investments	$(529.6)	$36.1

REQUIRED

a. Identify and discuss each item that caused a change in Pioneer Resource's net cash flows for each year.

b. Using only the cash flow statement, what do you think about Pioneer Resource's cash flow prospects for 1998?

c. Describe and evaluate Pioneer Resource's apparent strategy for financing its acquisitions. How do its dividend payments and its repurchases of common stock affect your conclusions about financing strategies?

Interpreting Financial Statements: Cash Flow Effects (continuation of Case 5–48)

5–49 Using the data from the Case 5–48, if you now know that Pioneer Resource's net income figures for 1997 and 1996 were, respectively, $1,253.8 and $1,238.2 ($ in millions), write a short essay explaining the relationship between net income and net cash flow provided by operating activities. Draw a simple graph to show how these amounts relate to each other. Explain your graph and any conclusions that may be drawn from it.

Interpreting Financial Statements: Cash Flow Effects (continuation of Cases 5–40, 5–48, and 5–49)

5–50 Compare Pioneer Resource's net income and cash provided by operating activities (see Cases 5–48 and 5–49) with Sigma Designs' net income (loss) and cash provided (or used) by operating activities (see Case 5–40). While these are two distinctly different companies, how do your conclusions about cash flows differ? Why do you think there are such vast differences?

Interpreting Financial Statements: Cash Flow Effects (continuation of Case 5–48)

5–51 With regard to Case 5–48, evaluate Pioneer Resource's category of cash flows labeled as "Other investing activities, net." What events or decisions seemed to occur each year? If you merged these two amounts (for each year), would the result be significant?

Interpreting Financial Statements: Cash Flow Effects (continuation of Case 5–48)

5–52 Why do you think that Pioneer Resource listed its changes in both short and long-term debt (see Case 5–48)? Why couldn't these amounts have been added, showing just the changes in all debt, each year?

Interpreting Financial Statements: Cash Flow Effects

5–53 Mitronics Corporation reported the following items (which are only partial excerpts) in its 1997 statement of cash flows (dollars in thousands).

	1997	1996
Net earnings	$788	$845
Increases (decreases) in current liabilities	(512)	532
Cash provided by operating activities	276	1,377

In the financial review section of Mitronics' annual report, management reported the following:

> Cash provided by operations was $276,000 in 1997 compared with $1,377,000 in 1996. The reduction was primarily due to lower earnings from operations and a reduction in current liabilities.

REQUIRED

a. What do you suppose Mitronics means in this note? Why might Mitronics' managers manage its cash in this manner?

b. What else would you like to know about Mitronics' cash flow from operating activities?

Interpreting Financial Statements: Cash Flow Effects

5–54 SILLA, Inc., reported the following items (which are partial excerpts) in its 1997 statement of cash flows ($ in thousands):

	1997	1996
Net loss	$ (81,542)	$(202,144)
Interest payments, net	(114,000)	(132,000)
Debt repayments	(214,000)	(7,100)
Cash provided by operating activities	36,548	15,432

Included in management's discussion of SILLA's annual results, they reported:

> During 1997, cash flows from operating activities included $31 million relating to net reductions in operating receivables and payables relating primarily to property sales of $35 million. Accordingly, operations provided enough cash flow for net interest costs but did not provide substantial additional cash for debt principal repayment or capital expenditures.

REQUIRED

a. Has SILLA improved its cash flow in the 1997 versus 1996? Why?

b. On what grounds would you agree, or disagree, with management's assertions about its cash flow from operating activities?

Interpreting Financial Statements: Cash Flow Effects

5–55 Woodway Company reported the following data in its 1997 statement of cash flows ($ in thousands):

	1997	1996
Net earnings	$ 1,654	$6,215
Cash provided by operating activities	26,118	1,984

REQUIRED

a. What are some likely explanations for the trend in cash provided by operating activities relative to the trend in net earnings?

b. Would you expect Woodway's cash balance at the end of 1997 to be higher or lower than that at the end of 1996? Why? What other information would you need before drawing definitive conclusions in this regard?

Interpreting Financial Statements: Cash Flow Effects

5–56 The following cash flow statement from Low-Down Industries is causing concern to its president, Ms. High-Flyer. She can't understand why Low-Down is having trouble meeting its debt obligations on a timely basis. She is further concerned about the long-term prospects of the company, especially since last year's net income was only $100,000.

Low-Down Industries
Statement of Cash Flows (abbreviated)
For the year ended, November 30, 1998

Net cash used by operating activities		$(23,000)
Proceeds from sale of building	125,000	
Purchase of equipment	(47,000)	
Net cash provided by investing activities		78,000
Dividends paid	(31,000)	
Payment on long-term note payable	(90,000)	
Net cash used by financing activities		(121,000)
Decrease in cash		$(66,000)

REQUIRED

a. Write a memo to Ms. High-Flyer addressing her concerns and your recommendations.

Interpreting Financial Statements: Cash Flow Effects (continuation of Case 5–56)

5–57 Assume that Low-Down Industries (Case 5–56) has no more land or buildings or other tangible assets to sell. Suppose also that Low-Down's operations will not substantially change.

REQUIRED

a. Prepare an approximate forecast of next year's cash flows, assuming no other major changes.

b. Identify several viable strategies for Ms. High-Flyer to consider for future years in order to alleviate these potential cash shortages.

Effects of Discounts on Net Income

5–58 Assume you are the controller of a publicly held company called Spring Corporation. The CEO and the CFO are quite concerned about financial analysts' assessments of Spring's prospects. Analysts have publicized their doubts about Spring's ability to generate cash from operating activities.

As is common, Spring pays for all of its inventory purchases almost immediately upon receipt of the appropriate bills. Because finance charges in this industry are exorbitant, you, as controller, are careful to make all payments within the allowable interest-free period. At year end, the CFO orders you to suspend temporarily all payments to suppliers. The obvious reason for this suspension is to enhance, that is to "window dress," Spring's CFOA in its statement of cash flows. It is also obvious that this action will cost Spring substantial future interest charges.

REQUIRED

a. How would you respond to the CFO's request? Why?

Preparing an Income Statement and a Statement of Cash Flows

5–59 Beth's Espresso Cart, first introduced in Chapter 4, is now in its second year of operation. Prepare an income statement and a statement of cash flows on the basis of the following data (assume all sales and purchases are for cash):

1. Cash collections from clients	$35,505
2. Payments to suppliers (beans, etc.)	17,347
3. Replacement of cups, pots, etc.	1,000
4. Depreciation of coffee cart	1,300
5. Withdrawals for personal use	6,000
6. Purchases of propane, electricity, etc.	510
7. Amortization of insurance (final year)	400
8. Repaid start-up loan (to her father)	4,000
9. Paid interest on above loan, three years at 10% per annum (interest is for last year, this year, and next year)	

Assume there have been no significant inventory changes (supplies, fuel, coffee beans, etc.) during the past two years.

Performance Evaluation (continuation of Case 5–59)

5–60 Based on your analysis of Case 5–59, what conclusions would you draw regarding the operating performance of Beth's Espresso Cart? Write a short memo evaluating the year's performance; provide suggestions you may have for next year.

Critical Essay: Effects on Net Income and Cash Flows

5–61 Jane Stallings is the vice-president of operations for the Floppy Disk Computer Company, which produces a wide variety of hardware and software for personal computers. This equipment is sold to other manufacturers and is also sold to business and personal (retail) customers through specialty computer suppliers in shopping malls and business centers throughout the United States and Europe.

Floppy Disk has been in business for about 15 years and its overall operating results have been generally satisfactory. However, because the product life cycle for floppy disks is reaching its end, the manufacturing of floppy disks is almost completely conducted in the Far East due to lower labor costs, and the Floppy Disk Divisions has had zero profits for the past three years, Jane Stallings has proposed eliminating the Floppy Disk Division.

Max Marcker, son of Floppy Disk's founder and holder of 45% of the company's shares, objected to this proposal at the last meeting of the board of directors. Max believes that a resurgence of interest in floppy disk technology will soon occur and that such products will soon be produced at a cost of 2 cents each. He suggested to the board that this division is still integral to the company's future, that it does contribute to its cash flows, and that better planning and budgeting will improve the company's future cash flows.

REQUIRED

a. Write a short memo to Max from Jane, explaining the difference between cash flows and profits.
b. Each of Floppy Disk's divisions has, in the past, been evaluated on the basis of net income and return on shareholders' equity. Jane Stallings has suggested that cash flows should now be viewed as just as important a performance measure as net income. Do you agree? Why? Suggest some cash-based ratios that would be more helpful and useful for annual performance evaluation of the divisions.
c. Jane has also suggested that each division be required to use the direct method in its cash flow statements. Do you agree? Explain why the direct method may be more helpful to the managers of each division, as well as for each of the persons who might be evaluating the divisions.

Critical Essay: Effects on Net Income and Cash Flows

5–62 Write a short essay describing the advantages and disadvantages of using the income statement and the cash flow statement as a basis for evaluating the performance of a firm. Specifically comment on the distinction between operating performance, based on cash provided by operations and on income from continuing operating activities and "bottom line" results on either the income statement or the cash flow statement.

Interpreting Financial Statements: Cash Flow Effects

5–63 Four Square Computer Company has provided the following (partial) income statement for the year ended 12-31-98:

Revenues	
Cash sales	$1,600,000
Sales on account	3,335,000
Subtotal	4,935,000
Expenses	
Salary expense	2,259,900
Supplies expense	300,550

Advertising expense	969,430
Rent	1,200,000
Miscellaneous	31,260
Subtotal	$4,761,140

REQUIRED

a. Calculate income before taxes, tax expense (at 28%), and net income after taxes.

b. About half of the sales on account have still not been collected, and are expected to be collected in January of the next fiscal year. Why are they included in this year's income statement?

c. Given that about half of this year's sales have not yet been collected, and represent all of the accounts receivable that are still outstanding, how would you view Four Square's profitability? On the basis of this limited information, what would you conclude about their operating cash flows for the year?

d. Assuming that all of the nonsalary expenses have been paid as they were incurred, and assuming that salaries for December have not been paid or accrued, what would you now conclude about Four Square's profitability and its operating cash outflows associated with expenses? Assume salaries were earned by employees evenly throughout the year.

e. Now, assume half of the advertising expense was incurred in December for a promotional campaign that was designed to boost sales in the post-holiday period. Do you think these expenses should have been omitted from this year's income statement and deferred until the following year? Why? If GAAP required that such advertising costs be expensed (that is, shown in this year's income statement), how do you feel that Four Square's managers might now view the results of 1998's operations? Why?

f. On December 31, Four Square purchased 1,000 shares of Microcell (a computer software company) at $121 per share. Why isn't this purchase reflected in the income statement?

g. In November, Four Square purchased 100,000 disk drive units at $12 per unit. These are very advanced disk drives that have not yet been sold. Why isn't this purchase shown on the income statement?

h. When the outstanding accounts receivable are collected in the next year, should those collections be shown on next year's income statement? Why?

i. When the disk drives are used to manufacture computers, should their cost be shown on the income statement for the month and year in which they are assembled into the finished product? Or, should they be shown on the income statement in the month and year when the computers (and their associated disk drives) are sold? Why?

Effects of Timing on Revenue Recognition

5-64 Key, Inc., manufactures key rings and "dummy" keys for football fans to shake and rattle at opportune times during football games, i.e., during "key" plays. These items are sold to sports specialty shops and sidewalk vendors during the football season. The company's fiscal year ends December 31 each year. In 1997, just before the "bowl" season, the company received orders, and payment, for $23,000 worth of keys and key rings. The goods will be manufactured and shipped on January 1, 1998, just in time for the bowl games later that day. Key recorded these orders in December 1997 on its balance sheet equation as follows:

WHAT WOULD
YOU DO?

ASSETS	=	LIABILITIES	+	SHAREHOLDERS' EQUITY
Cash + $23,000				Sales revenue + $23,000

The company's overall financial results, summarized under the accounting equation, were:

ASSETS	=	LIABILITIES	+	SHAREHOLDERS' EQUITY
$275,000		$266,000		$9,000

Its summarized income statement for 1997 was shown as:

Revenues	$115,000
Expenses	109,000
Net income	$ 6,000

REQUIRED

a. Show how the $23,000 in December 1997 orders should have been recorded.

b. Reconstruct the income statement, showing how it might have appeared without the inclusion of the $23,000 in December orders. For this purpose, assume the expenses associated with the orders were $11,000.

c. Show how the balance sheet would have changed if the $23,000 in orders had been recorded correctly. Why might Key management be unhappy with these results?

d. Discuss the ethical problems inherent in this situation for the company, for its financial managers, and for its auditors.

WHAT WOULD
YOU DO?

Effects of Returns on Net Income

5–65 VaporWare II, Inc. (VWIII), had spectacularly good financial results in 1997. However, in 1998, software "bugs" and other defects, and general customer dissatisfaction, resulted in returns of $3 million. These products had originally been expensed for $1 million. It cost $5 million to satisfy VWIII's irate customers. VWIII chose not to report any returns in 1998, while showing the $5 million as sales revenue in 1998.

REQUIRED

a. Show how the $3 million of returns should have been recorded.

b. If the defects had been properly anticipated, what impact would this have had on VWIII's 1997 income statement?

c. Show how the 1997 balance sheet would have changed if the returns had been recorded correctly. Why might VWIII's management be unhappy with these results?

d. Discuss how the 1998 financial statements will be affected by VWIII's treatment of these returns.

e. Discuss the ethical problems inherent in this situation, for the company, for its financial managers, and for its auditors.

Interpreting Financial Statements: Cash Flow Effects

5–66 From Appendixes C–F, select financial statements for two or three companies. Your instructor may specify which companies should be selected.

REQUIRED

a. Compare each company's cash flow from operations in tabular and graphical formats.

b. Compare each company's net operating income in tabular and graphical formats.

c. Identify the cash flow strategies of each company by examining the operating, financing, and investing sections of each cash flow statement.

d. Write a short memo to a potential investor in which you critique the cash flow strategies of each company. Identify which company might offer the most favorable prospects for increasing its operating cash flows.

Analyzing Financial Statements of Several Companies

5–67 Obtain recent financial statements for two or three companies. If possible, these companies should be in the same industry, or they should use the direct method in reporting their cash flows from operating activities.

REQUIRED

a. Compare each company's cash flow from operations in tabular and graphical formats.

b. Compare each company's net operating income in tabular and graphical formats.

c. Identify the cash flow strategies of each company by examining the operating, financing, and investing sections of each cash flow statement.

d. Write a short memo to a potential investor in which you critique the cash flow strategies of each company. Identify which company might offer the most favorable prospects for increasing its operating cash flows.

Research Project: Cash Flow Issues

5–68 Scan recent business publications, or use a business index in your library, to locate an article discussing a company's cash flow issues. Read the article and write a short summary discussing the managerial implications of the company's cash flow issues.

Research Project: Cash Flow Issues (continuation of Case 5–68)

5–69 With regard to Case 5–68, obtain the cash flow statements for the company described in your selected article. Conduct your own analysis of the company's cash flows, using the ratios described in this chapter. Rewrite the article on the basis of your analysis, clearly showing why you agree or disagree with the article's author.

Critical Essay: Using CFO and/or NI for Performance Evaluation

5–70 Write a short memo discussing the advantages of using operating cash flows as an indicator of success. Contrast the use of operating cash flows as a performance measure, with accrual-based net income measures. Indicate the circumstances under which managers might prefer to use both measures simultaneously.

USING
FINANCIAL
ACCOUNTING
ON THE
INTERNET

5–71 Locate the most recent financial statements for the computer manufacturing companies listed below. You may use either the 10-K available at EDGAR (**www.sec. gov/edgarhp.htm**) or the annual report available at the company page on the WWW. The annual report is usually located in the Investor Information section.

Corporation	Home Page Location
Ameritech	**www.ameritech.com**
U S West	**www.uswest.com**
Bell Atlantic	**www.bell-atl.com**
BellSouth	**www.bst.bls.com**

REQUIRED

a. Identify the amount of cash flow from operating activities.
b. Identify the amount of cash flow from investing activities.
c. Identify the amount of cash flow from financing activities.
d. Identify the amount of net cash flow.
e. Identify the amount of interest paid.
f. Identify the amount of taxes paid.
g. Compute cash return on assets.
h. Compute quality of sales.
i. Compute quality of income.
j. Compute cash interest coverage.

5–72 The 10-K for Oncogene Science, a biotechnology company, contains a thorough description of its main products. Locate the most recent 10-K from the EDGAR archives (**www.sec.gov/edgarhp.htm**).

REQUIRED

a. What are the main products of Oncogene Science?
b. Scroll down to the most recent set of financial statements. Using the income statement and the statement of cash flows, answer the following questions:

   1. What is the reported amount of net income?
   2. How much are net cash flows from operating activities?
   3. How much are net cash flows from investing activities? What is the primary component of this item?
   4. How much are net cash flows from financing activities?
   5. How does it cover its shortfall in cash flows from operating activities?

5–73 Locate the three 10-Q filings and the 10-K for the most recently completed fiscal year for Cedar Fair, L.P., and H&R Block. These statements can be retrieved from the EDGAR archives (**www.sec.gov/edgarhp.htm**).

REQUIRED

a. What is the main business of these two companies? What is the peak season for each of these two companies? Which quarter do you think will reflect this peak level of activity?
b. From the financial statements in the 10-K, identify the starting and ending dates for the most recently completed fiscal year.

PREPARING A STATEMENT OF CASH FLOWS

INTRODUCTION

Conceptually, the statement of cash flows could be prepared by analyzing the cash flow effects of each transaction and accumulating that information. Most accounting systems, however, are not designed to implement such an approach. Instead, cash flows are inferred from items on the balance sheet and income statement.

OPERATING ACTIVITIES

This section examines the income statement and balance sheet relationships that are relevant to determining cash flows from operating activities under the direct approach. The income statement and comparative balance sheets for the Peak Company that appear in Exhibits 5A–1 and 5A–2, respectively, are used to illustrate these relationships and to generate the statement of cash flows that appears in Exhibit 5–1.

Collections from Customers

Peak began 1998 with an accounts receivable balance of $4,000. Let us assume that Peak collected these receivables in 1998. (This is a reasonable assumption, but our result would not be affected by changing it.) The $4,000 is a cash inflow in 1998. Peak then made sales of $68,700 in 1998. What portion of these sales was collected in cash in 1998? Since we assumed that the beginning balance in accounts receivable has already been collected, the ending balance must have been part of 1998 sales. Therefore, all of 1998 sales have been collected in cash, except for the ending balance in accounts receivable. Accordingly, cash collected from customers can be computed as the beginning balance in accounts receivable plus the portion of 1998 sales that has been collected in 1998.

EXHIBIT 5A–1
INCOME STATEMENT

The Peak Company
Income Statement
For the Year Ended December 31, 1998

Revenues:

Sales	$68,700	
Interest revenue	1,100	
		$69,800

Expenses:

Cost of goods sold	42,500	
Salary expense	17,000	
Depreciation expense	2,000	
Interest expense	1,000	
Tax expense	2,000	
		64,500
Net Income		$ 5,300

$$\text{Cash collected from customers} = \text{Beginning balance in Accounts Receivable} + \text{Sales} - \text{Ending balance in Accounts Receivable}$$
$$= \$4,000 + \$68,700 - \$4,500$$
$$= \$68,200$$

Interest Received

A similar relationship can be used for cash collected in the form of interest on the firm's investments.

$$\text{Interest received} = \text{Beginning balance in Interest Receivable} + \text{Interest Revenue} - \text{Ending balance in Interest Receivable}$$
$$= \$300 + \$1,100 - \$100$$
$$= \$1,300$$

Payments to Employees

During 1998, Peak incurred a salary expense of $17,000. But how much cash did it actually pay to its employees in 1998? At the beginning of 1998, Peak had a liability to its employees of $400. Let us make the reasonable assumption that this amount was paid to employees in the early part of 1998, and thus constitutes a cash outflow in that year. This implies that the ending balance in salaries payable must have arisen from 1998's expense, and reflects that part of the expense that has not been paid at the end of 1998. Accordingly, cash payments to employees can be computed as the beginning balance in salaries payable plus the amount paid in 1998 for 1998's salary expense (salary expense minus the ending balance in salaries payable).

The Peak Company
Balance Sheet

	December 31	
	1998	**1997**
Cash	$33,600	$22,000
Accounts receivable	4,500	4,000
Interest receivable	100	300
Inventory	11,000	10,000
Property, plant, and equipment (net)	31,500	30,000
Investments	12,000	0
Total assets	$92,700	$66,300
Accounts payable	$ 6,000	$ 3,000
Salaries payable	300	400
Interest payable	200	0
Short-term debt	0	12,000
Long-term debt	30,000	5,000
Common stock	35,000	30,000
Retained earnings	21,200	15,900
Total liabilities and shareholders' equity	$92,700	$66,300

$$\begin{array}{ccc} \text{Payments to} \\ \text{employees} \end{array} = \begin{array}{c} \text{Beginning balance} \\ \text{in Salaries Payable} \end{array} + \begin{array}{c} \text{Salary} \\ \text{Expense} \end{array} - \begin{array}{c} \text{Ending balance in} \\ \text{Salaries Payable} \end{array}$$

$$= \quad \$400 \quad + \quad \$17,000 \quad - \quad \$300$$

$$= \quad \$17,100$$

Payments to Suppliers

Calculating cash paid to suppliers (for merchandise) is a bit more complex than the preceding illustrations. First, note that cost of goods sold is the income statement item related to cash paid to suppliers. However, the purchases for a period are more closely related to cash outflows than is cost of goods sold. How can purchases be computed based on the information contained in the financial statements? The following equation can help:

$$\text{Cost of goods sold} = \text{Beginning Inventory} + \text{Purchases} - \text{Ending Inventory}$$

The sum of beginning inventory plus purchases reflects the cost of goods available for sale. That is, this sum equals the cost of goods on hand during the year that could have been sold. All of these goods will have been sold by year-end, except for those that remain on hand at the end of the year (ending inventory). Thus, subtracting ending inventory from the sum of beginning inventory plus purchases yields the cost of goods that have been sold during the year.

The equation can be rearranged to solve for purchases:

$$
\begin{array}{rlll}
\text{Purchases} & = & \begin{array}{c}\text{Cost of} \\ \text{Goods Sold}\end{array} + \begin{array}{c}\text{Ending} \\ \text{Inventory}\end{array} - \begin{array}{c}\text{Beginning} \\ \text{Inventory}\end{array} \\
& = & \$42,500 + \$11,000 - \$10,000 \\
& = & \$43,500
\end{array}
$$

Because purchases can be made on credit, they do not necessarily reflect cash outflows. Assume that accounts payable relate solely to the acquisition of merchandise and that the beginning balance is paid in early 1998. This represents a cash outflow in 1998. Moreover, the ending balance in accounts payable must have arisen from 1998 purchases. Thus, all of the purchases made in 1998 have been paid for in that year, except for the ending balance in accounts payable. Therefore, cash paid to suppliers equals the beginning balance in accounts payable plus the portion of 1998's purchases that was paid in 1998 (purchases minus the ending balance in accounts payable).

$$
\begin{array}{rlll}
\begin{array}{c}\text{Payments to} \\ \text{suppliers}\end{array} & = & \begin{array}{c}\text{Beginning balance} \\ \text{in Accounts Payable}\end{array} + \text{Purchases} - \begin{array}{c}\text{Ending balance in} \\ \text{Accounts Payable}\end{array} \\
& = & \$3,000 + \$43,500 - \$6,000 \\
& = & \$40,500
\end{array}
$$

Payments for Interest

The previous discussions can be used to justify the following relationship regarding cash paid for interest:

$$
\begin{array}{rlll}
\begin{array}{c}\text{Interest} \\ \text{paid}\end{array} & = & \begin{array}{c}\text{Beginning balance} \\ \text{in Interest Payable}\end{array} + \begin{array}{c}\text{Interest} \\ \text{Expense}\end{array} - \begin{array}{c}\text{Ending balance in} \\ \text{Interest Payable}\end{array} \\
& = & \$0 + \$1,000 - \$200 \\
& = & \$800
\end{array}
$$

Depreciation

Although Peak's income statement contains a $2,000 depreciation charge, depreciation expense does not appear on the statement of cash flows prepared under the direct approach. This is because depreciation expense does not involve a cash outflow. Recall the analysis of depreciation:

Since cash is not affected, depreciation expense has no place in the direct approach to the statement of cash flows.

ASSETS	=	LIABILITIES	+	SHAREHOLDERS' EQUITY
Equipment				Retained earnings
− $2,000				− $2,000 (depreciation expense)

Taxes

Peak's 1998 tax expense of $2,000 happens to equal the amount of taxes paid on the statement of cash flows. Since no tax liability appears on either the beginning or the ending balance sheet, this makes sense. More generally, if the related balance sheet item has the same balance at the beginning and the end of the year, the cash flow statement amount will equal the expense reported on the income statement.

Other Items

Peak's income statement and balance sheets contain only a sampling of the accounts that could possibly appear. For example, the income statement could include selling expense and the balance sheet could include prepaid expenses and accrued liabilities. Accordingly, Peak's situation is only an illustration of the steps needed to adjust income statement numbers to cash flow figures.

As a general guide to preparing the operating activities section of the statement of cash flows under the direct approach, the following steps should be taken:

1. Ignore income statement items that are unrelated to cash flows (such as depreciation expense).
2. Ignore gains and losses associated with nonoperating activities (such as extraordinary gains and losses and gains and losses on disposals of noncurrent assets).
3. Adjust all the remaining income statement items by the changes in related balance sheet accounts. Be sure to include in the adjustments all balance sheet accounts related to operating activities.

Indirect Approach

As you know, the operating activities section can also be prepared under the indirect approach. The indirect approach starts with net income and makes adjustment to convert net income to cash flow from operating activities. Exhibit 5–3 contains Peak's cash flow statement using the indirect approach. The first adjustment is depreciation expense. Depreciation expense has been subtracted in calculating net income. Yet, it does not result in a cash outflow. Accordingly, net income understates the cash flow generated from operating activities. Therefore, to modify net income so that it reflects cash flow, depreciation expense must be added back.

The next adjustment relates to accounts receivable. Recall how Peak's sales were converted to a cash flow figure under the direct method:

$$\begin{array}{llll} \text{Cash collected} \\ \text{from customers} \end{array} = \begin{array}{l}\text{Beginning balance} \\ \text{in Accounts Receivable} \end{array} + \text{Sales} - \begin{array}{l}\text{Ending balance in} \\ \text{Accounts Receivable} \end{array}$$

$$= \qquad \$4,000 \qquad + \$68,700 - \qquad \$4,500$$

$$= \qquad \$68,200$$

Rearranging the equation slightly yields:

$$\begin{array}{llll}\text{Cash collected} \\ \text{from customers}\end{array} = \text{Sales} + \begin{array}{l}\text{Beginning balance in} \\ \text{Accounts Receivable}\end{array} - \begin{array}{l}\text{Ending balance in} \\ \text{Accounts Receivable}\end{array}$$

$$= \$68,700 + \qquad \$4,000 \qquad - \qquad \$4,500$$

$$= \$68,700 \qquad\qquad\qquad - \$500$$

$$= \$68,200$$

If the ending balance in accounts receivable is greater than the beginning balance, combining these components results in a negative number. Thus, to convert sales to a cash flow figure, sales must be reduced by the increase in accounts receivable. Since sales are included in net income, net income must be reduced by the increase in accounts receivable to compute a cash flow figure. More intuitively, an increase in accounts receivable suggests that not all of the current year's sales have been collected in cash. Therefore, sales (or net income) must be reduced by an increase in accounts receivable.

The other adjustments in Exhibit 5–3 are handled in a similar fashion.

INVESTING AND FINANCING ACTIVITIES

Although the information for preparing the operating activities section can often be obtained from the income statement and balance sheets, this is not usually the case for investing activities and financing activities. A detailed analysis of the relevant accounts is needed to identify the inflows and outflows of cash. This information is often readily available, since relatively few transactions are involved and documentation (such as bank notes) is easily accessible. Also note that the investing and financing activities sections are the same under both the direct and indirect approaches.

SUMMARY OF LEARNING OBJECTIVE

1. **Calculate cash flow from operating activities by using relationships among income statement and balance sheet items.**
Under the direct approach, individual income statement line items are adjusted by their related balance sheet accounts. For example, cash flow from operating activities is calculated by adjusting sales by the change in accounts receivable. Under the indirect approach, net income is adjusted for the change in these same balance sheet accounts. Additionally, nonoperating items and items with no cash flow consequence must also be eliminated from net income.

CASES AND EXTENSIONS

Using Direct Method to Calculate Cash Flow from Operating Activities

5A–1 Given the following two financial statements for Lucy Enterprises, prepare the cash flow from operating activities section of the statement of cash flows, using the direct method and the indirect method. The following classifications must be calculated when using the direct method:

- cash collections from customers
- cash payments to suppliers
- cash payments to employees
- taxes paid
- interest paid
- interest collected
- purchases

Income Statement for Year Ending December 31, 1998

Sales revenues	$550,000	
Cost of goods sold	210,000	
Gross margin		$340,000

Salary expenses	(115,000)	
Interest expense	(15,000)	
Interest revenue	20,000	110,000
Net income before taxes		230,000
Tax expense		92,000
Net income		$138,000

Balance Sheet at Year-End

	1998	1997		1998	1997
Cash	$225,000	$100,000	Accounts Payable	$ 30,000	$ 20,000
Accounts receivable	124,000	135,000	Salaries Payable	5,000	4,000
Inventory	35,000	21,000	Interest Payable	3,000	12,000
			Taxes Payable	2,500	3,500
	384,000	256,000		40,500	39,500
Property, plant,			Shareholders'		
and equipment	101,000	134,000	Equity	444,500	350,500
Totals	$485,000	$390,000		$485,000	$390,000

Using Direct Method to Calculate Cash Flow from Operating Activities

5A–2 The following condensed information ($ in thousands) is available from Mary's Muffins. Assume all sales are credit sales (accounts receivable) and all purchases are also on credit (accounts payable).

	December 31	
	Year 1	Year 2
Balance Sheet Data:		
Accounts receivable	$55	$ 53
Prepaid expenses	13	15
Salaries payable	22	25
Taxes payable	17	13
Inventory	32	26
Accounts payable	27	21
Income Statement Data:		
Sales revenues		$ 550
Cost of goods sold		210
Salaries expense		112
Tax expense		57
Depreciation expense		29
Other expense		$ 21

REQUIRED

a. Prepare the operating activities section of Year 2's statement of cash flows, using the direct method.

Preparation of the Statement of Cash Flows

5A–3 The following are comparative balance sheets for the Paulino Corporation for 1997 and 1996 and the income statement for the year ended December 31, 1997.

Paulino Corporation
Comparative Balance Sheets
December 31

Assets	1997	1996
Cash	$ 89,000	$ 60,000
Accounts receivable	65,000	50,000
Inventory	200,000	90,000
Land	100,000	225,000
Equipment, net	371,000	380,000
	$825,000	$805,000

Liabilities and Stockholders' Equity		
Accounts payable	54,000	32,000
Dividends payable	15,000	-0-
Interest payable	6,000	8,000
Mortgage payable	130,000	305,000
Invested capital	280,000	280,000
Retained earnings	340,000	180,000
	$825,000	$805,000

Paulino Corporation
Income Statement
For the Year Ended December 31, 1997

Sales		$1,200,000
Cost of good sold		(720,000)
Gross profit		480,000
Operating and other expenses		
Depreciation	(9,000)	
Other operating expenses	(275,000)	
Gain on sale of land	15,000	
Interest expense	(10,000)	(279,000)
Net income		$ 201,000

Additional Information:
1. Dividends declared during the year were $41,000.
2. Land at a cost of $125,000 was sold for $140,000.
3. The only change in equipment was the depreciation expense.
4. All other balance sheet account changes are from normal transactions.

REQUIRED

a. Prepare a statement of cash flows for Paulino Corporation.

STUDYING THIS CHAPTER
WILL ENABLE YOU TO

1. Identify the items included in cash.

2. Appreciate the need for cash planning and how firms exercise control over cash.

3. Comprehend the basic accounting for marketable securities and the limitations of generally accepted accounting principles in this area.

4. Determine if a firm is properly managing its accounts receivable.

5. Assess if a firm's allowance for uncollectible accounts is adequate.

6. Understand the various inventory cost flow assumptions and the effect that the firm's choice of inventory method has on its taxes, the quality of information in its financial statements, its management compensation, its loan covenants, and its stock price.

7. Analyze a firm's inventory management practices.

8. Appreciate the importance of prepaid expenses.

THE APPENDIX TO THIS CHAPTER WILL ENABLE YOU TO

1. Prepare a bank reconciliation.

CURRENT ASSETS

INTRODUCTION

This chapter examines five prominent current assets:

1. cash and cash equivalents
2. marketable securities,
3. accounts receivable,
4. inventories, and
5. prepaid expenses.

For each asset, we examine the accounting issues and the information contained in the financial statements.

CASH AND CASH EQUIVALENTS

Cash is the most liquid asset a business can own. Most firms devote considerable effort to the management and control of cash. Because a firm's creditors expect payment in cash, a sufficient amount of cash must always be available to meet obligations as they become due. This necessitates careful scheduling of cash inflows and outflows.

Although an adequate cash balance is essential, excessive holdings of cash should be avoided. Cash deposited in checking accounts (or even savings accounts) usually does not earn very much, if any, interest. Cash amounts over and above those needed to meet obligations due in the near future should be invested in assets earning higher returns.

The liquidity of cash also makes it easily pilfered. Firms must institute internal control procedures so that cash is properly accounted for and safeguarded. Failure to do so may tempt employees to misappropriate the firm's cash and may also result in various accounting errors.

Composition of Cash

Cash is composed of funds that are readily available. This includes cash on hand and cash on deposit in bank accounts that do not restrict the withdrawal of cash. Deposits in checking accounts would qualify, since those balances can be withdrawn on demand. Because banks rarely enforce restrictions on withdrawals from savings accounts, they are usually classified as cash. Also classified as cash are money market funds permitting withdrawal by check, checks from customers awaiting deposit, and foreign currency (converted to dollars). Items not classified as cash include certificates of deposit, stamps, and postdated checks.

Large corporations may have hundreds of checking accounts. Multiple accounts are needed because firms have numerous physical locations and each location makes expenditures. Firms also find it convenient to use separate accounts for specific purposes. For example, many firms use one or more checking accounts solely for payroll purposes. All checking accounts are condensed into the one cash item on the balance sheet.

Many firms keep **petty cash funds** on hand to pay for small, incidental expenditures, such as cab fare or delivery charges. These funds are included in the cash amount on the balance sheet. Many retailers also keep **change funds.** These funds enable cashiers to make change for their customers. Change funds are also included in the cash item on the balance sheet.

As a part of borrowing agreements with banks, firms sometimes agree to maintain **compensating balances.** These are minimum amounts the firm agrees to keep on deposit at the lending bank in accounts that pay little or no interest. As a result, the bank is able to use these funds interest free. This provides the bank with additional compensation for lending funds to the firm.

Compensating balances are usually included in the balance sheet cash amount and are disclosed in the notes to the financial statements. Exhibit 6–1 contains an illustration of such a disclosure for Pulitzer Publishing Company. The note indicates that Pulitzer must maintain a compensating balance of $200,000. This amount, however, is not material in relation to Pulitzer's $20,000,000 cash balance.

Instead of showing a cash item on their balance sheets, some firms use the term *cash and cash equivalents.* Recall from previous chapters that **cash equivalents** are short-term, highly liquid investments that will mature within three months. Examples include certificates of deposit, treasury bills, and commercial paper (short-term oblig-

EXHIBIT 6–1
DISCLOSURE OF
COMPENSATING BALANCES

Pulitzer Publishing Company
1991 Annual Report
Note 5 (partial)

At December 31, 1991, the Company has a $10,000,000 Line of Credit Agreement ("Credit Agreement") with a bank. The Credit Agreement provides for a short-term, variable-rate line of credit under which the Company may borrow and repay from time to time until maturity on May 31, 1992. The Credit Agreement requires the Company to maintain compensating balances of $200,000 with the bank in lieu of annual commitment fees. No borrowings were outstanding under the Credit Agreement as of December 31, 1991.

ations of corporations). Because cash equivalents can readily be converted into known amounts of cash, reporting a combined cash and cash equivalents figure is probably as informative as reporting each figure separately.

Control of Cash

As previously mentioned, because cash is so liquid and so easily transported, special care must be exercised to ensure that it is properly recorded and safeguarded. Most corporations follow several sound management practices that enhance their control over cash.

For example, employees who are permitted access to cash should not also have access to the accounting records for cash. Access to both cash and the accounting records might enable an employee to misappropriate cash and to conceal the theft by altering the records.

As an illustration, retail clerks (who have ready access to cash) should not "read" the cash register. That is, they should not have the responsibility of ascertaining the daily sales total from the register's internal record and recording this amount in the accounting records. As shown in Exhibit 6–2, clerks with such dual access could take some cash and hide the theft by reducing the firm's recorded cash collections.

Checking accounts with banks provide firms with several cash control advantages. First, cash receipts can be deposited daily. Limiting the amount of time cash is on the firm's premises reduces the possibility that it will be misappropriated.

Second, checks provide a written record of a firm's disbursements. Such a record would not necessarily exist if disbursements were made in currency. Moreover, most firms require that checks be supported by underlying documentation such as purchase orders, invoices, and receiving reports. This helps ensure that only valid expenditures are made and provides the basis for an analysis of costs and expenses.

Third, by limiting the number of people authorized to sign checks, firms restrict access to cash and reduce the possibility that cash will be used for unintended purposes.

Finally, bank statements provide a monthly listing of deposits and withdrawals. So not only does the firm keep track of its cash flows, but so does the bank. Thus, the bank statement can be used to verify the firm's cash records.

EXHIBIT 6–2
POOR CONTROL OVER CASH

This verification process is accomplished via a bank reconciliation, which is a detailed comparison of the firm's records and the bank statement. Since the bank reconciliation may uncover errors related to cash, it should be prepared by an employee who has no other cash-related responsibilities. The preparation of a bank reconciliation is illustrated in the appendix to this chapter.

➤ Analysis of Cash

The most informative analysis of cash pertains to cash flows. Chapter 5 examined the statement of cash flows, which summarizes the inflows and outflows of cash. A firm's ability to generate cash enables it to pay obligations as they become due, to replace and expand productive assets, and to provide a return to investors. Chapter 5 described analyses that provide insights into this capability.

The balance sheet does not contain information about a firm's cash *flows*. It simply indicates the amount of cash a firm holds on a given date. Nevertheless, some useful information about cash can be obtained from the balance sheet.

Exhibit 6–3 contains cash-related information for OshKosh B'Gosh, Inc. (OB). OB's cash position decreased substantially from 1993 to 1994. The cash balance declined from $17,853,000 to $10,514,000. Cash as a percentage of current liabilities also decreased significantly, from 44.6% to 26.4%.

Note that the cash to current liabilities ratio is a severe test of liquidity. To see this, compare OB's 1994 cash to current liabilities ratio to its current ratio, which was discussed in Chapter 3.

$$\text{Cash to current liabilities ratio} = \frac{\text{Cash}}{\text{Current liabilities}} \qquad \text{Current ratio} = \frac{\text{Current assets}}{\text{Current liabilities}}$$

$$= \frac{\$10,514}{\$39,844} \qquad\qquad = \frac{\$142,307}{\$ 39,844}$$

$$= 26.4\% \qquad\qquad\qquad = 357\% \text{ (or 3.57 to 1)}$$

Both ratios contain current liabilities in the denominator. However, since the cash to current liabilities ratio has a much smaller numerator, a lower ratio results.

OB's 1994 cash position is similar to that of its rivals in the apparel industry. Thus, OB's short-term creditors should be reasonably confident of its ability to honor obligations in the near future.

EXHIBIT 6–3
FINANCIAL STATEMENT INFORMATION

	OshKosh B'Gosh Selected Cash-related Information (dollars in thousands)	
	1994	**1993**
Cash and cash equivalents	$ 10,514	$ 17,853
Current assets	$142,307	$151,855
Current liabilities	$ 39,844	$ 40,061
Cash/current liabilities	26.4%	44.6%

Implications for Managers

Financial statements provide managers and others with historical information about cash. Managers must ensure that sufficient cash is available on an ongoing basis to enable the firm to meet its commitments. As in many cases, managers must be proactive, not reactive, and the historical information can help with decision making.

The management of cash begins with projecting the amount and timing of future cash flows. This enables firms to forecast their cash balances over the course of a specified time period. If positive net cash flows are expected, managers must identify profitable uses of that cash. Alternatively, if negative net cash flows are projected, managers must identify additional sources of cash. Possibilities include short-term debt, long-term debt, additional investments by owners, and the liquidation of assets. Other strategies might include attempting to speed up cash collections from customers and delaying payments to suppliers.

MARKETABLE SECURITIES

Many firms experience uneven cash flows during a year. Department stores, for example, make a large portion of their sales during November and December, resulting in significant cash inflows. In many instances, such large amounts of cash are not immediately needed to fund operations. Many firms elect to put excess cash balances into short-term investments. These investments typically produce higher earnings than those available from bank accounts, thus enabling firms to increase their earnings.

Types of Investments

Firms can choose from two general types of securities. **Equity securities** represent ownership interests in other corporations. For example, General Motors (GM) can purchase shares of IBM stock. This investment would be reflected on GM's balance sheet as an asset.

Firms can also invest in **debt securities,** which result from lending transactions. For example, if GM were to lend funds to IBM, IBM would probably issue a debt security as written evidence of the indebtedness. The security might be commercial paper (indicating short-term borrowing) or a bond (indicating long-term borrowing). In either case, the security would appear on GM's balance sheet as an asset.

This chapter deals primarily with investments in equity securities that are classified as current assets. As you know, current assets are either consumed or converted into cash within one year. Thus, we cover only investments that will be held a relatively short period of time. Long-term investments are covered in Chapter 13.

Marketability

This chapter also deals with securities that are **marketable.** A security is marketable if it is traded on a securities exchange registered with the Securities and Exchange Commission (SEC) or if its price is available through the National Association of Securities Dealers Automated Quotations systems or the National Quotation Bureau. Securities traded on foreign exchanges may also qualify.

Securities that are not readily marketable are unlikely candidates for short-term investments of excess cash. Nonmarketable securities cannot necessarily be liquidated when the investor desires to do so. Investments in nonmarketable securities are usually classified as long-term investments.

Basic Accounting

SFAS No. 115, *Accounting for Certain Investments in Debt and Equity Securities,* governs the accounting for short-term investments in marketable securities. This standard requires that a firm classify such investments as either **trading securities** or **available-for-sale securities.** Trading securities are intended to be held for brief periods of time; firms hold these securities to generate profits from short-term differences in price. For example, investment banks will often buy an entire stock issue from a corporation with the intent of almost immediately selling the stock to the public. The investment bank would classify the stock as a trading security.

Marketable equity securities not classified as trading securities are classified as available-for-sale. Nonfinancial organizations classify most of their investments in marketable equity securities as available for sale. Proper classification is important because the accounting treatment differs for the two categories. Since most corporations classify their securities as available-for-sale, this chapter emphasizes the accounting procedures for that classification.

Available-for-Sale Securities. Marketable equity securities classified as available-for-sale should be accounted for at market value on the balance sheet date. The difference between a security's historical cost and its market value is an *unrealized* gain or loss. The term *unrealized* indicates that the gain or loss has not been confirmed by an actual sale. However, since the securities are highly marketable, the value change is virtually certain, and, accordingly, the gain or loss is a valid and useful measure for financial statement users.

Unrealized gains and losses on available-for-sale securities do not, however, appear on the income statement. Instead, these gains and losses appear in a special section of shareholders' equity that is distinct from invested capital or retained earnings. Also note that the marketable securities account continues to reflect the historical cost of the securities. The adjustment to market value is made to a valuation account, often labeled **allowance for unrealized gain/loss.**

To illustrate, assume that on December 1, 1997, Mega Company purchased marketable securities for $1,000. This analysis is straightforward.

	ASSETS		= LIABILITIES +	SHAREHOLDERS' EQUITY
	Cash	Marketable securities		
Dec. 1	−$1,000	+$1,000		

On December 31 the securities are still on hand and have a market value of $980. To record the value change, reduce marketable securities and shareholders' equity by $20.

ASSETS		= LIABILITIES +	SHAREHOLDERS' EQUITY
Marketable securities $1,000	Allowance for unrealized loss		Unrealized loss on marketable securities
Bal. Dec. 31	−$20		−$20

In the asset section of the balance sheet, the $20 balance in allowance for unrealized loss would be subtracted from marketable securities to show a net asset of $980. The account **unrealized loss on marketable securities** is a separate component of shareholders' equity. Keep in mind that it is *not* an income statement account.

Assume further the securities are sold on January 10, 1998, for $990. Looking at the purchase and sale together, a $10 loss has been incurred. Since no loss was recognized on the income statement when the securities were revalued at the end of 1997, a $10 loss must now be reflected on the income statement.

The analysis is most easily completed in two steps. First, since the $20 loss is no longer unrealized, the entry to record that loss should be reversed. Second, cash is increased by $990, marketable securities are reduced by $1,000, and a $10 loss is recognized. This loss is termed *realized* because it has been confirmed by a cash transaction. This loss appears on the 1998 income statement.

	ASSETS			= LIABILITIES +	SHAREHOLDERS' EQUITY	
	Cash	Marketable securities	Allowance for unrealized loss		Unrealized loss on marketable securities	Retained earnings
Bal.		$1,000	−$20		−$20	
Jan. 10			+$20		+$20	
Jan. 10	+$990	−$1,000				−$10 (realized loss)

Trading Securities. Trading securities are also accounted for at market value. One major difference exists between the accounting for trading securities and that for securities classified as available-for-sale. Unrealized gains and losses on trading securities *are included* in net income, as opposed to being reflected in a special section of shareholders' equity. The FASB believed that, since trading securities are purchased to generate profits on short-term price changes, all unrealized gains and losses should be immediately reflected on the income statement.

Debt Securities. The accounting for debt securities is a bit more complex. If a firm intends to hold a debt security until its maturity date, the security is valued at historical cost. Debt securities not intended to be held until maturity appear on the balance sheet at market value. However, since debt securities classified as current assets will be liquidated within the next year, a large discrepancy between cost and market value is unlikely. Thus, in most cases, financial statement readers can view the marketable debt securities figure in the current asset section as a very close approximation to market value.

of business and that collection is extremely unlikely. The balances in the accounts receivable and allowance accounts would each be reduced by $450.

ASSETS		= LIABILITIES + SHAREHOLDERS' EQUITY
Accounts receivable	Allowance for uncollectible accounts	
Bal. $100,000	−$2,400	
−$ 450	+$ 450	
$ 99,550	−$1,950	

Since the balance in accounts receivable is reduced, as is the accompanying contra-asset, the write-off has no effect on total assets or expenses. This is proper, since the asset reduction and expense were previously recorded. Box's net receivable is $97,600, both before and after the write-off.

	Before	After
Accounts receivable, gross	$100,000	$99,550
Less allowance	2,400	1,950
Accounts receivable, net	$ 97,600	$97,600

The effect of the write-off is depicted graphically in Exhibit 6–5.

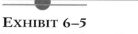

EXHIBIT 6–5
EFFECT OF WRITE-OFFS, ON ACCOUNTS RECEIVABLE

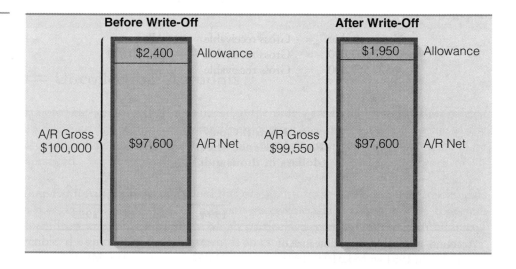

Estimation Methods. Firms can estimate the year-end adjustment for uncollectible accounts in several ways. One approach is the **aging method.** In its simplest form, the aging method classifies the year-end accounts receivable balance into two categories: (1) current and (2) past due. Suppose, for example, a firm's sales terms are 2/10, net 30. This indicates that all accounts are due within 30 days of sale. On the balance sheet date, accounts that have been outstanding 30 or fewer days are classified as current. The remainder are classified as past due.

Based on a firm's past experience, industry norms, and current trends, the firm estimates the percentage of each category that will not be collected. This is the step that requires the most judgment. Also, since older accounts are more likely not to be collected, the past-due category has a higher percentage of uncollectibles than the current category. These percentages are multiplied by each category's balance to estimate the allowance for uncollectible accounts.

Recall that Box Company estimated its allowance to be $2,400 at the *end* of 1997. The aging analysis necessary to obtain this amount is as follows:

Age Category	Balance	×	Percentage Estimated to Be Uncollectible	=	Estimated Amount Uncollectible
Current	$ 90,000		2%		$1,800
Past due	10,000		6%		600
Total	$100,000				$2,400

Although other estimation methods can yield different results on a year-to-year basis, over the long run their results will be quite similar.

Analysis of Accounts Receivable

The analysis of accounts receivable involves two issues: the relative size of accounts receivable and the adequacy of the allowance for uncollectible accounts. The financial statements of OB are used to illustrate these issues. Exhibit 6–6 contains some basic information about OB's receivables.

OshKosh B'Gosh
Selected Accounts Receivable-Related Information
(dollars in thousands)

	1994	1993
Accounts receivable, gross	$ 27,557	$ 22,787
Allowance for doubtful accounts	$ 3,700	$ 3,310
Sales	$363,363	$340,186
Accounts receivable as a percentage of sales	7.6%	6.7%
Collection period	28 days	24 days
Allowance as a percentage of accounts receivable	13.4%	14.5%

EXHIBIT 6–6
FINANCIAL STATEMENT
INFORMATION

Size of Accounts Receivable. Since accounts receivable earn no return after the discount period has expired, firms should limit their investment in this asset. The size of accounts receivable is usually assessed relative to the amount of credit sales. This seems appropriate since credit sales give rise to accounts receivable. Because most firms do not separately disclose credit sales, net sales are usually used. A straightforward analysis divides gross accounts receivable by sales:

$$\text{Accounts receivable as a percentage of sales} = \frac{\text{Accounts receivable (gross)}}{\text{Sales}}$$

OB's percentage increased from 6.7% in 1993 to 7.6% in 1994:

	1994	1993

$$\text{Accounts receivable as a percentage of sales} = \frac{\$\ 27{,}557}{\$363{,}363} = 7.6\% \qquad \frac{\$\ 22{,}787}{\$340{,}186} = 6.7\%$$

OB's trend is not favorable, since the percentage of its sales dollars tied up in receivables is higher. While the trend might be due to less effective management of accounts receivable, it could also be due to a changing sales pattern. If, in 1994, OB made a relatively larger proportion of its sales near year-end, we would expect to see an increase in year-end accounts receivable.

An alternative analysis involves calculating the average length of time it takes to collect a receivable. This is known as the **collection period.** It is calculated in two steps. First, calculate the average sales per day:

$$\text{Average sales per day} = \frac{\text{Sales}}{365}$$

Next, the collection period is calculated by dividing gross accounts receivable by average sales per day.

$$\text{Collection period} = \frac{\text{Accounts receivable (gross)}}{\text{Average sales per day}}$$

This ratio indicates the number of days sales in accounts receivable.

OB's collection period increased from 24 to 28 days. This is consistent with the analysis of accounts receivable as a percentage of sales.

	1994	1993
Average sales per day $=$	$\dfrac{\$363{,}363}{365} = \$996$	$\dfrac{\$340{,}186}{365} = \$932$
Collection period $=$	$\dfrac{\$\ 27{,}557}{\$996} = 28$ days	$\dfrac{\$\ 22{,}787}{\$932} = 24$ days

Exhibit 6–7 contains a comparison of OB's ratios with industry norms for apparel manufacturers and, as a point of contrast, food stores. OB's accounts receivable as a percentage of sales and its collection period are about one-half of its industry average.

EXHIBIT 6–7
COMPARISONS OF ACCOUNTS
RECEIVABLE RATIOS

Accounts Receivable Ratios Industry Comparisons			
	OB	Apparal Manufacturers	Food Stores
Accounts receivable as a percentage of sales	7.6%	13.5%	1.4%
Collection period	28 days	48 days	5 days
Allowance as a percentage of accounts receivable	13.4%	2.5%	0.9%

At least four interpretations are possible: (1) OB is doing an excellent job of quickly collecting its receivables and minimizing its investment in this asset; (2) OB's sales pattern during the year differs markedly from that of its competitors (that is, OB makes substantially fewer sales at year-end than its competitors do); (3) OB is inducing its customers to pay quickly either through strong pressure or steep discounts; or (4) OB factors more accounts receivable than its competitors.

Also note that food stores have a much shorter collection period than apparel maufacturers. This is due to the nature of food stores' credit sales. Most credit sales are made via customers' credit cards at major banks. Food stores are able to collect these receivables from the banks very quickly. Some credit sales are made to businesses (such as restaurants and caterers). These customers pay by check within a reasonable period of time.

Reality Check 6–1 summarizes an accounts receivable issue that arose for Topps Co., Inc. the sports card producer.

IS TOPPS ON TOP OF ITS RECEIVABLES?

Topps Co., Inc., produces sports cards. During two quarters in 1992, Topps' accounts receivable increased by more than 50%, while sales declined. Such a trend might indicate that Topps is experiencing difficulty collecting from its customers.

Topps asserts, however, that receivables have increased because of a change in its shipping schedule. It has begun to ship 50% of its cards in the final few weeks of a quarter. Thus, many of its accounts receivable are outstanding at quarter's end, and at the same time, are not yet past due.

REQUIRED

a. Does Topps' explanation make sense?
b. Can Topps' claim be verified with publicly available information?

Adequacy of Allowance for Uncollectible Accounts. Recall that writing off a specific account as uncollectible has no effect on total assets or net income. Assets and income are affected by the year-end adjustment in which uncollectible accounts are *estimated*. A great deal of judgment and discretion is used by management in making this estimate. Accordingly, analysts must carefully assess the reasonableness of the allowance for uncollectible accounts.

Few firms disclose their uncollectible accounts expense. However, most firms do disclose the year-end balance in the allowance for uncollectible accounts. The adequacy of this balance is usually assessed relative to the year-end accounts receivable balance. This is done by dividing the allowance by (gross) accounts receivable:

$$\text{Allowance for uncollectible accounts as a percentage of accounts receivable} = \frac{\text{Allowance for uncollectible accounts}}{\text{Accounts receivable (gross)}}$$

$$\text{Allowance for uncollectible accounts as a percentage of accounts receivable} = \frac{\overset{1994}{\$3,700}}{\$27,557} = 13.4\% \quad \frac{\overset{1993}{\$3,310}}{\$22,787} = 14.5\%$$

OB's percentage decreased from 14.5% in 1993 to 13.4% in 1994. The reason for such a decrease is not entirely apparent. Perhaps OB made a conscious decision to decrease its sales to customers with dubious credit ratings. Such a change in the customer base would allow a decrease in the allowance for uncollectible accounts.

Implications for Managers

As with any asset, managers should attempt to maximize the return on accounts receivable. One way to do this is to reduce the firm's investment in accounts receivable. Managers can employ several strategies to do this. Sales terms can be set so that the customer is obligated to make payment in a relatively short period of time. Managers should closely monitor accounts receivable collections to ensure that customers are paying within the agreed period.

Discounts for early payment can also induce customers to pay quickly. However, discounts large enough to prompt early payment may prove to be quite expensive for the seller.

Also keep in mind that sales terms may be constrained by industry practices. That is, a firm must provide terms that are competitive with those offered by its rivals. In general, sales terms are just one product attribute in a firm's overall promotional strategy.

Managers must also decide which customers will be granted credit. As mentioned previously, a trade-off exists between the amount of sales that can be generated and the level of uncollectible accounts expense incurred. Managers should set minimum credit ratings for its customers so that profitability is maximized.

INVENTORY

Inventory consists of products acquired for resale to customers. For many companies, inventory is a major asset and a significant source of revenue.

Basic Accounting

Assume that several items of inventory are acquired for a total price of $100. This transaction results in an increase in inventory and a decrease in cash.

ASSETS		=	LIABILITIES	+	SHAREHOLDERS' EQUITY
Cash	Inventory				
− $100	+ $100				

Now assume that half of the inventory is sold for $75. This transaction is analyzed in two steps. The revenue part increases cash and shareholders' equity by $75. The expense part decreases inventory and shareholders' equity by $50 (one-half of the $100 historical cost).

ASSETS		=	LIABILITIES	+	SHAREHOLDERS' EQUITY
Cash	Inventory				Retained earnings
+ $75					+ $75 (sales)
	− $50				− $50 (cost of goods sold)

The difference between the sales price of $75 and the cost of goods sold (CGS) of $50 is **gross profit** or **gross margin.**

 Cost Flow Assumptions

Most firms purchase inventory items on an ongoing basis. Usually, these purchases are not made at a uniform price. This poses an accounting problem when inventory is sold: What is the cost of the goods that were sold and what is the cost of the goods that remain on hand?

Some firms find it advantageous to keep a record of the cost of individual inventory items. These situations involve inventory units with a high dollar value and relatively few sales. Car dealerships are good illustrations. For example, when negotiating with a customer over the selling price of a given car, the cost of that particular car is important information for the dealer. Thus, these firms are motivated to keep a record of each car's cost. Moreover, a dealer's inventory consists of, perhaps, no more than 100 cars, and the dealer makes only a few sales per day. Such activity levels do not present a significant record-keeping challenge. The **specific identification method** maintains accounting records showing the cost of each inventory item.

For most businesses, however, the number of inventory units and the volume of purchases and sales are so large that the specific identification method would be very costly to implement. For example, a grocery store may sell 1,000 cereal boxes in one day. This requires firms to use one of the three inventory accounting procedures described in the next three subsections.

Average Cost. Consider the following summary of inventory acquisitions:

	# of Units	×	Unit Price	=	Total Cost
Beginning inventory	30		$4		$120
Purchase on February 18	10		5		50
Purchase on June 8	20		6		120
Purchase on October 22	20		8		160
Totals	80				$450

Assume 48 units were sold during the year and 32 units remain on hand at year-end. To prepare the financial statements, the cost of the ending inventory and the cost of goods sold must be determined.

The **average-cost method** calculates the weighted-average cost of an inventory item on hand during the period and applies this cost to the units sold and to the ending inventory. The average cost is calculated by dividing the cost of goods available for sale by the number of units available for sale. The **cost of goods available for sale** equals the cost of the beginning inventory plus the cost of all purchases during a period. It reflects the total cost of goods that were on hand at any time during the period and that were available to be sold:

$$\text{Average cost} \quad = \quad \frac{\text{Cost of goods available for sale}}{\text{Number of units available for sale}}$$

$$\frac{\$450}{\$\ 80} = \$5.625$$

To calculate the cost of the 48 units that have been sold, multiply the average cost of $5.625 by 48:

$$\text{Cost of goods sold} \quad = \quad \$5.625 \quad \times \quad 48 \quad = \quad \$270$$

To calculate the cost of the 32 units in ending inventory, multiply the average cost of $5.625 by 32:

$$\text{Ending inventory} \quad = \quad \$5.625 \quad \times \quad 32 \quad = \quad \$180$$

Alternatively, once either cost of goods sold or ending inventory has been calculated, the following equation can be used to compute the other.

$$\text{CGS} \quad = \quad \text{Beginning inventory} \quad + \quad \text{Purchases} \quad - \quad \text{Ending inventory}$$

Adding beginning inventory and purchases yields cost of goods available for sale. Subtracting the cost of goods that have not been sold (the ending inventory) from the cost of all goods available for sale results in CGS (the cost of the goods that have been sold). If ending inventory is calculated first, cost of goods sold can be computed as follows:

$$
\begin{aligned}
\text{CGS} \quad &= \quad \text{Beginning inventory} \quad + \quad \text{Purchases} \quad - \quad \text{Ending inventory} \\
&= \quad \$120 \quad\quad\quad\quad\quad + \quad \$330 \quad\quad - \quad \$180 \\
&= \quad \$270
\end{aligned}
$$

On the other hand, assuming that cost of goods sold was computed first, ending inventory can be calculated as follows.

$$
\begin{aligned}
\text{Ending inventory} \quad &= \quad \text{Beginning inventory} \quad + \quad \text{Purchases} \quad - \quad \text{CGS} \\
&= \quad \$120 \quad\quad\quad\quad\quad + \quad \$330 \quad\quad - \quad \$270 \\
&= \quad \$180
\end{aligned}
$$

This general equation can be used with all of the inventory methods described in this section.

WHAT WOULD YOU DO?

You are the sole owner of a local CPA firm. Your firm has been quite successful, primarily because of your hard work.

It is December 31 and you are working on the audit of The Boot Warehouse. Part of your audit program requires that you test count Boot's inventory. You have decided that counting seven sections of Boot's warehouse would provide sufficient assurance that the inventory is correctly stated.

There's just one problem. Because you have been so successful, and because you are so busy, you arrived at the warehouse late. Since Boot is scheduled to make a number of large shipments soon after midnight, there is not enough time to count the seven sections as you planned. Delaying the shipments would be very costly. In fact, Boot's lost profits would probably be greater than your audit fee. What would you do?

First-In, First-Out. Another commonly used inventory method is the First-in, First-out (or **FIFO**) method. This method *assumes* that *inventory costs* flow on a first-in, first-out basis. This implies that the cost of the beginning inventory and the cost of purchases made early in the period are the first to flow out of the firm and comprise cost of goods sold.

In our illustration, cost of goods sold under the FIFO method is based on the cost of the 48 units that were acquired first.

	# of Units	×	Unit Price	=	Total Cost
Beginning inventory	30		$4		$120
February 18	10		5		50
June 8	8		6		48
CGS	48				$218

Since cost of goods sold under the FIFO method is based on the cost of the earliest acquisitions, ending inventory must consist of the costs from the most recent purchases (those made closest to the period's end). Based on the inventory and purchase data given in the last subsection, ending inventory consists of the costs associated with the 32 units acquired closest to the end of the year. This includes the 20 units purchased on October 22 and 12 of the units purchased on June 8. Only 12 of the 20 units purchased on June 8 are included because the ending inventory consists of 32 units.

	# of Units	×	Unit Price	=	Total Cost
June 8	12		$6		$ 72
October 22	20		8		160
Ending Inventory	32				$232

Last-In, First-Out. The Last-in, First-out (**LIFO**) inventory method *assumes* that the *costs* associated with the purchases made closest to the period's end comprise the cost of goods sold. Therefore, cost of goods sold is based on the cost of the 48 units acquired most recently.

	# of Units	×	Unit Price	=	Total Cost
October 22	20		$8		$160
June 8	20		6		120
February 18	8		5		40
CGS	48				$320

Ending inventory, therefore, must be composed of the beginning inventory cost and the cost of the period's earliest acquisitions. Based on the preceding illustration, ending inventory is calculated by identifying the cost of the 32 units acquired the earliest.

	# of Units	×	Unit Price	=	Total Cost
Beginning inventory	30		$4		$120
February 18	2		5		10
Ending Inventory	32				$130

The difference between FIFO and LIFO can be described in terms of cost of goods available for sale. Recall that the cost of goods available for sale equals the cost of beginning inventory plus the cost of the year's purchases. FIFO assumes that the cost of goods sold consists of the costs of the beginning inventory and the earliest purchases and that the ending inventory is comprised of the more recent costs. In contrast, LIFO assumes that the cost of goods sold consists of the most recent costs and that the costs of beginning inventory and the earliest purchases are included in ending inventory. These partitions of cost of goods available for sale are depicted in Exhibit 6–8.

Financial Statement Effects of Inventory Method. The choice of inventory method can have significant effects on financial statements. In the Exhibit 6–8 illustration, the effects of inventory method choice can be summarized as follows:

	FIFO	Average Cost	LIFO
Cost of goods sold	$218	$270	$320
Ending inventory	$232	$180	$130

Notice that the illustration reflects a period of rising inventory costs, which is the typical situation for many firms. The conclusions drawn in this section are dependent on rising prices. Opposite conclusions would be warranted in periods of price declines.

LIFO results in the highest cost of goods sold because (1) it assumes the more recent costs are the first ones sold, and (2) these most recently acquired costs are the most expensive ones. FIFO results in the lowest cost of goods sold, and the average-cost method yields results between LIFO and FIFO. Since LIFO reports the highest cost of goods sold figure, it also results in the lowest reported net income number.

EXHIBIT 6–8
PARTITIONING COST OF GOODS AVAILABLE FOR SALE: FIFO VS LIFO

FIFO

Beginning inventory 30 × $4	Purchase of February 18 10 × $5	Purchase of June 8 20 × $6	Purchase of October 22 20 × $8

Cost of goods sold:
30 × $4 = $120
10 × 5 = 50
8 × 6 = 48
48    $218

Ending inventory:
12 × $6 = $ 72
20 × 8 = 160
32    $232

LIFO

Beginning inventory 30 × $4	Purchase of February 18 10 × $5	Purchase of June 8 20 × $6	Purchase of October 22 20 × $8

Ending inventory
30 × $4 = $120
2 × 5 = 10
32    $130

Cost of goods sold:
20 × $8 = $160
20 × 6 = 120
8 × 5 = 40
48    $320

LIFO results in the lowest ending inventory value because it assumes the earliest costs remain on hand at year-end, and these costs are the least expensive. FIFO yields the highest inventory value, and average cost falls between the two.

The Choice of Inventory Method

FIFO, LIFO, specific identification, and average cost are all acceptable inventory methods. Firms are free to choose one of these methods and consistently apply it across periods. Interestingly, GAAP does not require that the assumed flow of costs correspond to the actual flow of goods. Supermarkets, for example, put their older products on the front of shelves so that they will be sold before items acquired more recently; this helps preserve the general freshness of the merchandise available to customers. In this case, goods actually flow on a FIFO basis. However, supermarkets are not required to use FIFO in the preparation of their financial statements.

This raises a question about the factors that are considered by managers in selecting an inventory method. Because LIFO and FIFO yield the most dissimilar results, the following discussion focuses on them.

Taxes. The example we used to illustrate the various inventory methods was characterized by a period of rising prices. Many industries have experienced decades of inflation in inventory costs. In such periods, LIFO assigns the higher, recently acquired inventory costs to cost of goods sold. Of course, a higher cost of goods sold results in lower reported income. Thus, the selection of LIFO in inflationary periods reduces both reported pre-tax income and income taxes. Since a smaller check will be written to the IRS, the use of LIFO actually increases a firm's cash flow, even though reported net income is lower than under FIFO.

In general, firms are not required to select the same accounting principle for financial reporting and taxes. Since financial statements and tax returns serve different purposes, this makes sense. LIFO, however, is an exception to this general rule. If LIFO is used for tax purposes, it must be used for financial reporting. Many firms prepare their tax return using LIFO to obtain the associated tax savings and are thus required to use it for their financial statements.

Implementation Costs. Although we need not be concerned about the details, simply note that LIFO is more costly to implement than FIFO or average cost, especially for small firms. This may help explain why large firms tend to adopt LIFO more often than small firms. Managers must balance the tax savings from LIFO with the costs of implementation.

Quality of Financial Statement Information. LIFO and FIFO result in different financial statement numbers for inventory, cost of goods sold, and net income. Which method results in the most useful information? The answer is not clear-cut.

FIFO's ending inventory calculation is based on a firm's most recent acquisition costs. Thus, the inventory amount on the balance sheet is likely to be very close to current value. In contrast, LIFO's ending inventory is based on the costs of beginning inventory and the earliest acquisitions. Keep in mind that this occurs each year and that the beginning inventory may contain components carried forward from many years ago. Thus, in a period of rising prices, LIFO ending inventory values may be dramatically understated.

On the other hand, LIFO provides more informative income statement numbers because it matches current inventory costs with revenues. Cost of goods sold under LIFO consists of the costs of the most recent acquisitions. These costs approximate amounts necessary to replace inventory as it is depleted. Because of this, LIFO is more consistent with the matching principle. Furthermore, gross profit under LIFO is a useful measure of the resources generated from inventory sales that are available to cover other expenses and provide for net income. Managers may then view the gross profit measure as an indicator of "spendable" resources.

LIFO and Loan Agreements. As mentioned in previous chapters, many firms have loan agreements that require them to maintain certain levels of financial ratios. The current ratio is one example. Given that during a period of rising prices, LIFO results in a lower inventory figure, current assets will also be lower. This results in a lower current ratio and a greater likelihood of loan agreement violations. A number of other ratios will be similarly affected. When adopting LIFO, managers must be confident that the use of LIFO will not result in levels of financial ratios that violate existing loan agreements.

LIFO and Management Compensation. Since LIFO reduces reported net income in a period of rising prices, LIFO may also reduce the compensation of managers who have bonuses based on reported income. This could limit management's motivation to adopt LIFO.

LIFO and Stock Prices. LIFO results in lower *reported* net income during a period of rising prices. Some managers may fear that the stock market will react negatively to a lower income stream. Actually, the best evidence currently available suggests that the stock market responds favorably to LIFO adoptions. Financial statement readers realize that the underlying economic profitability of the firm is the same regardless of whether LIFO or FIFO is used. Moreover, since LIFO results in lower tax payments, the firm and its shareholders are better off.

Actual Usage of Inventory Methods. *Accounting Trends and Techniques* conducts an annual survey of 600 major U.S. corporations to ascertain their financial reporting practices. Exhibit 6–9 shows the number of firms using various inventory methods.

FIFO is the most frequently used method, followed by LIFO, with the average-cost method a distant third. The total number of firms exceeds the 600 that were surveyed because many firms use multiple inventory methods. Keep in mind that the results are for major corporations; as mentioned, because LIFO is relatively expensive to implement, smaller businesses utilize LIFO less frequently. Also, LIFO is not widely used outside the United States.

Valuation of Inventories at Lower of Cost or Market

Generally accepted accounting principles require that inventories be valued at **lower of cost or market (LCM)**. Inventory cost is determined based on one of the cost flow assumptions discussed earlier. Market is defined as current replacement cost, which is the amount that would be required to replace the firm's inventory on the balance sheet date.

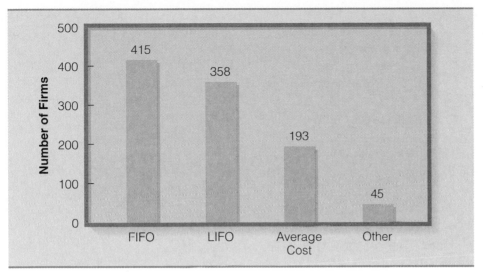

SOURCE: *Accounting Trends and Techniques,* 1993.

EXHIBIT 6–9
INVENTORY METHOD USAGE

The LCM rule is based on the rationale that a decline in replacement cost indicates that the inventory's utility to the firm has decreased. Conservatism would dictate that this loss should be reflected immediately in the financial statements, rather than postponing such recognition until the time of sale. When inventory is written down to market, the loss is sometimes disclosed separately on the income statement, but more frequently, it is included in the cost of goods sold.

Manufacturers

The inventories of manufacturers are comprised of three broad categories. **Raw materials** are the basic components of the inventory items produced by the firm. **Work-in-process** inventory consists of inventory items that are partially completed on the balance sheet date. **Finished goods** are completed inventory items that are awaiting sale.

Firms usually report just one total inventory figure on the balance sheet. The composition of the inventory is found in the notes to the financial statements. Exhibit 6–10 contains OB's inventory note. It shows the breakdown of inventory into the three basic components.

Analysis of Inventories

Both the income statement and the balance sheet contain useful information about inventories. The income statement contains information about cost of goods sold and gross profit. Gross profit is often expressed as a percentage of sales:

$$\text{Gross profit \%} = \frac{\text{Gross profit}}{\text{Sales}}$$

EXHIBIT 6–10
FINANCIAL STATEMENT
INVENTORY NOTE

OshKosh B'Gosh
Inventory Note
(dollars in thousands)

A summary of inventories follows:

	December 31,	
	1994	**1993**
Finished goods	$75,187	$82,737
Work in process	7,410	5,008
Raw materials	11,319	12,254
Total	$93,916	$99,999

The replacement cost of inventory exceeds the above LIFO costs by $16,122 and $14,716 at December 31, 1994 and 1993, respectively.

A higher gross profit percentage helps cover other expenses and contributes to net income. Exhibit 6–11 contains inventory-related information for OB. Its gross profit percentages for 1994 and 1993 are calculated as follows:

$$\text{Gross profit \%} = \quad \underset{1994}{\frac{\$103,947}{\$363,363}} = 28.6\% \quad \underset{1993}{\frac{\$95,260}{\$340,186}} = 28.0\%$$

OB's gross profit percentage increased modestly between 1993 and 1994. Several factors may have caused this. First, OB's inventory costs may have fallen. Second, competitive forces may have enabled OB to increase its selling prices. Finally, keep in mind that OB's different products probably have varying gross profit percentages. A change in the mix of products sold can affect the gross profit percentage.

OB's gross profit percentage is quite close to the industry norm for apparel manufacturers. In contrast, the pharmaceutical industry's average gross profit percentage exceeds 50%. Drug companies incur substantial costs when researching and develop-

EXHIBIT 6–11
FINANCIAL STATEMENT
INFORMATION

OshKosh B'Gosh
Selected Inventory-Related Information
(dollars in thousands)

	1994	**1993**
Inventory	$ 93,916	$ 99,999
Sales	$363,363	$340,186
Cost of goods sold	$259,416	$244,926
Gross profit	$103,947	$ 95,260
Gross profit %	28.6%	28.0%
Number of days sales in ending inventory	132	149

ing their products. Accordingly, they must sell their goods at relatively high markups so that they can cover these costs and remain profitable.

Reality Check 6–2 examines the effect of inventory write-downs on gross profit.

INVENTORY WRITE-DOWNS

Storage Technology Corporation (StorageTek) is a manufacturer of computer storage devices. StorageTek continually modifies its existing products and develops new ones. These improvements permit larger amounts of data to be stored and accessed more quickly.

One of StorageTek's new products is called **Iceberg.** An Iceberg system is composed of many small storage devices designed to work together. StorageTek is quite optimistic about Iceberg's future success.

Because Iceberg holds clear advantages over other systems that StorageTek sells, StorageTek may need to reduce the selling price of these other systems. Because of this, StorageTek must ensure that the recorded value of its inventory is not overstated. In fact, in the first quarter of 1994, shortly before Iceberg was marketed to the public, StorageTek reduced the recorded value of its older storage systems by $7,500,000. Write-downs such as this are rather common in industries that experience rapid technological change.

For the first quarter in 1994, StorageTek reported the following:

Revenue	$335,623,000
Cost of goods sold	$234,315,000

Assume the $7,500,000 charge was included in cost of goods sold.

REQUIRED

What effect did the write-down have on
a. gross profit?
b. gross profit percentage?

The balance sheet contains information about the cost of inventories remaining on hand at year-end. This provides insights into whether the level of inventory is adequate to meet customer demands. Inadequate levels may result in lost sales and reduced profitability. Excessive levels increase carrying costs, and this increase also has a negative impact on profitability. Carrying costs include storage, handling, insurance, and the opportunity cost of the funds invested in inventory. An opportunity cost exists because cash invested in inventory that remains on hand for several months cannot be invested in more profitable alternative opportunities.

The **number of days sales in ending inventory (NDS)** is frequently used to measure inventory levels. It is computed in two steps. First, divide cost of goods sold by 365. This indicates the cost of inventory sold in one day.

$$\text{CGS per day} = \frac{\text{CGS}}{365}$$

Next, divide ending inventory by CGS per day to obtain NDS. NDS reflects inventory size relative to the level of sales activity.

$$NDS = \frac{\text{Ending inventory}}{\text{CGS per day}}$$

OB's NDSs for 1994 and 1993 are calculated as follows:

		1994	1993
CGS per day (in thousands)	=	$\dfrac{\$259,416}{365} = 710.7$	$\dfrac{\$244,926}{365} = 671.0$
NDS	=	$\dfrac{\$\ 93,916}{\$\ 710.7} = 132$ days	$\dfrac{\$\ 99,999}{\$\ 671.0} = 149$ days

At the end of 1993, OB had nearly a one-half year's supply of inventory on hand. This seems high. While OB's inventory level had declined somewhat by the end of 1994, more than one-third of a year's supply still remained on hand.

It is interesting to contrast apparel manufacturers' NDS with that of food stores. Food stores maintain about 40 days sales of inventory on hand. This reflects the perishable nature of food stores' inventories, coupled with their high volume of sales.

Comparing LIFO and FIFO Firms

Comparing the financial statements of firms that use different inventory methods is troublesome. In these situations, differences in ratios might be due to the different accounting methods or to the different underlying economic conditions of the firms. Whenever possible in making interfirm comparisons, financial statement numbers should be recast to reflect the use of a uniform accounting method.

Although firms do not usually make disclosures enabling such analyses, companies using LIFO often reveal their FIFO-based net income and inventory values. In all likelihood, these firms are motivated to do this because FIFO results in a higher net income number than LIFO. Regardless of the motivation, the disclosures provide the basis to generate ratios on a FIFO basis for firms that actually use LIFO.

OB, which uses LIFO, elected to disclose the replacement cost of its inventories. Replacement cost approximates the FIFO cost of inventories, and allows the analyst to adjust OB's financial ratios for purposes of comparisons to FIFO firms. Recall the calculation for cost of goods sold:

CGS   =   Beginning inventory   +   Purchases   −   Ending inventory

Under LIFO, the calculation for 1994 was:

CGS	=	Beginning inventory	+	Purchases	−	Ending inventory
	=	$ 99,999,000	+	$253,333,000	−	$93,916,000
	=	$259,416,000				

The inventory disclosures indicate that under FIFO (or replacement costs), the beginning inventory would have been higher by $14,716,000 and the ending inventory would have been higher by $16,122,000. The only differences in the cost of goods sold calculations relate to the valuation of beginning and ending inventory. Therefore, FIFO-based cost of goods sold can be computed by adjusting LIFO-based cost of goods sold by these inventory valuation differences.

CGS under LIFO	$259,416,000
Plus the increase in the beginning inventory valuation under FIFO	14,716,000
Less the increase in the ending inventory valuation under FIFO	(16,122,000)
CGS under FIFO	$258,010,000

The difference in cost of goods sold between FIFO and LIFO is greater than the difference in net income. This is due to the tax effect. That is, a lower FIFO-based cost of goods sold results in a higher pre-tax income. However, a higher pre-tax income increases income tax expense, thus dampening the income-increasing effect of the lower cost of goods sold.

Exhibit 6–10 provides sufficient information to recalculate OB's ratios on a FIFO basis. OB's FIFO-based and LIFO-based ratios are summarized in Exhibit 6–12. As often happens, little difference exists in the gross profit percentages generated by the two methods. This occurs because the beginning and ending inventories are higher under FIFO by roughly the same amount; the previous calculation of FIFO cost of goods sold showed that these two inventory increases tend to cancel each other.

Inventory method has a more dramatic effect on NDS. The FIFO ratios indicate that OB has even more inventory on hand than suggested by the LIFO ratios. Given that most analysts believe FIFO yields more relevant balance sheet numbers, OB's inventory levels may be more problematic than they first appeared. Using FIFO, OB's NDS is 156, in contrast to the industry norm of 123. Since most firms in OB's industry use FIFO, this is a more valid comparison than the one based on OB's LIFO numbers. The comparison indicates that OB is carrying approximately 26% [(156 − 123)/123] more inventory than its average competitor. Accordingly, concern is warranted regarding OB's inventory levels.

EXHIBIT 6–12
INVENTORY RATIOS

OshKosh B'Gosh
Inventory Ratios

	1994	
	LIFO	FIFO
Gross profit %	28.6%	29.0%
Number of days sales in ending inventory	132	156

PREPAID EXPENSES

In many situations, firms pay for goods and services in advance. Insurance is a good example. Quite often, firms make full payment at the inception of a policy's term. The accounting issue involves the proper treatment of assets and expenses. At the beginning of a policy's term, an asset has been acquired: the right to be covered by insurance for the next year (or other time period). As the policy's term progresses, the asset is used up and an expense is incurred.

Prepaid expenses are recorded at their historical cost. Since prepaids usually have a short life, their cost corresponds closely to market value, and few analysts would object to this valuation practice.

Prepaid expenses generally constitute a very small proportion of a firm's assets. For example, in 1994 OB's prepaid expenses comprised 1.1% of its assets. Consequently, prepaids are not subjected to extensive analysis. Recall, however, that they are included in the numerator of the current ratio. Since prepaids will be utilized in the near future, most analysts feel that this is proper. Note that prepaids are not a source of future cash inflows. However, they do reflect the reduced need for future cash outflows.

SUMMARY OF LEARNING OBJECTIVES

1. Identify the items included in cash.

Cash includes funds on hand and cash on deposit in bank accounts that do not restrict withdrawals. Most firms also classify as cash amounts in money market funds on which checks can be drawn.

2. Appreciate the need for cash planning and how firms exercise control over cash.

Firms must carefully plan their cash inflows and outflows so that sufficient cash is available to meet obligations as they become due. At the same time, since cash earns virtually no return, excessive balances should be avoided. Also, since cash is easily misappropriated, management should take steps to safeguard cash and to ensure that the accounting for cash is proper. This can be accomplished through effective internal control procedures, including the use of checking accounts and bank reconciliations.

3. Comprehend the basic accounting for marketable securities and the limitations of generally accepted accounting principles in this area.

Marketable securities are shown on a balance sheet at market value. Revaluing marketable securities from their historical cost to market value requires that unrealized gains/losses be recorded. Most industrial firms own securities classified as available-for-sale. The rule for these securities requires that unrealized gains/losses not be shown on the income statement. Instead, they appear on the balance sheet in a separate component of shareholders' equity. This rule's major shortcoming is that the value change is not reflected in net income.

4. Determine if a firm is properly managing its accounts receivable.

Collections of accounts receivable should be made in a timely manner. This reduces the firm's investment in a nonproductive asset and reduces the opportunity for nonpayment. A firm's success at doing this is measured by its collection period.

5. Assess if a firm's allowance for uncollectible accounts is adequate.

On the balance sheet date, an adequate allowance for uncollectible accounts should be established. This is assessed by dividing the allowance by the ending accounts receivable balance.

6. Understand the various inventory cost flow assumptions and the effect that the firm's choice of inventory method has on its taxes, the quality of information in its financial statements, its management compensation, its loan covenants, and its stock price.

The most commonly used inventory cost flow assumptions are average cost, FIFO, and LIFO. FIFO (LIFO) assumes that the oldest (newest) costs are the first ones sold. The choice of inventory method can have a significant effect on the reported financial statement numbers. In a period of rising prices, LIFO results in the highest cost of goods sold and the lowest inventory value. The reverse is true for FIFO. The average-cost method yields results between LIFO and FIFO. Since LIFO has an adverse effect on net income and financial ratios, the adoption of LIFO may reduce managerial compensation and increase the likelihood of loan covenant violations. However, a lower reported net income number also reduces taxes. Because LIFO increases a firm's cash flows, adopting LIFO has a positive impact on stock prices.

Regardless of the direction of inventory prices, LIFO results in a cost of goods sold figure that reflects current costs, and FIFO results in an ending inventory value that reflects current costs.

7. Analyze a firm's inventory management practices.

To be profitable, a firm must sell inventory for more than its cost. The gross profit percentage measures a firm's success in doing this. A firm should also have an adequate, but not excessive, supply of inventory on hand. The amount of inventory on hand is measured by the number of days sales in ending inventory.

8. Appreciate the importance of prepaid expenses.

Prepaid expenses reflect payments made prior to the time that services are actually used. Prepayments often occur for insurance and rent. Prepayments are usually small in dollar amount and, accordingly, do not require detailed examination by analysts.

KEY TERMS

Accounts receivable (trade receivables)	Finished Goods
Aging method	Gross profit (margin)
Allowance for uncollectible accounts	FIFO
Allowance for unrealized gain/loss	Inventory
Available-for-sale securities	LIFO
Average-cost method	Lower of cost or market (LCM)
Cash	Marketable securities
Cash equivalents	Number of days sales in ending
Change funds	inventory (NDS)
Collection period	Petty cash funds
Compensating balances	Raw materials
Cost of goods available for sale	Specific identification method
Debt securities	Trading securities
Equity securities	Unrealized loss on marketable securities
Factor	Work-in-process

REALITY CHECK SOLUTIONS

SOLUTION TO REALITY CHECK 6–1

a. Topps' explanation may well make sense. Since sales and accounts receivable are recorded when goods are shipped, making shipments closer to a quarter's close will increase the accounts receivable balance on balance sheet dates.

b. Verifying Topps' claim would be difficult. Firms do not publish shipping schedules or any other information that might indicate when shipments occurred during a quarter. Perhaps the best source of information is Topps' customers. They would certainly know if shipping schedules have changed.

SOLUTION TO REALITY CHECK 6–2

Based on StorageTek's reported results, which include the effect of the charge, the following measures can be calculated:

Sales	$335,623,000
Less: Cost of goods sold	234,315,000
Gross profit	$101,308,000

$$\text{Gross profit percentage} = \frac{\text{Gross profit}}{\text{Sales}} = \frac{\$101,308}{335,623} = 30.2\%$$

Had the write-down not occurred, cost of goods sold would have been:

Cost of goods sold, as reported	$234,315,000
Less: Write-down	7,500,000
Cost of goods sold, adjusted	$226,815,000

Based on this, an adjusted gross profit and gross profit percentage can be calculated.

Sales	$335,623,000
Cost of goods sold, adjusted	226,815,000
Gross profit, adjusted	$108,808,000

$$\text{Adjusted gross profit percentage} = \frac{\text{Adjusted gross profit}}{\text{Sales}} = \frac{\$108,808}{335,623} = 32.4\%$$

As can be seen, the write-down had a modest downward effect on gross profit and the gross profit percentage.

QUESTIONS

6–1 What does the term *cash,* as shown on financial statements, usually include? Discuss *cash* and *cash equivalents* separately.

6–2 Why would a business usually want to have a positive cash balance? What does a firm usually do with cash? Describe how a firm might operate with a cash balance of zero in its accounting records.

6–3 Under what circumstances could a firm's cash balance be negative? Why?

6–4 Describe how market valuations are applied to short-term equity investments.

6–5 Explain the relationship between inventory cost flows and the actual flow of goods into and out of the firm's storeroom.

6–6 Why would a firm extend credit to its customers? Identify some firms that rarely offer credit terms. How have bank credit cards changed some of these credit practices? Identify some industries where credit is an essential part of daily business.

6–7 Discuss any relationship between inventory and accounts receivable. How are the dollar amounts reported in inventory related to those reported as accounts receivable? Are the dollar amounts comparable, or related to each other in any systematic manner? Under what circumstances could a firm have inventory, and not accounts receivable? What types of firms might have neither?

6–8 Identify which of the following items are classified as cash, and which are non-cash items.

a. Savings accounts

b. Postage stamps

c. Traveler's checks

d. Handwritten notes from employees promising to repay the firm for lunch money taken from the cash register

e. Travel advances provided to employees

f. Cash in a drawer waiting to be deposited at the bank

g. Customers' checks that have arrived in today's mail

h. A petty cash fund of $50 that is rarely used

i. Foreign currency

j. Foreign coins

k. U.S. savings bonds

l. 100 shares of IBM common stock

6–9 When does a firm recognize revenue? Does it depend on whether the transaction is a cash sale or a credit sale? Why?

6–10 What policies (within the firm) will help determine how quickly a firm collects cash on its credit sales? What customer attributes will also affect cash collections?

6–11 Describe one method that can be used to estimate a firm's uncollectible accounts expense.

6–12 Describe two different methods of accounting for marketable securities. Why is one method preferable?

6–13 Under what circumstances might cash not be considered a current asset?

6–14 Under what circumstances can accounts receivables be turned into cash, almost "overnight"?

6–15 Discuss the criterion "available-for-sale" as it is used in determining how marketable securities are reported in the firm's financial statements.

6–16 What steps can a firm take to protect cash held on its premises?

6–17 Discuss the relationships between "lower of cost or market" and the various methods that might be used to determine inventory costs, e.g., FIFO, LIFO.

6–18 Describe each of the following methods used to value inventories:

a. FIFO

b. LIFO

c. Weighted average

d. Specific identification

e. Lower of cost or market

6–19 Describe how LIFO provides better matching of revenues and expenses than FIFO. Why would such an attribute be desirable for income measurement?

6–20 Describe five general types of current assets. Why do you think managers and analysts might prefer that firms generally use these categories and definitions for current assets?

6–21 Define prepaid expenses and identify examples of two types of prepaid expenses.

6–22 If a firm purchased a three-year fire insurance policy on July 1, 1997, how would this policy be shown on the firm's balance sheet at December 31, 1998?

6–23 With regard to accounts receivable, explain how the average sales per day ratio and collection period ratio could be used. As a company relaxes its credit policies, how would the values of these ratios usually change? Why?

6–24 Discuss how and why accountants might use the accounts receivable contra-asset account Allowance for Uncollectible Accounts. Does such an account seem useful for managers and analysts? Why?

6–25 Firm A has an accounts receivable balance of $126,000 and a balance in its allowance for uncollectible accounts of $29,000. Contrast this situation with Firm B, which has corresponding balances of $963,000 and $865,000. Which firm is riskier? Why? Which firm do you think is doing a better job of managing its accounts receivable? Why?

6–26 Describe the circumstances under which a manager might want to change her firm's inventory method from FIFO to LIFO. Similarly, describe why a change from LIFO to FIFO might be desirable.

6–27 Answer each of the following multiple-choice questions:

To help achieve internal control over the assets of a company:

a. Segregate authorization and execution
b. Segregate authorization and review
c. Segregate custody and record keeping
d. Segregate custody and payment

Which of the following internal control statements is correct?

a. Internal control does not ensure that collusion will be detected.
b. Internal control design is the responsibility of the outside auditors.
c. The costs of internal control often exceed the benefits.
d. A strong system of internal control should be enough to show that the financial statements "present fairly."

EXERCISES

Analysis: Marketable Securities

6–28 The Amber Corporation purchased three different stocks during the year as follows:

- 100 shares of Fancy Corporation, cost $23 per share
- 250 shares of Traylor Corporation, cost $15 per share
- 180 shares of Sensor Corporation, cost $7 per share

Amber Corporation intends to sell these soon when its cash flow gets low. On the balance sheet date these securities had a market price as follows:

1. Fancy Corporation: $24 per share
2. Traylor Corporation: $12 per share
3. Sensor Corporation: $9 per share

REQUIRED

a. Assuming these securities are considered available-for-sale, what would be the effect on the financial statements of holding these securities?
b. Assuming these securities are considered trading securities, what would be the effect on the financial statements?
c. What if, after the balance sheet date, Amber decides to sell Traylor Corporation stock for a market price of $14 per share? What would be the effect on the financial statements if the security is (1) available-for-sale or (2) trading?

Cash, Cash Equivalents, and Short-Term Investment Classifications

6–29 The Simmons Corporation had the following investments at December 31:

1. 1000 shares of Hollings, Inc., purchased early in the year at $40 per share, and held as available-for-sale and with a year-end fair market value of $38 per share
2. $25,000 in U.S. three-month Treasury Bills
3. $15,000 commercial deposit with a maturity date of April 30 of the next year
4. $2,500 in postage stamps
5. $1,600 petty cash fund
6. $3,000 IOU from the president of Simmons Corporation
7. $12,000 money market account

REQUIRED

a. Describe where each item would be classified on the balance sheet.
b. At what amount should cash, cash equivalents, and short-term investments be reported?

Transactions Related to Accounts Receivable: Effects on Selected Financial Statement Items

6–30 Spit-Spot Cleaners, Inc., recognized the following events related to customer accounts receivable during 1997, the firm's first year of operation:

1. Sales on credit totaled $4,000,000 for the year.
2. The firm estimated that 2% of its receivables would ultimately prove to be uncollectible.
3. Cash collections of accounts receivable totaled $3,480,000 during 1997.
4. The firm wrote off uncollectible accounts of $75,000.

REQUIRED

a. Determine the effects of each of these events on the following financial statement items:

- Accounts receivable (net of allowance)
- Total assets
- Revenues
- Expenses

b. Determine the firm's balance of accounts receivable (net) at December 31, 1997.

Transactions Related to Accounts Receivable: Effects on Selected Financial Statement Items

6–31 Shard Crockery Co. recognized the following events related to customer accounts receivable during 1998. At the start of the year, the firm reported gross accounts receivable of $22,000,000 and an allowance for uncollectible accounts of $2,000,000.

1. Sales on credit totaled $60,000,000 for the year.
2. The company factored $18,000,000 of its receivables to a financial institution, and paid a fee of $700,000.

3. Uncollectible customer accounts totaling $3,200,000 were written off during the year.
4. Based on an aging of its remaining accounts receivable at year-end, the company estimates that 10% of its remaining receivables will ultimately be uncollectible.

REQUIRED

a. Determine the balance of accounts receivable (net of allowance) to be reported in Shard Crockery's balance sheet at the end of 1998.
b. Determine the effects of each of the events described above on the company's accounts receivable (net), total assets, revenues, and expenses.
c. How (if at all) would the factoring of accounts receivable during the year affect your calculation or interpretation of the company's accounts receivable collection period? Discuss.

Interpreting Financial Statements: Accounts Receivable

6–32 DSE is a world leader in the application of information technology. Excerpts from its 1997 financial statements disclosed the following information ($ in millions):

| | Years Ended December 31 | | |
	1997	1996	1995
Total revenues	$8,463.9	$8,154.3	$6,998.2
Accounts receivable	$1,325.6	$1,200.5	

REQUIRED

a. Since DSE did not separately disclose its allowance account balances, what interpretation must be given to the reported balances in accounts receivable?
b. What conclusions, based on the information available, can be drawn regarding DSE's management of accounts receivable?

6–33 Ratio Calculations: Accounts Receivable—Alternate Exercises (A) or (B)

Exercise (A)

Frosty King, Inc., reported the following information in its 1997 financial statements:

| | Years Ended November 30 | |
	1997	1996
Net sales	$228,542,157	$231,845,632
Accounts receivable, net	21,402,613	19,280,407
Allowance for uncollectible accounts	650,811	1,018,416

REQUIRED

a. Calculate the adequacy of Frosty King's allowance account for each year.
b. Calculate its average sales per day for each year.
c. Calculate its collection period for each year.
d. Calculate its accounts receivable as a percentage of sales for each year.
e. Based on your analyses, discuss Frosty King's management of accounts receivable.

Exercise (B)

StorageTek reported the following information in its 1993 financial statements ($ in thousands):

| | Years Ended December 31 | |
	1993	1992
Total revenue	$1,404,752	$1,550,945
Accounts receivable, net	218,701	313,350
Allowance for uncollectible accounts	12,452	11,949

REQUIRED

a. Calculate the adequacy of StorageTek's allowance account for each year.
b. Calculate its average sales per day for each year.
c. Calculate its collection period for each year.
d. Calculate its accounts receivable as a percentage of sales for each year.
e. Based on your analyses, discuss StorageTek's management of accounts receivable.

Gross Profit Ratio Calculations

6–34 Calculate the gross profit percentages for each of the following situations and, based on these results, identify which situations are most preferable:

a. Sales of $500,000, cost of goods sold of $300,000
b. Sales of $600,000, gross profit of $300,000
c. Sales of $600,000, cost of goods sold of $250,000
d. Sales of $500,000, cost of goods sold of $100,000

Gross Profit Ratio Calculations

6–35 Calculate the gross profit percentages for each of the following situations and, based on these results, identify which situations are most preferable:

a. Sales of $450,000, cost of goods sold of $300,000
b. Sales of $660,000, gross profit of $230,000
c. Sales of $700,000, cost of goods sold of $330,000
d. Sales of $800,000, cost of goods sold of $250,000

Turnover Ratios for Accounts Receivable and Inventory

6–36 Ken's and Den's Recreational Products, Inc., reports the following information in its 1998 financial statements:

| | Balance (dollars in millions) | |
	January 1, 1998	December 31, 1998
Accounts receivable (gross)	$14	$12
Allowance for uncollectible accounts	1	2
Inventory	20	26
During 1998:		
Sales		80
Cost of goods sold		55

REQUIRED

a. Determine Ken's and Den's accounts receivable collection period ratio and the number of days sales in ending inventory during 1998.

Inventory Valuation Error Effects on Financial Statements

6–37 Illusory Products Co. began operations early in 1997, and reported the following items in its financial statements at the ends of 1997 and 1998 ($ in millions):

	1997	1998
Ending inventory	$18	$22
Gross margin	62	75
Retained earnings	54	66

Early in 1999, management discovered that the ending inventory for 1997 was overstated by $7 million, and the ending inventory for 1998 was correctly measured. The company's income tax rate in both years was 40 percent.

REQUIRED

a. Determine the effects, if any, of the overstatement of 1997's ending inventory on Illusory Products' gross margin and retained earnings for 1997 and 1998.

Footnote Disclosures: Convert from LIFO to FIFO-Based Measures of Cost of Goods Sold

6–38 Dolo's Building Block Company uses LIFO costing and reports the following information in a footnote to its financial statements: "If Dolo had used FIFO costing during 1998, the beginning and ending inventories would have been higher by $50 million and $70 million, respectively."

REQUIRED

a. Determine how much higher or lower would be Dolo's cost of goods sold during 1998 if the firm had used FIFO in costing its inventories.
b. Assume that all of Dolo's income is taxed at 40%. How much higher or lower would be Dolo's income tax expense during 1998 if the firm had used FIFO?
c. What has been the total savings in income tax expenses through the end of 1998 due to the use of LIFO costing by Dolo?

Financial Statement Effects of Inventory Costing Methods, First Year of Operations

6–39 Tom Hanky, a financial analyst specializing in the toy industry, has provided the following comments concerning the 1997 financial statements of Toys-U-Must:

Toys-U-Must began operations in 1997 and uses the LIFO method in costing its inventories. Because the typical firm in the industry uses FIFO costing, it is desirable to adjust the company's financial statements "as if" FIFO costing had been used. Footnotes to the financial statements reveal that the use of FIFO would increase the company's inventory valuation by $150 million, and that the company's income is taxed at 40%.

REQUIRED

Based on Hanky's comments, explain how each of the following items would be adjusted in Toys-U-Must's 1997 financial statements:

a. Inventory
b. Working capital (current assets less current liabilities)
c. Gross margin
d. Income tax expense
e. Net income
f. Retained earnings

Financial Statement Effects of Inventory Costing Methods, Second Year of Operations (continuation of Exercise 6–39)

6–40 At the end of 1998, Toys-U-Must's financial statement footnotes reveal that the use of FIFO costing would increase the company's ending inventory valuation by $200 million (the effects on the beginning inventory are described in Exercise 6–39). Explain how each of the following items would be adjusted in order to convert the company's reported accounts "as if" the firm had used FIFO costing during 1998:

a. Inventory
b. Working capital
c. Gross margin
d. Income tax expense
e. Net income
f. Retained earnings

6–41 Ratio Calculations: LIFO and FIFO—Alternate Exercises (A), (B), or (C)

Exercise (A)

Teddie Bower, Inc., reported the following data in its annual financial statements ($ in thousands):

	1997	1998
Sales	$333,667	$313,456
Cost of goods sold— LIFO	32,587	44,690
Cost of goods sold—FIFO	30,198	45,833
Ending inventory—LIFO	11,189	10,567
Ending inventory—FIFO	15,999	14,234
Net income—LIFO	34,000	33,500
Net income—FIFO	38,980	37,765

REQUIRED

a. Calculate the number of days sales in ending inventory (NDS) under both LIFO and FIFO.
b. Calculate the gross profit percentage under both LIFO and FIFO.

c. Discuss the differences in inventory levels, income, and gross profit under both LIFO and FIFO.

d. Discuss why a firm might prefer LIFO under these circumstances.

Exercise (B)

Jeans R'Us, Inc., reported the following data in its annual financial statements ($ in thousands):

	1997	1998
Sales	$336,337	$367,336
Cost of goods sold—LIFO	31,678	44,690
Cost of goods sold—FIFO	31,089	41,656
Ending inventory—LIFO	12,298	13,365
Ending inventory—FIFO	14,888	18,989
Net income—LIFO	30,500	37,775
Net income—FIFO	37,895	40,876

REQUIRED

a. Calculate the number of days sales in ending inventory (NDS) under both LIFO and FIFO.

b. Calculate the gross profit percentage under both LIFO and FIFO.

c. Discuss the differences in inventory levels, income, and gross profit under both LIFO and FIFO.

d. Discuss why a firm might prefer LIFO under these circumstances.

Exercise (C)

Peggy Ashley, Inc., reported the following data in its annual financial statements ($ in thousands):

	1997	1998
Sales	$447,556	$898,445
Cost of goods sold—LIFO	55,986	98,234
Cost of goods sold—FIFO	46,567	110,935
Ending inventory—LIFO	31,097	65,434
Ending inventory—FIFO	56,709	78,345
Net income—LIFO	230.500	342,886
Net income—FIFO	378,634	554,678

REQUIRED

a. Calculate the number of days sales in ending inventory (NDS) under both LIFO and FIFO.

b. Calculate the gross profit percentage under both LIFO and FIFO.

c. Discuss the differences in inventory levels, income, and gross profit under both LIFO and FIFO.

d. Discuss why a firm might prefer LIFO under these circumstances.

Potential LIFO Liquidation: Effect on Profits

6–42 El Puerto Company uses LIFO to cost its inventories. Information regarding 1998's beginning inventory and purchases up until December 15, 1998, is shown below:

Beginning inventory (January 1, 1998) 500,000 units @ $10 $ 5 million
Purchases during 1998: 1,200,000 units @ an average cost of $20 $24 million

El Puerto sold 1,500,000 units up to December 15, and expects that very few, if any, additional sales will occur before year-end. Inventory purchase costs are $25 per unit at December 15, and prices are not expected to change over the remainder of 1998. The company's income tax rate is 40%.

REQUIRED

a. Determine El Puerto Company's ending inventory value and cost of goods sold for 1998 assuming (1) no additional purchases are made during 1998 and (2) an additional 400,000 units are purchased at $25 per unit before year-end.

b. Based on these calculations, would you advise the company to purchase additional inventory before year-end? Explain.

PROBLEMS

Comprehensive Marketable Securities, Accounts Receivable, Inventory

6–43 Pratsky, Inc., had the following account balances:

December 31, 1996

Assets		Liabilities	
Cash	$12,500	Accounts payable	$10,000
Accounts Receivable	22,400		
Allowance for		**Stockholders' Equity**	
uncollectible accounts	(3,400)	Invested capital	20,000
Inventory	17,500	Retained earnings	19,000
		Total stockholders' equity	39,000
	$49,000		$49,000

During 1997, the corporation had the following transactions:

1. Issued common stock for $40,000 cash.
2. Purchased inventory on account; 200 units @ $38 then 150 units @ $39. Note: Beginning inventory was comprised of 500 units @ $35.
3. Purchased 200 shares of IBM for $45/share and purchased 100 shares of Microsoft for $90/share.
4. Sales at retail during 1997 were $75,000 (half received in cash, and the balance on account).
5. Write-offs of uncollectible accounts totaled $2,600.
6. Received $38,000 from receivable customers.
7. Paid creditors on account $18,000. Paid operating expenses for the current period of $51,000.

8. At year-end, a physical inventory equaled 225 units. The company uses the LIFO inventory costing method.
9. Assume marketable securities are "available-for-sale," and the market price at December 31, 1997, for IBM is $42/share, and for Microsoft $102/share.
10. Based on the accounts receivable aging, management feels that the allowance for uncollectible accounts should have a balance of $5,700 at year end.

REQUIRED

a. Set up the beginning balances in the balance sheet equation. Leave enough room to add new accounts.
b. Record transactions 1–10 using the balance sheet equation.
c. Calculate the following ratios for 1996 and 1997 and evaluate the company's management of its accounts receivable:

- Accounts receivable/sales
- Sales/day (assume sales in 1996 = $125,786)
- Collection period
- Allowance as a percentage of accounts receivable

6–44 Ratio Calculations: Comprehensive Problem Including LIFO and FIFO—Alternate Problems (A) or (B)

Problem (A)

Two similar companies use different inventory valuation methods. In fact, the companies are identical except for inventory method. L Co. uses the LIFO inventory valuation method, and F Co. uses FIFO.

Income Statements	L Co.	F Co.
Sales	$ 30,000	$30,000
Cost of goods sold	(21,280)	(19,200)
Gross profit	8,720	10,800
Selling, general and administrative	(6,000)	(6,000)
Income before interest expense	2,720	4,800
Interest expense (12%)	(960)	(960)
Income before taxes	$ 1,760	$ 3,840

Balance Sheets	L Co.	F Co.
Assets		
Cash	$ 4,000	$ 4,000
Accounts receivable	5,000	5,000
Inventory	2,720	4,800
Total current assets	11,720	13,800
Fixed assets (net)	30,000	30,000
Total assets	$41,720	$43,800
Equities		
Current liabilities	$ 3,200	$ 3,200
Long-term liabilities	8,000	8,000
Total liabilities	11,200	11,200
Shareholders' equity	30,520	32,600
Total equities	$41,720	$43,800

REQUIRED

Using the financial statements from L Co. and F Co., calculate the following ratios (assume an income tax rate of 20%):

a. Current ratio
b. Accounts receivable as a percentage of sales
c. Average sales per day
d. Collection period
e. Gross profit percentage
f. Cost of goods sold per day
g. Number of days sales in ending inventory
h. Operating income ratio
i. Return on equity (assume average shareholders' equity for L and F Co. are $30,000 and $32,000, respectively)
j. Return on assets (assume average total assets for L and F Co. are $41,000 and $43,000, respectively)

Based on these results (a–j, above), which company represents:

k. The best lending alternative? Why?
l. The best investment alternative? Why?
m. The best acquisition alternative? Why?

Problem (B)

Two similar companies use different inventory valuation methods. LL Co. uses the LIFO inventory valuation method, and FF Co. uses FIFO. Ignore the effect of income taxes on each company.

Income Statements	LL Co.	FF Co.
Sales	$35,000	$35,000
Cost of goods sold	(20,350)	(18,200)
Gross profit	14,650	16,800
Selling, general and administrative	(6,000)	(6,000)
Income before interest expense	8,650	10,800
Interest expense (12%)	(960)	(960)
Income before taxes	$ 7,690	$ 9,840

Balance Sheets	LL Co.	FF Co.
Assets		
Cash	$ 4,100	$ 5,000
Accounts receivable	4,500	4,000
Inventory	1,720	3,870
Total current assets	10,320	12,870
Fixed assets (net)	29,000	31,000
Total assets	$39,320	$43,870
Equities		
Current liabilities	$ 3,120	$ 3,270
Long-term liabilities	8,000	8,000
Total liabilities	11,120	11,270
Shareholders' equity	28,200	32,600
Total equities	$39,320	$43,870

REQUIRED

Using the financial statements from LL Co. and FF Co., calculate the following ratios:

a. Current ratio
b. Accounts receivable as a percentage of sales
c. Average sales per day
d. Collection period
e. Gross profit percentage
f. Cost of goods sold per day
g. Number of days sales in ending inventory
h. Operating income ratio
i. Return on equity (use ending shareholders' equity in the denominator)
j. Return on assets (use ending total assets in the denominator)

Based on these results (a–j, above), which company represents:

k. The best lending alternative? Why?
l. The best investment alternative? Why?
m. The best acquisition alternative? Why?

Accounts Receivable: Effects on Allowance for Uncollectibles

6–45 Becca's Finance and Collection Company has had a lot of trouble collecting its receivables recently. Discuss how each of the following circumstances might be reflected in the Allowance for Uncollectible Accounts:

1. Dagwood Bumpstead has an "open" account, that is always overdue. Dagwood makes regular payments of $500 each month, but the balance in his account is always about $4,000.
2. Blondie purchased a car using $4,000 borrowed from Becca's. Blondie has not made any payments for six months, and her overdue balance exceeds $1,200.
3. Sad Sack has just borrowed $4,000 from Becca's, has excellent credit references, and, after borrowing the money, has sent Becca's a change-of-address notification showing a new address in Brazil.
4. Blondie paid her overdue balance.
5. Dagwood's son purchased a car using $4,000 borrowed from Becca's. He has no credit references, other than the family connections and circumstances discussed earlier. Becca's is unable to get Dagwood to co-sign the note!
6. Blondie's daughter purchased a new sound system for her house and car using $4,000 borrowed from Becca's. She has an excellent credit history, but after purchasing the sound system, it failed; she informed Becca's that since the seller provided no warranty, she was not going to make any payments on the defective sound system.

Accounts Receivable: Effects on Allowance for Uncollectibles (continuation of Problem 6–45)

6–46 Becca's Finance and Collection Company has the following year-end balances in its financial statements.

	1997	1998
Accounts receivable	$300,000	$500,000
Allowance for uncollectibles	(50,000)	(50,000)
Interest and finance revenue	150,000	300,000

REQUIRED

a. Assess the adequacy of the 1998 balance in the allowance for uncollectibles.
b. Describe the interest and finance revenue account. What does this account include? On which financial statement does it appear?
c. Calculate the accounts receivable as a percentage of revenues for each year. Evaluate the trends in this ratio.
d. Refer to Problem 6–45. If all of these circumstances happened in the last month of 1998, assess the adequacy of the 1998 balance in the allowance for uncollectibles account.

Accounts Receivable: Effects on Allowance for Uncollectibles

6–47 David's Finance and Collection Company has the following year-end balances in its financial statements.

	1998	1999
Accounts receivable	$950,000	$500,000
Allowance for uncollectibles	(65,000)	(50,000)
Interest and finance revenue	355,000	300,000

REQUIRED

a. Assess the adequacy of the 1999 balance in the allowance for uncollectibles account.
b. Describe the interest and finance revenue account. What does this account include? On which financial statement does it appear?
c. Calculate the accounts receivable as a percentage of revenues for each year. Evaluate the trends in this ratio.
d. If you now find that David's has made numerous high-risk loans at the end of 1999, assess the adequacy of the 1999 balance in the allowance for uncollectibles account.

Transaction Analysis: Accounts Receivable

6–48 S. Claus Company ended the 1997 season with an accounts receivable balance of $375,000, less allowance for uncollectible accounts of $37,500. Use the accounting equation to reflect each of the following situations, and calculate the 1998 season's end balance in accounts receivable and the allowance account.

a. Revenues in 1998 were $4,500,000, half of which were collected in cash, with the balance on account.
2. Cash collections of accounts receivable in 1998 were $2,375,000.
3. Write-offs of delinquent accounts in 1998 were $2,000. (Most people are not willing to offend S. Claus!)

4. S. Claus wants its allowance account, at the end of 1998, to have the same proportionate relationship reflected at the end of 1997.

Transaction Analysis: Accounts Receivable

6–49 Elfin Company ended the 1997 season with an accounts receivable balance of $288,000, less allowance for uncollectible accounts of $23,040. Use the accounting equation to reflect each of the following situations, and calculate the 1998 season's end balance in accounts receivable and the allowance account.

1. Revenues in 1998 were $8,400,000, half of which were collected in cash, with the balance on account.
2. Cash collections of accounts receivable in 1998 were $4,067,000.
3. Write-offs of delinquent accounts in 1998 were $9,500. (Most people are not willing to offend S. Claus's helpers!)
4. Elfin wants its allowance account, at the end of 1998, to have the same proportionate relationship reflected at the end of 1997.

Analyzing Accounts Receivable

6–50 The Atlas Tile Company has an accounts receivable balance, at December 31, of $376,000. Its allowance for uncollectible accounts, before adjustment, has a balance of $37,000. Credit sales for Atlas, for the year just ended, were $2,700,000. Using its credit history, Atlas decides to increase its allowance account by 3% of credit sales.

REQUIRED

a. Calculate the allowance for uncollectible accounts as a percentage of the accounts receivable ratio, both before and after the 3% adjustment was made.
b. Now, assume that the firm's auditors have conducted an aging analysis and recommend that the allowance account balance be increased to $96,000. Recalculate the allowance for uncollectible accounts as a percentage of accounts receivable ratio, after this alternative adjustment has been made.
c. Compare and contrast these results.

6–51 Transaction Analysis: Accounts Payable—Alternate Problems (A) or (B)

Problem (A)

S. Claus Company ended the 1996 season with an inventory balance of $667,000, and an accounts payable balance of $438,500. Use the accounting equation to reflect each of the following situations, and calculate the 1997 season's ending inventory and accounts payable balances.

1. S. Claus purchased merchandise totaling $1,875,000, on account, in 1997.
2. Cash payments on accounts payable in 1997 were $2,123,000.
3. All of S. Claus's payables are current, i.e., less than 30 days old. (Santa does not offend most people!)
4. S. Claus did have problems with one supplier, which resulted in a return of merchandise of $100,000 and a reduction in the balance due at the end of 1997.

5. Cost of goods delivered (Santa doesn't "sell" anything) in 1997 was $2,326,000.

Problem (B)

Elfin Company ended the 1997 season with an inventory balance of $888,000, and an accounts payable balance of $444,400. Use the accounting equation to reflect each of the following situations, and calculate the 1998 season's ending inventory and accounts payable balances.

1. Elfin purchased merchandise totaling $4,526,000, on account, in 1998.
2. Cash payments on accounts payable in 1998 were $4,442,000.
3. All of Elfin's payables are current, i.e., less than 30 days old. (Elves do not offend most people!)
4. Elfin did have problems with one supplier, which resulted in a return of merchandise of $250,000 and a reduction in the balance due at the end of 1998.
5. Cost of goods delivered (Elves don't "sell" anything) in 1998 was $4,242,000.

6–52 Calculating Ending Inventory: FIFO, LIFO, and Average-Cost Method—Alternate Problems (A) or (B)

Problem (A)

S. Claus Company makes toys and gifts. At the beginning of July, it owned 200 gallons of red paint, which were recorded on the balance sheet at $4.00 per gallon. The following events occurred in the next quarter.

1. Purchased 300 gallons on July 1 at $4.25 each.
2. Purchased 500 gallons on August 1 at $4.50 each.
3. Purchased 800 gallons during September at $4.75 each.
4. Used 1,430 gallons during July through September.

REQUIRED

a. Calculate the inventory balance at the end of September and the cost of goods used (not sold) during these three months using FIFO accounting.
b. Calculate the inventory balance at the end of September and the cost of goods used (not sold) during these three months using LIFO accounting.
c. Calculate the inventory balance at the end of September and the cost of goods used (not sold) during these three months using the average cost method to determine inventory balances.
d. Explain and discuss the differences shown under each method. Explain why the total costs of goods available for delivery (not for sale) must be identical under all methods.
e. Under what circumstances would S. Claus prefer one method to the others? Under what circumstances would S. Claus prefer one result to the others? Discuss how S. Claus might make a choice between inventory costing methods.

Problem (B)

Elfin Company makes toys and gifts. At the beginning of July, it owned 350 gallons of green paint, which were recorded on the balance sheet at $5.00 per gallon. The following events occurred in the next quarter:

1. Purchased 400 gallons on July 1 at $5.30 each.
2. Purchased 600 gallons on August 1 at $5.70 each.
3. Purchased 900 gallons during September at $4.75 each.
4. Used 1,750 gallons during July through September.

REQUIRED

a. Calculate the inventory balance at the end of September and the cost of goods used (not sold) during these three months using FIFO accounting.
b. Calculate the inventory balance at the end of September and the cost of goods used (not sold) during these three months using LIFO accounting.
c. Calculate the inventory balance at the end of September and the cost of goods used (not sold) during these three months using the average cost method to determine inventory balances.
d. Explain and discuss the differences shown under each method. Explain why the total costs of goods available for delivery (not for sale!) must be identical under all methods.
e. Under what circumstances would Elfin prefer one method to the others? Under what circumstances would Elfin prefer one result to the others? Discuss how Elfin might make a choice between inventory costing methods.

Interpreting Financial Statements: LIFO Versus FIFO

6–53 Elfin Company and S. Claus company perform similar functions; they had identical balance sheets at the beginning of 1998, and each made exactly the same purchases and sales during 1998. Elfin's net income was twice as high, and its inventory balance was twice as much, compared to the results shown by S. Claus Company. Assume there was an upward inflationary trend and one company used FIFO, the other, LIFO.

REQUIRED

a. Identify which inventory method was used by each company.
b. Discuss the advantages and disadvantages of having such latitude in choosing how to value your inventory and cost of goods sold, when such wide differences could occur in otherwise similar companies.
c. If you now find that one company used the average-cost method, how would that change the relative differences between net income and inventory balances?

CASES AND EXTENSIONS

Conceptual Discussion: Discounts

6–54 What are the differences among a sales discount, a wholesale ("trade") discount, and a quantity discount? From the customer's perspective, which of these differences are most important? **Note:** You may need to consult a business dictionary if you do not understand the two terms trade discount and quantity discount.

Conceptual Discussion: Marketable Securities

6–55 Marketable securities are usually shown on the balance sheet as current assets. Based on what you have learned, under what circumstances might they be shown as noncurrent assets? Why do you think a firm might hold its investments in marketable securities for more than a year?

Conceptual Discussion: Credit Management

6–56 The manager of Rob's Shoe Store has been congratulated by her division manager for almost completely eliminating all bad debts. She now conducts extensive credit checks on all prospective credit customers and rejects most applications. The cost of each credit report is $50 and the store's profits have declined significantly since she adopted this policy. Identify the circumstances under which this might be an acceptable policy. Under what circumstances might this be an unwise, or unacceptable, policy?

Conceptual Discussion: Credit Management (continuation of Case 6–56)

6–57 The manager of Rob's Shoe Store is considering conducting her own credit checks and preparing her own credit reports in order to avoid the $50 cost of credit reports on each prospective credit customer. Why might this not be a cost-effective practice?

Conceptual Discussion: Inventory Management (continuation of Cases 6–56 and 6–57)

6–58 Why would the manager of Rob's Shoe Store want to have large inventories on hand? Why would her division manager want to curtail these desires? Could a firm ever have too much inventory? If so, what undesirable consequences might occur?

Financial Statement Effects: Prepaid Insurance

6–59 Firefly Beach Cottages, Inc., purchased a three-year fire insurance policy for $4,800. The policy was purchased on July 1, 1996, and financial statements are prepared as of December 31 each year.

REQUIRED

a. Show the effects of this insurance policy on the balance sheets for each of the following years during which this policy would have an effect.
b. Similarly, calculate the effects on the income statement in each year.

Accounts Receivable Management

6–60 Sheila Glow sells advertising for KBOL, a local radio station. She receives a small monthly salary plus a commission of 20% of all advertising contracts that she negotiates and that are billed by KBOL. KBOL conducts an informal credit review on all new clients, but relies extensively on the salesperson's recommendations.

Since Sheila interviews the owner and chief financial officer (CFO) of all her new clients, she feels that her credit screening should be an adequate basis on which KBOL could reliably determine whether to accept or reject a potential client's credit request.

One potential new client, Atlas Tile Company, has been experiencing financial difficulties and several letters to the editors from disgruntled customers have recently appeared in the local newspaper. While Sheila knows

WHAT WOULD YOU DO?

that Atlas needs many new customers, her commissions have not been strong this month compared to prior months.

KBOL always has the right to reject Atlas's credit application. Sheila knows that if the credit application contains favorable information, it is likely to be accepted. In the process of helping Atlas' CFO complete the application, she suggests that City Bank's rejection of Atlas' loan application for $5,000 worth of working capital not be shown on the current application for KBOL's credit. She reasons that Atlas needs her help, and it is not her job to collect the bills; it is only her job to sell radio advertising.

REQUIRED

a. What are the ethical ramifications of Sheila's actions?
b. What are the likely business results of Sheila's actions?
c. How does KBOL's commission policy affect Sheila's incentives?
d. How might the commission policy be changed to more closely align Sheila's incentives with KBOL's goals?
e. If the radio station's managers find that Sheila helped falsify the credit report, what should they do? Why?

Interpreting Financial Statements: Current Assets

6–61 Refer to Bristol-Myers Squibb (BMS) financial statements in Appendix E. Review the balance sheet to determine how and where current assets were reported.

REQUIRED

a. Read Notes 1 and 8. Trace any numerical disclosures of current assets in the notes to corresponding disclosures in the financial statements.
b. Determine whether BMS has any unusual current assets. If so, discuss how they might be interpreted by financial analysts. Discuss how BMS's managers might view such assets.
c. Why do you suppose BMS reports cash equivalents separate from time deposits and marketable securities?
d. What method does BMS use to value its ending inventory? Compare their use of this method versus the methods used by Reebok (Appendix F) and OshKosh (Appendix C).

Interpreting Financial Statements: Current Assets

6–62 Refer to the Bristol-Myers Squibb (BMS) financial statements in Appendix E. Review the financial statements to determine how and where current assets have been reported.

REQUIRED

a. Can you determine which method BMS uses to calculate its allowance for uncollectible accounts? Is it essential for a financial analyst to know which method has been used? What reliance can an analyst place on the firm's disclosure of its allowances?
b. If the allowance amounts were not separately disclosed, discuss how they have been included in the firm's balance sheet.

c. Calculate the following accounts receivable ratios:

- Accounts receivable as a percentage of sales
- Average sales per day
- Collection period
- Allowance for uncollectible accounts as a percentage of accounts receivable

d. Based on these results, what conclusions can be drawn regarding BMS's accounts receivable?

e. Calculate the following inventory ratios:

- Gross profit percentage
- Cost of goods sold per day
- Number of days sales in ending inventory (NDS)

f. Based on these results, what conclusions can be drawn regarding BMS's inventories and cost of goods sold?

g. Discuss any other unusual concerns regarding BMS's current assets. What other related information might an external analyst require, or prefer?

Interpreting Financial Statements: Current Assets

6–63 Refer to Reebok's financial statements in Appendix F. Review the balance sheet to determine how and where current assets were reported.

REQUIRED

a. Read Note 1. Why does Reebok report cash and cash equivalents?

b. What is the gross amount of accounts receivable at the end of 1994 and 1993? Why do you suppose the allowance for doubtful accounts has decreased?

c. Discuss how "inventory" may differ from "prepaid expenses." In your opinion, should they be disclosed separately? Why?

d. Discuss any other unusual concerns regarding Reebok's current assets. What other related information might an external analyst require, or prefer?

Interpreting Financial Statements: Current Assets

6–64 Refer to Reebok's financial statements in Appendix F. Review the financial statements to determine how and where current assets have been reported.

REQUIRED

a. Calculate the following accounts receivable ratios:

- Accounts receivable as a percentage of sales
- Average sales per day
- Collection period
- Allowance for uncollectible accounts as a percentage of accounts receivable

b. Based on these results, what conclusions can be drawn regarding Reebok's accounts receivable?

c. Calculate the following inventory ratios:

- Gross profit percentage
- Cost of goods sold per day
- Number of days sales in ending inventory (NDS)

d. Based on these results, what conclusions can be drawn regarding Reebok's inventories and cost of goods sold?

e. Discuss any other unusual concerns regarding Reebok's current assets. What other related information might an external analyst require, or prefer?

Interpreting Financial Statements: Current Assets

6–65 Refer to OshKosh B'Gosh's financial statements in Appendix C. Review the balance sheet to determine how and where current assets were reported.

REQUIRED

a. Read Notes 1 and 3. Identify and discuss any unusual terms. Trace any numerical disclosures of current assets in the notes to corresponding disclosures in the financial statements.

b. Discuss how "prepaid expenses" may differ from "other current assets." In your opinion, should they be disclosed together? Why?

c. Discuss any other unusual concerns regarding OshKosh B'Gosh's current assets. What other related information might an external analyst require, or prefer?

Interpreting Financial Statements: Current Assets

6–66 Refer to OshKosh B'Gosh's financial statements in Appendix C. Review the financial statements to determine how and where current assets have been reported.

REQUIRED

a. What are the gross amounts of accounts receivable at December 31, 1994 and 1993? Why do you suppose the allowance increased, and the allowance balance is so small?

b. Calculate the following accounts receivable ratios:

- Accounts receivable as a percentage of sales
- Average sales per day
- Collection period
- Allowance for uncollectible accounts as a percentage of accounts receivable

c. Based on these results, what conclusions can be drawn regarding OshKosh B'Gosh's accounts receivable?

d. Calculate the following inventory ratios:

- Gross profit percentage
- Cost of goods sold per day
- Number of days sales in ending inventory (NDS)

e. Based on these results, what conclusions can be drawn regarding OshKosh B'Gosh's inventories and cost of goods sold?

f. Discuss any other unusual concerns regarding OshKosh B'Gosh's current assets. What other related information might an external analyst require, or prefer?

Interpreting Financial Statements: Current Assets

6–67 Refer to Wendy's financial statements in Appendix D. Review the balance sheet to determine how and where current assets were reported.

REQUIRED

a. Read Notes 1 and 8. Identify and discuss any unusual terms.
b. Why does Wendy's separate cash equivalents from short-term investments? Why are these reported at market value?
c. Discuss how "inventories" may differ from "other current assets." In your opinion, should they be disclosed separately? Does the distinction seem to be significant? Why?
d. Discuss any other unusual concerns regarding Wendy's current assets. As part of your discussion calculate their liquidity ratios.

Interpreting Financial Statements: Current Assets

6–68 Refer to Wendy's financial statements in Appendix D. Review the financial statements to determine how and where current assets have been reported.

REQUIRED

a. Did Wendy's disclose how it calculated the allowance for uncollectible accounts? Is it essential for a financial analyst to know which method has been used? What reliance can an analyst place on the firm's disclosure of its allowances?
b. If the allowance amounts were not separately disclosed, discuss how they have been included in the firm's balance sheet.
c. Calculate the following accounts receivable ratios (assume the doubtful account amounts pertaining to royalties are netted in the accounts receivable):

  • Accounts receivable as a percentage of sales
  • Average sales per day
  • Collection period (*Note:* Wendy's uses a 52/53 week year.)
  • Allowance for uncollectible accounts as a percentage of accounts receivable

d. Based on these results, what conclusions can be drawn regarding Wendy's accounts receivable?
e. Calculate the following inventory ratios:

  • Gross profit percentage
  • Cost of goods sold per day
  • Number of days sales in ending inventory (NDS) (use the caption "inventory and other" line item for inventory)

f. Based on these results, what conclusions can be drawn regarding Wendy's inventories and cost of goods sold?
g. Discuss any other unusual concerns regarding Wendy's current assets. What other related information might an external analyst require, or prefer?

Interpreting Financial Statements: Liquidity

6–69 Kesler Inc. is a research-based, health care company whose objectives include the application of scientific knowledge to help people enjoy longer, healthier, and more productive lives. Its balance sheets for 1997 and 1996 show the following amounts ($ in millions):

	1997	1996
Cash and cash equivalents	$1,295.0	$1,384.7
Short-term investments	502.4	307.6

In the Summary of Significant Accounting Policies in its Notes to Consolidated Financial Statements, Kesler reported:

> The Company considers demand deposits, certificates of deposit and certain time deposits with maturities of three months or less at the date of purchase to be cash equivalents. Certain items which meet the definition of cash equivalents but are part of a larger pool of investments are included in Short-term investments.

REQUIRED

a. Describe, in your own words, what Kesler may have done with some of its cash equivalents between 1996 and 1997.
b. Is Kesler's reporting of cash and cash equivalents consistent with your understanding of the balance sheet category "Cash and cash equivalents"? Why?
c. How would you feel about Kesler's treatment if you later found out that the *second* category of cash equivalents, described by Kesler as "Certain items . . . included in Short-term investments" was only about $2.5 (million) each year? What if it were more than $200 (million) each year?
d. How would you evaluate Kesler's treatment of cash and cash equivalents if the following amounts had been reported?:

	1997	1996
Cash and cash equivalents	$880	$ 165
Short-term investments, *at cost*	$445	$1,257

e. Based on this hypothetical situation, what actions did Kesler probably take in 1997 to improve its cash position?
f. Given Kesler's inclusion of some cash and cash equivalents on *two separate lines* of its balance sheet, how should an external analyst use this data in analyzing Kesler's liquidity? In other words, what should an analyst do to comprehensively interpret Kesler's liquidity?

Interpreting Financial Statements: Inventory Methods

6–70 Pioneer Resource, Inc., reported the following in its Notes to Consolidated Financial Statements for 1997.

> *Material and Supplies:* Inventories of new and reusable material and supplies are stated at the lower of cost or market with cost determined on a first-in, first-out or average cost basis. For certain large individual items, however, cost is determined on a specific identification basis.

REQUIRED

a. List and explain in your own words, all of the inventory costing methods used by Pioneer Resource.
b. Why do you suppose that Pioneer Resource is using all of these different methods? Does this seem to enhance the internal consistency and usability of Pioneer Resource's financial data? Why?
c. If inventories comprised only 1% of Pioneer Resource's assets, how would that change your opinion of these different inventory costing methods? What if inventories were 15% of Pioneer Resource's assets?

d. If the inventory balances reported by Pioneer Resource in 1997 and 1996 were $212.3 and $212.2 million, respectively, how would that change your view of Pioneer Resource's choice of reporting methods? Note that Pioneer Resource's 1997 total assets exceeded $22.4 billion. If in subsequent years you found that Pioneer Resource's inventories had increased by 300%, how would that change your views of these diverse inventory costing methods?

Interpreting Financial Statements: Current Assets

6–71 Entertainment Office Group is a leading producer of film (and video) entertainment. Its 1997 and 1996 consolidated balance sheets reported the following assets ($ in thousands):

	1997	1996
Cash and short-term investments	$ 37,015	$ 38,402
Accounts receivable, net	66,241	32,659
Film costs and program rights, net	180,501	130,204
Property, plant, and equipment, net	5,231	7,124
Other assets	—	14,050
Current liabilities	120,507	156,419

REQUIRED

a. Evaluate Entertainment's liquidity, on the basis of the above information.
b. If you were told that Entertainment's revenues had doubled between 1996 and 1997, how would you view the change in accounts receivable? Why? If Entertainment's revenues were constant, how would that affect your conclusions about accounts receivable?
c. What does the term "net" mean in each of the cases shown above?
d. Why do you suppose there are no "Other assets" in 1997?
e. What do you suppose is meant by the term "Film costs and program rights"? Could this be viewed as a type of inventory? If these were stocks of films and scripts, how would the fickle nature of public opinion and personal tastes affect your views of Entertainment's assets? Why?

Interpreting Financial Statements: Specialized Current Assets (continuation of Case 6–71)

6–72 With reference to Case 6–71, Entertainment's Notes to Consolidated Financial Statements contained the following item:

Program Rights

Advance payments to producers are recorded as program rights in the balance sheet and are stated at the lower of cost or estimated net realizable value.

REQUIRED

a. How does this knowledge of how program rights are created change your view of Entertainment's assets? Can its program rights still be viewed as inventory? Why?
b. If these advance payments will not be refunded by the producers, under any circumstances, how does that change your opinion concerning the program rights?

c. Does the fickle nature of public opinion and personal taste affect your view of these assets? Why?

d. What other information about the producers, the films, and the scripts would you need to have before coming to a final conclusion about the program rights?

e. Does the relative proportion of the program rights cause any concern about Entertainment's asset management? Why? Note that Entertainment's total assets were between $450 million and $475 million, each year.

f. If the program rights were less than $10,000,000 each year, would that change your conclusions about Entertainment's assets?

Interpreting Financial Statements: Specialized Current Assets (continuation of Cases 6–71 and 6–72)

6–73 With reference to Cases 6–71 and 6–72, suppose that you later find another note in Entertainment's annual report as follows:

Film Costs and Program Rights:
Film costs and program rights, net of amortization, comprised the following at December 31 ($ in thousands):

	1997	1996
Film costs:		
Released	$ 68,304	$ 60,028
In process and other	8,863	13,723
Program rights	103,334	56,453
	$180,501	$130,204

It is estimated that approximately one-half of the film cost associated with released product will be amortized in the next three years.

In October 1997, Entertainment purchased from Oroco Television, Inc. domestic television rights to Oroco's film library of more than 142 feature films and related receivables for approximately $45 million plus the assumption of approximately $10 million in liabilities.

REQUIRED

a. How does this new information about program rights affect your conclusions in Case 6–72? Does the fact that a substantial portion of these amounts relates to released films affect your conclusions? How?

b. Explain, in your own words, what happened in October 1997.

c. Where is the Oroco purchase recorded in Entertainment's assets?

d. Given this new knowledge about the Oroco purchase, what final conclusions can be drawn about Entertainment's film costs and program rights?

Conceptual Discussion: Factoring Accounts Receivable

6–74 Describe the concept of factoring accounts receivable. If necessary, conduct further research in a finance text to determine what functions a factor performs. Consider the following factoring issues:

a. Why would a company sell its receivables to a factor?

b. If these receivables were 180 days old, why do you think that a factor might not be interested in purchasing them?

c. Who do you think bears the risk in factoring? How can these risks be shifted?

d. What industries do you think might be more involved in factoring?

e. Why wouldn't a convenience store or a discount store be able to factor its accounts receivable, even if it had such receivables?

USING FINANCIAL ACCOUNTING ON THE INTERNET

6–75 Owens-Corning values its inventories using LIFO. This presents a problem when comparing its current ratio against that of a company using FIFO. Locate the latest financial statements for Owens-Corning at the company page (**www.owens-corning.com/**) or from the 10-K filed in the EDGAR archives (**www.sec.gov/edgarhp.htm**).

REQUIRED

a. Compute the current ratio and the number of days sales (NDS) in ending inventory based on numbers reported on the balance sheet.

b. Find the FIFO value of inventory reported in the Notes to the Financial Statements and recompute the current ratio and NDS.

c. Compare the ratios based on LIFO to those based on FIFO. How different are they? Do you think that the observed differences are great enough to have an impact on a decision?

6–76 Locate the latest available set of financial statements for Oncogene Science, Inc., from the 10-K on file in the EDGAR archives (**www.sec.gov/edgarhp.htm**).

REQUIRED

a. In what types of short-term securities does Oncogene invest? (The information needed to answer this question can be found in the Notes to the Financial Statements.)

b. According to STAS No. 115, what alternatives are available to Oncogene for reporting its investments in short-term securities?

c. Does Oncogene classify its short-term investments as trading securities, available-for-sale securities, or held-to-maturity securities?

d. Describe how Oncogene's investments are reflected on the income statement, balance sheet, statement of shareholders' equity, and statement of cash flows.

6–77 The Center for Inventory Management (CIM) publishes quarterly inventory ratios for manufacturing industry groups.

REQUIRED

a. How does CIM (**www.mindspring.com/~cim/cimhpirs.htm**) compute its inventory ratio? What shortcomings are implicit in its calculations?

b. How would you convert CIM's inventory ratio to the number of days sales in ending inventory described by this textbook?

c. Access the latest Inventory Ratio Study reported on the CIM home page (**www.mindspring.com/~cim/**) and identify the inventory ratios for two types of transportation equipment industries: motor vehicles and aircraft. Why are the ratios so different?

6–78 For HMOs, accounts receivable represent one of the major assets. HMOs provide medical services to patients and then bill insurance companies and Medicare/Medicaid agencies. Timely collection is important to maintaining adequate liquidity. Locate the latest 10-K filings for Columbia/HCA Healthcare and FHP International using the EDGAR archives (**www.sec.gov/ edgarhp.htm**).

REQUIRED

a. What is the value of net accounts receivable? What percent of total assets and current assets do they represent for each company?
b. What is the value of allowance for uncollectible accounts and what percentage of gross accounts receivable does it represent?
c. What are the net revenues for each HMO? Which HMO is larger?
d. Calculate the accounts receivable collection period for both companies.
e. Which company is doing a better job with its accounts receivable?

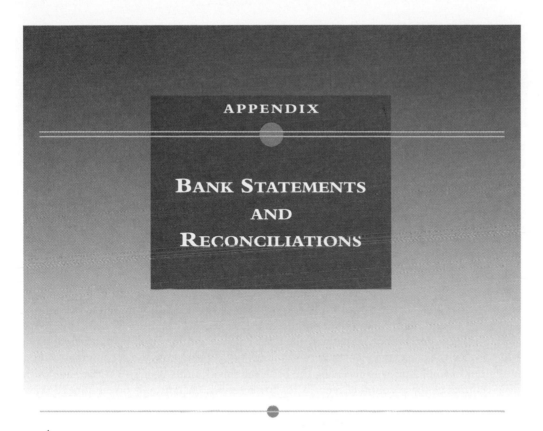

APPENDIX

BANK STATEMENTS AND RECONCILIATIONS

An earlier part of the chapter noted that bank statements provide an accounting of cash that is independent of the accounting undertaken by the firm. Exhibit 6A–1 contains an illustration of Quick Company's bank statement for the month of April. It contains three columns. One column shows withdrawals, one column reflects deposits, and the final column keeps a running total of the account's balance. This particular bank statement contains check numbers, which makes comparing the bank statement and the accounting records much easier. Notice that two withdrawals were not made by check. One withdrawal was preauthorized. This means that Quick has previously instructed the bank to make certain payments. A monthly loan payment is a good example. The other direct withdrawal was the service charge assessed by the bank for processing checks, making preauthorized payments, and so on.

As of any given date (e.g., April 30), the cash balance reported on the bank statement might not agree with the balance in the firm's accounting records (often called the book balance). This situation can arise for three general reasons. First, some transactions may be reflected in the accounting records, but not on the bank statement. For example, after a check is written and mailed to the payee, several days (or weeks) may elapse before the payee cashes the check and the check clears through the banking system. Until this happens, the bank is unaware of the check. Checks that are included in the accounting records, but not shown on the bank statement, are called **outstanding checks.**

A **deposit-in-transit** is another reconciling item that is recorded in the accounting records, but not yet recorded on the bank statement. Most banks delay, by one business day, processing deposits made after a certain time of day (say, 3 P.M.). These cash receipts are, however, already recorded in the firm's accounting records. Therefore,

EXHIBIT 6A–1
BANK STATEMENT

	Quick Company Bank Statement April 1998			
Date	Description	Withdrawals	Deposits	Balance
4–1	Balance			$7,780
4–6	Check # 210	$ 180		7,600
4–10	Check # 212	500		7,100
4–13	Check # 213	1,000		6,100
4–15	Deposit		$2,300	8,400
4–21	Check # 215	200		8,200
4–25	Check # 216	400		7,800
4–30	Preauthorized	140		7,660
4–30	Service charge	10		7,650

deposits made after 3 P.M. on the last business day of a month will be included in the month-end book balance, but not the bank balance.

The second major reason why the bank balance and the book balance might differ is that the bank statement may reflect items not yet shown in the accounting records. For example, prior to receiving the bank statement, firms usually will not have made entries in the accounting records for bank service charges and preauthorized withdrawals.

Errors, either in the accounting records or on the bank statement, are the third reason why the bank balance and the book balance might differ. If errors are unintentional and occur infrequently, they are not a cause for alarm; they simply need to be corrected. However, frequent or intentional errors involving cash warrant careful investigation.

EXHIBIT 6A–2
ACCOUNTING RECORDS
FOR CASH

	Quick Company Internal Cash Records	
Date	Description	Amount
4–1	Balance	$7,780
4–2	Check # 210	− 180
4–3	Check # 211	− 750
4–5	Check # 212	− 500
4–8	Check # 213	− 1,000
4–12	Check # 214	− 300
4–14	Deposit	2,300
4–17	Check # 215	− 200
4–22	Check # 216	− 400
4–26	Check # 217	− 50
4–28	Check # 218	− 250
4–30	Deposit	1,000
4–30	Balance	$7,450

Quick Company
Bank Reconciliation
April 30, 1998

Bank Balance		$7,650
Plus: Deposit-in-transit		1,000
		$8,650
Less: Outstanding checks		
# 211	$750	
# 214	300	
# 217	50	
# 218	250	
		(1,350)
Corrected balance		$7,300
Book balance		$7,450
Less: Preauthorized withdrawal		(140)
Service charge		(10)
Corrected balance		$7,300

Exhibit 6A–2 contains Quick Company's April accounting records for cash, and Exhibit 6A–3 illustrates Quick's April 30 bank reconciliation. Several valid approaches exist for preparing a bank reconciliation. The approach in Exhibit 6A–3 modifies both the bank and the book balances to obtain a corrected balance. The goal of the reconciliation is for the two corrected balances to agree. If this is accomplished, all the differences between the two sets of records have been identified, and the firm can have increased confidence that the accounting for cash is proper.

To prepare a reconciliation, compare the bank statement and the accounting records to identify those items appearing on one but not the other. These items result in differences between the book and the bank balances and must be included in the reconciliation.

Exhibit 6A–2 shows that Quick received $1,000 on April 30. That amount does not appear on the bank statement. Evidently, it was deposited after the close of business on April 30. This deposit-in-transit must be added to the bank balance.

Exhibit 6A–2 also shows that Quick wrote nine checks during April. However, checks 211, 214, 217, and 218 do not appear on the bank statement. Accordingly, these outstanding checks are subtracted from the bank balance.

Quick's bank statement (Exhibit 6A–1) contains two entries that do not appear in the accounting records: the preauthorized withdrawal and the service charge. The book balance should be reduced by these amounts. Also note that when Quick receives the bank statement and discovers the preauthorized withdrawal and the service charge, the accounting records should be adjusted, accordingly.

At this point in the reconciliation, the book balance and the bank balance have been adjusted and show the same corrected balance. This indicates that the reconciliation is complete.

One final point must be made about the Quick Company illustration. All of the reconciling items for the April 30 reconciliation arose during the month of April. This is not always the case. For example, Quick could have written a check in March that did not clear the bank by the end of April. This check would be outstanding at the end of April and would need to appear on the April 30 reconciliation. In general, items from the immediately preceding reconciliation should be reviewed to ascertain if they should be carried forward to the current month's reconciliation.

SUMMARY OF LEARNING OBJECTIVES

1. Prepare a bank reconciliation.

A bank reconciliation explains why a firm's bank statement balance differs from its book balance. Differences arise for three general reasons: (1) transactions were recorded in the accounting records but not the bank statement; (2) transactions were recorded on the bank statement but not the accounting records; and (3) errors.

KEY TERMS

Deposit-in-transit
Outstanding checks

PROBLEM

Bank Statement Reconciliation

6A–1 Theraux Corporation received its bank statement for the month ended October 31, 1997. Contained in the bank statement were the following items:

	Check #	$ Amount
Checks cleared:	1140	$100
	1156	400
	1159	250
	1161	500
	1162	183
	1163	175
	1165	194

	Date	$ Amount
Deposits cleared:	10/3/97	$1,250
	10/5/97	480
	10/16/97	1,595
	10/25/97	942
	10/28/97	2,106

Other Items:

(NSF) from J. Strauss	$ 275
Bank charges	80
Note receivable collected	640
Interest on note receivable	15
Beginning bank balance	$ 5,300
Ending bank balance	10,171

Theraux's check register showed the following during October:

	Check #	$ Amount
Checks written:	1140	$100
	1155	65
	1156	400
	1157	320
	1158	82
	1159	520
	1160	125
	1161	500
	1162	183
	1163	175
	1164	104
	1165	194
	1166	220

	Date	$ Amount
Deposits:	10/3	1,250
	10/5	480
	10/12	1,190
	10/16	1,595
	10/20	1,800
	10/25	942
	10/28	2,106
	10/31	745

Other Items:

- Outstanding check from September's bank reconciliation: #1142 for $195.
- Beginning checking balance: $5,105
- Ending checking balance: $12,225

REQUIRED

a. Prepare a bank reconciliation for October, 1997. (Be aware of transposition errors.)

b. What adjustment to the accounting equation is necessary for October?

Studying this chapter
will enable you to

1. Identify three major types of noncurrent assets: (1) property, plant, and equipment, (2) intangible assets, and (3) natural resources.

2. Explain how to account for the acquisition of these assets.

3. Describe the procedures for depreciation, amortization, and depletion.

4. List the factors affecting managers' selection of depreciation methods.

5. Determine which postacquisition expenditures should be expensed and which should be capitalized.

6. Explain the accounting issues associated with asset write-downs and disposals.

7. Interpret financial statement disclosures about noncurrent assets.

NONCURRENT ASSETS

INTRODUCTION

Chapter 6 dealt with current assets. Recall that current assets will be converted into cash or used in operations within a year or the firm's operating cycle, whichever is longer. **Noncurrent assets** are not expected to be fully utilized within that period. They are long-lived assets.

This chapter examines three noncurrent assets: 1) property, plant and equipment, 2) intangible assets and 3) natural resources.

PROPERTY, PLANT, AND EQUIPMENT

Property, plant and equipment (PPE) are tangible, long-lived assets used by a firm. Tangible assets derive value from their physical substance. These assets include land, land improvements (such as parking lots and roads), office buildings, office equipment, manufacturing facilities (factories), and factory equipment. These assets are sometimes referred to as **fixed assets.**

Initial Valuation

Property, plant, and equipment are initially valued at their historical cost. This includes all costs incurred to acquire the asset, place it in its desired location, and make it operational. Costs include invoice amounts (less any discounts), sales taxes, transportation charges, installation costs, costs of trial runs to adjust equipment, and costs to refurbish equipment purchased in a used condition.

As an example, assume a machine was purchased at an invoice price of $5,000. Sales tax was 7% and transportation charges were $145. The machine required a concrete base, which cost $80 for materials and $120 for labor. The machine's total cost is calculated as follows:

Invoice cost		$5,000
Sales tax ($5,000 × .07)		350
Transportation		145
Concrete base ($80 + $120)		200
Total cost		$5,695

To record the purchase, increase the asset machine and decrease the asset cash.

ASSETS		=	LIABILITIES	+	SHAREHOLDERS' EQUITY
Cash	Machine				
−$5,695	+$5,695				

Initially valuing property, plant, and equipment at historical cost is quite reasonable. Since a firm's managers have paid this amount, they certainly expect at least this level of benefits. Otherwise, the assets would not have been acquired. Moreover, historical cost is an objective valuation basis; it can easily be verified by examining invoices and canceled checks.

Sometimes, however, the proper accounting for asset acquisition and development is not obvious. Consider Chambers Development, Inc., which develops landfill sites for waste disposal. In developing its sites, Chambers incurs public relations and legal costs, as well as costs to pay its executives who work on various projects. Conceptually, two accounting alternatives are possible for these costs. One option is to expense them immediately. The analysis involves a decrease in cash and a decrease in shareholders' equity via an expense.

ASSETS	=	LIABILITIES	+	SHAREHOLDERS' EQUITY
Cash				Retained earnings
−$xxx				−$xxx (various expenses)

Since net income and shareholders' equity are reduced, this approach is quite conservative.

The second option views these expenditures as part of the cost of the asset landfill sites. Accordingly, these costs are **capitalized;** that is, the asset *landfill sites* is increased as these costs are incurred. The analysis decreases cash and increases landfill sites.

ASSETS		=	LIABILITIES	+	SHAREHOLDERS' EQUITY
Cash	Landfill sites				
−$xxx	+$xxx				

This is a much less conservative, perhaps even an aggressive, approach.

GAAP requires that costs be capitalized only when they reflect future economic benefits. Thus, the question involves how closely tied these expenditures are to future economic benefits. Prior to 1991, Chambers capitalized these costs. Beginning in that year, however, Chambers expensed those costs and restated prior years' financial statements to reflect the more conservative accounting alternative.

Accounting issues can have serious consequences. Chambers' accounting practices were the subject of an SEC probe and a criminal investigation by the U.S. Attorney General's Office.

WHAT WOULD YOU DO?

As chief accountant for the Craig Manufacturing Company (CMC), you oversee all accounting functions. Both you and Mr. Craig are very concerned about this year's financial statements. CMC will probably violate its loan covenant dealing with the debt to assets ratio. CMC's loan agreement specifies that CMC must maintain a ratio of .4 or lower. Failure to do so will result in a renegotiation of the loan's terms. Interest rates have risen since the loan was obtained, and there is every reason to believe that the bank would require a higher interest rate. This additional cash drain could force CMC to lay off up to 100 workers.

CMC, like most corporations, has an accounting policy regarding the capitalization of fixed assets. All fixed assets costing $100 or more are capitalized and depreciated. Fixed assets costing less than $100 are expensed immediately. The **materiality principle** justifies CMC's policy. This principle states that items that are sufficiently small in dollar value need not be treated in strict accordance with GAAP. Most accountants feel that the clerical costs of capitalizing modest expenditures, developing depreciation schedules, and making annual depreciation adjustments outweigh the benefits of small increases in the precision of the financial statements.

Mr. Craig has just suggested that CMC change its capitalization policy. He wants CMC to capitalize all fixed asset acquisitions. Mr. Craig states that this policy is not forbidden by the materiality principle and that more accurate financial statements would result.

Why do you think that Mr. Craig really wants to change this policy? What are the ethical implications of a policy change?

Depreciation

Many fixed assets have extended, but limited lives. Since these assets help generate revenues throughout their useful lives, their costs must be reflected as expenses in those years. **Depreciation** is the process of allocating the cost of a fixed asset as an expense in the years during which the asset helps generate revenue. Depreciation is an application of the matching principle. Because land has an unlimited life, it is not depreciated.

GAAP permits the use of any depreciation method that is systematic and rational. Methods differ in the *timing* of expense recognition during an asset's life. However, over the course of an asset's entire life, total depreciation expense will be the same under all methods. Three commonly used methods are illustrated here: the straight-line, sum-of-the-years'-digits, and declining-balance methods.

Straight-Line Method. The **straight-line (SL) method** allocates an equal amount of depreciation expense to each year in an asset's life. This method is based on the rationale that each year benefits equally from the asset's services.

To illustrate, assume a machine has a cost of $4,900, an economic life of five years, and an estimated residual value of $400. **Residual value** (or **salvage value**) is the amount the firm expects to receive from selling the asset at the end of its useful economic life.

Useful economic lives and residual values are estimates. Both are affected by the physical deterioration an asset is expected to undergo, and by technological obsolescence. The effect of technological obsolescence is well illustrated by computers. Computers can physically perform their tasks for extended periods of time (perhaps a decade or more). However, due to rapid advances in the computer industry, computers frequently become outdated. This affects both the length of time a firm expects to use a computer (its economic life) and the estimated residual value when the computer is taken out of service.

Annual straight-line depreciation expense is calculated by first subtracting the residual value from the cost. This difference is the **depreciable basis.** Next, divide the depreciable basis by the number of years in the asset's estimated useful life:

$$\text{Annual depreciation expense} = \frac{\text{Historical cost} \quad - \quad \text{Residual value}}{\text{Number of years}}$$

$$= \frac{\$4,900 \quad - \quad \$400}{5 \text{ years}}$$

$$= \$900 \text{ per year}$$

To record depreciation expense, the asset is decreased and shareholders' equity is decreased by an expense. Although Chapter 2 suggested that the asset account should be decreased, actual practice uses a contra-asset account called **accumulated depreciation.**

ASSETS		= LIABILITIES +	SHAREHOLDERS' EQUITY
Equipment	Accumulated depreciation		Retained earnings
Bal. $4,900			−$900 (depreciation expense)
	−$900		

On the balance sheet, accumulated depreciation is deducted from the cost of property, plant, and equipment, and the difference, called the **book value** (or net book value), is included in total assets. For example, after the preceding analysis, the book value is $4,000:

Historical cost	$4,900
Less accumulated depreciation	(900)
Book value	$4,000

Depreciation expense, accumulated depreciation, and book value over the five years can be summarized as follows:

Date	Depreciation Expense	Accumulated Depreciation	Book Value
At acquisition	$ 0	$ 0	$4,900
End of year 1	900	900	4,000
End of year 2	900	1,800	3,100

End of year 3	900	2,700	2,200
End of year 4	900	3,600	1,300
End of year 5	900	4,500	400

Sum-of-the-Years'-Digits Method. The **sum-of-the-years'-digits (SYD) method** is one of several accelerated methods. Accelerated methods result in relatively large depreciation charges in the early years of an asset's life. Such a pattern can be justified by the notion that some assets are more efficient in the earlier years of their life and, therefore, render greater services. That is, they help generate more revenue. To properly match costs with revenues, expenses should be larger in those early years.

Annual depreciation expense is calculated by multiplying an asset's depreciable basis by a fraction that varies from year to year. The denominator is always the sum of the years' digits in the useful life of the asset. For an asset with a five-year life, this denominator would be $5 + 4 + 3 + 2 + 1 = 15$. The sum of the years' digits can be computed with the following formula:

$$\text{Sum of the years' digits} = \frac{N \times (N + 1)}{2}$$

where N equals the number of years in the asset's life. For an asset with a five-year life, the computation is

$$\text{Sum of the years' digits} = \frac{5 \times (5 + 1)}{2}$$
$$= 15$$

The fraction's numerator is the number of years remaining in the asset's useful life as of the beginning of the year for which depreciation is being calculated. Therefore, depreciation expense for years 1 and 2 would be $1,500 and $1,200, respectively.

Year 1	Year 2

Depreciation expense $= \$4,500 \times \dfrac{5}{15} = \$1,500$ $\$4,500 \times \dfrac{4}{15} = \$1,200$

Under the sum-of-the-years'-digits method, depreciation expense declines each year. At the end of the fifth year, the entire depreciable basis of $4,500 will be depreciated.

Date	Depreciation Expense	Accumulated Depreciation	Book Value
At acquisition	$ 0	$ 0	$4,900
End of year 1	1,500	1,500	3,400
End of year 2	1,200	2,700	2,200
End of year 3	900	3,600	1,300
End of year 4	600	4,200	700
End of year 5	300	4,500	400

To make sure you understand this concept, verify the calculation of year 5's depreciation expense of $300.

Declining-Balance Methods. **Declining-balance (DB) methods** also result in accelerated depreciation charges. Annual depreciation expense is calculated by multiplying an asset's book value (cost − accumulated depreciation) at the beginning of the year by a percentage. The percentage equals a multiple of the straight-line *rate*.

Frequently used multiples are 200% and 150%. Residual values are not used in the initial determination of declining-balance depreciation rates or depreciation expense.

Since the asset in our illustration has a five-year life, the straight-line rate is 20% (1/5 = 20%). Using a multiple of 200% (200% = 2.0) results in a declining-balance rate of 40% (20% × 2.0). A multiple of 200% is referred to as the **double-declining-balance method (DDB)**. Depreciation charges for the first two years are $1,960 and $1,176, respectively:

$$\begin{aligned} \text{Depreciation expense, year 1} &= (\text{Cost} - \text{Accumulated Depreciation}) \times .4 \\ &= (\$4,900 - \$0) \times .4 \\ &= \$1,960 \end{aligned}$$

$$\begin{aligned} \text{Depreciation expense, year 2} &= (\text{Cost} - \text{Accumulated Depreciation}) \times .4 \\ &= (\$4,900 - \$1,960) \times .4 \\ &= \$1,176 \end{aligned}$$

A depreciation schedule for the five years is:

Date	Depreciation Expense	Accumulated Depreciation	Book Value
At acquisition	$ 0	$ 0	$4,900
End of year 1	1,960	1,960	2,940
End of year 2	1,176	3,136	1,764
End of year 3	706	3,842	1,058
End of year 4	423	4,265	635
End of year 5	235	4,500	400

To be sure that you understand declining-balance depreciation, verify the calculation of year 3's depreciation expense of $706.

Depreciation expense in the fifth year is not calculated in the typical way. The conventional calculation multiplies the book value at the end of year 4 ($635) by 40%. This yields an expense of $254. However, that expense would result in total accumulated depreciation of $4,519 ($4,265 + $254) and a book value of $381. Since an asset should not be depreciated to an amount below its residual value, depreciation in year 5 is limited to $235 (the amount that would leave a book value of $400).

Residual value is not utilized in the original determination of declining-balance depreciation because the computations themselves include an implicit residual value. That is, by setting depreciation expense equal to a percentage of book value, a book value will always remain. Thus, there is no need to consider residual value explicitly until the end of an asset's depreciation schedule; residual value must then be considered so that an asset's book value is not depreciated below its residual value.

Exhibit 7–1 summarizes the results of the three depreciation methods discussed in this section.

Tax Depreciation. Tax law requires firms to use the Modified Accelerated Cost Recovery System (MACRS). This system specifies the useful lives to be assigned to different types of assets, and also indicates the depreciation method to be used. For example, cars are assigned a 5-year life and double-declining-balance depreciation is required. Therefore, cars are depreciated at a 40% declining-balance rate. As another example, land improvements, such as sidewalks and fences, are assigned a 15-year life and a 150% declining-balance is used. Sidewalks and fences would then be depreciated at a 10% rate (1/15 × 150% = 10%).

EXHIBIT 7–1 SUMMARY OF DEPRECIATION METHODS

Assumptions

Cost	$4,900
Residual value	$ 400
Estimated life	5 years

Summary

End of Year	SL Deprec. Expense	SL Accum. Deprec.	SL Book Value	SYD Deprec. Expense	SYD Accum. Deprec.	SYD Book Value	DDB Deprec. Expense	DDB Accum. Deprec.	DDB Book Value
0	$ 0	$ 0	$4,900	$ 0	$ 0	$4,900	$ 0	$ 0	$4,900
1	900	900	4,000	1,500	1,500	3,400	1,960	1,960	2,940
2	900	1,800	3,100	1,200	2,700	2,200	1,176	3,136	1,764
3	900	2,700	2,200	900	3,600	1,300	706	3,842	1,058
4	900	3,600	1,300	600	4,200	700	423	4,265	635
5	900	4,500	400	300	4,500	400	235*	4,500	400

*Assets should not be depreciated below their residual value.

NOTE: Total depreciation expense over the five years combined is the same under all methods. The methods differ only in the timing of depreciation charges. Also note that since total depreciation expense is the same across the five years, total net income over the five years will also be the same.

Selection of Depreciation Method. Several factors influence managers' selection of a depreciation method for financial reporting. Managers might wish to provide financial statement readers with useful information. This would prompt them to select a depreciation method that best reflects the pattern of benefit usage. For example, if an asset is uniformly productive throughout its life, the straight-line method would be chosen.

Additionally, however, some economic issues may influence their decisions. If managers' compensation is tied to reported accounting earnings, managers are likely to prefer the straight-line method, since it results in lower depreciation charges and higher reported income. Lending agreements may also play a role. For example, some agreements require the firm to keep its debt to assets ratio below a specified value. This ratio contains total assets in the denominator. Since recorded asset values decline more quickly under accelerated depreciation methods, managers can reduce the likelihood of violating such agreements by selecting the straight-line method.

Firms do not generally use the same depreciation method for both financial reporting and tax purposes. MACRS is required for tax purposes, but is not always acceptable for financial reporting. This is partially due to the permissive nature of MACRS. For example, under MACRS, cars are given a five-year life and a zero residual value. These may not be realistic assumptions for many firms and might yield misleading financial statements. As mentioned earlier, firms frequently wish to report the lower depreciation expense associated with the straight-line method on their financial statements. In fact, as Exhibit 7–2 shows, the vast majority of publicly held companies use the straight-line method for financial reporting.

EXHIBIT 7–2
SELECTION OF DEPRECIATION
METHODS

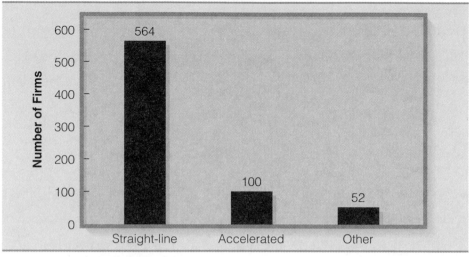

SOURCE: *Accounting Trends and Techniques,* 1993.

Some Misconceptions About Depreciation. Two misconceptions frequently arise regarding depreciation. First, some people believe that depreciation is a valuation procedure. That is, they believe the book value that results from depreciation reflects an asset's market value. It does not. Book value results from the application of a rather mechanical depreciation method. No attempt is made to estimate the current market value of an asset by surveying recent transactions.

Second, depreciation expense is alleged to be a source of cash. This misconception is due to the format of the statement of cash flows. Recall that under the indirect approach, depreciation expense is added to net income in calculating cash provided by operating activities. Depreciation expense is added, not because it is a source of cash, but because (1) it was previously subtracted in determining net income and (2) it does not involve a cash outflow. Be especially careful not to fall into this "cash flow trap"; depreciation, by itself, can never generate cash.

Expenditures After Acquisition

Firms often make expenditures during a fixed asset's life. Frequently, the expenditures are for routine repairs and maintenance. Since these expenditures merely maintain the economic benefit already contained in the asset, they do not enhance the asset's value. Accordingly, these expenditures are immediately expensed. Usually, cash is decreased and shareholders' equity is decreased by an expense.

Some expenditures, however, do enhance an asset's value. For example, Northwest Airlines recently renovated 40 of its DC-9 twinjets. The renovations included engine modifications to reduce jet noise, new seats, and new carpeting. These changes extended each jet's life by 15 years. Other expenditures can expand an asset or make it more efficient and productive. For example, a personal computer's hard drive can be replaced with a larger one, and new chips can be installed that enable the computer to perform tasks more quickly. Since all of these expenditures increase an asset's value, they should be capitalized. That is, the asset's recorded value should be increased.

Note that a change in an asset's book value or remaining estimated life will necessitate a change in the periodic depreciation charge.

Disposals

Firms frequently sell fixed assets when needs change or when assets age or become obsolete due to technological advances. To illustrate the accounting for a disposal, assume the machine described in the previous section was depreciated for two years using the straight-line method. At that point, the machine's book value is $3,100 ($4,900 − $1,800). Also assume the asset was sold at the beginning of year 3 for $2,500. Because an asset with a book value of $3,100 was sold for $2,500, the firm incurred a $600 loss. The analysis increases cash by $2,500, reduces the asset machine by $4,900, eliminates accumulated depreciation of $1,800, and decreases shareholders' equity via a $600 loss.

	ASSETS			=	LIABILITIES	+	SHAREHOLDERS' EQUITY
	Cash	Machine	Accumulated depreciation				Retained earnings
Beginning Balance		$4,900	−$1,800				
	+$2,500	−$4,900	+$1,800				$600 (loss on sale)
Ending Balance	$ 0	$ 0					

Gains and losses on sales of property, plant, and equipment are included in the income statement. If material, they are separately disclosed; otherwise, they are combined with other items.

These gains and losses must be interpreted carefully. First, note that the loss just illustrated is associated with a cash *inflow*. Therefore, the firm's overall cash position has improved, even though a loss was reported on the income statement.

Second, gains and losses on fixed asset disposals do not necessarily reflect good or poor managerial performance in the year of the disposal. They may be more a function of poorly estimated depreciation changes. Finally, managers have considerable discretion over the timing of these transactions. Therefore, whenever gains or losses appear on the income statement, the reader must always assess the possible reasons for and motivations behind such gains or losses.

Write-Downs

As discussed earlier, most firms value property, plant, and equipment at depreciated historical cost. However, when a fixed asset's utility drops below its book value, the asset should be written down. The purpose of this principle is to avoid overstating asset values.

Write-downs of fixed assets often occur when firms restructure their operations. Restructurings involve the elimination and consolidation of facilities, as well as layoffs of personnel. For example, in 1992 Hughes Aircraft Co. took a $749,400,000 restructuring charge. The charge was necessitated by reduced post–Cold War national defense spending.

If we assume that $300,000,000 of the charge was to write down fixed assets, the analysis would be:

ASSETS	=	LIABILITIES	+	SHAREHOLDERS' EQUITY
Fixed assets				Retained earnings
−$300,000,000				−$300,000,000
				(loss on restructuring)

Most analysts applaud the conservative nature of write-downs. However, the implementation of write-downs involves significant ambiguities. For example, GAAP provides limited guidance. A write-down is required only when the estimated future cash flows from using the asset fail to cover the book value of that asset.*

Because GAAP in this area is ill defined, managers enjoy a great deal of discretion and are accordingly provided with a tool for earnings manipulation. When it is in their best interest, managers can often successfully argue with their auditors to delay a write-down. Alternatively, managers sometimes engage in a *big bath.* Recall that a big bath involves recording large charges to income in a single year. Managers do this to relieve future years' income of these charges and to pave the way for reporting improved financial performance.

Financial Statement Presentation

Most balance sheets contain only one line item for property, plant, and equipment. This line shows acquisition cost less accumulated depreciation for all fixed assets. Notes to the financial statements contain more detailed information.

Exhibit 7–3 contains a partial balance sheet for OshKosh B'Gosh, Inc. (OB). OB's balance sheet contains the conventional one-line presentation. Exhibit 7–3 also contains excerpts from OB's notes. Note 1 indicates that OB uses straight-line depreciation. The note also discloses OB's estimates of its assets' useful lives. By comparing these estimates to industry norms, analysts can ascertain if a firm is overstating its earnings by selecting useful life estimates that are unduly long. Such estimates understate depreciation expense and overstate net income.

A breakdown of OB's property, plant, and equipment is provided in Note 4. It discloses the cost of the major types of fixed assets, as well as accumulated depreciation. Notice that the differences between cost and accumulated depreciation agrees with the amounts appearing on the balance sheet.

---

*In cases where a write-down is indicated, the asset should be written down to the present value of its cash flows. Present value techniques are discussed in the appendix to Chapter 8.

EXHIBIT 7–3 PARTIAL BALANCE SHEET AND RELATED NOTES

OshKosh B'Gosh, Inc.
Selected Financial Statement Information

	December 31	
	1994	**1993**
Property, plant and equipment	$69,829	$71,755

Related Notes

Note 1. Property, plant and equipment

Property, plant and equipment are carried at cost. Depreciation and amortization for financial reporting purposes is calculated using the straight line method based on the following useful lives:

	Years
Land improvements	10 to 15
Buildings	10 to 40
Leasehold improvements	5 to 10
Machinery and equipment	5 to 10

Note 4. Property, plant and equipment

A summary of property, plant and equipment follows:

	December 31	
	1994	1993
Land and improvements	$ 4,139	$ 4,172
Buildings	37,442	37,640
Leasehold improvements	7,862	5,268
Machinery and equipment	70,498	67,026
Construction in progress	9	291
Total	119,950	114,397
Less: Accumulated depreciation and amortization	50,121	42,642
Property, plant and equipment, net	$ 69,829	$ 71,755

Analysis

The analysis of property, plant, and equipment deals with two issues. First, is PPE effectively utilized? Second, what is the age of the assets? That is, is the firm replacing its productive capacity in a timely manner?

Utilization. Utilization is measured by **fixed asset turnover.** To calculate fixed asset turnover, divide sales by the average book value of property, plant, and equipment. In 1994, OB's sales were $363,363,000. Recall that book value equals historical cost less accumulated depreciation. It is also referred to as PPE-net. The average is calculated by adding beginning and ending PPE-net, and dividing by two.

Fixed asset turnover reflects the number of sales dollars generated by a $1 investment in PPE. OB's 1994 fixed asset turnover was 5.13:

$$\text{Fixed asset turnover} = \frac{\text{Net sales}}{\text{Average PPE-net}}$$

$$= \frac{\text{Net sales}}{(\text{Beginning} + \text{Ending PPE-net})/2}$$

$$= \frac{\$363,363}{(\$71,755 + \$69,829)/2}$$

$$= 5.13$$

Exhibit 7–4 summarizes selected ratios for OB, the apparel industry, and the steel industry, as a point of contrast. OB's fixed asset turnover is slightly below the 6.24 average of other apparel manufacturers. A lower fixed asset turnover might suggest that OB is underutilizing its property, plant, and equipment and may have excess capacity. On the other hand, OB may have elected to rely heavily on new, efficient, and costly equipment in the hope of reducing labor and other costs. Yet another possibility is that OB's competitors lease, rather than own, a larger component of their productive capacity. Since some leased assets might not appear on balance sheets, firms using leased assets might have a smaller denominator and a correspondingly higher turnover.

Some additional factors might also affect fixed asset turnover. Accelerated depreciation methods reduce PPE-net, more quickly than straight-line depreciation, and would result in a higher turnover ratio. Price changes and the maturity of a firm might also affect fixed asset turnover. For example, assume fixed asset prices are increasing over time. New entrants into an industry will be forced to acquire their productive capacity at higher costs than firms that are already established. New entrants, therefore, would have a higher PPE-net and a lower turnover. In summary, although fixed asset turnover is intended to measure asset utilization, other factors such as those just described can also affect it.

Also notice from Exhibit 7–4 that the steel industry has a relatively low fixed asset turnover. This is because the steel industry is capital intensive. Greater amounts of property, plant, and equipment are needed to manufacture steel than to produce clothing.

Percentage of PPE Depreciated (Age). Financial statements contain information about the original cost of property, plant, and equipment, as well as the depreci-

EXHIBIT 7–4
SELECTED RATIOS

OshKosh B'Gosh Inc. Selected Ratios and Industry Comparisons			
	OB	Apparal Manufacturers	Steel Manufacturers
Fixed asset turnover	5.13	6.24	1.50
Percentage of PPE depreciated	41.8%	51%	39%

ation that has been taken since the assets' acquisition. This permits an assessment of the relative age of a firm's assets. The calculation involves dividing accumulated depreciation by PPE-gross. PPE-gross is simply the assets' historical cost. Older assets have larger proportions of PPE-gross that have already been depreciated. OB's ratio for 1994 is 41.8%:

$$\text{Percentage of PPE depreciated} = \frac{\text{Accumulated depreciation}}{\text{PPE-gross}}$$

$$= \frac{\$\ 50,121}{\$119,950}$$

$$= 41.8\%$$

This is considerably below the industry norm of 51% that appears in Exhibit 7–4 and suggests that OB replaces its equipment more quickly than its competitors. That is, OB might have depreciated a lower percentage of its total property, plant, and equipment because it recently acquired fixed assets that have not yet generated much depreciation. Another interpretation might be that OB is a relatively young entrant into the apparel industry; an examination of OB's history, however, indicates that this is not the case.

Evaluation of the Accounting for Property, Plant, and Equipment. GAAP requires the use of depreciated historical cost. As previously mentioned, this valuation does not reflect current market value. Accordingly, care must be taken when using this information. For example, lending institutions sometimes require loan applicants to pledge assets as collateral. In evaluating the adequacy of the pledged assets, historical cost is not particularly relevant; the loan officer would be more interested in current market value.

Although the financial statements of U.S. companies do not disclose the market value of fixed assets, a few countries do permit the use of market value. Exhibit 7–5 contains a note from the annual report of Arrowfield Group Limited, an Australian company. The note shows that Arrowfield revalued its land, building and improvements in 1989. In this particular case, market value significantly exceeds historical cost. Since such differences can dramatically affect a number of ratios, care must be taken when comparing the financial statements of U.S. firms to those in countries that permit asset revaluations.

INTANGIBLE ASSETS

Intangible assets are long-lived assets whose values do not depend on their physical substance. Rather, their value is based on the legal rights they convey. Various intangible assets are described in this section. They are summarized in Exhibit 7–6.

Patents, granted by the federal government, convey the exclusive right to use a product or process for a period of 17 years. Patents are intended to promote innovation by ensuring that the firm that discovers and applies new knowledge reaps the benefits of its efforts.

Copyrights, also granted by the federal government, convey the exclusive right to use artistic or literary works for a period of 75 years. Common examples of works that can be copyrighted include books, songs, and movies. The economic life of a copyright may be considerably shorter than its legal life.

EXHIBIT 7–5
AUSTRALIAN FIRMS WRITE
UP FIXED ASSETS

a) The stud property (including fixed improvements) and the winery and vineyards were independently valued by Colliers International Property Consultants Pty. Limited in June 1989.

Arrowfield Group Limited
Property, Plant and Equipment Note

	1989	1988
Note 14—Property, Plant and Equipment		
Freehold land		
At cost	412	3,182
At independent valuation 1989[a]	11,173	—
	11,585	3,182
Buildings and improvements		
At cost	526	2,973
Accumulated depreciation	(73)	(217)
	453	2,756
At independent valuation 1989[a]	9,691	—
	10,144	2,756
Leasehold improvements, at cost	136	106
Accumulated amortisation	(28)	(1)
	108	105
Plant and equipment, at cost	4,091	1,956
Accumulated depreciation	(543)	(356)
	3,548	1,600
Plant and equipment under lease	722	1,021
Accumulated amortisation	(247)	(249)
	475	772
Capital works in progress, at cost	—	7,801
	25,860	16,216

EXHIBIT 7–6
SUMMARY OF
INTANGIBLE ASSETS

Asset	Description
Patents	Patents are granted by the federal government. They convey the exclusive right to use a product or process for a period of 17 years.
Copyrights	Copyrights are granted by the federal government. They convey the exclusive right to use a work of art (a book, movie, etc.) for a period of 75 years.
Trademarks	Trademarks are words, symbols, or other distinctive ways of identifying a particular company's product. Trademarks are issued by the federal government and have unlimited legal lives.
Franchises and licenses	Franchises and licenses are rights granted by contracts. The contracts convey the right to market products or engage in specified activities. The legal life of a franchise or license is stated in the contract.
Goodwill	Goodwill is the excess of the purchase price of a business over the fair value of its identifiable assets.

Trademarks are words, symbols, or other distinctive elements used to identify a particular firm's products. You are probably familiar with Kleenex tissue. Kleenex is a registered trademark of the Kimberly-Clark Corporation. McDonald's Golden Arches and MGM's Lion are well-known symbols established and protected by their corporations as trademarks. Trademarks have unlimited legal lives. However, their economic lives may be limited.

Franchises and licenses are rights to market a particular product or service or to engage in a particular activity. For example, Pizza Hut sells franchises to various individuals and businesses. A franchise permits the holder to operate a Pizza Hut restaurant at a specified location. This right has economic value to the holder and would be reflected as an asset. As another example, some pharmaceutical companies acquire the right to sell the products of other companies. This right also has value and would be shown as an asset (see the following discussion on research and development costs).

For accounting purposes, the intangible asset **goodwill** can only arise in one situation: acquiring an ongoing business. In many such acquisitions, the purchase price exceeds the total fair value of the separately identifiable assets. The higher purchase price reflects the willingness of the buyer to pay for loyal customers, trained workers, and the like, that many ongoing businesses possess. Goodwill equals the excess of the purchase price over the total fair value of all specifically identifiable assets acquired. As an illustration, in 1992 Storage Technology Corporation (StorageTek) acquired Edata Scandinavia AB for $75,000,000 and recorded $44,700,000 of goodwill. In other words, more than half of the purchase price was recorded as goodwill.

Acquisition

Intangible assets acquired from others are initially recorded at their historical cost. For example, if a company acquires a patent for $300,000, cash would decrease and patents would increase by $300,000.

ASSETS		=	LIABILITIES	+	SHAREHOLDERS' EQUITY
Cash	Patents				
−$300,000	+$300,000				

Because the patent has already been developed, future economic benefits seem probable and recording an asset is proper.

As another illustration, StorageTek's purchase of Edata is recorded as follows (in thousands):

ASSETS			=	LIABILITIES	+	SHAREHOLDERS' EQUITY
Cash	Various assets	Goodwill				
−$75,000	+$30,300	+$44,700				

Research and Development Costs. Many firms internally develop new products, as opposed to purchasing patents from others. Since large expenditures can be made without the assurance of ultimate success, this strategy is more risky. Substantial uncertainty exists regarding future economic benefits. Because of this, GAAP requires that all research and development costs be expensed immediately. **Research and development costs** are those incurred to generate new knowledge or to translate knowledge into a new product or process. Most countries follow the practice of immediately expensing these costs.

The divergence in the accounting rules for externally acquired versus internally developed patents can reduce the interfirm comparability of financial statements, particularly in research-intensive industries such as pharmaceuticals. For example, Roberts Pharmaceutical Corporation's intangible assets increased from $23,742,100 in 1991 to $116,817,400 in 1992. Since Roberts' strategy is to acquire already-established pharmaceutical products from other companies, the acquisition cost of those products are capitalized as assets.

Exhibit 7–7 contains Roberts' financial statement notes regarding intangible assets. The largest intangible asset is product rights acquired. These rights were obtained in one of two ways: (1) the direct purchase of a patent from the holder or (2) a licensing agreement with the holder of the patent.

In contrast, Merck, Inc., internally develops its pharmaceutical products. Accordingly, the $1.1 billion Merck spent to develop new products in 1992 was expensed immediately, even though some of those products proved successful and resulted in patents.

EXHIBIT 7–7
INTANGIBLE ASSETS

Roberts Pharmaceutical Corporation
Excerpts from Financial Statement Notes

Note 1 (partial)
Intangible assets are stated at cost less accumulated amortization. Amortization is determined using the straight-line method over the estimated useful lives of the related assets which are estimated to range from ten to thirty-five years.

Note 4
Intangible assets consisted of (dollars in thousands):

| | December 31, | |
	1991	1992
Product rights acquired	$22,637.7	$101,023.9
Goodwill	1,160.6	14,759.8
Other assets	695.3	3,408.9
	24,493.6	119,192.6
Less: Accumulated amortization	751.5	2,375.2
	$23,742.1	$116,817.4

Special accounting rules exist for software development costs. For a given project, these costs are expensed until *technological feasibility* is demonstrated. Costs incurred after that point are capitalized. To some extent, these rules are inconsistent with the general procedures for research and development.

Exhibit 7–8 contains a note from StorageTek's financial statements. The note describes StorageTek's accounting for software development costs.

Storage Technology Corporation
Excerpt from Financial Statement Notes

Capitalized Software Costs
The Company capitalized costs of $23,092,000 in 1993, $9,148,000 in 1992, and $7,486,000 in 1991 associated with acquiring and developing software products to be marketed to customers. Other assets as shown on the Consolidated Balance Sheet include unamortized software product costs of $36,068,000 as of December 31, 1993, and $20,461,000 as of December 25, 1992. Amortization is based on the greater of straight-line amortization over estimated useful lives, generally four years, or the percentage of actual revenue versus total anticipated revenue. Amortization of software costs was $7,485,000 in 1993, $6,818,000 in 1992, and $2,877,000 in 1991.

EXHIBIT 7–8
SOFTWARE DEVELOPMENT
COSTS

 Amortization

Like many fixed assets, intangible assets have limited useful lives. Accordingly, the cost of these assets must be allocated as an expense to the years during which they help generate revenue. With fixed assets, this expense was labeled depreciation. **Amortization expense** is the term used for intangible assets. It is usually calculated on a straight-line basis, and the maximum amortization period is 40 years.

Suppose, for example, the patent acquired above for $300,000 was estimated to have a six-year life. Amortization expense in the amount of $50,000 ($300,000/6) would be recorded each year.

ASSETS	=	LIABILITIES	+	SHAREHOLDERS' EQUITY
Patents				Retained earnings
−$50,000				−$50,000
				(amoritization expense)

Unlike fixed assets, no contra-asset account is used. The asset account patents is reduced directly. Reality Check 7–1 addresses the issues of capitalization and amortization.

REALITY CHECK 7–1

As described in Exhibit 7–8, StorageTek capitalizes certain software development costs. Since firms outside of the computer industry expense all of their research and development costs, StorageTek's financial statements may not be comparable to those of firms in other industries.

In 1992, StorageTek reported the following results (dollars in thousands):

Income before taxes	$27,034
Provision for income taxes	17,700
Net income	$ 9,334

REQUIRED

a. Based on the information contained in Exhibit 7–8, recalculate StorageTek's net income to reflect the immediate expensing of all software development costs.

NATURAL RESOURCES

Natural resources are assets such as mines containing gold, silver, copper, or other minerals, wells containing oil or gas, and timberlands. Natural resources (also called wasting assets) are important assets of firms in the extractive industries.

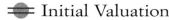 Initial Valuation

Natural resources acquired from others are valued at their historical cost. However, many firms self-explore and develop natural resource sites. The accounting for this type of situation is somewhat controversial. The issue involves the treatment of exploration costs associated with unsuccessful sites.

One approach, the **full cost method,** capitalizes as an asset the exploration costs of both successful and unsuccessful sites. This approach recognizes that a firm cannot expect success every time it attempts to locate valuable resources. Accordingly, the expenditures associated with both successful and unsuccessful sites are viewed as costs incurred to obtain successful sites.

The **successful efforts method** expenses immediately the cost of unsuccessful sites. Only the costs directly associated with locating and developing successful sites are capitalized. Since assets are recorded at lower amounts and expenses are recognized more quickly, successful efforts is the more conservative method. Reality Check 7–2 describes how the Newmont Mining Corporation accounts for its exploration costs.

GAAP permits the use of either method. Large firms (e.g., Exxon) tend to use successful efforts, while small firms tend to use full cost. Small firms select full cost because higher net income and larger asset values make them appear more profitable in the short term. The higher net income and larger asset values under the full cost method also reduce the likelihood of violating loan covenants based on accounting ratios. Large, established firms are in much less danger of violating loan covenants. They select the conservative successful efforts method because the lower reported net income helps reduce the political costs of the very visible oil industry. That is, lower net income numbers help the oil industry to argue that it is not unduly profiting at the public's expense.

NEWMONT MINING CORPORATION
EXCERPT FROM FINANCIAL STATEMENT NOTES

Mineral exploration costs are expensed as incurred. When it has been determined that a mineral property has proven or probable ore reserves, the costs of subsequent reserve definition and the costs incurred to develop such property, including costs to remove overburden to initially expose the ore body, are capitalized. Such costs, and estimated future development costs are amortized using a units-of-production method over the estimated life of the ore body. On-going development expenditures to maintain production are generally charged to operations as incurred.

Significant payments related to the acquisition of exploration interests are capitalized. If a mineable ore body is discovered, such costs are amortized using a units-of-production method. If no mineable ore body is discovered, such costs are expensed in the period in which it is determined the property has no future economic value.

REQUIRED

a. Does Newmont use the full cost or the successful efforts method? Why?

Depletion

Depletion is quite similar to depreciation and amortization. As with all long-lived assets, natural resources help generate revenue over their useful lives. Accordingly, the cost of those resources must be matched as an expense to that revenue.

As an illustration, assume an oil well was acquired for $255,000. The analysis increases the asset oil well and decreases cash.

ASSETS		=	LIABILITIES	+	SHAREHOLDERS' EQUITY
Cash	Oil well				
−$255,000	+$255,000				

Further assume the well is estimated to contain 45,000 barrels of oil, and that the property can probably be sold for $30,000 after all the oil is extracted. Depletion is calculated on a per-unit basis. Subtract the residual value from the historical cost and then divide by the estimated number of barrels in the well:

$$\text{Depletion per barrel} = \frac{\text{Historical cost} - \text{Residual value}}{\text{Estimated number of barrels}}$$

$$= \frac{\$255,000 - \$30,000}{45,000} = \$5$$

The depletion charge per barrel is $5. If during the first year of operation 8,000 barrels were extracted and sold, the depletion charge would be $40,000 ($5 × 8,000). The analysis would decrease the recorded value of the oil well; shareholders' equity would be reduced via depletion expense.

ASSETS	=	LIABILITIES	+	SHAREHOLDERS' EQUITY
Oil well				Retained earnings
−$40,000				−$40,000
				(depletion expense)

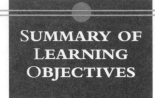

SUMMARY OF LEARNING OBJECTIVES

1. **Identify three major types of noncurrent assets: (1) property, plant, and equipment, (2) intangible assets, and (3) natural resources.**

   Property, plant, and equipment (fixed assets) are tangible, long-lived assets. These assets consist of land, land improvements, buildings, factories, furniture, and equipment. Intangible assets have no physical substance. Rather, their value derives from the legal rights they convey to firms. Intangible assets include patents, copyrights, and franchises. Natural resources are important assets to firms in the extractive industries. Natural resources include oil and gas wells, timberlands, and mines containing gold, copper, and other minerals.

2. **Explain how to account for the acquisition of these assets.**

   Fixed assets and intangible assets acquired from others are initially valued at their historical cost. The accounting for intangible assets developed internally is more problematic. Given that intangible assets have no physical substance, it is sometimes difficult to verify that expenditures made to develop them really reflect future economic benefits. Because of this, the FASB provides specific guidance in certain situations. For example, all research and development expenditures must be expensed immediately. Natural resources acquired from others are recorded at their historical cost. Two methods are available to account for natural resources obtained through self-exploration: the full cost method and the successful efforts method. The successful efforts method is the more conservative one because assets are valued at lower amounts and expenses are recognized more quickly.

3. **Describe the procedures for depreciation, amortization, and depletion.**

   Many fixed assets have limited useful lives, and they help generate revenue only during that period. Accordingly, the matching principle requires that these assets (except land) be depreciated. That is, the cost of fixed assets must be allocated as an expense over their useful lives. Managers are free to choose from a number of generally accepted depreciation methods. Since intangible assets have limited lives, they are amortized. This is a procedure very similar to depreciation. Amortization is usually calculated on a straight-line basis over a maximum period of 40 years. Since natural resources are consumed over their useful lives, they are subject to depletion charges. Depletion charges are calculated on a per-unit (ton, barrel, etc.) basis.

4. List the factors affecting managers' selection of depreciation methods.

Managers might want to provide financial statement users with useful information. If so, they would select the depreciation method that best reflects the expiration of benefits contained in the firm's assets. Since the choice of depreciation method affects reported net income, some managers might be motivated to select the straight-line method, which results in the lowest depreciation expense and the highest net income. This tends to increase managers' bonuses and decrease the chances of violating loan covenants.

5. Determine which postacquisition expenditures should be expensed and which should be capitalized.

Expenditures that extend an asset's life, enlarge the asset, or make the asset more efficient are capitalized. Expenditures that merely maintain the value already contained in an asset are expensed.

6. Explain the accounting issues associated with asset write-downs and disposals.

Asset write-downs are needed when an asset's utility falls below its book value. The associated loss appears on the income statement, often labeled as a restructuring charge. Asset disposals often give rise to gains and losses. These gains and losses do not necessarily reflect the performance of management in the year in which the gain or loss is recorded. Rather, they more frequently reflect faulty estimates used in previous depreciation calculations. Since managers can influence the timing (and perhaps the amount) of gains and losses recognized from write-downs and disposals, these items must be carefully evaluated.

7. Interpret financial statement disclosures about noncurrent assets.

Analyses of noncurrent assets provide insights into how effectively these assets are being used; firms naturally want to generate as many sales as possible with a given fixed asset base. A firm's success doing this is measured by fixed asset turnover. Financial statements also provide information about assets' ages. This is measured by the percentage of PPE depreciated. Firms with older assets will find it difficult to compete with firms that have newer, more efficient assets.

KEY TERMS

Accumulated depreciation	Goodwill
Amortization expense	Intangible assets
Book value	Materiality principle
Capitalize	Natural resources
Copyrights	Noncurrent assets
Declining-balance methods (DB)	Patents
Depletion	Property, plant, and equipment
Depreciable basis	Research and development costs
Depreciation	Residual value
Double-declining-balance method (DDB)	Salvage value
	Straight-line method (SL)
Fixed assets	Successful efforts method
Fixed asset turnover	Sum-of-the-years'-digits method (SYD)
Franchises and licenses	Trademarks
Full cost method	

REALITY CHECK SOLUTIONS

SOLUTION TO REALITY CHECK 7–1

a.   ($ in thousands)

Income before taxes as reported	$27,034
Less: Costs capitalized	(9,148)
Plus: Amortization of previously capitalized costs	6,818
Income before taxes, adjusted	24,704
Provision for income taxes*	(16,058)
Income, adjusted	$ 8,646

*Using StorageTek's approximate effective tax rate $= \dfrac{\$17,700}{\$27,034} = .65.$

Provision for income taxes = $24,704 × .65 = $16,058

SOLUTION TO REALITY CHECK 7–2

a. Newmont uses the successful efforts method. There are two indications of this:

1. Exploration costs are expensed as incurred. No costs are capitalized until it is probable that a property has valuable reserves.
2. Costs incurred to acquire exploration interests are capitalized. However, if no reserves are found, the costs are expensed immediately.

QUESTIONS

7–1 Define the following terms related to noncurrent assets:

   a. Depreciation expense
   b. Intangibles
   c. Amortization
   d. Straight-line method versus sum-of-the-years'-digits method
   e. Wasting assets
   f. Depletion

7–2 Discuss the differences between depreciation and amortization.

7–3 Discuss the differences between property, plant, and equipment (PPE) and intangible assets.

7–4 Discuss the differences between current assets and noncurrent assets.

7–5 Current assets, such as inventory, are not depreciated. Why should noncurrent assets be depreciated, amortized, or depleted?

7–6 Discuss the differences between the full cost method and the successful efforts methods when accounting for natural resources. Why do you suppose large firms might prefer one method, and small firms the other?

7–7 Discuss the term *accumulated depreciation*. How does this differ from depreciation expense? Why is accumulated depreciation treated as a contra-asset? Why is this often called a "negative" asset?

7–8 Under what circumstances could the sum-of-the-years'-digits depreciation method produce the same pattern of total annual expenses as would the straight-line method?

7–9 Discuss two different types of noncurrent assets that may be found on a typical balance sheet.

7–10 Discuss three different types of intangible assets, indicating what types of firms might hold such assets.

7–11 Why do accountants write off, or reduce, noncurrent asset? Why might such write-offs be confusing? How could these possibly confusing effects be reduced?

7–12 Some finance texts suggest that depreciation is a source of cash. Refute this assertion.

7–13 Some finance texts suggest that balance sheets reflect the true value (the market value) of noncurrent assets. Refute this assertion.

7–14 When depreciation expense is shown in a firm's financial statements, does it represent a source of cash? How does depreciation expense affect cash flows?

7–15 When accumulated depreciation is shown on a balance sheet, do changes in accumulated depreciation represent a source or use of cash? How is cash affected by changes in accumulated depreciation? What other events result in changes to accumulated depreciation?

7–16 Identify the only times when noncurrent assets have an effect on cash flows.

7–17 How does depletion of natural resources affect cash flows? When does cash change as a result of transactions involving natural resources?

7–18 How does amortization of an intangible asset affect cash flows? When does cash change as a result of transactions involving intangibles?

7–19 Discuss the following proposition: Intangible assets have no substance; therefore, they have no value and should not be shown on the firm's balance sheet.

7–20 Discuss the following proposition: Intangible assets reflect so much uncertainty that they should not be shown on the firm's balance sheet.

7–21 Discuss the following proposition: Intangible assets may last one year, or they may last indefinitely; therefore, no one can determine the proper amortization schedule until the asset is exhausted or retired.

7–22 Discuss the differences between the three depreciation methods—straight-line, sum-of-the-years'-digits, and declining-balance—presented in this chapter.

7–23 Why would a firm choose one depreciation method over another?

7–24 Discuss the following proposition: GAAP should only include one depreciation method: options give managers too much flexibility and too many opportunities to manipulate net income.

7–25 Discuss the following proposition: GAAP should permit managers the flexibility to choose from among several depreciation methods; each firm is unique and may require the flexibility to match its depreciation method to its own unique circumstances.

Classifying and Capitalizing Costs

EXERCISES

7–26 Identify which of the following costs could be capitalized on the firm's balance sheet. That is, which costs could be shown as part of property, plant, and equipment (PPE)?

 a. New windshield wiper blades on the company's truck

 b. New sidewalks in front of the firm's factory

c. Freight expenses for new equipment installed in the factory
d. Installation costs for the new equipment
e. Realtor's fees on the purchase of land
f. Minor engine repair on the truck
g. Engine replacement on the truck
h. Razing or demolishing a building on newly acquired land
i. Design costs for a new building

Calculating Property, Plant, and Equipment Cost

7-27 A firm purchased machinery on account with an invoice price of $15,000. The terms of payment were 2/10, net 30. In addition, transportation of $250, installation of $420, and sales tax of $1,000 were paid in cash. While installing the machinery, an employee's negligence caused $150 worth of damage to the machine, which was repaired and paid in cash.

REQUIRED

a. Calculate the total cost of the machinery.

Calculating Property, Plant, and Equipment Cost

7–28 A firm purchased land for a purchase price of $150,000. Broker commissions of $3,000 and other closing costs of $1,800 were paid in acquiring the land. An old building that was on the land was demolished. The demolition costs were $4,500. However, some of the demolished building scrap parts were sold for $2,200. In addition, there were delinquent real estate taxes owing on the land of $800 that the firm had to pay to acquire the land.

REQUIRED

a. Calculate the total cost of the land.

Graphing Depreciation Cost Flows

7–29 Draw a freehand graph, with dollars on the vertical axis and time (years) on the horizontal axis, showing the pattern of depreciation expenses that would be expected under each of the following depreciation methods:

a. Straight-line depreciation
b. Double-declining-balance depreciation
c. Sum-of-the-years'-digits depreciation

Classifying and Capitalizing R&D Costs

7–30 Firm A purchased a patent from another firm at a cost of $1 million. Firm B spent the same amount in developing a patent through its own internal research and development (R&D) efforts.

REQUIRED

a. Describe the accounting treatment for each firm. That is, show the balance sheet and income statement effects for each firm.
b. Why might a firm prefer one method over the other?

Calculating Depletion Expense

7–31 A firm has an oil well costing $2,600,000, which is expected to produce 5 million barrels of oil and can probably be sold for $100,000 after all of the oil is extracted. If 500,000 barrels of oil were extracted and sold this year, what is the depletion expense?

Income Statement Effects of Capitalizing Installation Costs

7–32 A firm acquires a machine for $150,000 and spends $50,000 to install it. The machine has a five-year life and a zero residual value. The firm is considering the possible effects on net income if it chooses to capitalize or expense the installation costs. Calculate the effect on net income each year if the firm uses straight-line depreciation.

Three Methods of Calculating Depreciation Expense

7–33 A firm purchased computer-aided drafting and machining equipment at the beginning of 1998 for $420,000. The machine has an expected useful life of six years, and a $38,000 residual value.

REQUIRED

a. Calculate the annual depreciation expense for the first four years of the equipment's life using the straight-line method.
b. Calculate the annual depreciation expense for the first four years of the equipment's life using the double-declining-balance method.
c. Calculate the annual depreciation expense for the first four years of the equipment's life, using the sum-of-the-years'-digits method.
d. Comment on the differences in your results. Which method would managers prefer if they are trying to maximize their net income? Which method would they prefer if the objective is to minimize income taxes? Why?
e. Using double-declining-balance depreciation, calculate depreciation expense through the sixth year. Why did you have to adjust depreciation in the sixth year?

Transaction Analysis: Disposal of Fixed Assets

7 34 A firm acquired a $650,000 fixed asset that has a four-year life and a residual value of $50,000. Show the effects on the balance sheet equation of the asset's disposal at the end of the fourth year, assuming the following separate circumstances:

a. The asset is sold for its estimated residual value.
b. The asset is sold for $75,000.
c. The asset is sold for $35,000.
d. The asset is scrapped (junked) and disposal costs are $10,000.

Transaction Analysis: Sum-of-the-Years'-Digits Depreciation

7–35 A firm acquired a $24,000 truck that has a three-year life and an estimated residual value of $6,000. Using the balance sheet equation, record the truck's purchase and depreciation using sum-of-the-years'-digits depreciation. Show the effects in each year, and be sure to include separate accounts for accumulated depreciation and retained earnings in your equation.

Transaction Analysis: Double-Declining-Balance Depreciation

7–36 A firm acquired a $20,000 computer, along with $14,000 of related ancillary equipment that can only be used on this machine. The computer and the related equipment have an estimated life of five years and a residual value of $2,000. Using the balance sheet equation, record the computer's purchase and depreciation using the double-declining-balance method. Show the effects in each year, and be sure to include separate accounts for accumulated depreciation and retained earnings in your equation.

Transaction Analysis: Disposal of Fixed Assets (continuation of Exercise 7–36)

7–37 With regard to Exercise 7–36, show the effects on the balance sheet equation of disposing of the computer, and the related equipment, under each of the following separate circumstances:

a. Selling at the end of the fifth year for $2,000.
b. Selling at the end of the fifth year for $6,000.
c. Selling at the end of the fourth year for $8,000.

Financial Statement Effects: Recognizing Patents

7–38 A firm acquired a patent for $125,000 and expected its economic useful life to be 15 years.

REQUIRED

a. What is the correct useful life?
b. Show the balance sheet effects of holding the patent for three years.
c. What if the firm had to defend its patent in a lawsuit at the beginning of year 4? Assume the firm spent $5,000 on legal fees and lost the lawsuit.

Financial Statement Effects: Depletion

7–39 A firm spent $1,500,000 for an oil well that is expected to produce 3,000,000 barrels of oil. During the first year no oil is extracted. During the second year 1,000,000 barrels are extracted and sold.

REQUIRED

a. Show the effects on the balance sheet equation of the oil well acquisition and depletion during these two years.
b. Discuss the impact on both the income statement and the balance sheet during each year.

Financial Statement Effects: Depletion

7–40 A firm acquired a $4.5 million gold mine that is expected to yield 500,000 ounces of gold. During each of the first two years, 100,000 ounces of gold are mined and sold.

REQUIRED

a. Show the effects on the balance sheet equation from the mine acquisition and depletion for each of these two years.
b. Discuss the impact on the income statement and balance sheet at acquisition and at the end of each year.
c. What would be the depletion during each of the first two years if the firm estimated it would cost $200,000 to clean up the mine at the end of its productive life? (Note that the mine has a negative residual value.)

Financial Statement Effects: Disposing of Natural Resources (continuation of Exercise 7–40)

7–41 With regard to the original information in Exercise 7–40, show the effects of the following two possibilities at the beginning of the third year of owning the gold mine. Discuss the effects on the income statement and the balance sheet of the gains or losses that may occur:

a. The gold mine is sold for $5 million.
b. The gold mine is fully exhausted and declared worthless.

PROBLEMS

7–42 Balance Sheet Effects of Alternative Depreciation Methods— Alternate Problems (A) or (B)

Problem (A)

A firm purchased a computer-controlled drill press at the beginning of 1998 for $360,000. The drill press has an expected useful life of 10 years and a $40,000 residual value. Assume the firm begins the year prior to the purchase of the drill press with the following balance sheet items:

Plant and equipment	$3,500,000
Less: Accumulated depreciation	(1,235,000)
Plant and equipment, net	$2,265,000

REQUIRED

a. Determine the correct ending balances in each of these balance sheet elements, after including the annual depreciation, using straight-line depreciation, for the first three years of the drill press's life. Ignore depreciation on the existing plant and equipment.

b. Determine the correct ending balances in each of these items, after including the annual depreciation, using double declining-balance depreciation, for the first three years of the drill press's life. Ignore depreciation on the existing plant and equipment.

c. Calculate the effects on net income if the firm used double-declining-balance depreciation, instead of straight-line depreciation. Calculate these differences for each of the first three years for the drill press, and combined, for the same three years. Ignore depreciation on the existing plant and equipment.

d. Comment on the net income differences. Do they seem significant, each year, or in total?

e. After the firm has owned the drill press for 10 years, what effects will any of these depreciation methods have on the firm's net income? Why?

f. Using double-declining-balance depreciation, calculate depreciation expense through the tenth year. Why did you have to adjust the depreciation in the tenth year?

Problem (B)

A firm purchased computer-aided drafting and machining (CAD-CAM) equipment at the beginning of 1998 for $420,000. The machine has an expected useful life of six years and a $38,000 residual value. Assume that the firm begins the year prior to the purchase of CAD-CAM equipment with the following balance sheet items:

Plant and equipment	$6,250,000
Less: Accumulated depreciation	(1,145,000)
Plant and equipment, net	$5,105,000

REQUIRED

a. Determine the correct ending balances in each of these balance sheet elements after including the annual depreciation, using straight-line depreciation, for the first four years of the equipment's life. Ignore depreciation on the existing plant and equipment.

b. Determine the correct ending balances in each of these items, after including the annual depreciation, using double-declining-balance depreciation, for the first four years of the equipment's life. Ignore depreciation on the existing plant and equipment.

c. Calculate the effects on net income if the firm used double-declining-balance depreciation, instead of straight-line depreciation. Calculate these effects for each of the first four years of the equipment's life, and combined, for the same four years. Ignore depreciation on the existing plant and equipment.

d. Comment on the net income differences. Do they seem significant, each year, or in total?

e. After the firm has owned the CAD-CAM machine for six years, what effects will any of these depreciation methods have on the firm's net income? Why?

7–43 Two Methods of Calculating Depreciation Expense—Alternate Problems (A) or (B)

Problem (A)

A firm purchased a computer-controlled drill press at the beginning of 1998 for $480,000. The drill press has an expected useful life of 10 years, and zero residual value. Assume the firm begins the year with the following balance sheet items:

Cash and other assets		$8,115,000
Plant and equipment	$3,500,000	
Less: Accumulated depreciation	(1,040,000)	
Plant and equipment, net		$2,460,000
Liabilities		$1,000,000
Shareholders' equity		$9,575,000

REQUIRED

Ignore depreciation on the existing plant and equipment.

a. Show the effects of the drill press purchase on the firm's balance sheet equation. Assume the firm borrowed the money to purchase the drill press.

b. Show the effects of straight-line depreciation on the balance sheet equation for the first two years of the drill press's life.

c. Show the effects of double-declining-balance depreciation on the balance sheet equation for the first two years of the drill press's life.

d. Comment on these differences. Do you think the firm's balance sheet will be stronger under either method? Why?

Problem (B)

A firm purchased computer-aided drafting and machining (CAD-CAM) equipment at the beginning of 1998 for $630,000. The machine has an expected useful life of seven years and a zero residual value. Assume that the firm begins the year with the following balance sheet items:

Cash and other assets		$8,001,000
Property, plant and equipment	$4,750,000	
Less: accumulated depreciation	(2,635,000)	
Property, plant and equipment, net		$2,115,000
Liabilities		$2,000,000
Shareholders' equity		$8,116,000

REQUIRED

Ignore depreciation on the existing plant and equipment.
a. Show the effects of the CAD-CAM machine's purchase on the firm's balance sheet equation. Assume the firm borrowed the money to purchase the machine.
b. Show the effects of straight-line depreciation on the balance sheet equation for the first two years.
c. Show the effects of double-declining balance depreciation on the balance sheet equation for the first two years.
d. Comment on these differences. Do you think the firm's balance sheet will be stronger under either method? Why?

7–44 Gain or Loss on Disposal of Fixed Assets—Alternate Problems (A) or (B)

Problem (A)

Swen and Jerry are twins who each own an ice cream company. Four years ago, they each purchased an ice cream mixer. Each mixer was identical in all respects, including the cost of $35,000. Each had an estimated useful life of five years and an estimated residual value of $5,000.

The only difference between the two mixers was in the depreciation method chosen. Swen chose the straight-line method, whereas Jerry chose the double-declining balance method.

Because of the intense competition in the ice cream business and the resulting rapid changes in technology and mixing methods, Swen and Jerry each decided to replace their mixers on the same day at the end of the fourth year, and, being brothers, they sold their old mixers to two other twins in the neighboring state, Haskin and Dobbins, for exactly the same price, $10,000.

Later, at a family reunion, Swen mentioned that he had sold his mixer at a loss of $1,000. Jerry, while smiling under his beard, said that he had done better than that, and that Swen should check with his accountant because Jerry had realized a gain on the sale of his mixer.

REQUIRED

a. Explain how Swen could have had a loss on the sale of the same mixer on which Jerry had a gain.

Problem (B)

Hand and Hammer are twins who each own a baking soda company. Four years ago, they each purchased a baking soda mixer. Each mixer was identical in all respects, including the cost of $45,000. Each had an estimated useful life of five years and an estimated residual value of $5,000.

The only difference between the two mixers was in the depreciation method chosen. Hand chose the straight-line method, whereas Hammer chose the double-declining balance method.

Because of the intense competition in the baking soda business and the resulting rapid changes in technology and mixing methods, Hand and Hammer each decided to replace their mixers on the same day at the end of the fourth year, and, being sisters, they sold their old mixers to two other twins in the neighboring state, White and Black, for exactly the same price, $9,000.

Later, over cocktails, Hand mentioned that she had sold her mixer at a loss of $4,000. Hammer, while smiling under her cowboy hat, said that she had done better than that, and that Hand should check with her accountant, because she had realized a gain of $3,168 on the sale of her mixer.

REQUIRED

a. Explain how Hand could have had a loss on the sale of the same mixer on which Hammer had a gain.

7–45 Gain or Loss on Disposal of Fixed Assets—Alternate Problems (A) or (B)

Problem (A)

Warhol Enterprises purchased a spray painter at the beginning of 1996 at a cost of $150,000. Warhol estimated that the spray painter would last five years and have a residual value of $30,000. Warhol decided to use straight-line depreciation. Two years later, at the end of 1997, Warhol sold the spray painter for $100,000.

REQUIRED

a. Calculate the book value of the spray painter at the end of 1996 and the end of 1997, prior to its sale.
b. Calculate the gain or loss on the sale of the spray painter.
c. Calculate the income statement effect if Warhol had decided to give the spray painter to a charitable foundation.

Problem (B)

Johns Inc. purchased a canvas stretcher at the beginning of 1997 at a cost of $16,000. Johns estimated that the canvas stretcher would last four years, and have no residual value. Johns decided to use straight-line depreciation. Two years later, at the end of 1998, Johns sold the canvas stretcher for $10,000.

REQUIRED

a. Calculate the book value of the canvas stretcher at the end of 1997 and the end of 1998, prior to its sale.

b. Calculate the gain or loss on the sale of the canvas stretcher.

c. Calculate the income statement effect if Johns had decided to give the canvas stretcher to a charitable foundation.

d. Calculate the gain or loss on the sale of the canvas stretcher, if Johns had originally decided to use the sum-of-the-years'-digits depreciation method.

e. Next, assume Johns originally thought that the stretcher would have only a two-year life, but that its residual value would be $10,000; in other words, Johns made perfect predictions in 1997 about the life and value of the canvas stretcher at the end of 1998. Compute the gain or loss and compare it with your answer in part d.

WHAT WOULD YOU DO?

7–46 Asset Valuations: Book vs. Tax Reporting—Alternate Problems (A) or (B) (continuation of Problem 7–45)

Problem (A)

Consider Problem 7–45(A), where Warhol might have given the spray painter to a charitable foundation. What if through this gift Warhol would realize significant tax benefits, especially by claiming that the market value of the spray painter was actually $250,000? This high value could presumably be justified because of its collectible value, having been used by such a popular artist. Comment on the ethical implications of the disposal decision and of the valuation decision.

Problem (B)

Consider Alternate Problem 7–45(B), where Johns might have given the canvas stretcher to a charitable foundation. What if, through this gift, Johns would realize significant tax benefits, especially by claiming that the market value of the canvas stretcher was actually $50,000? This high value could presumably be justified because of its collectible value, having been used by such a popular artist. Comment on the ethical implications of the disposal decision and of the valuation decision.

Property, Plant, and Equipment Ratio Analysis

7–47 The following financial statement information is from TRW, Inc. TRW is a global company specializing in high-tech components for the automotive, space, and computer industries.

Property, plant, and equipment on the basis of cost (in millions)

	1994	1993
Land	$ 104	$ 104
Buildings	1,527	1,461
Machinery and equipment	3,925	3,555
	5,556	5,120
Less: Accumulated depreciation	3,067	2,793
Total property, plant, and equipment	2,489	2,327

Other Information

Sales revenue	$9,087	$7,948

REQUIRED

a. Comment on the changes in the property, plant, and equipment accounts.
b. Calculate fixed asset turnover (1994 only) and % of PPE depreciated (both years).
c. Comment on the results you calculated in part b.

Amortization of Intangibles

7–48 Bishop Corporation had the following intangible assets on December 31, 1997:

1. A patent was acquired from another company on January 1, 1997, for $25,000. The patent had been registered with the U.S. Patent Office on January 1, 1993. Assume the legal life is the useful life.
2. On April 2, 1997, the company was successful in obtaining a patent. The legal fees paid to an outside law firm were $8,400. The development costs paid to engineers who were employees of Bishop were $75,000. The patent's estimated useful life is its legal life.
3. On July 1, 1997, Bishop acquired all of the assets net of the liabilities of Fargo Company. The identifiable net assets' market values at the time of purchase totaled $100,000. Bishop acknowledged the superior earnings and loyal customer following of Fargo Company. Therefore, Bishop and Fargo agreed on a total purchase price of $145,000. Any goodwill arising from the purchase is to be amortized over 40 years.
4. On December 31, 1997, Bishop paid a consulting firm $17,000 to develop a trademark. In addition, legal fees paid in connection with the trademark were $3,000. Assume a useful life of 20 years.

REQUIRED

a. Determine the amortization expense for 1997 and the book value of each of the intangible assets listed above.

CASES AND EXTENSIONS

Financial Statement Effects: Amortizing Intangible Assets

7–49 Assume you are the manager of a small firm that has an intangible asset valued at $10 million. You believe that the firm's earnings prospects are quite favorable during the next five years. You also learn that you have a choice in selecting the amortization period for this intangible, which can range from 5 years to 40 years in length.

REQUIRED

a. Choose an amortization period of either 5 or 40 years, and defend your choice.

Financial Statement Effects: Amortizing Intangible Assets (continuation of Case 7–49)

7–50 With regard to Case 7–49, suppose the firm's earnings prospects for the next five years are very unfavorable. In fact, you discover that the amortization period of five years for this intangible will certainly result in a net loss (negative net income) over the next five years.

REQUIRED

a. Choose an amortization period either of 5 or 40 years and defend your choice.

b. Discuss any other viable options and why another option might be preferable.

Conceptual Discussion: Recognizing Gain or Loss on Disposal

7–51 Discuss the concept of recognizing a gain or loss at the time an asset is sold. Is such a gain or loss a function of good management, or is it a function of improper estimates of residual values? Why do you think that such gains or losses should be shown on the income statement? How do they affect your evaluation of the current year's net income?

Conceptual Discussion: Choosing a Depreciation Method

7–52 A firm acquired a $26,000 computer, including software, with an estimated useful life of four years and an estimated residual value of $6,000. The firm's financial vice president is trying to choose between using straight-line depreciation and double-declining-balance depreciation. It is rumored that the computer will be obsolete at the end of the second year. She also believes that the firm will have relatively high profits during the next two years. Provide advice to the CFO regarding your recommendation about the preferred depreciation method.

Financial Statement Effects: Depreciation Costs (continuation of Case 7–52)

7–53 With regard to Case 7–52, calculate the effects on the balance sheet equation for the first two years, using each depreciation method. Be sure to include separate accounts for accumulated depreciation and retained earnings in your balance sheet equation.

Financial Statement Effects: Fixed Asset Disposal (continuation of Cases 7–52 and 7–53)

7–54 With regard to Cases 7–52 and 7–53, assume that the computer is sold on the first day of the third year for $4,000 because it is obsolete and no longer useful for any purpose in this firm.

REQUIRED

a. Calculate the effect on net income from the computer's disposal using each depreciation method.

b. Assuming these experiences are typical for most computers, what advice would you now give the CFO regarding depreciation methods that should be used for computers?

c. Under what circumstances might the controller still want to use straight-line depreciation for computer equipment?

Financial Statement Effects: Land Ownership

7–55 Answer the following questions:

a. How would land owned by a manufacturer be shown on its balance sheet?

b. Would land owned by a real estate investment company, perhaps, have a different purpose than land occupied by a factory? Contrast the balance sheet presentation of land as a fixed asset and as some other type of asset.

c. Create a numerical example showing two ways a firm may report land on its balance sheet, depending on the proposed use of the land. How much discretion do you suppose that managers might have in making this choice?

Conceptual Discussion: Recognizing Estimated Residual Value

7–56 Estimating an asset's residual value incorporates significant uncertainties into the financial statements. Discuss the proposition that residual values should be ignored when an asset is depreciated.

Conceptual Discussion: Recognizing Asset Write-Downs

7–57 Discuss the concept of write-downs, that is, writing down the value of noncurrent assets on the firm's balance sheet. Why do write-downs provide managers with flexibility to manipulate earnings?

Conceptual Discussion: Recognizing Asset Write-Downs

7–58 Defend the statement that write-downs are an essential part of the conservative nature of accounting. Defend the notion that write-downs should be permitted whenever the firm, or its accountants, believe that an asset's value has been permanently impaired.

Conceptual Discussion: Recognizing Asset Write-Ups

7–59 Asset write-ups are permitted in Australia. That is, when managers of an Australian firm believe that an asset's market value has increased, they are permitted to increase the asset's reported value on the balance sheet. Defend or refute asset write-ups.

Interpreting Financial Statements: Fixed Assets

7–60 Refer to the Bristol-Myers Squibb (BMS) financial statements in Appendix E. Review the balance sheet to determine how and where fixed assets and the associated accumulated depreciation were reported.

REQUIRED

a. Read Notes 1, 3, 6, and 9. Identify and discuss any unusual terms.
b. Determine whether BMS has any unusual fixed assets. If so, discuss how they might be interpreted by financial analysts. Discuss how BMS's managers might view such assets.
c. Discuss how investments differ from advances. In your opinion, should they be disclosed together? Which is more liquid?
d. Identify BMS's accumulated depreciation balances at the end of each year. If these items are not disclosed, what effects will this have on your analysis of their financial statements?
e. Calculate the following ratios for BMS:

- Fixed asset turnover
- Percentage of PPE depreciated

f. Based on your answer above, how effectively is BMS managing its long-term assets?

Interpreting Financial Statements: Disposal of Fixed Assets

7–61 Refer to the Bristol-Myers Squibb (BMS) financial statements in Appendix E. Review the financial statements to determine how and where any disposals of fixed assets were reported.

REQUIRED

a. Refer to Note 3. Were the gains or losses on disposals of fixed assets clearly reported?

b. Why are no specific dollar amounts given for gain or losses on the various fixed asset disposals in Note 3?

c. Refer to the statement of cash flows. How much cash was received from the sale of businesses? How much cash was spent on capital expenditures?

d. Discuss any other unusual concerns regarding BMS's fixed assets. What other related information might an external analyst require, or prefer?

Interpreting Financial Statements: Fixed Assets

7–62 Refer to Reebok's financial statements in Appendix F. Review the balance sheet to determine how and where fixed assets and the associated accumulated depreciation were reported.

REQUIRED

a. Read Notes 1 and 3. Identify and discuss any unusual terms. Trace any numerical disclosures of fixed asset costs in the notes to corresponding disclosures in the financial statements.

b. Determine whether Reebok has any unusual fixed assets. If so, discuss how they might be interpreted by financial analysts. Discuss how Reebok's managers might view such assets.

c. Identify Reebok's accumulated depreciation balances at the end of each year. If these items are not disclosed, what effects will this have on your analysis of their financial statements?

d. Calculate the following ratios for Reebok:

- Fixed asset turnover
- Percentage of PPE depreciated

e. Based on your answers above, how effectively is Reebok managing its long-term assets?

Interpreting Financial Statements: Fixed Assets

7–63 Refer to OshKosh B'Gosh's financial statements in Appendix C. Review the balance sheet to determine how and where fixed assets and the associated accumulated depreciation were reported.

REQUIRED

a. Read Notes 1, 2, and 4. Identify and discuss any unusual terms. Trace numerical disclosures of fixed asset costs in the notes to corresponding disclosures in the financial statements.

b. Determine whether OshKosh B'Gosh has any unusual fixed assets. If so, discuss how they might be interpreted by financial analysts. Discuss how OshKosh B'Gosh's managers might view such assets.

c. Identify OshKosh B'Gosh's accumulated depreciation balances at the end of each year. If these items are not disclosed, what effects will this have on your analysis of their financial statements?

d. Calculate the following ratios for OshKosh B'Gosh:

- Fixed asset turnover
- Percentage of PPE depreciated

e. Based on your answers above, how effectively is OshKosh B'Gosh managing its long-term assets?

Interpreting Financial Statements: Disposal of Fixed Assets

7–64 Refer to OshKosh B'Gosh's financial statements in Appendix C. Review the financial statements to determine how and where any disposals of fixed assets were reported.

REQUIRED

a. Where were the disposals of fixed assets reported? Trace numerical disclosures of such items in the notes to corresponding disclosures in the financial statements.

b. Calculate the effects of disposals of fixed assets on net income. In other words, how much of OshKosh B'Gosh's net income can be attributed to the disposal of fixed assets?

c. Discuss any other unusual concerns regarding OshKosh B'Gosh's fixed assets. What other related information might an external analyst require, or prefer?

Interpreting Financial Statements: Fixed Assets

7–65 Refer to Wendy's financial statements in Appendix D. Review the balance sheet to determine how and where fixed assets and the associated accumulated depreciation were reported.

REQUIRED

a. Read all notes concerning fixed assets. Identify and discuss any unusual terms. Trace numerical disclosures of fixed asset costs in the notes to corresponding disclosures in the financial statements.

b. Determine whether Wendy's has any unusual fixed assets. If so, discuss how they might be interpreted by financial analysts. Discuss how Wendy's managers might view such assets.

c. Identify Wendy's accumulated depreciation balances at the end of each year. If these items are not disclosed, what effects will this have on your analysis of their financial statements?

d. Calculate the following ratios for Wendy's:

- Fixed asset turnover
- Percentage of PPE depreciated

e. Based on your answers above, how effectively is Wendy's managing its long-term assets?

Interpreting Financial Statements: Disposal of Fixed Assets

7–66 Refer to Wendy's financial statements in Appendix D. Review the financial statements to determine how and where any disposals of fixed assets were reported. Also identify how and where any gains or losses on disposals of fixed assets were reported.

REQUIRED

a. Were the gains or losses on disposals of fixed assets clearly reported?
b. How much of Wendy's income before income taxes can be attributed to the disposal of fixed assets?
c. Refer to the statement of cash flows. How much cash was received from restaurant dispositions? How much cash was spent on capital expenditures?

Comprehensive Analysis: Fixed Assets

7–67 Pfizer Inc. reported the following information in its property, plant, and equipment note to the 1994 financial statements ($ in millions):

	1994	1993	1992
Land	$ 85.2	$ 81.8	$ 71.7
Buildings	1,218.6	1,093.8	953.9
Machinery and equipment	2,108.4	1,897.8	1,706.9
Furniture, fixtures and other	940.2	812.8	698.3
Construction in progress	640.5	414.5	385.6
Total PPE	4,992.9	4,300.7	3,816.4
Less accumulated depreciation	1,919.7	1,668.2	1,511.3
Book value PPE	$3,073.2	$2,632.5	$2,305.1

REQUIRED

Part I

a. Identify and describe each term in this note.
b. During which year(s) did Pfizer acquire substantial fixed assets? How do you know?
c. During which year(s) did Pfizer sell some fixed assets? How can you tell?
d. Did Pfizer's construction change markedly during these three years? What evidence supports your conclusion?
e. Calculate the percentage of PPE depreciated for each year. Discuss the meaning and implications of your results.

Part II

Given the following additional information from Pfizer's 1994 annual report ($ in millions):

	1994	1993	1992
Net sales	$8,281.3	$7,477.7	$7,230.2
Income from operations	1,972.5	913.3	1,553.9

f. Calculate fixed asset turnover for 1994 and 1993.
g. Evaluate and discuss your results.

Part III

h. If you now learn that the average fixed asset turnover is 1.4 for the chemical industry, reevaluate and discuss your earlier results.

Part IV

Pfizer Inc. reported the following summary of significant accounting policies in its 1994 annual report:

Property, plant, and equipment are recorded at cost. Significant improvements are capitalized. In general, the straight-line method of depreciation is used for financial reporting purposes and accelerated methods are used for U.S. and certain foreign tax reporting purposes.

i. Discuss each part of this note, indicating how it relates to the concepts described in this chapter.

Part V

j. Identify and discuss areas where managers have some discretion to choose between alternative accounting policies or methods.
k. Similarly, identify areas where substantial judgment and subjectivity may be used.
l. What opportunities may Pfizer use to adjust or to manipulate net income? Are they significant? Why?

Comprehensive Analysis: Fixed Assets

7–68 Spelling Entertainment, which produces films and videos and other entertainment media, lists the following items in its 1994 annual report ($ in thousands):

	1994	1993	1992	1991
Property, plant, and equipment, net	$ 16,161	$ 4,770	$ 4,834	$ 6,331
Other assets	19,678	4,562	6,512	13,879
Net assets held for disposition	0	0	0	16,475
Intangibles, net of accumulated amortization of $17,671, $10,527, $6,713 and $2,626	400,751	1,549,983	159,291	154,946
Revenues	$599,839	$ 274,899	$257,546	$122,748
Operating income	50,743	39,727	25,315	13,987

REQUIRED

Part I

a. Describe each of Spelling's noncurrent assets.
b. Identify any unusual trends or unusual items.
c. Calculate fixed asset turnover for 1993 and 1994. Use property, plant, and equipment, net.

Part II

d. How does Spelling seem to be managing its fixed assets? What evidence supports your conclusion?

e. Why are intangibles Spelling's largest noncurrent asset? What problems might this create, especially if these intangibles represent copyrights and trademarks that are no longer fashionable?

Part III

f. What additional information is needed before you can calculate Spelling's percentage of PPE depreciated?
g. Where might you find such information?
h. Upon carefully reading the notes to Spelling's 1994 financial statements, you do not find the requisite information. What would you do next to find this information?

Part IV

Further review of Spelling's notes reveals the following additional information about its asset disposal strategy, or the effects thereof.

Net assets (liabilities) held for disposition consisted of the following at December 31, ($ in thousands):

	1994	1993	1992	1991
Receivables, net	$ 608	$ 2,714	$ 7,445	$40,282
Investments	0	0	0	2,600
Property, plant, and equipment, net	3,161	4,467	4,572	23,050
Other assets	0	0	247	5,280
Accounts payable and other accruals	(1,749)	(1,780)	(4,023)	(16,681)
Notes payable	0	0	0	(19,500)
Other liabilities	0	0	(1,090)	(4,707)
	$ 2,020	$ 5,401	$ 7,151	$30,324
Less allowance for estimated estimated losses on disposal of segment	(20,368)	(29,621)	(15,058)	(13,849)
	$(18,348)	$(24,220)	$ (7,907)	$16,475

i. Describe each item in the above note. Note that only one of the above subtotals was reported in Spelling's balance sheet (see above, Part I). Where were the other subtotals reported? Why?
j. Discuss the implications of this note. What does this note imply about the valuations of Spelling's other assets? Why?
k. How have Spelling's perceptions regarding its asset disposal activities changed over the years? Why?
l. Would an external analyst view Spelling's note as optimistic, or worse? Why?
m. If Spelling completes its disposition program in 1995, what is the likely effect on 1995's net income? Why?

Comprehensive Analysis: Noncurrent and Intangible Assets

7–69 Boudreaux Group is an international biochemical and pharmaceutical firm, headquartered in Switzerland. Its 1997 annual report includes the following (Swiss francs in millions):

	1997	1996	1995
Property, plant, and equipment, net	$ 7,010	$ 6,319	$ 5,815
Intangible assets	1,895	2,050	2,200
Other long-term assets	1,583	1,313	1,064
Total long-term assets	$10,488	$ 9,682	$ 9,079
Sales	$13,576	$12,702	$11,840
Gross profit	8,145	7,139	6,295
Gross (original) cost PPE	13,077	11,950	10,905

Intangible assets

Intangible assets comprise acquired intellectual property (including patents, technology and know-how), trademarks, licenses, and other similarly identified rights. They are recorded at their acquisition cost and are amortized over the lower of their legal or estimated economic lives up to a maximum of ten years. Costs associated with internally developed intangible assets are expensed as incurred.

REQUIRED

a. Describe each of Boudreaux's disclosures related to noncurrent assets.
b. For 1996 and 1997, calculate the fixed asset turnover.
c. For 1996 and 1997, calculate the percentage of PPE depreciated.
d. Discuss and interpret the results of these ratio computations.
e. With regard to intangibles, how has Boudreaux constrained some of the discretion and subjectivity that it might have had otherwise?
f. What impact does the term *know-how* have on your analysis of Boudreaux's noncurrent assets?

Financial Statement Interpretation: R&D Costs

7–70 Beaubox, one of Europe's leading packaging manufacturers, is headquartered in Paris. Its 1997 annual report contains the following note.

Research and Development Expenditure

Such expenditure is charged to the profit and loss account in the year in which it is incurred. Tangible assets related to research and development are depreciated over the expected useful lives of the assets.

REQUIRED

a. Discuss the meaning and possible interpretation of this note.
b. Rewrite this note to clarify its meaning.
c. Does this treatment of R&D seem consistent with U.S. GAAP? In what ways?

Financial Statement Interpretation: Depreciation and Depletion

7–71 Inco Limited, headquartered in Toronto, is one of the world's premier mining and metals companies. Its 1994 annual report contains the following note:

Depreciation and Depletion

Depreciation is calculated using the straight-line method and, for the nickel operations in Indonesia, the unit-of-production method, based on the estimated economic lives of property, plant, and equipment. Such lives are generally limited to a maximum of 20 years and are subject to annual review. Depletion is calculated by a method that allocates mine development costs ratably to the tons of ore mined.

Upon further study, you learn that the unit-of-production depreciation method is very similar to the methods described in this chapter to determine depletion allowances.

REQUIRED

a. Identify and discuss each term in this note.
b. Why would a company want to use more than one depreciation method?
c. Does the 20-year limitation on useful lives result in more conservative, or less conservative, measures of net income? What other information would you need to better assess this issue?
d. What choices does Inco Limited have during its annual review of useful lives? What would be the most likely balance sheet and income statement effects of such a review? Why?
e. What is the potential impact of not distinguishing between acquired and developed natural resources?

Financial Statement Interpretation: Cash Flow Effects

7–72 Sigma Designs is a diversified graphic systems corporation. Its statement of cash flows follows:

Sigma Designs, Inc.
Statement of Cash Flows
For the Years Ended January 31, 1995 and 1994

	1995	1994
	(dollars in thousands)	
Cash Flows from Operating Activities		
Net loss	$ (8,773)	$ (29,546)
Adjustments to reconcile net loss to net cash provided by operating activities (summary of all net adjustments)	(110)	15,885
Net cash provided by (used for) operating activities	(8,883)	(13,661)
Cash Flows from Investing Activities		
Purchases of marketable securities	(25,350)	(22,542)
Sales of marketable securities	22,296	33,355
Equipment additions	(721)	(612)
Software development costs (capitalized)	(1,255)	(494)
Other asset transactions	0	183
Net cash provided (used for) investing activities	(5,030)	9,890
Cash Flows from Financing Activities		
Common stock sold	13,201	493
Repayment of long-term obligations	1,710	0
Other financing transactions	(1,925)	0
Net cash provided (used for) financing activities	12,986	493
Decrease in cash and equivalents	$ (927)	$ (3,278)

REQUIRED

a. What do you think is represented by the category of cash flows shown as "Software development costs (capitalized)"? Who has received these cash payments?

b. Do these "Software development costs" payments seem material, relative to the size of Sigma Designs? How would you feel about this type of cash payment if it were $3,000,000 each year?

Conceptual Discussion: Loss of Fixed Assets

7–73 Becky's Courier Service is a one-person, one-bicycle operation. Her only capital equipment is a highly specialized, custom-designed mountain bike that can be used throughout the urban jungle.

REQUIRED

a. Assume her mountain bike broke, and she is very sad over its loss. What accounting recognition should be given to this tragedy?

b. Would your answer change if the bike had been stolen? Why?

c. Assume her mountain bike was destroyed in a fire while chained in a bike rack at a client's site. The client's insurance company provided Becky with a check for the replacement cost of the bicycle, which was twice its original price. What accounting recognition should be given to this event?

WHAT WOULD YOU DO?

Capitalizing or Expensing Decisions

7–74 The president of your company has made it clear that he wants to report as large a net income number as possible. Part of your responsibility as the controller is to determine if certain expenditures should be expensed or capitalized. Knowing the president's wishes, which of the following expenditures would you capitalize?

a. Painting costs (part of the factory and office building are painted each year)

b. Costs to repair cracks in the parking lot

c. Cost of tree pruning on corporate grounds

d. Cost to produce brochures that will be given to prospective customers next year

e. Costs to replace an engine in a company truck

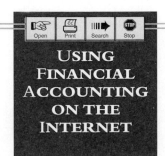

USING FINANCIAL ACCOUNTING ON THE INTERNET

7–75 Locate the most recent set of financial statements for the computer manufacturers listed below. You may use either the 10-K available at EDGAR (**www.sec.gov/edgarhp.htm**) or the annual report available at the company page on the WWW.

Corporation	Home Page Location
Compaq	**www.compaq.com** (under "contents")
Gateway	**www.gw2k.com** (under "Tell Me About Gateway")
IBM	**www.ibm.com/IBM/**
Dell	**www.us.dell.com/us/**

REQUIRED

a. What is the total value of the property, plant, and equipment owned by each corporation? What percentage of total assets do they represent?
b. What is the composition of the property, plant, and equipment account (i.e., what percentage is land, etc.)? What is the method of depreciation used for each fixed asset class?
c. Calculate the fixed asset turnover and the percentage of PPE depreciated for each company.

7–76 For each of the following companies, locate the most recent 10-K available using the EDGAR database (**www.sec.gov/edgarhp.htm**): Walt Disney Corp., Schering Plough, Oncogene Science, Chicago Tribune, John Wiley & Co., RJR Nabisco, Macromedia Inc.

REQUIRED

a. Identify a unique intangible asset owned by each company.
b. For each intangible asset you have listed, identify (1) its value in both dollars and as a percentage of total assets and (2) the method of amortization used. (*Hint:* You will find much useful information in the Notes to the Financial Statements.)

7–77 Companies in different industries naturally use different assets in daily operations. The differences are reflected in both type and amount of long-term tangible assets. Locate, from 10-Ks on file with EDGAR (**www.gov.sec/edgar-hp.htm**), the latest balance sheet and Notes to the Financial Statements for the following companies:

- Ameritech (telecommunications)
- Banc One (banking)
- Boeing (airplane manufacturing)
- Dole (food products)
- Southwest Airlines (air transportation)

REQUIRED

a. Before looking at the 10-Ks, list those types of long-term tangible assets you believe should be included on each company's balance sheet.
b. Identify the primary long-term tangible assets for each company and determine the percent of total assets it represents.
c. Comment on the differences you observe due to industry influences.

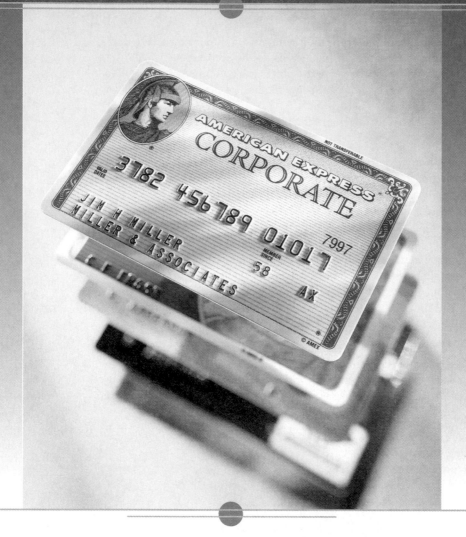

CHAPTER 8

STUDYING THIS CHAPTER
WILL ENABLE YOU TO

1. Recognize the types of current liabilities that are reported on the balance sheets of most business firms.
2. Understand the types of business transactions and events that create current liabilities.
3. Appreciate how liability reporting often depends on estimates and judgments.

STUDYING THE APPENDIX WILL ENABLE YOU TO

1. Determine the future value, or compound amount, of dollars that are invested or borrowed today.
2. Determine the value today, or present value, of dollars that are to be received or paid in the future.
3. Understand how the concept of present value is used to calculate interest expense.

CURRENT
LIABILITIES

INTRODUCTION

Chapters 6 and 7 discussed accounting and reporting for assets. Our focus now shifts to the sources of the funds that are invested in assets. The balance sheet equation indicates that the firm's economic resources or assets are obtained from two sources: creditors and investors, i.e.,

$$\text{ASSETS} = \text{LIABILITIES} + \text{SHAREHOLDERS' EQUITY}$$

Chapters 8 and 9 examine liability accounting and reporting issues. Chapter 10 discusses shareholders' equity.

TYPES OF CURRENT LIABILITIES

Liabilities or "borrowed capital" constitutes a major source of funds for business firms. In fact, the average corporation relies on debt for more than half of the funds it has invested in assets. In some industries (e.g., public utilities and financial institutions), debt financing may exceed 90 percent of total assets. Financial statement users pay careful attention to the sources of financing because the success of a firm depends as much on the effective management of its liabilities and shareholders' equity as it does on the efficient utilization of its assets. The firm's liability management also affects the risks and the returns available to the firm's creditors and shareholders.

Exhibit 8–1 shows the current liabilities section of a recent balance sheet for Rockwell International Corporation, a firm doing business in the electronics, aerospace, and automotive components industries. The items and amounts shown in the exhibit are typical of those reported by business firms. The next section discusses the accounting and reporting issues associated with each major current liability shown on Rockwell International's balance sheet.

EXHIBIT 8–1
CURRENT LIABILITIES

Rockwell International Corporation Current Liabilities at September 30, 1993 (dollars in millions)	
Current Liabilities	
Accounts payable–trade	$ 859.8
Short-term debt	166.4
Accrued compensation and benefits	710.1
Current portion of long-term debt	7.4
Advance payments from customers	362.7
Accrued product warranties	165.6
Accrued income taxes	94.1
Accrued restructuring costs	62.1
Other	562.7
Total current liabilities	$2,990.9

Current liabilities are short-term obligations that usually must be paid from current assets within a year. They can be of several types: (1) obligations to pay cash to other entities, such as accounts payable, notes payable, and accrued liabilities; (2) obligations to provide other entities with goods or services for which payment has already been received, such as revenues received in advance; and (3) obligations to honor product warranties (guarantees). Examples of each are discussed next.

LIABILITIES REQUIRING CASH PAYMENTS

 Accounts Payable

The largest single item listed among Rockwell's current liabilities is accounts payable–trade. **Accounts payable** represent debts that the firm incurs in purchasing inventories and supplies, as well as amounts that the firm owes for other services used in its operations, such as rentals, utilities, insurance, and so on. Most business transactions with suppliers involve short-term credit, for which payments are due within a designated period such as 30 or 60 days. To illustrate, assume a firm purchased inventory for $100,000 to be paid within 30 days. The purchase of inventory would increase inventory and accounts payable.

At the date of purchase:

ASSETS	=	LIABILITIES	+	SHAREHOLDERS' EQUITY
Inventory +$100,000		Accounts payable +$100,000		

The $100,000 payment to the supplier would decrease cash and eliminate the accounts payable.

At the date of payment:

ASSETS	=	LIABILITIES	+	SHAREHOLDERS' EQUITY
Cash		Accounts payable		
−$100,000		−$100,000		

⬤ Discounts

Suppliers frequently offer discounts for early payment. The discount rates are usually high enough to induce customers to pay promptly. If the buyer intends to pay within the discount period, then the inventory is usually recorded at its cost, net of the discount. In the preceding example, if the supplier offered a 2% discount for early payment, and the purchaser intends to pay within the discount period, then the inventory would be recorded initially at a cost of $98,000 ($100,000 invoice price, minus a $2,000 discount).

At the date of purchase:

ASSETS	=	LIABILITIES	+	SHAREHOLDERS' EQUITY
Inventory		Accounts payable		
+$98,000		+$98,000		

If the account subsequently is paid *after* the discount period has expired, then the purchaser would incur an interest expense of $2,000 ($100,000 − 98,000).

At the date of payment:

ASSETS	=	LIABILITIES	+	SHAREHOLDERS' EQUITY
Cash		Accounts payable		Retained earnings
−$100,000		−$98,000		−$2,000 (interest expense)

In times of low liquidity, some managers are tempted to "stretch out" their payments to suppliers and thereby forgo the available purchase discounts. Such a tactic represents a very high cost of borrowing and should be avoided. For example, recall from Chapter 6 that discount terms of 2/10, net 30 imply an annual interest rate of about 36%. Firms can usually borrow from other sources at rates much lower than this. Consequently, most firms pay their accounts within the discount period and rely instead on other, less costly sources of borrowed capital to raise cash.

⬤ Notes Payable

Rockwell's current liabilities include $166.4 million of short-term debt, which consists mainly of notes payable to financial institutions. Business firms frequently borrow funds from banks or other lenders by signing a formal **note payable** with a fixed repayment date. Notes payable may be either interest bearing or discounted. To illustrate the accounting for an interest-bearing note, assume that a firm borrows $200,000 from a bank, to be repaid in six months at an interest rate of 12% per year. Interest rates are usually stated on a yearly basis, even if the loan is for a shorter time period. This transaction increases cash and notes payable by $200,000.

At the date of borrowing:

ASSETS	=	LIABILITIES	+	SHAREHOLDERS' EQUITY
Cash		Notes payable		
+$200,000		+$200,000		

Recall that the principal amount *(P)*, the interest rate *(r)*, and the time period *(t)* of the loan are used to determine the interest expense *(I)* in the following way:

$$\text{Interest} = \text{Principal} \times \text{Rate} \times \text{Time}$$
$$I = P \times r \times t$$
$$= \$200,000 \times 12\% \times 1/2 \text{ year}$$
$$= \$12,000$$

When the note is repaid with interest, cash is reduced by $212,000, the notes payable balance is eliminated, and the firm incurs interest expense of $12,000.

At the date of payment:

ASSETS	=	LIABILITIES	+	SHAREHOLDERS' EQUITY
Cash		Notes payable		Retained earnings
−$212,000		−$200,000		−$12,000 (interest expense)

To illustrate the accounting for a discounted note, assume that the firm signs a note promising to pay the bank $200,000 in six months. The bank will *discount* the note by deducting the interest charge in advance. Assuming the interest rate is 12 percent, the bank will deduct interest of $12,000 ($200,000 × 12% × 1/2 year = $12,000) in advance. The amount paid to the borrower upon signing the note is then $188,000 ($200,000 − $12,000 = $188,000). This transaction increases cash and notes payable by $188,000.

At the date of borrowing:

ASSETS	=	LIABILITIES	+	SHAREHOLDERS' EQUITY
Cash		Notes payable		
+$188,000		+$188,000		

When the note is repaid, cash is reduced by $200,000 (the face amount of the note), the note payable balance is eliminated, and the firm incurs interest expense of $12,000.

At the date of payment:

ASSETS	=	LIABILITIES	+	SHAREHOLDERS' EQUITY
Cash		Notes payable		Retained earnings
−$200,000		−$188,000		−$12,000 (interest expense)

Accrued Compensation and Benefits

Rockwell International's current liabilities listed in Exhibit 8–1 include $710.1 million in accrued compensation and benefits. **Accrued liabilities** represent expenses that have been incurred prior to the balance sheet date that have been neither paid nor included with liabilities as of the balance sheet date. An adjustment must be made to recognize the expense and the related obligation at the balance sheet date.

Rockwell's accrued compensation benefits consist primarily of (1) wages and salaries earned, but unpaid, at the balance sheet date and (2) vacation and holiday pay. To illustrate an adjustment to recognize accrued wages and salaries, assume that Rockwell has a weekly payroll of $400 million, and that Rockwell's balance sheet date of September 30, 1993, falls on a Tuesday. In such a situation, Rockwell's employees have earned two days' pay, or $160 million (2 days ÷ 5 days = 40%; $400 million weekly payroll × 40% = $160 million), as of the balance sheet date. If so, it is necessary for Rockwell to accrue the expense and liability as of September 30, 1993:

ASSETS	=	LIABILITIES	+	SHAREHOLDERS' EQUITY
		Accrued compensation		Retained earnings
		+$160 million		−$160 million
				(compensation expense)

As a result, $160 million of compensation expense would be recognized in 1993, and the current liabilities reported at September 30, 1993, would include an accrued liability for this amount. When the weekly payroll ($400 million) is paid to the employees on October 3, 1993, the following balance sheet effects occur:

ASSETS	=	LIABILITIES	+	SHAREHOLDERS' EQUITY
Cash		Accrued compensation		Retained earnings
− $400 million		−$160 million		−$240 million
				(compensation expense)

Note that this accrual of compensation expense is used to achieve the objective of matching costs and benefits that was discussed earlier (especially in Chapters 2 and 4). The total compensation expense of $400 million has been appropriately divided between the fiscal years ending on September 30 of 1993 and 1994, in proportion to the benefits obtained each year.

To illustrate the accrual of vacation benefits, assume Rockwell's employees earn vacation benefits evenly over the period July 1 through June 30, and the firm incurs total vacation expenses each year of $2 billion. In this case, at the balance sheet date of September 30, 1993, Rockwell's employees would have earned three months (July, August, and September) of vacation benefits, or $500 million (3 months ÷ 12 months = 25%; $2 billion annual expense × 25% = $500 million). For this reason, Rockwell's 1993 income statement would include an expense and the balance sheet at September 30, 1993, would include a current liability for accrued employee benefits of $500 million.

Current Maturities of Long-Term Debt

A variety of long-term borrowing arrangements will be discussed in Chapter 9. For the present, bear in mind that, as time goes by, long-term debts become short-term debts. For this reason, the current liabilities of many firms include the portion of long-term debt that matures within the coming year. Note in Exhibit 8–1 that Rockwell International reports $7.4 million among its current liabilities, described as the current portion of long-term debt. This amount is a claim against the company's current assets in the coming year and is therefore a current liability.

Accrued Income Taxes

Rockwell's current liabilities shown in Exhibit 8–1 include accrued income taxes in the amount of $94.1 million. Business corporations are taxable entities and must file tax returns with the federal and state governments. In fiscal 1993, Rockwell reported income before taxes of $904.1, and was assessed $343.4 million in income taxes. Of this amount, $94.1 million remains unpaid at September 30, 1993. Similar to individual taxpayers, corporations are on a "pay-as-you-go" system for the payment of income taxes. Rockwell has been making regular payments to government taxing authorities throughout the year, based on estimates of its 1993 taxable income.

Accrued Restructuring Costs

Rockwell's current liabilities shown in Exhibit 8–1 include $62.1 million in accrued restructuring costs. During the difficult economic climate of the late 1980s and early 1990s many major corporations decided to *restructure,* i.e., to downsize and to refocus their operations. Corporate downsizing often entails the retraining, layoff, or termination of many employees, and the associated costs to the firms may be substantial. Corporations that refocus their operations may discontinue various lines of business, often at considerable losses. The process of restructuring a firm may take several years.

When a firm decides to restructure, the total estimated costs of restructuring are expensed in the current year. For example, Rockwell embarked on a restructuring program in fiscal 1991 and in that year reported an expense and an accrual of restructuring costs of $271.5 million.

During fiscal 1991:

ASSETS	=	LIABILITIES	+	SHAREHOLDERS' EQUITY
		Accrued restructuring costs		Retained earnings
		+$271.5 million		−$271.5 million
				(restructuring expense)

During fiscal 1992 and 1993, the firm made expenditures of $209.4 million in its attempts to downsize and refocus operations.

During fiscal 1992 and 1993:

ASSETS	=	LIABILITIES	+	SHAREHOLDERS' EQUITY
Various assets		Accrued restructuring costs		
−$209.4 million		−$209.4 million		

As a result, the remaining obligation for restructuring costs is $62.1 million ($271.5 − $209.4 = $62.1) at the end of fiscal 1993. Bear in mind that this amount is based on estimates made in 1991, when the restructuring program was undertaken. If the actual restructuring costs incurred (in the future) differ from this estimated amount, Rockwell will need to make adjustments to income reported in future periods.

Accounting for restructuring costs is a controversial issue in financial reporting, because the dollar amounts are often material, and require difficult estimates of costs to be incurred over several years in the future. Moreover, in many cases the costs are related to actions that are planned by management in future periods, rather than being based on completed agreements or transactions. Some investors and analysts suggest that current accounting practices in reporting restructuring costs give managers too much discretion in shaping the numbers that will appear on the present and future income statements. Several of the cases at the end of this chapter and in subsequent chapters illustrate how managers have chosen to report restructuring expenses. Reality Check 8–1 shows footnote disclosures of restructuring changes reported by a major corporation.

OBLIGATIONS TO PROVIDE GOODS OR SERVICES

In many industries customers pay in advance for goods and services to be provided at future dates. Education, transportation, magazine publishing, advertising, and construction are all examples of industries where advance customer payments are often required. For instance, the current liabilities of Rockwell International at the end of

H. J. HEINZ COMPANY
RESTRUCTURING CHARGES

REALITY CHECK 8–1

The fiscal 1993 annual report of H. J. Heinz Company, an international food processing and food service firm, included a liability for accrued restructuring costs of $179.3 million. Footnotes contain the following explanation:

> In 1992, restructuring charges of $88.3 million on a pre-tax basis ($0.20 per share) were reflected in operating income to provide for the consolidation of functions, staff reductions, organizational reform, and plant modernizations and closures.
>
> In 1993, restructuring charges of $192.3 million on a pre-tax basis ($0.45 per share) were reflected in operating income. The major components of the restructuring plan related to employee severance and relocation costs ($99 million) and facilities consolidation and closure costs ($73 million). Upon completion of all of the projects in 1995, it is anticipated that the total headcount reduction will be achieved.

REQUIRED

a. Why do firms accrue restructuring costs before such costs are actually incurred? Do such costs satisfy the definition of liabilities that was presented in Chapter 3 of this text?

b. Based on the footnote information, H. J. Heinz has recognized restructuring costs of $280.6 million ($88.3 in 1992 plus $192.3 in 1993 equals $280.6). How will these charges affect the amounts of income reported by the firm in future years? How would these charges influence your comparison of the firm's profit trend between 1993 and 1994?

1993 shown in Exhibit 8–1 include an obligation of $362.7 million, described as advance payments from customers.

To illustrate the accounting for such advance customer payments, assume that during 1993 Rockwell received $800 million as advance payments from customers. Assume also that $437.3 million of this amount is earned by September 30, 1993, and the remainder is earned in the following fiscal year. These events are recognized in each year.

In 1993, on receiving the customers' deposits, the entire $800 million is unearned, and the company has an obligation to perform future services.

Upon receipt of customer deposits:

ASSETS	=	LIABILITIES	+	SHAREHOLDERS' EQUITY
Cash		Advance payments from customers		
+$800 million		+$800 million		

Because $437.3 million of the payments has been earned by the end of fiscal 1993, this amount is recognized as revenue in 1993:

ASSETS	=	LIABILITIES	+	SHAREHOLDERS' EQUITY
		Advance payments from customers		Retained earnings
		−$437.3 million		+$437.3 million (revenue)

Because $800 million was received in advance from customers and $437.3 million has been earned during 1993, the balance sheet at September 30, 1993, would show a remaining obligation of $362.7 million. When these amounts are earned in the following year, the remaining obligation will be eliminated, and revenues of $362.7 million will be recognized.

As revenues are earned in 1994:

ASSETS	=	LIABILITIES	+	SHAREHOLDERS' EQUITY
		Advance payments from customers		Retained earnings
		−$362.7 million		+$362.7 million (revenue)

Reality Check 8–2 shows how a major airline reports obligations to provide transportation services to its customers, for which payment has been received in advance.

REALITY CHECK 8–2

DELTA AIR LINES
CURRENT LIABILITIES FOR AIR TRAFFIC
AND FREQUENT FLYERS

Delta Air Lines is one of the world's largest airlines and provides scheduled passenger service, air freight, mail, and other related aviation services. Delta's current liabilities at the end of fiscal 1993 include over $1 billion in obligations for air traffic liabilities and a frequent flyer program. Accompanying footnotes provide the following explanations:

Passenger revenue: Passenger ticket sales are recorded as revenue when the transportation is provided. The value of unused tickets is included in current liabilities as air traffic liability.

Frequent flyer program: The company sponsors a travel incentive program whereby frequent travelers accumulate mileage credits that entitle them to certain awards, including free travel. The company accrued the estimated incremental cost of providing free travel awards under its Frequent Flyer program when free travel award levels are achieved. The accrued incremental cost is recorded in current liabilities.

REQUIRED

a. In what way does Delta's air traffic liability differ from accounts payable included in current liabilities? In what ways are the two items similar?
b. Contrast the ways that Delta measures its air traffic and frequent flyer liabilities. Attempt to justify the differences in the two measurements.

Notice in this case that although Rockwell's balance sheet at the end of 1993 reports a $362.7 million obligation for advance payments, this does not represent a dollar amount that the company must pay to outside entities. Rather, it represents resources that Rockwell has received from customers, but has not yet earned. Rockwell must earn these payments in future periods, and the resulting revenues (together with any related expenses) will be recognized in these future periods. If Rockwell does not fulfill this obligation, the advances would be returnable and then would be a liability payable in cash.

OBLIGATIONS FOR WARRANTIES

It is common business practice for companies to stand behind the quality of their products by offering assurances of repairs, replacements, and/or refunds in the event of product failures or customer dissatisfaction. Although the eventual costs of such **obligations for warranties** cannot be known with certainty at the date of sale, those costs are associated with current sales revenues. For revenues and expenses to be properly matched, the future costs of warranties and guarantees associated with the current period revenues must be estimated and recorded in the current period. Also, the related obligations must be reported on the balance sheet.

As an example, Rockwell International provides warranties on many of its sales. Exhibit 8–1 shows that Rockwell reports among its current liabilities an obligation for product warranties in the amount of $165.6 million. This implies that Rockwell's managers estimate that the company will eventually make expenditures of about $165.6 million related to merchandise sold prior to the balance sheet date. If we assume that the entire obligation relates to 1993 sales and no costs have yet been incurred for warranties on 1993 sales, the company must have recognized the following event in 1993:

ASSETS	=	LIABILITIES	+	SHAREHOLDERS' EQUITY
		Warranty obligation +$165.6 million		Retained earnings −$165.6 million (warranty expense)

In subsequent years, the firm will spend cash or use other resources to perform warranty repairs. As the warranty repairs occur in subsequent periods, the liability will be eliminated.

In subsequent periods:

ASSETS	=	LIABILITIES	+	SHAREHOLDERS' EQUITY
Cash (or other resources) −$165.6 million		Warranty obligation −$165.6 million		

Note that no additional expenses are recognized at these points because the warranty expenses were matched against sales in 1993.

Of course, the cost to be incurred for product warranties cannot be known for certain in the period of sale. For this reason, Rockwell must rely on its past experience and on information from other firms engaged in similar activities to make a reasonable estimate of its obligations for warranties. If the amounts of warranty expenses and obligations are potentially significant to users of Rockwell's financial statements, the firm's auditors will carefully evaluate the assumptions used to estimate this obligation.

SUMMARY OF LEARNING OBJECTIVES

1. **Recognize the types of current liabilities that are reported on the balance sheets of most business firms.**
   Current liabilities belong to one of three broad categories: (1) obligations to pay cash to other entities at specific dates, such as accounts payables, and notes payable, and accrued liabilities; (2) obligations to provide goods or services for which payment has been received in advance; and (3) estimated costs to be incurred that are associated with revenues recorded in earlier periods, such as warranty obligations. Each of these three categories of current liabilities shows a common characteristic: Each obligates the firm to use current assets within the coming year or operating cycle.

2. **Understand the types of business transactions and events that create current liabilities.**
   Most businesses purchase inventories, supplies, and services using short-term credit, or accounts payable. Also, firms frequently borrow operating funds through short-term loans, or notes payable. At the end of an accounting period, firms usually require accruals to recognize expenses and current obligations for expenses such as wages and salaries, income taxes, and other items. In addition, firms often guarantee their products and services and must report obligations for the estimated costs of warranties of past sales.

3. **Appreciate how liability reporting often depends on estimates and judgments.**
   The matching concept that underlies the measurement of income requires that all costs associated with current revenues be recognized in the current period. In some cases (e.g., product warranties, restructuring costs), the actual expenditures will be made in future years, and the dollar amounts to be incurred are not known with certainty. For this reason, currently reported expenses and liabilities are the results of estimates, based on past experience, industry norms, and professional judgments.

Accounts payable
Accrued liabilities
Current liabilities

Note payable
Obligations for warranties

KEY TERMS

SOLUTION TO REALITY CHECK 8–1

a. Firms accrue restructuring costs in their attempt to match revenues and expenses. Because the decision to restructure operations is made in the current period, all of the estimated associated expenses are recognized in the current period. It may be argued that such costs meet the definition of current liabilities because (1) the firm

REALITY CHECK SOLUTIONS

is presently obliged to make the future transfers, (2) the obligation is unavoidable, and (3) the event causing the liability has already occurred.

b. Because these costs have already been recognized as expenses by H. J. Heinz in 1992 and 1993, they will not result in expenses in future periods. Income in future years will be higher as a result. The income reported in 1993 is lower by the after-tax amount of the restructuring costs recorded in that year, and income reported in subsequent years will be higher. Analysts may find it useful to adjust the reported income numbers to reflect earnings before the impact of the restructuring charges is taken into account.

SOLUTION TO REALITY CHECK 8–2

a. Delta's air traffic liability obligates the firm to provide passenger services in the future. Assuming that Delta operates at a profit, the cost of satisfying the liability will be less than the reported amount of the liability. Accounts payable, on the other hand, are recorded at the actual amounts that are expected to be paid to creditors.

The two items are similar in the sense that both items obligate Delta to disburse current assets or to provide services in the near-term future (i.e., within the longer of a year or operating cycle).

b. Delta measures its air traffic liability based on the value of the unused tickets. In contrast, Delta's frequent flyer liability is measured at the estimated incremental cost of providing travel. As a result, Delta will report revenues, costs, and operating profits when the air traffic liability is satisfied.

It is difficult to justify the different methods used in measuring these two obligations. Both represent liabilities to provide future air travel service. Airline company managements prefer measuring frequent flyer obligations at incremental cost, because this results in a lower reported obligation than would measurements based on the value of frequent flyer awards.

QUESTIONS

8–1   Define a liability. What is the difference between liabilities and shareholders' equity?

8–2   If liabilities represent amounts owed to others, why is judgment needed in determining the amount of some liabilities? Identify several cases where the accountant cannot just look up the amount due on a bill or other document, and then enter that amount in the financial statements.

8–3   a. Identify three different types of liabilities.
       b. Indicate how they are created, and how they are then reduced. What does it mean to reduce a liability?
       c. How else might you describe a reduction of a liability?
       d. What generally happens when a liability "matures" or reaches its maturity date?

8–4   Why do you suspect that firms want to have liabilities? Could a firm operate without liabilities? Who would be advantaged or disadvantaged if there were no opportunities for a firm to incur liabilities? Under what circumstances might a firm be unable to obtain or incur a liability?

8–5   a. Discuss the differences between current and long-term liabilities.
       b. Identify three types of current liabilities.
       c. Indicate how such current liabilities reduce a firm's need for cash.

8–6 a. Describe how three different types of current liabilities might be created.
    b. What, or who, restricts the growth of current liabilities?
    c. How might current liabilities be abused or misused?

8–7 List and describe four separate items that are typically included in the current liability section of the balance sheet.

8–8 Evaluate the following statement: "The success of a firm depends as much on the effective management of its liabilities and shareholders' equity as it does on the efficient utilization of its assets."

8–9 Explain why most business firms pay their accounts payable within the discount period. As a manager, in what circumstance might you decide to pay after the discount period has expired?

8–10 Discuss the similarities and differences between notes payable and accounts payable.

8–11 Explain why the matching concept that guides the measurement of periodic net income often entails the reporting of accrued liabilities on the balance sheet.

8–12 How do restructuring costs originate? Discuss your agreement or disagreement with the reporting of liabilities related to restructuring activities that will be undertaken in future years.

8–13 Various current liabilities reported in the balance sheet require that managers make estimates and assumptions concerning future events. Identify several such liabilities. If certain of these estimates and assumptions are subsequently found to be wrong, how should this be reflected in the financial statements? Discuss.

8–14 Indicate which, if any, of the following items would be reported as a current liability:

    a. Advance payments from customers for services to be performed at future dates.
    b. Agreements signed with suppliers to purchase inventory at future dates.
    c. Agreements signed with customers to deliver completed products at future dates.
    d. Advance payment to suppliers for inventory to be shipped at future dates.

8–15 Explain your agreement or disagreement with the inclusion of the following items among a firm's current liabilities:

    a. Estimated future expenditures to provide warranty repairs on items sold prior to the balance sheet date.
    b. Estimated future expenditures for legal costs to be incurred in defending the firm from product liability suits filed before the balance sheet date.

8–16 Explain why each of the following items should (or should not) be reported as liabilities in the financial statements:

    a. Estimated future repair and maintenance costs for equipment that is owned by the firm at the balance sheet date.
    b. Estimated employee retraining costs related to a plant closing that management has planned to occur late in the year subsequent to the balance sheet date.

8–17 What dollar amount of liability would you recognize in this case: A firm has sold 1,000,000 units of a product that has a one-year warranty. Management estimates that about 5% of the units will require repairs, and the costs per repair will average about $12.

8–18 To reduce insurance costs, a firm insures its sales automobile fleet with a $1,000 deductible per vehicle (i.e., the insurance company will only reimburse losses in excess of $1,000 per accident). The firm insures 800 vehicles, and estimates that about 50 of these will be involved in accidents with substantial collision damages in the coming year. What dollar amount (if any) of liability would you recognize on the firm's current balance sheet?

8–19 What dollar amount of liability would you recognize in this case: An airline's passengers have accumulated 20 million frequent flyer miles at the balance sheet date, which could be exchanged for about 1,000 "free" domestic round-trip tickets. Similar tickets are sold at an average price of $600, and the company incurs an incremental cost of about $200 for each passenger carried. Management believes that about 75% of these tickets will ultimately be issued.

8–20 Deltoid Health Club has received $2.5 million in prepaid annual membership fees from its members, and estimates that its cost of providing services to these customers over the coming year will be $1.6 million. How much of a liability should Deltoid report in its financial statements?

8–21 Manuel's Transmission Shoppe, Inc., is comparing price quotations from two potential suppliers of a similar component part. The first supplier quotes a price of $100, with payment in cash on delivery. The second supplier quotes a price of $105, with full payment due in 60 days. The second supplier also offers a 4% discount for payment within 30 days. Discuss how Manuel should evaluate these competing price quotations.

8–22 Bob's Steakhouse may either pay its suppliers within 30 days at a 1% discount, or pay the full amount due in 60 days. The firm also may borrow from banks by signing short-term notes payable at an interest rate of 10% per year. Pat Forebode, the firm's treasurer, advises that the firm pay all of its bills in full in 60 days, thereby taking full advantage of "interest-free" supplier accounts payable. Evaluate Pat's proposal.

EXERCISES

8–23 Transaction Analysis: Inventory and Accounts Payable—Alternate Exercises (A) or (B)

Exercise (A)

Use the accounting equation to show the effects of each of the following transactions on the firm's balance sheet:

1. Purchased $250,000 of inventory on account.
2. Paid creditors $125,000 on account.
3. Purchased $200,000 of inventory on account, at a 2% discount.
4. Paid creditors the amount due from transaction 3.
5. Purchased $300,000 of inventory, half for cash, half on account.
6. Paid creditors the amount due from transaction 5.
7. Purchased $400,000 of inventory all at a 3% discount, half on account, half for cash.

Exercise B

Use the accounting equation to show the effects of each of the following transactions on the firm's balance sheet:

1. Purchased $350,000 of inventory on account, terms 2/10, net 30. The firm records the inventory net of the discount.
2. Paid the creditors in transaction 1 within the discount period.
3. Purchased $300,000 of inventory on account, terms 3/15, net 45. The firm records the inventory net of the discount.
4. Purchased $400,000 of inventory, no terms, half for cash and half on account.
5. Paid creditors the amount due from transaction 4.
6. Paid the creditors in transaction 3 *after* the discount period.

Transaction Analysis: Inventory and Current Liabilities

8–24 Use the accounting equation to analyze the effects of the following transactions on Jack's Shoe Company:

1. Jack's Shoe Company acquires 300 pairs of shoes at a billed cost of $18,000. Jack's has not yet paid for the shoes.
2. Jack's Shoe Company makes a partial payment of $6,000.
3. Jack's Shoe Company returns 10 pairs of shoes with a note requesting a credit to their account of $610.
4. Jack's pays the net balance due on its account.

Transaction Analysis: Continuation of Exercise 8–24

8–25 With reference to Exercise 8–24, assume that Jack's Shoe Company has been offered a 10% discount for prompt payment of all amounts that are due. Assume Jack's intends to take advantage of all discounts and that all payments are made within the discount period. Record all of the transactions in Exercise 8–24 using the balance sheet equation and this new set of information regarding the 10% discount.

Transaction Analysis: Notes Payable and Interest

8–26 Use the accounting equation to show the effects of each of the following transactions on the firm's balance sheet:

1. Borrowed $20,000 cash from First Bank and signed an interest-bearing 120-day note (12% annual interest rate) on October 1.
2. On November 1, borrowed cash from Interwest Bank. Signed a note with a face value of $18,000 and a maturity of 90 days. The bank discounted the note at a 10% annual interest rate and issued the net proceeds to the firm.
3. At December 31 (year-end), record the following adjustments:

   • Accrue interest on the note in transaction 1 plus the interest.
   • Record interest incurred on the note in transaction 2.

4. Paid the note in transaction 1 plus interest at maturity.
5. Paid the note in transaction 2 at maturity.

8–27 Transaction Analysis: Unearned Revenue and Interest—Alternate Exercises (A) or (B)

Exercise (A)
Use the accounting equation to show the effects of each of the following transactions on the firm's balance sheet:

1. Received subscription orders and cash of $360,000, representing 160,000 magazines.
2. Mailed 30,000 magazines (ignore any inventory effects).
3. Borrowed $100,000 at 6% annual interest for one year.
4. Mailed 30,000 magazines (ignore any inventory effects).
5. Mailed 70,000 magazines (ignore any inventory effects).
6. Accrued interest on the loan for six months (Set up an interest payable account).
7. Accrued interest on the loan for the following six months.
8. Repaid the loan, plus accrued interest.
9. Discuss the implications and meaning of the remaining subscriptions. What aspects of these subscriptions will most concern the firm's managers?

Exercise (B)

Use the accounting equation to show the effects of each of the following transactions on the firm's balance sheet:

1. Received subscription orders and cash of $600,000, representing 200,000 magazines.
2. Mailed 40,000 magazines (ignore any inventory effects).
3. Borrowed $250,000 at 8% annual interest for one year.
4. Mailed 40,000 magazines (ignore any inventory effects).
5. Mailed 88,000 magazines (ignore any inventory effects).
6. Accrued interest on the loan for six months (Set up an interest payable account).
7. Accrued interest on the loan for the following six months.
8. Repaid the loan, plus accrued interest.
9. Discuss the implications and meaning of the remaining subscriptions. What aspects of these subscriptions will most concern the firm's managers?

Transaction Analysis: Warranties and Interest

8–28 Use the accounting equation to analyze the effects of the following transactions on Town Floral, Inc.:

1. Acquired 2,000 floral bouquets at a billed cost of $15 per bouquet. Terms of payment are 2/10, n/30. Town Floral records purchases, net of the discount.
2. Signed a 120-day note for $15,000. The bank discounted the note at an annual rate of 10% and deposited the proceeds in Town Floral's bank account.
3. Extended warranties of $18,000. The company accrued this cost.
4. Paid the bills to the suppliers of the bouquets after the discount period had lapsed.
5. Paid $10,000 in warranty claims during the year.
6. Recorded interest incurred for 90 of the 120 days on the note described in transaction 2.

Multiple Choice

8–29 Circle the correct response to the following multiple choice questions:

1. All of the following are current liabilities except:

   a. Unearned revenue   c. Prepaid insurance
   b. Accrued liabilities   d. Current maturities of long-term debt

2. Jason Company received $5,000 from customers in advance. The company recorded this receipt to cash and to sales revenue. What effect does this incorrect entry have on the company's financial position?

   a. Assets are overstated; liabilities are understated; stockholders' equity is overstated.
   b. No effect on assets; liabilities are understated; stockholders' equity is overstated.
   c. Assets are understated; liabilities are understated; stockholders' equity is overstated.
   d. No effect on assets; no effect on liabilities; no effect on stockholders' equity.

3. At December 31, Daniels Chocolate Company owes $200,000 under a 20-year mortgage to Interstate Industrial Bank. Approximately $11,000 of principal is due and payable the next year. How should the liability be reported on the December 31 balance sheet?

   a. All of the $200,000 should be reported as a long-term liability and nothing reported as a current liability.
   b. All of the $189,000 should be reported as a long-term liability and $11,000 as a current liability.
   c. All $200,000 should be reported as a current liability.
   d. Of the $200,000, only report $189,000 as a long-term liability and nothing as a current liability.

Transaction Analysis: Warranties and Interest

8–30 Use the accounting equation to show the effects of each of the following transactions on the firm's balance sheet:

   1. Accrued warranties estimated at $1,200,000 at December 31, 1996.
   2. Paid warranty claims costing $1,300,000 in cash during 1997.
   3. Borrowed $10,000,000 at 9% annual interest for 240 days on September 30, 1997. Assume 360 days in a year.
   4. Sold goods costing $12,000,000 for $25,000,000 cash during 1997.
   5. Accrued interest on the loan at year-end December 31, 1997 (Set up an interest payable account).
   6. Estimated warranties at year-end 1997. Record the adjustment based on past sales and warranty claims of $1,500,000. Why was there a negative balance in the warranty payable account before your adjustment?
   7. Repaid the loan, plus interest at maturity. What is the maturity date?

Transaction Analysis: Warranties and Interest

8–31 Use the accounting equation to show the effects of each of the following transactions on the firm's balance sheet:

   1. Accrued estimated warranties of $3,375,000.
   2. Paid warranty claims costing $1,500,000 cash.
   3. Signed a short-term one-year note for $150,000,000 that was discounted at 8% annual interest and received the proceeds.
   4. Accrued interest on the loan for three months.

5. Accrued interest on the loan for three more months.
6. Paid additional warranty claims costing $1,500,000 cash.
7. Accrued interest on the loan for the following six months.
8. Repaid the loan, plus accrued interest.
9. Paid additional warranty claims costing $300,000 cash.
10. Discuss the meaning of the unexpired warranty obligation. What might the firm do if it expects warranty claims to continue at the same rate for another year?

Transaction Analysis: Loans and Interest

8–32 Assume Jill's Slipper Shop takes out a short-term bank loan of $32,000 to pay for merchandise. This bank loan carries a simple interest rate of 12% per year.

REQUIRED

a. Use the balance sheet equation to show the effect of this bank loan on Jill's financial statements.
b. Show the effect of using the loan proceeds to pay for merchandise inventory.
c. Also show the effects on the balance sheet equation of the interest expense at the end of the first and second months, assuming the loan has not yet been repaid.
d. Finally, assume the loan is repaid at the end of the third month. Show the effects of the loan repayment, and interest for three months, on the balance sheet equation.

Transaction Analysis: Subscriptions

8–33 Maggie's Millinery Magazine (MMM) is very popular among the jet set who rely on her exotic hats and other fine apparel for every film premiere and Academy Award ceremony. MMM is only available by subscription at an annual rate of $360 for 12 monthly issues. Show the effects of the following events using the balance sheet equation:

1. MMM receives orders for 10 annual subscriptions, with full payment enclosed.
2. MMM sends six issues to each of these subscribers during the current year. Ignore inventory effects.
3. These subscribers have all failed to win an Oscar, so they cancel their subscriptions after the first six months, and MMM sends them a refund for the remaining issues.

Transaction Analysis: Subscriptions

8–34 Maggie's Millinery Magazine (MMM) has many satisfied subscribers who have now realized their objectives of fame, fortune, and glory. Show the effects of the following transactions on MMM's balance sheet:

1. As a result of its popularity, MMM receives subscription renewals of $36 million, for 1997, at the end of 1996.
2. During the first quarter of 1997, MMM receives additional subscriptions of $55 million, all for 1997.
3. At the end of the first quarter of 1997, MMM decides to prepare quarterly financial statements. What is the financial statement effect of transactions 1 and 2?

4. What will be the effects on the financial statements at the end of 1997?
5. What would have been the effect on MMM's financial statements if you had not properly recorded the 1997 subscriptions?
6. How could MMM mislead itself or others by not properly recording subscriptions in the appropriate time period?

PROBLEMS

Transaction Analysis: Warranties and Interest

8–35 Set up the following accounts and balances at December 31, 1996, in an accounting equation:

Cash	$ 5,000,000
Inventory	10,000,000
Warranty obligation	2,250,000
Notes payable	-0-
Interest payable	-0-
Common stock	500,000
Retained earnings	12,250,000

REQUIRED

a. Show the effects of each of the following transactions on the firm's balance sheet.

   1. Borrowed $150,000,000 cash on June 1, 1997 and signed a nine-month note at an 8% annual interest rate.
   2. Sold goods during 1997 costing $8,000,000 for $18,000,000 cash.
   3. Paid warranty claims during 1997 of $1,600,000.
   4. Accrued interest on the note at December 31, 1997.

b. Discuss the meaning of the remaining warranty obligation. What might the firm do if it expects warranty claims to continue at the same rate for another year?

c. What is the maturity date of the note? Assuming no additional interest has been accrued since December 31, 1997, what is the effect on the balance sheet when the firm pays the note plus interest?

Transaction Analysis: Inventory and Current Liabilities

8–36 Use the balance sheet equation to analyze the effects of the following transactions:

   1. Jill's Slipper Shop is formed with an original investment of $100,000 in exchange for common stock.
   2. Jill's signs a 12-month lease for its retail shop and pays a deposit of $2,000, along with the first month's rent of $2,000.
   3. Jill's orders and receives merchandise for resale on account at an invoice cost of $32,000.
   4. Jill's returns $1,800 worth of merchandise because it has been waterstained in transit.
   5. Jill's pays the balance of its liability for the merchandise.
   6. Jill's two employees have worked in the shop for the first month, but Jill's decides that it cannot pay them until the end of the next month. Each employee has earned a salary of $2,000 and commissions of $1,200. Ignore

any payroll tax or other implications of withholdings that may normally be recorded in conjunction with payroll transactions.

7. What effect does not paying the employees have on Jill's balance sheet? What effect is it likely to have on the employees? Which is more significant?

8. What is the long-term effect of not paying employees? What are the possible, and likely, long-term effects of not paying suppliers? In other words, if Jill's continues to defer its employees' salaries and commissions, and if Jill's fails to pay for its merchandise, what will happen to Jill's Slipper Shop?

Transaction Analysis: Comprehensive Problem

8–37 In its first year, Sam's Subway Emporium engaged in the following transactions. Indicate the effects of each transaction on Sam's balance sheet by using the balance sheet equation.

1. Sam's was formed with a cash investment of $50,000 in exchange for common stock.

2. Sam's purchased a lunch cart for $10,000 cash.

3. Sam's ordered food and other supplies at a cost of $13,500, not yet received.

4. Sam's received the food and supplies, but intended to pay later.

5. Sam's felt quite generous and gave its employees an advance on their first month's salaries of $2,500.

6. Sam's then got a bit nervous about whether it could pay its employees and suppliers in subsequent months, so a bank loan of $100,000 was acquired at an annual interest rate of 10%.

7. Sam's failed to pay for its first month's food and other supplies; the supplier billed Sam's a 20% late fee.

8. Sam's paid the employee's salaries of $27,500 during the year and also recognized the wages that were paid in advance as expenses.

9. Assume an entire year has passed and Sam's has made no payments on the loan or the supplier's bill. Assume the late fee is assessed quarterly; i.e., four times each year if the account is not paid. Accrue interest on the loan. Use an interest payable account for both the late fees and the interest on the loan.

10. On the first day of the next year, record the effects of Sam's repayment of the bank loan. Also, record Sam's payment of the supplier's bill.

Changes in Various Current Liabilities

8–38 The Distraught Novelty Co. reports the following current liabilities in its balance sheet at December 31, 1997:

Accounts payable to suppliers	$2,500,000
Revenues received in advance	920,000
Income taxes payable	480,000
Warranty obligations	650,000
Total current liabilities	$4,550,000

The firm's current liabilities changed during 1998 for the following reasons:

1. Additional credit purchases from suppliers totaled $10,300,000, and cash payments to suppliers totaled $9,800,000.

2. Revenues received in advance were fully earned during 1998. The associated

expenses, paid in cash, were $570,000.

3. The firm recognized $1,500,000 in income tax expense during 1998, and made total tax payments of $1,350,000.

4. For merchandise sold prior to 1998, warranty services costing a total of $575,000 were performed during 1998. There are no additional warranty obligations for pre-1998 sales, and the company estimates that its warranty obligation for 1998 sales is approximately $700,000 at December 31, 1998.

REQUIRED

a. Determine how each of the described events affects the firm's balance sheet in 1998.

b. Determine the composition of Distraught's current liabilities at December 31, 1998.

Transactions Affecting Various Current Liabilities

8–39 Antic Evenings, a local catering service, had the following transactions during December 1998:

1. Purchased decorative paper products on credit for $75,000, to be paid in full in 60 days.

2. On December 20, purchased cutlery and chinaware on credit for $120,000, at terms of 2/30, net 90 (i.e., a 2% discount is allowed if the bill is paid within 30 days). The company intends to pay this bill prior to January 18, 1999.

3. Received a property tax bill for $12,000, covering the period December 1, 1998–November 30, 1999.

4. Received a deposit of $5,000 for catering services to be performed in February 1999.

REQUIRED

a. Show how each of the described transactions would affect Antic Evening's balance sheet equation.

WHAT WOULD YOU DO?

REQUIRED

a. Determine the Estimated Warranty Obligations balance to be reported on the balance sheet at the end of each year. Does the assumption that warranty expenses will average about 5% of sales appear to be justified?

b. Tim Plistic, general manager of Tenuous Products, makes the following observation upon seeing your response to part a: "Clearly we are too conservative in estimating our warranty expenses. Every year we are estimating greater expenses than we are actually incurring, and this creates an ever-increasing overstatement of our warranty obligations." Comment on this inference.

c. On further inquiry among the factory service personnel, you learn that products sold in a given year are likely to require about 20% of their warranty repairs in the year of sale, and the remaining 80% of their repairs in the year after the sale. How does this information affect your assessment of the adequacy of Tenuous Products' reported liability for warranty expenses as of the end of the fourth year?

d. Based on your analysis in part c, what is your estimate of the amount of warranty expense that should be reported in Tenuous Products' income statement during the fourth year?

e. Assume that no changes are made to the warranty expenses that are shown above (i.e., the four-year total expenses remains at $9,500,000). If sales in the fifth year are $70,000,000, what will be the year-end balance in the Estimated Warranty Obligation account? In this case, what financial reporting action do you recommend?

Revenues Received in Advance and Warranty Obligations

8–41 Road Scholars offers a program of study leading to its E.Z. MBA degree. Classes are offered during commuting hours in a leased car traveling from suburban areas to urban business centers. The firm has received $400,000 in tuition payments for classes to be taught during the Fall 1997 and Spring 1998 semesters. The Fall semester lasts from October through January, and the Spring semester lasts from March through June.

REQUIRED

a. On the basis of the information given, determine the amounts of tuition revenue to be recognized in the firm's income statements during 1997 and 1998, and any liability for revenues received in advance to be reported in the balance sheet at December 31, 1997.

b. Upon further inquiry you have learned that the firm offers students three basic core-level courses during the Fall semester, and two more advanced courses during the Spring semester. How, if at all, does this information affect your answers to part a?

c. To attract additional students, Road Scholars is offering students a rebate of one-half of their tuition if their salaries have not increased by at least 50% within five years after completing their degrees. How would such a guarantee affect your answers to part a?

**CASES AND
EXTENSIONS**

Current Liabilities: Interpreting Financial Statements

8–42 Refer to the Bristol-Myers Squibb (BMS) financial statements in Appendix E. Review the balance sheet to determine how and where current liabilities were reported.

REQUIRED

a. Read Notes 10 and 11. Identify and discuss any unusual terms. Trace any numerical disclosures of current liabilities in the notes to corresponding disclosures in the financial statements.

b. Determine whether BMS has any unusual current liabilities. If so, discuss how they might be interpreted by financial analysts. Discuss how BMS's managers might view such liabilities.

c. In general, discuss how customer advances are related to deferred income. In your opinion, should they be disclosed together? Why?

d. Discuss how short-term borrowings are related to current maturities of long-term debt. In your opinion, should they be disclosed separately? Why?

e. Discuss any other unusual concerns regarding BMS's current liabilities. What other related information might an external analyst require, or prefer?

Current Liabilities: Interpreting Financial Statements

8–43 Refer to Reebok's financial statements in Appendix F. Review the balance sheet to determine how and where current liabilities were reported.

REQUIRED

a. Read Notes 5 and 7. Identify and discuss any unusual terms. Trace any numerical disclosures of current liabilities in the notes to corresponding disclosures in the financial statements.

b. Determine whether Reebok has any unusual current liabilities. If so, discuss how they might be interpreted by financial analysts. Discuss how Reebok's managers might view such liabilities.

c. Discuss how accounts payable are related to accrued expenses. In your opinion, should they be disclosed together? Why?

d. Discuss how income taxes payable are related to dividends payable. In your opinion, should they be disclosed separately? Why?

e. Discuss any other unusual concerns regarding Reebok's current liabilities. What other related information might an external analyst require, or prefer?

Current Liabilities: Interpreting Financial Statements

8–44 Refer to OshKosh B'Gosh's financial statements in Appendix C. Review the balance sheet to determine how and where current liabilities were reported.

REQUIRED

a. Read Notes 1, 5, 6, and 7. Identify and discuss any unusual terms. Trace any numerical disclosures of current liabilities in the notes to corresponding disclosures in the financial statements.

b. Determine whether OshKosh B'Gosh has any unusual current liabilities. If so, discuss how they might be interpreted by financial analysts. Discuss how OshKosh B'Gosh's managers might view such liabilities.

c. Discuss how accounts payable are related to accrued liabilities. In your opinion, should they be disclosed separately? Why?

d. Discuss any other unusual concerns regarding OshKosh B'Gosh's current liabilities. What other related information might an external analyst require, or prefer?

Current Liabilities: Interpreting Financial Statements

8-45 Refer to Wendy's financial statements in Appendix D. Review the balance sheet to determine how and where current liabilities were reported.

REQUIRED

a. Read Notes 2 and 3. Identify and discuss any unusual terms. Trace any numerical disclosures of current liabilities in the notes to corresponding disclosures in the financial statements. (*Note:* Combine the information in both notes.)

b. Determine whether Wendy's has any unusual current liabilities. If so, discuss how they might be interpreted by financial analysts. Discuss how Wendy's managers might view such liabilities.

c. Discuss how accrued salaries and wages are related to accounts payable. In your opinion, should they be disclosed separately? Why?

d. Discuss any other unusual concerns regarding Wendy's current liabilities. What other related information might an external analyst require, or prefer?

WHAT WOULD YOU DO?

Financial Statement Effects: Warranty Recognition

8–46 Hiram's Hi-Tech Industries assembles specialized electronic interfaces that are used in hand-held computers and communications devices (PDAs). Hiram's has had significant warranty claims on its interfaces and is wondering what liability recognition would be appropriate for 1998. Hiram's 1997 statements showed a warranty liability of $12 million, which had been totally exhausted at the end of 1998. Hiram's sales have doubled during 1998, while its quality enhancement efforts have been having little effect. In fact, Hiram's president privately admits that quality may have significantly declined in 1998. The president also wonders whether Hiram's should shorten its typical two-year warranty period.

Hiram's controller is arguing for recognition of warranty obligations of $12 million because that amount appeared to be adequate for the prior year. Hiram's auditors are arguing for a liability recognition of $30 million on the grounds that $12 million was not adequate for the prior year and that, with an increase in sales, more warranty claims are likely.

Hiram's balance sheet equation, without any liability recognition, is as follows:

ASSETS	=	LIABILITIES	+	SHAREHOLDERS' EQUITY
$100,000,000	=	$35,000,000	+	$65,000,000

REQUIRED

a. Indicate the effect on the balance sheet equation of the controller's recommendation.

b. Indicate the effect on the balance sheet equation of the auditor's recommendation.

c. Calculate the debt to total assets ratios under each recommendation.

d. How do you think an external user of these financial statements will view the differences between a 35% debt to assets ratio and the ratios that you calculated in part c?

e. Now, assume that the actual warranty costs in 1998 were $25 million. Show the effects on the balance sheet equation under both the controller's recommendation and the auditor's recommendation. How has matching been affected by following the controller's recommendation?

f. While the controller has obviously underestimated these warranty claims, do you feel that the auditor has, conversely, overestimated the warranty claims? Why?

g. What other recommendations regarding quality and warranty issues might you make to Hiram's Hi-Tech Industries?

Financial Statement Effects: Warranty Recognition

8–47 The following summary data are available for Hilary's Lo-Tech Health Care Concern.

	1997	1998
Total liabilities	$ 3,500,000	$ 4,600,000
Warranty obligations (unrecorded)	750,000	850,000
Stockholder's equity	10,000,000	12,000,000
Total assets	13,500,000	16,600,000

REQUIRED

a. Compute the debt to total assets ratio for each year, assuming no recognition of warranty obligations.

b. Compute the debt to total assets ratio for each year, assuming warranty obligations have been recorded.

c. Compute the debt to total assets ratio for each year, assuming warranty obligations have been underestimated and a more realistic estimate would require that they be quadrupled.

d. Explain why total assets have not changed under either of the changes suggested in parts b and c.

e. Identify the effects on the income statement (that is, on warranty expenses) of each of the changes suggested in parts b and c.

f. Why do you think managers might want to underestimate warranty liabilities? Discuss both balance sheet and income effects.

WHAT WOULD
YOU DO?

Warranty Costs

8–48 Sigma Designs does not report any warranty costs on its income statement, nor does it report any warranty obligations on its balance sheet. Sigma reports only the following four types of costs and expenses in its income statement:

- Costs of sales,
- Sales and marketing,
- Research and development, and
- General and administrative.

Its sales decreased significantly from 1991 to 1992 while they were quite stable from 1992 to 1993.

REQUIRED

a. Assuming Sigma offers warranties to its clients, where do you suppose its warranty costs were reported on the income statement? Why do you imagine they are not separately reported?

b. Suppose you find that Sigma's warranty costs increased significantly from 1991 to 1993. Suppose its board must decide whether to recognize current warranty obligations of $5 million or $10 million. Show the effects on Sigma's balance sheet equation (dollars in millions) at the end of 1993 under each of these proposals.

ASSETS	=	LIABILITIES	+	SHAREHOLDERS' EQUITY
$44,267	=	$6,479	+	$37,788

c. Calculate the effects of each proposal on Sigma's debt to total assets ratio.

d. Assume Sigma's CEO estimated, and had strong evidence, that warranty costs would be $10 million. Prepare a one-paragraph memo that justifies the CEO's recommendations for recognizing warranty obligations of $10 million. In what way is this treatment the most conservative possible?

e. Assume Sigma's controller is very liberal and wants to recognize no additional warranty costs. Write a one-paragraph memo justifying this position.

f. Which position (part d or e) would you approve or support? Why? Discuss the ethical implications of each choice.

Financial Statement Effects: Warranty Costs

8–49 Engineering Group, Inc., is a major British international engineering firm with the following liabilities shown on its 1997 balance sheet:

Loans and other borrowings	$392,000,000
Other creditors	31,000,000
Provisions for liabilities and charges	130,500,000

REQUIRED

a. Where do you suppose its warranty obligations, if any, are included in these accounts?

b. Now suppose you examine a note to these financial statements titled "Provisions for Liabilities and Charges" showing the following items:

Recognition of postretirement benefits	$ 32,900,000
Exchange rate adjustments	15,200,000
New subsidiaries (reorganization costs)	71,400,000
Profit and loss account	11,000,000
Total	$130,500,000

Where do you suppose its warranty obligations, if any, are included in these accounts?

c. Why do you suppose Engineering Group does not make any more explicit mention of warranty obligations?

d. Describe some of the typical warranty obligations of an engineering consulting firm.

Liabilities: Interpreting Financial Statements

8–50 Cabot Corporation is principally involved in the manufacture of carbon black and other specialty chemicals. Its 1994 financial statements have an accrued liability for environmental proceedings related to cleanup as a result of divesting businesses worth $44,000,000.

REQUIRED

a. Why do you suppose this liability is now included on Cabot Corporation's balance sheet?

b. Would you suspect these costs will all be paid on the same date in the future?

c. If not, would you recommend that this liability be shown at its expected future cost, or at the present value of its expected future cost? Why? (You may need to refer to the appendix to answer this part).

Liabilities: Interpreting Financial Statements

8–51 Tyler Corporation is a diversified company that provides goods and services through three major operating subsidiaries: (1) a retailer of auto parts and supplies; (2) a marketer of products for fund-raising programs in schools; and (3) a manufacturer of cast iron pipe and fittings for waterworks applications. Its 1994 financial statements include the following current liabilities:

	1994	1993
Accounts payable	$20,083,000	$11,675,000
Accrued customer discounts	4,204,000	4,055,000
Accrued insurance	4,181,000	4,780,000
Accrued wages and commissions	5,133,000	1,736,000
Income tax	967,000	1,250,000
Other accrued liabilities	16,991,000	12,408,000
	$51,559,000	$35,904,000

REQUIRED

a. Describe each of the liabilities shown on Tyler's balance sheet.

b. Why do you suppose Tyler is accruing customer discounts?

c. Tyler's total current assets were $102,878,000 and $75,395,000 for 1994 and 1993, respectively. Included in these amounts are inventories, prepaids, and deferred taxes totaling $61,761,000 and $39,424,000 for 1994 and 1993, respectively. Calculate current and quick ratios and comment on your results.

d. At the end of 1994 Tyler accrued an estimated contingent liability of $3,953,000 for environmental contamination. This amount is included in other accrued liabilities. As an investor, is this disclosure adequate on the balance sheet? Why haven't they separately disclosed this obligation? What concerns do you have and what other information would you want to see?

Liabilities: Interpreting Financial Statements

8–52 Oncogene Science, Inc., is a biopharmaceutical company involved in developing innovative products for the diagnosis and treatment of cancer, cardiovascular disease, and a number of other important human illnesses. Its proprietary core technologies include oncogenes, tumor suppressor genes, and gene transcription. Its 1994 financial statements include the following current liabilities and no (zero) other liabilities:

	1994	1993
Accounts payable and accrued expenses	$2,522,171	$2,202,060
Unearned revenue, current portion	457,384	258,000
Total current liabilities	$2,979,555	$2,460,060

REQUIRED

a. Describe each of the liabilities shown on Oncogene's balance sheet.
b. Why do you suppose Oncogene is now reporting unearned revenues?
c. From a lender's or an investor's viewpoint, how would you evaluate Oncogene's liability disclosures? Are there any missing categories of information for which you would prefer to have additional disclosures?
d. Why might you suspect that these liabilities, which are relatively immaterial in amount, could reflect high risks for an investor or a lender?

Liabilities: Interpreting Financial Statements

8–53 Polygram is an international entertainment company, which has published such recent hits as Billy Ray Cyrus' *Achy Breaky Heart.* Polygram is headquartered in Amsterdam. It lists the following current liabilities in a note to its 1994 annual report (stated in millions of Netherlands guilders):

	1993	1994
Payables to banks	25	155
Short-term notes	459	749
Accounts payable to trade creditors	665	798
Accounts payable to other companies	41	20
Income taxes payable	106	139
Dividend payable (to shareholders)	135	153
Other accrued expenses	1931	2167
Total	3,362	4,181

REQUIRED

a. Identify and describe each of Polygram's current liabilities.
b. Identify and discuss any unusual trends in its current liabilities.

c. Given that Polygram's total assets and net sales increased by only about 5%, how does that affect your evaluation of its current liabilities?

d. Assume that most of the other accrued expenses are comprised of accrued license fees. Why would such a firm have almost half of its current liabilities in accrued license fees? Are such fees due as quickly or as soon as are Polygram's debts to banks or to trade creditors? Why?

USING FINANCIAL ACCOUNTING ON THE INTERNET

8–54 Locate the most recent set of financial statements for the regional telecommunications companies listed below. You may use either the 10-K available at EDGAR (**www.sec.gov/edgarhp.htm**) or the annual report available at the company page on the WWW. The annual report is usually located in the Investor Information section.

Corporation	Home Page Location
Ameritech	**www.ameritech.com**
U S West	**www.uswest.com**
Bell Atlantic	**www.bell-atl.com**
BellSouth	**www.bst.bls.com**

REQUIRED

Identify or compute the following for each corporation:

a. Total current liabilities and current liabilities as a percentage of total liabilities
b. Composition of current liabilities
c. Income tax payable and income tax payable as a percent of current liabilities

8–55 Locate the most recent set of financial statements for the companies listed below. You may use either the 10-K available at EDGAR (**www.sec.gov/edgarhp.htm**) or the annual report available at the company page on the WWW. The annual report is usually located in the Investor Information section.

Corporation	Home Page Location
Dell Computers	**www.dell.com**
Ben & Jerrys	**www.benjerry.com**
Lewis Galoob Toys	**www.galoob.com**

REQUIRED

a. For each company, what is the percentage of accrued liabilities to current liabilities?
b. List any unusual accrued liabilities. Explain what these items represent, given the main business of each company.

8–56 Locate the 10-K filing for the following companies from EDGAR (**www.sec.gov/edgarhp.htm**). Scroll down to the Notes to the Financial Statements sections where the following current liabilities are explained:

Corporation	Current Liability
Novell	Deferred revenue
Browning-Ferris	Deferred revenue

Reader's Digest   Unearned revenue

FHP International   Unearned premium, medical claims payable

REQUIRED

a. Describe the nature of the liability that each of the above terms represents.
b. Why has revenue recognition been deferred for each of the above cases?

8–57 In 1995, Sundstrand Corporation decided to, among other things, shut down and dispose of its Lima, Ohio, manufacturing facility. The company recognized the costs associated with this decision as restructuring charges and expensed the costs in 1995. Locate the 1995 10-K for Sundstrand Corporation from EDGAR (**www.sec.gov/edgarhp.htm**). Scroll down to the financial statements.

REQUIRED

a. Locate the income statement and identify the total amount of the restructuring charge shown on the 1995 income statement. Also, calculate its impact as a percentage of net income.
b. Based on the information provided in the Notes to the Financial Statements, determine why the charge was taken and what it includes. When did the company plan to complete shutdown and disposition of the Lima facility?
c. Refer to the balance sheet and determine the amount of the restructuring charge that has been accrued as a current liability. What percentage of current liabilities does this represent? Based on the time frame for the shutdown and disposition of the Lima facility, is it reasonable to classify the accrued restructuring costs as a current liability?

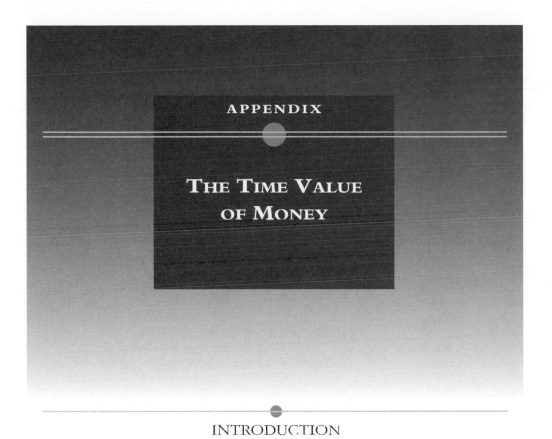

INTRODUCTION

Chapter 9 will discuss accounting for noncurrent liabilities, which obligate the firm to transfer assets or provide services to other entities beyond the period used to define current liabilities. Because noncurrent liabilities entail payments to be made more than one year in the future, it is necessary to consider the concept of present and future values, or the **time value of money,** prior to discussing the accounting and reporting of noncurrent liabilities.

FUTURE VALUE AND PRESENT VALUE

Future Value

Money deposited to an interest-earning bank account will "grow" over time. For example, $1,000 deposited in an account earning 8% per year will amount to $1,080 ($1,000 × 1.08 = $1,080) after one year. If the total amount is left on deposit for a second year, it will grow to $1,166 rounded ($1080 × 1.08 = $1,166). Because the interest is not withdrawn from the account, in each successive year the account earns "interest on interest," and the account grows by a larger dollar amount each year. This notion of earning interest on interest is referred to as **compound interest.** The growth in the account balance can be depicted in the following way:

Initial deposit	$1,000
Amount in one year	$1,000 × (1.08) = $1,080.00
Amount in two years	$1,000 × (1.08) × (1.08)
or	$1,000 × (1.08)^2
=	$1,000 × (1.166) = $1,166

More generally, let P represent the initial deposit, let i represent the interest rate, let n represent the number of periods (e.g., years) over which the deposit is allowed to grow, and let A represent the **future value** of the deposit. The relationship may be written in this way:

$$A = P \times (1 + i)^n$$

In our earlier example, $P = \$1,000$, $i = 8\%$, and $n = 2$, so

$$\begin{aligned} A &= P \times (1 + i)^n \\ &= \$1000 \times (1.08)^2 \\ &= \$1000 \times (1.166) \\ &= \$1,166 \end{aligned}$$

If the deposit were allowed to grow for 10 years, the future value would be $2,159, i.e.,

$$\begin{aligned} A &= P \times (1 + i)^n \\ &= \$1000 \times (1.08)^{10} \\ &= \$1000 \times (2.159) \\ &= \$2,159 \end{aligned}$$

This simple formula may be used for any values of P (the initial deposit), i (the interest rate), and n (the number of periods) in order to obtain the future value of the deposit. The expression $(1 + i)^n$ is referred to as the **future value factor** because it converts the initial deposit to its future value for given values of i and n.

Future values frequently must be computed in business and finance, and special tables have been prepared showing the future value factors for various interest rates and numbers of periods. As a practical matter, financial calculators or personal computers are used to make these calculations. The tables included in this text are useful as a way of introducing you to the concepts of future values and present values. Exhibit 8A–1 contains future value factors, and you can use this table to verify the calculations that were made earlier. For example, refer to the 8% column in Exhibit 8A–1; the entries in this column show the future amounts for $1 invested today at 8% per period. The factors for 1-, 2-, and 10 periods are 1.080, 1.166, and 2.159, respectively, the same as those used in our previous calculations.

Present Value

In the preceding examples, we determined the future value of a cash deposit made today. Business decisions often require that we determine the value today, or **present value,** of an amount to be received or paid in the future. For example, suppose we need $10 million in three years to pay for new plant and equipment. How much would we need to deposit today in order to have $10 million in three years, assuming that the interest rate is 10% per year? In this case we know the future amount ($10 million), the interest rate (10%) and the number of periods (three years). We need to determine the value today, or the present value, of $10 million to be paid three years in the future. Recall our earlier expression for calculating future values:

EXHIBIT 8A–1 FUTURE VALUE OF $1

Periods	1%	2%	4%	6%	8%	10%	12%	14%	16%	18%	20%
1	1.010	1.020	1.040	1.060	1.080	1.100	1.120	1.140	1.160	1.180	1.200
2	1.020	1.040	1.082	1.124	1.166	1.210	1.254	1.300	1.346	1.392	1.440
3	1.030	1.061	1.125	1.191	1.260	1.331	1.405	1.482	1.561	1.643	1.728
4	1.041	1.082	1.170	1.262	1.360	1.464	1.574	1.689	1.811	1.939	2.074
5	1.051	1.104	1.217	1.338	1.469	1.611	1.762	1.925	2.100	2.288	2.488
6	1.062	1.126	1.265	1.419	1.587	1.772	1.974	2.195	2.436	2.70	2.986
7	1.072	1.149	1.316	1.504	1.714	1.949	2.211	2.502	2.826	3.186	3.583
8	1.083	1.172	1.369	1.594	1.851	2.144	2.476	2.853	3.278	3.759	4.300
9	1.094	1.195	1.423	1.689	1.999	2.358	2.773	3.252	3.803	4.436	5.160
10	1.105	1.219	1.480	1.791	2.159	2.594	3.106	3.707	4.411	5.234	6.192
11	1.116	1.243	1.539	1.898	2.332	2.853	3.479	4.226	5.117	6.176	7.430
12	1.127	1.268	1.601	2.012	2.518	3.138	3.896	4.818	5.936	7.288	8.920
13	1.138	1.294	1.665	2.133	2.720	3.452	4.363	5.492	6.886	8.599	10.70
14	1.149	1.319	1.732	2.261	2.937	3.798	4.887	6.261	7.988	10.15	12.84
15	1.161	1.346	1.801	2.397	3.172	4.177	5.474	7.138	9.266	11.97	15.41
16	1.173	1.373	1.873	2.540	3.426	4.595	6.130	8.137	10.75	14.13	18.49
17	1.184	1.400	1.948	2.693	3.700	5.054	6.866	9.276	12.47	16.67	22.19
18	1.196	1.428	2.026	2.854	3.996	5.560	7.690	10.58	14.46	19.67	26.62
19	1.208	1.457	2.107	3.026	4.316	6.116	8.613	12.06	16.78	23.21	31.95
20	1.220	1.486	2.191	3.207	4.661	6.728	9.646	13.74	19.46	27.39	38.34
21	1.232	1.516	2.279	3.400	5.034	7.400	10.80	15.67	22.57	32.32	46.01
22	1.245	1.546	2.370	3.604	5.437	8.140	12.10	17.86	26.19	38.14	55.21
23	1.257	1.577	2.465	3.820	5.871	8.954	13.55	20.36	30.38	45.01	66.25
24	1.270	1.608	2.563	4.049	6.341	9.850	15.18	23.21	35.24	53.11	79.50
25	1.282	1.641	2.666	4.292	6.848	10.83	17.00	26.46	40.87	62.67	95.40

$$A = P \times (1 + i)^n$$

If we know A, the future value, and wish to determine P, the present value, we need only rearrange the expression as follows:

$$P = A \times 1/(1 + i)^n$$

In the present example, the future payment is known to be $10 million; the time period is three years, and the interest rate is 10%:

$$
\begin{aligned}
P &= A \times 1/(1 + i)^n \\
&= \$10,000,000 \times 1/(1.10)^3 \\
&= \$10,000,000 \times (.751) \text{ (rounded)} \\
&= \$7,510,000
\end{aligned}
$$

In other words, if you were to deposit $7,510,000 into an account earning 10% interest, then the account balance would accumulate to $10 million at the end of three years. You can verify this result by using the future value factors in Exhibit 8A–1. Note that the future value factor at 10% for three periods is 1.331:

$$A = P \times (1 + i)^n$$
$$= \$7,510,000 \times (1.10)^3 = \$7,510,000 \times (1.331)$$
$$= \$10,000,000 \text{ (rounded)}$$

In financial terms, you would be equally as well off if you were to receive (or pay) $10 million in three years or to receive (or pay) $7,510,000 today.

In this case, the future value, *A,* is multiplied by a **present value factor,** $1/(1 + i)^n$, in order to obtain its present value. Exhibit 8A–2 contains present value factors. Notice that the future value factors in Exhibit 8A–1 and the present value factors in Exhibit 8A–2 have a *reciprocal* relationship, i.e., present value factors are the inverses of future value factors:

$$\text{Present value factor} = \frac{1}{\text{Future value factor}}$$

EXHIBIT 8A–2 PRESENT VALUE OF $1

Periods	1%	2%	4%	6%	8%	10%	12%	14%	16%	18%	20%
1	0.990	0.980	0.962	0.943	0.926	0.909	0.893	0.877	0.862	0.847	0.833
2	0.980	0.961	0.925	0.890	0.857	0.826	0.797	0.769	0.743	0.718	0.694
3	0.971	0.942	0.889	0.840	0.794	0.751	0.712	0.675	0.641	0.609	0.579
4	0.961	0.924	0.855	0.792	0.735	0.683	0.636	0.592	0.552	0.516	0.482
5	0.951	0.906	0.822	0.747	0.681	0.621	0.567	0.519	0.476	0.437	0.402
6	0.942	0.888	0.790	0.705	0.630	0.564	0.507	0.456	0.410	0.370	0.335
7	0.933	0.871	0.760	0.665	0.583	0.513	0.452	0.400	0.354	0.314	0.279
8	0.923	0.853	0.731	0.627	0.540	0.467	0.404	0.351	0.305	0.266	0.233
9	0.914	0.837	0.703	0.592	0.500	0.424	0.361	0.308	0.263	0.225	0.194
10	0.905	0.820	0.676	0.558	0.463	0.386	0.322	0.270	0.227	0.191	0.162
11	0.896	0.804	0.650	0.527	0.429	0.350	0.287	0.237	0.195	0.162	0.135
12	0.887	0.788	0.625	0.497	0.397	0.319	0.257	0.208	0.168	0.137	0.112
13	0.879	0.773	0.601	0.469	0.368	0.290	0.229	0.182	0.145	0.116	0.093
14	0.870	0.758	0.577	0.442	0.340	0.263	0.205	0.160	0.125	0.099	0.078
15	0.861	0.743	0.555	0.417	0.315	0.239	0.183	0.140	0.108	0.084	0.065
16	0.853	0.728	0.534	0.394	0.292	0.218	0.163	0.123	0.093	0.071	0.054
17	0.844	0.714	0.513	0.371	0.270	0.198	0.146	0.108	0.080	0.060	0.045
18	0.836	0.700	0.494	0.350	0.250	0.180	0.130	0.095	0.069	0.051	0.038
19	0.828	0.686	0.475	0.331	0.232	0.164	0.116	0.083	0.060	0.043	0.031
20	0.820	0.673	0.456	0.312	0.215	0.149	0.104	0.073	0.051	0.037	0.026
21	0.811	0.660	0.439	0.294	0.199	0.135	0.093	0.064	0.044	0.031	0.022
22	0.803	0.647	0.422	0.278	0.184	0.123	0.083	0.056	0.038	0.026	0.018
23	0.795	0.634	0.406	0.262	0.170	0.112	0.074	0.049	0.033	0.022	0.015
24	0.788	0.622	0.390	0.247	0.158	0.102	0.066	0.043	0.028	0.019	0.013
25	0.780	0.610	0.375	0.233	0.146	0.092	0.059	0.038	0.024	0.016	0.010

For example, when $i = 8\%$ and $n = 2$

$$Present value factor = .857$$
$$Future value factor = 1.166$$
$$and .857 = 1/1.66$$

Let's use the present value factors in Exhibit 8A–2 to determine the present value of $100,000 to be received in five periods, assuming alternatively that the appropriate interest rate is 4, 8, and 12%. When interest rates are used to compute present values instead of future values, the interest rate is usually referred to as the **discount rate.**

Discount Rate (%)	Future Cash Receipt ($)	×	Present Value Factor for $n = 5$ (Exhibit 8A–2)	=	Present Value ($)
4	100,000	×	.822	=	82,200
8	100,000	×	.681	=	68,100
12	100,000	×	.567	=	56,700

As you might expect, the same future cash flow ($100,000 in this example) has differing present values depending on the discount rate used. A larger discount rate produces a smaller present value. This is a sensible result because a higher interest rate indicates that interest earnings will be greater. Accordingly, the required initial deposit is smaller. The choice of a suitable discount rate to use in finding the present value of expected future cash flows requires considerable judgment. In general, discount rates that are used by lenders and investors vary directly with risk. For instance, riskier loans and investments require higher discount rates.

Present Value and Series of Future Payments

Imagine for a moment you have won a million-dollar lottery and will receive payments of $200,000 at the end of each year for five years (5 years × $200,000 = $1 million). Could you use your lottery prize immediately to pay for a million-dollar house? You soon would realize that the lottery prize is worth less than $1 million because the payments will be received at various future dates. To find the prize's real value, you would need to determine the present value of each payment. Then you would add the present values of the individual payments in order to obtain the total present value. Assuming a 10% interest rate, the calculation is as follows:

Date of Payment	Cash flow ($)	×	Present Value Factor (Exhibit 8A–2)	=	Present Value ($)
End of:					
Year 1	200,000	×	.909	=	181,800
Year 2	200,000	×	.827	=	165,400
Year 3	200,000	×	.751	=	150,200
Year 4	200,000	×	.683	=	136,600
Year 5	200,000	×	.621	=	124,200
Total			3.791		$758,200

This result shows that the series of five payments of $200,000 has a value today of $758,200, even though the total of the five payments is $1 million. In other words, if you were to receive $758,200 today and deposit this amount in a bank account earning 10% per year, you would be able to withdraw $200,000 at the end of each year for five years. In this sense, you would be just as well off receiving $758,200 immediately as if you received the five lottery payments (totaling $1 million) over five years. Instead of buying a million-dollar house today, you can only afford to spend $758,200.

In this lottery example, the cash flows are equal in dollar amount and are paid at the end of each period. The term **annuity** is used to describe equal cash flows over uniform time intervals. Such cash flow patterns are found frequently in business contracts. For this reason, special present value tables have been prepared for evaluating annuities. Exhibit 8A–3 contains present value factors for this purpose. If we use the notation S to indicate the dollar amount of each of a series of cash flows and PVAF (i percent, n periods) to indicate the present value factor for an annuity of n periods at interest rate i, and if the interest rate is 10%, then your lottery winnings may be valued as follows using Exhibit 8A–3:

EXHIBIT 8A–3 PRESENT VALUE OF AN ANNUITY

Periods	1%	2%	4%	6%	8%	10%	12%	14%	16%	18%	20%
1	0.990	0.980	0.962	0.943	0.926	0.909	0.893	0.877	0.862	0.847	0.833
2	1.970	1.942	1.886	1.833	1.783	1.736	1.690	1.647	1.605	1.566	1.528
3	2.941	2.884	2.775	2.673	2.577	2.487	2.402	2.322	2.246	2.174	2.106
4	3.902	3.808	3.630	3.465	3.312	3.170	3.037	2.914	2.798	2.690	2.589
5	4.853	4.713	4.452	4.212	3.993	3.791	3.605	3.433	3.274	3.127	2.991
6	5.795	5.601	5.242	4.917	4.623	4.355	4.111	3.889	3.685	3.498	3.326
7	6.728	6.472	6.002	5.582	5.206	4.868	4.564	4.288	4.039	3.812	3.605
8	7.652	7.325	6.733	6.210	5.747	5.335	4.968	4.639	4.344	4.078	3.837
9	8.566	8.162	7.435	6.802	6.247	5.759	5.328	4.946	4.607	4.303	4.031
10	9.471	8.983	8.111	7.360	6.710	6.145	5.650	5.216	4.833	4.494	4.192
11	10.368	9.787	8.760	7.887	7.139	6.495	5.938	5.453	5.029	4.656	4.327
12	11.255	10.575	9.385	8.384	7.536	6.814	6.194	5.660	5.197	4.793	4.439
13	12.134	11.348	9.986	8.853	7.904	7.103	6.424	5.842	5.342	4.910	4.533
14	13.004	12.106	10.563	9.295	8.244	7.367	6.628	6.002	5.468	5.008	4.611
15	13.865	12.849	11.118	9.712	8.559	7.606	6.811	6.142	5.575	5.092	4.675
16	14.718	13.578	11.652	10.106	8.851	7.824	6.974	6.265	5.669	5.162	4.730
17	15.562	14.292	12.166	10.477	9.122	8.022	7.120	6.373	5.749	5.222	4.775
18	16.398	14.992	12.659	10.828	9.372	8.201	7.250	6.467	5.818	5.273	4.812
19	17.226	15.678	13.134	11.158	9.604	8.365	7.366	6.550	5.877	5.316	4.844
20	18.046	16.351	13.590	11.470	9.818	8.514	7.469	6.623	5.929	5.353	4.870
21	18.857	17.011	14.029	11.764	10.017	8.649	7.562	6.687	5.973	5.384	4.891
22	19.660	17.658	14.451	12.042	10.201	8.772	7.645	6.743	6.011	5.410	4.909
23	20.456	18.292	14.857	12.303	10.371	8.883	7.718	6.792	6.044	5.432	4.925
24	21.243	18.914	15.247	12.550	10.529	8.985	7.784	6.835	6.073	5.451	4.937
25	22.023	19.523	15.622	12.783	10.675	9.077	7.843	6.873	6.097	5.467	4.948

$$P = S \times \text{PVAF}_n^i \quad (i \text{ percent, } n \text{ periods})$$
$$= \$200{,}000 \times \text{PVAF}_5^{.10} \quad (10\%, 5 \text{ periods})$$
$$= \$200{,}000 \times 3.791 \text{ (from Exhibit 8A–3)}$$
$$= \$758{,}200$$

This is the same result as the one we obtained earlier by finding the present values of each payment and adding them to obtain the total present value of the series of five payments. In fact, the present value factors for annuities are equal to the sum of the present value factors for the individual cash flows. Refer to our previous calculation. The total of the five present value factors from Exhibit 8A–2 is the same as present value factor for a five-period annuity from Exhibit 8A–3.

Future Value and Series of Future Payments

Firms sometimes arrange to make a series of cash payments over several periods to a special fund referred to as a **sinking fund.** The ending balance of the sinking fund is usually designated for a special purpose, such as the retirement of outstanding debt or the replacement of operating assets. To illustrate, let us continue with your imagined lottery winnings. Assume you deposit in a retirement fund the $200,000 payments received at the end of each of the next five years. You expect to earn 10% each year. At the end of the fifth year, what would be the balance in your retirement fund? To find the future value of the fund, you would determine the future value of each deposit. Then you would add these future values in order to determine the total future value of your fund in the following manner:

Date of Deposit	Cash flow ($)	×	Future Value Factor (Exhibit 8A–1)	=	Future Value ($)
End of:					
Year 1	200,000	×	1.464	=	292,800
Year 2	200,000	×	1.331	=	266,200
Year 3	200,000	×	1.210	=	242,000
Year 4	200,000	×	1.100	=	220,000
Year 5	200,000	×	1.000	=	200,000
	Total		6.105		$1,221,000

Because each deposit is made at the end of the year, the first deposit earns interest for four years, the second deposit earns interest for three years, and so on. The last deposit is made at the end of the fifth (and last) year and so earns no interest at all. Since each of the cash flows is the same ($200,000), the cash flows are an annuity. That is, they are equal in dollar amount and are deposited each period. Because sinking funds with equal annual deposits are found frequently in business contracts, special future value tables have been prepared containing the appropriate annuity factors. Exhibit 8A–4 contains such factors. If we use the notation S to indicate the dollar amount of each of a series of future cash flows and FVAF (i percent, n periods) to indicate the future value factor for an annuity of n periods at interest rate i, and if the interest rate is 10%, then after five periods your retirement fund will amount to $1,221,000, computed as follows using Exhibit 8A–4:

EXHIBIT 8A–4   FUTURE VALUE OF AN ANNUITY

Periods	1%	2%	4%	6%	8%	10%	12%	14%	16%	18%	20%
1	1.000	1.000	1.000	1.000	1.000	1.000	1.000	1.000	1.000	1.000	1.000
2	2.010	2.020	2.040	2.060	2.080	2.100	2.120	2.140	2.160	2.180	2.200
3	3.030	3.060	3.122	3.184	3.246	3.310	3.374	3.440	3.506	3.572	3.640
4	4.060	4.122	4.246	4.375	4.506	4.641	4.779	4.921	5.067	5.215	5.368
5	5.101	5.204	5.416	5.637	5.867	6.105	6.353	6.610	6.877	7.154	7.442
6	6.152	6.308	6.633	6.975	7.336	7.716	8.115	8.536	8.978	9.442	9.930
7	7.214	7.434	7.898	8.394	8.923	9.487	10.09	10.73	11.41	12.14	12.92
8	8.286	8.583	9.214	9.897	10.64	11.44	12.30	13.23	14.24	15.33	16.50
9	9.369	9.755	10.58	11.49	12.49	13.58	14.78	16.09	17.52	19.09	20.80
10	10.46	10.95	12.01	13.18	14.49	15.94	17.55	19.34	21.32	23.52	25.96
11	11.57	12.17	13.49	14.97	16.65	18.53	20.65	23.04	25.73	28.76	32.15
12	12.68	13.41	15.03	16.87	18.98	21.38	24.13	27.27	30.85	34.93	39.58
13	13.81	14.68	16.63	18.88	21.50	24.52	28.03	32.09	36.79	42.22	48.50
14	14.95	15.97	18.29	21.02	24.21	27.98	32.39	37.58	43.67	50.82	59.20
15	16.10	17.29	20.02	23.28	27.15	31.77	37.28	43.84	51.66	60.97	72.04
16	17.26	18.64	21.82	25.67	30.32	35.95	42.75	50.98	60.93	72.94	87.44
17	18.43	20.01	23.70	28.21	33.75	40.54	48.88	59.12	71.67	87.07	105.9
18	19.61	21.41	25.65	30.91	37.45	45.60	55.75	68.39	84.14	103.7	128.1
19	20.81	22.84	27.67	33.76	41.45	51.16	63.44	78.97	98.60	123.4	154.7
20	22.02	24.30	29.78	36.79	45.76	57.28	72.05	91.02	115.4	146.6	186.7
21	23.24	25.78	31.97	39.99	50.42	64.00	81.70	104.8	134.7	174.0	225.0
22	24.47	27.30	34.25	43.39	55.46	71.40	92.50	120.4	157.4	206.3	271.0
23	25.72	28.85	36.62	47.00	60.89	79.54	104.6	138.3	183.6	244.5	326.2
24	26.97	30.42	39.08	50.82	66.76	88.50	118.2	158.7	214.0	289.5	392.5
25	28.24	32.03	41.65	54.86	73.11	98.35	133.3	181.9	249.2	342.6	472.0

$$\text{Future value} = S \times \text{FVAF}^i_n \ (i \text{ percent, } n \text{ periods})$$
$$= \$\ 200{,}000 \times \text{FVAF}^{.10}_5 \ (10\%, 5 \text{ periods})$$
$$= \$\ 200{,}000 \times 6.105 \ (\text{from Exhibit 8A–4})$$
$$= \$1{,}221{,}000$$

In other words, $200,000 per year for five years at 10% interest has the same value as a single receipt of $1,221,000 at the end of five years. From our earlier example, recall that the same five-year $200,000 annuity has a present value of $758,200. From this, it follows that a single payment of $1,221,000 to be received in five years has the same value as $758,200 to be received immediately.[1]

At this point, you have acquired a useful set of tools for dealing with the time value of money. You are able to determine the future amount, or compound value, of an

---

[1]The future value factor for five periods at 10% is 1.611 (from Exhibit 8A–1).

$$A = P \times (1 + i)^n$$
$$= \$758{,}200 \times (1.10)^5$$
$$= \$758{,}200 \times (1.611)$$
$$= \$1{,}221{,}000 \ (\text{rounded})$$

amount deposited today at a specified interest rate and number of time periods. Conversely, you are able to determine the value today, or present value, of an amount to be received at a specified future date, given the prevailing interest rate. Also, you are able to determine both the present value and the future value of an ordinary annuity or a series of periodic cash flows that are equal in dollar amount. The discussion of noncurrent liabilities in Chapter 9 will give you a chance to put these tools to good use.

This appendix has explained the time value of money and has illustrated the techniques of compound interest that are used widely in accounting for long-term financial assets and liabilities. Present value is the term used to denote the value today of cash to be received or paid in future periods. Future value is the term used to denote the expected maturity value of cash that is deposited (or otherwise invested) today at a specified rate of interest for a given number of future periods. Special tables have been constructed containing present value and future value factors for single cash flows, and the use of these tables has been illustrated in this appendix.

Business cash flows are often in the form of annuities, which are a series of cash flows that are equal in dollar amount and occur over uniform time intervals. Present value and future value calculations for annuities have been explained in the appendix. Special tables also have been constructed for evaluating annuities, and their use has been illustrated.

SUMMARY OF LEARNING OBJECTIVES

1. Determine the future value, or compound amount, of dollars that are invested or borrowed today.

Compound interest calculations were explained using the following notation:

A = future value
P = present value
S = dollar amount of each of a series of cash flows (an annuity)
i = periodic interest rate
n = number of time periods

Future value, single cash deposit:

$$A = P \times (1 + i)^n \text{ (requires use of Exhibit 8A–1)}$$

Future value, series of equal cash flows (an annuity):

$$A = S \times \text{FVAF}_n^i \ (i \text{ percent, } n \text{ periods) (requires use of Exhibit 8A–4)}$$

2. Determine the value today, or present value, of dollars that are to be received or paid in the future.

Present value, single future cash flow:

$$P = A \times 1/(1 + i)^n \text{ (requires use of Exhibit 8A–2)}$$

Present value, series of equal cash flows (an annuity)

$$P = S \times \text{PVAF}_n^i \ (i \text{ percent, } n \text{ periods) (requires use of Exhibit 8A–3)}$$

3. Understand how the concept of present value is used to calculate interest expense.

When a firm borrows money, the amount received is the present value of the dollar amounts that will be repaid to the lender in the future. In other words, the future repayments are discounted at a suitable interest rate, to determine the present value of the loan. For this reason, interest expense is determined each period by multiplying the present value of the loan at the start of the period, by the interest rate that was used in discounting the future repayments.

Future Value (

8A–13 Calcula
annual

a. Dep
b. Depo
$10,
of th
c. Mak
year.
four

Present Value

8A–14 Calcula
12% in

a. A ce
at th
b. A $1
c. An i
the

Future Value (

8A–15 You hav
for $25
for thro
deposit
the end

Present Value

8A–16 At the
specifie

a. Assu
b. Assu
c. Why
diffe
valu
why

Present Value

8A–17 A firm
$300,0
bility?

a. Assu
b. Assu

c. Why should a reader of financial statements be concerned about the interest rate that the firm may have used in calculating the present values of various financial contracts?

PROBLEMS

Time Value Calculations

8A–18 Evaluate each independent situation using the appropriate table and an interest rate of 12%.

a. You would like to relax and not work for the next six years. However, you would like to withdraw $25,000 at the end of each year. How much must you have in your investment account now to be able to do this?

b. You would like to have $100,000 upon graduation. How much should you invest in a fund at the end of each year for the next four years?

c. Your firm signs a contract to repay $1,000,000 in five years. How much will the firm receive today in exchange for this promised future payment?

d. You have found some wonderful mountain property. You're thinking if you could invest a single sum of $50,000 for five years you might be able to buy a parcel of land that costs $70,000. However, the land cost is expected to appreciate compounded at 4% per year. Can you afford the land?

Time Value Calculations

8A–19 Evaluate each independent situation, using the appropriate table and an interest rate of 8%.

a. A retirement fund is set up to pay $15,000 per year for the next 20 years. How much is in the fund at the beginning?

b. A company is required, as part of their loan restrictions, to set up a sinking fund account (an investment account) and invest $5,000 at year-end for four years. How much will be in the fund at the end of four years to provide for the debt payoff? Identify two alternative ways of using the tables to calculate your answer.

c. How much should you invest now to have $60,000 at the end of nine years? Would your answer be different if interest is compounded semiannually during these nine years?

d. How much will your fund grow to in 10 years if you invest $20,000 today? Would your answer be different if interest is compounded semiannually during these 15 years?

Annuity Necessary to Meet Future Cash Objective

8A–20 A firm promises to pay its CEO a bonus of $1,000,000 on her retirement at the end of eight years. How much must the firm put aside at the end of each year at an interest rate of 10% in order to meet its commitment? Identify two alternative ways of using future value tables to analyze this problem.

Future Value of Annuity Deposits

8A–21 A large chemical firm has just lost a major lawsuit under which it must make 20 payments of $1,000,000 at year-end to the survivors of its chemical factory explosion. Using an 8% interest factor, how much must be in the fund to provide for these payments?

Present Value Calculations

8A–22 Calculate the present value of the following cash flows, using a 10% interest rate:

   a. Your rich uncle promises to give you $1,000,000 in 10 years, when you are more mature and able to handle such sums.
   b. Your rich aunt promises to give you $3,000,000 in 20 years, when she is sure you are mature enough to handle such sums.
   c. Evaluate which of the two promises you prefer, and describe why you prefer it.

Present Value Calculations

8A–23 Calculate the present value of the following cash flows, using an 8% interest rate:

   a. Your rich uncle promises to give you $100,000 for each of the next five years, and $1,000,000 at the end of the tenth year.
   b. Your rich aunt promises to give you $3,000,000 in 20 years, when she is sure that you will need the money!
   c. Evaluate which of the two promises you prefer, and describe why you prefer it.

Present Value Calculations

8A–24 Calculate the present value of the following cash flows, using a 12% rate of interest:

   a. Your rich uncle promises to give you $100,000 for each of the next five years, $200,000 for the following five years, and $1,000,000 at the end of the tenth year.
   b. Your rich aunt promises to give you $3,000,000 in 20 years, when she is sure that she will have enough money to afford this gift.
   c. Evaluate which of the two promises you prefer, and describe why you prefer it.

Present Value Calculations

8A–25 Calculate the present value of the cash flows associated with a life insurance policy that you inherited, using a 10% interest rate.

   a. The life insurance policy offers a payout option of $300,000 at the end of each of the next three years.
   b. A second option, under the same policy, is to receive $100,000 at the end of each year, for the next 12 years.
   c. Identify which option you prefer, and describe why you prefer it.

Present Value Calculations

8A–26 Calculate the present value of the cash flows associated with the retirement options under your pension plan, using an 8% interest rate.

a. One retirement option under the pension plan is to receive 90% of your current annual salary of $80,000 at the end of the year, for life, which is expected to be 20 years.
b. Another option is to receive a lump sum distribution of $1,300,000 immediately.
c. A third option is to receive five annual (year-end) payments of $300,000.
d. Evaluate which option you prefer, and describe why you prefer it.

Present Value Calculations

8A–27 Calculate the present value of the cash flows associated with the retirement options under your pension plan, using a 10% interest rate.

a. One retirement option under the pension plan is to receive 90% of your current annual salary of $100,000 at the end of the year, for life, which is expected to be 20 years.
b. Another option is to receive a lump sum distribution of $1,000,000 immediately.
c. A third option is to receive five annual (year-end) payments of $250,000.
d. Evaluate which option you prefer, and describe why you prefer it.

Present Value Calculations

8A–28 Calculate the present value of the cash flows associated with a life insurance policy that you inherited, using a 12% interest rate.

a. The life insurance policy offers a payout option of $500,000 at the end of each of the next four years.
b. A second option, under the same policy, is to receive $245,000 per year, for each of the next 12 years.
c. Identify which option you prefer, and describe why you prefer it.

CASES AND EXTENSIONS

Present Values: Interpreting Financial Statements

8A–29 Refer to Wendy's financial statements in Appendix D. Review the financial statements to determine how and where present value calculations may have been used.

REQUIRED

a. Were present value calculations disclosed?
b. If the present value calculations were not separately disclosed, discuss areas where you infer that such calculations must have been used.

Present Values: Interpreting Financial Statements

8A–30 Refer to Reebok's financial statements in Appendix F. Review the financial statements to determine how and where present value calculations may have been used.

REQUIRED

a. Were present value calculations disclosed?

b. If the present value calculations were not separately disclosed, discuss areas where you infer that such calculations must have been used.

Present Values: Interpreting Financial Statements

8A–31 Refer to OshKosh B'Gosh's financial statements in Appendix C. Review the financial statements to determine how and where present value calculations may have been used.

REQUIRED

a. Were present value calculations disclosed?
b. If the present value calculations were not separately disclosed, discuss areas where you infer that such calculations must have been used.

Present Values: Interpreting Financial Statements

8A–32 Refer to Bristol-Myers Squibb's financial statements in Appendix E. Review the financial statements to determine how and where present value calculations may have been used.

REQUIRED

a. Were present value calculations disclosed?
b. If the present value calculations were not separately disclosed, discuss areas where you infer that such calculations must have been used.

CHAPTER 9

STUDYING THIS CHAPTER WILL ENABLE YOU TO

1. Recognize the types of noncurrent obligations that are reported by business firms.

2. Comprehend features of long-term borrowing contracts, i.e., notes and bonds payable.

3. Determine periodic interest expense and the valuation of noncurrent obligations in financial reports.

4. Be alert to additional business obligations that presently are unreported.

5. Appreciate why income is measured differently for income tax and financial reporting purposes.

6. Understand why the tax basis and the financial reporting basis of assets and liabilities may differ.

7. Interpret financial statement measurements of income tax expense and deferred income tax liability.

NONCURRENT LIABILITIES

INTRODUCTION

Noncurrent liabilities represent obligations of the firm that generally are due more than one year after the balance sheet date. The major portion of noncurrent liabilities consists of notes and bonds payable. In addition, deferred income tax payments are an important component of liabilities for many companies. Each of these types of liabilities is discussed in the following sections. Note that this chapter relies on the present value concepts developed in the appendix to Chapter 8.

LONG-TERM NOTES PAYABLE

Interest-Bearing Notes

One way a firm borrows funds is by signing an **interest-bearing note.** A bank or other lender will loan the face amount, or principal, of the note for a specified period. The borrower will pay interest periodically and will repay the principal when the note becomes due (i.e., at its **maturity date**). For example, if Random Enterprises, Inc., borrows $10 million at the beginning of 1998 for two years at a market interest rate of 12% per year, the financial statements would reflect the following events.

Upon receipt of the loan proceeds at the beginning of 1998, cash and long-term notes payable are each increased by $10 million:

ASSETS	=	LIABILITIES	+	SHAREHOLDERS' EQUITY
Cash		Long-term notes payable		
+$10 million		+$10 million		

In *each* of the years 1998 and 1999, as the periodic interest payments are made, cash is decreased by $1.2 million ($10 million × 12% = $1.2 million) and interest expense is recognized.

ASSETS	=	LIABILITIES	+	SHAREHOLDERS' EQUITY
Cash				Retained earnings
−$1.2 million				−$1.2 million (interest expense)

When the loan is repaid at maturity at the end of 1999, cash and long-term notes payable are each decreased by $10 million.

ASSETS	=	LIABILITIES	+	SHAREHOLDERS' EQUITY
Cash		Long-term notes payable		
−$10 million		−$10 million		

The net result of these three transactions is that $10 million cash has been borrowed, and later $12.4 million was repaid. The firm has incurred interest expense of $1.2 million each year, or a total interest expense of $2.4 million, for the privilege of using the $10 million for two years.

▬ Discounted Notes

In the previous example Random Enterprises borrowed $10 million by signing an interest-bearing note. Suppose the note did not require periodic payments of interest. Instead, assume that Random Enterprises signs a note on January 1, 1998, promising to pay the lender $10 million in two years, and will not make periodic interest payments. In this case, the lender will be unwilling to provide Random the full $10 million face value of the note. No one is willing to loan money without interest. All long-term financing arrangements involve interest, even if it is not separately identified.

If a prospective lender instead invested some smaller amount (as yet to be determined) for two years to earn 12%, that initial investment would grow to $10 million by the end of 1999. How much would a lender be willing to loan in return for Random's noninterest-bearing note? To answer this question, we must discount the note. Random Enterprises will receive only the present value of the note (Chapter 8 appendix), computed at the current lending rate of 12%. The present value of the note is $7,970,000, computed as follows:

$$
\begin{aligned}
P &= A \times PVF^i_n \\
&= \$10 \text{ million} \times PVF^{12\%}_{2 \text{ years}} \\
&= \$10 \text{ million} \times (.797) \text{ (from Exhibit 8A–3)} \\
&= \$7,970,000
\end{aligned}
$$

In other words, if the prospective lender instead deposited $7,970,000 in a bank account for two years to earn 12% per year, the initial deposit would grow to $10 million by the end of 1999. For this reason, lenders would be unwilling to loan more than $7,970,000 for Random Enterprise's note. As a result, Random Enterprises must issue the note at a discount of $2,030,000 ($10,000,000 − $7,970,000 = $2,030,000).

The discount on Random's note payable represents the interest that is associated with this transaction. It should be recognized as interest expense by Random

Enterprises over the two-year term of the note. The discount also represents interest income to the lender over the same period. In each year, the amount of interest to be recognized is 12% of the value of the note at the start of the year. The yearly amounts of interest are calculated as follows:

Amount received from lender,	
January 1, 1998	$ 7,970,000
Interest during 1998 ($7,970,000 × .12)	956,400
Loan balance, January 1, 1999	$ 8,926,400
Interest during 1999 ($8,926,400 × .12)	1,073,600*
Loan balance, January 1, 2000	$10,000,000

*Rounded

Notice that the amount of interest expense increases between 1998 and 1999. This occurs because Random Enterprises makes no interest payment to the lender in 1998. As a result, the amount of the loan increases to include the unpaid interest. In other words, the lender is earning compound interest (interest on interest) in 1999. These events would affect Random Enterprise's financial statements in the following manner.

The receipt of cash from the lender at the beginning of 1998 in exchange for Random's note payable will increase cash and noncurrent liabilities:

ASSETS	=	LIABILITIES	+	SHAREHOLDERS' EQUITY
Cash		Long-term notes payable		
+$7,970,000		+$7,970,000		

Interest expense during 1998 and 1999 will decrease retained earnings and increase the reported value of noncurrent liabilities:

ASSETS	=	LIABILITIES	+	SHAREHOLDERS' EQUITY
		Long-term notes payable		Retained earnings
		+$956,400		−$956,400
				(interest expense)

At January 1, 1999, the carrying value of the note is $8,926,400 ($7,970,000 + $956,400). In 1999, interest is again added to the loan balance:

ASSETS	=	LIABILITIES	+	SHAREHOLDERS' EQUITY
		Long-term notes payable		Retained earnings
		+$1,073,600		−$1,073,600
				(interest expense)

At January 1, 2000, the maturity date of the note, the carrying value of the note has been increased to $10,000,000 ($8,926,400 + $1,073,600). This amount is eliminated, and the lender is paid cash of $10 million.

ASSETS	=	LIABILITIES	+	SHAREHOLDERS' EQUITY
Cash		Long-term notes payable		
−$10 million		−$10 million		

The net result of these transactions is that slightly less than $8 million has been borrowed and used by Random Enterprises for two years and interest expense of slightly more than $2 million has been incurred for the privilege of using the $8 million for two years. In the end, Random has repaid $10 million, which included both principal and interest.

BONDS PAYABLE

Bonds payable represent a major source of borrowed capital for U.S. firms. **Bonds** are notes, sold to individual investors as well as to financial institutions. Managers may prefer to issue bonds to investors rather than to borrow directly from financial institutions for a variety of reasons. Bond financing may offer advantages in terms of the availability and cost of borrowing and the managers' subsequent flexibility in making business decisions. For example, the amount that financial institutions are willing to loan to a single firm may be limited because the lender aims to diversify its risks by loaning smaller amounts to many different borrowers. The sale of bonds, on the other hand, enables the borrower to obtain access to much larger amounts of loanable funds from large institutional investors and also from thousands of individual investors.

In addition, for some firms, bond financing may be less expensive. The interest rates that prevail in the bond market may be less than the rate available from financial institutions. Finally, bond financing may offer managers greater flexibility in the future. A direct lending agreement often imposes various restrictions on managers' investing and financing activities until the loan is repaid. As examples, a lending agreement may restrict the firm's dividend payments or may limit the amounts that the firm may borrow from other lenders until the debt is repaid. Although bond issuances also may entail similar restrictions, they may be less onerous than the restrictions imposed by financial institutions.

A bond is a contract that is sold to investors. Bonds obligate the borrower (the issuing corporation) to make periodic interest payments, usually every six months, and to pay the principal or face value of the bond at a specified maturity date. Prior to issuing bonds, managers meet with financial advisers to decide on the maturity value and other terms of the bond contract, and also to predict the market interest rate at which the bonds can be sold. The predicted interest rate usually becomes the **coupon rate** or face rate (or nominal rate) that is contained in the bond contract. This rate, in conjunction with the face value, determines the cash interest to be paid periodically to bondholders.

The **market rate** of interest cannot be known with certainty until the date on which the bonds are sold. Market interest rates are the "cost of money" and are determined by the forces of supply and demand in the financial markets. The federal government, through the actions of the Federal Reserve, also influences interest rates. Because the market rate constantly changes, and the coupon rate is fixed when the bonds are printed, it is rare that the bond coupon rate will coincide exactly with the market interest rate when the bonds are sold. The following sections illustrate the issuance and reporting for bonds when the market interest rate in turn equals, exceeds, or falls below the coupon rate of interest.

Issuance of Bonds at Par

If the coupon rate of a bond coincides with the market rate of interest when the bonds are actually sold to investors, then the bonds will sell at **par value** or face value. To illustrate the sale of bonds at par, assume Marley Company issues bonds on January 1, 1997, with a principal amount of $100 million, to be repaid in 10 years and a 12% coupon rate of interest payable semiannually. The bond contract obligates Marley to make the following payments:

Principal: $100,000,000 due in 10 years (after 20 six-month periods),

Interest: $6,000,000 due at the end of each six-month period, for 10 years ($100,000,000 × 12% × 6/12 = $6,000,000).

Since the market rate and the coupon rate of interest are the same, the bonds will sell at their face value of $100 million. Because the bonds pay interest each six months, the quoted annual interest rate of 12% is actually 6% each six-month period. When interest is paid each six months, the interest rate is said to be compounded semiannually. To use the present value tables, bonds with a 12% semiannual interest coupon are regarded as outstanding for a number of six-month periods (20 in this case), and the interest rate is 6% per period. In general, when interest is compounded n times each year, the periodic interest rate is i/n, and the number of periods is $n \times years$. In the present case, the periodic interest rate is 6% (i/n or 12%/2 = 6%), and the number of periods is 20 ($n \times$ years or 2 × 10 = 20).

The following events would be reported in the financial statements over the life of the bond. On January 1, 1997, Marley Co. receives $100 million in cash, and bonds payable are recorded in this amount:

ASSETS	=	LIABILITIES	+	SHAREHOLDERS' EQUITY
Cash		Bonds payable		
+$100 million		+$100 million		

Each six months for 10 years, Marley Co. recognizes interest expense and pays $6 million to the bondholders, i.e., each June 30 and December 31, from 1997 through 2006:

ASSETS	=	LIABILITIES	+	SHAREHOLDERS' EQUITY
Cash				Retained earnings
−$6 million				−$6 million
				(interest expense)

At the maturity date, December 31, 2006, Marley Co. pays $100 million in bond principal and retires the bonds:

ASSETS	=	LIABILITIES	+	SHAREHOLDERS' EQUITY
Cash		Bonds payable		
−$100 million		−$100 million		

To recap, Marley Company received $100 million from investors when the bonds were issued and paid a total of $220 million to bondholders over the life of the bond issue. The total interest expense was, therefore, $120 million ($220 million in payments minus $100 million in receipts), and the interest expense each year was $12 million (2 × $6 million).

Sale or Issuance of Bonds at a Discount

In cases where the coupon rate of interest differs from the market rate on the date that bonds are sold, the present value of the bond issue will not equal the face amount of the bond. Consider, for example, an investor buying a bond when the *coupon rate is below the market rate of interest*. Because the coupon rate does not provide the investor with a rate of return equal to that available on other similar investments, the investor will buy the bonds only if they are sold at a **discount** from the par or face value. Bear in mind that the bond contract represents a fixed series of cash payments to bondholders. The present value of any fixed series of cash payments will depend on the discount rate, which in this case is the market rate of interest.

To illustrate the accounting for bonds sold at a discount, assume that the Marley Company bonds described earlier were sold on January 1, 1997, and that the market rate of interest was 16% (compounded semiannually) on that date. Investors will discount the bonds' cash flows at the current market rate of interest. Because the coupon rate is only 12%, the bonds will sell at a discount. Note, however, that the interest coupon payments will still be $6 million because that is the amount stated in the bond contract. The present value is computed as follows.

Principal, due in 20 six-month periods at 8% (one-half of the 16% annual rate):

Amount	× Present value factor (Exhibit 8A–2) $n = 20$, $i = 8\%$	
$100,000,000	× 0.215	= $21,500,000

Interest payments, due each six months for 20 periods:

$$
\begin{array}{lll}
& \text{(Exhibit 8A-3)}\ n = 20,\ i = 8\% & \\
\$6,000,000 & \times\ 9.818 & =\ \underline{58,908,000} \\
& \text{Total present value} & \underline{\$80,408,000}
\end{array}
$$

Consequently, the bonds will sell at $80,408,000 ($100 million face value, minus $19,592,000 discount). If prospective bondholders were to deposit $80,408,000 in an account earning interest at 16% compounded semiannually, they would be able to withdraw $6 million each six months and $100 million at the end of 10 years. For this reason, bond investors would be unwilling to pay more than $80,408,000 for the Marley Company bonds.

Upon issuing the bonds, Marley Company's cash and bonds payable (net of the bond discount) will increase by $80,408,000:

ASSETS	=	LIABILITIES	+	SHAREHOLDERS' EQUITY
Cash		Bonds payable		
+$80,408,000		+$80,408,000		

In effect, the discount represents additional interest paid to bondholders. This compensates for the fact that the coupon interest payments are lower than those provided by competing investments. The total interest expense is determined as follows:

Total explicit interest payments	$120,000,000
Add: Bond discount	19,592,000
Total interest expense	$139,592,000

The amount of this interest expense to be recognized each interest period (an interest period is six months in this example) is based on the reported value of the bonds at the start of the interest period, and the market rate of interest when the bonds were issued. Because Marley Company's bonds were sold on January 1, 1997, when the market rate of interest was 16% compounded semiannually, or 8% each six-month period, the interest expense during 1997 and 1998 would be determined as shown in Exhibit 9–1.

Whenever the periodic interest expense differs from the periodic cash payments to the bondholders, the reported value of the bonds will be adjusted for the difference. This adjustment is termed **amortization.** In Exhibit 9–1, note that the interest expense recorded in each period exceeds the cash interest ($6,000,000) that is paid to the bondholders. Because the actual interest expense incurred each period is greater than the amount that is paid currently to the bondholders, the reported value of the bonds (i.e., bonds payable, minus discount) increases each period. In fact, as shown in Exhibit 9–1, the reported value of the bonds will increase to exactly $100,000,000, the principal amount of the bonds, by the date that the bond issue matures (i.e., at the end of the year 2006). In other words, the discount on the bonds will be completely amortized by that date, so the bonds will be reported at their face value of $100 million. The interest expense and bond coupon payment for the first six months in 1997 would be recorded in the following way:

ASSETS	=	LIABILITIES	+	SHAREHOLDERS' EQUITY
Cash		Bond payable		Retained earnings
−$6,000,000		+$432,640		−$6,432,640
				(interest expense)

As you can see, because the cash payment required by the coupon rate of interest is less than the actual interest expense for the period, the amount of the liability must be increased for the difference. During the first interest period (January 1–June 30, 1997), $432,640 of the bond discount has been amortized.

EXHIBIT 9–1   CALCULATION OF INTEREST EXPENSE

Marley Company
Calculation of Interest Expense
Bonds Sold at a Discount

Six-month Period Beginning	(1) Reported Value of Bonds, Beginning	(2) Interest Expense (1) × 8%	(3) Interest Payment	(4) Increase in Reported Value (2) − (3)	(5) Reported Value of Bonds End of Period (1) + (4)
Jan. 1, 1997	$80,408,000	$ 6,432,640	$6,000,000	$ 432,640	$80,840,640
July 1, 1997	80,840,640	6,467,251	6,000,000	467,251	81,307,891
Total expense, 1997		$12,899,891			
Jan. 1, 1998	81,307,891	$ 6,504,631	6,000,000	504,631	81,812,522
July 1, 1998	81,812,522	6,545,000	6,000,000	545,000	82,357,523
Total expense, 1998		$13,049,631			
.	.	.		.	.
.	.	.		.	.
.	.	.	.	.	.
July 1, 2006	$98,148,114	$ 7,851,886	$6,000,000	$1,851,886	$100,000,000

NOTE: The reported value of the bonds increases each period because the interest expense exceeds the amount paid to the bondholders, which increases the company's obligation to the bondholders. At the maturity date of the bonds, the reported value will equal the principal (face) amount of $100 million.

 ## Sale or Issuance of Bonds at a Premium

Suppose the market rate of interest on January 1, 1997, when the Marley Company bonds were sold, is *below* the coupon rate of 12%. In this case investors would find the bonds to be quite attractive, because *the coupon rate is higher than the market interest rate* available on other investments of equivalent risk. As a result, the market price of Marley's bonds would increase. The bonds would be issued at a **premium,** i.e., at an amount greater than the principal amount of $100 million. For example, if the market interest rate is 8% when the bonds are issued, investors will be willing to pay $127,140,000, determined as follows.

Principal, due in 20 six-month periods at 4% (one-half of the 8% annual rate):

Amount	× Present value factor (Exhibit 8A–2) $n = 20, i = 4\%$	
$100,000,000	× 0.456	= $ 45,600,000

Interest payments, due each six months for 20 periods:

	(Exhibit 8A–3) $n = 20, i = 4\%$	
$6,000,000	× 13.590	= 81,540,000
	Total present value	$127,140,000

Consequently, the bonds will sell at $127,140,000 ($100,000,000 face value + $27,140,000 premium). The total interest expense over the life of the bonds is determined as follows:

Total explicit interest payments	$120,000,000
Less: Bond premium	− 27,140,000
Total interest expense	$ 92,860,000

The amount of interest expense to be recognized each interest period (each six months in this example) is based on the reported value of the bonds at the start of the interest period. Exhibit 9–2 shows how the interest expense during 1997 and 1998 would be determined.

EXHIBIT 9–2 CALCULATION OF INTEREST EXPENSE

Marley Company
Calculation of Interest Expense
Bonds Sold at a Premium

Six-month Period Beginning	(1) Reported Value of Bonds, Beginning	(2) Interest Expense (1) × 4%	(3) Interest Payment	(4) Decrease in Reported Value (3) − (2)	(5) Reported Value of Bonds End of Period (1) + (4)
Jan. 1, 1997	$127,140,000	$ 5,085,600	$6,000,000	$ 914,400	$126,225,600
July 1, 1997	126,225,600	5,049,024	6,000,000	950,976	125,274,624
Total expense, 1997		$10,134,624			
Jan. 1, 1998	125,274,624	$ 5,010,985	6,000,000	989,015	124,285,609
July 1, 1998	124,285,609	4,971,424	6,000,000	1,025,576	123,257,033
Total expense, 1998		$ 9,982,409			
.	.	.	.	.	.
.	.	.	.	.	.
July 1, 2006	$101,923,307	$ 4,076,693	$6,000,000	$1,923,307	$100,000,000

NOTE: The reported value of the bonds decreases each period because the amount paid to the bondholders exceeds the interest expense, which decreases the company's obligation to the bondholders. At the maturity date of the bonds, the reported value will equal the principal (face) amount of $100 million.

The amount of this interest expense to be recognized in each period would be determined as before, i.e., the reported value of the bonds at the start of each interest period would be multiplied by the market rate of interest when the bonds were issued. The logic of this calculation is the same as that shown in Exhibit 9–1 for the case of bonds sold at a discount.

The total interest expense incurred by Marley Company over the life of bonds sold at a premium will be less than the total interest coupons paid. In effect, the premium represents a reduction in interest paid to the bondholders, to compensate for the fact that the coupon rate is too high.

Early Retirement of Bonds

After bonds are sold to investors, they are often subsequently traded (bought and sold) among investors. The market value of bonds that are traded among investors vary from day to day as prevailing interest rates rise and fall. This occurs because the bond contract specifies a set of cash payments to be made to bondholders, and the present value of a given set of future cash flows changes whenever there is a change in the rates used to make the present value calculations. For example, market interest rates on corporate bonds fell dramatically in the early 1990s and, as a result, the value of existing bonds increased substantially. As the monetary authorities began to tighten money and increase interest rates in subsequent years, the market value of existing bonds declined.

Fluctuations in the market prices of outstanding bonds do not result in additional cash inflows and outflows for the issuing company. Consistent with the historical cost principle, the reported value of bonds in the financial statements of the issuing company are *not* revised to reflect changes in market interest rates and market prices of the outstanding bonds.

For this reason, changes in market rates of interest may motivate firms to buy back their outstanding bonds prior to their scheduled maturity dates. If market rates of interest have changed subsequent to the issuance of the bonds, then the current market prices of the bonds may differ substantially from values shown on the books of the issuing firm. If the firm does repurchase its own bonds, any difference between the reported value and the repurchase price must be recognized as an extraordinary gain or loss by the issuer when the transaction is completed.

To illustrate this point, assume Marley Company issued bonds at par early in 1997, and that interest rates have risen subsequently. When interest rates rise, the market values of outstanding bonds decline because the remaining cash payments (principal and interest coupons) are discounted by lenders at higher rates. If we assume Marley repurchases bonds with a $100 million reported value at a market value of $85 million, the firm would report a gain of $15 million:

Reported value of bonds payable	$100,000,000
Cost to repurchase bonds payable	− 85,000,000
Gain on repurchase of bonds	$ 15,000,000

This transaction would be recognized in Marley's financial statements in the following way:

ASSETS	=	LIABILITIES	+	SHAREHOLDERS' EQUITY
Cash		Bonds payable		Retained earnings
−$85,000,000		−$100,000,000		+$15,000,000 (gain)

The financial reporting of such gains or losses upon early retirement of bonds has been a matter of sharp debate. Managers argue that in cases where bonds are retired at less than their reported values, there is an economic gain to the firm. Liabilities have been eliminated for less than their reported values and net assets have been increased. Analysts and accounting policy makers, on the other hand, observe that managers are able to decide whether and when to repurchase outstanding bonds, and for this reason have considerable control over the time periods in which the resulting gains or losses are recognized. Reality Check 9-1 shows the composition of long-term debt for a major company that has debt issued at a variety of different interest rates.

REALITY CHECK 9-1

EASTMAN KODAK COMPANY LONG-TERM BORROWINGS

Eastman Kodak Company, developer and manufacturer of imaging and health products for commercial and medical customers, includes the following information in a footnote describing the long-term debt reported in its 1993 financial statements:

Long-term debt (partial)

Issue:	(Dollars in Millions)
10.05% notes due 1994	$ 350
7⅞% notes due 1997	135
8.55% notes due 1997	200
6⅜% convertible debentures due 2001	278
Zero-coupon convertible debentures due 2011 ($3,680 face value)	1,127

REQUIRED

a. Why do the interest rates differ among the various debt issues reported by Kodak?

b. Why is the information concerning the due dates of Kodak's debt useful to the analyst?

c. Assume that the prevailing market interest rate is 8.25% at the balance sheet date, and that each of the first four issues listed was initially issued by Kodak at par (face) value. Which of these issues would you expect to have a current market value above par? Which issues would have a market value below par value?

d. Based on your response to part c, if Kodak's management wished to report a gain on early debt retirement, which of the issues would be retired?

e. Why would lenders be willing to invest in zero-coupon bonds (i.e., bonds that do not pay interest periodically to bondholders)?

Managers may use bond repurchases as a means of "smoothing" fluctuations in income. For example, in periods of poor operating performance, managers may improve reported income merely by repurchasing outstanding bonds with market values below their reported values. Moreover, firms that retire bonds early often issue additional bonds in order to replace the retired debt. This practice has the appearance of "paper shuffling" because the firm's debt position is essentially unchanged, but substantial gains have been included in income. Also, because firms must issue new debt at higher interest rates in order to retire older debt bearing lower interest rates, future periods will report higher interest expenses and lower net income.

In response to this issue, the FASB requires that material gains and losses from the early retirement of debt be reported as extraordinary items on the income statement. Recall, from our discussion of the income statement in Chapter 4, that extraordinary gains and losses are reported in a separate section of the income statement, separate from the calculation of the firm's income from ongoing or recurring operations. This separation is useful to financial statement users who want to assess the firm's ability to generate profit from its ongoing operations in future periods.

OTHER ASPECTS OF BORROWING AGREEMENTS

In addition to specifying payments of principal and interest, borrowing agreements (**indentures**) may include a variety of other provisions that are important to users of financial statements. These provisions are added to make the debt issues more attractive to prospective lenders. Common provisions include restrictive covenants, collateral, and convertibility. Each of these features is described briefly in this section.

Restrictive Covenants

Borrowers may agree to various restrictions on management's ability to invest, pay dividends, incur additional debt, or take other actions that may affect the firm's ability to meet its repayment obligations. Such **restrictive covenants** are often based on accounting measurement of assets, liabilities, and/or income. Violation of these restrictions constitutes technical default on the debt and may allow lenders to increase interest rates or impose other penalties on the borrower.

For example, Exhibit 9–3 shows a portion of the footnote disclosures included in Jackpot Enterprise's 1991 financial statements, describing restrictive covenants related to the company's lines of credit and long-term debt. These agreements require Jackpot to maintain minimum levels of cash, working capital and net worth; restrict future borrowing by the firm; and constrain management's discretion in mergers, sales of assets, payments of dividends to stockholders, and repurchases of its common stock.

The existence and the nature of restrictive covenants are an important concern to analysts of financial reports. Restrictions that are based directly on accounting measurements, e.g., working capital (current assets minus current liabilities) and net worth (total assets minus total liabilities, which we have already described as net assets) may affect the choice of accounting methods in use by the firm.

To illustrate, recall that, in periods of rising costs, the FIFO method of inventory costing results in higher reported profits and inventory valuations than does LIFO. Also, the straight-line method of depreciating plant and equipment results in lower depreciation charges and higher asset valuations than do accelerated methods of

EXHIBIT 9–3

SAMPLE OF FOOTNOTE
DISCLOSURES

**Jackpot Enterprise, Inc.
1991 Annual Report**

Note 7—Line of Credit (partial)

To be able to draw under the line, or if borrowings are outstanding, the agreement with the bank requires, among other things, Jackpot to maintain certain minimum levels of cash, cash equivalents and/or certain marketable securities, working capital and net worth. As of June 30, 1991, Jackpot was in compliance with all the requirements. The agreement also provides that, except for borrowings represented by the 8.75% Convertible Subordinated Debentures due May 14, 2014 (the "Debentures") (see Note 8), additional institutional borrowings cannot exceed $2,000,000 and seller or assumed financing of future acquisitions, if any, cannot exceed $5,000,000.

Note 8—Long-Term Debt (partial)

The Debentures were issued under an indenture (the "Indenture") containing a number of restrictive covenants, including restrictions on mergers and sales of assets and the creation of liens on assets; limitations on payments of cash dividends and purchases of Jackpot's common stock (see Note 9); and the use of the Debenture proceeds by Jackpot and its subsidiaries, which are reserved for the acquisition of gaming businesses ("Gaming Businesses"), as defined, and, pending such acquisition, certain short-term investments.

---

depreciation. Consequently, managers who face restrictive covenants that are based on asset values, income, or net worth would be more likely to choose FIFO rather than LIFO costing for inventories, despite possibly paying higher taxes. They would also probably choose straight-line rather than accelerated depreciation methods for long-lived assets.

Debt covenant restrictions may be affected by changes in generally accepted accounting principles, such as new statements of the FASB. For instance, if a firm is approaching the minimum limits of working capital or net worth specified in its lending agreements, then management is likely to favor accounting standards that increase reported asset valuations and net worth. Management is also likely to oppose prospective new accounting standards that would make violations of these restrictions more likely. Some debt contracts provide for exceptions or adjustments to the restrictions if there are subsequent changes in generally accepted accounting principles. An example of restrictive covenants on long-term borrowings is provided in Reality Check 9–2.

Collateral

Debt agreements sometimes require that specific assets of the firm be pledged as security in the event of default by the borrower. These assets are termed **collateral.** Mortgages on office buildings, plant, and equipment are frequent examples, especially in transportation industries such as airlines, railroads, and trucking companies. On the other hand, lenders are sometimes reluctant to accept as collateral a business asset that has limited resale value or alternative use. In these cases the lender may require that a sinking fund be established to secure the debt. The sinking fund is segregated cash

**NUCLEAR METALS, INC.
RESTRICTIVE COVENANTS ON DEBT**

REALITY CHECK 9–2

Nuclear Metals, Inc., a metallurgical technology firm, provides the following information concerning restrictive covenants in its 1993 footnotes to the financial statements:

All long-term obligations contain restrictive covenants including, among others, a requirement to maintain minimum working capital of $17,000,000, consolidated net worth . . . of not less than $25,000,000 and current assets greater than 200% of current liabilities. . . .

The following amounts appear on the year-end balance sheet:

Current assets	$41,289,000
Total assets	$65,091,000
Current liabilities	$ 8,209,000
Total liabilities	$22,054,000

REQUIRED

a. Is Nuclear Metals, Inc. in compliance with its restrictive covenants at the end of 1993?
b. By how much might the firm's current assets decrease and still not violate the working capital restriction? (Assume current liabilities remain constant.)
c. By how much might the firm's current assets decrease and still not violate the current ratio constraint? (Assume current liabilities remain constant.)
d. Why do you suppose the firm's borrowing agreements restrict both the dollar amount of working capital *and* the current ratio?

and/or other liquid temporary investments, usually administered by an independent trustee or financial institution and pledged as collateral to retire a specific bond or note.

Convertibility

An attractive feature to many investors is the right to exchange debt instruments for other securities, usually common stock of the borrowing firm. **Convertible bonds** give the bondholder the option to exchange bonds for a predetermined number of shares of stock. If the stock price subsequently increases above the value of the bonds, the bondholders will be likely to convert their holdings to stock. Conversely, if the stock price remains below the value of the debt, the bondholders will continue to collect interest and will receive the bond principal at maturity. Convertible debt is examined in more detail in Chapter 10, which discusses shareholders' equity.

COMMITMENTS AND CONTINGENCIES

Most financial statements include a footnote captioned "commitments and contingencies." The purpose of this note is to alert financial statement users to the fact that a variety of actual and potential future claims exist that do not meet the FASB's criteria for recognition as liabilities at the balance sheet date. Yet, these claims may be important to users in assessing the firm's debt position.

Commitments are agreements with suppliers, customers, employers, or other entities that are not yet completed transactions and consequently have not been recognized in the accounts. If such agreements are significant, they should be disclosed in the notes to the financial statements. **Contingencies** are existing conditions whose resulting gains and losses are currently uncertain, but will be resolved by the occurrence of future events. Commitments and contingencies may be referenced in either the current or the noncurrent liability sections depending on when they are likely to require payment, or they may only be disclosed in the notes.

Exhibit 9–4 includes portions of the note discussing commitments and contingencies included in the 1991 annual report of Chevron Corporation. The first portion of the exhibit illustrates a commitment. The company has signed a variety of contracts related to its future operations. Because these contracts are not yet executed, they are not valued in the financial statements.

The second portion of Exhibit 9–4 illustrates a significant contingent obligation of Chevron Corporation. Similar obligations are faced by many firms in the chemical, petroleum refining, nuclear power, and special metals fabrication industries. This is the requirement, pursuant to environmental laws, to correct the effects of past disposals of toxic wastes. Although Chevron's managers are currently unable to put a "price tag" on the ultimate amount of the liability, the dollar magnitude is potentially substantial.

EXHIBIT 9–4
SAMPLES OF COMMITMENTS
AND CONTINGENCIES

Chevron Corporation
1991 Annual Report
Disclosures of Commitments and Contingencies

Note 18—Commitments (partial)

The company also has certain long-term fixed or minimum commitments under agreements negotiated to assist suppliers in obtaining facilities financing. In addition, the company has contractual commitments to certain companies in which it has equity interests to pay minimum shipping and processing charges or advance funds that can be applied against future charges. Payments and future commitments under all these arrangements are not material in aggregate.

Note 18—Contingencies (partial)

The company is subject to loss contingencies pursuant to environmental laws and regulations that in the future may require the company to take action to correct or ameliorate the effects on the environment of prior disposal or release of chemical or petroleum substances by the company or other parties. Such contingencies may exist for various sites including, but not limited to: Superfund sites, operating refineries, closed refineries, oil fields, service stations, terminals and land development areas. The amount of such future cost is indeterminable due to such factors as the unknown magnitude of possible contamination, the unknown timing and extent of the corrective actions that may be required, the determination of the company's liability in proportion to other responsible parties and the extent to which such costs are recoverable from insurance.

Financial Reporting of Income Taxes

Corporations measure income for financial reporting purposes and for income tax purposes, and the objectives of these measurements differ. Income measures for financial reporting purposes should help financial analysts to assess the firm's future ability to generate cash. Income measures for income tax purposes, on the other hand, must comply with the relevant provisions of the Internal Revenue Service (IRS) tax code. IRS regulations reflect the objectives of government fiscal policy, rather than the objectives of financial analysis and reporting.

Book and Tax Differences

Because of these differing objectives, revenue and expense measurements that are used to determine taxable income may differ from those used in financial reporting. Accountants in these cases distinguish between book and tax measurements: Book measurements are used for financial reporting purposes, while tax measurements must comply with income tax laws.

In most cases, differences between book and tax measurements are **temporary** in nature. For example, in order to stimulate purchases of property, plant, and equipment, the U.S. government allows firms to depreciate such assets quickly for tax purposes. Firms can thereby reduce their income taxes in the earlier years after purchasing such assets. This accelerated depreciation usually exceeds the amount of depreciation expense that is used for financial accounting measurements of income. In later years, however, the situation is reversed. Financial statements continue to report depreciation expense although for tax purposes the asset is already fully depreciated.

Accounting standards for reporting income tax expenses and liabilities reflect a basic premise: all events that affect the tax impact of temporary differences should be recognized currently in the financial statements. Broadly, two types of events can affect these expected tax impacts: (1) a change in the amount of temporary differences between the book and the tax bases of a firm's assets (or liabilities) and (2) a change in tax rates that will apply to those temporary differences.

To illustrate the measurement of income tax expenses and liabilities, consider the information provided in Exhibit 9–5 about the financial statement and income tax accounting used by Dorian Company to account for its plant and equipment. As shown in Exhibit 9–5, Dorian uses the straight-line method of depreciation for financial reporting purposes and an accelerated method of depreciation for income tax purposes. As a result, the financial statement carrying value, or book basis, of these assets is $700 million at December 31, 1997, and the tax basis of these assets is $300 million. The book and tax bases of Dorian's plant and equipment differ by $400 million:

Book basis of plant and equipment	$700 million
Tax basis of plant and equipment	300 million
Difference (book basis exceeds tax basis)	$400 million

Deferred Tax Liability. Because temporary differences such as those resulting from accelerated tax depreciation only allow a firm to postpone its tax payments to later years, the postponed taxes will be paid eventually. For this reason, accounting standards require that firms recognize a liability for such future income taxes, i.e., those will be paid as a result of present differences between the tax and the book bases of assets. (Note that the tax and the book bases of liabilities also may differ for tax purposes. Although such differences may give rise to deferred tax assets, this possibility is not discussed here. However, the impact of such deferred tax assets is illustrated in many of the actual financial statements shown in the cases as part of this chapter, as well as in the appendixes to this text.)

The liability for future income taxes is referred to as a **deferred income tax liability.** The measurement of a firm's deferred income tax liability is obtained by multiplying the difference between the asset's book and tax bases by the appropriate income tax rate.

Dorian Company's income tax rate is expected to be 35% over the relevant future. Consequently, Dorian's deferred tax liability at December 31, 1997, is $140 million, computed as follows:

Excess of book over tax basis of plant and equipment	$400 million
Multiplied by income tax rate	× 35%
Deferred tax liability, December 31, 1997	$140 million

Income tax expense reported in the financial statements is computed in the following manner:

Income tax actually payable	$XXX
Increase (decrease) in deferred tax liability	YYY
Total income tax expense	$ZZZ

To illustrate, refer again to Exhibit 9–5, which shows that during 1998 Dorian's tax depreciation exceeds the book depreciation of the plant and equipment by $90 million ($150 million − $60 million = $90 million). As a result, the difference between the tax and book bases of these assets has increased by $90 million, and the amount of the deferred tax liability has increased by $31.5 million, computed as follows:

Book basis of plant and equipment, December 31, 1998	$ 640 million
Less: Tax basis of plant and equipment, December 31, 1998	− 150 million
Difference at December 31, 1998	490 million
Multiplied by income tax rate	× 35%
Deferred tax liability, December 31, 1998	$171.5 million
Less: Deferred tax liability, December 31, 1997	− 140.0 million
Increase in deferred tax liability during 1998	$ 31.5 million

Dorian's 1998 income tax expense is the sum of the amount actually payable, $35 million (shown in Exhibit 9–5), and the increase in the deferred tax liability during 1998 computed above, i.e.:

Income tax payable (Exhibit 9–5)	$35.0 million
Plus: Increase in deferred tax liability	31.5 million
Total income tax expense	$66.5 million

Note that in the resulting statements, $66.5 million is equal to 35% of Dorian's reported pre-tax income of $190 million (35% × $190 million = $66.5 million). This relationship occurs because our example assumes that tax rates remain stable at 35%. On the other hand, the rate for the income tax actually payable, $35 million, on pre-tax income is just 18.4% ($35 million ÷ $190 million = 18.4%). If this amount were

Exhibit 9–5
Depreciation for Book
and Tax Purposes

Dorian Company
Depreciation of Plant and Equipment for Book
and Tax Purposes, 1996 and 1997

At December 31, 1997:	Book	Tax
Plant and equipment, original cost	$900 million	$900 million
Accumulated depreciation	200 million[a]	600 million[b]
Basis	$700 million	$300 million
During 1998:		
Income tax rate	35%	35%
Income before depreciation	$250 million	$250 million
Depreciation	$ 60 million	$150 million
Pre-tax income	$190 million	$100 million
At December 31, 1998:	Book	Tax
Plant and equipment, original cost	$900 million	$900 million
Accumulated depreciation	260 million	750 million
Basis	$640 million	$150 million

Income tax actually payable for 1998:	
Income before depreciation	$250 million
Tax depreciation	−150 million
Taxable income	100 million
Multiplied by tax rate	× 35%
Tax actually payable	$ 35 million

(a) Straight-line depreciation is used for financial reporting.
(b) Accelerated depreciation is used for tax reporting.

to be reported as income tax expense on the income statement, investors might be misled about Dorian's true tax burden. Deferred tax accounting appears to provide a better matching of expenses on the income statement, at least when tax rates are expected to be stable over time.

Historically, tax rates in the United States have been relatively stable. In the third quarter of 1993, however, a new deficit-reduction law raised the corporate tax rate from 34 to 35%. This apparently minor adjustment in tax rates required that firms revalue their deferred tax liabilities upward by about 2.9% (1% rate increase ÷ 34% old rate = 2.9%). Because accounting standards require this adjustment to be included in the calculation of tax expense for the quarter in which the new tax law is signed, many firms experienced a considerable drop in the forecast for third-quarter profits. As examples, International Paper's profit forecast fell by 50.8%, and Georgia Pacific's forecasted profits were revised to a forecasted loss ("New Tax Rate to Push Profits Below Forecasts," *Wall Street Journal,* September 17, 1993).

Other Aspects of Income Tax Reporting

The foregoing discussion of income tax reporting has emphasized the issue of accelerated depreciation. This focus is appropriate because the predominant portion of temporary differences between the book and the tax bases of corporate assets of U.S. firms is due to differences in tax and book depreciation.

There are many other reasons why tax and book income measurements differ, however. For example, revenue and expense measurements in areas such as leasing, warranties, debt refinancing, exchanges of assets, and various other areas are treated differently for tax and book purposes. In some cases, the differences result in postponements of taxable income (as with accelerated depreciation). In other cases, however, the different treatments result in earlier recognition of taxable income. As a result, some firms may report deferred tax assets, rather than deferred tax liabilities.

Although further discussion of these other types of temporary differences is too specialized for this text, the basic framework that was used in calculating tax differences due to differences in depreciation methods applies in many other areas.

Deferred Taxes and the Liability Concept

Present financial reporting standards emphasize that deferred tax obligations are liabilities. In some respects, however, the manner in which deferred tax obligations are classified and measured is inconsistent with liability reporting.

Generally, business liabilities are classified as current or noncurrent based on the length of time to repayment. Deferred tax obligations, in contrast, are classified based on the current versus noncurrent classification of the related asset. For example, depreciating assets are classified as noncurrent assets, and for this reason the related deferred tax obligations are also classified as noncurrent. Accounting literature does not provide any compelling reason for this practice.

Generally, long-term obligations are reported at their present values, i.e., the future payments are discounted to the present at an appropriate rate of interest. Deferred tax obligations are not discounted, however, even in cases where the temporary differences are not expected to reverse for many years. Consequently, managers and investment analysts often argue that the amounts reported as deferred tax obligations are substantial overstatements of the economic value of these liabilities.

Other Liabilities

This chapter has examined various types of noncurrent liabilities that are included in financial reports. Other types of liabilities are more controversial in nature. The acceptable methods of accounting and reporting for these controversial items have changed substantially in recent years and are continuing to evolve. For this reason, Chapter 12 is devoted to a discussion of controversial areas in liability reporting. That chapter discusses accounting for leases, pensions, and postemployment benefits.

1. **Recognize the types of noncurrent obligations that are reported by business firms.**
   The major portion of long-term debt that is reported on corporate balance sheets consists of notes and bonds payable. Many corporations also report substantial obligations for deferred income taxes.

2. **Comprehend the features of long-term borrowing contracts, i.e., notes and bonds payable.**

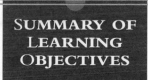

SUMMARY OF LEARNING OBJECTIVES

Notes payable represent direct borrowings by the firm from banks or other lenders. The note is a formal contract to repay a specific amount at a definite future date. Most notes require interest payments periodically over the life of the loan. Some notes do not entail periodic interest payments and instead are sold at a discount to compensate lenders for the use of their funds.

Bonds payable constitute a major form of borrowed capital for business corporations. Bonds are contracts that obligate the issuing corporation to make periodic interest payments and to repay the principal at a specified maturity date. Bonds are sold to investors and are actively traded among investors subsequent to their issuance. The amount that the issuing firm receives for its bonds depends on the relationship between the coupon or face rate of interest and the market rate of interest when the bonds are issued. Bonds will sell at par (face) value if the coupon and market rates are equal; at a discount if the market interest rate exceeds the coupon rate; or at a premium if the coupon rate exceeds the market rate.

3. **Determine periodic interest expense and the valuation of noncurrent obligations in financial reports.**

Firms use compound interest calculations to determine the periodic interest expense and balance sheet valuation of bonds payable. Fluctuations in the market prices of bonds payable that occur subsequent to their issuance are not reflected in the financial statements. If firms retire bonds early, i.e., before the maturity date, any difference between the carrying value and the cost to retire the bonds is reported as an extraordinary gain or loss.

4. **Be alert to additional business obligations that presently are unreported.**

In addition to long-term liabilities that are valued and reported on the balance sheet, firms disclose additional information in footnotes regarding actual and potential future claims that do not presently meet the FASB's criteria for recognition as liabilities at the balance sheet date. In some cases, these commitments and contingencies may be important in assessing the future solvency of the firm.

5. **Appreciate why income is measured differently for income tax and financial reporting purposes.**

Income measurement for tax purposes must comply with income tax laws, and income measurement for financial reporting purposes must comply with current accounting standards. Because these two income measures serve different purposes, the resulting pre-tax book (financial reporting) income and tax (tax return) income will differ.

6. **Understand why the tax basis and the financial reporting basis of assets and liabilities may differ.**

Differences between book and tax income imply differences in the book and tax bases (or carrying values) of the related assets. These differences are usually temporary in nature because total taxable income over the entire useful life of an asset will usually be the same for tax and book purposes. In other words, timing differences may allow a firm to postpone tax payments to future years, but not to avoid the tax payments. Consequently, firms must recognize an obligation for deferred (postponed) taxes.

7. **Interpret financial statement measurements of income tax expense and deferred income tax liability.**

Income tax expense reported in the financial statements is computed by adding income tax payable and any change in the total amount of deferred tax liability to get the total expense:

Income tax actually payable		$XXX
Increase (decrease) in deferred tax liability	+ (−)	YYY
Total income tax expense		$ ZZZ

Deferred tax obligations are reported in the balance sheet as part of a firm's total debt. Unlike other long-term obligations, however, they are not shown at their present values and, therefore, may reflect an overstatement of a firm's liabilities.

KEY TERMS

Amortization	Indentures
Bond	Interest-bearing notes
Bonds payable	Market rate
Collateral	Maturity date
Commitments	Noncurrent liabilities
Contingencies	Par value (bonds)
Convertible bonds	Premium on bonds
Coupon rate	Restrictive covenants
Deferred income tax liability	Temporary differences
Discount on bonds	

REALITY CHECK SOLUTIONS

SOLUTION TO REALITY CHECK 9–1

a. The primary reason that interest rates differ among debt issues is that interest rates prevailing in financial markets change over time. Consequently, some debt is issued when interest rates in general are relatively high, and other debt is issued when interest rates in general are relatively low.

In addition, interest rates may differ because of the features of individual debt issues. For example, Kodak's convertible debentures have a relatively low interest rate (6 ⅜%). A convertible debenture allows the holder to exchange the debt issue for a designated number of shares of common stock. This conversion feature is usually attractive to investors, so lenders are willing to accept a lower rate of interest.

b. The information about the maturity dates of Kodak's outstanding debt is useful to the analyst in predicting the firm's future cash flows. Kodak must generate sufficient cash to retire the debt, from operating cash flows and/or from additional borrowings and shareholders' investments.

c. If the prevailing market interest rate is 8.25%, then the issues that were sold at lower interest rates (the 7 ⅞% and the 6 ⅜% issues) would be valued below par, i.e., at a *discount*. The issues that were sold at higher interest rates (the 10.05% and 8.55% issues) would be valued above par, i.e., at a *premium*. As discussed in part a, the current market value of the convertible debt would also be affected by the value of the conversion privilege.

d. If Kodak's management desires to report a gain due to early retirement of debt, the issues that are presently selling below par (and reported value on the balance sheet) might be retired. Kodak would then report a gain on debt retirement equal to the difference between current market value and the reported value. This gain would be classified as extraordinary in the income statement.

e. Creditors are willing to buy zero-coupon bonds at a discount from face value. The difference between the face value and the issue price will provide interest income to the creditors over the term of the debt issue. For example, Kodak's zero-coupon bonds are reported at a discount of $2,553 ($3,680 face value minus $1,127 reported value). If the bonds are held to maturity in 2011, investors will earn approximately 6.75% per year as interest income. Note also that the zero-coupon bonds are convertible. For this reason, lenders may also be willing to accept a lower interest rate.

SOLUTION TO REALITY CHECK 9–2

a. Evaluation of compliance with restrictive covenants:

Minimum working capital of $17,000,000:

Current assets	$41,289,000
Less: Current liabilities	− 8,209,000
Working capital	$33,080,000

Therefore, the firm complies with the minimum working capital restriction.

Current ratio of 200% (or, 2.0):

$$\text{Current ratio} = \frac{\text{Current assets}}{\text{Current liabilities}}$$
$$= \$41,289,000/\$8,209,000$$
$$= 502.9\% \text{ (or, 5.029)}$$

Therefore, the firm complies with the current ratio restriction.

Net worth of $25,000,000:

$$\text{Net worth} = \text{Total assets less total liabilities}$$
$$= \$65,091,000 - \$22,054,000$$
$$= \$43,037,000$$

Therefore, the firm complies with the net worth restriction.

b. The firm's current assets might decrease up to $16,080,000 before violating the working capital restriction:

Actual working capital (see calculation in part a)	$33,080,000
Working capital restriction	−17,000,000
Excess over restriction	$16,080,000

c. The firm's current assets might decrease up to $24,871,000 before violating the current ratio restriction:

Actual current assets	$41,289,000
Current liabilities × 200% ($8,209,000 × 2)	−16,418,000
Difference	$24,871,000

d. Lenders may restrict *both* the current ratio and the dollar amount of working capital for the following reason. Long-term borrowings extend over many years, and during that time the firm's operating level may change substantially. For lower levels of output, the firm may have relatively small amounts of current assets and liabilities, and a high current ratio would not provide much protection for long-term lenders. In this case, the dollar amount of working capital is an important feature.

At higher levels of output, when current assets and liabilities are relatively large, a high current ratio offers stronger protection to the long-term creditors.

9–1 Define a long-term or noncurrent liability. Describe the differences between a current and noncurrent liability.

9–2 Identify some of the reasons why a firm may prefer to have some current and some noncurrent liabilities.

9–3 If a firm has noncurrent liabilities with a fixed interest rate, what will happen to the firm's financial statements when market interest rates increase? Decrease? When interest rates on a firm's financial instruments are fixed, why don't financial statements generally reflect the actual current market interest rates, which may vary on a daily basis?

9–4 Under what circumstances would managers prefer fixed interest rates and when might they prefer to have variable interest rates on their noncurrent liabilities? Discuss several choices that managers might make in these circumstances. What are the financial statement outcomes or consequences of these choices? Under what circumstances do managers have the opportunity to adjust the valuation of their liabilities to reflect market conditions?

9–5 Describe the major differences between a bond discount and a bond premium. Include the distinction between coupon (or nominal) interest rates and market interest rates at the bond issuance date.

9–6 If a long-term bond is issued at a discount, both the carrying value of the bond and the recognized interest expense will increase in each successive period during which the bond is outstanding. Explain why this occurs.

9–7 If a long-term bond is issued at a premium, both the carrying value of the bond and the recognized interest expense will decrease in each successive period during which the bond is outstanding. Explain why this occurs.

9–8 Evaluate the following statement: "When a firm issues bonds at a discount, in effect the firm is paying the lender some of the bond interest expense in advance. The difference between the bond principal and the amount paid to the issuer should be reported on the balance sheet as prepaid interest expense, and be listed as an asset."

9–9 Provide several reasons why managers may prefer to issue long-term bonds to a number of investors, rather than to borrow directly from financial institutions.

9–10 Discuss reasons why lenders may incorporate various restrictive covenants in a lending agreement. Provide several examples of restrictive covenants.

9–11 Assume that a firm has several long-term bonds outstanding, at various different interest rates. Explain the relationship between bond coupon rates and current market interest rates that would cause the bonds to sell at par, below par, and above par value.

9–12 Assume that a firm has bonds outstanding with a principal amount of $100 million, and a carrying value of $105 million, and a current market value of $112 million. What amount of gain or loss would the firm report if the bonds were to be retired today (ignore transactions costs)? Do you consider this to be a "real" gain or loss? Explain.

9–13 Discuss the purposes of income measurement for financial reporting. Then, discuss why income taxes, both as an expense and as a liability are included in a firm's financial statements.

9–14 Most firms keep at least two "sets of books," in the sense that a given transaction may be interpreted differently for "book" (i.e., financial reporting) and "tax" (i.e., income tax calculations) purposes. Is this ethical? Discuss.

9–15 Suppose the U.S. Congress decides to stimulate business investment in new plant and equipment by providing a reduction in income taxes equal to 10% of the costs of eligible new investments. If a firm acquires $100 million in new plant and equipment, and consequently receives a $10 million dollar reduction in income taxes, should the $10 million be interpreted (a) as income, (b) as a reduction in the cost of the acquired assets, or (c) in some other manner? Discuss.

9–16 Explain the nature of *temporary* differences between book and tax measurements of assets and liabilities. Why is this concept important for financial reporting of income tax expense? Why is it important for reporting a firm's liabilities?

9–17 Whether a firm uses straight-line or accelerated depreciation in accounting for a long-lived depreciable asset, the total amount of depreciation expense over the entire service life of the asset will be the same. If so, why is the choice among these depreciation methods for financial statement purposes important? Why is the timing of depreciation expense on a firm's tax return important?

9–18 Discuss the meaning of a deferred income tax liability. In your discussion, address the following points:

a. Why does a deferral exist?
b. Do these obligations satisfy the definition of liabilities that was provided in Chapter 3?
c. How (if at all) would the carrying value of these liabilities be affected by changes in income tax rates?
d. How (if at all) would the carrying value of these liabilities be affected by changes in interest rates?

9–19 Provide a reply to the following: "If a firm does not earn taxable income in future periods, then it will not pay taxes. For this reason, it makes no sense to report deferred tax liabilities. These amounts will only be payable if the firm earns future taxable income, and that is an event that has not yet happened. Financial accounting is supposed to be historical in nature. Deferred tax accounting does not fit into the historical cost framework."

9–20 Evaluate the following proposal: "If an asset is fully depreciated for income tax purposes, it is less valuable than an asset that has a substantial undepreciated cost for tax purposes. This implies that the valuation of assets on the balance sheet should be adjusted as their tax bases are reduced."

9–21 Comment on the following observation: "Mammoth Company is not paying its fair share of the national budget. The firm reported income before taxes of $4 billion in 1994, and paid only $40 million in income taxes. That is only 1% of its income. Even the middle-class pay more tax than that. I suppose it's legal, but it's sure not ethical. That company's management should be removed from office."

9–22 Assume U.S. (enacted) income tax rates are increased from 35 to 40%. How would this increase affect a firm that presently reports a deferred tax liability of

$700 million? Specifically, how would the firm's net income be affected in the period in which the rate increase was enacted, and how would the carrying value of the deferred tax liability be changed? Do you agree with these financial statement effects? Discuss.

9–23 Current financial accounting standards do not permit the discounting of deferred tax obligations, even in cases where the deferred obligations are not expected to be paid for many years. Evaluate this practice. Your evaluation should address the following points:

a. Is it consistent to discount some long-term debt (e.g., bonds payable), and not other long-term liabilities (e.g. tax deferrals), and then add these amounts together in order to measure total liabilities?

b. If deferred tax obligations were to be discounted, would you suggest using a current market interest rate or some other rate? On the other hand, could you argue that tax deferrals are essentially an "interest-free" loan from the government, and therefore require discounting at zero interest?

c. If deferred tax obligations were to be discounted, and interest rates in general were subsequently to rise, how (if at all) would the carrying values of the deferred tax obligations be adjusted?

EXERCISES

Transaction Analysis: Long-Term Notes Payable

9–24 Use the balance sheet equation to analyze the effects of the following transactions involving noncurrent liabilities. Set up separate accounts under each heading.

ASSETS = LIABILITIES + SHAREHOLDERS' EQUITY

1. The firm signs a long-term note for $5 million for three years at an interest rate of 8%. The firm receives the $5 million in cash.
2. The first interest payment is due and is paid at the end of the first year.
3. The interest payment at the end of the second year is due, but is not paid.
4. The note is completely satisfied (paid) at the end of the third year, including the accrued interest from year 2. Show the effects of each interest payment and the repayment separately. Assume that interest on any unpaid balances compounds; that is, interest will accrue on the unpaid interest carried over from year 2.

Transaction Analysis: Notes Payable and Simple Interest

9–25 Use the balance sheet equation to analyze the effects of the following transactions involving noncurrent liabilities. Set up separate accounts under each heading.

ASSETS = LIABILITIES + SHAREHOLDERS' EQUITY

1. Sally Shrimpton wants to expand her pottery business, but is very cash poor. She borrows $150,000 from her local banker and signs a note when she receives the cash.
2. Sally purchases a new kiln for $50,000 cash.
3. Sally purchases clay, paint, and other supplies for $20,000 cash.
4. Sally pays herself a bonus of $25,000 because she wants to remodel her kitchen.
5. Interest for the first six months is now due, at an annual rate of 15%.
6. Sally pays the interest due.
7. Interest for the second six months is due.
8. Interest for the third six-month period is due.
9. Sally pays the interest for the second and third six-month periods and makes partial payment on the loan of $50,000.
10. Interest for the fourth six-month period is due.
11. Interest for the final year (two six-month periods) is due.
12. Sally fully repays the note, along with all of the accumulated interest.

Transaction Analysis: Noninterest Bearing Notes

9–26 Sally Shrimpton's pottery business has been quite successful and she wants to expand again. However, she hates to make interest payments to the bank. She recently saw an ad for discounted notes and decides that she much prefers a discounted note, as compared to an interest-bearing note. Show the effects of each of the following transactions on the balance sheet equation. Set up separate accounts under each heading.

ASSETS = LIABILITIES + SHAREHOLDERS' EQUITY

1. Sally signs a discounted, three-year, $200,000 note (see Chapter 8) and receives the proceeds from her banker. When she gets home, she reads the fine print and finds that the note does not require any periodic interest payments, which was her intent. However, she does find that the note includes interest at a rate of 12% and she wonders if the banker made a mistake. When she gets her next bank statement, she is surprised and shocked to find that the banker did not deposit $200,000 in her account on the day she signed the note; in fact, the deposit was much less! Calculate the loan proceeds and determine the effects of the loan on the balance sheet equation.
2. Sally now understands that interest is included in all notes, whether she makes any monthly or annual payment of the interest. Record the interest for the first year.
3. Record the interest for each of the next two years.
4. Record the final payment on the note.
5. What payment would Sally have been required to make, if she had repaid the note at the end of the second year? Why doesn't she have to pay the entire $200,000 at this point, if she repaid the note at the end of the second year?

Transaction Analysis: Noninterest Bearing Notes

9–27 On June 1, 1996, the Brewer Company signed a $450,000, five-year note, discounted (16% compounded rate) payable to First Bank. The $450,000 is due and payable June 1, 2001.

REQUIRED

Set up an accounting equation and record the following:

a. Cash proceeds received by Brewer Company.
b. Interest for each of the five years.
c. The final payment of the note.

Issuing Noninterest Bearing Notes

9–28 Calculate the financial statement effects, at the date of issue, of each of the following discounted notes (see Chapter 8):

a. $10,000,000 note for one year at a 10% market interest rate.
b. $20,000,000 note for three years at a 12% market interest rate.
c. $5,000,000 note for 10 years at a 10% market interest rate.
d. What amount of cash is necessary to repay these notes at maturity, assuming no other changes during the term of the notes? (*Hint:* No further calculations are necessary to answer this question.)

Transaction Analysis: Issuing Bonds

9–29 Use the balance sheet equation to analyze the effects of issuing the following long-term bonds (assume semiannual compounding). Assume a coupon rate of 8%. Set up separate accounts under each heading.

ASSETS = LIABILITIES + SHAREHOLDERS' EQUITY

a. $10,000,000 bonds for one year at a 8% market interest rate.
b. $20,000,000 bonds for three years at a 12% market interest rate.
c. $5,000,000 bonds for 10 years at a 8% market interest rate.

Transaction Analysis: Issuing Bonds

9–30 Use the balance sheet equation to analyze the effects of issuing the following long-term bonds, assuming a market interest rate of 12% and semiannual compounding in each case. Set up separate accounts under each heading.
a. $10,000,000 bonds for one year, with a coupon interest rate of 10%.
b. $20,000,000 bonds for three years, with a coupon interest rate of 12%.

ASSETS = LIABILITIES + SHAREHOLDERS' EQUITY

c. $5,000,000 bonds for 10 years, with a coupon interest rate of 10%.

d. Discuss why each of these bonds was issued at a premium or a discount.

Transaction Analysis: Issuing Bonds

9–31 Use the balance sheet equation to analyze the effects of issuing the following long-term bonds, assuming a market rate of interest of 8% and semiannual compounding in each case. Set up separate accounts under each heading.

ASSETS	=	LIABILITIES	+	SHAREHOLDERS' EQUITY

a. $10,000,000 bonds for one year, with a coupon interest rate of 10%.

b. $20,000,000 bonds for three years, with a coupon interest rate of 12%.

c. $5,000,000 bonds for 10 years, with a coupon interest rate of 10%.

d. Discuss why each of these bonds was issued at a premium or a discount.

Transaction Analysis: Bond Principal and Interest

9–32 Use the balance sheet equation to analyze the financial statement effects of the following transactions involving long-term bonds, assuming semiannual compounding in each case. Set up separate accounts under each heading.

ASSETS	=	LIABILITIES	+	SHAREHOLDERS' EQUITY

a. Issue $10,000,000 of five-year bonds carrying a coupon interest rate of 8%, payable semiannually. The market rate of interest at the time of issuance, for similar bonds, was 4%.

b. Record the interest due and paid after the first six months.

c. Record the interest due and paid at the end of the first year.

d. Record the interest due and paid during each six-month period during the second year.

e. How much cash will be paid at maturity (at the end of the fifth year)?

f. Show the effects of the bond repayment on the financial statements at the end of the fifth year.

g. Discuss why these bonds were issued and recorded at a premium or discount.

Transaction Analysis: Bond Principal and Interest

9–33 Use the balance sheet equation to analyze the financial statement effects of the following transactions involving long-term bonds, assuming semiannual compounding in each case. Set up separate accounts under each heading.

ASSETS	=	LIABILITIES	+	SHAREHOLDERS' EQUITY

a. Issue $20,000,000 of five-year bonds carrying a coupon interest rate of 8%, payable semiannually. The market rate of interest at the time of issuance, for similar bonds, was 12%.
b. Record the interest paid after the first six months.
c. Record the interest due and paid at the end of the first year.
d. Record the interest due and paid during each six-month period during the second year.
e. How much cash will be paid at the end of the fifth year?
f. Show the effects of the bond repayment on the financial statements at the end of the fifth year.
g. Discuss why these bonds were issued and recorded at a premium or discount.

Income Tax Expense, Tax Payable, and Deferred Tax Liability

9–34 Selected information from the income statements and tax returns of Buchanan Trading Co. are provided below for 1998 and 1999, the firm's first two years of operations ($ in millions):

	Income Statement Items	
	1998	**1999**
Income before depreciation and taxes	$1000	$1100
Depreciation expense	400	450
Pre-tax income	600	650
Income tax expense (35%)	210	227.5

	Tax Return Items	
	1998	**1999**
Income before depreciation and taxes	$1000	$1100
Depreciation expense	700	800
Taxable income	300	300
Income tax payable (35%)	105	105

REQUIRED

Determine the following amounts for 1998 and 1999:

a. Difference between the tax basis and book basis of Buchanan's assets at the end of each year.
b. Deferred tax liabilities at the end of each year.

Change in Enacted Tax Rates (continuation of preceding exercise)

9–35 In the year 2000, Buchanan Trading Co. reported $800 million of depreciation in its income statement, and $600 million of depreciation on its tax return. The firm's income before depreciation and income taxes was $950 million. Enacted income tax rates applicable to firms such as Buchanan were increased to 45% effective at the beginning of the year 2000.

REQUIRED

a. Based on the information provided above and in the preceding exercise, determine Buchanan's income tax expense and net income after tax reported on its income statement for the year 2000, and the amount of deferred tax liability to be reported on its balance sheet at December 31, 2000.

9–36 Tax Expense, Tax Payable, and Deferred Tax Liability, Stable Tax Rate—Alternate Exercises (A) or (B)

Exercise (A)

Wilbur Mills, Inc., began operations in early 1998. The firm recognized $12 million of depreciation expense on its income statement and reported $20 million as depreciation on its tax return for 1998. The 1998 income statement shows pre-tax income of $10 million and the income tax rate is 40%.

REQUIRED

Determine the following amounts for 1998:

a. Income tax expense.
b. Income tax payable.
c. Difference between the book and tax bases of Wilbur Mills' assets at year-end.
d. Deferred tax liability at year-end.

Exercise (B)

Rosty Co. began operations in early 1997. The firm recognized $30 million of depreciation expense on its income statement, and reported $50 million as depreciation on its 1997 tax return. The firm's income was taxed at 30%. The 1998 income statement shows pre-tax income of $25 million.

REQUIRED

Determine the following amounts:

a. Tax liability for 1997.
b. Deferred tax liability at the end of 1997.
c. Difference between the book and tax bases of Rosty's assets at the end of 1997.
d. Income tax expense for 1997.

9–37 Tax Expense, Tax Payable, and Deferred Tax Liability, Changing Tax Rate (continuation of Exercise 9–36)—Alternate Exercises (A) or (B)

Exercise (A)

During 1999, Wilbur Mills, Inc., recognized an additional $12 million of depreciation expense on its income statement and reported $16 million as depreciation on its tax return. During 1999 the enacted income tax rate was reduced from 40 to 35%, effective at the beginning of 1999. The 1999 income statement shows pre-tax income of $14 million.

REQUIRED

Determine the following amounts for 1999:

a. Income tax expense.
b. Income tax payable.
c. Difference between the book and tax bases of Wilbur Mills' assets at year-end.
d. Deferred tax liability at year-end.
e. Percentage relationship between pre-tax income and income tax expense reported in the income statement for 1999.

Exercise (B)

During 1998, Rosty Co. recognized an additional $30 million of depreciation expense on its income statement, and reported $40 million as depreciation on its tax return. During 1998, the enacted income tax rate applicable to firms such as Rosty Co. was increased from 30 to 40%. The 1998 income statement shows pre-tax income of $12 million.

REQUIRED

Determine the following amounts:

a. Difference between the book and tax bases of Rosty's assets at the end of 1998.
b. Deferred tax liability at the end of 1998.
c. Tax liability for 1998.
d. Income tax expense for 1998.
e. Percentage relationship between pre-tax income and income tax expense reported in the 1998 income statement.

PROBLEMS

9–38 Issue Bonds, Calculate Interest, Amortize Premium or Discount—Alternate Problems (A) or (B)

Problem (A)

Zany Sam's issued $600,000 of six-year, 8% bonds at a time when the market demanded a yield of 12% (on similar bonds). The bonds were issued on January 1 and require interest payments on each subsequent June 30 and December 31, until maturity.

REQUIRED

a. Compute the issue price, and determine the amount of any premium or discount at issue date.
b. Using the balance sheet equation, show the effects of issuing the bonds on the financial statements.
c. Prepare a table showing the amortization of the discount or premium at each of the first four semiannual periods.
d. Under normal circumstances, how much cash will be paid at each interest date?
e. Determine the carrying value two years after the date of issue. (*Reminder:* The carrying value or book value of the bonds equals the face amount of the bonds plus premium, or minus discount.)
f. Assume the bonds can be retired two years after issue at 98 (98% of par value). Show the effects on the financial statements of this early retirement.
g. Why would a firm want to retire bonds early? Why would a firm pay more than book value to retire bonds early?

Problem (B)

Zany Sam's No. 2 issued $800,000 of 10-year, 8% bonds at a time when the market demanded a yield of 4% (on similar bonds). The bonds were issued on January 1 and require interest payments on each subsequent June 30 and December 31, until maturity.

REQUIRED

a. Compute the issue price, and determine the amount of any premium or discount at issue date.

b. Show the effects on the financial statements, using the balance sheet equation, of the bond issue.

c. Prepare a table showing the amortization of the discount or premium at each of the first four semi-annual periods.

d. Under normal circumstances, how much cash will be paid at each interest date?

e. Determine the book value (face amount, plus premium or minus discount) two years after the date of issue.

f. Assume the bonds can be retired two years after issue at 102 (102% of par value). Show the effects on the financial statements of this early retirement.

g. Why would a firm want to retire bonds early? Why would a firm pay more than book value to retire bonds early?

Contingencies

9–39 How should the following contingencies be treated on the annual report of Akronite Corporation at December 31, 1997?

a. The corporation is presently being sued for patent infringement. The damages are estimated to be $12 million and Akronite's attorneys feel this will probably be the amount required to be paid. However, the court date is set for June of the following year.

b. The corporation is being sued by the federal government for environmental pollution. The damages alleged by the federal government will probably be assessed against the corporation. However, no estimate has been determined at this point.

c. The corporation is suing another corporation for various infringements. The court date is scheduled for March 1998. The lawsuit total is $15 million and it is almost a sure thing that Akronite will prevail and collect $15 million.

Financial Statement Effects of Deferred Taxes

9–40 Gottlieb Enterprises is concerned about whether its balance sheet properly discloses its deferred tax liabilities. Gottlieb's preliminary balance sheet at the end of 1997 can be summarized as follows:

Current assets	$ 400,000	Current liabilities	$ 250,000
Fixed assets, net	1,400,000	Long-term debt	500,000
		Shareholders' equity	1,050,000
Total assets	$1,800,000	Total liabilities and	
		shareholders' equity	$1,800,000

Gottlieb's tax return shows that the net book value of its fixed assets, for tax purposes, is only $900,000.

REQUIRED

a. Based solely on the above information, compute Gottlieb's deferred tax liability at the end of 1997, assuming a 38% average tax rate.

b. Now, if you found that Gottlieb had already calculated a deferred tax liability of $250,000 at the beginning of 1997, and included it erroneously in shareholders' equity, calculate the change in Gottlieb's deferred tax liability.

c. Based on your answer in part b, indicate how Gottlieb's 1997 income tax expense must have been affected by these tax deferrals.

d. Based on your answers above, correctly prepare Gottlieb's balance sheet for the end of 1997.

e. Discuss why it is important for a firm to disclose its deferred tax liabilities. To illustrate this importance, compare Gottlieb's balance sheet shown in the problem statement with your new balance sheet from part d.

Financial Statement Effects of Deferred Taxes

9–41 Motherwell, Inc., is concerned about whether its balance sheet properly discloses its deferred tax liabilities. Motherwell's preliminary balance sheet at the end of 1997 can be summarized as follows:

Current assets	$ 600,000	Current liabilities	$ 333,000
Fixed assets, net	1,550,000	Long-term debt	666,000
		Shareholders' equity	1,151,000
Total assets	$2,150,000	Total liabilities and	
		shareholders' equity	$2,150,000

Motherwell's tax return shows that the net book value of its fixed assets, for tax purposes, is only $850,000.

REQUIRED

a. Compute Motherwell's deferred tax liability, assuming a 35% average tax rate.

b. Now, if you found that Motherwell had already calculated a deferred tax liability of $335,000 at the beginning of 1997, and included it erroneously in current liabilities, calculate the change in Motherwell's deferred tax liability.

c. Based on your answer in part b, indicate how Motherwell's 1997 income tax expense must have been affected by these tax deferrals.

d. Based on your answers above, correctly prepare Motherwell's balance sheet for the end of 1997.

e. Discuss why it is important for a firm to disclose its deferred tax liabilities. To illustrate this importance, compare Motherwell's balance sheet shown in the problem statement with your new balance sheet from part d.

Long-term Debt: Interpreting Financial Statements

9–42 Cabot Corporation is a specialty chemicals company. Its 1994 annual report contains a note on long-term debt. A partial list of the long-term debt follows ($ in thousands) exclusive of current maturities:

	1994	1993
Notes due 1997, 9.875%	$150,000	$150,000
Notes due 2002–2022, 8.07%	105,000	105,000
Overseas Private Investment Corp		
due 2002, floating rate 6.5%	15,000	—
Industrial revenue bonds, due		
1997–2014, 9.35%–14%	5,000	6,000

REQUIRED

a. Comment on why Cabot might have long-term debt with such different interest rates and different maturities.

b. Based on current interest rates, which of these do you think would sell above or below par values? Why?

c. Discuss how managers might use an aggressive debt retirement strategy to increase or decrease net income.

Financial Statement Effects of Deferred Taxes

9–43 Tyler Corporation's statement of operations is summarized below ($ in thousands):

	1994	1993	1992
Net sales	$357,850	$282,403	$286,206
Costs and expenses:			
Cost of sales	256, 195	221,024	223,826
Selling, general, and administrative expense	103,402	57,972	55,667
Interest expense, net	3,820	487	608
Total costs and expenses	363,417	279,483	280,101
Income (loss) before income tax (benefit)	(5,567)	2,920	6,105
Income tax (benefit)			
Current	(859)	2,649	4,051
Deferred	(7)	(1,067)	(1,181)
	(866)	1,582	2,870
Income (loss) before cumulative changes	(4,701)	1,338	3,235
Cumulative effect of changes in accounting principles		(3,601)	
Net income (loss)	($4,701)	$ (2,263)	$ 3,235

REQUIRED

a. Explain the item "Income tax (benefit)." How can income tax be positive? That is, how can income tax be deducted from income before tax in 1992 and 1993, and added in 1994?

b. Calculate the following ratios for 1994 and 1993:

1. Operating income.
2. Net income.
3. ROE; assume average stockholders for 1994 and 1993 are $114,000 and $117,000 ($ in thousands) *Note:* You may want to take out nonrecurring items before calculating the ratios.

c. Evaluate Tyler's performance during 1993 and 1994.

Deferred Taxes: Interpreting Financial Statements

9–44 Refer to Wendy's financial statements in Appendix D. Review the balance sheet to determine how and where deferred taxes were reported.

REQUIRED

a. Read Note 4. Identify and discuss any unusual terms. Trace disclosures of deferred taxes in the notes to corresponding disclosures in the financial statements.

b. Determine whether Wendy's has a net long-term deferred tax liability. If it is not a liability, determine what it is and how Wendy's managers might view the income tax carryforward.

c. Identify the years where Wendy's income taxes paid (shown at the bottom of the cash flow statement) as a percentage of income before tax were close to the statutory rate. Identify the years where Wendy's paid less. Did it ever pay more than the overall statutory rate?

d. Discuss any other unusual concerns regarding Wendy's deferred taxes. What other related information might an external analyst require, or prefer?

Long-Term Debt: Interpreting Financial Statements

9–45 Refer to Wendy's financial statements in Appendix D. Review the balance sheet to determine how and where long-term liabilities were reported.

REQUIRED

a. Read Notes 2 and 3. Identify and discuss any unusual terms. Trace numerical disclosures of long-term liabilities in the notes to corresponding disclosures in the financial statements.

b. Discuss any other unusual concerns regarding Wendy's long-term liabilities. What other related information might an external analyst require, or prefer?

c. Read Note 8 concerning commitments and contingencies. Identify and discuss any unusual terms. Discuss how Wendy's future income might be affected by the situations described in the note.

Deferred Taxes: Interpreting Financial Statements

9–46 Refer to Reebok's financial statements in Appendix F. Review the balance sheet to determine how and where deferred taxes were reported.

REQUIRED

a. Read Notes 1 and 13. Identify and discuss any unusual terms. Trace disclosures of deferred taxes in the notes to corresponding disclosures in the financial statements.

b. Determine whether Reebok has a deferred tax liability. If it is not a liability, determine what it is and how Reebok's managers might view its deferred income taxes.

c. Identify the years where Reebok's income taxes paid (shown at the bottom of the cash flow statement) as a percentage of income before taxes were close to the statutory rate. Identify any years where Reebok paid less. Did it ever pay more than the overall statutory rate?

d. Discuss any other unusual concerns regarding Reebok's deferred taxes. What other related information might an external analyst require, or prefer?

Long-Term Debt: Interpreting Financial Statements

9–47 Refer to Reebok's financial statements in Appendix F. Review the balance sheet to determine how and when long-term liabilities were reported.

REQUIRED

a. Read Note 7. Identify and discuss any unusual terms. Trace numerical disclosures of long-term liabilities in the notes to corresponding disclosures in the financial statements.

b. Discuss any other unusual concerns regarding Reebok's long-term liabilities. What other related information might an external analyst require, or prefer?

c. Read Note 15 concerning contingencies. Discuss how Reebok's future income might be affected by the situation described in the note.

Deferred Taxes: Interpreting Financial Statements

9–48 Refer to OshKosh B'Gosh's financial statements in Appendix C. Review the balance sheet to determine how and when deferred taxes were reported.

REQUIRED

a. Read Notes 1 and 9. Identify and discuss any unusual terms. Trace numerical disclosures of deferred taxes in the notes to corresponding disclosures in the financial statements.

b. Determine whether OshKosh B'Gosh has a net long-term deferred tax liability. If it is not a liability, determine what it is and how OshKosh B'Gosh's managers might view its deferred income taxes.

c. Identify the years where OshKosh B'Gosh's income taxes paid (shown at the bottom of the cash flow statement) as a percentage of income before tax were close to the statutory rate. Identify the years where OshKosh B'Gosh paid less. Did it ever pay more than the overall statutory rate?

d. Discuss any other unusual concerns regarding OshKosh B'Gosh's deferred taxes. What other related information might an external analyst require, or prefer?

Long-Term Debt: Interpreting Financial Statements

9–49 Refer to OshKosh B'Gosh's financial statements in Appendix C. Review the balance sheet to determine how and where long-term liabilities were reported.

REQUIRED

a. Read Note 7. Identify and discuss any unusual terms. Trace numerical disclosures of long-term liabilities in the notes to corresponding disclosures in the financial statements.

b. Discuss any other unusual concerns regarding OshKosh B'Gosh's long-term liabilities. What other related information might an external analyst require, or prefer?

Deferred Taxes: Interpreting Financial Statements

9–50 Refer to Bristol-Myers Squibb's (BMS) financial statements in Appendix E. Review the balance sheet to determine how and where deferred taxes were reported.

REQUIRED

a. Read Note 7. Identify and discuss any unusual terms. Trace numerical disclosures of deferred taxes in the notes to corresponding disclosures in the financial statements.

b. Determine whether BMS has a net long-term deferred tax liability. If it is not a liability, determine what it is and how BMS managers might view its deferred income taxes.

c. Identify the years where BMS paid income taxes at a rate close to the statutory rate. Use the taxes paid, as shown at the bottom of the cash flow statement, to calculate the tax rate percentage of income before taxes. Identify the years where BMS paid less. Did it ever pay more than the overall statutory rate?

d. Discuss any other unusual concerns regarding BMS's deferred taxes. What other related information might an external analyst require, or prefer?

Long-Term Debt: Interpreting Financial Statements

9–51 Refer to the Bristol-Myers Squibb's (BMS) financial statements in Appendix E. Review the balance sheet to determine how and where long-term liabilities were reported.

REQUIRED

a. Read Note 11. Identify and discuss any unusual terms. Trace numerical disclosures of long-term liabilities in the notes to corresponding disclosures in the financial statements.

b. Discuss any other unusual concerns regarding BMS long-term liabilities. What other related information might an external analyst require, or prefer?

c. Read Note 18 concerning contingencies. Identify and discuss any unusual terms. Discuss how BMS's future income might be affected by the situation described in the note.

CASES AND EXTENSIONS

Conceptual Discussion: Variable Versus Fixed Interest Rates

9–52 If a firm has noncurrent liabilities with floating (variable) interest rates, what will happen to the firm's financial statements when the market rate of interest increases? Decreases? Why is there more consistency in this case, than in the case of fixed interest rates?

Written Memo: Bond Terms

9–53 Write a short memo describing the key features of long-term bonds. Include at least the following terms in your memo: par or face value, collateral, restrictive covenants, coupon rate, maturity date, and semiannual compounding.

Issuing Bonds, Premium or Discount

9–54 Maggie Markel's Moving Emporium needs to acquire additional capital in order to purchase new trucks and warehouse storage space, and to conduct a national advertising campaign. Maggie has heard of bonds and thinks that her friends and relatives would buy them if they were especially attractive. Although she knows that bonds issued by other similar moving companies are currently yielding about 8% compounded semiannually, she decided to be kind to her friends and relatives and offer an interest rate of 10% compounded semiannually on the bonds. Maggie has never heard of premiums or discounts on bonds and intends to sell the bonds at their face amount (par).

REQUIRED

a. How many $1,000 bonds must Maggie issue, *at par,* in order to raise $1,000,000?

b. Write a memo to Maggie explaining the possible effects and consequences of selling $1,000,000 of 5% bonds, at par, when similar bonds yield 4%.

c. If Maggie sold the bonds at their market value, including an appropriate premium or discount, how much would Maggie receive for the $1,000,000 bonds? (Assume five-year bonds.) How realistic is this assumption? Why?

d. Write a short memo summarizing your recommendations to Maggie about issuing these bonds.

Issuing Bonds, Premium or Discount (continuation of Case 9–54)

9–55 With regard to the previous case, revise your answers, assuming that you now learn that bonds similar to those issued by Maggie Markel's Moving Emporium are very risky and require an interest rate of 12% compounded semiannually (6% each six months) before they can be sold to anyone, even to Maggie's friends and relatives.

Interpreting Financial Statements: Long-Term Liabilities

9–56 Hansel, Inc., is an international company specializing in debt collection, with a range of complementary credit management services. It is headquartered in Amsterdam and aims to maintain and enhance its position as Europe's leading force in debt collection. Its 1996 financial statements list bank loans of £17,000,000 (£ = pounds sterling) with the following related note:

> BANK LOANS
> The company has entered into a syndicated loan facility of £25,400,000 of which £20,000,000 has been used as of December 31, 1996 (December 31, 1995: £13,000,000). £17,000,000 has been classified as long-term (1995: £13,000,000). The facility expires on December 16, 1998. The interest is calculated at 1.5% over LIBOR. A fee of 0.5% p.a. over the non-utilized part of the facility is payable. There are no additional costs on an early redemption.

REQUIRED

a. Explain each of the unusual terms or provisions described in this footnote.

b. Determine what LIBOR is, using a finance text or a finance glossary. Note that "p.a." means "per annum" or annually.

c. Calculate the annual fee on the unused portion of this credit arrangement, assuming the above balances were all outstanding during 1996.

d. Assuming no changes in monetary amounts, will these liabilities be shown as a current liability at the end of 1997? What must happen for them to remain as a long-term liability?

e. What amount must be included as the long-term liability on the balance sheet at the end of 1995? Why?

f. From the perspective of management, what else would you like to know about these long-term debts that is not shown in the financial statements?

g. For an investor evaluating a large international company, do these seem like significant and unusual long-term debts?

h. How does the accounting disclosure of these long-term debts compare to the treatment of 30-year bonds discussed in this chapter?

Interpreting Financial Statements: Ratio Calculations

9–57 Oncogene Science, Inc., shows no long-term debt in its 1994 financial statements. Its subtotals for liabilities and stockholders' equity follow:

	1994	1993
Total current liabilities	$ 2,979,555	$ 2,460,060
Total long-term debt	405,031	109,875
Total stockholders' equity	38,656,314	45,044,603
Total liabilities and equity	$42,040,900	$47,614,538

REQUIRED

a. Calculate Oncogene's debt and equity composition ratios using the capital composition ratios first introduced in Chapter 3.

b. Using only the information shown above, what does this evidence say, pro and con, about Oncogene's ability to meet its liabilities? Would this suggest a high or low likelihood of bankruptcy? Why?

c. What other information would you need to assess the firm's liquidity? Its default risk?

Interpreting Financial Statements: Ratio Calculations

9–58 Sigma Designs indicates that it has repaid much of its long-term debt, between January 31, 1994, and January 31, 1995. Its subtotals for liabilities and stockholders' equity at January 31 follow ($ in thousands):

	1995	1994
Total current liabilities	$13,564	$ 8,622
Total long-term liabilities	1,102	1,518
Total shareholders' equity	18,721	16,499
Total liabilities and equity	$33,387	$26,639

REQUIRED

a. Calculate Sigma Designs' debt and equity composition ratios.

b. Using only the information shown above, what does this evidence say, pro and con, about Sigma Designs' ability to meet its liabilities? Would this suggest a high or low likelihood of bankruptcy? Why?

c. What other information would you need to assess the firm's liquidity? Its default risk?

Interpreting Financial Statements: Compare and Contrast (continuation of Cases 9–57 and 9–58)

9–59 Contrast the debt management strategies of Oncogene Science and Sigma Designs (see data in the preceding two cases). Which company seems to be the most conservative in managing its liabilities? Why? Is there anything unusual about changes in their stockholders' equity accounts that might make them somewhat noncomparable?

Interpreting Financial Statements: Ratio Calculations

9–60 Pfizer, Inc. reports the following subtotals in its 1995 annual report ($ in millions):

	1995	1994	1993
Total current liabilities	$ 4,421.3	$ 4,176.0	$ 3,854.7
Total liabilities	5,945.2	5,742.5	5,042.8
Total shareholders' equity	8,504.5	8,254.9	8,200.1
Total liabilities and equity	$18,871.0	$18,173.4	$17,097.6

REQUIRED

a. Calculate the debt and equity composition ratios for Pfizer for each year.
b. What factors would indicate that Pfizer is a very stable company, especially with respect to its management of debt and equity? Would a more stable company generally have high or low risk of default? Why?
c. What else might you want to examine before concluding that Pfizer was a stable company with low default risk?

Interpreting Financial Statements: Ratio Calculations

9–61 Exabyte Corporation reports the following subtotals in its 1994 annual report, in thousands of dollars, year-ending December 31, 1994, and January 1, 1994 (note that these dates still represent two consecutive fiscal years):

	December 31 1994	January 1 1994
Total current liabilities	$ 45,621	$ 38,318
Long-term obligations	237	454
Total stockholders' equity	196,907	158,535
Total liabilities and equity	$242,765	$197,307

REQUIRED

a. Calculate Exabyte's debt and equity composition ratios.
b. What factors would indicate that Exabyte has a low risk of default on its long-term debt?
c. What debt management strategy does Exabyte seem to use?
d. What else might you examine in order to assess Exabyte's risk of default?
e. Can the most recent year be compared with fiscal year ended January 1, 1994? Why would a company change its year-end by a few days? What other information would you like to have before feeling comfortable about this issue?

Interpreting Financial Statements: Compare and Contrast (continuation of Cases 9–60 and 9–61)

9–62 Compare and contrast the composition ratios of Exabyte and Pfizer (see the preceding two cases). Which company seems to be the most conservative in managing its liabilities? Why? Which company seems to have the higher default risk? Why? Does the relative difference in size of these two companies have an impact on your relative assessments? Why?

Comprehensive Financial Statement Analysis

9–63 Using library or other information sources, obtain financial statements or summaries of financial information for one set of the following companies:

1. IBM	Storagetek	Digital
2. UAL (United Airlines)	American Airlines (AMR)	Delta Air Lines
3. General Motors	Ford Motor Company	Chrysler

REQUIRED (for each company)

a. Examine the liability section of the balance sheet. Calculate the relevant subtotals for current liabilities, noncurrent liabilities, and shareholders' equity.

b. Identify any unusual accounts and any unusual patterns.

c. Read the relevant notes and discuss them with a colleague or with your instructor.

d. Calculate the debt and equity composition ratios.

e. Assess the relative changes in debt and equity and the relative default and any other risks that may emerge in these statements.

f. Calculate the liquidity ratios that have been introduced thus far in this text, and comment on any significant differences.

g. Calculate any other ratios or financial comparisons that would help you analyze the differences in your companies.

h. Identify any factors that may inhibit the comparability of these companies. Identify any other information that you may need to make a more useful comparison between your selected companies.

WHAT WOULD YOU DO?

9–64 Tall Tree Timber, Inc., issued $10 million in long-term bonds that contained the following restrictive covenants:

- Current ratio must exceed 2.0.
- Return on assets must exceed 2%.
- Net income ratio must exceed 2%.
- Debt composition ratio must be less than 60%.

Tall Tree Timber's most recent financial results ($ in millions) follow:

Current assets	$ 40	Current liabilities	$ 10
Property, plant, and equipment	55	Long-term debt	9
Other assets	10	Stockholders' equity	86
Total assets	$105	Total liabilities	
		and stockholders' equity	$105
Net revenues	$600	Income tax rate	20%
Net income	$ 30	Interest expense	$ 5

REQUIRED

a. Compute the appropriate ratios described in the loan covenants and evaluate whether they have been met. Use ending total assets for average total assets.

b. Now, suppose the auditors find that revenues have been overstated by $38 million, thereby reducing revenues and reducing net income by $28 million net of tax. This new calculation will reduce stockholders' equity and current assets by $28 million. Recalculate the appropriate ratios and test whether the loan covenants have been met.

c. Alternatively, suppose Tall Tree changes its depletion (of natural trees) allowance calculations. This new calculation will reduce stockholders' equity (net income) and property, plant, and equipment by $50 million. Again, recalculate the appropriate ratios and test whether the loan covenants have been met.

d. Alternatively, suppose Tall Tree Timber decides to switch from FIFO to LIFO and that such a switch will reduce current assets and stockholders' equity (net income) by $30 million. Again, recalculate the appropriate ratios and test whether the loan covenants have been met.

e. Which of the above scenarios would cause the greatest concern to bond-holders? Would any of these likely result in default proceedings to redeem or "call" the bonds? Why?

WHAT WOULD YOU DO?

9–65 Tall Tree Timber issued $10 million in bonds with a nominal interest rate of 8%, at a time when the market rate for similar bonds was 4%. The bonds have a four-year maturity and pay interest semiannually.

a. Calculate the premium or discount at the issue date. Indicate how the bonds would be shown on Tall Tree Timber's balance sheet at the date of issue.

b. Calculate the interest expense and the cash outflows that would occur at the end of each semiannual period.

Additional Data: Tall Tree Timber now anticipates refinancing the bonds at the end of the second year; in other words, after four semiannual periods have expired. To do so, it would issue $10 million of new 5% bonds at par. The firm has sufficient operating resources to pay for any other redemption costs, including the call premium of 2% over par.

c. Calculate all of the cash flows associated with refinancing or refunding of the old bonds. Also, calculate the gain or loss to be recognized.

d. Evaluate whether the proposed refunding is advantageous for the firm's shareholders? Why?

e. Discuss the advantages and disadvantages of a GAAP requirement that all long-term debt be shown at its current market value, rather than at its market value only at the issue date.

Interpreting Contingency Disclosures

9-66 The following excerpts from the Commitments and Contingencies Notes were reported by three different companies:

PolyGram N.V.

PolyGram has extensive international operations, and is subject to a number of legal proceedings incidental to these operations. PolyGram does not expect that the outcome of currently pending proceedings against PolyGram will, either individually, or in the aggregate, have a material adverse effect upon the financial condition of PolyGram.

Oncogene Science, Inc.

The Company has received several letters from other companies and universities advising the Company that various products being marketed and research being conducted by the Company may be infringing on existing patents of such entities. These matters are presently under review by management and outside counsel for the Company. Where valid patents of other parties are found by the Company to be in place, management will consider entering into licensing arrangements with the universities and/or other companies or discontinuing the sale or use of any infringing products. Management believes that the ultimate outcome of these matters will not have a material adverse effect on the financial position of the Company.

Sigma Designs, Inc.

The Company pays royalties for the right to sell certain products under various license agreements. During fiscal 1995, 1994, and 1993, the Company incurred royalty expense of $508,040, $181,405, and $275,000, respectively.

At January 31, 1995, the Company had letters of credit outstanding in the amount of $941,000, maturing at various dates up to June, 1996.

The Company sponsors a 401(k) savings plan in which most employees are eligible to participate. The Company is not obligated to make contributions to the Plan and no contributions have been made by the Company.

REQUIRED

a. Compare and contrast these three notes.
b. Do you believe that companies should be more specific, or more general, in such notes? Why?
c. Which of these companies do you think faces the greatest risk, based only on the information presented herein? Why?

Long-Term Debt: Interpreting Financial Statements

9–67   Pfizer is a research-based global health care company. Its 1994 annual report contains a note on Long-Term Debt as follows: Long term debt, exclusive of current maturities . . . , is summarized as follows (dollars in millions).

	1994	1993	1992
7⅛% notes due 1996	$250.0	$250.0	$250.0
6½% notes due 1997	250.0	250.0	250.0
10¼% industrial development bonds due 2001	22.0	22.0	22.0
7% solid waste disposal facilities revenue bonds due 2025	18.0	—	—
Other borrowings and mortgages	64.2	48.5	49.3
	$604.2	$570.5	$571.3

REQUIRED

a. Comment on why Pfizer might have long-term debt with such different interest rates and different maturities.
b. Based on current interest rates, which of these do you think would sell above or below par values at today's rates? Why?
c. Discuss how managers might use an aggressive debt retirement strategy to increase or decrease net income.

Effects of Changing Debt Strategies

9–68 ALZA Corporation develops, manufactures, and markets therapeutic products that incorporate drugs into advanced dosage forms designed to provide controlled, predetermined rates of drug release for extended time periods. ALZA may be best known for its Nicoderm nicotine transdermal system. It reported the following liabilities in its 1994 and 1993 balance sheet:

Liabilities	1994	1993
	(dollars in thousands)	
Short-term debt	$ —	$249,520
Accounts payable	20,006	11,678
Accrued liabilities	18,773	17,415
Deferred revenue	16,340	6,698
Current portion of long-term debt	869	867
Total current liabilities	$ 55,988	$286,178
5¼% zero coupon convertible subordinated debentures	$344,593	$ —
Other long-term liabilities	41,192	28,969
Total long-term liabilities	$385,785	$ 28,969

REQUIRED

a. Identify and describe any unfamiliar terms in ALZA's balance sheet (excerpts).

b. What strategic decision did ALZA implement in 1994? How do you know this?

c. Describe how this decision will affect ALZA's current ratio. How are its capital composition ratios affected?

d. Should ALZA's investors or creditors be unduly concerned about the decision of part b? Why?

e. Suppose you now examine ALZA's financial highlights to determine that its net income for 1994 and 1993, respectively, was $58,120,000 and $45,612,000. You also examine the "fine print" at the bottom of the financial highlights and find that ALZA's 1993 net income includes ". . . a $3.8 million ($.05 per share) extraordinary charge relating to the redemption of ALZA's 5¼% zero-coupon convertible subordinated debentures." Does this new information change any of your conclusions regarding ALZA's decision (see part b)? Why?

f. How would your conclusions differ if ALZA's net income had only been $5 million each year?

Interpreting Deferred Taxes

9–69 Sigma Designs' statement of operations is summarized below ($ in thousands):

	1995	1994	1993
Net sales	$43,700	$ 34,989	$27,058
Costs and expenses:			
Cost of sales	36,980	27,538	23,045
Restructuring charges	(517)	13,654	0
Sales and marketing	9,022	9,448	7,476

Research and development	4,349	11,988	5,043
General and administrative	3,521	2,718	1,951
Total cost and expenses	53,355	65,346	37,515
Income (loss) from operations	(9,655)	(30,357)	(10,457)
Interest income-net	336	699	1,207
Other net	546	(39)	(67)
Income (loss) before income taxes	(8,773)	(29,697)	(9,317)
Provision (credit) for income taxes	—	(151)	(2,151)
Net income (loss)	$ (8,773)	$(29,546)	$ (7,166)

REQUIRED

a. Explain the item "Provision (credit) for income taxes." How can income taxes be positive? That is, how can income taxes be added to income?

b. How does this new interpretation about deferred taxes (see part a) affect your evaluation of Sigma Design's profitability? Calculate relevant income statement ratios using both "bottom line" net income and any other income figures that you deem relevant. Be sure to calculate the net income ratio on an after-tax basis. Calculate any other appropriate ratios. Evaluate Sigma Design's performance for 1995. Assume interest expense is $200 ($ in thousands).

Interpreting Deferred Taxes

9–70 Waco Rubber, Inc., disclosed the following items in its 1997 financial statements:

	1997	1996
Current Assets		
Deferred income tax benefit	$1,894,550	$4,139,205
Current Liabilities		
Deferred income taxes payable	—	236,543

REQUIRED

a. Discuss the nature of each of these deferred tax items. How should an analyst use these data?

b. Upon further examination of Waco's notes to its financial statements, you find the following additional disclosures:

At December 31, 1997, the Company had NOL [non-operating loss] carryforwards for Federal income tax and financial reporting purposes of approximately $15,000,000 and $34,000,000, respectively, available to offset future taxable income. These carryforwards will expire at various dates between 2002 and 2000. The usage of a portion of both the Federal income tax carryforward and the financial reporting loss is restricted based upon the purchase price of two subsidiaries of the Company.

Based on this new information, reconsider the two items shown in Waco's balance sheet. Why might they be so different? How much future benefit might really occur?

c. Upon further examination of Waco notes to its financial statements, you find no further disclosures or explanations of the above items shown on its balance sheet. In fact, the company only disclosed details relating to $338,000 of deferred tax provisions in 1997 and to $(839,000) of deferred tax provisions (benefits) in 1996. What other information would you find helpful in order to analyze and interpret Waco's financial statements?

USING FINANCIAL ACCOUNTING ON THE INTERNET

9–71 Retrieve the most recent 10-K filings for Kmart, Wal-Mart, Gillette, and Mem Co. from the EDGAR archives (**www.sec.gov/edgarhp.htm**). Examine the long-term debt section of the Notes to the Financial Statements and answer the following questions:

REQUIRED

a. Calculate the ratio of long-term debt to total assets for each company for the last two years. Comment on any changes that you observe.
b. Analyze the long-term debt for each company using the following format:

Term to Maturity	Interest Rates (Range)
Due within 1 year	
Due in 2 years	
Due in 3 years	
Due in 4 years	
Due in 5 years and beyond	

Comparing Kmart to Wal-Mart and Gillette to Mem, which company do you believe obtained better terms for its debt?

9–72 Locate the most recent set of financial statements for the companies listed below. You may use either the 10-K available at EDGAR (**www.sec.gov/edgarhp.htm**) or the annual report available at the company page on the WWW. The annual report is usually located in the Investor Information section.

Corporation	Home Page Location
Owens Corning	**www.owens-corning.com**
Rohm & Haas	**www.rohmhaas.com**
Utilicorp	**www.utilicorp.com/ucu/ucu1.htm**
Eli Lilly	**www.lilly.com**

The Notes to the Financial Statements contain a section on contingencies.

REQUIRED

a. Describe at least one contingency faced by each company.
b. Has each corporation accrued for its loss contingency, or is it only mentioned in the Notes to the Financial Statements? If it is only mentioned in the notes, is a dollar amount disclosed?
c. If a dollar amount for contingent liabilities is available, calculate the percentage of shareholders' equity it represents for each company. In your opinion, is this a significant amount?

9–73 Many corporations retired part of their long-term debt prematurely in 1994. Two such corporations are Kodak and Scotts Co. For each company, locate the

10-K filing for fiscal 1994 from the EDGAR archives (**www.sec.gov./ edgarhp.htm**). For each company determine:

a. Cash outflow for the debt retired
b. Face value of the debt retired and its associated stated interest rate
c. Impact of the retirement on the income statement
d. Long-term debt-to-total assets ratio for 1993 and 1994 (What impact did the retirement have on this ratio?)
e. Net income as a percentage of sales for 1993 and 1994 (What impact did the retirement have on this ratio?)

CHAPTER 10

STUDYING THIS CHAPTER
WILL ENABLE YOU TO

1. Understand why large business firms prefer to organize as corporations.
2. Comprehend the types of transactions and events that affect
the components of shareholder's equity.
3. Interpret shareholders' equity ratios that are helpful in
analyzing financial statements.

SHAREHOLDERS' EQUITY

INTRODUCTION

Corporations are the dominant form of business organization in advanced industrial nations such as the United States. Although they only represent about 25% of business firms, they generate about 80% of business revenues. A corporation is an entity that is owned by its shareholders and raises **equity capital** by selling shares of stock to investors. Equity capital is an ownership interest in the corporation: Each share of stock represents a fractional interest in the issuing firm. Equity capital is *not* a liability to be repaid at a future date.

Shares of stock of most major corporations are traded (bought and sold) on major security exchanges, such as the New York and American Stock Exchanges. For business managers, a primary advantage of the corporate form of organization is the ability to raise large amounts of cash by selling shares of stock to many different individuals and institutions (e.g., mutual funds, insurance companies, and pension plans), rather than relying on the investments of a few owners and lenders.

Stockholders expect to earn returns on their investments, in the form of **dividends** and **capital gains.** Dividends are distributions of assets, usually cash, that the corporation elects to make periodically to its stockholders. Capital gains (or losses) result from increases (or decreases) in the market price of stocks over the period during which an investor holds them. Neither the payment of dividends nor the appreciation in stock prices is guaranteed to the equity investor. Instead, the ability of a corporation to generate cash through profitable operations determines its ability to pay dividends and also influences the market price of its stock.

A corporation comes into existence when its **charter** is approved by the state in which it chooses to locate and incorporate. State laws vary, so that many features of corporations depend on the state in which a firm incorporates. Among other things, the charter will indicate the corporation's business purpose, and will authorize the firm to issue one or more types of ownership shares. The most basic type of ownership share is **common stock.** Common shareholders are the true **residual owners** of a corporation; after all other claims against a firm's assets have been satisfied, the common shareholders own what remains. This view of shareholders' equity is apparent when we write the basic balance sheet equation in the following way:

SHAREHOLDERS' EQUITY = ASSETS − LIABILITIES

This expression shows that the value of shareholders' equity reported on a firm's balance sheet is determined by the valuation of its assets and liabilities. Recall that financial accounting reports use historical costs rather than current market prices in valuing the firm's assets and liabilities. For this reason the reported value of shareholders' equity does not attempt to measure the market value of the firm's outstanding shares of stock.

Shareholders' equity comes from two sources: **invested (paid-in) capital** and **retained earnings.** Invested capital is the amount received by the corporation upon the sale of its stock to investors. Note that invested capital usually includes two components: **par value** and **additional paid-in capital.** For our purposes, we will concentrate on the sum of these parts, not on the individual components. Retained earnings is the amount of prior earnings that the firm has reinvested in the business, that is, the portion that has not been paid to shareholders as dividends. Exhibit 10–1 shows the shareholder's equity section from a recent balance sheet reported by E. I. Du Pont de Nemours and Company (Du Pont). Note that Du Pont's total shareholders' equity at that date (in millions of dollars) was $12,822. Of that amount, $5,416 was received from the sale of stock to investors, and $7,406 represents past earnings that have been reinvested in the firm's operations. For most profitable firms, retained earnings represents the major part of shareholders' equity.

EXHIBIT 10–1
SHAREHOLDERS' EQUITY
COMPONENTS

	Du Pont Company 1994 Annual Report Shareholders' Equity (partial) (Dollars in Millions)	
	December 31, 1994	December 31, 1993
Shareholders' equity:		
Preferred stock	$ 237	$ 237
Common stock: $0.60 par value; 900,000,000 shares authorized; 681,004,944 shares and 677,577,437 shares issued and outstanding	408	407
Additional paid-in capital	4,771	4,660
Reinvested earnings	7,406	5,926
Total shareholders' equity	$12,822	$11,230

The description of DuPont's common stock in Exhibit 10–1 distinguishes between the number of common shares that are **authorized, issued,** and **outstanding.** Authorized shares are those that the firm is permitted to issue according to its corporate charter; the outstanding shares are those that are presently held by investors. Some of the issued shares may have been repurchased and held as treasury stock, as is explained later in the chapter. Treasury stock *is not* considered to be outstanding.

Exhibit 10–1 also shows that Du Pont's common stock has been assigned a par value of $0.60 per share, and the total par value of the outstanding shares is reported separately on the balance sheet. Although for legal purposes the shares of most firms have a designated par or stated value, the par or stated value is usually a minor amount compared to the actual market price of the stock. For example, although Du Pont's common stock has a par value of just $0.60 per share, the stock had a market price per share of about $60 at the end of 1994.

Three basic transactions account for most of the changes that occur in shareholders' equity: (1) sale of stock to investors, (2) recognition of periodic net income or loss, and (3) declaration of cash dividends to shareholders. Each of these transactions is examined in this section. Other, less frequent types of transactions are discussed in a subsequent section.

**BASIC
TRANSACTIONS
AFFECTING
SHAREHOLDERS'
EQUITY**

Sale of Stock to Investors

Suppose that Du Pont's management decides to issue an additional 10 million shares of stock to investors, and the market price is $70 per share of stock. In this case, Du Pont would receive a total of $700 million ($70 × 10 million shares) from investors. In this example, note that we are ignoring any transactions costs, such as fees and commissions incurred by the issuing firm. The transaction would increase cash and invested capital by $700 million. The invested capital would consist of $6 million in par value (10 million shares × 0.60 par value per share), and $694 million in capital invested in excess of par value ($700 million total invested minus $6 million recorded as par value).

ASSETS	=	LIABILITIES	+	SHAREHOLDERS' EQUITY	
Cash				Par value	Additional paid-in capital
+$700 million				+$6 million	+$694 million

Managers would immediately put these funds to work to earn returns for the shareholders, e.g., by investing in additional plant and equipment. That is, the transaction to issue shares of stock is immediately followed by many other transactions where the money is used for some corporate purpose.

In some instances noncash items may be received when stock is issued to investors. Examples include noncash assets, such as property or intangible assets, and services, such as from a company's attorneys.

Recognition of Periodic Net Income or Loss

Business firms must periodically determine the amount of net income (or loss) from their activities. Net income (loss) represents an increase (decrease) in a firm's shareholder equity, or net assets, due to its revenues, expenses, gains, and losses during the period. For example, Du Pont earned net income of $2,727 million during 1994, and paid $1,247 million as dividends. As a result, its retained earnings increased by $1,480 million ($2,727 million − $1,247 million) over the year. Note the amounts of Du Pont's retained earnings shown in Exhibit 10–1 at the beginning and the end of 1994. These amounts are related in the following way, where the retained earnings balances are all shown in Exhibit 10–1 (millions of dollars):

Retained earnings, December 31, 1993	$ 5,926
Add: Net income during 1994	+ 2,727
Less: Dividends declared during 1994	− 1,247
Retained earnings, December 31, 1994	$ 7,406

Declaration and Payment of Cash Dividends

Du Pont paid dividends of $1,247 million to its shareholders in 1994. On the **date of declaration,** the dividend became a liability, because Du Pont obligated itself to make the dividend payment. On that date, retained earnings were decreased and liabilities were increased by $1,247 million:

ASSETS	=	LIABILITIES	+	SHAREHOLDERS' EQUITY
		Dividends payable		Retained earnings
		+$1,247 million		−$1,247 million

Management also specifies a **date of record,** and the dividend is paid to investors who own the shares on that specific date. Subsequently, the stock is considered *ex dividend,* i.e., subsequent purchasers are not entitled to receive the previously declared dividend. On the **date of payment,** Du Pont's cash and dividends payable (liability) are reduced by $1,247 million:

ASSETS	=	LIABILITIES	+	SHAREHOLDERS' EQUITY
Cash		Dividends payable		
−$1,247 million		−$1,247 million		

Observe that the change in retained earnings over a period is the difference between a firm's net income and dividends during the period. The ending balance in retained earnings reflects the total net income of the firm in all past periods, less the total amount of dividends to shareholders.

ADDITIONAL TRANSACTIONS AFFECTING SHAREHOLDERS' EQUITY

In addition to the three basic transactions discussed in the last section, a variety of other, less frequent occurrences may affect the reported amount and composition of shareholders' equity. This section examines several of these additional types of transactions and events.

Stock Dividends

On occasion, firms distribute additional shares of stock to shareholders, in proportion to the number of shares presently owned. For example, if a firm declares a 1% **stock**

dividend, this means that existing shareholders will receive additional shares equal to 1% of their present holdings. In this case a shareholder with 100 shares would receive an additional share (1% × 100 shares) as a stock dividend.

Stock dividends reduce retained earnings in an amount equal to the value of the stock that is distributed. For example, assume Flotsam Company has 10 million common shares issued and outstanding, and declares a 2% stock dividend when the market price of its stock is $45 per share. The firm will distribute an additional 200,000 shares (2% × 10 million shares = 200,000 shares), and the total value of the dividend is $9 million ($45 × 200,000 shares = $9 million). Retained earnings will decrease, and paid-in capital will increase, by $9 million. The number of shares outstanding will also increase by 2%.

ASSETS	= LIABILITIES +	SHAREHOLDERS' EQUITY	
		Invested capital	Retained earnings
		+$9 million*	−$9 million

*This amount would be apportioned between par value and additional paid-in capital, based on the company's par value per share.

Notice that this transaction does not affect the firm's assets and liabilities, and so does not affect total shareholders' equity. The composition of shareholders' equity is affected, however. The transaction decreased retained earnings and created an offsetting increase in paid-in capital.

As a stockholder of 100 shares of Flotsam Company, would you be better off as a result of the stock dividend? Although it is true that you have received two additional shares of stock, your proportionate interest in Flotsam remains unchanged. Moreover, because the company's assets and liabilities are unchanged, the stock dividend has no direct effect on Flotsam's operating ability. In fact, the market price of each share of stock could decline just enough to leave the total value of your investment unchanged (i.e., 100 shares × old price = 102 shares × new price).

Surprisingly, stock dividends do appear to benefit existing shareholders. The market price per share of existing shares usually does not decline sufficiently to offset the effect of issuing additional shares. Some analysts suggest that this otherwise puzzling result may be due to the use of stock dividends as a "signal to the market" by managers that the firm expects higher profits and cash flows in the future. Managers may be reluctant to make public forecasts about future earnings increases, and may instead prefer to communicate their favorable expectations by less direct actions such as stock dividends.

Stock Splits

Stock splits are distinct from stock dividends, and involve an exchange of multiple shares of stock for existing outstanding shares. For example, a two-for-one stock split exchanges two "new" shares for each "old" share held by existing shareholders. Unlike stock dividends, stock splits do not entail a reduction in retained earnings nor an increase in paid-in capital. In fact, stock splits do not change any of the elements in the financial statements. Only the description of the firm's stock is amended to reflect the new number of shares authorized, issued, and outstanding.

Managers may split a firm's stock when they believe that the price per share has risen beyond the range that is attractive to smaller investors. Therefore, splitting the shares is expected to reduce the share price and increase demand. Similar to stock dividends, stock splits also seem to be interpreted by investors as favorable signals by management about future operating performance. Stock splits usually result in an increase in the total market value of the firm's outstanding shares, because the price per share typically does not decline sufficiently to offset the increase in the number of shares. For example, a 2-for-1 stock split usually does not cut the price per share in half.

Reality Check 10–1 shows how a stock split was reported by one major corporation.

REALITY CHECK 10–1

GENERAL DYNAMICS CORPORATION STOCK SPLIT

A footnote to the 1993 financial statements of General Dynamics Corporation, a major producer of nuclear submarines, armored vehicles and other weapons systems for the U.S. Government, includes the following information:

> Stock split: On 4 March 1994, the Company's Board of Directors authorized a two-for-one stock split effected in the form of a 100% stock dividend to be distributed on 11 April 1994 to shareholders of record on 21 March 1994. Shareholders' equity has been restated to give retroactive recognition to the stock split for all periods presented by reclassifying from retained earnings to common stock the par value of the additional shares arising from the split. In addition, all references in the financial statements to number of shares, per share amounts, stock option data, and market prices of the Company's common stock have been restated.

REQUIRED

a. Explain why the accounting treatment described by General Dynamics is not typical of either a stock split or a stock dividend, as these events are described in this chapter.

b. Why does General Dynamics give retroactive recognition to the stock split in all related financial statement references?

c. Why do you suppose General Dynamics' management decided to split the company's stock?

d. As an existing General Dynamics shareholder, would you be pleased by management's decision to split your stock? Explain.

Treasury Stock

Firms sometimes repurchase their own outstanding shares and hold them for future use. Repurchased shares are termed **treasury stock,** and are no longer outstanding, although they continue to be labeled as "issued." A variety of motives lead managers to acquire treasury stock. For example, managers may consider the stock to be undervalued in the stock market, and to be a "good buy" that can be resold later at a higher price. Also, treasury stock purchases may in some cases be preferable to dividend payments as a way of reducing a firm's shareholders' equity. Note that this use of treasury stock depends on income tax features that are beyond the scope of this text. In addition, treasury stock purchases may enable managers to "buy out" certain groups of shareholders in order to realign votes on future issues of corporate policy. Treasury stock may also be distributed to employees under an employee stock option plan.

The acquisition of treasury stock reduces cash and shareholders' equity. In this sense, treasury stock acquisitions are the opposite of a shareholder investment. The cost of treasury shares is usually subtracted from total shareholders' equity. For this reason, the purchase price of treasury stock is a **contra-equity account.**

To illustrate the reporting of treasury stock, Exhibit 10–2 shows the shareholders' equity portion of Tyler Corporation's balance sheet at the end of 1994. Note that Tyler refers to its additional paid-in capital as *capital surplus.* Other companies may use other terminology to describe this item. As of that date, Tyler has paid $6,722,000 to acquire its treasury stock. This amount is subtracted when computing Tyler's total shareholders' equity. We can infer that the treasury stock purchase had the following effect on Tyler's balance sheet.

ASSETS	=	LIABILITIES	+	SHAREHOLDERS' EQUITY
Cash				Treasury stock
−$6,722,000				−$6,722,000*

*Although treasury stock has been increased by $6,722,000, this represents a decrease in shareholders' equity because treasury stock is a contra-equity account. Also, note that the common stock account has not changed, since the repurchased stock has not been retired. It is being held for future use.

EXHIBIT 10–2
TREASURY STOCK REPORTING

Tyler Corporation
1994 Annual Report
Treasury Stock Reporting
(Dollars in Thousands)

	December 31, 1994	December 31, 1993
Shareholders' equity:		
Common stock: $.01 par value, 50,000 shares authorized, 21,309,277 shares issued	$ 213	$ 213
Capital surplus	48,587	49,109
Retained earnings	68,220	72,921
	117,020	122,243
Less 1,450,178 treasury shares in 1994 and 1,011,046 treasury shares in 1993, at cost	6,722	4,279
Total shareholders' equity	$110,298	$117,964

Suppose Tyler sold the treasury stock at a greater amount, say, $10 million, at a future date. Generally accepted accounting principles do not allow the recognition of gains or losses due to transactions in a firm's own stock. Consequently, Tyler's cash would increase by $10 million, the treasury stock would be eliminated, and paid-in capital would increase by the difference of $3,278,000 ($10,000,000 − 6,722,000 = $3,278,000).

ASSETS	=	LIABILITIES	+	SHAREHOLDERS' EQUITY	
Cash				Treasury stock	Invested capital
+$10,000,000				+$6,722,000*	+$3,278,000

*Although treasury stock has been decreased, this represents an increase in shareholders' equity because treasury stock is a contra-equity account.

Employee Stock Options

Stock options are rights to purchase a firm's stock at a specific price over some designated future period. Although stock options are sometimes sold directly to investors, they are usually granted as part of the compensation paid to key executives and other employees. For example, Exhibit 10–3 shows how stock options were reported in Walgreen Co.'s 1990 annual report. Note that Walgreen's options allow the recipients to purchase the firm's stock over a 10-year period, at a price equal to the stock's market price at the date of the grant. At the balance sheet date, outstanding options were exercisable at prices ranging from $10.81 to $50.13 per share. At that date, the firm's stock had a market price of $52 per share.

EXHIBIT 10–3
REPORTING OF STOCK OPTIONS

Walgreen Co.
1990 Annual Report
Footnote Disclosures of Stock Options (partial)

Stock Option Plan
The Executive Incentive Stock Option Plan provides for the granting to key employees of options to purchase Company common stock over a 10-year period, at a price not less than the fair market value on the date of grant. Options may be issued under the Plan until October 13, 1992, for an aggregate of 2,400,000 shares of common stock of the Company. The number of shares available for future grant was 1,478,004 at August 31, 1990. Optionees may exercise their options at any time, provided that options granted prior to July 13, 1988, be exercised in sequential order. All outstanding options are considered exercisable.

Stock options, as a means of compensation, offer several distinct benefits to firms and employees. Because the value of stock options depends on the future market price of the firm's stock, option holders are highly motivated to improve the performance of the firm. Actions that benefit the firm's stockholders also directly benefit the option holders. As a result, managers and other employees who hold stock options have the same objective as company shareholders: to make the firm's equity securities more valuable. In addition, although option holders gain if the price of the optioned stock subsequently rises, they avoid the "downside risk" of loss if the stock price declines. If the stock price is below the option price, the option simply will not be exercised.

A more arguable advantage of stock options from the firm's point of view is the way that options are currently handled in financial statements. Because most employee options are granted at market value, the firm does not recognize any compensation expense associated with the options.

To illustrate how stock options for employees are treated, assume Jetsom Inc. issued options to its employees to purchase one million shares of its common stock in 1994 at an option price of $10 per share, equal to the market price at the date of the grant. Subsequently in 1997, assume all of the options were exercised when Jetsom's market price per share had risen to $90.

For financial statement purposes, Jetsom would record no compensation expense in 1994, when the options were granted. In 1997, when the options are exercised, Jetsom would record the cash proceeds of $10 million ($10 × 1 million shares = $10 million) as an issuance of common stock for cash.

ASSETS	=	LIABILITIES	+	SHAREHOLDERS' EQUITY
Cash				Invested capital
+$10 million				+$10 million

This method of accounting for stock options is presently being debated by the accounting profession. Opponents of current practice argue that in situations like the Jetsom case, the granting of stock options in 1994 should entail the recognition of compensation expense. The grantees were given valuable rights that might otherwise have been sold to other investors. Moreover, in 1997 Jetsom's optioned shares had a market value of $90 million. Yet, these options had been issued to the option holders for only $10 million in cash. In retrospect, granting the options in 1994 seems to have cost Jetsom $80 million ($90 million market value, less $10 million proceeds). Consequently, some accountants believe that reported compensation expense is understated and reported net income is overstated.

At present there is little agreement among accounting regulators and preparers of financial statements concerning how to measure the compensation expense implicit in the granting of employee stock options. Until the conceptual and practical issues are resolved, the FASB has recently required that substantial additional information be included in the notes to the financial statements concerning the features of a firm's stock option plans. See Reality Check 10–2 for a sample of financial statement disclosures regarding stock options.

Preferred Stock

In addition to common stock, firms often issue **preferred stock,** which has a priority claim over common stock with respect to dividends. In addition, if the firm should liquidate its assets and cease to exist, preferred shareholders' claims would be satisfied before any assets were distributed to the common stockholders.

CROWN CORK AND SEAL COMPANY EXERCISE OF STOCK OPTIONS

Crown Cork and Seal Company, an international producer of metal and plastic packaging, reports the following information in its 1993 financial statements:

Stock issued under stock option and employee savings plans: 1,415,711 shares

Resulting changes in shareholders' equity:

Paid-in capital increase	$23,600,000
Treasury stock decrease	7,000,000
Total increase in shareholders' equity	$30,600,000

The market price of Crown's common stock averaged about $40 per share during 1993.

REQUIRED

a. What was the average amount of proceeds per share that Crown received for the stock issued in 1993 under its stock option and employee savings plans?
b. What was the aggregate market value of the shares issued by Crown during 1993 under these plans?
c. How would you interpret the difference between the aggregate market value and the aggregate proceeds received by Crown for the stock issued in 1993? Is your interpretation consistent with the accounting treatment? Explain.

The description of preferred stock in corporate financial reports discloses the special features of the stock issue. To illustrate, Exhibit 10–4 shows the description of Sequa Corporation's preferred stock contained in its 1990 annual report. Sequa's preferred shares have an annual dividend of $5 per share. Analysts would also note that Sequa's preferred shares are cumulative and convertible. **Cumulative** indicates that if the firm does not declare a dividend in any year, the amount accumulates and must be paid before any dividends are paid to common stockholders. For example, if Sequa did not pay dividends for three years, then a cumulative dividend of $15 per share ($5 × 3 years = $15) must be paid to preferred shareholders before dividends are paid to common shareholders.

Convertible preferred shares may be exchanged for common shares at the preferred shareholders' option. To illustrate, each share of Sequa's preferred stock is convertible into 1.322 shares of common stock. Presently, 797,000 shares of preferred stock have been issued. If the entire issue were to be converted to common stock, then Sequa would issue 1,053,634 common shares (797,000 preferred shares × 1.322 exchange ratio = 1,053,634 common shares) and would retire the preferred stock. In this case the preferred stock component of shareholders' equity would be eliminated, and transferred to common stock.

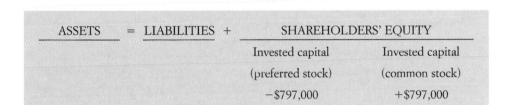

Sequa Corporation
1990 Annual Report
Footnote Disclosures of Preferred Stock (partial)

EXHIBIT 10–4
REPORTING OF
PREFERRED STOCK

Note 13. Capital Stock
The Company's capital stock consists of Class A and Class B common stock, and $5.00 cumulative convertible preferred stock.

Each share of $5.00 cumulative convertible preferred stock is convertible into 1.322 shares of Class A common stock. At December 31, 1990, 4,543,636 shares of Sequa Class A common stock were reserved for conversion of preferred and Class B common stock and stock options. At December 31, 1990, 5,724 Class B common shares were reserved for stock options. The preferred stock is redeemable, at the option of the Company, at $100 per share.

ASSETS	= LIABILITIES +	SHAREHOLDERS' EQUITY	
		Invested capital (preferred stock)	Invested capital (common stock)
		−$797,000	+$797,000

Note that the conversion of preferred stock does not change total shareholders' equity. Assets and liabilities are also unaffected. The number of common shares outstanding has increased, however, and the preferred stock's dividend requirement has been eliminated.

Convertible Debt

Firms that borrow by issuing bonds frequently include a conversion privilege in the bond contract. **Convertible bonds** allow the bondholder to exchange the bonds for a specified number of shares of stock. For example, in 1990 the Alcoa Company's long-term debt included $150 million principal in convertible bonds payable, exchangeable for common stock at $62 per share at any time before the year 2002. If all of the bondholders elected to convert to common stock, Alcoa would then issue 2,419,355 shares of common stock ($150 million bond principal ÷ $62 conversion price = 2,419,355 shares of common stock). Alcoa's bonds payable would be reduced, and paid-in capital would be increased by $150 million:

ASSETS	=	LIABILITIES	+	SHAREHOLDERS' EQUITY
		Bonds payable		Invested capital
		−$150 million		+$150 million

Note that the conversion of debt to common stock reduces the firm's liabilities and increases shareholders' equity. The number of common shares outstanding is increased, and the periodic interest expense is eliminated.

Convertible bonds such as those issued by Alcoa are **hybrid securities.** A hybrid security is neither clearly debt, nor clearly equity. Instead, it combines certain features of both types of securities. In the case of convertible bonds, the bondholder is, in one sense, a lender, and owns the firm's promise to make future interest and principal payments. In another sense, the holder of a convertible bond holds an option to acquire a specified number of common shares at a fixed price at any time over the life of the bond issue. In fact, investors in convertible bonds are willing to pay for this combination of debt and equity features. Convertible bonds generally are issued at higher prices (i.e., at lower interest rates) than is nonconvertible debt.

The proper way to account for hybrid securities is a matter of debate. Present accounting standards reflect the view that convertible debt is to be reported as debt until it is actually converted, and as equity thereafter. No recognition is given in the financial statements to the likelihood that conversion will actually occur, or to the relative values to investors of the debt and equity features of the hybrid security.

Opponents of present practice argue that it is misleading to ignore the hybrid nature of convertible securities. In the case of debt, they argue that the issue price should be apportioned between the amount the investor is paying for the debt features, and the additional amount being paid for the conversion privilege. Ignoring these separate elements, they contend, causes the financial statements to overvalue the firm's reported liabilities, undervalue its shareholders' equity, and understate periodic interest expense. To address these and related issues, the FASB has initiated a comprehensive financial instruments project. The project aims to identify the component claims that are bundled in hybrid financial assets and liabilities, and to develop appropriate methods of valuation for these components.

EARNINGS PER SHARE

Perhaps the most widely cited number in corporate financial reports is **earnings per share (EPS).** EPS focuses on the common stock. **EPS** indicates the portion of total company income that is applicable to a single share of common stock, and is computed in this manner:

$$\text{EPS} = \frac{\text{Net income available for common shareholders}}{\text{Average number of common shares outstanding}}$$

For example, assume that Starbright Company reported net income of $99 million in 1996, and had 45 million shares of common stock outstanding throughout the entire year. Starbright's 1996 EPS is $2.20, calculated as follows:

$$\text{EPS} = \frac{\$99 \text{ million}}{45 \text{ million shares}}$$

$$= \$2.20$$

EPS Calculations with Changes in Shares Outstanding

It is unusual for a large firm's outstanding shares to remain constant throughout the year. Additional stock issuances, transactions in treasury stock, exercises of stock options, conversions of debt and preferred stock, and other events cause the number of shares to vary over the year. In these cases the denominator in the EPS calculation is the **weighted average** of the common shares outstanding during the year. To illustrate, assume that Starbright reported net income of $118 million during 1997, and that the firm's common shares changed as shown in Exhibit 10–5.

EXHIBIT 10–5
COMMON SHARES
OUTSTANDING

Starbright Company
Common Shares Outstanding During 1997

Outstanding shares, January 1, 1997	45 million
Add: Additional shares issued May 1, 1997	+ 15 million
Balance, May 1, 1997	60 million
Less: Treasury shares purchased July 1, 1997	− 10 million
Balance, July 1, 1997	50 million
Add: Additional shares issued October 1, 1997	+ 16 million
Outstanding shares, December 31, 1997	66 million

To calculate Starbright's EPS for 1997, we need first to determine the firm's weighted average shares outstanding during the year. The calculation appears in Exhibit 10–6, and shows that each level of outstanding shares is weighted by the fraction of a year that it stayed constant. Exhibit 10–6 shows that Starbright's average shares outstanding in 1997 was 54 million. Accordingly, the firm's EPS in 1997 is:

$$\text{EPS} = \frac{\text{Net income \$118 million}}{\text{Weighted average shares, \$54 million}}$$

$$= \quad \$2.19 \text{ per share}$$

EXHIBIT 10–6
WEIGHTED AVERAGE
COMMON SHARES

Starbright Company
Weighted Average Common Shares During 1997

Period	Length	Fraction of a year	×	Shares Outstanding	=	Shares
January 1–April 30, 1997	4 months	4/12	×	45 million	=	15.0 million
May 1–June 30, 1997	2 months	2/12	×	60 million	=	10.0 million
July 1–Sept 30, 1997	3 months	3/12	×	50 million	=	12.5 million
October 1–Dec 31, 1997	3 months	3/12	×	66 million	=	16.5 million
Totals	12 months					54.0 million

EPS Calculations with Preferred Stock Outstanding

When a firm has both preferred and common stock outstanding, the preferred stock's share of net income must be subtracted in order to determine the EPS of the common stock. This is required because dividends must be paid to preferred shareholders before any earnings are available to common shareholders. Cumulative preferred stock always must be allocated its portion of net income. Noncumulative preferred stock is assigned a portion of income only in years when the firm actually declares a preferred stock dividend.

To illustrate, assume that Avalon Company reports net income $120 million in 1998, and has both preferred and common stock outstanding. Pertinent details about the stock issues appear in Exhibit 10–7. Avalon's income available for common stock is determined as follows:

Net income, 1998	$120 million
Less: Income applicable to preferred shares	
($10 per share × 2 million shares)	−20 million
Income applicable to common shares	$100 million

Consequently, the EPS of the common stock is $2.50 ($100 million of income ÷ 40 million common shares outstanding).

EXHIBIT 10–7
STOCK ISSUE DETAILS

> **Avalon Company**
> **Descriptions of Preferred and Common Stock**
> **Outstanding During 1998**
>
> Preferred stock, cumulative annual dividend of $10 per share, 2 million shares outstanding throughout all of 1998.
>
> Common stock, 40 million shares outstanding throughout all of 1998.

ANALYSIS BASED ON SHAREHOLDERS' EQUITY

The starting point in any analysis of a corporation's borrowed and equity capital is a careful reading of the descriptions provided in the body of the financial statements and the accompanying footnotes. As you have seen in this chapter, terms such as *convertible, cumulative, preferred,* and many others are critical in understanding the relative rights and priorities of the debt and equity claims on corporate assets.

The number and type of financial ratios that are based on shareholders' equity are constrained only by the imagination of the analyst. New ratios are continually being developed and tested by the "gurus of the day" quoted in the business press. This section discusses three ratios that seem to have stood the test of time: the financial leverage ratio, the market-to-book value ratio, and the price-to-earnings ratio.

Financial Leverage, or Debt-to-Assets Ratio

A basic decision faced by financial managers is the extent to which a firm should rely on borrowed capital. Shakespeare's adage "neither a borrower nor a lender be" is poor business advice. It is beneficial for most corporations to rely on debt to some extent. The degree of reliance on debt, or **financial leverage,** is measured as the ratio of debt to assets:

$$\text{Financial leverage} = \frac{\text{Total liabilities}}{\text{Total assets}}$$

Exhibit 10–8 shows financial leverage ratio calculations for two firms, based on financial reports for 1994. Wendy's International's debt is equal to about 37% of its total assets. This reflects Wendy's reliance mainly on the retention of its earnings to finance its growth. Bank of Boston Corporation provides a dramatic contrast: Borrowed capital is equal to more than 93% of its total assets. This reflects the fact that Bank of Boston is engaged in the banking industry. Banks accept deposits from customers, and report substantial liabilities for future withdrawals.

Financial Leverage Ratios, Two Firms **Measured at December 31, 1994** **(Dollars in Thousands)**	
Wendy's International Corporation (Restaurants)	
Debt	$ 404,594
Equity	681,498
Total assets (equals debt plus equity)	$ 1,086,092
Financial leverage ratio: $404,594/$1,086,092 = .373	
Bank of Boston Corporation (Banking)	
Debt	$41,488,000
Equity	3,142,000
Total assets (equals debt plus equity)	$44,630,000
Financial leverage ratio: $41,488,000/$44,630,000 = .930	

EXHIBIT 10–8
FINANCIAL LEVERAGE RATIO
CALCULATIONS

The lesson to be learned in comparing Wendy's and Bank of Boston in Exhibit 10–8 is that comparisons of financial leverage ratios across companies in different industries must be undertaken with caution. To some extent differences in financial leverage reflect management's willingness (or reluctance) to rely on borrowed capital. To a large extent, however, financial leverage is determined by industry characteristics and practices.

Financial leverage ratios are widely used by analysts to assess the risks of debt and equity securities. Firms with debt percentages that are substantially above their industry averages tend to have a higher likelihood of default on debt payments. As a result, high financial leverage is associated with lower bond quality ratings and therefore higher borrowing (interest) costs. Equity investments have also been found to be riskier for firms with high financial leverage. The share prices of highly leveraged firms tend to be more volatile than the share prices of firms with lower financial leverage.

Market-to-Book Value Ratio

Analysts often compare the market value of a firm's outstanding common stock to the reported value (i.e., book value) of common shareholders' equity. For example, at the end of 1994 Compaq Computer had 86,089,647 shares of stock outstanding, and the market price per share was about $60. Compaq reported total shareholders' equity of

$2,717,529,000, or $31.57 per share ($2,717,529,000 total shareholders' equity ÷ 86,089,647 shares outstanding). Accordingly, Compaq's **market-to-book value ratio** is computed as follows:

$$\text{Market-to-book value ratio} \quad = \quad \frac{\text{Market price per share}}{\text{Book value per share}}$$

$$= \quad \frac{\$60}{\$31.57}$$

$$= \quad 1.9$$

Why would investors be willing to buy Compaq's stock at over 1.9 times its underlying book value? The answer rests on the fact that the current market price of Compaq's stock depends on the future cash flows (dividends and resale price) that stockholders expect. In this sense, market price measures the **economic value** of Compaq's stock. The book value of Compaq's stock, on the other hand, reflects the methods used to identify and measure Compaq's assets and liabilities. Accounting measurements are based largely on historical costs, and do not purport to reflect contemporary expectations about future cash flows. Despite its popularity, the market-to-book value ratio appears to be comparing "apples to oranges."

Price-to-Earnings Ratio

The ratio of a stock's market price per share to its EPS is termed its **price-to-earnings (P/E) ratio.** For example, Compaq Computer's market price per share at the end of 1994 was $60, and its 1994 EPS was reported at $5.14. The resulting P/E ratio is

$$\text{P/E} \quad = \quad \frac{\text{Price per share}}{\text{EPS}}$$

$$= \quad \$60/\$5.14$$

$$= \quad 11.7$$

This result indicates that Compaq's stock was selling at a price that is 11.7 times its earnings per share.

P/E ratios are often used to assess growth, risk, and earnings quality. To illustrate, at the end of 1994 the average firm in the personal computer industry had a P/E ratio of about 8.5. Why would Compaq's stock have a greater P/E multiple than the industry average? To answer this question, we must consider the effects of growth, risk, and earnings quality on interfirm comparisons of P/E ratios.

Growth and the P/E Ratio

P/E ratios vary directly with expected future growth rates in earnings. If investors expect a firm's future earnings to grow rapidly, then current earnings understate the future earning power of the firm. Stock price, on the other hand, reflects investor expectations of future earnings and cash flows. Consequently, the ratio of prices to earnings will be relatively high for firms with high expected rates of earnings growth.

Risk and the P/E Ratio

It is well established among investors that riskier investments require higher returns. Lenders require higher interest payments from borrowers with lower credit ratings, and equity investors demand greater returns, and therefore pay lower prices, for the stocks of risky firms. For this reason high-risk firms are expected to have lower-than-average P/E multiples, and low-risk firms are expected to exhibit higher than average P/E multiples.

Earnings Quality and the P/E Ratio

Earnings quality refers to the sustainability of currently reported earnings in future periods. Firms that use conservative methods of income measurement (e.g., LIFO inventory costing, accelerated depreciation, and amortization) are more likely to be viewed as having higher earnings quality than firms that use more liberal income measurement methods. The securities market is likely to place a higher share price on firms with quality earnings. In other words, P/E multiples should vary directly with firms' earnings quality.

Let's return to the earlier observation that Compaq's P/E ratio is higher than average for firms in the personal computer industry. We may now interpret this finding as follows: investors expect that Compaq will have higher earnings growth, lower investment risk, and/or higher earnings quality than other firms in its industry. The market price, and therefore the P/E ratio, is based on the *expectations* of investors about a company's future performance.

SUMMARY OF LEARNING OBJECTIVES

1. **Understand why large business firms prefer to organize as corporations.**

   Major business firms prefer to organize as corporations. The ability of a corporation to sell its ownership shares to a large number of individual an institutional investors allows the firm to invest in large-scale operations. The basic ownership shares in a corporation are referred to as common stock, which represents a residual interest in the assets of the firm. Some corporations also issue preferred stock, which has priority over common stock in receiving dividends and other distributions of assets.

2. **Comprehend the types of transactions and events that change the components of shareholders' equity.**

   Corporate shareholders' equity arises from both the sale of ownership shares and the retention of profits in the business. Most changes that occur in shareholders' equity arise from three basic transactions:

   a. Issuance of stock to investors, which increases paid-in capital.
   b. Recognition of periodic income (loss), which increases (decreases) retained earnings.
   c. Declaration of cash dividends, which decreases retained earnings.

   Other events that affect shareholders' equity include the following:

   d. Stock dividends, which are distributions of additional shares to investors. These dividends decrease retained earnings and increase paid-in capital, but have no effect on total shareholders' equity or total assets.

e. Stock splits, which are exchanges in which multiple "new" shares of stock are received for each "old" share. These exchanges do not change any of the components of shareholders' equity.

f. Purchase of treasury shares, the cost of which is subtracted from shareholders' equity, and the subsequent resale of treasury shares.

g. Issuance of stock options, which are rights to purchase the firm's stock at a specified price over a designated future period.

h. Conversion of securities, such as bonds payable or preferred stock, that allow the holder to exchange the securities for a predetermined number of common shares.

3. **Interpret shareholders' equity ratios used in analyzing financial statements.**

Shareholders' equity is used extensively in ratio analysis of financial statements. Four widely employed measures are the following:

$$\text{Earnings per share (EPS)} = \frac{\text{Net income}}{\text{Weighted average number of common shares outstanding}}$$

$$\text{Debt-to-assets or financial leverage ratio} = \frac{\text{Total debt}}{\text{Total assets}}$$

$$\text{Market-to-book value ratio} = \frac{\text{Market price per share}}{\text{Book value per share}}$$

$$\text{Price-to-earnings ratio} = \frac{\text{Market price per share}}{\text{EPS}}$$

The proper interpretation of each of these ratios requires that you be familiar with the conventions and the limitations of historical-cost-based financial accounting methods.

KEY TERMS

Additional paid-in-capital	Financial leverage ratio
Authorized shares	Hybrid securities
Capital gains	Invested capital
Charter	Issued shares
Common stock	Market-to-book value ratio
Contra-equity account	Outstanding shares
Convertible bonds	Paid-in capital
Convertible preferred stock	Par value
Cumulative preferred stock	Preferred stock
Date of declaration	Price-to-earnings (P/E) ratio
Date of payment	Residual owners
Date of record	Retained earnings
Dividends	Stock dividend
Earnings per share (EPS)	Stock option
Earnings quality	Stock split
Economic value	Treasury stock
Equity capital	Weighted average

SOLUTION TO REALITY CHECK 10–1

a. Typical accounting for a two-for-one stock split does not entail any reclassification of retained earnings. Rather, a two-for-one stock split simply reduces per share par value by 50%, so the total par value of the issued shares remains constant. Typical accounting for a stock dividend entails a reclassification of an amount from retained earnings equal to the market value of the shares distributed as a dividend.

General Dynamics uses neither method. Instead, an amount equal to the par value of the additional shares issued is reclassified from retained earnings to paid-in capital. As a result, the par value per share is the same before and after the "split," and the total par value is doubled.

b. General Dynamics gives retroactive recognition to the stock split in order to aid analysts in making comparisons with prior years. For example, if net income was unchanged from the prior year and the number of shares was *not* retroactively adjusted, the earnings per share would appear to decrease by 50%

c. The company may have split the stock in order to reduce the per-share price, and thereby make the stock more accessible for smaller investors. Alternatively, management may use stock splits as an indirect way to "signal" investors that management expects higher per share earnings and dividends in the future.

d. Generally, existing shareholders benefit from stock splits. Although each shareholder's fractional interest in General Dynamics is not changed by the stock split, the total value of existing shares usually increases around the date of such announcements. The increase in stock prices may reflect investor expectations of higher future cash flows.

SOLUTION TO REALITY CHECK 10–2

a. The average proceeds per share received by Crown on issuance of the shares is $21.61:

Total increase in shareholders' equity,	$30,600,000	
÷ Number of shares issued	1,415,711	
= Average proceeds per share		$21.61

b. The aggregate market value of the shares issued was $56,628,440 ($40 per share market value × 1,415,711 shares).

c. The difference between the aggregate market value and the proceeds received by Crown on issuance of these shares is $26,028,440 ($56,628,440 − $30,600,000). It is reasonable to interpret this difference as compensation expense, because Crown could have received the full aggregate market value if the shares had been sold to investors on the open market. The accounting treatment does not recognize this difference, however, because the issued shares are recorded at the exercise prices of the options. Some analysts argue that the accounting principles used in accounting for options result in an understatement of related expenses.

10–1 Describe the differences between shareholders' equity and liabilities.

10–2 Identify three components of shareholders' equity and describe each component.

10–3 Describe how dividends decrease shareholders' equity. Under what circumstances will dividends not reduce shareholders' equity?

10–4 Write a short memo explaining why large firms prefer to organize as corporations.

10–5 Describe why a firm's owners might prefer a corporate structure, rather than a partnership.

10–6 Under what circumstances might a partnership want to shift immediately to a corporate structure?

10–7 Describe the differences between common and preferred stock.

10–8 Write a short memo describing why a firm's financial statements do not reflect the market value of the firm's shares of common and preferred stock.

10–9 Describe the differences between an equity or ownership interest in a corporation as compared to a creditor interest. What different rights does each have?

10–10 Distinguish between dividends and other benefits that you might get by owning shares in a corporation. If you were an investor, why might you prefer a $100 noncash benefit, rather than $100 cash dividend? Under what circumstances would you prefer the $100 in cash?

10–11 Describe why retained earnings cannot be equated with cash. Why is it incorrect to consider any portion of shareholders' equity as cash?

10–12 Describe why shareholders' equity can be referred to as a residual interest in a corporation.

10–13 Distinguish between invested capital and retained earnings. What are the sources of each? Describe how each may be reduced.

10–14 With regard to common stock, distinguish among authorized, issued, and outstanding shares. Why would a firm never have more outstanding shares than authorized and issued shares?

10–15 Under what circumstances will a firm receive cash when it issues stock? Under what circumstances might it not receive cash?

10–16 Identify and describe the differences between a stock dividend and a stock split.

10–17 With regard to common stock, describe the concept of treasury stock. Describe why this is shown in a contra-equity account.

10–18 Distinguish between outstanding common stock and treasury stock. Why would a firm want to have treasury stock?

10–19 Describe the concept of employee stock options. Why might a firm want to issue stock options?

10–20 What are cumulative dividends as compared to noncumulative dividends?

10–21 Identify and describe the differences between convertible preferred stock and convertible bonds.

10–22 Why might a firm want to issue hybrid securities, such as convertible bonds or preferred stock with special preference rights?

10–23 a. Describe how earnings per share (EPS) is computed.
b. Why do you think that this is such an important ratio?
c. Describe what EPS represents.

10–24 Describe why the market-to-book value ratio is analogous to comparing apples to oranges. Accountants usually avoid inconsistent or noncomparable relationships; why do you think analysts have found this ratio to be useful?

10–25 Explain why price-to-earnings ratios may differ among firms. As an investor, would you prefer to buy a stock that has a relatively high or low price-to-earnings ratio? Discuss.

10–26 Assume that a firm uses relatively "conservative" methods of accounting (e.g., LIFO inventory costing; and/or accelerated depreciation methods). Describe how this would affect your interpretation of the following measures: EPS; financial leverage ratio; price-to-earnings ratio.

EXERCISES

Transaction Analysis: Shareholders' equity

10–27 Davidson Corp. has the following transactions. Use the balance sheet equation to analyze the financial statement effects of these transactions. Set up the following accounts: cash, patent, and stockholders' equity accounts, preferred stock, capital in excess of par, common stock, and treasury stock.

1. Issue 5 million shares of $2.00 par value preferred stock at a price of $10.00.
2. Issue 5 million shares of no-par common stock at a price of $20.00.
3. Purchase 100,000 shares of its own common stock as treasury stock at a market price of $35.00.
4. Issue 200,000 shares of no-par common stock in exchange for patent rights. The stock has a market price of $40.

Transaction Analysis: Shareholders' Equity

10–28 DWN Corporation began operations in 1998. Calculate the balances in each component of shareholders' equity at the end of 1998, after recognizing the following transactions:

1. Issue 1 million shares of $5.00 par value common stock at a price of $15.00.
2. Earn net income of $450,000.
3. Declare and pay dividends of $200,000.
4. Purchase 10,000 shares of its common stock as treasury stock at $25.00.
5. Sell 5,000 shares of treasury stock for $30.00.

Transaction Analysis: Shareholders' Equity

10–29 SKN Corporation began operations in 1998. Calculate the balances in each component of shareholders' equity at the end of 1998, after recognizing the following transactions:

1. Issue 2 million shares of $10.00 par value common stock at a price of $25.00.
2. Incur high R&D costs and show a net loss on its 1996 income statement of $1,500,000.
3. Issue 4 million shares of $25.00 preferred stock at a price of $30.00.

Transaction Analysis: Shareholders' Equity

10–30 RMN Corp. had a variety of shareholders' equity transactions in 1998. Record these transactions in each of the components of shareholders' equity, and in "Cash and other assets." Given the following balances in each account at the beginning of 1998, use the balance sheet equation to calculate the ending balance in each account.

ASSETS	=	LIABILITIES	+	SHAREHOLDERS' EQUITY

Beginning Balances

Cash and other assets	$78,000,000
Common stock, $1.00 par value	5,000,000
Capital in excess of par	25,000,000
Retained earnings	50,000,000
Treasury stock (40,000 shares)	(2,000,000)

1996 Transactions Affecting Shareholders' Equity

1. Issue 5 million shares of no-par preferred stock at a price of $4.00.
2. Sell the treasury stock for $4,500,000.
3. Earn net income of $35,000,000.
4. Declare and pay dividends of $10,000,000.
5. Employee stock options were granted for the purchase of 100,000 shares of common stock. The market price currently is $7 per share. The exercise price is $7 per share.
6. The stock options were exercised and the company issued the 100,000 shares. The current market price is $8 per share.

Earnings per Share Calculations

10–31 Calculate earnings per share (EPS) given the following information:

- Net income, $255,000,000
- Authorized common stock, 50,000,000 shares
- Common stock, 25,000,000 shares outstanding all year
- Bonds payable, $50,000,000

Earnings per Share Calculations

10–32 Calculate earnings per share (EPS) given the following information:

- Net loss, $20,000,000
- Common stock, 2,000,000 shares outstanding all year
- Preferred stock, 2,000,000 shares authorized, but none issued

Earnings per Share Calculations

10–33 Calculate earnings per share (EPS) given the following information:

- Net income, $345,000,000
- Authorized common stock, 20,000,000 shares, $1.00 par value
- Weighted average number of shares outstanding, 11,455,678
- Dividends paid, $35,000,000

Earnings per Share Calculations

10–34 Calculate earnings per share (EPS) given the following information:

- Net income, $65,100,000
- Common stock outstanding, 3,100,000 shares
- Preferred stock outstanding, 1,000,000 shares
- Dividends paid on preferred stock, $5,000,000
- Bonds payable, $40,000,000
- Retained earnings (ending balance), $45,679,000

Comprehensive Exercise: Stockholders' Equity

10–35 Swan and Duboner Corporation has the following stockholders' equity at December 31, 1996:

Contributed Capital	1996
6% Preferred stock: $100 par value, 20,000 shares authorized, 5,000 shares issued and outstanding	$ 500,000
Common stock: $5 par value, 1,000,000 shares authorized, 250,000 shares issued	1,250,000
Additional paid-in capital	1,740,000
Total contributed capital	3,490,000
Retained earnings	850,000
Total stockholders' equity	$4,340,000

The corporation had the following transactions during 1997:

1. *February 1:* Declared a dividend of $6 per share on the preferred stock, and $0.50 per share on the common stock.
2. *February 10:* The board of directors established this as the record date.
3. *February 25:* The dividends were paid.
4. *March 31:* A 2-for-1 stock split on the common stock was declared and issued.
5. *April 30:* The corporation bought back 100,000 shares of its common stock for $6 per share. These shares will be reissued in the future.
6. *June 30:* Employee stock options were granted for 10,000 shares. The current market price is $5.50 per share. The exercise price is $6 per share.
7. *August 15:* The corporation sold 20,000 shares of its treasury stock for $7 per share.
8. *October 31:* Employees exercise their stock options. The current market price is $7.50 per share.
9. *December 31:* The net income for the year is $600,000.

REQUIRED

a. Set up an accounting equation and record the above transactions.
b. Calculate EPS, assuming that the common weighted average shares outstanding were 380,000 shares.
c. Why do companies, in general, declare and issue a stock split?

Transaction Analysis: Shareholders' Equity

10–36 Calculate the ending balance in Retained Earnings. Record the effects of the following transactions using the balance sheet equation and "Cash and other assets."

ASSETS	=	LIABILITIES	+	SHAREHOLDERS' EQUITY

1. Beginning balance in retained earnings is $2,590,000: common stock $1 par $2,000,000; and cash and other assets are $4,590,000.

2. Earn net income of $3,560,000.
3. Declare and pay dividends of $2,000,000.
4. Issue 4 million shares common stock par value $1.00 at a price of $4.00.
5. Issue stock dividends in the amount of $3,000,000 representing 1,000,000 shares.

Earnings per Share Calculations

10–37 Calculate earnings per share (EPS) given the following information:

- Net income, $63,000,000
- Common stock outstanding, 3,000,000 shares
- Bonds payable, $35,000,000
- Retained earnings (ending balance), $42,300,000

Earnings per Share Calculations

10–38 Calculate earnings per share (EPS) given the following information:

- Common stock outstanding, 4,000,000 shares
- Net income, $55,000,000
- Bonds payable, $33,000,000
- Retained earnings (ending balance), $44,000,400
- Preferred shares outstanding, 1,000,000, $10.00 par value
- Preferred dividends, $2,000,000

PROBLEMS

Transaction Analysis: Shareholders' Equity

10–39 Use the balance sheet equation (and "Cash and other assets") to calculate the ending balances in each of the following accounts, given the beginning balances and various transactions during the year.

ASSETS	=	LIABILITIES	+	SHAREHOLDERS' EQUITY

Beginning Balances

Cash and other assets	$125,000,000
Convertible bonds payable	20,000,000
Convertible preferred stock, $10 par value	30,000,000
Common stock, $10 par value	40,000,000
Retained earnings	35,000,000

Transactions

1. Convert half of the convertible bonds payable to common stock at a conversion price of $40.00 per share.
2. Convert all of the convertible preferred stock to common stock at 1.5 shares of preferred stock for each share of common stock (conversion ratio).
3. Purchase 500,000 shares of its own common stock as treasury stock at a market price of $12.50.
4. Earn net income of $17,500,000.
5. Pay dividends of $5,000,000.
6. Issue 1,000,000 shares of common stock when the market price was $15.00 per share, in exchange for a parcel of land priced at $20,000,000.

Comprehensive Dividend Problem: Stockholders' Equity

10–40 Macintosh Browning Corporation has the following stockholders' equity at December 31, 1996:

Contributed Capital	1996
7% Cumulative preferred stock: $120 par, 50,000 shares authorized, 20,000 shares issued and outstanding	$2,400,000
Common stock: $10 par, 500,000,000 shares authorized, 300,000 shares issued	3,000,000
Additional paid-in capital	900,000
Total contributed capital	6,300,000
Retained earnings	1,200,000
Treasury stock (74,000 shares of common stock)	(1,110,000)
Total stockholders' equity	$6,390,000

REQUIRED

a. Why do you suppose Macintosh issued preferred stock? What does the 7% cumulative term indicate?
b. Assume the board of directors has not declared a dividend in the past several years and that the preferred stock has been outstanding during these years. What is the amount of dividends outstanding for previous years on these cumulative shares?
c. Why does this company have preferred stock and not additional debt?
d. If the board declared and paid dividends to the preferred and common shareholders during the year, show the effects (ignore $ amounts) on stockholders' equity on the date of declaration, date of record, and date of payment.

Comprehensive Problem: Stockholders' Equity

10–41 LP+G Corporation has the following stockholders' equity at December 31, 1996:

Contributed Capital	
Common stock: $20 par, authorized 700,000 shares, issued 200,000 shares	$ 4,000,000
Additional paid-in capital	3,200,000
Total contributed capital	7,200,000
Retained earnings	5,400,000
Total stockholders' equity	$12,600,000

During 1997, the following transactions occurred.

1. *January 31:* A 2-for-1 common stock split was declared by the board of directors. The shares were issued. The market price was $110 per share.
2. *March 15:* The corporation repurchased 50,000 shares of its common stock as treasury stock at $54 per share.
3. *May 31:* The board of directors declared a $2 cash dividend per share.
4. *June 10:* This is the date of record that the board of directors established.
5. *June 20:* The dividends were paid.

6. *August 30:* The corporation granted employee stock options of 20,000 shares. The market price was $54 per share. The exercise price is $54 per share.
7. *October 15:* The corporation sold 30,000 shares of its treasury stock for $55 per share.
8. *November 25:* Employee stock options were exercised. The market price was $56 per share.

REQUIRED

a. Set up an accounting equation and record the above transactions.
b. Why do you suppose the corporation issued a 2-for-1 stock split?
c. Why would a company issue a stock dividend instead of cash? What impact does a stock dividend have on overall stockholders' equity?

Conceptual Discussion: Preferred Stock

10–42 The H. Houdini Company's capital structure includes 10,000,000 of long-term debt, at an average rate of 12%. The capital structure also includes $3,000,000 of (cumulative) preferred stock, with stated dividends of 5%, and $6,000,000 of common stock. It has no retained earnings.

REQUIRED

a. How does the preferred stock affect the risk and potential returns of the long-term debt and the common stock?
b. In what ways might the preferred stock be considered debt? How might it be viewed as equity?

Financial Statement Impact: Debt Versus Equity

10–43 The Open Sesame Company has assets of $300,000,000, long-term debt of $100,000,000, common stock of $100,000,000, and retained earnings of $100,000,000. Most of the long-term debt consists of convertible debt carrying fairly high interest rates that are about five points above the current prevailing market. Open Sesame wants to issue $100,000,000 of new debt at current market rates. It will then "call," or retire, the existing convertible debt, using the money from the new debt. Since its share prices have also increased 40% over the past several years, Open Sesame is also considering raising additional funds by issuing new shares of common stock. Funds from the common stock issue would also be used to refinance the debt.

REQUIRED

a. If Open Sesame issued new debt, what would be the impact on its balance sheet? On its income statement?
b. If Open Sesame issued new common stock, what would be the impact on its balance sheet? What assumption is crucial to answering this question?
c. What other considerations might drive Open Sesame's decision about this possible refinancing of its long-term debt?
d. How might the current creditors be affected if Open Sesame tries to "call," or retire, its convertible debt? How might they feel? What actions might they take, immediately upon hearing of the call?

10–44 Financial Statement Impact: Debt Versus Equity—Alternate Problems (A), (B), or (C)

Problem (A)

Smith Smyth, Inc., has the following capital structure:

Current liabilities	$ 20,000,000
Long-term debt	30,000,000
Preferred stock ($10 par value)	40,000,000
Common stock ($1 par value)	40,000,000
Capital in excess of par	20,000,000
Retained earnings	15,000,000
Total liabilities and shareholders' equity	$165,000,000

REQUIRED

a. Determine the impact on Smyth's capital structure if it issues additional long-term debt of $20,000,000. In other words, show what Smyth's capital structure will be with the new debt.

b. Determine the impact on Smyth's capital structure if it converts half of the long-term debt, including that issued in part a, to common stock at a conversion price of $10.

c. Determine the impact on Smyth's capital structure if it converts all of its preferred stock to common stock. The conversion ratio is 2.5 shares of common stock for each share of preferred stock.

d. Determine the impact on Smyth's capital structure if it purchases 5,000,000 shares for its common stock at a market price of $12 per share.

e. Determine the impact on Smyth's capital structure if it suffers losses in the next fiscal year of $10,000,000.

f. Reconstruct the right side of the balance sheet, reflecting all of the above changes, as if they occurred simultaneously. (*Hint:* Set up an accounting equation and record all of the transactions.)

Problem (B)

Bitsy Betsy, Inc., has the following capital structure:

Current Liabilities	$35,000,000
Long-term debt	35,000,000
Preferred stock (no par)	45,000,000
Common stock (no par)	45,000,000
Retained earnings	10,000,000
Total liabilities and shareholders' equity	$170,000,000

REQUIRED

a. Determine the impact on Betsy's capital structure if it issues additional long-term debt of $25,000,000. In other words, show what Betsy's capital structure will be with the new debt.

b. Determine the impact on Betsy's capital structure if it converts half of the long-term debt, including that issued in part a, to common stock.

c. Determine the impact on Betsy's capital structure if it converts all of its preferred stock to common stock.

d. Determine the impact on Betsy's capital structure if it suffers losses in the next fiscal year of $10,000,000.

e. Reconstruct the right side of the balance sheet, reflecting all of the above changes, as if they occurred simultaneously.

Problem (C)

Snippy Sam, Inc., has the following capital structure:

Current liabilities	$ 15,000,000
Long-term debt	25,000,000
Preferred stock ($10 par value)	37,500,000
Common stock ($5 par value)	37,500,000
Capital in excess of par	10,000,000
Retained earnings	(15,000,000)
Total liabilities and shareholders' equity	$110,000,000

REQUIRED

a. Determine the impact on Sam's capital structure if it issues additional long-term debt of $15,000,000. In other words, show what Sam's capital structure will be with the new debt.

b. Determine the impact on Sam's capital structure if it converts half of the long-term debt, including that issued in part a, to common stock at a conversion price of $20.

c. Determine the impact on Sam's capital structure if it converts all of its preferred stock to common stock. The conversion ratio is 1.5 shares of common stock for each share of preferred stock. *Hint:* Set up an accounting equation and record all of the transactions.

d. Determine the impact on Sam's capital structure if it suffers further losses in the next fiscal year of $10,000,000.

e. Reconstruct the right side of the balance sheet, reflecting all of the above changes, as if they occurred simultaneously. *Hint:* Set up an accounting equation and record all of the transactions.

Effects of Events on Elements of Financial Statements

10–45 A list of business transactions and events follows:

1. Sale of common stock to investors
2. Sale of preferred stock to investors
3. Declaration of a cash dividend to common shareholders
4. Purchase of treasury stock
5. Sale of treasury stock
6. Issuances of options to employees, which will become exercisable in two years
7. Announcement of a 2-for-1 stock split

REQUIRED

Indicate how each of the items listed above would affect the following financial statement items or ratios:

a. Total assets
b. Liabilities

c. Shareholders' equity

d. Retained earnings

e. Earnings per share

f. Financial leverage (debt divided by total assets)

Comparing Financial Ratios of Two Firms Using Differing Accounting Methods

10–46 You have been provided with the following information for two firms at the end of 1998 ($ in millions):

	Adam Co.	Zachary Co.
Total assets	$105	$210
Total liabilities	$70	$120
Shareholders' equity	$35	$90
Net income during 1998	$15	$25
Shares outstanding during 1998	1 million	1.2 million
Market price per share	$125.00	$150.00

REQUIRED

a. Based on the information above, determine the following items for each firm:

- Earnings per share
- Price-to-earnings ratio
- Financial leverage (debt-to-assets ratio)

b. Upon further inquiry, you learn that Adam uses LIFO inventory costing and accelerated depreciation of plant and equipment costs. Zachary uses FIFO costing and straight-line depreciation. If Adam had been using the same inventory costing and depreciation methods as Zachary, then Adam's net income during 1998 would have been higher by $20 million, and the carrying value of Adam's total assets would have been higher by $85 million. Based on this information, recompute the three ratios above "as if" Adam and Zachary used the same accounting methods for inventory and depreciation.

Stock Options as Executive Compensation

10–47 Late in 1996 Natalie Attired, a recent MBA graduate, signed a three-year employment contract with Generic Co. that provides her with an annual salary of $90,000. In addition, at the start of each year 1997 through 1999, Natalie receives options to purchase 3,000 shares of Generic's common stock, at the market price when the options are received. These options are exercisable for four years from the date of receipt. Assume the following information related to these options:

Year	Market Price per Share, Beginning of Year	Options Exercised During the Year
1997	$ 50	None
1998	$ 80	4000*
1999	$130	2000†
2000	$ 90	None

*3,000 options at $50, and 1,000 options at $80.

†2,000 options at $80.

REQUIRED

a. Determine the total compensation expense to Natalie that would be reported by Generic in each of the years 1997 through 1999.

b. Determine the total economic benefit that Natalie has received (i.e., salary plus value of stockholding and options) from Generic over the three-year period.

c. Comment on any difference between your answers to parts a and b above.

CASES AND EXTENSIONS

Research Project: Forming a Corporation

10–48 Contact the appropriate state office, business research library, or other source to find out how a corporation is established. Write a short memo describing the important steps in establishing a corporation, concentrating on the possible financial statement effects.

Research Project: No Par Shares

10–49 Conduct whatever outside research is necessary to distinguish between par value shares and no-par shares. Why might a firm prefer to issue no-par (zero stated value) shares?

Research Project: Stock-based Compensation

10–50 Obtain and read the most recent FASB pronouncements on stock-based compensation. Write a memo describing the way you think this issue would most clearly be reflected or disclosed on a company's financial statements. Support your opinion.

Interpreting Financial Statements: Shareholders' Equity

10–51 Refer to Wendy's financial statements in Appendix D. Review the balance sheet to determine how and where shareholders' equity has been reported.

REQUIRED

a. Read the Consolidated Statement of Shareholders' Equity. Identify and discuss any unusual terms.

b. Determine whether Wendy's has any unusual types of shareholders' equity. If so, discuss how they might be interpreted by financial analysts. Discuss how Wendy's managers might view such equity items.

c. Discuss how "preferred stock" is related to "common stock." In your opinion, should they be disclosed separately? Why? Determine why Wendy's shows preferred stock on its balance sheet, but at zero amounts.

d. Discuss several reasons why Wendy's has treasury stock.

e. Discuss any other unusual concerns regarding Wendy's shareholders' equity. What other related information might an external analyst require, or prefer?

Interpreting Financial Statements: Equity Ratio Calculations

10–52 Refer to Wendy's financial statements in Appendix D. Review the financial statements to determine how and where shareholders' equity has been reported.

REQUIRED

a. Calculate the financial leverage, or debt, ratio for each year. Interpret your results.

b. Based on the notes, is there any other possible way in which the leverage ratio could be calculated? If so, do so by taking a more liberal (or more conservative) approach to reclassifying any convertible securities. Contrast these results with your earlier results. *Note:* Refer to Note 2 pertaining to convertible debentures (bonds).

c. Calculate the market-to-book value ratio. If market prices are not disclosed somewhere in the annual report, go to your library to determine the market price at the end of each fiscal year. Discuss your results.

d. Calculate the price-to-earnings ratio, using the market price determined above and primary earnings-per-share information. Discuss your results.

e. Discuss any other unusual concerns regarding Wendy's shareholders' equity. What other related information might an external analyst require, or prefer?

Interpreting Financial Statements: Shareholders' Equity

10–53 Refer to Reebok's financial statements in Appendix F. Review the balance sheet to determine how and where shareholders' equity has been reported.

REQUIRED

a. Read the Consolidated Statement of Stockholders' Equity. Identify and discuss any unusual terms. Trace any numerical disclosures of shareholders' equity in the notes to corresponding disclosures in the balance sheet.

b. Determine whether Reebok has any unusual types of shareholders' equity. If so, discuss how they might be interpreted by financial analysts. Discuss how Reebok's managers might view such equity items.

c. Discuss how "paid-in capital" is related to "common stock." In your opinion, should they be disclosed separately? Why?

d. Determine why Reebok had the same amount of "shares in treasury" each year. How many shares of common stock are outstanding?

e. Evaluate the increase in "unearned compensation." Why is this item shown as part of shareholders' equity? Is this account, or the increase, significant? Why?

f. Discuss any other unusual concerns regarding Reebok's shareholders' equity. What other related information might an external analyst require, or prefer?

Interpreting Financial Statements: Equity Ratio Calculations

10–54 Refer to Reebok's financial statements in Appendix F. Review the financial statements to determine how and where shareholders' equity has been reported.

REQUIRED

a. Calculate the financial leverage, or debt, ratio for each year. Interpret your results.

b. Based on the notes, is there any other possible way in which the leverage ratio could be calculated? If so, do so by taking a more liberal (or more conservative) approach to reclassifying any convertible securities. Contrast these results with your earlier results.

c. Calculate the market-to-book value ratio. If market prices are not disclosed somewhere in the annual report, go to your library to determine the market price at the end of each fiscal year. Discuss your results.

d. Calculate the price-to-earnings ratio, using the market price determined above. Discuss your results.

e. Discuss any other unusual concerns regarding Reebok's shareholders' equity. What other related information might an external analyst require, or prefer?

Interpreting Financial Statements: Shareholders' Equity

10–55 Refer to OshKosh B'Gosh's financial statements in Appendix C. Review the balance sheet to determine how and where shareholders' equity has been reported.

REQUIRED

a. Read Notes 1 and 11. Identify and discuss any unusual terms. Trace any numerical disclosures of shareholders' equity in the notes to corresponding disclosures in the financial statements.

b. Determine whether OshKosh B'Gosh has any unusual types of shareholders' equity. If so, discuss how they might be interpreted by financial analysts. Discuss how OshKosh B'Gosh's managers might view such equity items.

c. Discuss how "class A common stock" is related to "class B common stock." In your opinion, should they be disclosed separately? Why?

d. Determine why "additional paid-in capital" decreased in 1994.

e. There has been a decrease in the number of class A shares. Why isn't there a resulting treasury stock account?

f. Discuss any other unusual concerns regarding OshKosh B'Gosh's shareholders' equity. What other related information might an external analyst require, or prefer?

Interpreting Financial Statements: Equity Ratio Calculations

10–56 Refer to OshKosh B'Gosh's financial statements in Appendix C. Review the financial statements to determine how and where shareholders' equity has been reported.

REQUIRED

a. Calculate the financial leverage, or debt, ratio for each year. Interpret your results.

b. Based on Note 1, what do you think is meant by the company not having any common stock equivalents?

c. Calculate the market-to-book value ratio. If market prices are not disclosed somewhere in the annual report, go to your library to determine the market price at the end of each fiscal year. Discuss your results.

d. Calculate the price-to-earnings ratio, using the market price determined above. Discuss your results.

e. Discuss any other unusual concerns regarding OshKosh B'Gosh's shareholders' equity. What other related information might an external analyst require, or prefer?

Interpreting Financial Statements: Shareholders' Equity

10–57 Refer to the Bristol-Myers Squibb (BMS) financial statements in Appendix E. Review the balance sheet to determine how and where shareholders' equity has been reported.

REQUIRED

a. Read Notes 1 and 15. Identify and discuss any unusual terms. Trace any numerical disclosures of shareholders' equity in the notes to corresponding disclosures in the financial statements.

b. Determine whether BMS has any unusual types of shareholders' equity. If so, discuss how they might be interpreted by financial analysts. Discuss how BMS managers might view such equity items.

c. Discuss how "common stock" is related to "preferred stock." In your opinion, should they be disclosed separately? Why?

d. Determine why BMS had negative amounts of "treasury stock" each year. Why is treasury stock increasing?

e. Discuss why preferred stock shares have decreased over the years. What is meant by preferred stock having a liquidation value of $50 per share?

f. Discuss any other unusual concerns regarding BMS's shareholders' equity. What other related information might an external analyst require, or prefer?

Interpreting Financial Statements: Equity Ratio Calculations

10–58 Refer to the Bristol-Myers Squibb (BMS) financial statements in Appendix E. Review the financial statements to determine how and where sharcholders' equity has been reported.

REQUIRED

a. Calculate the financial leverage, or debt, ratio for each year. Interpret your results.

b. Based on the notes, is there any other possible way in which the leverage ratio could be calculated? If so, do so by taking a more liberal (or more conservative) approach to reclassifying any convertible securities. Contrast these results with your earlier results.

c. Calculate the market-to-book value ratio. If market prices are not disclosed somewhere in the annual report, go to your library to determine the market price at the end of each fiscal year. Discuss your results.

d. Calculate the price-to-earnings ratio, using the market price determined above. Discuss your results.

e. Discuss any other unusual concerns regarding BMS's shareholders' equity. What other related information might an external analyst require, or prefer?

Interpreting Financial Statements: Shareholders' Equity

10–59 Vicorp Restaurants, Inc., headquartered in Denver, operates or franchises 408 midscale restaurants, primarily under the names Bakers Square and Village Inn. Its 1994 balance sheet included the following shareholders' equity section (in thousands):

Shareholders' Equity	1994	1993	1992
Common stock: $0.05 par value, 20,000,000 shares authorized, 9,509,426. 9,911,536, and 10,189,066 issued	$ 476	$ 496	$ 509
Additional paid-in capital	91,544	98,338	105,701
Retained earnings	42,846	49,484	32,960
Treasury stock, at cost (0,0, and 212,851 shares)	0	0	(3,725)
Total shareholders' equity	$134,866	$148,318	$135,445

REQUIRED

a. Explain each item in the shareholders' equity section of Vicorp's balance sheet.
b. Why is there such a large discrepancy between the amounts assigned to common stock versus the additional paid-in capital?
c. Assuming zero dividends, did Vicorp have positive or negative net income in 1993? in 1994? Why?
d. How many shares of its own common stock did Vicorp purchase in 1992? At what price? Assume that Vicorp did not sell any additional shares in 1992.
e. Could Vicorp issue 10,000,000 shares of common stock to quickly raise additional funds? In which years?
f. Calculate the amount of dividends paid by Vicorp, if any, in 1993 and 1994. For this purpose, assume that Vicorp's net income was $16,524,000 in 1993, and they had a net loss of $6,638,000 in 1994.

Interpreting Financial Statements: Earnings per Share

10–60 Pierre's, headquartered in Paris, reports the following note to its 1996 financial statements:

Share Capital: The share capital comprises fully paid shares with a nominal value of FRF [French franc] 10. Changes in the number of shares (in number of shares) are as follows:

	1996	1995
At 1 January	75,452,501	74,442,637
In lieu of cash (stock) dividends	—	725,402
Exercise of stock options	112,095	140,550
Conversion of bonds	745	3,324
Exercise of staff (employee) options	—	25,733
At 31 December	75,565,341	75,337,646

Information relevant to the earnings per share calculations is as follows:

	1996	1995
Average outstanding	75,422,540	75,122,483
Profit attributed to shareholders (FRF)	965,000,000	841,000,000

REQUIRED

a. Explain each item in Pierre's note.
b. What differences might exist between stock options and staff options?
c. Why does the average number of shares outstanding differ from the balances at January 1 and December 31?
d. Calculate Pierre's earnings per share (EPS).

Interpreting Financial Statements: Shareholders' Equity

10–61 Exabyte Corporation reported the following information in its 1994 balance sheet ($ in thousands and shares in thousands as well):

Stockholders' Equity	1994	1993
Preferred stock: $0.001 par value; 14,000 shares authorized, no shares issued and outstanding	—	—
Common stock: $0.001 par value, 50,000 shares authorized; 21,657 and 21,190 shares issued	22	21
Capital in excess of par value	57,208	51,242
Treasury stock, at cost, 15 and 15 shares	(9)	(9)
Retained earnings	139,686	107,281
Total stockholders' equity	$196,907	$158,535
Total assets	$242,765	$197,307
Common and common equivalent shares	21,965	21,399
Net income	$ 32,405	$ 16,182

REQUIRED

a. Explain each of Exabyte's stockholders' equity items.
b. What significance is there to the equality of par values for both the preferred and common stock?
c. How many shares of stock were actually owned by the public at the end of each year?
d. Why does Exabyte disclose preferred stock even though no shares have been issued?
e. Why does the number of shares listed as "Common and common equivalent shares" differ from the number of shares outstanding?
f. Using the information on treasury stock, determine the price paid for treasury shares. Does it concern you that this price is so much higher than the shares' par value?
g. Calculate the earnings per share (EPS).
h. On the basis of the above information, how would you assess Exabyte's profitability?
i. If you learned that Exabyte paid no dividends in 1994, would that concern you?

Cash Flow Impact on Shareholders' Equity

10–62 Sigma Designs is a high-tech software development company specializing in imaging and multimedia computer applications. Sigma Designs' statement of cash flows is presented below:

Sigma Designs, Inc.
Statement of Cash Flows
For the Years ended January 31, 1995 and 1994
(dollars in thousands)

	1995	1994
Cash flows from operating activities		
Net loss	$(8,773)	$(29,546)
Adjustments to reconcile net loss to net cash provided by operating activities (summary of all adjustments, net)	(110)	15,885
Net cash provided by (used for) operating activities	(8,883)	(13,661)
Cash flows from investing activities		
Purchases of marketable securities	(25,350)	(22,542)
Sales of marketable securities	22,296	33,355
Equipment additions	(721)	(612)
Software development costs (capitalized)	(1,255)	(494)
Other asset transactions	0	183
Net cash provided (used for) investing activities	(5,030)	9,890
Cash flows from financing activities		
Common stock sold	13,201	493
Repayment of long-term obligations	1,710	0
Other financing transactions	(1,925)	0
Net cash provided (used for) financing activities	12,986	493
Decrease in cash and equivalents	$ (927)	$ (3,278)

REQUIRED

a. If you now learned that the majority of payments included in the caption "Other financing transactions" in 1995 were for repurchasing common stock owned by officers and their family members, how would you feel about investing in Sigma Designs?

b. As a banker, would you loan money to Sigma Designs? Why or why not?

c. How would these conclusions change if the repurchases of stock were $100,000?

d. What if you learned that Sigma planned to repurchase shares for $2,000,000 and needed to sell more shares, or borrow funds, to accomplish this objective?

Interpreting Financial Statements: Shareholders' Equity

10–63 Consider Sigma Designs' balance sheets for 1995 and 1994 ($ in thousands). Sigma Designs is a high-tech software development company specializing in imaging and multimedia computer applications.

	1995	1994
Assets		
Cash and equivalents	$ 881	$ 1,808
Marketable securities	7,349	3,514
Accounts receivable, net of allowances	11,958	7,246
Inventories	9,736	10,602
Prepaid expenses and other	1,086	569
Total current assets	31,010	23,739
Equipment, net	1,343	1,200
Other assets	1,034	1,700
Total assets	$33,387	$26,639
Liabilities and Shareholders' Equity		
Current Liabilities		
Bank lines of credit	$ 1,710	$ 0
Accounts payable	9,333	4,207
Accrued salary and benefits	1,748	2,313
Other accrued liabilities	773	2,102
Total current liabilities	13,564	8,622
Long-term liabilities	1,102	1,518
Shareholders' Equity		
Common stock	38,820	27,544
Retained earnings (deficit)	(20,099)	(11,045)
Shareholders' equity	18,721	16,499
Total liabilities and shareholders' equity	$33,387	$26,639

REQUIRED

a. Concentrate on the equity section of the balance sheet. What major changes have occurred in this section? What may have caused these changes?

b. Since Sigma had a net loss each year, what can you conclude about its return on equity ratios?

International Comparisons: Shareholders' Equity

10–64 BF Group, a British company, reported the following components of shareholders' equity in its 1996 balance sheet (the relative size of each account balance is also shown):

- Called up share capital (large balance)
- Share premium account (small balance)
- Capital reserve (large balance)
- Profit and loss account (small balance, but much larger than the current year's net income

REQUIRED

a. Compare and contrast each of these terms with corresponding terms typically shown on a U.S. firm's balance sheet.

b. Why do you suppose that a British firm would show both a reserve account and a profit and loss account?

Comprehensive Evaluation

10–65 The Nothing But Cheese (NBC) Company is a small, but successful, family-owned business that specializes in family photography in wholesome circumstances. The company conducts still and video photography of individuals and families in settings that can best be described as "heartwarming." NBC's photographic techniques are unique, incorporating several patented photographic equipment innovations and improvements. The company fully expects to dominate its market niche within the region for the foreseeable future.

The firm has been in existence for over 40 years and has had a long-term philosophy of "no debt" and "family control." There are currently 5,000 shares of $1 par value common stock outstanding, all of which are held by family members. NBC's shareholders' equity section of its December 31, 1996, balance sheet contained the following data:

Common stock: $1 par value, 100,000 shares authorized, 5,000 shares issued	$ 5,000
Additional paid-in capital in excess of par value	595,000
Retained earnings	9,898,000
Total shareholders' equity	$10,498,000

Sophia Fuji, NBC's current president, has found three alternative ways of raising additional capital, which would be used both for current operating purposes, as well as expansion to neighboring regions.

- *Alternative 1:* Issue 40,000 shares of 6%, $100 par value cumulative preferred stock to a local, but very wealthy, investor. Each share could be converted to 4 shares of common stock, anytime after the year 2000.
- *Alternative 2:* Borrow $4,000,000 from a local bank at 10%, with a maturity date at the end of the year 2000.
- *Alternative 3:* Transform NBC immediately into a public company by issuing 500,000 shares of common stock at an estimated price of $8 per share. Of course, any member of the Fuji family could purchase stock on the open market at the issue date, or at any later date.

REQUIRED

a. Has NBC been successful in the past? Has it been profitable? What information is needed to answer these questions?

b. How can it obtain cash for expansion or operating purposes if none of these options is successful? In other words, what other options could Sophia also pursue?

c. Show the effects on the shareholders' equity section of NBC's balance sheet of each of the three alternatives identified earlier by Sophia.

d. Noting that interest is deductible for tax purposes, while dividends are not, evaluate the advantages and disadvantages of each of the three options. Show the effects on net income of each option.

e. Write a short memo from Sophia to her relatives recommending one of the three options, while at the same time criticizing the other two options.

f. One of Sophia's more vocal and complaining relatives responds to your memo and suggests that each of the three options is too expensive and threatens the loss of family control. He suggests that the family members must invest the additional $4,000,000 through purchase of additional shares. Since Sophia has already been told that other Fuji family members will not consider this option, write a short, but tactful, memo from Sophia to the dissenting family indicating why your recommendation above (part e) is still preferable.

Conceptual Discussion: Exchanges of Debt or Equity

10–66 Many U.S. firms have recently completed exchanges or swaps of stock for debt. Collectively, such swaps often retire more debt than the value of the stock that is exchanged. In other words, the face value of the debt often exceeds the market value of the stock that is exchanged. Typical swaps might include:

- Convertible preferred stock for common stock
- Debt for convertible preferred stock
- Convertible debt for common stock
- Debt for cash and common stock

REQUIRED

a. What do you suppose are the incentives or motivations for such swaps? Why would an investor or owner give up something with a historical cost higher than its current market value?
b. What is the effect of such swaps on a firm's balance sheet?

Conceptual Discussion: Risk Associated with Debt or Equity

10–67 Consider the following assertion and write a short essay explaining why a firm's risk would change under these circumstances:

> Another way to minimize the apparent riskiness of an enterprise as judged from its financial statement is to make its debt look like equity.

Conceptual Discussion: Debt Disguised as Equity

10–68 An American Accounting Association Committee suggests the following in a committee report subtitled "Debt Disguised as Equity" (*Accounting Horizons,* September 1991, p. 88):

> . . . is to make its debt look like equity. If this can be done while at the same time retaining the tax-deductibility of the interest on the debt, so much the better. Complex schemes have been thought up to secure these ends, and even relatively simple steps may be taken to disguise a liability as equity. . . . One proposal that the FASB is exploring is to get rid of the distinction altogether.

REQUIRED

a. Identify two ways in which a firm might disguise or transform its debt into equity.
b. Identify two reasons why a firm might want to disguise its debt as equity. Identify two reasons why a firm might not want to do this.
c. Discuss the ethical implications of disguising debt as equity.
d. Who do you think should set rules to control firm's choices regarding the disclosure of debt and equity? Why?

e. What recommendations would you propose to solve these issues?

Research Project: Shareholders' Equity

10–69 Locate recent annual reports for three companies in the same industry. If such reports are not conveniently available, use a business reference service, such as *Moody's, Standard & Poor's,* or *Compustat* to obtain the following information:

- Company name and industry designation
- Preferred stock (number shares outstanding and dollar amount)
- Common stock (number shares outstanding and dollar amount)
- Retained earnings
- Total shareholders' equity
- Total current liabilities
- Total long-term liabilities
- Total assets
- Earnings per share
- Market price (year-end or representative price)

REQUIRED

a. For each company, compute the financial leverage ratios.
b. For each company, compute the composition ratios (% total assets).
c. For each company, compute the price-to-earnings ratio and the market-to-book value ratio.
d. Identify any other useful ratios or relationships.
e. Write a short memo comparing and contrasting the financial structure and risks associated with the three companies.

Interpreting Financial Statements: Shareholders' Equity

10–70 DUD Computer is a private company. DUD's major product lines are CAD/CAM Computervision design systems, midrange computers, and computer services. DUD had $1.26 billion in debt at the end of 1995. DUD's losses were more than half a billion dollars and its net worth (retained earnings) was a negative $674.9 million. It will be in default on its loan covenants if it fails to secure new financing by the end of 1997. Its summary financial trends were:

	1995	1994
Revenue ($ billions)	$1.44	$1.55
Net (loss) ($ millions)	($562.8)*	($172.8)
Loss per share	($9.02)	($3.21)

*Includes nonrecurring charges of $352.2 million.

REQUIRED

a. A recent comment was made that the company is still in peril from too much debt. On what basis do you suppose this comment was made?
b. Construct a scenario where this level of debt and the comment above would be premature.
c. Using the data given above, calculate the net loss and loss per share after *excluding* the nonrecurring charges.

d. The company's president and CEO suggested that DUD had positive cash flow and would have been profitable if it weren't for huge debt payments and write-downs. Critique the president's conclusions. Is it possible for a company with such huge losses to have positive cash flows? Why? Is it also possible for a company's debt payments to affect its net income? Why?

Financial Statement Impact: Earnings per Share

WHAT WOULD YOU DO?

10–71 Premier Anesthesia is a high-tech health services provider that transformed itself from a private company to a public company in 1992. At the end of 1992, its price-to-earnings ratio was 45.0, based on *estimated* 1992 earnings. Its quarterly earnings for the first and second quarter of 1992 were, respectively, 3 cents and 6 cents a share. Curiously, its year-to-date EPS at the end of the second quarter of 1992 was 11 cents per share (*WSJ*, December 8, 1992, p. C1). Premier Anesthesia's market price more than doubled during the last half of 1992 (from less than $6.00 per share to more than $14 per share).

REQUIRED

a. Comment on the discrepancy between the reported earnings-per-share data.
b. Comment on Premier Anesthesia's spectacular share prices relative to its earnings.

Additional Data

A reporter, Mr. Craig Torres, reported that ". . . much of Premier's interest earnings come from high interest loans to a group of clinics" owned and controlled by Premier's chairman and largest stockholder (*WSJ*, December 8, 1992, p. C1). These loans carried interest rates ranging from 12% to 24%. Premier also booked management fees from the clinics as operating income. Mr. Torres suggested that ". . . Premier's earnings come not from the hospital world, but from collecting interest income. . . ." The article was headlined as "Premier Anesthesia's Earnings are Bloated by Interest Income" and "Premier Anesthesia's Earnings Get a Big Boost from Large Injection of Loan-Interest Income." Approximately 42% of the firm's earnings were derived from these related-party loans.

c. Conduct a library search for one to two articles on "related-party" issues. Summarize the key issues, as they reflect financial reporting and ethics.
d. Describe how a company may earn interest income from another company, particularly one that it controls. Comment on the ethical issues of such loans and the reporting of such income, particularly given the market's response to Premier Anesthesia's earnings. Also, comment on the interest rates, given that the prime rate during this period was around 6%.

Additional Data

Mr. Torres also reported that no buyer had been found for the clinics, so that the loans were essentially "bridge" financing until Premier Anesthesia could acquire the clinics. He reported that "Some analysts suspect Premier is deliberately delaying the deal's closing to keep collecting interest income, and thus avoid losing an important source of earnings in its first year as a public company" (*WSJ,* December 8, 1991, p. C2).

e. Reassess your conclusions about the sources of Premier's earnings, and about the ethics of its earnings management tactics.

f. What might you recommend in similar circumstances? Why?

WHAT WOULD YOU DO?

Transfer of Cash to Related Companies

10–72 Philip Morris was the founder and chairman of Lollipops, Inc., until his death in 1994. The company's performance had been sharply declining during the early 1990s. Since Morris owned the majority of the shares in Lollipops, Inc., he was very concerned about the resultant decline in the share prices and market value of Lollipops. To protect his investments, he secretly funneled $300,000,000 from other companies that he owned into purchases of additional Lollipops' shares. These new shares were used by the other companies as collateral for bank loans; they were used to finance the purchase of the shares and to support the operations of the other companies. After his death, this series of stock purchases and bank loans was revealed in the financial press, and Lollipops' shares plummeted in value!

REQUIRED

a. In what ways were these transactions unethical?

b. How might Lollipops have survived this calamity?

Research Project: Corporate Restructuring

10–73 Scan the recent financial press, such as *Business Week, Forbes,* or the *Wall Street Journal,* to identify a company that has recently changed its capital structure. Read one or more recent articles on this company and write a short summary of the restructuring, addressed as a memo to your instructor. In your memo, include all of the company's stated reasons for the restructuring, as well as any other reasons that you might consider relevant and rational. To the extent possible, show how the company's capital structure appeared before and after the restructuring.

Research Project: Changes in Capital Structure

10–74 Choose one of the companies whose financial statements appear in the Appendixes C through F. Obtain the company's most recent financial statement, or get a summary of its balance sheet in your library. Obtain any recent articles about the company that describe changes in its capital structure.

REQUIRED

a. Compare the company's capital structure as of the original financial statements (in the appropriate appendix) to the company's most recent capital structure.

b. Document or identify any possible reasons for changes in the company's capital structure.

c. Identify any problems in the firm's original capital structure, or in its most recent capital structure. What might the firm's managers do to resolve these problems?

d. Identify any inconsistencies in the firm's behavior. That is, were its actions consistent with the problems that you identified? Discuss these inconsistencies, particularly from the viewpoint of an external analyst who has to make predictions about the future success of the company.

Research Project: Changes in Capital Structure

10–75 Choose an industry that interests you. Identify the three largest firms in that industry. Obtain their most recent financial statements, or summaries thereof. Obtain any recent articles on this industry, or on the three firms you have selected.

REQUIRED

a. Discuss the similarities and differences in the three firms' capital structures.

b. Discuss how these firms might be changing their capital structure, especially in response to industry or market factors.

c. Discuss how the firms' capital structures might reflect problems or opportunities in this industry.

d. Identify any inconsistencies in the firms' management of their capital structures. That is, discuss how each firm's capital structure is responsive to both its particular circumstances, and to industry and market factors. Discuss how the firm might be acting consistently and rationally relative to these factors. Discuss any inconsistencies, particularly from the viewpoint of an external analyst who has to make predictions about the future success of the company.

USING FINANCIAL ACCOUNTING ON THE INTERNET

10–76 Clorox and Lubrizol repurchased some common stock in 1995. Locate their 10–K filings for 1995 from the EDGAR archives (**www.sec.gov/edgarhp.htm**).

REQUIRED

a. For each company, list the number of shares of common stock authorized, issued, and outstanding. Do they hold any treasury stock?

b. How many shares of common stock did each of these companies repurchase in 1995? What was the cash outflow for shares repurchased?

c. What was the impact of the repurchase program on shareholders' equity?

10–77 The web page of the NETWorth Equities Center (**networth.galt.com/www/home/equity/irr/**) contains information on several hundred corporations. In addition to links to corporate home pages or financial information, it also provides current and historical stock price data (as well as other market-related data). Access the market related data for Hewlett-Packard, Bell Atlantic, and Oracle.

REQUIRED

a. Which stock exchange is each company listed on, and what is its ticker symbol?

b. Identify the most recent stock price and price-to-earnings ratio for each company.

c. Examine the latest set of financial statements for each company from either the corporate home page or EDGAR (**www.sec.gov/edgarhp.htm**). What is the EPS and book value per share for each company?

d. For each company, compute the market-to-book value ratio and the price-to-earnings ratio (based on the annual EPS identified in part c). Based on these two ratios, which company do you believe has the highest growth expectations as per the market?

10–78 Access the web page of the NETWorth Equities Center (**networth.galt.com/ www/home/equity/irr/**), which provides links to corporate pages and market-related data. Locate the links for Applied Materials, and "click" on the ticker symbol to access information on its stock price. The menu at the page bottom contains one option labeled "Action?" Select the first down arrow and choose "graph." If you click on the "submit" button the service should return a stock price chart for the last 15 days. You have the option to expand the time horizon to any number of weeks or years.

REQUIRED

a. Set the time horizon so that it will capture enough price history to include the stock prices of October 12, 1995. Your chart should show a marked price drop for October 1995. What were the share prices before and after the drop?

b. Use the EDGAR archives (**www.sec.gov/edgarhp.htm**) to locate the 10–K filings for Applied Materials for fiscal 1994 and 1995. Examine the shareholders' equity section of the consolidated balance sheet for each year. Determine the par value of the common stock and the number of shares of common stock issued and outstanding for each year. Note your observations and check the Notes section for any explanations.

c. Is the stock price reaction consistent with the information provided in the financial statements?

S T U D Y I N G T H I S C H A P T E R
WILL ENABLE YOU TO

1. Understand why financial statements are analyzed.

2. Know where to obtain financial information.

3. Determine when financial information is comparable; alternatively, learn how to enhance the comparability of financial information that may appear to be noncomparable.

4. Identify, calculate, use, and interpret appropriate ratios.

5. Identify limitations of financial statement analyses.

A FRAMEWORK
FOR FINANCIAL
STATEMENT
ANALYSIS

INTRODUCTION

Accountants produce financial information in the form of financial statements. We have previously shown you many different excerpts from annual financial reports. In this chapter, we link many of the ratios and analytical concepts that have been previously introduced. The purpose of this chapter is to show how a comprehensive financial statement analysis can be conducted. To accomplish this purpose, we will use the entire set of financial statements from Wendy's International, Inc., which is one of the United States' largest restaurant chains, with more than 4,000 company- and franchise operated restaurants.

In order for financial information to be useful, it must be interpreted. A comprehensive set of ratios, in an organized framework, enhances the usefulness and interpretability of financial statements and eases the communication of financial information between firms and users.

USERS OF FINANCIAL STATEMENTS

Users of financial statements can be found in many sectors of the economy. Typical users include the firm's owners, creditors, managers, employees, customers, and suppliers. Users of financial statements include those who already have an economic link to the firm, as well as those who may want to have a future economic relationship.

Most users have, or intend to have, a transactional relationship with the firm. Some users may be able to obtain information directly from the firm. For example, a potential creditor can request that a credit application be prepared according to its own specifications. Potential customers or potential suppliers may also request special information as they see fit. Most users, however, will use the annual financial statements, as well as quarterly and other interim reports.

Each of these users may have different objectives while analyzing financial statements. For example:

- *Investors* will use financial statement information to help decide whether to increase or decrease their ownership interests in the firm. These decisions are based on projections of investment risks and returns. Financial ratios are widely used in making these projections.
- *Managers* will use financial statement information in many different ways, but one of the most important is in setting goals. Managerial goals may be stated in terms of increasing various profitability ratios. Goals may be stated in terms of maintaining or increasing the firm's liquidity, or they may be stated in terms of changing the capital structure in favor of more debt or more equity.
- *Customers* will often use the annual financial statements to evaluate the firm's stability and its ability to deliver, on a timely basis, the quantity and quality of goods or services that may be purchased.
- *Potential suppliers and creditors* will often be most interested in whether the firm can pay its bills.
- *Other users* of financial statements have a more distant relationship with the firm. These users include government regulators in areas such as securities trading, taxation, environmental protection, occupational health and safety, insurance and other financial markets, and foreign trade. Other interactions could occur with employee trade unions or public interest and other community groups. Finally, various economic and public policy analysts might review a firm's financial statements in their quest to create or improve legislation affecting many broad areas of commerce and social welfare. Any of these groups might want to explore how the firm has affected various components of society.

SOURCES OF FINANCIAL INFORMATION

In addition to the basic business financial statements and disclosures that we have described in earlier chapters, various other types of financial information are available to financial analysts. These other types of information may be used in combination with financial statements. For example, most regulatory agencies require firms to prepare special-purpose regulatory reports, such as tax returns or environmental impact statements. The SEC also requires special reports each year and each quarter. The SEC's annual report is called a Form 10-K, which is discussed more thoroughly in Chapter 14. This is an expanded variation on the firm's annual report, which can frequently be used to clarify issues of concern or ambiguity in the annual report.

In addition to annual reports filed with the SEC, public companies must also file quarterly reports, which are less detailed than the annual reports. Further, whenever major events occur that require public disclosure, public firms are also required to file special reports with the SEC designed to provide immediate information to any interested party. Events that must be reported include replacement of the firm's auditor, a major acquisition or disposition of a business segment, or any major news announcement.

Other sources of public information that are more readily available include various business periodicals such as the *Wall Street Journal, Business Week, Forbes, Fortune, Barron's,* or various newsletters that specialize in certain industries or locales. Even your local newspaper will often have a business section on either a weekly or daily basis.

Investment advisory services also publish summary information about specific firms and industries. Some of the more well known of these include *Standard & Poors, Moody's, Value Line, Dun & Bradstreet's,* and *Robert Morris and Associates.* Such services provide condensed information from company annual reports. This information is usually prepared in a standardized format. The process of "homogenizing" the information from the annual report, however, may obscure some of the important insights that could have been obtained from the report itself. One advantage of these services is their inclusion of interpretations of the financial results and their opinions regarding the future prospects of the companies.

The major source of financial information with which we will be concerned is the firm's **annual report.** A major portion of the 1994 annual report of Wendy's is included in Appendix D, and will be referenced throughout our discussion. Such reports, in their entirety, usually contain the following elements (see Appendix D for examples of each):

1. Management discussion and analysis (MDA), which is a narrative report providing a qualitative description of the year's highlights. This section may also include a letter from the CEO.
2. Independent accountant's report (auditor's report), which is usually presented as an unqualified opinion, or in some version of a qualified opinion regarding the financial statements (see Chapter 14). Annual reports generally include management's statement of responsibility for the information contained in the financial statements.
3. Primary financial statements, which include the balance sheet, the income statement, and the statement of cash flows.
4. Secondary financial statements, which may include the statement of shareholders' equity, other reconciliations related to the cash flow statement, and other disclosures regarding the primary financial statements.
5. Notes to the financial statements, which include a variety of supplementary disclosures, such as quarterly data, business segment information, and trend information in the form of 5- or 10-year comparisons of selected financial data or key ratios.

This set of information in the annual report provides the basis for much of the analysis conducted by users of financial statements. Little formal analysis can be applied to the qualitative statements contained in the discussion sections and in the notes. However, the qualitative and narrative discussions can provide much insight into many of the relationships that are revealed by the ratio calculations. Both the quantitative and qualitative information must be reviewed by the conscientious analyst.

Later in this chapter, we provide a framework for reviewing this information in order to assess the firm's past performance and its future potential. For the remainder of the chapter, we focus exclusively on financial statement analysis from the perspective of an equity investor. Although many of the same ratios would be used by creditors and many of the other financial statement users identified earlier, we will take an *investor focus* as we develop and illustrate our framework.

BASIS OF COMPARISON

One of the analyst's first decisions must be to identify the basis of comparison. That is, what data are to be used to compare and evaluate the target firm? Financial data do not exist in a vacuum. Analyzing financial statements for a single year for one firm is like reporting only part of a football score (e.g., 14)! Therefore, financial statement analysis is often concerned with comparing the current year's results with other, related results. The choices include:

1. the prior year(s),
2. another similar firm in the same industry,
3. another firm in which the analyst may invest,
4. all firms in the same industry and/or industry averages, or
5. benchmarks or targets that have been previously established, e.g., lending or investing criteria.

The analyst must determine that a comparable and useful reference is available with which to compare the target firm. Usually, the prior year or years are a good reference point with which to begin. Any statements that include the effects of a major financial restructuring or merger or similar nonrecurring event would generally be noncomparable. In other words, before comparing a firm's results with the prior year, the analyst must examine both sets of statements and notes to determine whether a significant unusual event occurred.

If significant unusual events have occurred that would distort comparisons, then the financial statements may need to be restated or rearranged to make them more comparable. Restatements may be necessary in the following situations:

- mergers or major acquisitions,
- discontinued operations or major dispositions,
- changes in accounting principles or estimates,
- extraordinary items (on the income statement),
- changes in account classifications,
- changes in reporting periods (e.g., fiscal periods),
- shifts in industry structure or classification, or
- any other unusual or nonrecurring event.

It is beyond the scope of this text to illustrate all of these possible restatements, but several examples are given in the case discussion in the latter part of this chapter. The primary guideline is that "more comparability is better." Financial information from firms might be comparable if the firms:

- operate in the same country,
- follow similar accounting practices,
- are of similar size (revenues and/or assets),
- produce similar products or services, and
- have a similar capital structure.

Although other important dimensions of comparability may be available, size, capital structure, and product mix are the most important for our purposes. The analyst must decide whether differences in these areas are material, or whether they might have an impact on the final conclusions. Comparability is a subjective and qualitative issue that can never be quantified by a numerical index.

Thus far, we have identified four major steps that must be accomplished before starting to calculate financial statement ratios:

1. Identify the purpose and objectives of the analysis.
2. Review the financial statements, notes, and audit opinion to identify any unusual events or characteristics and to become familiar with the nature of the firm's operations.
3. Determine whether any restatements due to mergers, discontinued operations, etc., are necessary to enhance the comparability of the firm's financial statements.

4. Determine whether the firm's size, capital structure, and product mix are sufficiently comparable (between firms or time periods) to proceed with the ratio calculations.

The next major step is to conduct horizontal and vertical analyses of the financial statements. Usually, this analysis begins with the income statement, including all of its major revenue and expense items. **Horizontal analysis** focuses on year-to-year changes or growth for each major element in the income statement. Common-size financial statements, a tool employed in **vertical analysis,** examine the percentage composition of the income statement. Percentages are calculated on the basis of net revenues, where each item on the income statement is separately analyzed.

Horizontal and vertical analyses of the major subtotals in the balance sheet and in the cash flow statement should also be conducted. The results of these analyses will focus attention on areas of significant changes. Such analyses do not provide complete answers. Rather, they indicate areas of concern that require further investigation. Therefore, step 5 in our framework is:

5. Conduct horizontal and vertical analyses of each financial statement, with special emphasis on the income statement. Identify any unusual trends.

Categories of Financial Ratios

Analysts find it useful to classify ratios into broad groupings, based on the characteristics that particular ratios are intended to measure. In this section, we discuss ratios under four major headings that are widely employed by analysts: liquidity, profitability, capital structure, and investor ratios.

Liquidity Ratios. Liquidity ratios indicate the short-term solvency of the firm. They also indicate how effectively the firm is managing its working capital. Exhibit 11–1 shows the formulas used in computing a representative set of liquidity ratios. Each of these ratios has been described earlier in the text, as indicated by the chapter references in the exhibit. The **current ratio** and **quick ratio** are measures of solvency. Other measures of cash availability might also be used to indicate how many days the firm could operate using only its current cash balances. A limitation of these ratios is that they do not reflect the availability of short-term credit. Many firms operate with decreasing levels of liquidity as they rely more heavily on "lines of credit" that can be used, or repaid, on a daily basis. Humana, Inc. (a health care insurance and hospital company), reported zero cash on its balance sheet for three years (1990–1992)! In many cases, high current or quick ratios will indicate mismanagement or wasteful investment in working capital. Some firms may just have too much liquidity!

The **number of days in inventory** indicates how quickly the firm is "turning" its inventory. Comparative industry statistics can often be used to evaluate the days in inventory. Certainly, comparisons with the prior periods will indicate whether the turnover has increased or decreased. Changes in product mix will dramatically affect the inventory ratios.

EXHIBIT 11–1
SUMMARY OF LIQUIDITY RATIOS

$$\text{Current ratio} = \frac{\text{Current Assets}}{\text{Current Liabilities}}$$
(Chapter 3)

$$\text{Quick ratio} = \frac{(\text{Cash + Cash Equivalents + Accounts Receivable})}{\text{Current Liabilities}}$$
(Chapter 3)

$$\text{Average sales per day} = \frac{\text{Sales Revenue}}{365}$$
(Chapter 6)

$$\text{Collection period} = \frac{\text{Accounts Receivable}}{\text{Average Sales per Day}}$$
(Chapter 6)

$$\text{Cost of goods sold per day} = \frac{\text{Cost of Goods Sold}}{365}$$
(Chapter 6)

$$\text{Number of days' sales in ending inventory (NDS)} = \frac{\text{Ending Inventory}}{\text{Cost of Goods Sold per day}}$$
(Chapter 6)

Step 6 in our framework encompasses liquidity ratios:

6. Calculate the basic liquidity ratios. In cases where liquidity seems to be too high, or too low, conduct further analyses as necessary.

Profitability Ratios. Profitability ratios are the second major focus of analysis for any investor. Without profits, there will be no return to the investor. Without profits, the investor would usually not want to invest. The primary profitability ratios are defined in Exhibit 11–2; they are referenced to the earlier chapters in which they were initially discussed.

The **gross profit percentage** is the first source of profitability for a manufacturing or merchandising firm. The data for the gross profit margin are found in the first sections of the income statement. These data indicate the level of profits earned from buying and reselling goods. A decreasing gross profit percentage may indicate decreased sales prices, higher costs of production, or a shift from high-profit to low-profit products.

The **operating income ratio** is the second indicator of profitability because it includes all of the other normal and recurring operating costs. Increasing or stable levels of operating income indicate sustainability of the firm's profits. Decreasing operating income ratios usually indicate a need for the firm to examine its production efficiency, its marketing strategies, and its control of administrative costs.

The most important profitability ratio from an investor's viewpoint is the **return on equity (ROE) ratio.** It is often called ROI, return on investment ratio, because it indicates the annual rate of return to the firm's investors or owners. Return on equity represents the residual return that is available to owners after deducting all other financing costs.

The **return on assets (ROA) ratio** indicates the rate of return on the firm's assets. It can be used to compare rates of return with alternative investments that could be

Gross Profit Percentage	=	$\dfrac{\text{Gross Profit}}{\text{Net Sales Revenue}}$ (Chapter 6)
Operating Income Percentage	=	$\dfrac{\text{Operating Income}}{\text{Sales Revenue}}$ (Chapter 4)
Return on Equity	=	$\dfrac{\text{Net Income}}{\text{Average Shareholders' Equity}}$ (Chapter 4)
Return on Assets	=	$\dfrac{\text{Net Income} + (\text{Interest Expense} \times [1 - \text{Tax Rate}])}{\text{Average Total Assets}}$ (Chapter 4)
Cash Return on Assets	=	$\dfrac{\text{Cash Flow from Operating Activities} + \text{Interest Paid}}{\text{Average Total Assets}}$ (Chapter 5)
Quality of Income	=	$\dfrac{\text{Cash Flow from Operating Activities}}{\text{Net Income}}$ (Chapter 5)

EXHIBIT 11–2
SUMMARY OF PROFITABILITY RATIOS

undertaken. Just as in the adjusted net income percentage described earlier, ROA adjusts for the effects of debt financing by removing the after-tax effects of interest expense. It can be used to compare profitability across firms and over different time periods.

Some analysts may prefer to analyze the firm's profitability and financial returns in terms of cash, and not in terms of accrual-based net income. The **cash return on assets ratio** should be compared with the corresponding profitability ratios based on net income, and ROA. Results that appear to be inconsistent should be examined carefully. These ratios look at financial returns to the firm in terms of cash, and not in terms of accrual-based net income. As such, the cash-based profitability ratios are often viewed as more objective by analysts.

The final profitability ratio, **quality of income,** is a direct comparison between cash flows from operating activities (CFOA) and net income (NI). The analyst must examine trends within the same company to determine that CFOA is not decreasing relative to NI. Therefore, step 7 in our financial statement analysis framework is:

7. Calculate profitability ratios based on net income and on cash flows from operating activities. Evaluate trends in profitability. Compare the appropriate NI and CFOA ratios for consistency. Compare profitability ratios across similar companies and against industry averages.

Capital Structure. Capital structure analysis assesses the firm's strategies for financing its assets. Capital structure indicates the relative amounts of debt and equity capital. The analyst evaluates how those sources change, and how they compare with other firms in the same industry. The analyst tries to gain insight into the firm's decisions about capital sources in order to predict future capital financing decisions. An investor would surely like to know whether the firm is likely to issue new debt or sell additional shares of stock. Identifying shifts in capital structure over time may indicate how the firm will make future decisions about sources of capital. The major ways to examine capital structure are summarized in Exhibit 11–3.

EXHIBIT 11–3
SUMMARY OF CAPITAL
STRUCTURE RATIOS

Percentage Composition = The results of the vertical analysis of right side of the balance sheet, such that the sum of all sources of capital must be 100%: (Chapter 3)

$$\frac{\text{Current Liabilities}}{\text{Total Liabilities and Shareholders' Equity}}$$

$$\frac{\text{Long-term Debt}}{\text{Total Liabilities and Shareholders' Equity}}$$

$$\frac{\text{Deferred Taxes + Other Similar Liabilities}}{\text{Total Liabilities and Shareholders' Equity}}$$

$$\frac{\text{Shareholders' Equity}}{\text{Total Liabilities and Shareholders' Equity}}$$

Financial Leverage (also called Debt to Assets) = $\dfrac{\text{Total Liabilities}}{\text{Total Assets}}$ (Chapters 3, 10)

Times Interest Earned = $\dfrac{\text{Earnings Before Interest and Taxes (EBIT)}}{\text{Interest Expense}}$ (Chapter 4)

Percentage composition analysis is the starting point for any analysis of capital structure. It provides a description of the relative amounts of capital obtained from each major source of financing. The analyst will examine the percentage composition results to note changes from the prior year. The analyst will also compare percentage composition ratios with similar firms and with industry averages.

Note that the **financial leverage ratio** is simply a variation on percentage composition analysis. All liabilities are added, and then divided by total assets (which, by definition, must equal total liabilities and shareholders' equity). It is not always clear whether to include deferred taxes and other similar liabilities. In many cases, because of recent changes in accounting rules regarding deferred taxes, the analyst will find that this category of liabilities may be dominant as a source of capital.

The other capital structure ratio is also informative about the financing strategies that the firm has chosen. The **times interest earned ratio** is an indicator of relative risk. The lower the times interest earned, the higher the risk of bankruptcy or other default.

Times interest earned indicates the "cushion" or margin of safety that the firm enjoys in meeting its interest expenses. A ratio close to 100% indicates that the firm is barely covering its interest expenses. Any slight decrease in earnings would then result in an inability to cover the interest expenses. As usual, trends in this ratio should be monitored. Therefore, step 8 in our financial statement analysis framework is:

8. Evaluate the firm's capital structure with special emphasis on trends in the percentage composition ratios.

Investor Ratios. Investor ratios were introduced in Chapter 10. These ratios all relate to an external dimension of ownership interest. Most indicate how the firm is performing with regard to the market value of its shares. A listing of investor ratios appears in Exhibit 11–4.

EXHIBIT 11–4
SUMMARY OF INVESTOR RATIOS

$$\text{Earnings per Share (EPS)} = \frac{\text{Net Income}}{\substack{\text{Weighted Average Number of} \\ \text{Shares Outstanding}}}$$
(Chapter 10)

$$\text{Market to Book Value} = \frac{\text{Market Price per Share}}{\text{Book Value per Share}}$$
(Chapter 10)

$$\text{Price-to-Earnings (P/E)} = \frac{\text{Market Price per Share}}{\text{Earnings per Share}}$$
(Chapter 10)

The **earnings-per-share (EPS) ratio** indicates the net income earned by each share of outstanding stock. It is most often used by investors as a primary comparison of performance and profitability across different companies. However, we believe that it is overemphasized. It should not be used in isolation outside the context of other dimensions of financial performance. Furthermore, it should only be used in conjunction with EPS from prior years and/or with EPS for other comparable firms.

The **market-to-book value ratio** indicates the relationship between the market's valuation of the firm and the book values shown in the firm's financial statements. It is often used by investors to select targets of opportunity where the market is thought to undervalue a particular firm. It can also be used to influence an investor's decision to sell shares in a firm, where the market may overvalue the firm's assets. On the other hand, a high market-to-book ratio may reflect the fact that financial accounting may undervalue the firm's recorded assets—many valuable economic resources of the firm may not even appear on the balance sheet.

The **price-to-earnings (P/E) ratio** indicates the relationship between market prices and earnings and is widely used to compare firms. Investors will often establish guidelines, or cutoffs, such that they only purchase shares with a P/E of less than 30. In any event, the P/E ratio indicates the interaction between stock market prices and the income statement. As such, it is a convenient and widely accessible way to compare alternative investment opportunities.

Finally, Step 9 in our financial statement analysis framework is:

9. Examine the firm's market performance using EPS, P/E, and market-to-book value ratios.

Final Steps

After assembling this myriad of ratios, the astute analyst must ask a series of questions:

So what?   What's missing?   How do we predict the future?

Obviously, there are no easy recipes in this area! The analyst must look for inconsistencies and ambiguities that are evidenced in peculiar trends or unusual ratio results. Many ratios merely provide clues that require the analyst to look further at the notes to determine events and accounting treatments that are the cause of the numbers in the financial statements. The thoughtful analyst will always go back and forth between the numerical calculations and the underlying information in the notes, while trying to decipher reality. Therefore, the last step is:

10. Examine any inconsistencies in the ratio results, and review the notes for further clarification. Then, recalculate the ratios based on new insight and information obtained from the notes. Finally, try to estimate how the firm's liquidity, profitability, capital structure, and investor performance may change in the future.

Financial Statement Analysis Framework

In summary, our entire financial statement analysis framework is:

1. Identify the purpose and objectives of the analysis. Who is the user, and what decisions are to be made after the analysis?
2. Review the financial statements, notes, and audit opinion to identify any unusual events or characteristics.
3. Determine whether any restatements due to mergers, discontinued operations, accounting changes, or other factors are necessary to enhance the comparability of the statements.
4. Determine whether the firm's size, capital structure, and product mix are appropriate to proceed with the ratio calculations.
5. Conduct horizontal and vertical analyses of each financial statement, with special emphasis on the income statement. Identify any unusual trends.
6. Calculate the basic liquidity ratios. In cases where liquidity seems to be too high, or too low, conduct further analyses as necessary.
7. Calculate profitability ratios based on net income and on cash flow from operating activities. Evaluate trends in profitability. Compare the appropriate NI and CFO ratios for consistency. Compare profitability ratios across similar companies and against industry averages.
8. Evaluate the firm's capital structure with special emphasis on trends in the percentage composition ratios.
9. Examine the firm's market performance using EPS, P/E, and market-to-book value ratios.
10. Examine any inconsistencies in the ratio results. Review the notes for further clarification. Recalculate the ratios based on new insight and information obtained

from the notes. Try to estimate how the firm's liquidity, profitability, capital structure, and investor performance may change in the future.

In this section, we apply our financial statement analysis framework to Wendy's International, Inc. We chose the Wendy's statements because they are representative of how most large companies present their financial data and because their statements include a variety of interesting, but typical, complications. For instance, the OshKosh B'Gosh statements that you have examined already present fairly straightforward financial reporting formats. In contrast, Wendy's provides an interesting dose of real-world complexity where we can concentrate as much on the sources of information as on the numerical calculations. We have taken an investor focus to this analysis, concentrating on information that might be useful to someone contemplating purchasing shares of Wendy's common stock.

FINANCIAL STATEMENT ANALYSIS, WENDY'S INTERNATIONAL, INC.

Initial Review of Wendy's International, Inc.

The independent auditor's report by Coopers & Lybrand is a fairly typical, unqualified opinion (Appendix D). Note that the fiscal year ended on different dates in 1995 and 1994. It is somewhat unusual to have a different fiscal year-end each year; however, in an industry that is open and available for business each day, the number of days in each fiscal period may be significant. Because Wendy's financial statements are based on 52 weeks in both 1995 and 1994, each year includes the same number of weekdays and weekends.

Although some unique events occurred during each year, the statements have sufficient detail to permit comparison across the 1995 and 1994 fiscal years. We do not extend this analysis to industry comparisons because that is a topic for more advanced courses. We note also that all of the dollar amounts, except the per-share amounts, are stated in thousands of dollars. As you have already seen, this type of rounding is quite typical in financial reporting. Such rounding will make no significant difference in the ratio results.

Horizontal and Vertical Analyses of Wendy's International, Inc.

Horizontal and vertical analyses of Wendy's income statements for fiscal 1995 and 1994 appear in Exhibits 11–5 and 11–6, respectively. The corresponding analyses of Wendy's balance sheets are presented in Exhibits 11–7 and 11–8.

The horizontal analysis for Wendy's income statement, Exhibit 11–5, indicates that net sales grew about 4.8% in fiscal 1995. Expenses grew in a smaller proportion than net sales (3.7% vs. 4.8%). The more interesting comparison relates to net earnings, which increased 22.5% in 1995. Normally, earnings will grow faster than sales because at least some of the firm's expenses, such as depreciation and administrative costs, do not vary directly with sales from year to year. Large swings in income are major indicators of unusual events affecting the firm.

EXHIBIT 11–5
HORIZONTAL ANALYSIS OF
INCOME STATEMENT

Wendy's International, Inc.
Income Statement: Horizontal Analysis
Fifty-Two Weeks Ended January 1, 1995, and January 2, 1994
(In Thousands, Except Per-Share Data)

	1995	Percent Change	1994
Revenues			
Retail sales	$1,256,192	+ 4.8%	$1,198,777
Royalties	113,558	+ 8.5	104,663
Other	28,107	+ 68.7	16,655
	1,397,857	+ 5.9	1,320,095
Costs and expenses			
Cost of sales	731,691	+ 3.7	705,671
Company restaurant operating costs	330,480	+ 3.5	319,367
General and administrative expenses	108,254	+ 6.0	102,161
Depreciation and amortization of property and equipment	68,070	+ 3.7	65,655
Interest, net	9,891	– 15.5	11,706
	1,248,386	+ 3.6	1,204,560
Income before income taxes	149,471	+ 29.4	115,535
Income taxes	52,315	+ 44.2	36,268
Net income	$ 97,156	+ 22.5%	$79,267
Primary earnings per share	$.93	+ 20.8%	$.77
Dividends per share	$.24		$.24
Primary shares	104,238		102,897

EXHIBIT 11–6 VERTICAL ANALYSIS OF INCOME STATEMENT

Wendy's International, Inc.
Income Statement: Vertical Analysis
Fifty-Two Weeks Ended January 1, 1995, and January 2, 1994
(In Thousands, Except Per-Share Data)

	1995		1994	
	Dollars	**%**	**Dollars**	**%**
Revenues				
Retail sales	$1,256,192	89.9%	$1,198,777	90.8%
Royalties	113,558	8.1	104,663	7.9
Other	28,107	2.0	16,655	1.3
	1,397,857	100.0	1,320,095	100.0
Costs and expenses				
Cost of sales	731,691	52.3	705,671	53.4
Company restaurant operating costs	330,480	23.7	319,367	24.2
General and administrative expenses	108,254	7.7	102,161	7.7
Depreciation and amortization of property and equipment	68,070	4.9	65,655	5.0
Interest, net	9,891	.7	11,706	.9
	1,248,386	89.3	1,204,560	91.2
Income before income taxes	149,471	10.7	115,535	8.8
Income taxes	52,315	3.7	36,268	2.8
Net income	$97,156	7.0%	$79,267	6.0%

The vertical analysis for Wendy's income statement, Exhibit 11–6, indicates that cost of sales has actually declined as a percent of net sales (revenue). This is a desirable trend and one that is difficult to accomplish in most retail industries, especially in food sales. Total costs and expenses have also declined in percentage terms. Net earnings, as a percent of net sales, increased slightly in 1995.

EXHIBIT 11–7
HORIZONTAL ANALYSIS
OF BALANCE SHEET

Wendy's International, Inc.
Balance Sheet: Horizontal Analysis
January 1, 1995 and January 2, 1994
(dollars in thousands)

	January 1 1995	Percent Change 1994 to 1995	January 2 1994
Assets			
Current assets			
Cash and cash equivalents	$ 119,639	+66.8%	$ 71,698
Short-term investments, at market	15,292	−62.4	40,647
Accounts receivable, net	28,015	+2.3	27,381
Notes receivable, net	7,446	+41.6	5,259
Deferred income taxes	13,067	+6.7	12,244
Inventories and other	19,702	−8.3	21,478
	203,161	+13.7	178,707
Property and equipment, at cost			
Land	222,671	+9.3	203,651
Buildings	359,503	+9.3	329,023
Leasehold improvements	189,243	+3.7	182,519
Restaurant equipment	335,474	+16.0	289,242
Other equipment	53,265	−18.3	65,197
Capital leases	63,531	−1.0	64,148
	1,223,687	+7.9	1,133,780
Accumulated depreciation and amortization	(457,368)	+7.3	(426,496)
	766,319	+8.3	707,284
Cost in excess of net assets acquired, net	30,780	+26.6	24,314
Deferred income taxes	16,142	+5.8	15,250
Other assets	69,690	−1.7	70,931
	$1,086,092	+9.0%	$ 996,486

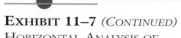

Exhibit 11–7 (*Continued*)
Horizontal Analysis of
Balance Sheet *Continued*

	January 1 1995	Percent Change 1994 to 1995	January 2 1994
Liabilities and shareholders' equity			
Current liabilities			
Accounts and drafts payable	$ 69,845	+1.6%	$ 68,735
Accrued expenses			
Salaries and wages	22,173	+36.1	16,288
Taxes	15,248	+2.1	14,935
Insurance	26,037	+22.0	21,345
Other	11,409	+2.2	11,160
Income taxes	1,683	−41.9	2,896
Deferred income taxes	3,108	+35.2	2,299
Current portion of long-term obligations	57,674	+927.9	5,611
	207,177	+44.6	143,269
Long-term obligations			
Term debt	104,842	−33.1	156,741
Capital leases	40,018	−8.8	43,892
	144,860	−27.8	200,633
Deferred income taxes	39,799	−2.6	40,859
Other long-term liabilities	12,758	+16.7	10,930
Commitments and contingencies			
Shareholders' equity			
Preferred stock, authorized: 250,000 shares			
Common stock: $0.10 stated value, authorized: 200,000,000 shares			
Issued: 101,787,000 and 100,823,000 shares, respectively	10,179	+1.0	10,082
Capital in excess of stated value	171,004	+6.1	161,238
Retained earnings	503,712	+16.9	430,866
Translation adjustments	(19)	−100.1	1,347
Pension liability adjustment	(3,212)	−24.9	(2,572)
	681,664	+13.4	600,961
Treasury stock at cost: 29,000 shares	(166)		(166)
	681,498	+13.4	600,795
	$1,086,092	+9.0%	$996,486

EXHIBIT 11–8
VERTICAL ANALYSIS
OF BALANCE SHEET

Wendy's International, Inc.
Balance Sheet: Vertical Analysis
January 1, 1995, and January 2, 1994
(dollars in thousands)

	January 1, 1995		January 2, 1994	
	Dollars	%	Dollars	%
Assets				
Current assets				
Cash and cash equivalents	$ 119,639	11.0%	$ 71,698	7.2%
Short-term investments, at market	15,292	1.4	40,647	4.1
Accounts receivable, net	28,015	2.6	27,381	2.7
Notes receivable, net	7,446	.7	5,259	.5
Deferred income taxes	13,067	1.2	12,244	1.2
Inventories and other	19,702	1.8	21,478	2.2
	203,161	18.7	178,707	17.9
Property and equipment, at cost				
Land	222,671	20.5	203,651	20.4
Buildings	359,503	33.1	329,023	33.0
Leasehold improvements	189,243	17.4	182,519	18.3
Restaurant equipment	335,474	30.9	289,242	29.0
Other equipment	53,265	4.9	65,197	6.5
Capital leases	63,531	5.9	64,148	6.4
	1,223,687	112.7	1,133,780	113.8
Accumulated depreciation and amortization	(457,368)	(42.1)	(426,496)	(42.8)
	766,319	70.6	707,284	71.0
Cost in excess of net assets acquired, net	30,780	2.8	24,314	2.4
Deferred income taxes	16,142	1.5	15,250	1.5
Other assets	69,690	6.4	70,931	7.1
	$1,086,092	100.0%	$ 996,486	100.0%

 Liquidity Analysis of Wendy's International, Inc.

Wendy's liquidity ratios for each fiscal year are calculated in Exhibit 11–9, and provide the following insights. Wendy's current ratio and quick ratio have declined somewhat. This is partly due to the significant increase in current maturities of long-term debt. Another factor affecting the current ratio is a decrease in the number of days' sales in inventory, from 11 days to less than 10 days. On the whole, Wendy's liquidity ratios have declined. An analyst must consider these liquidity issues in the context of profitability and other ratios.

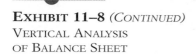

EXHIBIT 11–8 (*CONTINUED*)
VERTICAL ANALYSIS
OF BALANCE SHEET

	January 1, 1995		January 2, 1994	
	Dollars	%	Dollars	%
Liabilities and shareholders' equity				
Current liabilities				
Accounts and drafts payable	$ 69,845	6.4%	$ 68,735	6.9%
Accrued expenses				
Salaries and wages	22,173	2.0	16,288	1.6
Taxes	15,248	1.4	14,935	1.5
Insurance	26,037	2.2	21,345	2.1
Other	11,409	1.1	11,160	1.1
Income taxes	1,683	.2	2,896	.3
Deferred income taxes	3,108	.3	2,299	.3
Current portion of long-term obligations	57,674	5.3	5,611	.6
	207,177	19.1	143,269	14.4
Long-term obligations				
Term debt	104,842	9.6	156,741	15.7
Capital leases	40,018	3.7	43,892	4.4
	144,860	13.3	200,633	20.1
Deferred income taxes	39,799	3.7	40,859	4.1
Other long-term liabilities	12,758	1.2	10,930	1.1
Commitments and contingencies				
Shareholders' equity				
Preferred stock, authorized: 250,000 shares				
Common stock: $0.10 stated value, authorized: 200,000,000 shares Issued: 101,787,000 and 100,823,000 shares, respectively	10,179	.9	10,082	1.0
Capital in excess of stated value	171,004	15.7	161,238	16.2
Retained earnings	503,712	46.4	430,866	43.2
Translation adjustments	(19)	(.0)	1,347	.0
Pension liability adjustment	(3,212)	(.3)	(2,572)	(.2)
	681,664	62.7	600,961	60.3
Treasury stock at cost: 29,000 shares	(166)	(.0)	(166)	(.0)
	681,498	62.7%	600,795	60.3%
	$1,086,092	100.0%	$996,486	100.0%

EXHIBIT 11–9   LIQUIDITY ANALYSIS

		Wendy's International, Inc. Liquidity Ratios, 1995 and 1994 (dollars in thousands)		
Ratio		**Formula**	**1995**	**1994**
Current ratio	=	$\dfrac{\text{Current assets}}{\text{Current liabilities}}$ =	$\dfrac{\$203{,}161}{\$207{,}177}$	$\dfrac{\$178{,}707}{\$143{,}269}$
		=	.98	1.25
Quick ratio	=	$\dfrac{\substack{\text{Cash and equivalents,}\\\text{short-term}\\\text{investments, and}\\\text{accounts receivable}}}{\text{Current liabilities}}$ =	$\dfrac{\$119{,}639 + 15{,}262 +\ 28{,}015}{\$207{,}177}$	$\dfrac{\$71{,}698 + 40{,}647 +\ 27{,}381}{\$143{,}269}$
		=	.79	.98
Average sales per day	=	$\dfrac{\text{Sales revenue}}{\text{Days in the year}^*}$ =	$\dfrac{\$1{,}256{,}192}{364}$	$\dfrac{\$1{,}198{,}777}{364}$
		=	$3{,}451	$3{,}293
Collection period	=	$\dfrac{\text{Accounts receivable}^\dagger}{\text{Average sales per day}}$ =	$\dfrac{\$28{,}015}{\$3{,}451}$	$\dfrac{\$27{,}381}{\$3{,}293}$
		=	8.1 days	8.3 days
Cost of goods sold per day	=	$\dfrac{\text{Cost of goods sold}}{\text{Days in the year}^*}$ =	$\dfrac{\$731{,}691}{364}$	$\dfrac{\$705{,}671}{364}$
		=	$2{,}010	$1{,}939
Number of days' sales in ending inventory	–	$\dfrac{\text{Ending inventory}}{\text{Cost of goods sold per day}}$ =	$\dfrac{\$19{,}702}{\$2{,}010}$	$\dfrac{\$21{,}478}{\$1{,}939}$
		=	9.8 days	11.1 days

*The number of days in the reporting years is 364 days (52 weeks × 7 days = 364).

†Because gross receivables are used in this ratio, the balances in the Allowance for uncollectible accounts usually must be added to the net accounts receivable. Because this adjustment is not material for Wendy's, we have used net accounts receivable in the calculation.

Profitability Analysis of Wendy's International, Inc.

Wendy's profitability ratios are calculated in Exhibit 11–10. The operating income ratio indicates an increase in profitability. Return on equity and return on assets have both increased as a result. These trends in profitability ratios would be encouraging for most investors.

On the other hand, the cash-based profitability ratios indicate mixed trends. The statement of cash flows (Appendix D) shows that operating cash flows increased from $146,676,000 in 1994 to $165,711,000 in 1995. Wendy's cash return on assets increased slightly, from 16.9% to 17.0%. Its quality of income declined, from 185% to 171%.

These results dictate that the investor look more closely at the sources of cash flow from operations to determine whether they are likely to continue at these same levels. As we indicated earlier, most investors prefer cash flows to net income, if they have to make a choice. Wendy's exhibits increasing trends in profitability based on net earnings and accrual-based calculations. On the other hand, the cash flow-based ratios seem mixed. The investor must decide on which set of profitability ratios to rely most heavily.

EXHIBIT 11–10   PROFITABILITY ANALYSIS

Ratio		Formula		1995	1994
		Wendy's International, Inc. **Profitability Ratios, 1995 and 1994** **(Dollars in Thousands)**			
Operating income percentage	=	$\dfrac{\text{Operating income}}{\text{Sales revenue}}$	=	$\dfrac{\$149,471}{\$1,256,192}$	$\dfrac{\$115,535}{\$1,198,777}$
			=	11.9%	9.6%
Return on equity	=	$\dfrac{\text{Net income}}{\text{Shareholders' equity}}$	=	$\dfrac{\$97,156}{\$681,498}$	$\dfrac{\$79,267}{\$600,795}$
			=	14.3%	13.2%
Return on assets†	=	$\dfrac{\text{Net income} + [\text{Interest expense} \times (1 - \text{tax rate})]}{\text{Average total assets}}$	=	$\dfrac{\$103,585}{\$1,086,092}$	$\dfrac{\$87,297}{\$996,486}$
			=	9.5%	8.8%
Cash return on assets	=	$\dfrac{\text{Cash flow from operating activities} + \text{Interest paid}}{\text{Average total assets}}$	=	$\dfrac{\$165,711 + 19,236}{\$1,086,092}$	$\dfrac{\$146,676 + 21,874}{\$996,486}$
			=	17.0%	16.9%
Quality of income	=	$\dfrac{\text{Cash flow from operating activities}}{\text{Operating income}}$	=	$\dfrac{\$165,711}{\$97,156}$	$\dfrac{\$146,676}{\$79,267}$
			=	171%	185%

†Calculated using Wendy's effective tax rates shown in the notes, 35.0% in 1995 and 31.4% in 1994. In 1995, the numerator is $103,585 ($97,156 + $9,891 × (1−.350)), and in 1994 the numerator is $87,297 ($79,267 + $11,706 × (1−.314)).

Capital Structure Analysis of Wendy's International, Inc.

Wendy's capital structure can be described by the ratios in Exhibit 11–11. The vertical analysis of Wendy's liability and shareholders' equity indicates a modest decline in long-term debt. Deferred taxes and other similar liabilities were minor portions of total debt in both years. Shareholders' equity increased in percentage terms, reflecting decreases shown in long-term liabilities. These results are due mainly to the reclassification of a portion of Wendy's long-term debt in 1994 as a current liability in 1995, because the debt will be paid during 1995.

Wendy's times interest earned increased from 10.9 to 16.1. A times interest earned in excess of 16 is a healthy margin of safety. On the whole, after considering the decrease in debt and associated interest expenses, Wendy's capital structure analysis does not indicate any major concerns.

EXHIBIT 11–11 CAPITAL STRUCTURE ANALYSIS

Wendy's International, Inc.
Capital Structure Ratios, 1995 and 1994
(dollars in thousands)

Composition analysis: Percentage of total financing provided by each type of debt and shareholders's equity.

	1995		1994	
	Amount	%	Amount	%
Total assets (equals total liabilities and shareholders' equity)	$1,086,092	100.0	$996,486	100.0
Financed by:				
Current liabilities	$ 207,177	19.1%	$143,269	14.4%
Long-term debt + capital leases	144,860	13.3	200,633	20.1
Deferred taxes and other debt	52,557	4.8	51,789	5.2
Total liabilities	404,594	37.2	395,691	39.7
Shareholders' equity	681,498	62.8	600,795	60.3
Total	$1,086,092	100.0%	$996,486	100.0%

Additional Ratio Analysis:

Ratio	Formula		1993	1994
Financial leverage	$\dfrac{\text{Total liabilities}}{\text{Total assets}}$	=	37.2% (above)	39.7% (above)
Times interest earned	$\dfrac{\text{Earnings before interest and taxes}}{\text{Interest expense}}$	=	$\dfrac{\$159,362}{\$9,891}$	$\dfrac{\$127,241}{\$11,706}$
		=	16.1 times	10.9 times

 Investor Ratios, Wendy's International, Inc.

Wendy's investor ratios are calculated in Exhibit 11–12. Before arriving at final conclusions regarding the market's valuation of Wendy's, calculations based on year-end prices should be conducted. Based on the ratios shown, it appears that the market is reassured by Wendy's performance in 1995. Its market-to-book value ratio has remained steady. Further evaluations based on trends should also be conducted. The price-to-earnings ratio has declined moderately, from 21.4 to 19.4. The analyst would need to separate out the effects of economy-wide influences on P/E ratios (e.g., changes in interest rates or other factors causing changes in the overall market prices of equity securities) in order to interpret this change in Wendy's P/E ratio.

EXHIBIT 11–12 INVESTOR ANALYSIS

	Wendy's International, Inc. Investor Ratios, 1995 and 1994			
Ratio	Formula		1995	1994
Earnings per share	Provided directly on the income statement (Exhibit 11–5)	=	$.93	$.77
Market-to-book value*	$\dfrac{\text{Market price per share}}{\text{Book value per share}}$	=	$\dfrac{\$18.06}{\$6.70}$	$\dfrac{\$16.44}{\$5.96}$
		=	2.70	2.76
Price-to-earnings*	$\dfrac{\text{Market price per share}}{\text{Earnings per share}}$	=	$\dfrac{\$18.06}{\$.93}$	$\dfrac{\$16.44}{\$.77}$
		=	19.4	21.4

*We have used the fiscal year-end market price per share, and computed book value per share using the number of shares shown on the balance sheet.

Summary, Wendy's International, Inc.

The results of our analysis of Wendy's financial statements are cautiously positive. The primary weak indicators were in the areas of liquidity and profitability (based on accrual-based earnings). There were significant positive trends in profitability, slightly negative trends in liquidity, and stability in investor ratios. Further examination of supplementary information, as well as subsequent quarterly results for 1996 and 1997, could be used to support or challenge these conclusions.

LIMITATIONS OF FINANCIAL STATEMENT ANALYSIS

Financial statement analysis is limited on several dimensions. GAAP, and its underlying accounting conventions and measurement rules and principles, present some limits. Managers often have the ability to select favorable accounting methods. They can make choices as to the timing for reporting favorable or unfavorable results. A close reading of the notes may indicate where some of these choices have had an impact on the financial ratios. However, many of these managerial choices will not be revealed to external users of financial statements. Investors, in particular, must rely on independent accountants' assessments of the suitability of management's accounting choices.

A second major limitation of financial statement analysis concerns the "What's missing?" factor. Many major factors affecting profitability and survival of the firm are just not included in accrual accounting, nor in the financial statements. Examples of such omissions include changes in the firm's market share, changes in customer relations or preferences, changes in the firm's labor productivity, other changes in its human resources or human resource management systems, innovations or structural changes in technology, changes in the environment, changes in legislation or public policy, changes in competitors, or changes in substitute products or services. Sometimes these factors are discussed in the narrative sections of the annual report. They are often mentioned in the CEO's letter. Wendy's Management Review section (see Appendix D) alludes to some of these qualitative factors.

A third concern in financial statement analysis is that "real" events are often hard to distinguish from the effects of alternative accounting methods or principles. By focusing more on cash flows, the investor or other analyst can identify cases where financial reports based on accrual accounting may diverge from the cash flows or inadequately reflect other pertinent economic events.

A fourth, and final, limitation of financial statement analysis concerns predictability. The past may not be a reliable indicator of the future. Stable trends may be reversed tomorrow! Financial statements are just one of the important inputs that the investor must use as a basis for investing decisions. Further study of finance and accounting will give you additional tools on which to rely. Appendix B of this text gives you some ideas on how you might pursue your study of these important topics.

SUMMARY OF LEARNING OBJECTIVES

1. **Understand why financial statements are analyzed.**

   Investors comprise the primary audience of financial reporting. Financial analysts use financial accounting reports in order to assess the potential risks and returns from investing in debt and equity securities.

2. **Know where to obtain financial information.**

   Although financial statement analysis begins with the set of financial statements included in published financial reports, analysts gather additional information from a variety of sources, including the financial sections of major newspapers, specialized business periodicals, reports of changes in governmental fiscal and monetary policies, conferences and addresses by business leaders, and many other sources.

3. **Determine when financial information is comparable; alternatively, learn how to enhance the comparability of financial information that may appear to be noncomparable.**

   The analyst must determine that a comparable and useful reference is available with which to compare the target firm. Usually, the prior year or years are a good reference point with which to begin. Before comparing a firm's results with the prior year, the analyst must examine both sets of statements and notes to determine whether an unusual event occurred. If significant unusual events have occurred that would distort comparisons, then the financial statements for any of these years may need to be restated or rearranged to make them more comparable. The primary guideline is "more comparability is better." Financial information is more comparable if the firms:

   - operate in the same country,
   - follow similar accounting practices,

- are of similar size (revenues and/or assets),
- produce similar products or services, and
- have a similar capital structure.

4. **Identify, calculate, use, and interpret appropriate ratios.**

We have operationalized this objective by developing a general framework that can be used to conduct a comprehensive financial statement analysis. Financial analysis relies on both qualitative and quantitative analyses, and cannot be reduced to a simple set of recipes. The techniques summarized in this chapter merely provide a point of departure for the analyst in assessing the investment worth of a given firm.

A summary of our financial statement analysis framework follows:

a. Identify the purpose and objectives of the analysis.
b. Review the financial statements, accompanying notes, management letters, and other commentary, and the report of the independent auditor. Be alert to any unusual events that may affect your interpretations of the numerical items in the financial statements.
c. Determine whether any adjustments are needed to make the financial statements comparable to those of the previous year, or to financial statements of other, supposedly similar firms. Be especially aware of mergers, discontinued operations, changes in methods of accounting, or major shifts in product mix.
d. Conduct horizontal and vertical analyses of each financial statement. The horizontal analysis will aid you in discussing major changes in financial statement items compared to previous periods. The vertical analysis will help you to focus on variations in the composition of the firm's assets, and the relative proportions of its debt and equity financing. A vertical analysis will also help you focus on causes of variation in net income.
e. Organize your ratio calculations under the broad headings of liquidity, profitability, capital structure, and investor performance. Compute the standard financial ratios in each of these categories.
f. Compare the financial ratios to prior years and to industry norms. If the firm's ratios depart from its past history or prevailing norms, attempt to explain these departures by reviewing other supplementary disclosures in the financial statements. Remember that there are often excellent reasons why a firm will differ from its competitors, and may alter its policies over time. These steps have been illustrated using Wendy's financial statements.

5. **Identify limitations of financial statement analyses.**

A variety of judgments are used to decide how to calculate a given financial ratio. Rarely do the line items that are reported in the financial statements fit neatly into a standard formula. Often the results of the ratio calculations provide more questions than answers. The most useful product of ratio analysis may well be the list of intelligent questions that result.

KEY TERMS

Capital structure	Financial leverage ratio
Cash return on assets ratio	Horizontal analysis
Current ratio	Gross profit percentage
Earnings-per-share (EPS) ratio	Investor ratios

Liquidity ratios
Market-to-book value ratio
Number of days in inventory
Operating income ratio
Percentage composition analysis
Price-to-earnings (P/E) ratio
Profitability ratios

Quality of income ratio
Quick ratio
Return on assets (ROA) ratio
Return on equity (ROE) ratio
Times interest earned ratio
Vertical analysis

QUESTIONS

11-1 Describe several basic goals of financial statement analysis.

11-2 Identify several users of financial statement analysis. Discuss the differences between users who have regular interaction with the firm versus those who may have less frequent interactions.

11-3 Identify and describe several sources of financial information for publicly traded U.S. companies.

11-4 Discuss why it is so important that financial information be comparable before conducting analysis and computing ratios.

11-5 Discuss several ways that comparability between firms can be enhanced.

11-6 Discuss several aspects of noncomparability that the analyst cannot overcome.

11-7 Identify several bases of comparability that might be established before attempting to compare ratio results.

11-8 Identify the major elements of financial statements that form the basis for an investor's analysis.

11-9 Describe several situations that may require restatement of the financial statements prior to conducting ratio calculations.

11-10 Describe the benefits of conducting horizontal and vertical analyses.

11-11 Describe why one must analyze both cash and accounts receivable as part of a liquidity analysis.

11-12 Describe why one must analyze both cash flows and net income as part of a profitability analysis.

11-13 Describe the similarities between collection period and the number of days' sales in ending inventory.

11-14 Describe the relationship between return on equity (ROE) and cash return to shareholders.

11-15 Describe the relationship between return on assets (ROA) and cash return on assets.

11-16 Describe the relationship between quality of sales and accounts receivable as a percent of sales.

11-17 Discuss the differences between cash flow from operating activities (CFOA) and cash collections from customers.

11-18 Compare and contrast the quality of the income ratio with dimensions of income quality.

11-19 Discuss why a tax adjustment is necessary as part of return on assets (ROA).

11-20 Discuss the relationship between financial leverage and percentage composition.

11-21 Under what circumstances might the percentage composition ratios not sum to 100%?

11–22 Describe why the percentage composition ratios might have three or four components. Why might they have less than three components? Why might they have more than four such components?

11–23 Describe the relationships between cash interest coverage and times interest earned.

11–24 Why would a lender not be too concerned about market-to-book value and price-to-earnings (P/E) ratios?

11–25 Why would a lender and an investor be equally concerned with earnings per share (EPS)?

11–26 Discuss why the financial leverage ratio may be confusing and less useful than the percentage composition ratios.

11–27 Discuss why the "What's missing?" question is so crucial during all phases of financial statement analysis.

11–28 Describe several limitations of financial statement analysis. What can be done to minimize these limitations?

Note: Exercises 11–29 through 11–35 are based on the summarized financial statements of International Dairy Queen, Inc., which are provided in Exercise 11–29.

Introductory Problem and Data Set

11–29 International Dairy Queen, Inc., reported the following results for 1994, as summarized below:

	1994	1993
Revenues:		
Net sales	$268,804,179	$241,611,862
Service fees	54,170,022	51,601,113
Franchise sales (fees)	8,627,218	7,625,539
Property management	8,081,030	8,988,027
Other	1,150,051	1,267,434
	340,832,500	311,093,975
Costs and expenses:		
Cost of sales	242,412,898	217,154,994
Property management expenses	7,571,984	8,441,375
Selling, general & administrative	40,494,230	37,515,701
Interest expense (income)	(1,577,511)	(1,425,788)
	288,901,601	261,686,282
Income before income taxes	51,930,899	49,407,693
Income taxes	20,510,000	19,520,000
Net income	$ 31,420,899	$ 29,887,693
Earnings per common share	$1.30	$1.19

International Dairy Queen's Consolidated Balance Sheet is summarized below:

	1994	1993
Assets		
Current assets:		
Cash and cash equivalents	$ 31,766,220	$ 21,188,062
Marketable securities	6,956,192	9,989,490

Notes receivable, net	7,318,076	3,411,747
Accounts receivable, net	25,089,704	23,247,355
Inventories	5,403,560	4,560,714
Prepaid expenses	2,372,108	1,086,561
Miscellaneous	1,346,037	1,476,043
Total current assets	80,251,897	64,959,972

Other assets:

Notes receivable, net	14,484,091	21,406,772
Miscellaneous	1,305,087	1,630,849
Total other assets	15,789,178	23,037,621

Other revenue-producing assets:

Franchise rights, net	87,754,481	83,770,710
Rental properties, net	2,894,628	3,241,108
Miscellaneous	22,999	39,036
Total other assets	90, 672,108	87,050,854

Property, plant, and equipment, net	9,783,053	9,349,670
Total assets	$196,496,236	$184,398,117

Liabilities and Stockholders' Equity	1994	1993
Current liabilities:		
Drafts and accounts payable	$17,127,108	$16,791,824
Committed advertising	1,108,279	2,092,851
Other liabilities	7,318,827	6,761,960
Income taxes payable	438,753	1,017,626
Current maturities (L-T debt)	367,462	1,913,481
Total current liabilities	26,360,429	28,577,742
Deferred franchise income	435,983	278,917
Deferred income taxes	14,995,000	14,955,000
Long-term debt	23,343,752	23,901,770
Contingencies and commitments (Note 4)		
Stockholders' equity:		
Class A common stock	149,172	156,594
Class B common stock	88,160	90,291
Paid-in capital	4,109,104	3,957,075
Retained earnings	129,232,252	114,377,927
Equity adjustments	(2,217,616)	(1,897,199)
Total stockholders' equity	131,361,072	116,684,688
Total liabilities and shareholders' equity	$196,496,236	$184,398,117

A summary of International Dairy Queen's cash flow statement shows the following ($ in thousands):

	1994	1993
Net cash provided by operating activities	$ 33,760	$ 34,997
Net cash provided by (used in) investing activities	(4,550)	(17,206)
Net cash used in financing activities	(18,527)	(27,543)
Other adjustments	(104)	(302)
Net (decrease) increase in cash	$ 10,579	($10,054)
Cash payments for income taxes	$21,063	$18,798
Cash payments for interest	$ 1,930	$ 2,545

REQUIRED

a. Identify any unusual terms in International Dairy Queen's summarized financial statements.

Horizontal Analysis

11–30 With regard to the preceding financial statements from International Dairy Queen, Inc., prepare a horizontal analysis of the income statement.

Vertical Analysis

11–31 With regard to the preceding financial statements from International Dairy Queen, Inc., prepare a vertical analysis of the income statement.

Liquidity Ratios

11–32 With regard to the preceding financial statements from International Dairy Queen, Inc., calculate the appropriate liquidity ratios.

Profitability Analysis

11–33 With regard to the preceding financial statements from International Dairy Queen, Inc., conduct a profitability analysis.

Capital Structure Analysis

11–34 With regard to the preceding financial statements from International Dairy Queen, Inc., conduct a capital structure analysis.

Summary and Conclusions

11–35 With regard to our analysis of International Dairy Queen, Inc., write a short memo summarizing your conclusions. Indicate why International Dairy Queen might be facing financial threats or opportunities. Also, indicate what additional data you might need to refine your analyses or conclusions.

Note: Exercises 11–36 through 11–42 are based on the summarized financial statements of General Cinema Companies, Inc., which are provided in Exercise 11–36.

Introductory Problem and Data Set

11–36 General Cinema Companies, Inc., reported the following results for 1994 as summarized below ($ in thousands except for per-share amount):

Years Ended October 31	1994	1993
Revenues	$452,563	$495,031
Costs applicable to revenues	188,616	214,653
Selling, general and administrative expenses	241,435	260,128
Corporate expenses	5,646	1,900
Operating earnings (loss)	16,866	18,350

Investment income	1,640	96
Interest expense	(648)	(605)
Other income (expense), net	5,188	(600)
Earnings (loss) before income taxes, and cumulative effect of accounting change	23,046	17,241
Income tax expense	9,449	6,738
Net earnings (loss)	$ 13,597	$ 10,503
Amounts applicable to common shareholders:		
Net earnings (loss)	$1.73	NA

General Cinema's consolidated balance sheet is summarized below ($ in thousands):

October 31	1994	1993
Assets		
Current assets:		
Cash and equivalents	$ 85,021	$ 7,790
Deferred income taxes	2,090	0
Other current assets	5,722	2,622
Total current assets	92,833	10,412
Property and equipment:		
Land, buildings and improvements	32,411	38,675
Equipment and fixtures	130,016	131,710
Leasehold improvements	151,442	159,289
	313,869	329,674
Less accumulated depreciation and amortization	136,174	130,349
Total property and equipment, net	177,695	199,325
Other assets:		
Other	26,130	798
Total assets	$296,658	$210,535

October 31	1994	1993
Liabilities		
Current liabilities:		
Current maturities of long-term liabilities$ 722	$ 637	
Trade payables	39,065	34,028
Other current liabilities	59,972	53,956
Total current liabilities	99,759	88,621
Long-term liabilities:		
Capital lease obligations	4,179	4,756
Other long-term liabilities	28,016	27,551
Total long-term liabilities	32,195	32,307
Deferred income taxes	15,181	17,376
Commitments and contingencies	—	—
Total liabilities	147,135	138,304

Balance sheet continued on page 492

Shareholders' Equity

Common stock: $0.01 par value; authorized 25,000; issued and outstanding 7,802, 0	78	—
Paid-in capital	135,848	—
Retained earnings	13,597	—
Investment by Harcourt General	—	72,231
Total shareholders' equity	149,523	72,231
Total liabilities and equity	$296,658	$210,535

General Cinema's cash flow statement is summarized below ($ in thousands):

Year ended October 31	1994	1993
Net cash provided by operations	$28,512	$53,849
Net cash used by investment activities	(14,949)	(16,322)
Net cash (used) provided by financing transactions	63,668	(35,288)
Net increase (decrease) in cash during the year	$77,231	$ 2,239

Supplemental schedule of cash flow information

Cash paid for interest	$ 610	$ 720
Cash paid for income taxes	$ 13,100	$ 9,500

REQUIRED

a. Identify any unusual terms in General Cinema's summarized financial statements.

Horizontal Analysis

11–37 With regard to the preceding financial statements from General Cinema Companies, Inc., prepare a horizontal analysis of the income statement.

Vertical Analysis

11–38 With regard to the preceding financial statements from General Cinema Companies, Inc., prepare a vertical analysis of the income statement.

Liquidity Ratios

11–39 With regard to the preceding financial statements from General Cinema Companies, Inc., calculate the appropriate liquidity ratios.

Profitability Analysis

11–40 With regard to the preceding financial statements from General Cinema Companies, Inc., conduct a profitability analysis.

Capital Structure Analysis

11–41 With regard to the preceding financial statements from General Cinema Companies, Inc., conduct a capital structure analysis. Discuss why General Cinema reported no EPS in 1993.

Summary and Conclusions

11–42 With regard to your analysis of General Cinema Companies, Inc., write a short memo summarizing your conclusions. Indicate why General might be facing financial threats or opportunities. Also, indicate what additional data you might need to refine your analyses or conclusions.

Note: Exercises 11–43 through 11–49 are based on the summarized financial statements of Electronic Fab Technology, which are provided in Exercise 11–43.

Introductory Problem and Data Set

11–43 Electronic Fab Technology (EFT) is a leader in information technology. EFT reported the following results for 1994, as summarized below ($ in millions):

Year Ended December 31	1994	1993
Net sales	$52,541,842	$29,816,626
Cost of goods sold	47,123,066	25,688,263
Gross profit	5,418,776	4,128,363
Selling, general and administrative	2,395,164	1,842,442
Operating income	3,023,612	2,285,921
Other income (expense):		
Interest expense	(175,400)	(236,917)
Interest income	78,933	0
Other, net	31,187	(11,723)
Total other income (expense)	(65,280)	(248,640)
Income before income taxes	2,958,332	2,037,281
Income tax expense	1,041,415	736,612
Net income	$ 1,916,917	$ 1,300,669
Weighted average shares outstanding	3,626,845	2,483,000

EFT reported the following consolidated balance sheets, as summarized below ($ in millions):

December 31	1994	1993
Assets		
Current assets:		
Cash and cash equivalents	$ 153,483	$ 43,879
Accounts receivable, net	3,858,523	2,480,421
Inventories	7,479,374	4,639,969
Income taxes receivable	64,655	0
Deferred income taxes	85,847	85,490
Prepaids and others	49,467	49,165
Total current assets	11,691,349	7,298,924

Balance sheet continued on page 494

Property and equipment, net:

Land	662,098	161,903
Buildings	4,779,049	1,589,865
Machinery and equipment	8,395,468	3,763,995
Furniture and fixtures	1,043,098	328,555
	14,879,713	5,844,318
Less accumulated depreciation	3,162,155	2,188,893
Property plant and equipment	11,717,558	3,655,425

Other assets:

Cash surrender value of life insurance	36,248	41,750
Other assets	33,929	176,067
Total assets	$23,479,084	$11,172,166

December 31	1994	1993

Liabilities and Shareholders' Equity

Current liabilities:

Notes payable	$ —	$ 300,000
Current portion of long-term debt	170,000	244,433
Accounts payable	3,606,645	3,273,461
Income taxes payable	—	611,790
Accrued compensation	813,788	326,869
Other accrued expenses	356,598	138,827
Total current liabilities	4,947,031	4,895,380

Long-term debt, net of current portion	3,230,000	2,539,337
Deferred income taxes	312,660	190,918
Commitments and contingencies	—	—

Shareholders' equity:

Preferred stock: $0.01 par value,
  authorized 5,000,000 shares — —
Common stock; $0.01 par value,
  authorized 45,000,000 shares, issued

3,891,000 and 2,368,500 shares	38,911	23,685
Additional paid-in capital	10,016,035	505,316
Retained earnings	4,934,447	3,017,530
Total shareholders' equity	14,989,393	3,546,531
Total liabilities and		
shareholders' equity	$23,479,084	$11,172,166

EFT's consolidated statements of cash flow disclosed the following summary information:

December 31	1994	1993
Net cash provided by operating activities	$ (697)	$ 814
Net cash used in investing activities	(9,035)	(870)
Net cash used in financing activities	9,842	59
Net increase (decrease) in cash	$ 110	$ 3
Cash paid for:		
Income taxes (refund)	$ 1,596,475	$ (16,591)
Interest	$ 175,400	$236,917

REQUIRED

a. Identify any unusual terms in EFT's summarized financial statements.

Horizontal Analysis

11–44 With regard to the preceding financial statements from EFT, prepare a horizontal analysis of the income statement.

Vertical Analysis

11–45 With regard to the preceding financial statements from EFT, prepare a vertical analysis of the income statement.

Liquidity Ratios

11–46 With regard to the preceding financial statements from EFT, calculate the appropriate liquidity ratios.

Profitability Analysis

11–47 With regard to the preceding financial statements from EFT, conduct a profitability analysis.

Capital Structure Analysis

11–48 With regard to the preceding financial statements from EFT, conduct a capital structure analysis.

Summary and Conclusions

11–49 With regard to your analysis of EFT, write a short memo summarizing your conclusions. Indicate why EFT might be facing financial threats or opportunities. Also, indicate what additional data you might need to refine your analyses or conclusions.

PROBLEMS

Note: Problems 11–50 through 11–56 are based on the financial statements of Reebok International, which are included in Appendix F.

Applying the Financial Statement Analysis Framework: Reviewing the Notes

11–50 Review Reebok International's financial statements to determine whether any unusual or noteworthy events may limit the scope or comparability of financial statement analysis. Review Ernst & Young's report. Determine whether any restatements might be necessary, and determine whether there are any barriers that would restrict the comparability of Reebok's performance. In other words, conduct the first four steps in our financial statement analysis framework.

Applying the Financial Statement Analysis Framework: Horizontal and Vertical Analyses

11–51 Prepare horizontal and vertical analyses of Reebok's income statement for 1994 and 1993 (step 5 of our financial statement analysis framework).

Applying the Financial Statement Analysis Framework: Liquidity Analysis

11–52 Conduct an analysis of Reebok's liquidity for 1994 and 1993 (step 6 of our financial statement analysis framework).

Applying the Financial Statement Analysis Framework: Profitability Analysis

11–53 Conduct an analysis of Reebok's profitability for 1994 and 1993 (step 7 of our financial statement analysis framework).

Applying the Financial Statement Analysis Framework: Capital Structure Analysis

11–54 Analyze Reebok's capital structure for 1994 and 1993 (step 8 of our financial statement analysis framework).

Applying the Financial Statement Analysis Framework: Investor Analysis

11–55 Calculate Reebok's investor ratios for 1994 and 1993 (step 9 of our financial statement analysis framework).

Applying the Financial Statement Analysis Framework: Overall Conclusions

11–56 Review your results from the previous six problems, state your overall conclusions regarding Reebok's performance in 1994 and 1993, and then determine whether your results are consistent (step 10 of our financial statement analysis framework). Recalculate, as necessary, any ratios that could be restated based on new information found in the notes. Identify any additional information that you may require before making an investment in Reebok.

Note: Problems 11–57 through 11–63 are based on Wendy's financial statements, which are contained in Appendix D.

Applying the Financial Statement Analysis Framework: Reviewing the Notes

11–57 Review Wendy's financial statements to determine whether any unusual or noteworthy events may limit the scope or comparability of financial statement analysis. Review Coopers and Lybrand's audit report. Determine whether any restatements might be necessary, and determine whether there are any barriers that would restrict the comparability of Wendy's performance. In other words, conduct the first four steps in our financial statement analysis framework.

Applying the Financial Statement Analysis Framework: Horizontal and Vertical Analyses

11–58 Prepare horizontal and vertical analyses of Wendy's income statement for 1994 and 1993 (step 5 of our financial statement analysis framework).

Applying the Financial Statement Analysis Framework: Liquidity Analysis

11–59 Conduct an analysis of Wendy's liquidity for 1994 and 1993 (step 6 of our financial statement analysis framework).

Applying the Financial Statement Analysis Framework: Profitability Analysis

11–60 Conduct an analysis of Wendy's profitability for 1994 and 1993 (step 7 of our financial statement analysis framework). Note that Wendy's operating earnings and net earnings were negative in 1994 and 1993.

Applying the Financial Statement Analysis Framework: Capital Structure Analysis

11–61 Analyze Wendy's capital structure for 1994 and 1993 (step 8 of our financial statement analysis framework).

Applying the Financial Statement Analysis Framework: Investor Analysis

11–62 Calculate Wendy's investor ratios for 1994 and 1993 (step 9 of our financial statement analysis framework).

Applying the Financial Statement Analysis Framework: Overall Conclusions

11–63 Review your results from the previous six problems, state your overall conclusions regarding Wendy's performance in 1994 and 1993, and then determine whether your results are consistent (step 10 of our financial statement analysis framework). Recalculate, as necessary, any ratios that could be restated based on new information found in the notes. How does this possible restatement change your conclusions about Wendy's profitability? Identify any additional information that you may require before making an investment in Wendy's.

CASES AND EXTENSIONS

Research Project: Interviewing a User

11–64 Interview a local stockbroker or financial analyst to determine what financial ratios he/she finds most useful.

Research Project: User Interviews and Industry Comparisons

11–65 Go to your local business library. Examine the industry averages for the food service industry and compare them to Wendy's reported ratio results shown in this chapter.

Research Project: Interviewing a User

11–66 Interview a local stockbroker or financial analyst and discuss the differences between liquidity and profitability ratios. Identify the three most important ratios in each area used by this stockbroker, and describe why they are important.

Research Project: Interviewing a User

11–67 Interview a local stockbroker or financial analyst and discuss the differences between the debt-to-equity ratio and financial leverage (debt/assets). At the same time, discuss the percentage composition ratios and determine whether he/she would find them more helpful than debt-to-equity (or similar) ratios.

Evaluating Choices Among Accounting Methods

11–68 Describe several possible choices of accounting methods that managers may make in an effort to manipulate or influence reported earnings. What can the analyst do to combat these earnings manipulation possibilities?

Evaluating Possibilities for Bias and Manipulation of Net Income

11–69 Describe how managers may affect the timing of earnings recognition. What can the analyst do to combat these earnings manipulation possibilities?

Evaluating Possibilities for Bias and Manipulation of Net Income

11–70 Describe how managers may make biased estimates that will cause net income to be overstated or understated. What can the analyst do to combat these earnings manipulation possibilities?

Research Project: Comparing Two Companies in the Same Industry

11–71 Obtain financial statements from two companies in the same industry. Conduct a comprehensive financial statement analysis of each company. Compare each company on dimensions where they are significantly different. Write a short report indicating why you would, or would not, invest in either company.

Research Project: Comparing Two Companies in the Same Industry

11–72 Obtain financial statements from two companies in the same industry. Go to your business library and get industry statistics and ratios on this industry. Conduct a comprehensive financial statement analysis of each company. Compare each company to each other and to the industry averages. Write a short report describing the positive and negative aspects of each firm with respect to its past performance, relative to each other and its industry.

Research Project: Financial Statement Analysis and Interviewing Company Managers

11–73 Obtain financial statements from a local company. Conduct a comprehensive financial statement analysis of this company using our framework. After completing your analysis, conduct an interview with a financial manager (e.g., CFO) and a general manager (e.g., CEO or operating vice president) using your ratio results and initial conclusions as a basis for learning more about the company's performance. After your interview(s), write a report describing your conclusions regarding the company's performance. Indicate why you would, or would not, invest in this company.

Research Project: Financial Statement Analysis Applied to Nonprofit Organization

11–74 Review the financial statement ratios in this chapter and consider which might apply to a nonprofit organization. Write a short report indicating why each of these ratios would (or would not) apply to a nonprofit organization.

Research Project: Financial Statement Analysis Applied to a Nonprofit Organization

11–75 Obtain the audited financial statements of a local nonprofit organization. Apply our financial statement analysis framework, as appropriate, to this organization. Write a short report describing your conclusions regarding this organization's performance. Indicate why you would, or would not, make a contribution to this organization.

Research Project: Comparing Two Companies in the Same Industry and Evaluating a Possible Merger Strategy

11–76 Obtain the financial statements from two companies in the same industry. Conduct a comprehensive financial statement analysis of each company. Next, consider a scenario under which the largest of these two companies would consider acquiring, or merging with, the smaller company. Write a short report evaluating the advantages and disadvantages of this hypothetical merger or acquisition.

Financial Statement Analysis: Notes

11–77 Refer to the following excerpts from Fiddler Capital Management Incorporated's 1996 financial statements. You have been provided with the independent auditor's report, financial statements, and Notes 1 and 2.

INDEPENDENT AUDITORS' REPORT

Board of Directors
Fiddler Capital Management Inc.
Edina, Minnesota

We have audited the accompanying statement of financial condition of Fiddler Capital Management Inc. (the Company), wholly owned by HHS Companies, Inc., as of September 30, 1996. This financial statement is the responsibility of the Company's management. Our responsibility is to express an opinion on this financial statement based on our audit.

We conducted our audit in accordance with generally accepted auditing standards. Those standards require that we plan and perform the audit to obtain reasonable assurance about whether the statement of financial condition is free of material misstatement. An audit includes examining, on a test basis, evidence supporting the amounts and disclosures in the financial statement. An audit also includes assessing the accounting principles used and significant estimates made by management, as well as evaluating the overall financial statement presentation. We believe that our audit of the statement of financial condition provides a reasonable basis for our opinion.

In our opinion, such financial statement presents fairly, in all material respects, the financial position of Fiddler Capital Management Inc. as of September 30 1996, in conformity with generally accepted accounting principles.

Touch, Rose, & Thorne
March 1, 1997

FIDDLER CAPITAL MANAGEMENT INCORPORATED
(wholly owned by HHS Companies Inc.)
STATEMENT OF FINANCIAL CONDITION
September 30, 1996

ASSETS:

Cash	$ 5,100,000
Advisory fees receivable (Note 3)	5,567,000
Expense reimbursements receivable	1,076,000
Net receivable from Parent and Affiliate	12,851,000
Prepaid expenses	135,000
Furniture and equipment at cost	
(net of 1,041,000 accumulated depreciation)	1,577,000
Other assets	288,000
	$26,594,000

LIABILITIES AND STOCKHOLDERS' EQUITY

LIABILITIES:

Employee compensation and related benefits payable (Note 5)	$ 8,347,000
Accounts payable and accrued expenses	1,618,000
Total liabilities	9,965,000

STOCKHOLDERS' EQUITY:

Common stock, $1 par value; 10,000 shares authorized, issued, and outstanding	10,000
Additional paid-in capital	2,239,000
Retained earnings	14,380,000
Total stockholders' equity	16,629,000
	$26,594,000

See notes to statement of financial condition.

NOTES TO STATEMENT OF FINANCIAL CONDITION
September 30, 1996

1. Summary of Significant Accounting Practices

Fiddler Capital Management Inc. (the Company) is a wholly owned subsidiary of HHS Companies Inc. (the Parent) and is an investment advisor registered under the Investment Advisors Act of 1940. The Company furnishes investment advice to profit sharing and pension plans, financial institutions, corporate funds, management investment companies, and individuals. As of September 30, 1996, the Company managed over $14 billion of assets with approximately $118 million managed by a foreign sub-advisor and $848 million managed by two affiliates.

The Company is charged various expenses, including rent, by the Parent based on specifically identified charges and other cost allocations. The effect of these charges on retained earnings is not necessarily indicative of the costs that would have been incurred had the Company operated independently.

Depreciation of furniture and equipment is provided using accelerated methods over estimated useful lives of five or seven years.

Statement of Financial Accounting Standards (SFAS) No. 106, *Employer's Accounting for Postretirement Benefits Other than Pension,* requires the Company to change the way it accounts for the cost of postretirement benefits other than pensions. Currently, the Company's Parent follows the pay-as-you-go (cash basis) accounting practice which records as expense the postretirement benefits in the year they are paid. SFAS No. 106 requires accrual of the expected costs to provide postretirement benefits (such as health care benefits) during the years that employees render the service necessary to become eligible for the benefits. Under the new rules, the Company's statement of financial condition will include an allocation of the Parent's liability for the obligation to provide postretirement benefits, and the Company will be charged for its portion of the net periodic cost of those benefits. The Parent has not yet determined how much of the liability would be allocated to the Company; however, adoption of this standard is not expected to materially increase the Company's annual expense for postretirement benefits. The Parent currently estimates that it will have a transition obligation for postretirement benefits at the date of adoption of the standard of approximately $14 million, a portion of which would be allocated to the Company. However, it is expected the amount allocated would not significantly impact the Company's financial condition. The Company's Parent is required to adopt this statement in the first quarter of fiscal 1997.

The Company files consolidated federal and state income tax returns with its Parent and affiliates. Payments are made to the Parent for income taxes computed on pretax book income using the consolidated effective tax rate under Accounting Principles Board Opinion No. 11. The Company expects to adopt the provisions of Financial Accounting Standards Board Statement No. 109, *Accounting for Income Taxes,* in fiscal year 1997.

Adoption of the statement is not expected to have a material impact on the financial condition of the Company.

2. Canadian Accounting Principles

The financial statements have been prepared in accordance with accounting principles generally accepted in the United States which, in the case of the Company, conform in all material respects with those in Canada.

REQUIRED

a. Identify what is missing in these excerpts. What items would you normally expect to find in a typical annual report that have not been provided by Fiddler?

b. Review Note 1, and discuss each item in your own words.

c. Write a short memo responding to Note 2, describing the ways that you agree and disagree with the assertions in Note 2, regarding generally accepted accounting principles in the United States. Ignore the reference to Canadian accounting principles.

Research Project: New Ratios

11–78 In your business library, find several recent articles that discuss financial statement analysis.

REQUIRED

a. Compare and contrast the ratios presented in this text with those in the articles you selected.

b. Discuss the advantages and disadvantages of any new ratios that were described in these articles. If the authors of these articles agree on several ratios, focus your attention on the new ratios (where there is commonality).

c. Apply these new ratios from part b to the text's discussion of Wendy's. Compare the results of using these new ratios with the results obtained using the ratios described in this text.

Research Project: New Ratios

11–79 In your business library, find several recent articles that discuss financial statement analysis.

REQUIRED

a. Compare and contrast the ratios presented in this text with those in the articles you selected.

b. Discuss the advantages and disadvantages of any new ratios that were described in these articles. If the authors of these articles agree on several ratios, focus your attention on the new ratios (where there is commonality).

c. Apply these new ratios from part b to an analysis of one of the companies in the appendixes. Compare the results of using these new ratios with the results obtained using the ratios described in this text.

Research Project: New Cash Flow-Based Ratios

11–80 In your business library, find several recent articles discussing cash flow-based ratios that can be used in financial statement analysis.

REQUIRED

a. Compare and contrast the cash flow-based ratios presented in this text with those in the articles you selected.

b. Discuss the advantages and disadvantages of any new cash flow-based ratios that were described in these articles. If the authors of these articles agree on new cash flow-based ratios, focus your attention on these new ratios (where there is commonality).

c. Apply these new ratios from part b to an analysis of Wendy's (Appendix D). Compare the results of using these new cash flow-based ratios with the results obtained using the ratios described in this text.

Research Project: New Cash Flow-Based Ratios

11–81 In your business library, find several recent articles discussing cash flow-based ratios that can be used in financial statement analysis.

REQUIRED

a. Compare and contrast the cash flow-based ratios presented in this text with those in the articles you selected.

b. Discuss the advantages and disadvantages of any new cash flow-based ratios that were described in these articles. If the authors of these articles agree on new cash flow-based ratios, focus your attention on the new ratios (where there is commonality).

c. Apply these new ratios from part b to an analysis of one of the companies in the appendixes. Compare the results of using these new cash flow-based ratios with the results obtained using the ratios described in this text.

Research Project: Ratio Analysis of Service Firm

11–82 Review the financial statement ratios in this chapter and consider which might apply to a service organization, such as a law firm or an accounting firm. Write a short report indicating why each of these ratios would apply to a service firm.

Research Project: Ratio Analysis of Service Firm

11–83 Obtain the audited financial statements of a local service firm. Apply our financial analysis framework, as appropriate, to this firm. Write a short report describing your conclusions regarding this firm's performance. Indicate why you would, or would not, be concerned about the long-term success of this firm.

USING FINANCIAL ACCOUNTING ON THE INTERNET

11–84 Access the EDGAR archives (**www.sec.gov/edgarhp.htm**) to locate the latest available 10-K filings for Kmart and Wal-Mart. Scroll down to the Summary of Key Financial Information and calculate the following ratios for the most recent two years. *Hint:* Some data must be obtained from the consolidated financial statements:

a. *Liquidity ratios:* current ratio, quick ratio, average sales per day, collection period, number of days' sales in ending inventory, and cost of sales per day.

b. *Profitability ratios:* gross profit percentage, operating income percentage, net income percentage, return on equity, and return on assets.

c. *Capital structure ratios:* debt to assets, capital composition analysis, and times interest earned.

d. *Earnings-per-share, market-to-book value, and price-to-earnings ratio* for the most recent year only: Use **http://quotes.galt.com** for the latest market price of each stock.

e. In your opinion, which company is doing a better job of managing its business? Which company has better growth prospects?

11–85 Locate the latest available 10-K filing (**www.sec.gov/edgarhp.htm**) of Diebold, Inc., an Ohio-based manufacturer of automated teller machines. Scroll down to the Management Analysis of Results of Operations where vertical and horizontal analyses of the results have been included and answer the following questions:

REQUIRED

a. Describe the products and services in which the company deals. Which item (products or services) is growing at the fastest rate? Which item constitutes the largest percentage of sales revenue?

b. For both products and services, how has the cost of sales as a percentage of revenue changed during the last year? Do products or services have a higher gross margin percentage in the most recent year?

c. Have operating and sales expenses been increasing as a percentage of sales?

d. What is the operating income percentage (of net sales) for each of the three years? Comment on the causes of the year-to-year changes.

This chapter consists of two parts, each of which may be read independently. Part I deals with financial reporting of lease obligations.

STUDYING PART I WILL ENABLE YOU TO

1. Distinguish between leases that are ordinary rentals, and those that are in substance a purchase of assets.
2. Understand how leases impact the measurement of financial position and operating performance.

Part II discusses financial reporting of obligations for retirement benefit plans, mainly pensions and medical benefits.

STUDYING PART II WILL ENABLE YOU TO

3. Know the difference between defined contribution and defined benefit pension plans.
4. Appreciate the impact of retirement benefit liabilities on reported financial position and operating results.
5. Understand the key assumptions necessary to measure postretirement obligations and expenses.

Additional Issues in Liability Reporting

Introduction to Part I:
Financial Reporting of Lease Obligations

Business firms obtain the right to use property, plant, and equipment by means of either a purchase or a lease. A **lease** is an agreement between an owner (or **lessor**) and a renter (or **lessee**) that conveys the right to use the leased property for a designated future period (typically several years). The lessee makes periodic payments, usually of the same dollar amount each time, over the term of the lease. Leases may be relatively short term, e.g., three or four years, or may extend over the entire economic life of the leased asset.

Leasing is an increasingly popular way of obtaining business assets. In fact, leasing is one of the fastest growing industries in the United States. In recent years leasing has accounted for more than one-third of all new equipment investment in this country. The U.S. Department of Commerce projects that leasing will grow more quickly than other types of asset acquisition throughout the 1990s.

Benefits of Leasing

From a lessee's perspective, there are many potential advantages to leasing, rather than purchasing, an asset. Some of these advantages are based on sound economic incentives, and others are based on the methods used to report leases in financial statements.

Leases offer financial flexibility beyond that available with other borrowing arrangements. For example, loan agreements sometimes impose considerable restrictions on borrowers. These restrictions may concern key financial ratios, profitability requirements, dividend payments, and other financial actions. Lease agreements, on the other hand, do not generally give the lessor the power to impose such restrictions. Instead, the lessor's claim is secured by the leased asset.

Leasing may also reduce the lessee's risks of equipment obsolescence. A lessor may have less risk than a lessee if the asset has a well-developed secondary market so that the lessor may resell or re-lease the used equipment. The economic life of an asset depends on its uses; e.g., national airlines cannot use outdated airplanes, but many regional carriers regularly use them for short-haul flights. Consequently, new passenger airplanes are usually first leased to major airlines, and after the initial leasing period, they are then leased to regional carriers. Leases can reduce financial risk as well. Unlike some forms of debt financing that carry variable interest rates, lease payments normally are uniform each month or year. This feature insulates the lessee from the effects of interest rate increases. On the other hand, the lessee will not benefit if interest rates decline.

ANALYZING LEASES

To provide a framework for discussing the financial statement effects of leasing, we consider first the case in which a firm borrows in order to purchase a long-lived asset. Exhibit 12–1 provides pertinent information about a jet aircraft to be acquired by the Exec Perk Company. The company will finance the purchase by installment debt, and will make a series of $2 million repayments at the end of each of the next six years. You will recognize this payment pattern as an ordinary annuity, which may be evaluated using present value methods (Chapter 8).

Present value	=	Periodic loan payment	×	Annuity present value factor, six periods at 12%
	=	$2 million	×	4.111 (Exhibit 8A–3; $i = 12\%$, n = six periods)
	=	$8,222,000		

Because the present value of the loan payments is $8,222,000, this is a suitable measure of the cost of the aircraft to Exec Perk Company. Upon purchasing the aircraft, Exec Perk would increase both its noncurrent assets and noncurrent liabilities by $8,222,000.

ASSETS	=	LIABILITIES	+	SHAREHOLDERS' EQUITY
Equipment		Installment debt		
+$8,222,000		+$8,222,000		

EXHIBIT 12–1
PURCHASE OF A
LONG-LIVED ASSET

Exec Perk Company
Information Regarding Installment Purchase of an Asset

Asset to be purchased	Jet aircraft
Estimated useful life	6 years
Benefit pattern	Straight line
Residual value	Zero
Method of financing	Installment debt
Annual payments (end of year)	$2 million
Borrowing rate	12%

Over the six-year estimated useful life of the aircraft, the cost will be systematically expensed. Assuming a straight-line benefit pattern, the annual depreciation expense is $1,370,333 ($8,222,000 cost ÷ 6 years).

ASSETS	=	LIABILITIES	+	SHAREHOLDERS' EQUITY
Equipment, net of accumulated depreciation				Retained earnings
−$1,370,333				−$1,370,333 (depreciation expense)

In addition, Exec Perk has borrowed the money ($8,222,000) from the seller in order to purchase the asset, at an interest rate of 12%. For this reason the firm must also recognize interest expense of $986,640 ($8,222,000 × 12% = $986,640) during the first year of the loan.

ASSETS	=	LIABILITIES	+	SHAREHOLDERS' EQUITY
		Installment debt		Retained earnings
		+$986,640		−$986,640 (interest expense)

Exec Perk will also make the first installment payment at the end of the year:

ASSETS	=	LIABILITIES	+	SHAREHOLDERS' EQUITY
Cash		Installment debt		
−$2,000,000		−$2,000,000		

As a result of these events, Exec Perk has recognized total aircraft-related expenses of $2,356,973:

Depreciation expense	$1,370,333
Interest expense	986,640
Total expense	$2,356,973

In each of the remaining five years, Exec Perk would continue to record depreciation expense of $1,370,333, and interest expense computed at 12% of the carrying value of the installment debt. Because the debt is being repaid in installments, the interest expense would be smaller in each successive year.

In summary, the installment purchase of the aircraft has affected Exec Perk's financial statements in the following ways: long-term assets and long-term debt have increased to reflect the cost of the asset and the firm's obligation to make installment payments. Also, the income statement includes both depreciation expense and the interest expense on the amount borrowed.

CAPITAL AND OPERATING LEASES

If a firm decides to lease an asset, the impact on the financial statements depends on how the lease is classified according to rules established by the FASB. Accountants must classify leases as either capital leases or operating leases. A **capital lease** is interpreted "as if" it is essentially a purchase of an asset, financed by debt to be repaid in installments. Consequently, a capital lease will affect the financial statements in the same way an installment purchase would. It will increase the amounts of reported long-term assets and long-term debt, as shown earlier. An **operating lease,** on the other hand, is interpreted as an ordinary rental, where the asset is merely used by the lessee. Operating leases do not entail increases in reported long-term assets and debt. Instead, the lease payments are merely reported as rent expense.

A lease is classified as a capital lease if it meets one or more of the following criteria:

1. The lease transfers ownership of the property to the lessee by the end of the lease.
2. The lease gives the lessee an option to purchase the leased asset at a bargain price.
3. The lease term is equal to 75% or more of the estimated economic life of the leased property.
4. The present value of the lease payments is 90% or more of the fair value of the property at the inception of the lease.

Note that any of these criteria recognize that ownership rights have, in substance, been transferred from the lessor to the lessee. Only if a lease meets **none** of these four criteria will it be classified as an operating lease.

To show the accounting treatment of capital leases, consider Exhibit 12–2, describing Rapid Dispatch's prospective lease of a mainframe computer. Note that the first three criteria for a capital lease are not met in this case. The lease does not transfer ownership (first criterion). There is no bargain purchase option (second criterion). The lease term of six years is less than 75% of the estimated economic life (75% of 10 years = 7.5 years) of the leased property (third criterion).

To evaluate the fourth criterion, that the present value of the lease payments must equal or exceed 90% of the fair value of the leased property, the lease payments must be discounted using the lessee's borrowing rate (assumed at 12%). Note that the lease obligates Rapid Dispatch to make payments of $2 million to the lessor at the end of each year for six years. You will recognize that this lease payment pattern is an ordinary annuity, which may be evaluated using present value methods (Chapter 8).

EXHIBIT 12–2
PROSPECTIVE LEASE INFORMATION

Rapid Dispatch Company	
Information Regarding Prospective Lease Agreement	
Property to be leased	Mainframe computer
Lessor's fair value of property	$9 million
Economic life of property	10 years
Annual lease payment (due at the end of each year)	$2 million
Term of lease	6 years
Lessee's incremental borrowing rate	12%
Renewal or purchase options	None
Ownership transfer to lessee	No

$$
\begin{aligned}
\text{Present value} \quad &= \quad \text{Periodic lease payment} \quad \times \quad \text{Annuity present value} \\
&\qquad\qquad\qquad\qquad\qquad\qquad\qquad \text{factor, six periods at 12\%} \\[6pt]
&= \quad \$2 \text{ million} \qquad\qquad\quad \times \quad 4.111 \text{ (Exhibit 8A-3;} \\
&\qquad\qquad\qquad\qquad\qquad\qquad\qquad i = 12\%, n = \text{six periods)} \\[6pt]
&= \quad \$8,222,000
\end{aligned}
$$

Since the present value of the lease payments is $8,222,000 and the fair value of the property at the inception of the lease is $9 million (Exhibit 12–2), we can see that the present value of the lease payments exceeds the 90% test ($8,222,000 ÷ $9,000,000 = 91.3%). Consequently, Rapid Dispatch must capitalize the lease. Capitalization will increase both the firm's noncurrent assets and noncurrent liabilities by $8,222,000 when the lease is signed.

ASSETS	=	LIABILITIES	+	SHAREHOLDERS' EQUITY
Leased assets		Lease obligations		
+$8,222,000		+$8,222,000		

Over the six-year term of the lease, the asset cost will be systematically expensed. Because the lease is an intangible asset, the term *amortization* is used, rather than depreciation. Assuming a straight line benefit pattern, the annual lease amortization expense is $1,370,333 ($8,222,000 cost ÷ 6 years):

ASSETS	=	LIABILITIES	+	SHAREHOLDERS' EQUITY
Leased assets				Retained earnings
−$1,370,333				−$1,370,333
				(amortization expense)

In addition, Rapid Dispatch has in effect borrowed the money ($8,222,000) needed to purchase the asset from the lessor at an interest rate of 12%. For this reason, the firm must also recognize interest expense of $986,640 ($8,222,000 × 12% = $986,640). Rapid Dispatch will also make the first $2 million lease payment at year-end.

ASSETS	=	LIABILITIES	+	SHAREHOLDERS' EQUITY
Cash		Lease obligations		Retained earnings
		+$986,640		−$986,640
−$2,000,000		−$2,000,000		(interest expense)

As a result of these events, Rapid Dispatch has recognized total lease-related expenses during the first year of $2,356,973:

Amortization expense	$1,370,333
Interest expense	986,640
Total expense	$2,356,973

The reported value of the lease obligation at year-end, after the first lease payment, is $7,208,640:

Lease obligation, beginning of the year	$8,222,000
Add: Interest expense	986,640
Less: Lease payment	(2,000,000)
Lease obligation, end of the year	$7,208,640

The reported value of the leased assets at the end of this first year is $6,851,667 ($8,222,000 original cost, less $1,370,333 amortization).

If Rapid Dispatch's lease contract had qualified as an operating lease, then no asset or liability would have been recognized at the inception of the lease. Instead, each year the firm would recognize a rental expense of $2,000,000, paid in cash to the lessor at year-end.

ASSETS	=	LIABILITIES	+	SHAREHOLDERS' EQUITY
Cash				Retained earnings
−$2,000,000				−$2,000,000 (rent expense)

Exhibit 12–3 contrasts the impact of capital versus operating lease treatments on Rapid Dispatch's balance sheet and income statement over the life of the lease. Note the following:

1. Capital and operating leases both will result in total expense of $12 million over the entire term of the lease, because this is the total amount to be paid to the lessor ($2 million × 6 years = $12 million).
2. Under a capital lease, the total yearly expense (amortization plus interest) is higher in the earlier years, and lower in the later years. This occurs because the interest expense declines as the lease debt is partially repaid in installments. In contrast, the operating lease shows a constant annual expense of $2 million.
3. The capital lease is reported as a leased asset on the balance sheet. The asset is systematically amortized over the lease term. A lease obligation, to be repaid in installments, is also reported as a liability. In contrast, the operating lease treatment reports neither an asset nor a liability.

IMPACT OF LEASES ON RATIO RELATIONSHIPS

The differences in the financial reporting of capital and operating leases may have a major impact on financial ratios for firms with many leases. Recall that capital leases result in higher asset values and greater amounts of debt than do operating leases. Also, capital leases initially result in lower incomes (because total lease expenses are

EXHIBIT 12–3   CAPITAL VERSUS OPERATING LEASE TREATMENTS

Rapid Dispatch Company
Comparison of Capital and Operating Leases Effects on
Selected Financial Statement Items

Capital Lease Effects:

	Balance Sheet		Income Statement, Year Ended				
Date	Leased Assets	Lease Obligation	Amortization Expense	+	Interest Expense	=	Total
Inception (Jan. 1)	$8,222,000	$8,222,000					
December 31, year 1	6,851,667	7,208,640	$1,370,333	+	$ 986,640	=	$2,356,973
year 2	5,481,334	6,073,677	1,370,333	+	865,037	=	2,235,611
year 3	4,111,001	4,802,518	1,370,333	+	728,841	=	2,099,429
year 4	2,740,668	3,378,820	1,370,333	+	576,302	=	1,946,904
year 5	1,370,335	1,784,278	1,370,333	+	405,458	=	1,776,076
year 6	-0-	-0-	1,370,335*	+	215,722*	=	1,584,777
		Totals	$8,222,000	+	$3,778,000	=	$12,000,000

Operating Lease effects:

Balance Sheet		Income Statement
Leased Assets	Lease Obligation	Rental expense: $2,000,000 each year
-0-	-0-	Total: $2,000,000× 6 years = $12,000,000

higher in the earlier years of the lease). Consequently, ratios that use net income, total assets, or debt in their calculations will be affected. As examples, return on assets, the debt-to-assets ratio, and earnings per share will all appear less favorable in the earlier years under capital leases, because capital leases must be shown as both an asset and a liability.

Operating leases, on the other hand, are accounted for as rentals, so that neither the leased property nor the liability for future lease payments is shown on the balance sheet. For this reason, operating leases are often referred to as "off-balance-sheet" financing. Accounting standards, however, require that footnotes to the financial statements include substantial disclosures about operating leases. Financial analysts, if they desire, may use this supplementary information to recast the balance sheet "as if" the operating leases were treated similarly to capital leases. Reality Check 12–1 illustrates how financial analysts may use supplementary information regarding operating leases, in evaluating a firm's indebtedness.

DELTA AIR LINES, INC., CAPITALIZATION EFFECTS FOR OPERATING LEASES

Delta Air Lines is one of the largest airlines in the world. It provides scheduled passenger service, air freight, mail, and other related aviation services. Selected balance sheet information from Delta's 1992 annual report is given here along with Note 4 to the financial statements, describing Delta's lease obligations.

Like most of the airline industry, Delta leases the major portion of its aircraft, airport terminal and maintenance facilities, ticket offices, and other property, plant, and equipment. Most of these leases are structured to meet the FASB's criteria for operating leases. Accounting standards require that the minimum annual rental commitments under both capital and operating leases be disclosed for the ensuing five years, and in the aggregate for later years.

Delta Air Lines, Inc.
Selected Financial Information, 1992 Annual Report
(Dollars in Thousands)

Balance sheet	
Current assets	$ 1,698,444
Property and equipment	7,093,312
Other assets	1,369,818
Total	$10,161,574
Current liabilities	$ 3,542,814
Noncurrent liabilities and other credits	4,724,692
Total liabilities	8,267,506
Common stockholders' equity	1,894,068
Total	$10,161,574
Net loss	$ 506,318

Delta Air Lines, Inc.
Footnote Disclosures of Lease Obligations
1992 Annual Report

Note 4. Lease Obligations:

The company leases certain aircraft, airport terminal and maintenance facilities, ticket offices, and other property and equipment under agreements with terms of more than one year. Rent expense is generally recorded on a straight-line basis over the lease term. Amounts charged to rental expense for operating leases were $997,326,000 in fiscal 1992; $668,848,000 in 1991; and $545,542,000 in fiscal 1990.

INTRODUCTION TO PART II:
POSTRETIREMENT BENEFIT OBLIGATIONS

Most medium and larger sized business firms provide retired employees with pensions and other postretirement benefits, mainly medical insurance coverage. The costs of these postretirement benefits are a component of employee expenses incurred during the **service lives** of the

At June 30, 1992, the Company's minimum rental commitments under capital leases and noncancelable operating leases with initial or remaining terms of more than one year were as follows:

Years Ending June 30	Capital Leases	Operating Leases
	(dollars in thousands)	
1993	$19,708	$906,698
1994	20,565	896,793
1995	18,323	880,980
1996	18,274	894,651
1997	17,530	901,514
After 1997	72,842	12,851,687
Total minimum lease payments	167,242	$17,332,323
Less: Amounts representing interest	47,423	
Present value of future minimum capital lease payments	119,819	
Less: Current obligations under capital leases	10,321	
Long-term capital lease obligations	$109,498	

Special facility revenue bonds have been issued by certain municipalities and airport authorities to build or improve airport terminal and maintenance facilities that are leased under operating leases by Delta. Under these lease agreements, the Company is required to make rental payments sufficient to pay principal and interest on the bonds as they become due. At June 30, 1992, Delta had guaranteed $679,505,000 principal amount of such bonds.

Note 4 on lease obligations shows that Delta's existing operating leases require total minimum lease payments exceeding $17 billion dollars in future years. These operating lease obligations are more than 100 times the company's capital lease obligations of $167.2 million.

REQUIRED

a. Assume that for purposes of financial analysis, you wish to treat Delta's operating leases "as if" they were capital leases. Develop an approximation of the capitalized value of Delta's leases, based on the information provided in Note 4.

b. Show how your approximation of the capitalized values of Delta's operating leases would affect your measurements of total assets, total liabilities, property and equipment, ratio of liabilities to assets, ratio of property, plant, and equipment to assets, and net income.

SOURCE: Delta Air Lines, Inc., 1992 *Annual Report.*

---

retirees, which are the working years prior to retirement. For this reason, the periodic expenses and obligations for postretirement benefits must be estimated to measure the operating performance and financial position of the employer firms.

Standards for measurement and reporting of postretirement expenses and obligations have tightened considerably during the past decade. Separate standards govern reporting for pensions, and reporting for other (nonpension) postemployment benefits. The following sections describe and contrast the financial reporting standards for both types of retiree benefits.

PENSION EXPENSES AND OBLIGATIONS

Pension plans are either defined contribution plans or defined benefit plans. A **defined contribution pension plan** specifies the periodic amount, usually a percentage of an employee's current salary, that the firm must contribute to a pension fund. The employee's retirement benefit depends on how well the pension fund invests the contributions that it has received. In any event, the employer's only obligation is to make the agreed-on contributions to the plan. In effect, the employee bears all of the risks and rewards of the investment performance of the pension fund. The financial reporting effects of defined contribution plans are straightforward and noncontroversial.

Defined benefit pension plans, in contrast, specify the benefits that employees will receive at retirement. The employer makes periodic contributions to a pension fund in order to set aside funds to pay these benefits. The amounts of these periodic contributions are influenced by income tax rules and other government regulations.

Because defined benefit plans specify the dollar amounts of the pensions to be paid to retirees, the employer assumes all of the risks and rewards associated with the pension fund investments. For instance, if pension fund assets are insufficient to pay the agreed-on benefits, then the employer must make additional payments. On the other hand, if the pension fund's assets exceed the amounts required for benefits, the employer will be able to reduce its contributions, and in some cases may even withdraw the excess funds from the pension fund.

Defined benefit pension plans have proven to be especially popular in U.S. industries that have strong labor union representation. Unions usually favor labor agreements that offer security and low risk to their members. Managers in these industries also have tended to favor labor contracts that postpone the cash impact of labor costs. Defined benefit plans, therefore, are prevalent in unionized industries (e.g., automobiles, chemicals, machinery, steel, paper, and transportation). Among firms with less labor union representation, the current trend has been away from defined benefit plans, to defined contribution plans.

Exhibit 12–4 shows the relationships among the employer, the pension plan, and the retirees in a typical defined benefit pension plan. The employer makes contributions to the pension fund, and the pension fund ultimately makes payments to retirees as specified in the employer's labor agreements. Unlike a defined contribution plan, however, the employer's pension obligation is to pay the benefits promised by the pension plan. In substance, the employer has an obligation to the beneficiaries, and the pension fund itself is just an intermediary.

BASIC ACCOUNTING FOR PENSIONS

To illustrate financial reporting for a defined benefit pension plan, refer to Exhibits 12–5 and 12–6, which contain portions of the pension footnote disclosures from Bethlehem Steel's annual report for 1992. Bethlehem Steel's pension benefits are based

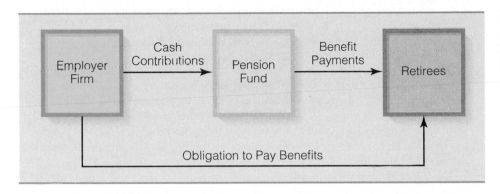

EXHIBIT 12–4
DEFINED BENEFIT PENSION
PLANS

both on the employees' years of service and highest earnings levels in the years preceding retirement. The reader of Bethlehem Steel's pension disclosures would give special attention to the measurements of pension obligations and annual pension cost. Both items are discussed in the following sections.

Measurement of Benefit Obligations

Exhibit 12–5 explains the measurement of Bethlehem Steel's pension obligations. Because pension benefits will be paid in future years, it is necessary to estimate the future payments and discount these to present values using an appropriate rate of interest. Bethlehem Steel uses a discount rate of 8.5% to measure its pension obligations.

The choice of a discount rate is crucial in evaluating pension obligations because minor variations in discount rates cause large variations in present values. Analysts often use the following rule of thumb: A 1% variation in the assumed discount rate will cause about a 20% variation in the valuation of pension obligations.

Observe that Bethlehem Steel reports three present value measurements. The **vested benefit obligation** indicates amounts to which employees have irrevocable rights, even if they leave the firm prior to retirement. The **accumulated benefit obligation** shows the amount of pension benefits that employees have earned to date, based on current salary levels. The **projected benefit obligation** measures the amount of pension benefits that employees have earned to date, based on the expected future salary levels that will determine these pension benefits.

Bethlehem Steel's disclosures indicate that 97% of the company's benefits were vested at the end of 1992 ($4,357.9 vested benefit ÷ $4,490.1 accumulated benefit = 97%). Inclusion of expected future salary levels in the calculation increases the pension obligation by only 7.4% ($4,822.7 projected benefit ÷ $4,490.1 accumulated benefit = 107.4%). These relationships reflect the fact that Bethlehem Steel has a stable and mature workforce.

Exhibit 12–5 also shows that the total market value of Bethlehem Steel's pension plan assets was $3.3 billion at the end of 1992. This amount is less than the pension liability, and indicates that Bethlehem Steel's pension plan was substantially underfunded at that date. Accounting standards require that Bethlehem Steel report the unfunded liability in the balance sheet. The liability is measured as the difference between the firm's accumulated benefit obligations and the fair value of the plan assets, as follows:

EXHIBIT 12–5
PENSION LIABILITY
FOOTNOTE DISCLOSURES

Bethlehem Steel Corporation
Pension Liability Recognized in Consolidated Balance Sheet
(1992 Annual Report)

We have noncontributory defined benefit pension plans which provide benefits for substantially all employees. Defined benefits are based on years of service and the five highest consecutive years of pensionable earnings during the last ten years prior to retirement or a minimum amount based on years of service. We fund annually the amount required under ERISA minimum funding standards plus additional amounts as appropriate.

The following sets forth the plan's actuarial assumptions used and funded status at year-end together with amounts recognized in our consolidated balance sheets:

	December 31	
	1992	1991
	(dollars in millions)	
Assumptions:		
Discount rate	8.50%	8.50%
Average rate of compensation increase	4.4%	4.5%
Actuarial present value of benefit obligations:		
Vested benefit obligation	$4,357.9	$4,324.4
Accumulated benefit obligation	4,490.1	4,457.2
Projected benefit obligation	4,822.7	4,769.6
Plan assets at fair value:		
Fixed income securities	1,979.8	2,090.3
Equity securities	1,006.0	1,187.1
Cash and marketable securities	315.6	214.9
Total plan assets	3,301.4	3,492.3
Projected benefit obligation in excess of plan assets	1,521.3	1,277.3
Unrecognized net gain	(58.3)	87.8
Remaining unrecognized net obligation resulting from adoption of Statement No. 87	(339.0)	(378.0)
Unrecognized prior service cost from plan amendments	(174.9)	(194.2)
Adjustment required to recognize minimum liability—intangible asset	239.6	172.0
Balance sheet liability	$1,188.7	$964.9

SOURCE: Abridged from note to Bethlehem Steel Corporation's *1992 Annual Report.*

Accumulated benefit obligation (Exhibit 12–5)	$ 4,490.1
Less: plan assets at fair value (Exhibit 12–5)	−3,301.4
Balance sheet liability	$ 1,188.7

Consequently, Bethlehem Steel reported a pension liability of almost $1.19 billion dollars at the end of 1992.

Measurement of Pension Expenses

Exhibit 12–6 shows the components of the pension expense reported in Bethlehem Steel's income statement, defined as follows:

- **Service cost,** also called the "normal cost," is the value of future pension benefits that employees have earned during the current year.
- **Interest cost** is the interest on the projected benefit obligation for the year. Recall that the projected benefit obligation is a present value, the discounted value of future payments. Each year this present value increases because the payment date is closer.
- **Return on plan assets** is a reduction in pension expense for the return that is expected on the plan's assets. This component is based on anticipated, not actual, return so that pension costs are not severely influenced by variations in investment values.
- **Other items (net)** includes systematic amortization of liabilities existing when present pension reporting standards were adopted, obligations resulting from subsequent changes in pension benefits, revisions in various assumptions underlying the pension valuation, and other factors.

Pension reporting continues to be an area of controversy in financial accounting. The basic issues center on (1) the assumptions used in measuring pension obligations and expenses, (2) the appropriate definition of pension obligations, and (3) whether pension funds are entities distinct from the employer firms.

EVALUATION OF PENSION REPORTING

EXHIBIT 12–6
PENSION EXPENSE
FOOTNOTE DISCLOSURES

Bethlehem Steel Corporation
Pension Expense Recognized in Consolidated Income Statement
(1992 Annual Report)

The assumptions used in each year and the components of our annual pension cost are as follows:

	1992	1991
	(Dollars in Millions)	
Assumptions:		
Return on plan assets	9.50%	10.25%
Discount rate	8.50%	9.25%
Defined benefit plans:		
Service cost—benefits earned during the period	$ 45.0	$ 45.6
Interest on projected benefit obligation	394.2	386.6
Return on plan assets	(312.2)	(317.2)
Other items (net)	63.4	71.7
Total cost	$190.4	$186.7

SOURCE: Abridged from note to Bethlehem Steel Corporation's *1992 Annual Report.*

Assumptions

A myriad of actuarial and economic assumptions underlie the estimation of pension obligations. **Actuarial assumptions** (e.g., employee turnover, service lives, longevity, etc.) are fairly standardized and noncontroversial. The major controversies concern the **economic assumptions,** particularly the assumed interest rate used to discount future pension benefits, and the anticipated rate of return on pension plan assets.

Employers are often slow to revise their expected investment returns or their discount rates. Many pension funds have not significantly reduced either of these rates since the mid-1980s, when stocks and bonds experienced extraordinary gains. In the early 1990s, however, interest rates declined to much lower levels.

When lower interest rates are used in pension calculations, the present value of future benefits is larger and the expected investment return on plan assets is lower. These effects may be dramatic. For example, in 1992 General Motors Corporation assumed an 11% rate of return but earned only 6.4%. In that year, General Motors' unfunded pension obligation increased by about $5 billion because of lower interest rates. It is estimated that in 1994, as a result of lower interest rates, more than half of the 200 largest corporate pension funds were underfunded ("Retirees at Risk: Hopeful Assumptions Let Firms Minimize Pension Contributions," *The Wall Street Journal,* September 2, 1993). Accordingly, the analyst must be alert to differences among firms in the discount rates and interest rate assumptions embedded in their pension measurements.

Measurements of Pension Obligations

Exhibit 12–5 shows three separate measures of Bethlehem Steel's pension obligation, i.e., vested, accumulated, and projected benefit obligations. Managers and analysts often disagree about which of these best represents the firm's pension obligation. Managers sometimes assert that vested benefits are the best measure of the obligation, because this is the amount that must be paid to employees, even if the firm were to discontinue its operations immediately. Bear in mind, however, that financial statements reflect a "going concern" assumption, unless the firm is actually expected to liquidate in the near-term future. Alternatively, some firms argue that the accumulated benefit amount is a suitable measure, because it assumes continuity of the firm, but does not incorporate salary increases that have yet to occur.

Finally, analysts frequently argue that the projected benefit obligation is most realistic, because it is based on expected pension payments (assuming normal rates of salary increase). Moreover, analysts argue that the accumulated benefit measurement is not meaningful because future salary increases are ignored in estimating future pension payments. Future inflation is reflected in the discount rates used to compute present values.

Present accounting standards do not aim to resolve these disputes. In fact, as discussed earlier, balance sheet disclosures of minimum pension obligations use the accumulated benefits measure, whereas income measures are based on the projected benefits measure. Accounting standards reflect a compromise that discloses two types of pension costs, along with extensive supplementary disclosures.

Pension Fund As a Distinct Entity

The pension fund is merely an intermediary between the employer and the pension beneficiary, as depicted in Exhibit 12–4. The employer is ultimately liable for all pension benefits, and bears all of the risks associated with the pension fund's investments. Consequently, many analysts do not regard the pension fund as an entity distinct from the employer firm, and suggest that pension plan assets and obligations should be included (consolidated) with those of the employer for financial reporting purposes.

The consolidation of the employer firm and its pension plan would dramatically alter the financial statements of most industrial firms. For example, Bethlehem Steel's pension plan had $3.3 billion in assets and $4.8 billion in obligations at the end of 1992. Bethlehem Steel itself had about $4.8 billion in assets (exclusive of pension amounts) at that date, and only $379 million in shareholders' equity. In this case, inclusion of the pension fund assets and obligations on Bethlehem Steel's balance sheet would almost double the apparent size of the company, and more than double its reported debt financing.

Pension Obligations and Financial Ratios

To illustrate the impact of pension obligations on financial ratios, consider Bethlehem Steel's ratio of debt to total assets at the end of 1993. Exhibit 12–7 summarizes pertinent information from Bethlehem Steel's financial statements.

Bethlehem Steel Corporation Selected Information for Financial Ratio Calculations (1993 Annual Report) (dollars in millions)	
Balance sheet items:	
Total assets (includes pension assets of $600.6 million)	$5,876.7
Total liabilities (includes pension liabilities of $1,613.6 million)	$5,180.1
Footnote disclosures:	
Plan assets at fair value	$3,365.8
Projected benefit obligations	$5,208.6

EXHIBIT 12–7
INFORMATION FOR FINANCIAL RATIO CALCULATIONS

If the analyst ignores the footnote disclosures of Bethlehem's pension assets and liabilities, and uses only the information in the balance sheet, then the company's debt-to-total assets ratio at the end of 1993 is 88.1%, computed as follows:

$$\frac{\text{Total liabilities (Exhibit 12–7)}}{\text{Total assets (Exhibit 12–7)}} = \frac{\$5,180.1}{\$5,876.7}$$

$$= 88.1\%$$

If instead the analyst does not consider the pension plan to be a distinct economic entity (for the reasons discussed earlier), the measurements of Bethlehem's assets and liabilities might be adjusted as follows (all dollar amounts are provided in Exhibit 12–7):

	($ in millions)
Total assets, as reported in the balance sheet	$5,876.7
Less: Pension assets included in the above amount	(600.6)
Pension plan assets at fair value, reported in note	3,365.8
Total assets, as adjusted	$8,641.9
Total liabilities, as reported in the balance sheet	$5,180.1
Less: Pension liabilities included in the above amount	(1,613.6)
Pension plan liabilities, reported in note	5,208.6
Total liabilities, as adjusted	$8,775.1

As a result of these adjustments made to Bethlehem's assets and liabilities, Bethlehem's adjusted ratio of debt to total assets at the end of 1993 is 101.5%, computed as follows:

$$\frac{\text{Total liabilities, as adjusted}}{\text{Total assets, as adjusted}} = \frac{\$8,775.1}{\$8,641.9}$$

$$= \quad 101.5\%$$

In this case, incorporation of pension plan assets and liabilities with those of Bethlehem Steel's indicates that the firm's adjusted liabilities exceed its adjusted assets. Thus, shareholders' equity would be negative at the end of 1993.

OTHER POSTRETIREMENT EXPENSES AND OBLIGATIONS

Approximately one-third of all U.S. workers are covered by employer medical plans that continue the employee's coverage after retirement. The costs of retiree medical benefits is substantial, and is expected to continue to increase as people live longer. Also, inflation and improvements in medical technology will contribute to rising health costs.

Until recently, the predominant way of reporting these nonpension postretirement benefits was **pay-as-you-go:** Expenses were reported on a cash basis, and no obligations were recognized for future payments. New accounting standards became mandatory in 1993, however, which require that firms currently report their obligations to provide future benefits and accrue the expenses during the years that employees provide service (*SFAS No. 106,* "Employers' Accounting for Postretirement Benefits Other Than Pensions," December 1990). For most affected firms, conversion to an accrual basis increased the amount of expenses currently recognized for medical benefits by two to three times (200 to 300%). As a result, adoption of the new standard in 1993 reduced profits at the 100 largest U.S. corporations by about 33%. Moreover, recognition of the related obligations reduced shareholders' equity an average of 20%. For example, at General Motors Corporation the reduction in shareholders' equity exceeded 80% ("Retiree Benefits to Take Bigger Bite of Profits," *The Wall Street Journal,* September 1, 1993).

Illustration of Nonpension Postretirement Benefit Disclosure

Bethlehem Steel Corporation chose to adopt the new standard early in 1992. Exhibit 12–8 contains excerpts of Bethlehem Steel's related disclosures, and will serve as a basis for our discussion. Observe that the overall format and content of these disclosures parallels that shown earlier for pension benefits (Exhibits 12–5 and 12–6). The

Bethlehem Steel Corporation
Postretirement Benefits Other Than Pension
Obligations and Expenses Recognized in Financial Statements
(1992 Annual Report)

EXHIBIT 12–8
NONPENSION
POST–RETIREMENT EXPENSES

1. Postretirement Benefits Other Than Pensions

In addition to providing pension benefits, we currently provide healthcare and life insurance benefits for most retirees and their dependents. Effective January 1, 1992, we adopted Statement No. 106 *Employers' Accounting for Postretirement Benefits Other Than Pensions* (see Note A). We previously accounted for such benefits generally on claims incurred basis and prior year financial statements have not been restated. We continue to fund healthcare benefits through various third-party administrators based on claims incurred. Therefore, the adoption of this statement has no effect on our cash flow. Life insurance benefits have been funded on an actuarial basis which amounted to $7.9 million in 1992.

Information regarding our plan's actuarial assumptions, funded status, liability and transition obligation follows:

	1992 December 31 (dollars in millions)
Accumulated postretirement benefit obligation:	
Retirees	$1,413.7
Fully eligible active plan participants	105.1
Other active plan participants	176.2
Total	1,695.0
Plan assets at fair value:	
Fixed income securities	159.6
Accumulated postretirement benefit obligation in excess of plan assets	1,535.4
Unrecognized net gain	4.5
Balance sheet liability	$1,539.9

The components of our postretirement benefit cost follow:

	1992 (dollars in millions)
Service cost	$ 9.0
Interest on accumulated postretirement benefit obligation	139.0
Return on plan assets—actual	(18.4)
—deferred	4.5
Multiemployer plans	7.1
Total cost	$141.2

The assumed weighted average healthcare trend rate used to calculate the accumulated postretirement benefit obligation and 1992 expense was 9.5%, declining gradually until it reaches an ultimate average rate of 5.5% in the year 2000. A 1% increase in the assumed healthcare trend rate would increase the accumulated postretirement benefit obligation by $147 million and 1992 expense by $14 million. The discount rate used in calculating the obligation and 1992 expense was 8.5% and the assumed earnings on plan assets was 9.5%.

SOURCE: Excerpts from Note I to Bethlehem Steel Corporation's *1992 Annual Report.*

analyst would focus on the measurement of the firm's obligation and the determination of the annual expense.

Bethlehem Steel reports a liability of $1.5 billion for nonpension postretirement benefits at the end of 1992. As shown in Exhibit 12–8, this amount represents the difference between the present value of these benefits ($1,695.0 million) and the plan assets at fair value ($159.6 million).

Although this measurement is similar to the measurement of pension obligations shown earlier (Exhibit 12–5), there are two notable differences. First, the **accumulated postretirement benefit obligation** measures the present value of the future benefits that employees and retirees have earned to date. The calculation incorporates future medical cost changes, based on an assumed average health care trend rate. This contrasts sharply with the calculation of the minimum pension liability, which ignores expected future price changes. The future price of medical inflation is admittedly hard to predict, and Bethlehem Steel also provides the analyst with an estimate of the sensitivity of the measurements to a 1% increase in the assumed rate.

Second, the fair values of the plan assets are minor, relative to the accumulated benefit obligation. Few firms fund any of their nonpension retirement benefits. There are no regulatory funding requirements or income tax advantages to motivate early funding, and most firms opt instead to simply pay the medical and life insurance premiums when they become due.

Measurement of Nonpension Postretirement Benefit Expense

The cost components shown in Exhibit 12–8 for the nonpension expenses follow the same format as those for pension costs (Exhibit 12–5). The **service cost** represents the amount of the accumulated benefit obligation that was earned by employees over the current year. The **interest cost** is the beginning of the year obligation multiplied by the discount rate. For firms like Bethlehem Steel, with mature employee groups, interest cost is the largest component of the net expense because the benefit obligation is so large. Because the benefits are not substantially funded, the **return on plan assets** provides only a minor offset to the other cost components.

A comparison of the financial statement impacts of pension and nonpension benefits for Bethlehem Steel indicates that both types of postretirement benefits have similar effects on the firm's financial position and operating results. Although the total obligations for pensions are much greater than those for nonpension benefits, the pension benefits are substantially funded, while the nonpension benefits are not. As a result, the unfunded obligations are approximately the same for both types of benefits (about $1.5 billion each) at the end of 1992. Similarly, the firm's expenses in 1992 were approximately the same for pension and nonpension benefits, because pension costs were substantially offset by investment returns on the pension fund assets.

As noted earlier, standards for the measurement and reporting of postretirement benefits in financial statements have changed considerably in recent years. As a result, financial analysts must reconsider the usefulness of conventional financial ratio calculations, in light of these new employee benefits measurements and disclosures. There are no simple recipes for modifying the typical ratios. The informed user of financial reports must be aware that financial statement analysis is more art than science, and that much of the information that is pertinent to a decision may not appear in the body of the financial statements. Recognition of these new financial reporting standards may require modification of analysts' traditional rules of thumb regarding trends and changes in a firm's performance.

Reality Check 12–2 contrasts the disclosures related to pensions and non–pension post–employment benefits for a major U.S. corporation.

MERCK & CO., INC., SELECTED POSTEMPLOYMENT BENEFIT DISCLOSURES

REALITY CHECK 12–2

Merck and Co., Inc. is the world's largest pharmaceutical company. The firm designs, develops and markets human and animal health products and specialty chemicals. The following information has been abstracted from the notes to Merck's 1993 financial statements.

	Pension Benefits		Other Postretirement Benefits	
	1993	1992	1993	1992
	(dollars in millions)		(dollars in millions)	
Funded status of benefit plans:				
Plan assets at market value	$1,329.6	$1,411.8	$310.2	$ 30.4
Accumulated benefit obligation	1,364.3	1,193.9	979.6	758.4
Projected benefit obligation	1,834.2	1,573.2	—	—
Components of annual expense:				
Service cost	97.4	86.4	31.0	31.2
Interest cost	135.7	123.7	69.2	62.9
Actual return on assets	(61.5)	(94.1)	(22.4)	(1.8)
Other	(74.6)	(34.7)	2.1	(1.9)
Total cost	$ 97.0	$ 81.3	$ 79.9	$ 90.4
Underlying assumptions:				
Discount rate	7.5%	9.0%	7.5%	9.0%
Expected return on plan assets	10.0%	10.0%	10.0%	10.0%
Future compensation increases	5.0%	6.0%	—	—
Health care cost trend	—	—	12.0%	13.0%

REQUIRED

a. Do you consider Merck's pension benefits and other postemployment benefits to be overfunded or underfunded at the end of 1993? Explain.
b. Distinguish between the "accumulated benefit obligation" amounts reported for each type of plan.
c. With respect to the components of the annual costs, why is interest expense included? Why does the return on plan assets appear as a negative component?
d. The disclosure of assumptions reveals three changes between 1993 and 1992: (1) the discount rate has been decreased from 9 to 7.5%, (2) the rate of future compensation increases has been revised from 6 to 5%, and (3) the health care cost trend rate has been changed from 13 to 12%. Explain how each of these changes would affect your comparisons of postemployment liabilities and costs between 1993 and 1992.

1. Distinguish between leases that are ordinary rentals, and those that are in substance a purchase of assets.

A lease is an agreement between an owner (or lessor) and a renter (or lessee) that conveys the right to use the leased property for a designated future period. Accountants classify leases as either capital leases or operating leases. A capital lease is interpreted as essentially a purchase of the leased asset, while an operating lease is reported on the same basis as an ordinary rental.

Accounting standards provide a set of explicit criteria to identify capital leases. Essentially, a capital lease transfers the potential risks and rewards of ownership to the lessee. A capital lease is reported as an asset financed by installment debt.

2. Understand how leases impact the measurement of financial position and operating performance.

Capital leases affect the balance sheet and income statement in the same manner as would an installment purchase of the asset. Noncurrent assets and lease obligations are reported based on the present value of the series of lease payments. The annual expense (lease amortization expense and interest expense) is relatively higher in the earlier years, and declines as the lease obligation is reduced over time. By contrast, operating leases are reported as ordinary rentals. Neither assets nor liabilities are recognized in the balance sheet when the lease is signed. The annual expense is generally equal to the annual lease payments.

Extensive disclosures in the Notes to Financial Statements are provided for all long-term leases, both capital and operating, indicating the amount and timing of future minimum lease payments. Financial statement analysts must use these "off-balance-sheet" amounts in order to aid in assessments of liquidity and solvency of lessee firms.

3. Know the difference between defined contribution and defined benefit pension plans.

Pension plans are either defined contribution or defined benefit plans. Defined contribution plans specify the employer's required payments to the pension fund, and do not present any special reporting issues. Defined benefit plans, on the other hand, specify the future pension payments to which an employee will be entitled. Both types of plans require that the employer make periodic payments to a pension fund, but under a defined benefit plan the employer assumes all of the risks associated with pension fund investments.

4. Appreciate the impact of retirement benefit liabilities on reported financial position and operating results.

Firms with defined benefit plans must report on the balance sheet a minimum liability equal to the difference between pension obligations and the value of pension fund assets. Pension expense reported on the income statement consists mainly of current service costs plus interest on the pension obligation minus returns expected to be earned on the pension fund's assets.

5. Understand the key assumptions necessary to measure postretirement obligations and expenses.

Measurements of pension obligations and expenses are based on a variety of assumptions, including assumptions about future earnings of pension fund investments and future salary increases of covered employees. The critical assumptions are disclosed in footnotes to the financial statements. Financial analysts must be alert to variations in assumptions used by different firms to measure pension obligations and expenses.

Standards for the financial reporting of nonpension postretirement benefits have been adopted recently and are similar to the standards used for reporting pensions. The future trend of medical costs must be considered in predicting future benefits. Such costs are difficult to predict due to changes in medical technology, medical cost inflation, changing standards of medical care, the potential impact of a national health plan, and other factors. For this reason, the liabilities and expenses associated with nonpension retiree benefits are difficult to measure. Financial analysts must be creative as well as cautious when incorporating these measurements in financial ratio analysis.

KEY TERMS

Accumulated benefit obligation	Lessee
Accumulated postretirement benefit obligation	Lessor
	Operating lease
Actuarial assumptions	Other items (net)
Capital lease	Pay-as-you-go
Defined benefit pension plan	Projected benefit obligation
Defined contribution pension plan	Return on plan assets
Economic assumptions	Service cost
Interest cost	Service lives
Lease	Vested benefit obligation

REALITY CHECK SOLUTIONS

SOLUTION TO REALITY CHECK 12–1

a. The present values of Delta's capital leases are included in the asset and liability totals reported in its balance sheet (and in our summary balance sheet information). If financial analysts also desire to incorporate Delta's operating leases "as if" they were capital leases, it is necessary first to discount the future minimum lease payments at Delta's borrowing rate. The borrowing rate is not disclosed in the financial statements, however. If it may be assumed that Delta's capital and operating leases have relatively similar cash flow patterns, then an approximate present value for the operating leases may be computed as follows:

Present value of capital lease payments (Note 4)	$ 119,819
Total minimum capital lease payments (Note 4)	$ 167,242
Percentage of present value to total payments:	

$$\frac{\$119,819}{\$167,242} \;=\; 71.6\%$$

Total minimum operating lease payments	$17,332,323
× Percentage of present value to total payments (above)	71.6%
Estimated present value of operating lease payments	$12,409,943

b. This approximation indicates that capitalization of the operating leases would increase Delta's reported property, plant and equipment as well as debt by about

$12.4 billion. Selected financial statement relationships would be affected by capitalizing leases as follows:

Delta Air Lines, Inc.
Selected Financial Ratios Before and After
Capitalization of Operating Leases

	Before Capitalization (See Reality Check 12–1)	After Capitalization[a]	% Change
Total assets	$10,161,574	$22,561,574	+ 122%
Total liabilities	$ 8,267,506	$20,667,506	+ 150%
Property and equipment	$ 7,093,312	$19,493,312	+ 175%
Liabilities/assets	81.4%	91.6%	
Property and equipment/assets	69.8%	86.4%	
Net loss	$ 506,318	?[b]	?[b]

[a]The amounts after capitalization are determined by adding $12.4 billion to debt and property, plant, and equipment, based on the approximate present value of the operating lease commitments earlier.

[b]Lease expense is generally higher in the earlier years for capital leases. While the income effect is not readily calculable given the information in Delta's financial report, Delta's reported net loss would certainly have increased if leases had been capitalized.

As shown in the preceding calculations, capitalization of Delta's operating leases would increase the reported amount of total assets, liabilities, and property and equipment by 122%, 150%, and 175%, respectively. We do not include any income-based ratios (e.g., return on assets) because Delta operated at a loss in 1993.

SOLUTION TO REALITY CHECK 12–2

a. *Pension plans:* Merck's accumulated benefit obligation exceeds plan assets by $34.7 million ($1,364.3 million, less $1,329.6 million), and Merck's projected benefit obligation exceeds plan assets by $504.6 million ($1,834.2 million, less $1,329.6 million). By either measure, Merck's plans are underfunded at the end of 1993. The projected benefit obligation, which includes projected rates of compensation increases, is a more meaningful definition of the pension obligation.

   Other (nonpension) plans: Merck's accumulated benefit obligation exceeds plan assets by $699.4 million ($979.6 million, less $310.2 million), so these benefits are underfunded at the end of 1993. (See the following discussion also.)

b. The "accumulated benefit obligation" has a different interpretation for pension obligations than for other postretirement obligations. For pension obligations, the accumulated benefit obligation assumes that present salary levels will continue through the employee retirement dates, i.e., future rates of compensation increases are ignored. For nonpension obligations, on the other hand, future rates of medical cost inflation are formally incorporated in the calculation of the accumulated benefit obligations. The financial statement analyst must be alert to the different meanings of "accumulated benefits."

c. Interest expense is a component of the annual cost of postretirement benefits because the obligations are reported at present value; the expected future benefit payments are discounted at an appropriate interest rate. As time passes, the present value of future payments increases. This increase in the value of liability is due to interest expense.

The return on plan assets represents amounts that have been earned on the invested plan assets. Increases in the value of the plan's investments reduce the amount of the unfunded pension obligation. For this reason, these returns constitute income (or a reduction in expense) related to pensions.

d. *Discount rate:* Expected future benefit payments are discounted to determine the present value of the pension obligation. Reductions in the discount rate increase the present value of the pension obligation.

Rate of compensation increases: The projected benefit obligation incorporates future compensation increases. As the assumed rate is lowered, the present value of the obligation decreases. In contrast, the accumulated benefit obligation for pensions ignores future compensation increases, so this measure is unaffected by the assumed change in compensation rates.

Health care cost trend rate: A decrease in this rate reduces the firm's estimated future payments for medical benefits, and thereby reduces the firm's obligation.

QUESTIONS

12–1 Discuss several reasons why business managers might choose to lease rather than to purchase operating assets (e.g., buildings and equipment).

12–2 Describe the key features that you would expect to find in a long-term lease agreement.

12–3 Distinguish between capital leases and operating leases as the terms are used in financial reporting. Is the distinction meaningful? Discuss.

12–4 What criteria are used in deciding whether a given lease agreement constitutes a capital lease or an operating lease? Do these criteria make economic sense? Discuss.

12–5 Contrast the effects that capital leases and operating leases have on the following financial statement elements and relationships. Discuss how each of these effects might influence a manager's decision about how to design a lease contract.

    a. Total assets
    b. Total liabilities
    c. Net income, earlier years
    d. Net income, later years
    e. Ratio of debt to total assets
    f. Ratio of operating income to total assets

12–6 Assume that a given lease contract qualifies as a capital lease.

    a. How would you determine the dollar amount to be reported in the balance sheet as an asset?
    b. How would this dollar amount change over successive balance sheets?
    c. How would you determine the amount to be reported in the balance sheet as a lease obligation?
    d. How would the amount of the obligation change over successive balance sheets? Would the balance sheet amounts reported as leased assets and lease obligations ever be the same? Explain.

12–7 Explain why the total annual expenses associated with capital leases are higher in the earlier years, and lower in the later years, of the lease term. Why is it necessary that the total expense over the entire life of the lease be the same for capital and operating leases?

12–8 Evaluate the following statement: Capitalizing a lease creates a fictitious asset. The lessee does not own the leased asset, because the lessor retains title and will repossess the asset at the end of the lease term. A lease is simply a rental, and this is true regardless of the length of the lease term.

12–9 Respond to the following statements: Firms have many different types of contracts that obligate them to make a series of cash payments at dates well into the future. For example, CEOs and other top managers often have multiyear contracts that guarantee substantial salaries even if the manager is terminated. Should the cash payments specified in these contracts also be capitalized? Would it make sense to put managers on the balance sheet as intangible assets? If not, why do we make an exception for leases?

12–10 Notes to financial statements include disclosures about operating leases, including minimum rental commitments, disclosed by year for the ensuing five years, and in the aggregate for later years. How do you think a financial analyst should use this supplementary (note) information when evaluating a firm's total debt? If you consider operating leases to be components of a firm's total debt, should the related amounts be reported in the body of the financial statements? Discuss.

12–11 For a capital lease, the amounts that are initially recorded as leased assets and lease obligations will depend on the interest rate used to discount the lease payments. In addition, the discount rate will also affect the periodic amounts of expense reported for capital leases.

a. Assume that a manger wishes to report relatively small amounts of leased assets and obligations. Would she prefer a low or a high discount rate? Explain.

b. Assume that a manager wishes to report relatively larger amounts of income in the earlier years of a lease. Would she prefer a low or a high discount rate? Explain.

c. Assume that a manager wishes to report a relatively high ratio of income to assets in the earlier years of a lease. Would she prefer a low or a high discount rate? Explain.

12–12 What types of postretirement benefits are usually provided to employees by larger sized business firms?

12–13 Why do firms provide postretirement benefits to employees?

12–14 When should the costs of postretirement benefits be reported as expenses on the income statement?

12–15 Distinguish between defined contribution and defined benefit pension plans. Which arrangement is riskier for the employee? Which is riskier for the employer? Explain.

12–16 A typical defined benefit pension plan involves three entities: the employer firm, the pension plan, and the covered employee. Describe the relationships among these three entities.

12–17 Firms with defined benefit pension plans report three separate liability amounts in the notes to the financial statements. These are the obligations for vested benefits, accumulated benefits, and projected benefits.

a. Describe how these amounts differ.

b. Identify which of these amounts best measures the employer's liability as of the balance sheet date. Explain the reasons for your choice.

12–18 Accounting standards require that firms report their unfunded pension liabilities on the balance sheet. Describe what is meant by an unfunded pension liability. Explain why you believe that such an amount should (or should not) be included on the balance sheet.

12–19 Pension expense includes three main components: service cost, interest cost, and a reduction in expense for the return on plan assets. Explain how each of these amounts is determined.

12–20 Distinguish between the actuarial assumptions and the economic assumptions that underlie the measurement of pension liabilities and expenses. Which of these types of assumptions is more controversial? Why?

12–21 Present accounting standards report only the amount of unfunded pension obligations on the balance sheet. Gross pension assets and liabilities are not reported on the financial statements. This practice is based on the premise that the pension fund is an entity distinct from the employer firm.

a. Do you agree with this premise? Why?

b. If the pension fund is not a distinct entity, how should pension assets and liabilities be reported in the financial statements?

c. Which key financial statement elements and ratios would be likely to change dramatically, if the pension fund were consolidated with (added to) the employer firm's financial statements?

12–22 Many firms provide their employees with other, nonpension postretirement benefits, primarily medical plans. Outline the similarities and differences in accounting for pensions and nonpension postretirement benefits, with respect to:

a. Liability measurement

b. Balance sheet reporting

c. Expense recognition

EXERCISES

12–23 Installment Purchase—Alternate Exercises (A) or (B)

Exercise (A)

Determine the first year's financial statement impact of the following purchase terms:

- Annual payments, at year-end, $15,000
- 5-year useful life and note term
- 10% borrowing rate
- Straight-line benefit pattern
- Zero residual value
- Installment purchase

Exercise (B)

Determine the first year's financial statement impact of the following purchase terms:

- Annual payments, at year-end, $25,000
- 10-year useful life and note term
- 12% borrowing rate
- Straight-line benefit pattern
- Zero residual value
- Installment purchase

12–24 Operating or Capital Lease—Alternate Exercises (A) or (B)

Exercise (A)
Determine the first year's financial statement impact of the following lease terms:

- Annual payments, at year-end, $15,000
- 5-year useful life
- 10% borrowing rate
- Straight-line benefit pattern
- Zero residual value
- 5-year lease term
- Lessor's fair value of property, $60,000

Exercise (B)
Determine the first year's financial statement impact of the following lease terms:

- Annual payments, at year-end, $25,000
- 10-year useful life
- 12% borrowing rate
- Straight-line benefit pattern
- Zero residual value
- 10-year lease term
- Lessor's fair value of property, $225,000

PROBLEMS

12–25 Lease versus Purchase—Alternate Problems (A) or (B)

Problem (A)
Consider the following terms:

- Annual payments, end of each year, $40,000
- 10-year useful life
- 10% borrowing rate
- Straight-line benefit pattern
- Zero residual value
- Lease purchase
- Initial deposit upon signing agreement, $20,000, refundable upon satisfying all purchase terms
- 5-year lease terms
- Lessor's fair value of property, $170,000

REQUIRED

a. How might you change the terms if you wanted to be sure this purchase would be reported as a capital lease?

b. Show the first year's financial statement impact of your revised terms, and compare it to the financial statement impact of the original terms.

Problem B

Consider the following terms:

- Annual payments, end of each year, $30,000
- 12-year useful life
- 8% borrowing rate
- Straight-line benefit pattern
- Zero residual value
- Lease purchase
- Initial fees paid upon signing agreement, $20,000
- 8-year lease term
- Lessor's fair value of property, $220,000

REQUIRED

a. How might you change the terms if you wanted to be sure this purchase would be reported as a capital lease?
b. Show the first year's financial statement impact of your revised terms, and compare it to the financial statement impact of the original terms.

Capital versus Operating Lease

12–26 Schott Sausages, in trying to lease a sausage machine, is concerned about whether the machine will be reported as a capital or operating lease. Consider the following facts in your deliberations:

- Annual lease payment required, $30,000
- Term of lease and useful life of machine, 5 years
- Discount rate, 10%

REQUIRED

a. Should the sausage machine be reported as a capital or operating lease? Why?
b. Calculate the annual expense for the first two years associated with a capital lease, using straight-line depreciation and zero residual value.
c. Why are the capital lease costs higher than the operating lease costs in part b?

Capital versus Operating Lease

12–27 Hannah Steel Corporation signed a five-year lease agreement on January 2, 1997, for the lease of equipment. The annual lease payment required at the end of each year is $4,000. The useful life of the equipment is five years and the fair market value is $18,000.

REQUIRED

a. Assume that Hannah's (lessee) incremental borrowing is 8%. Calculate the present value of the lease payments.
b. Is this a capital lease or an operating lease?
c. If the total lease payments are $4,000 × 5 years = $20,000, why isn't this the present value?
d. Advise Hannah on the advantages and disadvantages of a capital versus an operating lease.

Evaluation of Liabilities: Potential Creditor Viewpoint

12–28 L'alpane is a transportation company headquartered in Paris. Its 1996 annual report includes the following liabilities (all in French francs):

	1995	1996
Payables to:		
Affiliated companies	38,642,541	8,325,461
Third parties	5,162,034	3,705,679
Accrued expenses and provisions	22,655,420	37,042,469
Total liabilities	66,459,995	49,073,609

REQUIRED

a. Describe each of L'alpane's liabilities.

b. All other things being equal, would you consider L'alpane to be more, or less, liquid at the end of 1996? Why?

c. If you were a banker who had lent money to L'alpane, how would you feel about the firm's handling of its liabilities? Why?

d. If you were a creditor who had *leased an airplane* to L'alpane, and your account is 60 days past due, how would you feel about L'alpane's management of its liabilities? Why?

e. Relative to many other large companies, does L'alpane owe much money to external parties? How can you tell? Given a natural and long-standing aversion to debt by many French companies, does L'alpane's balance sheet suggest that this firm also avoids debt? Why, or why not?

12–29 Effect on Ratios: Lease–Purchase—Alternate Problems (A) or (B)

Problem (A)

Consider the following summary financial statements at the beginning of the period:

Current assets	$ 40,000	Current liabilities	$ 15,000
Other assets	110,000	Other liabilities	113,150
		Capital stock	10,000
		Retained earnings	11,850
Total	$150,000	Total	$150,000

Net income during the period (exclusive of the lease) was $35,000. Also, assume the company entered into a lease with the following terms:

- Annual payments, end of each year, $30,000
- 12-year useful life
- 8% borrowing rate
- Straight-line benefit pattern
- Zero residual value
- 6-year lease term
- Lessor's fair value of property, $240,000

REQUIRED

Use *beginning* balance sheet data to calculate the following requirements:

a. Calculate the return on equity (ROE) ratio at year end and the financial leverage ratio for this company, assuming that this new asset is reported on the financial statements as a capital lease.

b. Calculate the return on equity (ROE) ratio and the financial leverage ratio for this company, assuming that this new asset is reported on the financial statements as an operating lease.

c. Discuss the relative impact on these financial statements of acquiring this asset under an operating lease versus a capital lease.

Problem (B)

Consider the following summary financial statements at the beginning of the period:

Current assets	$1,050,000	Current liabilities	$ 650,000
Other assets	2,450,000	Other liabilities	1,500,000
		Capital stock	100,000
		Retained earnings	1,250,000
Total	$3,500,000	Total	$3,500,000

Net income (during the period exclusive of the lease) was $250,000. Also, consider the following lease terms:

- Annual payments, at year-end, $25,000
- 10-year useful life
- 12% borrowing rate
- Straight-line benefit pattern
- Zero residual value
- Lease purchase
- 8-year lease term
- Lessor's fair value of property, $225,000

REQUIRED

Use *beginning* balance sheet data to calculate the following requirements:

a. Calculate the return on equity ratio and the financial leverage ratio for this company, assuming that this new asset is reported on the financial statements as a capital lease.

b. Calculate the return on equity ratio and the financial leverage ratio for this company, assuming that this new asset is reported on the financial statements as an operating lease.

c. Discuss the relative impact on these financial statements of acquiring this asset under an operating lease versus a capital lease.

Interpreting Financial Statements: Postretirement Benefits

12–30 Review Wendy's financial statements in Appendix D.

REQUIRED

a. Read Note 9. Identify any unfamiliar or unusual terms. Match the terms presented in this chapter to the terms used by Wendy's.

b. Determine the firm's total obligations for pension benefits.

c. Determine the amount of the firm's unfunded obligations for pension benefits.

d. Determine the firm's expense for pension benefits and nonpension benefits.

e. Does the firm disclose any types of obligations that are not included in the financial statements? If so, evaluate the significance of these potential obligations, to the extent possible, using the information in the financial statements. Why were these potential obligations not included as liabilities?

Interpreting Financial Statements: Leases

12–31 Review Wendy's financial statements in Appendix D.

REQUIRED

a. Read Note 3. Identify any unfamiliar or unusual terms. Match the terms presented in this chapter to the terms used by Wendy's.

b. Do the firm's capital leases (the firm is the lessee) have any significant effect on its balance sheet? How?

c. Do the firm's operating leases (the firm is the lessee) have any significant effect on its balance sheet? How?

d. What proportion of the firm's total assets were financed by capital leases?

e. What other impact might leases have on the long-term success or failure of this firm?

Interpreting Financial Statements: Postretirement Benefits

12–32 Review Reebok's financial statements in Appendix F.

REQUIRED

a. Read Note 8 and scan the rest of the financial statement for other relevant information. Identify any unfamiliar or unusual terms. Match the terms presented in this chapter to the terms used by Reebok.

b. Why does Reebok have no pension liability?

c. What was the expense recorded for retirement plans?

d. Why do you suppose Reebok does not have a defined benefit plan?

Interpreting Financial Statements: Leases

12–33 Review Reebok's financial statements in Appendix F.

REQUIRED

a. Read Note 6. Identify any unfamiliar or unusual terms. Match the terms presented in this chapter to the terms used by Reebok.

b. Does the firm have any capital leases?

c. Do the firm's operating leases have any significant effect on its balance sheet? How?

d. What other impact might leases have on the long-term success or failure of this firm?

Interpreting Financial Statements: Postretirement Benefits

12–34 Review OshKosh B'Gosh's financial statements in Appendix C.

REQUIRED

a. Read Note 10. Identify any unfamiliar or unusual terms. Match the terms presented in this chapter to the terms used by OshKosh B'Gosh.
b. Determine the firm's total obligations for pension benefits and nonpension benefits.
c. Determine the amount of the firm's unfunded obligations for pension benefits and nonpension benefits.
d. Does the firm disclose any types of obligations that are not included in the financial statements? If so, evaluate the significance of these potential obligations, to the extent possible, using the information in the financial statements. Why were these potential obligations not included as liabilities?

Interpreting Financial Statements: Leases

12–35 Review OshKosh B'Gosh's financial statements in Appendix C.

REQUIRED

a. Read Note 8. Identify any unfamiliar or unusual terms. Match the terms presented in this chapter to the terms used by OshKosh B'Gosh.
b. Do the firm's operating leases have any significant effect on its balance sheet? How?
c. What proportion of the firm's total assets were financed by capital leases?
d. What other impact might leases have on the long-term success or failure of this firm?

Interpreting Financial Statements: Postretirement Benefits

12–36 Review Bristol-Myers Squibb's financial statements in Appendix E.

REQUIRED

a. Read Notes 13 and 14. Identify any unfamiliar or unusual terms. Match the terms presented in this chapter to the terms used by Bristol-Myers.
b. Determine the firm's total obligations for pension benefits and nonpension benefits.
c. Determine the amount of the firm's unfunded obligations for pension benefits and nonpension benefits.
d. Does the firm disclose any types of obligations that are not included in the financial statements? If so, evaluate the significance of these potential obligations, to the extent possible, using the information in the financial statements. Why were these potential obligations not included as liabilities?

Interpreting Financial Statements: Leases

12–37 Review Bristol-Myers Squibbs' financial statements in Appendix E.

REQUIRED

a. Read Note 16. Identify any unfamiliar or unusual terms. Match the terms presented in this chapter to the terms used by Bristol-Myers.
b. Do the firm's operating leases have any significant effect on its balance sheet? How?
c. What proportion of the firm's total assets were financed by capital leases?
d. What other impact might leases have on the long-term success or failure of this firm?

CASES AND EXTENSIONS

Postretirement Pension Plans

12–38 Du Pont Corporation is a diversified international company involved in selling petroleum and chemical products. In Note 26 of its 1994 annual report, Du Pont reported the following partial information regarding its noncontributory defined benefit retirement plans ($ in millions):

December 21	1994	1993
Actuarial present value of:		
Vested benefit obligation	$(10,342)	$(11,681)
Accumulated benefit obligation	(10,744)	(12,177)
Projected benefit obligation	$(12,303)	$(14,195)
Plan assets at fair value	14,223	15,250
Excess of assets over projected benefit obligation	$ 1,920	$ 1,055

REQUIRED

a. Determine whether the pension plan is overfunded or underfunded.

b. Comment on the ability of the plan assets to provide payments to future retirees.

c. What impact could a drastic increase (decrease) in the pension discount rate have on the figures above?

Postretirement Pension Plans

12–39 Cabot Corporation is a diversified, international company that manufactures and sells specialty chemical and petroleum products. In its 1994 annual report the following partial postretirement defined benefit plan information was disclosed in Note J ($ in thousands):

September 31	1994	1993
Actuarial present value of projected benefit obligations	$155,253	$144,254
Plan assets at fair value	163,651	150,659
Excess of plan assets over projected benefit obligations	$ 8,398	$ 6,405

REQUIRED

a. Determine whether the pension plan is overfunded or underfunded.

b. Comment on the ability of the plan assets to provide payments to future retirees.

c. The discount rate used in calculating the pension obligation was 8.0 and 7.2% for 1994 and 1993, respectively. The expected rate of return used on plan assets was 9.0 and 7.9% for 1994 and 1993, respectively. What if the discount rate on the pension plan should have been 12%? What impact on the financial information would this have? Similarly, what is the expected impact of a 6% discount rate? (Ignore dollar amounts.)

Capital versus Operating Lease

12–40 Movie Madness, Inc., sells and rents movies, video games, and VCRs. The company wanted to lease some video editing equipment in order to expand its market.

REQUIRED

a. Movie Madness is considering signing either an operating lease for the video editing equipment or a lease that meets one of the four criteria of a capital lease. What advice would you give the company?

Pension Plan Disclosures

12–41 Spelling Entertainment Group (SEI), specializing in film and video entertainment, reported the following liabilities on its 1993 balance sheet:

- Accounts payable, accrued expenses, and other liabilities
- Accrued participation expense
- Deferred revenue
- Bank and other debt
- Income taxes
- Net liabilities related to discontinued operations

Part I

REQUIRED

a. Describe each of these liabilities and the economic events from which they were derived.
b. Identify whether any of these liabilities pertain to pension and/or postretirement expenses. Why might a company not have such liabilities?

Part II SEI reported the following:

Benefit Plans: The Company maintained two defined contribution employee retirement plans which covered substantially all nonunion employees of SEI. Contributions by SEI were discretionary or set by formula. . . . Expenses under the various employee retirement plans were $463,000, $586,000, and $355,000 for the years ended. . . . A significant number of the Company's production employees are covered by union sponsored, collectively bargained, multiemployer pension plans. The Company contributed approximately $4,259,000, $3,714,000, and $1,383,000 for the years ended. . . . The Company does not have any postretirement or postemployment benefits.

REQUIRED

c. Explain, in your own words, Spelling's various pension plans.
d. Why doesn't Spelling report any pension or postretirement liabilities on its balance sheet? Explain why this might or might not be justified.

Pension Plan Disclosures

12–42 Public Service Company of Colorado, a major supplier of natural gas and electricity in Colorado, included the following amounts in its 1993 balance sheet ($ in thousands):

	1993	1992
Deferred Charges		
Employees' postretirement benefits, other than pensions (Note 10)	$ 25,855	—
Pension benefits (Note 10)	23,149	$ 15,629
Noncurrent Liabilities		
Defueling and decommissioning liability (Note 2)	140,008	140,008
Employees' postretirement benefits, other than pensions (Note 10)	42,878	43,078

Part I

REQUIRED

a. Describe each of the items excerpted from Public Service's balance sheet.
b. Why did Public Service show $25,855,000 of deferred charges for employees' postretirement benefits in 1993, but none in 1992?
c. Why do you suppose that Public Service's liability for defueling and decommissioning did not change during 1993?
d. Why did Public Service's deferred charges for pension benefits increase significantly in 1993?

Part II Public Service Company of Colorado also included Note 10 in its annual report, as shown in the excerpts on pages 540–542:

REQUIRED

e. Read Note 10 and identify any questions you may have regarding the interpretation or clarification of unusual terms in this note. See your instructor, or an accounting dictionary, regarding such terms.
f. With reference to Part I, trace each item from Public Service's balance sheet to Note 10 (ignore the defueling and decommissioning liability, Note 2).
g. After studying Note 10, reconsider your answer to part b regarding why Public Service reported more than $25 million of deferred postretirement benefits in 1993, and none in 1992.
h. After studying Note 10, describe why Public Service's deferred pension benefits increased significantly in 1993.
i. With reference to the first paragraph in Note 10, describe why Public Service's balance sheet does not show any "projected benefit obligation," and why it does not show the increase of $24.6 million in its projected benefit obligation.
j. Describe, in your own words, the implications of the very last paragraph in Note 10.
k. In Note 10, what does "OPEB" mean? What is its significance?

l. A short paragraph toward the end of Note 10 discusses the "OPEB expense" on a "pay-as-you-go" basis. Discuss the implication of this paragraph, and why this information might be relevant to analysts and employees.

m. Public Service Company's total assets at the end of 1993 and 1992, respectively, were $4,057,600,000 and $3,759,583,000. Furthermore, Public Service Company's net income in each year, respectively, was $157,360,000 and $136,623,000. Given the variety and multitude of information about Public Service Company's employee benefit costs in Note 10 and in the balance sheet excerpts (see Part 1), how important are the related assets and liabilities? How much impact do they have on the overall evaluation of the company? In other words, how significant, or material, are these items? Does their significance justify the more than three pages of detailed information in Note 10? Why?

USING FINANCIAL ACCOUNTING ON THE INTERNET

12–43 Access the EDGAR archives (**www.sec.gov/edgarhp.htm**) and locate the most recent 10 K filings for US Air Group and Southwest Airlines. Both these companies rely extensively on the use of leased assets. In this problem you will analyze the impact of lease commitments on the company's assets and liabilities.

REQUIRED

a. For each company, determine the total minimum lease payments for operating leases and capital leases, and the present value of the future minimum capital lease payments.

b. Calculate the percentage of present value of the minimum lease payments for capital leases to the total minimum lease payments. *Hint:* Refer to Chapter 12, page 525 of your textbook.

c. Estimate the present value of the operating lease payments for each company.

d. For each company, calculate the debt-to-assets ratios before including operating leases, and the debt-to-assets ratios after including operating leases. Note your observations. Which company shows the most significant shift in the debt-to-assets ratio?

12–44 Access the EDGAR archives (**www.sec.gov/edgarhp.htm**) and locate the most recent 10-K filing by Kmart. Information about Kmart's pension plan can be found in the Notes to the Financial Statements.

REQUIRED

a. What are the total pension assets and liabilities?

b. What is the funding status of the pension plan?

c. What discount rate and average rate of return have been adopted by the company?

d. Identify total assets and total debt as reported on the balance sheet, and calculate the debt-to-assets ratio. Then, including all retirement plan-related assets and liabilities, recalculate the values of total assets, total liabilities, and the debt-to-assets ratio. What do you observe?

e. Now examine the latest 10-K for Wal-Mart (available at EDGAR). Should you make the same adjustments for Wal-Mart that you made for Kmart? State your reasons.

NOTES TO CONSOLIDATED FINANCIAL STATEMENTS *Continued*
Public Service Company of Colorado and Subsidiaries

10. Employee Benefits

Pensions

The Company and its subsidiaries (excluding Natural Fuels) maintain a noncontributory defined benefit pension plan covering substantially all employees. During 1993, the Board of Directors of the Company approved amendments that: 1) eliminated the minimum age of 21 for receiving credited service, 2) provided for an automatic increase in monthly payments to a retired plan member in the event the member's spouse or other contingent annuitant dies prior to the member, and 3) provided for Average Final Compensation to be based on the highest average of three consecutive years compensation. These plan changes increased the projected benefit obligation by $24.6 million.

The Company and its subsidiaries' funding policy is to contribute annually, at a minimum, the amount necessary to satisfy the Internal Revenue Service (IRS) funding standards.

The net pension expense in 1993, 1992 and 1991 was comprised of:

	1993	1992	1991
		(Thousands of Dollars)	
Service cost	$ 15,868	$ 14,788	$ 12,196
Interest cost on projected benefit obligation	38,106	35,695	33,322
Return on plan assets	(52,369)	(34,317)	(79,467)
Amortization of net transition asset at adoption of Statement of Financial Accounting Standards No. 87	(3,674)	(3,674)	(3,673)
Other items	8,219	(6,317)	39,807
Net pension expense	$ 6,150	$ 6,175	$ 2,185

Significant assumptions used in determining net periodic pension cost were:

	1993	1992	1991
Discount rate	8.2%	8.2%	8.9%
Expected long-term increase in compensation level	5.5%	5.5%	5.5%
Expected weighted average long-term rate of return on assets	11%	11%	11%

Variances between actual experience and assumptions for costs and returns on assets are amortized over the average remaining service lives of employees in the plan.

A comparison of the actuarially computed benefit obligations and plan assets at December 31, 1993 and 1992, is presented in the following table. Plan assets are stated at fair value and are comprised primarily of corporate debt and equity securities, a real estate fund and government securities held either directly or in commingled funds.

	1993	1992
	(Thousands of Dollars)	
Actuarial present value of benefit obligations:		
Vested	$ 392,623	$ 336,632
Nonvested	39,343	29,800
	431,966	366,432
Effect of projected future salary increases	128,294	110,776
Projected benefit obligation for service rendered to date	560,260	477,208
Plan assets at fair value	(523,548)	(483,941)
Projected benefit obligation (in excess of) less than plan assets	(36,712)	6,733
Unrecognized net loss	58,252	34,763
Prior service cost not yet recognized in net periodic pension cost	34,673	10,870
Unrecognized net transition asset at January 1, 1986, being recognized over 17 years	(33,064)	(36,737)
Prepaid pension asset	$ 23,149	$ 15,629

Significant assumptions used in determining the benefit obligations were:

	1993	1992
Discount rate	**7.5%**	8.2%
Expected long-term increase in compensation level	**5.0%**	5.5%

On January 25, 1994, the Board of Directors approved an amendment to the Plan which offers an incentive for early retirement for employees age 55 with 20 years of service as well as a Severance Enhancement Program (SEP) option for these same eligible employees. The Plan amendment and the SEP are effective for the period February 4, 1994 to April 1, 1994. The Plan amendment generally provides for the following retirement enhancements: a) unreduced early retirement benefits, b) three years of additional credited service, and c) a supplement of either a one-time payment equal to $400 for each full year of service to be paid from general corporate funds or a $250 social security supplement each month up to age 62 to be paid by the Plan.

The SEP provides for: a) a one-time severance ranging from $20,000-$90,000, depending on an employee's organization level, b) a continuous years of service bonus (up to 30 years), and c) a cash benefit of $10,000.

Eligible employees may elect to participate in either program. The total cost of the programs is estimated to range between $25 to $32 million. The Company intends to amortize such cost to expense over a period not to exceed approximately five years in accordance with anticipated regulatory treatment of such costs.

Postretirement benefits other than pensions

The Company and its subsidiaries provide certain health care and life insurance benefits for retired employees. A significant portion of the employees become eligible for these benefits if they reach either early or normal retirement age while working for the Company or its subsidiaries. Historically, the Company has recorded the cost of these benefits on a pay-as-you-go basis, consistent with the regulatory treatment. Effective January 1, 1993, the Company and its subsidiaries adopted Statement of Financial Accounting Standards No. 106—"Employers' Accounting for Postretirement Benefits Other Than Pensions" (SFAS 106) which requires the accrual, during the years that an employee renders service to the Company, of the expected cost of providing postretirement benefits other than pensions to the employee and the employee's beneficiaries and covered dependents. The additional other postretirement employee benefits (OPEB) costs in 1993 resulting from this new accounting standard, which exceed amounts being recovered through rates, have been deferred for future recovery.

During 1991, the CPUC approved a rate Settlement Agreement (see Note 8) and the Fort St. Vrain Supplemental Settlement Agreement (see Note 2), both of which addressed the accounting and regulatory treatment of the costs of postretirement benefits other than pensions. The rate Set-tlement Agreement stipulated that the Company would continue to recover such costs as paid until the date new rates are effective. The Fort St. Vrain Supplemental Settlement Agreement stipulated that, on the effective date of new rates (December 1, 1993) the Company would be allowed to recover the costs of postretirement benefits other than pensions as accrued in accordance with the provisions of SFAS 106, modified as follows:

- the actuarial calculation of such liability would include a return on assets that reflects monthly contributions net of benefit payments throughout the year;

- the attribution period would reflect each employee's expected retirement date rather than the full eligibility date;

- a forty-year levelized principal and interest amortization will be used for the transition obligation; and

- the accounting and regulatory treatment for life insurance benefits would remain on an as paid basis.

Pursuant to the Fort St. Vrain Supplemental Settlement Agreement, the Company had anticipated that any difference in expense resulting from the CPUC prescribed approach and the expense required by SFAS 106 would be reflected as a regulatory asset in the consolidated balance sheet and would be recovered from customers over future periods.

In January 1993, however, the Emerging Issues Task Force (EITF) provided guidance as to what additional criteria or evidence is needed for a rate regulated enterprise to recognize a regulatory asset equal to the amount of OPEB costs for which rate recovery has been deferred. Generally, a utility must determine that it is probable that future rates will allow for the recovery of this OPEB regulatory asset. In addition, no later than approximately five years from the date of adoption, rates must include full SFAS 106 costs and the recovery of the regulatory asset established during the deferral period must be accomplished within approximately twenty years. The EITF's conclusions do not include the CPUC approach prescribed in the Fort St. Vrain Supplemental Settlement Agreement.

As a result, and under the provisions of the Fort St. Vrain Supplemental Settlement Agreement, the parties to this Agreement have initiated discussions and negotiations focused on resolving this issue to the mutual acceptance of all parties without disrupting the overall Agreement. These discussions are continuing, and the Company believes it is probable that the matter will ultimately be resolved in a manner that will comply with the conclusions reached by the EITF relative to the recognition of OPEB regulatory assets for which rate recovery has been deferred. Should the currently approved methodology not be modified to conform with the EITF consensus, the Company would be required to record as an expense the difference between the amounts allowed in rates and that required by SFAS 106.

NOTES TO CONSOLIDATED FINANCIAL STATEMENTS *Continued*
Public Service Company of Colorado and Subsidiaries

Effective December 1, 1993, the Company began recovering such costs based on the level of expense determined in accordance with the CPUC approach in the Fort St. Vrain Supplemental Settlement Agreement (approximately $18 million on an annual basis for retail jurisdiction). During 1993, the Company deferred $25.9 million of SFAS 106 costs for future recovery. The Company plans to file a FERC rate case in 1994 which will include a request for approval to recover all wholesale jurisdiction SFAS 106 costs. Effective January 1, 1993, Cheyenne began recovering SFAS 106 costs as approved by the WPSC. The Company and Cheyenne intend to fund this plan based on the amounts reflected in cost-of-service, consistent with the rate orders.

The OPEB expense on a pay-as-you-go basis was $9.1 million and $8 million for 1992 and 1991, respectively.

The net periodic postretirement benefit cost in 1993 under SFAS 106 was comprised of:

	(Thousands of Dollars) 1993
Service cost	$ 4,943
Interest cost on projected benefit obligation	20,828
Return on plan assets	(164)
Amortization of net transition obligation at January 1, 1993, assuming a 20 year amortization period	12,710
Net postretirement benefit cost required by SFAS 106	38,317
1993 OPEB expense recognized in accordance with current regulation	(12,462)
Regulatory asset at December 31, 1993	$ 25,855

The funded status of the plan at December 31, 1993 and January 1, 1993 is as follows:

	(Thousands of Dollars) December 31, 1993	January 1, 1993
Accumulated postretirement benefit obligation:		
Retirees and eligible beneficiaries	$ 86,718	$ 79,692
Other fully eligible plan participants	95,103	95,262
Other active plan participants	98,342	79,238
Total	280,163	254,192
Plan assets at fair value	(476)	—
Accumulated benefit obligation in excess of plan assets	279,687	254,192
Unrecognized net loss	(10,059)	—
Unrecognized transition obligation	(241,483)	(254,192)
Accrued postretirement benefit obligation	$ 28,145	$ —

Significant assumptions used in determining the accumulated postretirement benefit obligation were:

	December 31, 1993	January 1, 1993
Discount rate	7.5%	8.2%
Ultimate health care cost trend rate	5.3%	6.0%
Expected long-term increase in compensation level	5.0%	5.5%

The assumed health care cost trend rate for 1993 is 12%, decreasing to 5.3% in 0.5% annual increments. A 1% increase in the assumed health care cost trend will increase the estimated total accumulated benefit obligation by $37.7 million, and the service and interest cost components of net periodic postretirement benefit costs by $5.2 million.

Postemployment benefits
In November 1992, the Financial Accounting Standards Board issued Statement of Financial Accounting Standards No. 112–"Employers' Accounting for Postemployment Benefits" (SFAS 112) which establishes the accounting standards for employers who provide benefits to former or inactive employees after employment but before retirement (postemployment benefits). This statement became effective January 1, 1994 and the Company has estimated its benefit obligation to be approximately $32 million, assuming a 7.5% discount rate. The Company believes it is probable that it will receive CPUC approval to recover these costs in future rates and, therefore, the application of the new standard will not have a material impact on the Company's financial position or results of operations as a regulatory asset and a corresponding liability will be established on the consolidated balance sheet.

CHAPTER 13

This chapter consists of two parts, each of which may be read independently.

STUDYING PART I OF THE CHAPTER
WILL ENABLE YOU TO

1. Understand the reasons for reporting consolidated financial statements.
2. Appreciate how affiliated firms construct and report their consolidated financial statements.

STUDYING PART II OF THE CHAPTER
WILL ENABLE YOU TO

3. Understand how foreign exchange rate fluctuations affect the financial reporting of transactions conducted in foreign currencies.
4. Determine how financial statements prepared initially in foreign currencies are translated to U.S. dollars.
5. Appreciate the wide diversity of international accounting practices.

REPORTING ISSUES FOR AFFILIATED AND INTERNATIONAL COMPANIES

INTRODUCTION TO PART I:
FINANCIAL REPORTING FOR AFFILIATED FIRMS

Most large firms grow by a combination of internal and external expansion. **Internal expansion** occurs as firms invest in new plant and equipment, research, and other productive assets in order to serve growing markets or to extend the scope of their operations into new products and markets. **External expansion** occurs as firms take over, or merge with, other existing firms. The first part of the chapter discusses the reasons why corporate takeovers may be preferable to internal expansion. Financial reporting for affiliated firms is explained as of the date of acquisition and for subsequent periods.

MOTIVATIONS FOR BUSINESS COMBINATIONS

Business firms often expand by taking over existing corporations. These **business combinations** may be more attractive than direct investments in new plant and equipment for several reasons. For example, the buyer firm may believe that external expansion is less costly than purchasing new assets and competing for customers in new markets. Also, the acquired firm may offer other advantages, such as a stable and reliable network of suppliers, a seasoned workforce, and proven methods of production and distribution. As a consequence, expansion by combination may avoid many of the uncertainties and start-up costs encountered under internal expansion.

When existing firms are combined, it may enable them to eliminate duplicate facilities, or yield economies of scale in production, distribution, marketing, finance, and/or general corporate administration. A buyer company may believe that the acquired firm's assets are poorly managed and that more profits could be earned by improving its asset management. A purchaser may also feel that new management may introduce operating efficiencies that yield higher profits.

Business combinations also may permit a firm to diversify quickly. A buyer firm in a declining industry may attempt to redeploy its resources into other products and markets. For example, as cigarette smoking has declined among informed adults, many larger tobacco firms have diversified by acquiring firms in other industries. Many firms may attempt, through business combinations, to diversify their risks related to cyclical or seasonal demands.

A major factor in recent business combinations is the rapid pace of technological change in communications, which has created links between industries that were previously considered to be unrelated. The prospect of an "information superhighway" has inspired combinations of firms in areas as disparate as cable television, telecommunications, banking, cinema, and catalog retail sales. The ongoing information revolution promises to redefine the boundaries among industries and provide impetus to many additional unconventional business combinations.

FORMS OF BUSINESS COMBINATIONS

Business combinations occur in a variety of different ways. In a **merger,** a buyer firm acquires either the stock or the assets and liabilities of an investee firm. The investee is then dissolved and no longer exists as a separate corporation. Alternatively, firms may combine by **consolidation.** In a consolidation a new corporation is created to acquire the stock or the net assets of two or more existing companies. The original companies then cease to exist as separate corporations. Finally, a business combination may occur as an **acquisition.** In an acquisition a buyer firm acquires more than 50% of the voting stock of an investee firm and thereby controls the investee. The buyer firm is referred to as the **parent company,** and the acquired firm continues to exist and operate as a **subsidiary** of the parent company.

Acquisitions comprise a major portion of the business combinations that occur among larger corporations. This type of business combination offers several advantages over mergers and consolidations. Because the parent may obtain effective control of a subsidiary without the need to acquire 100% of the seller's shares, the required investment by the parent may be reduced substantially. Also, because the subsidiary continues to exist as a legally separate entity, the parent has only limited liability for the debts of the subsidiary. In addition, it is relatively easy for the parent to increase or decrease its investment at future dates by purchasing or selling the subsidiary's shares.

A parent company and the other firms that it influences or controls are referred to as affiliated companies. The remainder of the discussion in this part of the chapter will explain financial reporting for affiliated companies.

FINANCIAL REPORTING FOR CONTROLLING INTERESTS IN AFFILIATED FIRMS

When one firm acquires the stock of another firm, the value of the resources (e.g., cash, shares of stock, or debt) paid by the parent is used to measure the historical cost of the parent's investment. Because the parent's investment exceeds 50% of the affiliate's voting shares, the parent is assumed to control the affiliate. Subsequent accounting and reporting for the affiliated firm are based on the historical cost concepts that were explained in the earlier chapters of this text.

In some circumstances firms combine by an exchange of voting stock. These combinations are interpreted as a "uniting of ownership interests" rather than a purchase of one firm by another. The accounting treatment for such exchanges is termed a **pooling of interests.** Illustrating pooling is beyond the scope of this text.

Accounting for the Acquisition of a Subsidiary Firm

To illustrate a typical acquisition, refer to Exhibit 13–1, which shows the preacquisition balance sheets and other pertinent information for Pepper Company and Shaker Inc., on January 1, 1998. On that date, Pepper Company paid a total of $400 million ($100 million in cash and $300 million in common stock) in order to acquire from the existing shareholders all of Shaker's outstanding shares.

Note that Shaker's balance sheet at the date of combination shows net assets (and therefore shareholders' equity) of $310 million. Pepper's willingness to pay $400 million indicates that the carrying value of Shaker's net assets at the combination date is less than the economic value of those net assets by at least $90 million ($400 million − $310 million = $90 million). Indeed, the note to Exhibit 13–1 reveals that the firm has $90 million of internally generated goodwill that does not appear on the balance sheet.

The acquisition of Shaker's stock will increase Pepper's investment in affiliated companies by $400 million; cash will decrease by $100 million, and invested capital will increase by $300 million. Pepper's net assets increase by $300 million.

ASSETS		= LIABILITIES +	SHAREHOLDERS' EQUITY
Cash	Investments in affiliates		Invested capital
− $100 million	+ $400 million		+ $300 million

EXHIBIT 13–1 PREACQUISITION BALANCE SHEETS

Pepper Company and Shaker Inc.
Preacquisition Balance Sheets and Other Information, at January 1, 1998
(dollars in millions)

Pepper Company Balance Sheet at January 1, 1998				Shaker, Inc. Balance Sheet at January 1, 1998			
Current assets:		Current liabilities	$ 420	Current assets:		Current liabilities	$ 50
Cash	$ 150			Cash	$ 20		
Other current				Other current			
assets	520	Long-term debt	540	assets	1,260	Long-term debt	1,280
Total	670	Total liabilities	960	Total	1,280	Total liabilities	1,330
Noncurrent assets				Noncurrent assets			
Property, plant,				Property, plant,			
and equipment,		Shareholders' equity		and equipment,		Shareholders' equity	
(net)	1,230	Invested capital	280	(net)	320	Invested capital	150
Other	450	Retained earnings	1,110	Other	40	Retained earnings	160
Total	1,680	Total equity	1,390	Total	360	Total equity	310
		Total liabilities				Total liabilities	
Total assets	$2,350	and equity	$2,350	Total assets	$1,640	and equity	$1,640

NOTE: An independent appraisal of Shaker Inc.'s assets and liabilities on January 1, 1998, indicates that book values and fair market values are equal, except that Shaker has $90 million of internally generated goodwill that does not appear on the balance sheet.

Shaker's balance sheet will be unaffected by the acquisition. Because Pepper Company bought Shaker's shares directly from existing shareholders, Shaker was not a party to the transaction. Shaker Company has neither received any resources nor issued any additional shares of stock.

Reality Check 13–1 illustrates the effect of the acquisition of a subsidiary company at a cost in excess of the fair value of the net assets acquired.

MERCK & CO., INC., ACQUISITION OF A SUBSIDIARY COMPANY

REALITY CHECK 13–1

Merck & Co., Inc., is the world's largest pharmaceutical company. The firm discovers, develops, and markets human and animal health products and specialty chemicals. The following information has been abstracted from Merck's note disclosures concerning business combinations during 1993.

> On November 18, 1993, the Company acquired all the outstanding shares of Medco Containment Services, Inc. (Medco) for approximately $6.6 billion. The purchase price consisted of $2.4 billion in cash, 114 million common shares with a market value of $3.8 billion, and 36.1 million options valued at $387.1 million, net of tax. The acquisition was accounted for by the purchase method and, accordingly, Medco's results of operations have been included with the Company's since the acquisition date. The estimated fair value of assets acquired and liabilities assumed totaled $3.0 billion and $1.5 billion, respectively. The excess of the purchase price over the estimated fair value of net assets is being amortized on a straight-line basis over 40 years.

REQUIRED

a. Based on the above information, show how Merck's balance sheet was affected by the acquisition of Medco (assume that Medco continues in existence as a legally distinct company.)

b. Determine the excess of Merck's purchase price over the fair value of Medco's net assets (i.e., the goodwill) implicit in the Medco acquisition.

c. Why do you suppose that Merck was willing to pay a substantial premium over the fair value of the net assets in order to acquire Medco?

d. Assume that Merck prepares a consolidated balance sheet, immediately following the acquisition of Medco. Show how the balance sheet of Merck would differ before and after consolidation.

Financial Reporting Subsequent to the Acquisition

Because Pepper Company has effective control of Shaker through ownership of a majority (in this case, all) of Shaker's voting shares, generally accepted accounting practice requires that Pepper Company's financial statements be prepared on a consolidated basis. **Consolidated financial statements** report the combined financial position, cash flows, and operating results for all firms that are under the parent company's control. Consolidation looks beyond the fact that affiliated firms are distinct legal entities, and focuses on the fact that they constitute a single economic entity. Consolidation is mainly a process of adding together the financial statement elements of the parent and its controlled subsidiaries, with certain necessary adjustments as described later.

A consolidation of Pepper Company and Shaker Inc. at the acquisition date would entail only the preparation of a consolidated balance sheet because no combined operations or cash flows have yet occurred at that date. Exhibit 13–2 shows the consolidation process. Note the following:

1. The balance sheets of each firm are listed side by side in a vertical format to facilitate adding the elements across each row.
2. A firm does not report an investment in its own shares as an asset on the balance sheet. Therefore, the balance of the investment account that appears on the separate (unconsolidated) balance sheet of the parent company must be eliminated, because the investee firm is included in the consolidated entity.

EXHIBIT 13–2 CONSOLIDATION PROCESS

	Pepper Company[a]	Shaker, Inc.	Adjustments	Consolidated
Pepper Company and Shaker Inc. Consolidation at the Acquisition Date, January 1, 1998 (dollars in millions)				
Current assets				
Cash	$ 50	$ 20		$ 70
Other current assets	520	1,260		1,780
Total current assets	570	1,280		1,850
Noncurrent assets				
Property, plant, and equipment (net)	1,230	320		1,550
Investment in Shaker Inc.	400	—	− 400[b]	—
Goodwill	—	—	+ 90[b]	90
Other	450	40		490
Total noncurrent assets	2,080	360		2,130
Total assets	$2,650	$1,640		$3,980
Current liabilities	$ 420	$ 50		$ 470
Long-term debt	540	1,280		1,820
Total liabilities	960	1,330		2,290
Shareholders' equity				
Invested capital	580	150	− 150[b]	580
Retained earnings	1,110	160	− 160[b]	1,110
Total shareholder's equity	1,690	310		1,690
Total liabilities and equity	$2,650	$1,640		$3,980

[a]Pepper Company's balance sheet differs from Exhibit 13–1 because cash was reduced by $100 million and invested capital was increased by $300 million in order to acquire for $400 million the investment in Shaker Inc.
[b]Pepper's investment in Shaker is eliminated, as well as Shaker's shareholders' equity. The difference of $90 million ($400 less $310 million) results in a revaluation of goodwill (+90 million).

3. Shaker's shareholders' equity must be eliminated because from a consolidated point of view, its stock is not outstanding. All of Shaker's stock is held by Pepper, and none is held by outside investors.

4. Shaker's net assets are revalued in the process of consolidation in order to reflect their appraised values at the acquisition date. Recall that Pepper Company paid $400 million to acquire Shaker's shareholders' equity, which has a carrying value of $310. The $90 million difference is attributed to goodwill. From a consolidated perspective, Shaker's net assets are $90 million higher than they are from the perspective of Shaker as a separate company. Pepper incurred this additional cost by buying Shaker's shares at an amount in excess of book value.

As a result of these consolidating adjustments, the consolidated balance sheet of Pepper Company, shown on the right side of Exhibit 13–2, shows consolidated assets of $3.98 billion and consolidated liabilities of $2.29 billion. Both of these amounts are greater than those shown on Pepper's separate balance sheet. The shareholders' equity of Pepper, $1.69 billion, is the same before and after consolidation, however. This occurs because the shareholders' equity of the subsidiary has been eliminated in the consolidation process.

A further complication can occur whenever the parent does not own 100% of the subsidiary's stock. Because Pepper Company owns 100% of Shaker Inc., the subsidiary's entire shareholders' equity is eliminated. In cases where a parent achieves control by acquiring less than 100% of a subsidiary's stock, the book value of the remaining outstanding shares of the subsidiary will appear on the consolidated financial statements with the label **minority interest in consolidated subsidiaries.** This term often appears either as another category of shareholders' equity, or as a separate item between liabilities and shareholders' equity.

Equity Method of Accounting for Affiliate Subsequent to the Acquisition Date

After the acquisition date, a parent company will often account for its investment in affiliated firms using the **equity method of accounting.** The equity method requires that Pepper recognize its share of Shaker's subsequent reported income (or loss). Moreover, any dividends paid by Shaker to Pepper will be considered as a reduction of Pepper's investment cost. Because Pepper recognizes Shaker's income as it is earned, Pepper cannot also count Shaker's dividend payments as additional income. To do so, would be "double counting."

To illustrate the equity method, assume Shaker Inc. earned $12 million in 1998, and paid dividends of $6 million. All of the dividends are paid to Pepper, which owns all of Shaker's stock. Shaker's income would be recognized by Pepper Company as an increase in the carrying value of the investment and as income of $12 million:

ASSETS	=	LIABILITIES	+	SHAREHOLDERS' EQUITY
Investment in subsidiary				Retained earnings
+$12 million				+$12 million
				(income from investments)

Upon receipt of the dividend, Pepper Company would increase cash and reduce the investment balance by $6 million:

ASSETS		= LIABILITIES + SHAREHOLDERS' EQUITY
Cash	Investment in subsidiary	
+$6 million	−$6 million	

Recall that Pepper Company paid an amount that was $90 million in excess of the book value of Shaker's shareholders' equity at the acquisition date. This amount was attributed to goodwill. This asset is being used in Shaker's operations, and from Pepper Company's point of view the additional asset cost must be recognized as expense over the useful life of the asset. In other words, Pepper's income from its investment in Shaker is less than the $12 million recorded earlier. If we assume that goodwill has a useful life of 18 years, the annual amortization expense for goodwill is $5 million ($90 million cost ÷ 18 years of useful life). This additional annual expense of $5 million must be recognized by Pepper Company. Accordingly, each year the carrying value of the investment is reduced by $5 million, and income from the subsidiary is reduced by the same amount. The net result is that the investment carrying value increased by $1 million in the first year ($12 million income less $6 million dividends and $5 million goodwill amortization).

ASSETS	= LIABILITIES +	SHAREHOLDERS' EQUITY
Investment in subsidiary		Retained earnings
−$5 million		−$5 million
		(income from investments)

Other Types of Consolidation Adjustments

The consolidation of Pepper Company and its subsidiary Shaker Inc. required relatively few adjustments because we have assumed that the operations of both firms are completely independent. In many cases, however, numerous transactions take place between affiliated firms that require further adjustment as part of the consolidation process. Consider, for example, a parent firm that has acquired controlling ownership of a major supplier. After the acquisition the firms would certainly continue their existing business relationship. As a result, the subsequent consolidated financial statements of the parent firm would require the following types of adjustments:

1. The accounts payable of the parent would include amounts owed to the subsidiary. Correspondingly, the accounts receivable of the subsidiary would include amounts due from the parent. These **intercompany receivables and payables** would be eliminated in consolidation. It would make no sense to report amounts owed to and from oneself on a consolidated balance sheet.

2. The sales among companies included in a consolidation do not constitute sales to outside entities. As a result, unless these **intercompany sales** are eliminated in preparing the consolidation, both consolidated sales and cost of goods sold would be overstated in the financial statements.

3. The inventories reported by the parent would be very likely to include items purchased from the subsidiary at a profit to the subsidiary. From a consolidated point of view, however, these inventories have not been sold to outside entities at the balance sheet date. As a result, these **unrealized inventory profits** would be removed from the carrying value of the inventory, and from the subsidiary's income, in the process of consolidation.

Various other transactions between affiliated firms occur frequently and must be adjusted appropriately in preparing a set of consolidated financial statements. Bear in mind that a set of legally distinct companies is consolidated as a single economic or reporting entity. As a result, financial statement elements such as receivables, payables, revenues, and expenses must involve transactions only with other, outside entities.

FINANCIAL RATIOS AND CONSOLIDATED FINANCIAL STATEMENTS

Consolidated financial statements are prepared primarily to serve investors and financial analysts. A useful starting point in the analysis of financial statements is the calculation of a set of key financial ratios. Note that many of these ratios were first introduced in earlier chapters, and were summarized in Chapter 11. This section illustrates how the consolidation of affiliated companies affects selected financial statement ratios.

As seen earlier, some financial statement elements will change dramatically as a result of consolidation of subsidiary firms, while other items will be unaffected. To illustrate the effects of consolidation on selected financial ratios, Exhibit 13–3 repeats the financial statements of Pepper Company before and after consolidation, as developed earlier in the chapter. Exhibit 13–3 also shows the calculation of two widely used financial ratios. Note the following:

1. Pepper's debt-to-assets ratio increased markedly, from 36.2 to 57.5%, as a result of consolidation. This ratio increases whenever a consolidated subsidiary has debt financing.

2. In Pepper Company's case, the current ratio increased from 1.36 to 3.94 as a result of consolidation. This occurs because Shaker Inc., the subsidiary, has a higher current ratio than does the parent company.

These illustrative ratio calculations show that many of the ratios used by analysts will differ before and after consolidation. Analysts must be careful when examining ratio trends that cover periods when new subsidiaries are being consolidated (or when subsidiaries are being sold, or divested).

EVALUATION OF CONSOLIDATION ACCOUNTING

Financial accounting standards require the reporting of consolidated financial statements based on a presumption that investor analysts need to evaluate the total set of economic resources that are controlled by the parent company, as well as the total liabilities and other claims against those resources. Correspondingly, the consolidated

Selected Financial Ratios Before and After Consolidation Pepper Company and Shaker Inc. at January 1, 1998 (dollars in millions)		
	Pepper Company, Unconsolidated (from Exhibit 13–1)	**Pepper Company, Consolidated (from Exhibit 13–1)**
Current assets	$ 570	$1,850
Noncurrent assets	2,080	2,130
Total assets	$2,650	$3,980
Current liabilities	$ 420	$ 470
Long-term debt	540	1,820
Total liabilities	960	2,290
Shareholders' equity	1,690	1,690
Total liabilities and equity	$2,650	$3,980
Net income during 1998:	$30 million	

Ratio	Unconsolidated	Consolidated
Debt-to-assets	$960/$2,650 = 36.2%	$2,290/$3,980 – 57.5%
Current ratio	$570/$420 = 1.36	$1,850/$470 = 3.94

EXHIBIT 13–3
FINANCIAL RATIOS

income statement measures the total revenues and expenses attributed to these economic resources and claims.

Recently the FASB has initiated a comprehensive reexamination of the principles and assumptions that underlie consolidated financial statements. Two key issues are (1) the development of a meaningful measure of "control" for purposes of including an investee in the consolidation and (2) the extent to which consolidation may in some cases impair rather than enhance the usefulness of financial statements.

With respect to the issue of control, it is unclear that ownership of a majority of an investee's outstanding shares is a necessary threshold to establish control. For example, a substantial portion of the shares outstanding in widely held companies is not voted at stockholders' meetings. Smaller investors with minor shareholdings may lack the incentive to study the issues and participate in the governance of a corporation. As a consequence, a parent company owning much less than 50% of an affiliate's outstanding stock may still regularly cast a majority of the votes on matters of company policy. The issue of control is further muddied by the existence of convertible securities (such as convertible bonds and preferred stock, discussed in Chapter 10). If the holders of such securities may at any time convert their holdings to voting common stock, then the ownership percentages in an investee may shift dramatically on short notice.

The usefulness of consolidated financial statements has also been questioned on grounds that aggregations of information cause a loss of information. Some analysts and company managers argue that because consolidation often entails the adding together of financial statements of companies in diverse industries, the resulting totals are very difficult to interpret. For example, most automotive companies and other durable goods manufacturers have subsidiary companies that extend consumer credit to the parent company customers. It was a long-standing practice for the parent firms to exclude finance subsidiaries from their consolidations. This practice was defended on the grounds that analysts would be misled by an aggregation of manufacturing and financial companies. Subsequently the FASB issued a standard that requires the consolidation of all majority-owned subsidiaries (see *SFAS No. 92,* "Consolidation of All Majority-Owned Subsidiaries," October 1987).

INTRODUCTION TO PART II: INTERNATIONAL ASPECTS OF FINANCIAL REPORTING

Business activities are increasingly international. As tariff barriers dissolve through regional trade arrangements such as the North American Free Trade Agreement (NAFTA) and the European Union (EU), domestic business firms rely more extensively on international trade both for sources of supply and as markets for their products. The political and economic reshaping of Eastern Europe and the still embryonic modernization of China ensure that international trade will be a substantial and rapidly growing component in the business affairs of domestic firms.

As foreign suppliers and customers become more essential to business activities, companies frequently establish or acquire subsidiary companies that operate in foreign nations. To report financial statements on a consolidated basis to U.S. investors, the foreign operations of those affiliates need to be translated into U.S. dollars. Because most foreign currency exchange rates fluctuate over time, a variety of issues arise in the preparation of dollar-denominated financial reports.

This part of the chapter discusses three related aspects of financial reporting for firms engaged in international business:

1. the reporting of transactions between foreign and domestic firms, when the transactions are valued on the basis of the foreign currency;
2. the method used in translating into U.S. dollars the financial statements of foreign affiliates that have been prepared in other currencies; and
3. the diversity of accounting practices that exist among nations, and the emerging efforts to achieve international harmonization of accounting practices.

FOREIGN CURRENCY TRANSACTIONS

If a U.S. company either buys from or sells to a foreign company, the firms must specify the currency that will be used to settle the resulting accounts receivable or payable. **Foreign currency transactions** create receivables or payables that must be settled in a foreign currency. These balances are said to be **denominated** in the foreign currency.

When a U.S. firm collects an account receivable that is paid in a foreign currency, it will then convert the foreign currency to dollars. Conversely, in order for a U.S. firm to make payment of an account that is payable in a foreign currency, it must first convert U.S. dollars into the foreign currency. In either case, the U.S. firm must buy or sell foreign currency at the current **foreign exchange rate** between the U.S. dollar and the foreign currency. The foreign exchange rate specifies the number of U.S. dollars needed to obtain one unit of a specific foreign currency. Note that **direct rates** for foreign exchange quote the number of U.S. dollars required for one unit of a foreign currency. **Indirect rates** indicate the number of foreign currency units required for one U.S. dollar. The discussion in this chapter uses *only* direct quotations.

As a basis for discussion, hypothetical foreign exchange rates between the U.S. dollar ($) and the British pound (£) for various dates are provided in Exhibit 13–4. These rates show the number of U.S. dollars required to buy one British pound at the dates indicated. For example, if we assume the rate is 1.40 on April 1, 1998, then US$1.40 is needed to buy one British pound.

Foreign Exchange Rates Between the U.S. Dollar ($) and British Pound (£), Spot and Forward Rates			
Date			**$/£**
April 1, 1998	Spot rate:		1.40
	Forward rate:	30 days	1.395
		60 days	1.38
		90 days	1.37
May 30, 1998	Spot rate:		1.30

EXHIBIT 13-4
HYPOTHETICAL FOREIGN
EXCHANGE RATES

The information in Exhibit 13–4 includes **spot rates** and **forward rates.** A spot rate is the rate of exchange for immediate delivery of foreign currencies. A forward rate is the rate of exchange for future delivery of foreign currencies, and the market in which foreign currencies are bought and sold for future delivery is referred to as a **currency forward market.** For example, Exhibit 13–4 indicates that the 60-day forward exchange rate of dollars to pounds is 1.38. If a U.S. firm needed British pounds in 60 days, it could contract today with a foreign exchange broker to buy pounds 60 days hence, at a price of US$1.38 per pound. Alternatively, the firm could simply wait and buy the pounds in 60 days, at the prevailing spot rate on that date.

Firms frequently contract to buy or sell foreign currencies in the forward market in order to protect against the risks of foreign exchange rate fluctuations. The exchange rates between most pairs of currencies change frequently, in response to the forces of supply and demand. As the number of U.S. dollars needed to buy a unit of foreign currency increases (or decreases), that foreign currency is said to strengthen (or weaken) against the dollar. As a result, if a U.S. firm has a foreign currency–denominated receivable or payable, then the dollar value of the account will vary as foreign currency exchange rates fluctuate.

The existence of forward markets for the foreign currencies of most major U.S. trading partners allows managers to **hedge,** or protect against the risks of exchange rate fluctuations. To illustrate, assume that on April 1, 1998, the Reagan Company, a U.S. firm, sells merchandise to Thatcher, Ltd., a British firm. The sales agreement specifies that Thatcher will make payment of £150,000 to Reagan in 60 days, on May 30, 1998. Sales are recorded using the spot rate on the date of sale, rather than the forward rate for the date of anticipated collection. Because the spot rate of exchange at the transaction date, April 1, 1998, is 1.40 (Exhibit 13–4), Reagan would record the account receivable and sale at $210,000 ($1.40 × 150,000 = $210,000).

ASSETS	=	LIABILITIES	+	SHAREHOLDERS' EQUITY
Accounts receivable				Retained earnings
+$210,000				+$210,000 (sales revenue)

Exhibit 13–4 shows that the spot rate of exchange on May 30, 1998, when the receivable balance is paid by Thatcher, Ltd., has fallen to 1.30. This indicates that the U.S. dollar has strengthened against the British pound and it requires fewer dollars to buy British pounds. Conversely, because the Reagan Company has a pound-denominated account receivable, the dollar value of the receivable has declined, to $195,000 ($1.30 × £150,000 = $195,000). Reagan's collection of the receivable would increase cash by $195,000, but the entire receivable must be eliminated, so an exchange rate loss would be recognized for $15,000 ($210,000 − $195,000).

ASSETS		=	LIABILITIES	+	SHAREHOLDERS' EQUITY
Cash	Accounts receivable				Retained earnings
+ $195,000	− $210,000				− $15,000
					(foreign currency loss)

In this example, the Reagan Company was exposed to the risk of exchange rate fluctuations over the 60-day collection period. The firm held an accounts receivable denominated in a foreign currency, and incurred a loss because that foreign currency weakened against the dollar. Consequently, the dollar value of the receivable declined. Reagan could instead have chosen to protect itself against rate fluctuations at the date of sale, by contracting on April 1 with a foreign exchange broker to sell 150,000 British pounds in 60 days, at the 60-day forward exchange rate of 1.38.

Upon signing such a **hedging contract,** the Reagan Company would recognize an account receivable from the currency broker for $207,000 ($1.38 forward rate × 150,000), in dollars to be received in 60 days. Reagan would also recognize an account payable to the broker for $210,000 ($1.40 spot rate × 150,000), to be paid in British pounds in 60 days, and a hedging expense of $3,000 ($210,000 account payable, less $207,000 account receivable).

ASSETS	=	LIABILITIES	+	SHAREHOLDERS' EQUITY
Accounts receivable		Accounts payable		Retained earnings
+$207,000		+$210,000		−$3,000 (hedging expense)

In effect, Reagan would have paid $3,000 to protect itself from exposure to foreign currency rate fluctuations over the collection term of the account receivable. Reagan would have an account receivable from Thatcher, Ltd., in British pounds that is offset by a liability to the foreign exchange broker that also is denominated in British pounds.

When the spot rate of exchange subsequently falls from $1.40 on April 1 to $1.30 on May 30, the Reagan Company would revalue downward by $15,000 the British-pound denominated receivables and payables. Because the $15,000 loss on the account receivable is exactly offset by the $15,000 gain on the account payable, no net gain or loss would result.

ASSETS	=	LIABILITIES	+	SHAREHOLDERS' EQUITY
Accounts receivable		Accounts payable		
−$15,000		−$15,000		

In summary, when a U.S. firm contracts either to receive or to pay future accounts that are denominated in foreign currencies, there is an attendant risk of gains or losses from fluctuations in foreign exchange rates. Usually, firms are able to insulate themselves from risk by hedging. Hedging is accomplished by entering into contracts with foreign exchange brokers to buy or sell foreign currencies at future dates.

The illustration in this section has shown how a firm would hedge a foreign currency account receivable by contracting to sell foreign currency in the future. Firms with foreign currency accounts payable would hedge in the opposite fashion. They would hedge by contracting to buy foreign currency in the future. In either case, the objective is the same: to have offsetting receivables and payables in the foreign currency. Besides hedging foreign currency–denominated accounts receivables or payables, firms often hedge commitments to engage in future transactions. These may include purchase commitments, sales agreements, employment contracts, and so on.

Hedging one's exposure to foreign exchange rate fluctuations is similar in concept to the payment of an insurance premium in order to avoid risk. Firms engaged in international trade may have significant amounts of foreign currency–denominated financial assets and liabilities. If these are left unhedged, gains and losses caused by changes in exchange rates might account for a substantial portion of periodic profits and losses. Rather than speculate on the future strength or weakness of the dollar, most managers of industrial trading firms hedge to avoid exposure to exchange rate fluctuations. Reality Check 13–2 describes how one firm partially hedges its exposures to foreign exchange rate fluctuations.

TRANSLATION OF FOREIGN CURRENCY FINANCIAL STATEMENTS

Foreign subsidiaries of U.S. firms usually prepare their financial statements in the currencies in which they transact their business, which is referred to as their **functional currency.** The U.S. parent firm will prepare its financial reports in U.S. dollars. As a consequence, the financial statements of the foreign subsidiaries must be translated in to U.S. dollars, in order to be consolidated with those of the parent company.

To illustrate the process of translation of foreign currency financial statements, consider the balance sheets and income statements of Perot, Inc., a subsidiary of a U.S.

BOISE CASCADE CORPORATION FOREIGN EXCHANGE GAINS AND LOSSES

Boise Cascade Company is a major producer of paper, building, and office products. The company reported the following items related to foreign exchange gains and losses in its 1993 financial statements (dollars in thousands):

Income statement:	1993	1992
Foreign exchange gain	$1,610	$6,590

Notes:

Foreign currency translation. Foreign exchange gains and losses reported on the Statements of Income (Loss) arose primarily from activities of the Company's Canadian subsidiaries. At December 31, 1993, contracts for the purchase of 50,000,000 Canadian dollars were outstanding. Gains or losses in the market value of the forward contracts are recorded as they are incurred during the year and partially offset gains or losses arising from translation of the Canadian subsidiaries' net liabilities.

REQUIRED

a. The Note discussion indicates that the firm, through its Canadian subsidiaries, has *net liabilities,* in Canadian dollars. Explain the meaning of this term.
b. From the information provided, are you able to tell whether the U.S. dollar strengthened or weakened against the Canadian dollar during 1993? Explain.
c. Does Boise Cascade attempt to fully "hedge" its foreign currency transactions? Explain.

company, at the end of 1998 as shown in Exhibit 13–5. Perot, Inc., operates in Taiwan and prepares its financial statements in New Taiwan dollars, or NT$. Because Perot, Inc., is a subsidiary of a U.S. company, its financial statements must be translated into U.S. dollars prior to consolidation with those of the U.S. parent.

Foreign exchange rates between U.S. and New Taiwan dollars must be used to translate into U.S. dollars the various elements of Perot's financial statements. Accounting standards require the use of different rates for different financial statement elements. The FASB specifies the following rates for translation (*SFAS No. 52,* "Foreign Currency Translation"):

- The **average exchange rate** during the reporting period is used to translate income statement items. Average rates are appropriate when operating activities have been level throughout the year, and changes in exchange rates have occurred evenly throughout the year. Exhibit 13–5 shows that the average rate during 1998 was $0.04. Thus, it required US$0.04 to buy one NT$.
- The current exchange rate, i.e., the spot rate at the balance sheet date, is used to translate asset and liability items. Exhibit 13–5 shows that the current exchange rate was US$0.038 on December 31, 1998.
- Various **historical exchange rates** are used to translate the balances of invested capital, beginning retained earnings, and dividends. Exhibit 13–5 shows that the exchange rate when Perot's stock was issued was $.05, and the rate when dividends were declared in 1998 was 0.039. The balance of Perot's retained earnings, translated into U.S. dollars, was $40.5 million at the beginning of 1998.

EXHIBIT 13–5
TRANSLATION OF FOREIGN
CURRENCY FINANCIAL
STATEMENTS

Perot, Inc.
Summary Income Statement and Balance Sheet
Year Ended December 31, 1998
(all currencies in millions)

Income Statement, Year Ended December 31, 1998

Account	NT$	Translation Rate	US$
Revenues	5,000	.04[a]	200.0
Expenses	(4,200)	.04[a]	(168.0)
Net income	800		32.0

Balance Sheet, December 31, 1998

	NT$	Translation Rate	US$
Assets	8,500	.038[b]	323.0
Liabilities	4,600	.038[b]	174.8
Invested capital	2,500	.050[c]	125.0
Retained earnings	1,400	—	60.8
Translation adjustment	—	—	(37.6)
Total	8,500		323.0

Analysis of Retained Earnings Changes During 1998

	NT$	Translation Rate	US$
Beginning balance	900	—[d]	40.5
Net income	800	—[e]	32.0
Dividends	(300)	.039[f]	(11.7)
Ending balance	1,400		60.8

NOTES: [a]Average exchange rate during 1998.
[b]Current (spot) rate on December 31, 1998.
[c]Historical rate when capital stock was issued.
[d]Beginning balance in US$ is obtained from the translated balance sheet on January 1, 1998.
[e]See translated income statement, above.
[f]Historical rate when dividends were declared.

The ending balance in retained earnings is not translated directly from Perot Inc.'s foreign currency balance sheet. Instead, it is computed in the following manner:

	millions of US$
Retained earnings, beginning balance (January 1, 1998)	$40.5
Add: Translated amount of net income (Exhibit 13–5)	32.0
Less: Translated amount of dividends (Exhibit 13–5)	(11.7)
Retained earnings, ending balance (December 31, 1998)	$60.8

Note in Exhibit 13–5 that the translated balance sheet for Perot, Inc. requires a **translation adjustment** in order to remain in balance. This adjustment is required because not all balance sheet elements are translated at the same exchange rate. In Perot's case the translated amounts of total assets are less than the translated amounts of total liabilities and shareholders' equity (exclusive of the translation adjustment) by $37.6 million. For this reason, $37.6 million must be subtracted from shareholders' equity to restore the balance.

The interpretation of this translation adjustment is a matter of continuing controversy. The FASB suggests the following interpretation: When a foreign subsidiary of a U.S. firm has assets in excess of its liabilities, this is similar to a partially unhedged investment in a foreign currency. If a foreign currency strengthens (or weakens) against the U.S. dollar, then this unhedged investment gives rise to an unrealized gain (or loss). In Perot's case the foreign currency (NT$) has weakened against the U.S. dollar, and the translation adjustment may be interpreted as an unrealized loss. Because the parent company intends to maintain its investment in Perot, Inc. over the foreseeable future, and because foreign currency exchange rates are likely to continue to fluctuate, it would be premature to recognize such unrealized gains or losses in income.

Some analysts question the view that a firm's net asset position should be viewed as an unhedged foreign currency investment. Instead, they argue that investments in nonmonetary items such as inventories, property, plant, equipment, and other assets should be accounted for based on the historical cost concept that underlies the parent company's financial statements. Translation of asset costs at current exchange rates causes the U.S. dollar book values of the assets to change whenever the translation rate fluctuates. For this reason, the translated book values do not represent historical costs. In a partial recognition of this problem, the FASB has established a special set of "remeasurement" rules for foreign currency financial statements in high-inflation countries. These special rules are beyond the scope of this text.

Many analysts who otherwise accept the FASB's interpretation of the net assets reported in foreign currency financial statements object to the exclusion of gains or losses from net income. These critics suggest that financial accountants have no special expertise in identifying temporary versus permanent changes in currency exchange rates. If current exchange rates are determined in a well-functioning foreign exchange market, based on the trading activities of informed investors, these analysts argue that the gains or losses that result from unhedged net assets or liabilities should be reported as part of net income when they occur.

INTERNATIONAL VARIATIONS IN ACCOUNTING STANDARDS

Diversity pervades the world community. Variations in language, custom, cuisine, and architecture, as well as in business, political, and social organizations, give truth to the adage that "travel is broadening." Although tour books routinely ignore the fact, accounting standards also vary among nations. International diversity in accounting standards complicates the task for investor analysts when attempting to evaluate risks and returns based on comparable financial information. Moreover, disparate accounting standards and disclosure requirements impede the ability of firms to raise debt and equity capital across national boundaries.

The accounting standards that have developed in a given nation or region reflect, to some extent, the unique characteristics of the society and business community in which they have evolved. Accordingly, as business firms become more international in their activities, and as investors aim for greater international diversification of their investments, it becomes essential to understand the differences in accounting standards that exist among nations.

UNDERLYING CAUSES OF ACCOUNTING DIVERSITY

Differences in accounting standards originate mainly from differences in the objectives of financial reporting across nations. In turn, different objectives exist for financial reporting due to the differing characteristics of legal systems, the financial structure of business firms, the relation between financial and tax accounting, and other factors.

Legal System Influences

The legal system of a nation influences the extent to which accounting standards aim to establish general, flexible guides to reporting practice, as opposed to providing a complete set of detailed, rigid rules with minimal scope for professional judgment by reporting firms. For example, countries such as the United States and the United Kingdom have legal systems that rely on statutes, which are then interpreted by the courts in a flexible manner to deal with the unique circumstances in individual cases. Other nations, such as France and Germany, have legal systems in which laws are designed to cover virtually all possible circumstances.

Corresponding to these differing legal systems, accounting rules in France and Germany tend to be very detailed and explicit, leaving no scope for judgment: Accounting disputes are resolved by "looking up" the correct solution in the applicable rule books. By contrast, and with some notable exceptions, U.S. and British accounting standards tend to establish broad frameworks, and allow considerable room for interpretations and assumptions in individual cases.

Financial Structure Influences

The financial structure of a firm refers to the sources from which its investment capital is obtained. In the United States and the United Kingdom, a major portion of financing is obtained by the sale of equity shares on security exchanges. These securities are typically held by diverse individuals and institutions that rely on published financial reports for investment-relevant information. For this reason the focus of financial accounting standards is on the decision-making usefulness of published financial reports.

In many other nations, including Germany and Japan, corporate financing is obtained primarily from direct borrowings and sale of equity securities to banks and other financial institutions. In these cases the lenders and investors are able to demand relevant and timely financial information directly from the firm. Because major lenders and investors do not depend on public financial reports, accounting standards for public financial reports are determined by factors other than investor information, such as conformity with the tax rules or the information needs of government economic planners.

Taxation Influences

In countries such as Germany, Italy, France, and Japan, there is a very close correspondence between financial reporting standards and the rules used to determine taxable income. In these nations there is no distinction made between the possibly different measurements needed for purposes of government fiscal policy, and the information needs of investors. Revenues and expenses must be recognized for tax purposes in the same periods in which they are reported to investors. Not surprisingly, accounting standards in these countries tend to be very conservative relative to U.S. standards. For example, price-to-earnings multiples (the ratio of market price per share to earnings per share) are much higher in Germany and Japan than in the United States. This comparison suggests that investors consider German and Japanese earnings numbers to be of higher quality (more conservative) than reported earnings of U.S. firms.

INTERNATIONAL DIFFERENCES IN SELECTED ACCOUNTING PRACTICES

This section considers five specific areas of accounting practice: accounting for goodwill in business acquisitions, consolidation policy, accounting for leases, pension reporting, and departures from historical cost in valuing assets. In each case, U.S. standards are compared to those in several major industrial nations.

Goodwill

As discussed in the first part of this chapter, goodwill arises in a business acquisition when the buyer pays an amount that exceeds the fair value of the identifiable net assets of the seller. The amount assigned to goodwill often accounts for a major portion of the purchase price. For U.S. firms, reported earnings subsequent to the acquisition must be reduced by systematic amortization of the amount attributed to goodwill.

In several European nations, including the United Kingdom, Germany, the Netherlands, and Italy, goodwill may be charged immediately to shareholders' equity. As a result, the asset (goodwill) does not appear on the balance sheet, and subsequent earnings are not reduced by goodwill amortization. Managers of U.S. firms often claim that this difference in accounting standards causes an "uneven playing field," because their European counterparts will be able to report higher profits subsequent to business combinations.

Consolidations

Firms in the United States are required to consolidate all majority-owned subsidiaries. Except for Australia, most major industrial nations do not require the consolidation of **nonhomogeneous subsidiaries,** i.e., those whose major operating activities are in industries that differ from those of the parent company. For example, U.S. automobile manufacturers are required to consolidate their financing subsidiaries, even though the activities are quite distinct from those of the parent companies. American managers argue that a substantial portion of the assets and debt controlled by foreign parent companies may easily be hidden on the books of unconsolidated, controlled subsidiaries. As a consequence, financial ratio calculations that are based on published financial statements may appear to be less favorable for U.S. firms.

Leases

As discussed in Chapter 12, U.S. accounting standards require that long-term leases be **capitalized,** i.e., recorded as assets and liabilities based on present value measurements, when the lessee acquires both the risks and the rewards of ownership. Although many advanced industrial nations have similar standards, the criteria they use to identify a capital lease are considerably more flexible than those in the United States. As a result, most leases are interpreted as operating leases, i.e., ordinary rentals of assets, rather than as capital leases. In Japan, most leases are designed as operating leases in order to minimize taxes. In Italy, *all* leases are reported as operating leases. Therefore, lease disclosures are not comparable between firms in these countries.

Pensions

The defined benefit type of pension plan that has been widely adopted by U.S. firms, as discussed in Chapter 12, is relatively less important in other nations. In many countries, government-sponsored pension arrangements are more prominent than are company-sponsored plans, and most of the latter are defined contribution plans. Even in cases where defined benefits plans do exist, only the U.S. requires an annual evaluation of the discount rate that is used to estimate the value of the pension liability. This annual evaluation has in recent years caused the amounts of unfunded pension liabilities, and also the reported pension expense, to be more volatile for mature U.S. firms. Moreover, U.S. standards require much greater detail in the footnote disclosures of pension assumptions, funding status, cost components, and other items.

Asset Valuations

American accounting standards generally require that assets be valued at historical cost. Exceptions are the lower of cost or market (LCM) rules, which are applied in accounting for most current assets, and the fair market value rules for investments in marketable securities. In contrast, U.K. companies may choose to revalue tangible and intangible noncurrent assets at current replacement cost. Alternatively, tangible noncurrent assets may be valued at current market values. France allows current cost revaluations of tangible assets, but not intangibles. Because of extremely high inflation rates, South American countries require that the historical costs of most noncurrent assets be adjusted by a purchasing power index to reflect inflation.

INTERNATIONAL HARMONIZATION OF ACCOUNTING STANDARDS

Recent years have seen a burgeoning demand by foreign firms for debt and equity capital, which has been obtained by selling securities in other nations. This demand is partly attributable to the wave of **privatization** in Eastern and Western Europe and in South America. Privatization is the selling to private investors of government-owned or controlled enterprises, and the resultant demands for investment capital often exceed what is available in the local economies.

The demand for access to investment capital in other nations is also due in part to international differences in the cost of capital. For example, because of a rigorous and comprehensive set of financial reporting standards and well-regulated securities markets, the cost of investment capital in U.S. financial markets is generally lower than that in other Western nations. As a result, the overall value of foreign stock and bond issues traded in U.S. markets totaled more than $110 billion in 1993 alone.

It may be quite costly, however, for foreign companies that initially prepare financial statements in their domestic currencies, and apply domestic accounting standards, to expand and recast their financial reports in a manner that allows them to list their shares on foreign stock exchanges. As an example, in 1993 Daimler-Benz AG, a German automaker, decided to list its shares on the New York Stock Exchange. To comply with U.S. financial reporting standards, the company incurred expenses that were estimated to exceed $500 million ("Foreign Firms Raise More and More Money in the U.S. Markets," *The Wall Street Journal,* October 5, 1993).

The considerable amount of expense incurred by firms in preparing financial reports to comply with multiple sets of accounting standards, as well as the difficulties encountered by investor analysts in evaluating investment opportunities across national boundaries, has given impetus to efforts to harmonize accounting standards internationally. Harmonization would require that financial statements worldwide conform to a single set of accounting standards.

To promote harmonization of accounting standards throughout the world business community, the International Accounting Standards Committee (IASC) was formed in 1973. This committee is a joint effort, initially undertaken by professional accounting groups in 10 Western nations (including the AICPA in the United States). The IASC issues accounting pronouncements, termed International Accounting Standards (IAS). To date, more than 30 such standards have been issued.

The effectiveness of the IASC as a force for international harmonization is limited by several factors. First, the committee has no power to enforce its standards. Recall that in the United States, the authority of the FASB is backed by the endorsement of the SEC, and firms must follow FASB pronouncements in order to list and sell securities. No similar authority exists to give credibility to IASC standards.

A second reason why IASC standards have failed to achieve harmonization is the fact that the standards themselves usually fail to agree on a single method of accounting. Instead, most standards enumerate and endorse a variety of accounting methods that are used by member nations. Only in this manner has the IASC been able to achieve the consensus needed to issue its standards. There is no agreement among IASC members regarding the set of accounting standards that is "best" for the international financial market. For example, there is wide acknowledgment that U.S. accounting standards require more elaborate and comprehensive disclosures than do the standards in other nations. Yet, accounting groups in other nations argue that "more is not necessarily better": Financial reporting in the United States might be unduly complicated and expensive, thereby putting extra burdens on preparers and users alike.

It is questionable whether any international group, whatever its composition, will be able to achieve worldwide harmonization of accounting standards. Throughout the earlier chapters of this book we have considered many of the FASB standards that govern financial reporting in the United States. As you have seen, such standards are the result of a political process, which attempts to balance the economic impact of accounting rules on a variety of different constituencies. Similar processes exist in other nations. Accordingly, existing accounting standards may vary from those in the United States because a different political consensus has been achieved in those nations. It may be naive to believe that the FASB, or its counterpart groups in other countries, will modify their standards purely in the interest of international harmonization.

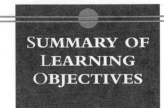

1. **Understand the reasons for reporting consolidated financial statements.**

Business firms often expand by taking over existing firms. Most takeovers occur as acquisitions, in which a buyer firm acquires a majority of the voting shares of a seller firm. The buyer is thereafter referred to as the parent company, and the seller as a subsidiary company. Both firms continue to exist as legally distinct corporations. Because they are under common control, their financial statements must be consolidated for financial reporting purposes.

2. **Appreciate how affiliated firms construct and report their consolidated financial statements.**

Consolidation requires adding together the assets, liabilities, revenues, and expenses of the parent and subsidiary firms. A variety of consolidation adjustments must be made to reflect the fact that both firms are now a single economic entity. The following adjustments characterize most consolidations:

a. The balance of the parent's investment account in the subsidiary must be eliminated, because from a consolidated perspective the subsidiary is not a distinct economic entity. The subsidiary's shareholder's equity also must be eliminated, because its shares are not held outside the consolidated entity.

b. The subsidiary's individual assets and liabilities may require revaluation in the process of consolidation in order to reflect differences between the parent's cost of acquisition and their carrying values at the acquisition date. In subsequent periods, these revaluations may require adjustments to the revenues and expenses used in computing consolidated income.

c. Intercompany borrowing and lending might result in accounts receivable and payable on the balance sheets of a parent and its consolidated subsidiaries. If so, these amounts must be eliminated.

d. Revenues and expenses reported on the consolidated income statement must reflect only transactions with outside entities, which are firms that are not included in the consolidation. Similarly, the carrying values of assets must exclude any unrealized profits for assets that have been transferred among the affiliated firms.

3. **Understand how foreign exchange fluctuations affect the financial reporting of transactions conducted in foreign currencies.**

Companies engaged in international trade often have accounts receivable or accounts payable that are denominated in foreign currencies. Fluctuations in foreign currency exchange rates affect the dollar value of such receivables and payables, resulting in gains or losses.

The existence of forward markets for foreign currencies allows managers to hedge and thereby protect against the risks of exchange rate fluctuations. Firms with foreign currency receivables may contract to sell foreign currency in the future, and firms with foreign currency payables may contract to buy foreign currency in the future. In either case, the firm's goal is to have offsetting amounts of receivables and payables denominated in a given foreign currency.

4. Determine how financial statements prepared initially in foreign currencies are translated to U.S. dollars.

Foreign subsidiaries of U.S. firms usually prepare their financial statements in the currencies in which they transact their business. These foreign currency financial statements must be translated into U.S. dollars in order to be consolidated with the U.S. parent for financial reporting purposes.

Generally, an average exchange rate for the period is used to translate the income statement; the current exchange rate at the balance sheet date is used to translate assets and liabilities; and historical exchange rates are used to translate most components of shareholders' equity. As a consequence of using a variety of exchange rates, the balance sheet requires a translation adjustment in order to balance. Currently, accounting standards do not recognize changes in this translation adjustment as gains or losses in the income statement. Instead, the adjustment is reported as a separate component of shareholders' equity.

5. Appreciate the wide diversity of international accounting practices.

Many different sets of accounting standards coexist in the world economy. In any given nation, local accounting standards are influenced by the unique characteristics of the society and business community. Because international diversity in accounting standards complicates the task of investment analysis and impedes the international flow of capital, there is widespread interest in the establishment of uniform worldwide accounting standards. Such efforts have had only limited success to date, however. There is no consensus internationally that any existing set of national standards would be "best" for all nations.

KEY TERMS

Acquisition	Hedging contract
Average exchange rate	Historical exchange rates
Business combination	Indirect rates
Capitalize	Intercompany receivables and payables
Consolidated financial statements	Intercompany sales
Consolidation	Internal expansion
Currency forward market	Merger
Current exchange rate	Minority interest in consolidated subsidiaries
Denominated	Nonhomogeneous subsidiaries
Direct rates	Parent company
Equity method of accounting	Pooling of interests
External expansion	Privatization
Foreign currency transactions	Spot rate
Foreign exchange rate	Subsidiary
Forward rate	Translation adjustment
Functional currency	Unrealized inventory profits
Hedge	

REALITY CHECK SOLUTIONS

SOLUTION TO REALITY CHECK 13–1

a. The total value of the consideration (cash plus common stock plus stock options) paid by Merck is $6,587.1 million, and would affect Merck's balance sheet as follows on November 18, 1993:

ASSETS		=	LIABILITIES	+	SHAREHOLDERS' EQUITY	
Cash	Investment in Medco				Invested capital (options)	Common stock
−$2,400.0 million	+$6,587.1 million				+$387.1 million	+$3,800.0 million

b. The goodwill implicit in the acquisition price is computed as follows ($ in millions):

Cost of investment in Medco (see above)		$6,587.1
Fair value of net assets:		
Fair value of assets acquired	$3,000.0	
Less: Fair value of liabilities assumed	(1,500.0)	
Net		−1,500.0
Excess of cost over fair value of net		
assets (goodwill)		$5,087.1

c. Merck's managers believe that the value of the future cash flows to be earned from the Medco acquisition justify the substantial acquisition premium. The economic values of many firms exceed the fair values of their identifiable net assets. This is especially true for firms such as Medco that have substantial investments in research and development, highly skilled employees, and a well-developed customer base.

d. Merck's balance sheet would be adjusted in the following manner in order to be consolidated with Medco at the acquisition date:

ASSETS	=	LIABILITIES	+	SHAREHOLDERS' EQUITY
Investment in Medco		Liabilities assumed		
−$6,587.1 million		+$1,500.0 million		
Goodwill				
+$5,087.1 million				
Other assets				
+$3,000.0 million				

In other words, the entire investment account would be eliminated; Medco's assets and liabilities, at their fair values when acquired, would be added to Merck's assets and liabilities; and the goodwill would be recognized explicitly on the consolidated balance sheet.

SOLUTION TO REALITY CHECK 13–2

a. The term *net liabilities* indicates that the firm's Canadian dollar–denominated liabilities exceed its Canadian dollar–denominated assets (e.g., currency, accounts and notes receivable, and other claims to fixed amounts of Canadian dollars).

b. Because Boise Cascade reports a foreign exchange gain in its 1993 income statement, and has a net liability in Canadian dollars, we can infer that the U.S. dollar strengthened relative to the Canadian dollar during 1993. The gain occurs because fewer U.S. dollars are needed to repay a debt denominated in Canadian dollars, as the U.S. dollar becomes stronger.

c. A company would be fully hedged if its foreign currency–denominated assets and liabilities were fully offsetting. In such a case, foreign currency gains and losses would cancel. Boise Cascade's note indicates that the firm is "partially hedged." The unhedged amount enables the firm to report a gain in 1993. If the U.S. dollar should weaken relative to the Canadian dollar, the firm would then incur a loss on its unhedged net Canadian liabilities.

QUESTIONS

13–1 Distinguish between business growth through internal and external expansion. Discuss several reasons why a firm might seek to expand externally, rather than internally.

13–2 Explain how a firm might attempt to diversify risks by combining with other business firms.

13–3 Business combinations usually occur in the form of mergers, consolidations, or acquisitions. How do each of these types of combinations differ?

13–4 What advantages might a business acquisition offer as opposed to a merger or a consolidation?

13–5 Evaluate the following statements: Accounting for goodwill makes no sense. If a firm generates goodwill internally, the costs are written off as expenses, and no related asset appears on the balance sheet. If, on the other hand, a firm purchases goodwill by acquiring another firm, the amount paid for goodwill is reported as an asset. How is an analyst supposed to make comparisons given these rules? Wouldn't it be more sensible to make *all* firms write off goodwill immediately?

13–6 Suppose that Psycho Company buys all of Somatic Inc.'s outstanding shares directly from Somatic's existing shareholders. Describe how Somatic's balance sheet would be affected by the acquisition.

13–7 Describe what is meant by consolidated financial statements. In what circumstances should a parent company's financial statements be prepared on a consolidated basis?

13–8 This chapter states that "consolidation is mainly a process of adding together the financial statement elements of a parent and its controlled subsidiaries, with certain necessary adjustments." Discuss why the following items may require adjustments in preparing a consolidated balance sheet.

a. Investment in a subsidiary (on the parent's balance sheet)
b. Shareholders' equity (on the subsidiary's balance sheet)
c. Accounts receivable
d. Accounts payable
e. Inventory
f. Goodwill
g. Property, plant, and equipment

13–9 Discuss why the following items may require adjustments when preparing a consolidated income statement:

a. Income from a subsidiary (on the parent's income statement)

b. Sales
c. Cost of goods sold
d. Depreciation and amortization expenses

13–10 Which of the following items would differ on a firm's financial statements before and after consolidation of its subsidiaries? Explain your answers.

a. Total assets
b. Total liabilities
c. Shareholders' equity
d. Sales
e. Expenses
f. Net income

13–11 Indicate how you would expect each of the following financial ratios to differ before and after a consolidation of a parent firm and its subsidiaries:

a. Debt-to-total assets ratio
b. Net income-to-sharcholders' equity ratio
c. Net income-to-total assets ratio
d. Net income-to-sales ratio
e. Current ratio

13–12 Respond to the following remarks: I just read in the financial pages that Whale company owns 60% of Minnow Inc.'s shares. Whale Company includes all of Minnow's assets and liabilities and all of Minnow's revenues and expenses in its consolidated financial statements. It seems to me that this is a misrepresentation. If Whale owns 60% of Minnow, then it should only reflect 60% of Minnow in its financial statements.

13–13 Is it necessary for one firm to own more than 50% of the voting stock of another firm in order to exert control over the investee firm? If not, how do you suggest that control be defined for purposes of deciding on the preparation of consolidated financial statements?

13–14 It is sometimes argued that consolidation may result in a loss of information, and produce aggregations in the financial statements that are difficult to interpret. Explain why you agree or disagree with this statement. Can you think of areas other than consolidations where accounting numbers may be too aggregated to serve investment analysts? Discuss.

13–15 Describe what is meant by a foreign currency transaction.

13–16 Which of the following events is a foreign currency transaction, from the point of view of the U.S. firm:

a. A U.S. firm purchases inventory from a British firm, with payment to be made in British pounds.
b. A U.S. firm sells to an Italian firm, with payment to be made in U.S. dollars.
c. A U.S. firm purchases from a Taiwanese firm, with payment to be made in Japanese yen.

13–17 Explain whether a U.S. firm would experience a gain or a loss related to its unhedged accounts receivable or payable in each of the following cases:

a. A U.S. firm has accounts receivable in British pounds, and the pound strengthens relative to the U.S. dollar.

b. A U.S. firm has accounts payable in Mexican pesos, and the peso weakens relative to the U.S. dollar.

c. A U.S. firm has accounts receivable in French francs, and the franc weakens relative to the U.S. dollar.

d. A U.S. firm has accounts payable in Canadian dollars, and the Canadian dollar strengthens relative to the U.S. dollar.

13–18 Explain what is meant by a "hedge" of a foreign currency–denominated account receivable or payable.

13–19 Assume that a U.S. firm has an account receivable in Swiss francs, with payment due in 90 days, and wishes to hedge its exposure to currency rate fluctuations. Explain the actions the U.S. firm would take to accomplish such a hedge. Describe how the U.S. firm's financial statements would be affected if the Swiss franc strengthened relative to the U.S. dollar before the account receivable was collected.

13–20 Distinguish between spot rates and forward rates of foreign currency exchange. Which rate would a U.S. firm use in order to report its balance sheet accounts receivable in foreign currencies?

13–21 Explain why the financial statements of U.S. firms' foreign subsidiaries must be translated to U.S. dollars in order to prepare consolidated financial statements.

13–22 The balance sheets of foreign firms, prepared in their local currencies, must be in balance (i.e., assets equal liabilities plus shareholders' equity). Yet, when such balance sheets are translated to U.S. dollars they usually require a "translation adjustment" in order to balance. Explain why this is so.

13–23 Identify the exchange rate (current, historical, or average) that would be used to translate to U.S. dollars each of the following elements of the financial statements of a foreign subsidiary:

a. Accounts receivable
b. Property, plant, and equipment
c. Total liabilities
d. Paid-in capital
e. Sales
f. Net income
g. Dividends

13–24 Assume that a foreign subsidiary of a U.S. firm acquired a parcel of land in 1996, and that each year thereafter the functional currency of the foreign subsidiary continues to weaken against the U.S. dollar. Describe how the carrying value of the land would change on successive translated balance sheets of the foreign subsidiary. Is the result sensible? What remedy do you propose?

13–25 Describe the main factors that cause differences in accounting standards across nations.

13–26 Do you agree that worldwide harmonization of accounting standards is a desirable objective? If so, prepare a memorandum that indicates how such accounting standards should be developed and enforced. If you do *not* agree, prepare a memorandum that identifies the major reasons why the costs of standardization outweigh its benefits.

13–27 Explain how the legal system of a nation may influence the types of accounting standards that are established.

13–28 Explain how the prevailing financial structure of business firms may affect the types of financial reports that are published.

13–29 Describe how taxation rules may influence the types of financial accounting standards that are developed. How might this influence differ in nations where there is no difference between income measurements for investor and taxation purposes?

13–30 Identify several areas of accounting practice where there are substantial differences among nations. In each case, defend what you consider to be the superior practice.

EXERCISES

Purchased goodwill

13–31 The following excerpt is from the acquisitions note contained in Tyler Corporation's 1994 annual report:

> On January 7, 1994, the company completed the purchase of Institutional Financing Services, Inc. (IFS). . . . IFS was acquired for approximately $50,000,000 and the assumption of seasonal working capital debt of $12,800,000. The purchase price and expenses associated with the acquisition exceeded the fair value of IFS's net assets by approximately $40,854,000 which has been assigned to goodwill.

REQUIRED

a. Why do you suppose Tyler Corporation paid over $40 million more than the fair value of the net assets of IFS?

b. If Tyler amortizes goodwill over 40 years, what would be the impact on the income statement for the annual amortization?

Consolidation

13–32 Goliath Corporation purchased all of the outstanding stock of the Masonry Corporation on January 1, 1996, for $6,000,000. The purchase price was paid as follows: Goliath Corporation issued 40,000 shares of its own common stock, par $1, with a market price of $102/share, and cash paid of $1,920,000. The acquisition was accounted for as a purchase and, therefore. Masonry's income statement has been included with Goliath's since the acquisition date. The estimated fair value and carrying value of the assets purchased and the liabilities assumed totaled $7,600,000 and $2,100,000. The excess of the purchase price over the fair value of the assets is being amortized over 40 years on a straight-line basis.

REQUIRED

a. According to the information given, use the balance sheet equation to show how Goliath's financial statements will be affected by its acquisition of Masonry. (Assume Masonry continues as a separate corporation.)

b. Determine any goodwill inherent in this acquisition.

c. Why do you suppose Goliath paid more than the fair value of Masonry's net assets?

Consolidation and goodwill

13–33 On January 1, 1997, Maplegrove Deli, Inc., purchased all of the outstanding stock of Biznos Sub Shops, Inc., for $4,500,000. Maplegrove paid $2,000,000 cash and issued 25,000 shares of its common stock, no par value, currently selling for $100 per share. The estimated fair value and carrying value of Biznos' assets (purchased by Maplegrove) and liabilities (assumed by Maplegrove) approximated $6,200,000 and $1,920,000. The excess of the purchase price over the fair value of the assets is being amortized over 40 years on a straight-line basis. During 1997, Biznos' earned net income of $3,400,000 and paid dividends of $230,000.

REQUIRED

a. Use the balance sheet equation to show how Maplegrove's financial statements are affected at the date of acquisition.
b. How is Maplegrove affected by Biznos' net income and dividends?
c. How much goodwill should Maplegrove amortize? Show the effect on Maplegrove's balance sheet equation.
d. What is the net amount Maplegrove earned from owning Biznos during the year?

Consolidation: Adjustment to the Income Statement

13–34 Presented below are condensed income statements for the MHL Company and its wholly owned subsidiary, PTE Inc., for the year ended December 31, 1998 ($ in millions) (MHL acquired its ownership of PTE in 1989.):

	MHL Company	PTE Inc.
Sales	$260	$180
Cost of sales	(110)	(75)
Other operating expenses	(145)	(85)
Net income*	5	20

---

*MHL has not recognized any income during 1998 related to its ownership of PTE's shares.

REQUIRED

Explain how each of the following items would affect your preparation of a consolidated income statement for MHL and PTE:

a. During 1998 PTE made sales to MHL totaling $40 million.
b. At the end of 1998, MHL's inventory includes $10 million for items purchased from PTE. The cost of these sales incurred by PTE was $4.5 million.
c. At the beginning of 1998, none of MHL's inventory consisted of goods purchased from PTE.

Consolidation (continuation of Exercise 13–34)

13–35 Based on the information provided in Exercise 13–34, prepare a consolidated income statement for MHL Company for the year 1998.

Consolidation: Adjustments to the Balance Sheet

13–36 Presented below are condensed balance sheets for the ASAP Company and its wholly owned subsidiary, BYOB Inc., at December 31, 1999 ($ in millions):

	ASAP Company	BYOB Inc.
Current assets	$ 30	$ 55
Noncurrent assets	210	95
Total	$240	$150
Liabilities	$110	$85
Shareholders' equity	130	65
Total	$240	$150

REQUIRED

Explain how each of the following items would affect your preparation of a consolidated balance sheet for ASAP and BYOB:

a. The noncurrent assets of ASAP include its investment in BYOB, at a value of $65 million.
b. The current assets of BYOB include an account receivable from ASAP of $9 million.
c. The noncurrent assets of BYOB include land purchased from ASAP for $25 million. The cost of the land to ASAP was $7 million.

Consolidation (continuation of Exercise 13–36)

13–37 Based on the information provided in Exercise 13–36, prepare a consolidated balance sheet for ASAP Company at December 31, 1999.

Consolidation of Balance Sheets

13–38 Selected items from the unconsolidated financial statements of Tipton Financial Services, Inc., and its wholly owned subsidiary are provided below. Tipton accounts for its investment in Smartcom, Inc., using the equity method. Its investment cost is equal to Smartcom's net asset book value (shareholders' equity).

	Tipton	Smartcom
	($ in thousands)	
Total assets (including the investment)	$420,000	$210,000
Total liabilities	230,000	190,000
Total shareholders' equity	190,000	20,000
Sales	1,200,000	575,000
Interest expense	40,000	30,000
Net income	24,000	100

REQUIRED

a. Combine the two unconsolidated companies' financial statements and show the *consolidated* financial statements of Tipton, similar to Exhibit 13–2. Remember to eliminate Tipton's investment against Smartcom's shareholders' equity.

Consolidation Ratios (continuation of Exercise 13–38)

13–39 Refer to Exercise 13–38 and the consolidated financial statements of Tipton Financial Services, Inc.

REQUIRED

a. Calculate the following ratios for Tipton *before* and *after* consolidation:

- Debt-to-total assets ratio
- Return on shareholders' equity ratio (use ending shareholders' equity to approximate the average)

b. Comment on any differences in these ratios before and after consolidation.

13–40 Foreign Currency Transactions—Alternate Exercises (A) or (B)

Exercise (A)

In each of the following examples, determine the gain or loss resulting from foreign exchange transactions. All exchange rates are shown as the number of U.S. dollars required to obtain one unit of foreign currency.

a. Bancroft Company purchases supplies and records an accounts payable of 100,000 Japanese yen. The exchange rate on the purchase date is $0.007. When the accounts payable is paid, the exchange rate has risen to $0.008.

b. Vaughn Enterprises sells services and records an accounts receivable of 12,000 British pounds when the exchange rate is $1.55. Vaughan receives payment in pounds from the British buyer when the exchange rate is $1.60.

c. Bishop Chess Company records an accounts payable of 60,000 Swiss francs when the exchange rate is $0.65. At payment date, the exchange rate has fallen to $0.62.

Exercise (B)

In each of the following examples, determine the gain or loss resulting from foreign exchange transactions. All exchange rates are shown as the number of U.S. dollars required to obtain one unit of foreign currency.

a. Shipley Company purchases supplies and records an accounts payable of 82,000 Japanese yen. The exchange rate on the purchase date is $0.009. When the accounts payable is paid, the exchange rate has risen to $0.006.

b. Cameron Enterprises sells services and records an accounts receivable of 38,200 British pounds when the exchange rate is $1.38. Vaughan receives payment in pounds from the British buyer when the exchange rate is $1.44.

c. Bishop Chess Company records an accounts payable of 82,000 French francs when the exchange rate is $0.56. At payment date, the exchange rate has fallen to $0.51.

Foreign Currency Transactions (continuation of Exercise 13–40)

13–41 In each of the examples in Exercise 13–40 (A) or (B), describe how the firm might have hedged its foreign currency exposure by transactions to buy or sell foreign currencies in futures markets.

PROBLEMS

Statement of Consolidation Policy

13–42 Cabot Corporation, a producer of specialty chemicals and materials, reports the following accounting policies for intercorporate investments:

Principles of Consolidation: The Consolidated Financial Statements include the accounts of Cabot Corporation and majority-owned and controlled domestic and foreign subsidiaries. Investments in majority-owned affiliates where control is temporary and investments in 20 percent to 50 percent-owned affiliates are accounted for on the equity method. All significant intercompany transactions have been eliminated.

REQUIRED

a. Cabot notes only "majority-owned and controlled" subsidiaries are included in the consolidation. Is it possible that majority (i.e., greater than 50%) ownership in a subsidiary would not constitute control? Discuss.

b. Why are subsidiaries that are less than 100% owned included in the consolidation?

c. Cabot uses the equity method to account for investments in 20 to 50% owned affiliates. Explain how consolidation of these affiliates would affect Cabot's reported total assets, total liabilities, shareholders' equity, and net income.

d. Cabot states that all significant intercompany transactions have been eliminated. Provide several examples of intercompany transactions that require elimination in order to consolidate affiliated firms.

Effects of Consolidation on Selected Accounts and Ratios

13–43 Selected items from the unconsolidated financial statements of Mammoth Motors Company and its wholly owned subsidiary, Chattel Credit Corp., are provided below. Mammoth accounts for its investment in Chattel using the equity method, and the investment cost is equal to Chattel's book value of shareholders' equity.

	Mammoth Motors Co.	Chattel Credit Corp.
	($ in millions)	
Total assets (including investments)	$29,000	$18,500
Total liabilities	15,500	17,700
Total shareholders' equity	13,500	800
Sales	54,000	10,200
Interest expense	4,000	—
Net income	3,000	1,100
Income tax rate	35%	30%

REQUIRED

a. Determine how the following items would be valued in Mammoth Motors' consolidated financial statements:

- Total assets
- Total liabilities
- Shareholders' equity
- Sales
- Net income

b. Contrast the following financial ratios of Mammoth Motors before and after consolidation with Chattel Credit:

- Debt-to-total assets ratio
- Return on assets ratio
- Return on shareholders' equity ratio
- Operating income ratio
- Asset turnover ratio

Foreign Currency Transactions: Unhedged Accounts Receivable and Payable

13–44 In each of the following cases, determine the amount of gain or loss to be reported in 1998 due to unhedged accounts receivable or payable that are denominated in foreign currencies. All exchange rates are stated as the number of U.S. dollars required to obtain one unit of foreign currency.

  a. Asebrook Company recorded an accounts receivable of 10,000 British pounds in 1998 when the exchange rate was $1.50. At year-end, the exchange rate had risen to $1.60.
  b. Baker Company recorded an accounts payable of 1,000,000 New Taiwan dollars in 1998 when the exchange rate was $0.04. At year-end, the exchange rate had risen to $0.05.
  c. Hanno Company recorded an accounts receivable of 100,000 Canadian dollars in 1998 when the exchange rate was $0.75. At year-end, the exchange rate had fallen to $0.68.
  d. Pfeiffer Company recorded an accounts payable of 50,000 Swiss francs in 1988 when the exchange rate was $0.60. At year-end, the exchange rate had fallen to $0.57.

Foreign Currency Transactions, Unhedged Accounts Receivable and Payable (continuation of Problem 13–44)

13–45 In each of the cases considered in Problem 13–44, describe how the U.S. firm might have insulated itself from foreign exchange gains and losses by transactions in the foreign exchange forward market.

Foreign Currency Transactions and Hedging Activities

13–46 On October 1, 1998, the Keaton Company, a U.S. firm, sold merchandise to Chaplin, Inc., a British firm. The sales agreement specifies that Chaplin will make payment of £500,000 to Keaton in 120 days, i.e., on February 1, 1999. Relevant exchange rates are shown in the following table:

Spot and Forward Rates, U.S. Dollar ($) and British Pound (£)

Date	Rate	$/£
October 1, 1998	Spot	$1.50
	30-day forward	1.48
	60-day forward	1.46
	90-day forward	1.42
	120-day forward	1.40
December 31, 1998	Spot	1.46
February 1, 1999	Spot	1.51

REQUIRED

a. Determine the amount of the account receivable and sales revenue to be recorded (in U.S. dollars) by the Keaton Company on the date of sale.
b. What amount of gain or loss would be reported by Keaton in 1998 and in 1999, if the foreign currency receivable is not hedged?
c. Describe how Keaton might hedge the above transaction in the forward market for British pounds. What is the amount of income or expense associated with the hedging transaction?
d. In retrospect on February 1, 1999, would it have been wise for Keaton to hedge the account receivable? Explain.

Interpreting Financial Statements: Affiliated Firms

13–47 Review the Bristol-Myers Squibb (BMS) financial statements in Appendix E.

REQUIRED

a. Read Notes 1 and 3. Identify any unfamiliar or unusual terms. Match the terms presented in this chapter to the terms used by BMS.
b. Determine whether BMS's relationships with its subsidiaries seem to have a significant effect on the firm's liquidity, profitability, capital structure, or other important dimensions of the firm's performance.
c. Does the firm use the equity method of accounting for its ownership of affiliated companies? How does the firm's choice of method affect its results?

Interpreting Financial Statements: Foreign Currency Translation

13–48 Review the Bristol-Myers Squibb (BMS) financial statements in Appendix E.

REQUIRED

a. Read Notes 5 and 12. Identify any unfamiliar or unusual terms. Match the terms presented in this chapter to the terms used by BMS.
b. Does the firm's treatment of foreign currency translations seem to have any significant effect on its balance sheet? How?
c. BMS has entered into foreign exchange contracts with foreign exchange brokers. Briefly explain the company's actions and give an example similar to the examples provided in the text as part of your explanation.

Interpreting Financial Statements: Affiliated Firms

13–49 Review Reebok's financial statements in Appendix F.

REQUIRED

a. Read Notes 1, 2, and 12. Identify any unfamiliar or unusual terms. Match the terms presented in this chapter to the terms used by Reebok.
b. Determine whether Reebok's relationships with its subsidiaries seem to have a significant effect on the firm's liquidity, profitability, capital structure, or other important dimensions of the firm's performance.
c. Does the firm use the equity method of accounting for its ownership of affiliated companies? How does the firm's choice of method affect its results? To the extent possible, characterize the method used as being either conservative, aggressive, or in between, in terms of its impact on net income.

Interpreting Financial Statements: Foreign Currency Translation

13–50 Review Reebok's financial statements in Appendix F.

REQUIRED

a. Read Notes 1 and 11. Identify any unfamiliar or unusual terms. Match the terms presented in this chapter to the terms used by Reebok.

b. Does the firm's treatment of foreign currency translations seem to have any significant effect on its balance sheet? On its income statement?

c. What other impact might foreign currency translations have on the long-term success or failure of this firm? On other aspects of its financial statements? On other aspects of the firm's performance?

Foreign Currency Hedging

13–51 In Du Pont Corporation's 1994 annual report, Note 27 contained the following (partial) information:

Principal foreign currency exposures and related hedge positions at December 31, 1994, were as follows:

Currency ($ in millions)	Net Monetary Asset (Liability) Exposure	Open Contracts to Buy (Sell) Foreign Currency After Tax	Net After-Tax Exposure
British pound	$(1,428)	$1,427	$(1)
Dutch gilder	$ 273	$(271)	$ 2
Italian lira	$ 205	$(206)	$(1)

REQUIRED

a. Discuss the impact that hedging has had on Du Pont's financial statements.

Allocation of Acquisition Cost in a Purchase

13–52 Ronco, Inc., purchased all of the outstanding voting stock of Nanco, Ltd., on January 1, 1997, at a cost of $750 million paid in cash. On the acquisition date, Nanco had the following assets and liabilities ($ in millions):

	Book Value	Fair Market Value
Cash	$ 55	$ 55
Other assets	820	950
Liabilities	430	364

REQUIRED

a. Explain why the fair market values of Nanco's identifiable assets and liabilities may differ from their book or carrying values at the acquisition date.

b. Determine the excess of Ronco's investment cost over the book value of Nanco's net assets.

c. Determine the excess of Ronco's investment cost over the fair market value of Nanco's net assets.

d. Is there goodwill implicit in the investment cost incurred by Ronco? If so, what amount would be reported as goodwill in Ronco's consolidated balance sheet on January 1, 1997?

Preparation of Consolidated Balance Sheet at Acquisition Date

13–53 On January 1, 1997, Tipper Company purchased all of the outstanding stock of Albert Inc. The post-combination balance sheets of both firms are listed below ($ in millions):

	Tipper Company	Albert Inc.
Cash	$ 20	$ 5
Accounts receivable	120	65
Other assets	950	330
Investment in Albert, Inc.	410	
Total assets	$1500	$400
Liabilities	$650	160
Shareholders' equity	850	240
Total liabilities and shareholders' equity	$1500	$400

Additional information:

1. On the date of acquisition, Albert Inc.'s other assets had a fair market value of $380 million. All other components of net assets had fair market values approximately equal to book values.
2. Albert's accounts receivable include $25 million that is due from Tipper Company.

REQUIRED

a. Assume Tipper Company will report a consolidated balance sheet on January 1, 1997. Indicate how each of the following items would be valued in the consolidated statement:

- Accounts receivable
- Other assets
- Investment in Albert Inc.
- Goodwill
- Liabilities
- Shareholders' equity

Valuation and Amortization of Goodwill

13–54 a. In a recent takeover battle between Viacom and QVC over Paramount, the potential cost of acquiring Paramount varied between $8 and $11.5 billion. How do you suppose a potential buyer (e.g., Viacom) would determine how much to pay in order to acquire another firm (e.g., Paramount)? To what extent would the assets and liabilities reported in Paramount's balance sheet influence the amounts offered for Paramount's ownership shares?

b. Assume that Viacom purchases Paramount for $11 billion, and that the recorded value of Paramount's net assets at that date is $6.5 billion. For purposes of subsequent financial reports, how would Viacom account for the difference of $4.5 billion ($11 billion − $6.5 billion = $4.5 billion)? How would this difference affect the balance sheets and the income statements of Viacom in subsequent years?

CASES AND EXTENSIONS

Advantages and Disadvantages of Comprehensive Disclosures

13–55 a. Managers of U.S. firms sometimes allege that they are at a disadvantage when selling securities in international markets because U.S. disclosure and measurement standards are more comprehensive, stringent, and costly than are those of most other nations. Assume that these managers are correct and propose a solution to the problem.

b. Managers of non-U.S. firms sometimes argue that they are impeded from selling securities in U.S. financial markets because U.S. reporting standards are extensive and costly to implement. Propose a diplomatic solution to the problem, with due consideration of the costs and benefits to foreign and domestic business firms.

Translation of Foreign Currency Financial Statements

13–56 The balance sheet and income statement of Buchanen, Inc., a subsidiary of a U.S. company, is shown below. Buchanen, Inc., operates in New Zealand, and prepares its financial statements in New Zealand dollars (NZ$).

Buchanen, Inc.
Balance Sheet and Income Statement
December 31, 1998
(NZ$ in millions)

Income Statement		Balance Sheet			
Revenues	NZ$ 1,200	Assets	NZ$ 1,500	Liabilities	NZ$ 600
Expenses	(900)			Paid-in capital	150
Net income	NZ$ 300			Retained earnings	750
			NZ$ 1,500		NZ$ 1,500

Supplementary information:

Exchange rates (US$/NZ$):
Average during 1998	.55
Spot rate, December 31, 1998	.60
Historical rate when capital stock was issued	.75
Beginning balance in retained earnings, in US$	$500

No dividends to shareholders were declared during 1998.

REQUIRED

a. Translate Buchanen's financial statements into U.S. dollars, so that they may be consolidated with those of the U.S. parent firm.

b. Has the U.S. dollar strengthened or weakened relative to the New Zealand dollar during 1998? Explain how this change has affected Buchanen's translated balance sheet.

c. Explain why a translation adjustment is required in order to bring the translated balance sheet into balance.

Reconciliation of Income and Shareholders' Equity: The United States and the United Kingdom

13–57 Foreign companies whose shares are registered on U.S. security exchanges must file with the SEC a description of significant differences between U.S. and domestic accounting principles, as well as a reconciliation of net income and shareholders' equity under domestic and U.S. GAAP.

Antic Knights, plc, a British firm, included the following information in its SEC filings for 1998.

1. Summary of Differences Between United Kingdom and United States Generally Accepted Accounting Principles:

   (a) *Acquisition Cost*
   Under United Kingdom GAAP there are certain acquisition-related costs which may be immediately charged to retained earnings. Under United States GAAP these costs are charged to the statement of earnings as incurred. Examples of such items include certain costs related to the closure of facilities which will not be operated and severance of individuals terminated.

   (b) *Deferred Taxation*
   United Kingdom GAAP allows for no provision for deferred taxation to be made if there is reasonable evidence that such taxation will not be payable in the foreseeable future. United States GAAP requires provisions for deferred taxation be made for all differences between the tax basis and book basis of assets and liabilities.

   (c) *Goodwill and Other Intangibles*
   The Company writes off certain intangible assets, which include goodwill, covenants not to compete and favorable lease rights, directly to retained earnings in the year of acquisition. Under United States GAAP these intangible assets would be capitalized as assets and amortized over their estimated useful lives.

2. Reconciliations of Net Income and Shareholders' Equity:

Net Income Reconciliation For the year ended March 31, 1998 (pounds in thousands)		Shareholders' Equity Reconciliation March 31, 1998 (pounds in thousands)	
Net earnings before extraordinary items	£ 19,726	Shareholders' equity	£ 8,652
Amortization of goodwill	(10,292)	Goodwill	13,312
Acquisition costs	(3,012)	Deferred taxes	(509)
Deferred income taxes	(333)	Other	1,172
Other	(1,895)	Shareholders' equity	
Estimated earnings, U.S. GAAP	£ 4,194	U.S. GAAP	£22,627

REQUIRED

a. For each of the indicated differences between U.S. and U.K. GAAP, indicate which method of accounting you consider to be more suitable to the needs of investor analysts. Explain your reasoning.

b. Based on the information provided by Parker, do you consider U.K. or U.S. GAAP to be more conservative? Explain.

c. Based on Parker's explanations of differences between U.K. and U.S. GAAP, explain why each of the individual reconciling items is added (or subtracted) to convert to U.S. GAAP (e.g., why is goodwill subtracted in the income reconciliation and added in the shareholders' equity reconciliation?).

Reconciliation of Income and Shareholders' Equity: The United States and Chile

13–58 Foreign companies whose shares are registered on U.S. security exchanges must file with the SEC a description of significant differences between U.S. and domestic accounting principles, as well as a reconciliation of net income and shareholders' equity under domestic and U.S. GAAP.

Goldplate Company, Inc., a Chilean firm, included the following information:

1. *Differences in Measurement Methods*
   The principal methods applied in the preparation of the accompanying financial statements which have resulted in amounts which differ from those that would have otherwise been determined under accounting principles generally accepted in the United States, are as follows:

   (a) *Inflation Accounting*
   The cumulative inflation rate in Chile, as measured by the Consumer Price Index, for the three-year period ended December 31, 1998 was approximately 85%.

   Chilean accounting principles require that financial statements be restated to reflect the full effects of loss in the purchasing power of the Chilean peso on the financial position and results of operations of reporting entities. The method is based on a model which enables calculation of net inflation gains or losses caused by monetary assets and liabilities exposed to changes in the purchasing power of local currency, by restating all non-monetary accounts of the financial statements.

   The inclusion of price-level adjustments in the accompanying financial statements is considered appropriate under the prolonged inflationary conditions affecting the Chilean economy.

   (b) *Revaluations of Property, Plant, and Equipment*
   Certain property, plant and equipment are reported in the financial statements at amounts determined in accordance with a technical appraisal carried out in 1994. Revaluation of property, plant and equipment is an accounting principle not generally accepted in the United States.

   (c) *Vacation Expense*
   The cost of vacations earned by employees is generally recorded by the Company on a pay-as-you-go basis. Accounting principles generally accepted in the United States require that this expense be recorded on the accrual basis as the vacations are earned.

   (d) *Inventory Valuation*
   Finished and in process products are reported in the financial statements at the replacement cost of the raw materials included therein and therefore exclude labor and overhead, which practice is contrary to the accounting principles generally accepted in the United States.

   (e) *Write-up of Noncurrent Asset*
   Net income reported in the Chilean GAAP financial statements as of December 31, 1998, includes the effects of the reversal of a valuation

allowance recorded in prior years to write-down the carrying value of disposable land to estimated market value.

2. Reconciliations of Net Income and Shareholders' Equity:

Net Income Reconciliation Year ended December 31, 1998 (CH$ in thousands)		Shareholders' Equity Reconciliation December 31, 1998 (CH$ in thousands)	
Net income, Chilean GAAP	CH$ 14,201,342	Shareholders' equity	CH$ 36,773,825
Depreciation on revaluation	43,188	Property revaluations	(4,259,726)
Provision for vacations	(58,984)	Inventory costing	67,592
Reverse asset write-up	(1,744,402)	Other	(2,154,501)
Other	627,904	Shareholders'	
Net income, U.S. GAAP	CH$ 13,069,048	equity, U.S. GAAP	CH$ 30,427,190

REQUIRED

a. For each of the individual differences between U.S. and Chilean GAAP, indicate which method of accounting you consider to be the more useful to investor analysts. Explain your reasoning.

b. Based on the information provided above, do you consider Chilean or U.S. GAAP to be more conservative? Explain.

c. Discuss why each of the individual reconciling items is added (or subtracted) in converting from Chilean to U.S. GAAP.

Interpreting Financial Statements: Affiliated Firms

13–59 The PolyGram Group includes businesses around the world that are chiefly involved in the acquisition, production, and marketing of repertoire as well as the manufacture, sales, and distribution of prerecorded sound carriers, such as compact disks, music cassettes, and records. In addition PolyGram is engaged in activities with respect to music video, in the production of films and television programming, and in music publishing. Its income statements are summarized below (in millions of Netherlands guilders):

	1992	1991
Net sales	6,617	6,326
Direct costs of sales	(3,502)	(3,391)
Gross income	3,115	2,935
Selling, general and administrative expenses	(2,326)	(2,200)
Income from operations	789	735
Financial income and expenses	(9)	18
Income before taxes	780	753
Income taxes	(226)	(238)
Income after taxes	554	515
Equity in income of nonconsolidated companies	(18)	(28)
Group income	536	487
Minority interests	(30)	(41)
Net income	506	446

REQUIRED

a. Discuss any unusual terms, or disclosure practices, in PolyGram's income statement.
b. Discuss how, and why, PolyGram's income has been reduced due to minority and other interests in affiliated companies.
c. Did these interests have a significant effect on PolyGram's income? Why?
d. What other information would you like to have about PolyGram's interests in affiliated companies? Why?
e. Evaluate PolyGram's profitability. Consider its operating income separately from group income and from net income.

WHAT WOULD
YOU DO?

Interpreting Financial Statements: Effects of U.S. GAAP (continuation of Case 13–59)

13–60 Consider Case 13–61 concerning PolyGram. In its 1992 financial statements, you find the following page labeled "Application of Generally Accepted Accounting Principles in the USA." This statement includes the following:

The calculation of Net income . . . , substantially in accordance with U.S. GAAP, is as follows (in millions of Netherlands guilders):

	1992	1991
Net income as per Consolidated Statements of Income of the PolyGram Group	506	446
Adjustments to reported income:		
a. amortisation of goodwill	(24)	(19)
b. amortisation of intangible assets	(53)	(37)
c. remeasurement of financial statements of entities in hyper-inflated countries	(2)	(16)
d. transactions with Philips	—	(27)
e. other	8	6
Approximate Net income in accordance with U.S. GAAP	435	353

REQUIRED

a. Discuss any unfamiliar terms used by PolyGram in this note.
b. How have the applications of U.S. GAAP affected PolyGram's reported net income? Do these differences seem significant? Why?
c. Reevaluate PolyGram's profitability (see preceding case). Does this new information change your assessment of PolyGram's profitability? How?
d. Why do you think PolyGram reports net income at higher levels in its primary financial statements, and then at lower levels after applying U.S. GAAP?
e. Which of PolyGram's disclosures of net income is more conservative? Which is more comparable to other U.S. companies? Which would you prefer as a manager? As an investor? As a financial analyst? Discuss these differences.

Interpreting Financial Statements: Affiliated Firms (Case 13–59 updated)

13–61 The PolyGram Group includes businesses around the world that are chiefly involved in the acquisition, production, and marketing of repertoire as well as the manufacture, sales, and distribution of prerecorded sound carriers, such as compact disks, music cassettes, and records. In addition PolyGram is engaged in activities with respect to music video, in the production of films and television programming, and in music publishing. Its income statements are summarized below (in millions of guilders):

	1994	1993
Net sales	8,600	7,416
Direct costs of sales	(4,543)	(3,909)
Gross income	4,057	3,507
Selling, general and administrative expenses	(2,988)	(2,575)
Income from operations	1,069	932
Financial income and expenses	8	(5)
Income before taxes	1,077	927
Income taxes	(302)	(264)
Income after taxes	775	663
Equity in income of non-consolidated companies	(9)	(20)
Group income	766	643
Minority interests	(28)	(29)
Net income	738	614

REQUIRED

a. Discuss any unusual terms, or disclosure practices, in PolyGram's income statement.

b. Discuss how, and why, PolyGram's income has been reduced due to minority and other interests in affiliated companies.

c. Did these interests have a significant effect on PolyGram's income? Why?

d. What other information would you like to have about PolyGram's interests in affiliated companies? Why?

e. Evaluate PolyGram's profitability. Consider its operating income separately from group income and from net income.

Interpreting Financial Statements: Effects of U.S. GAAP (continuation of Case 13–61)

13–62 Consider Case 13-61 concerning PolyGram. In its 1994 financial statements, you find the following page labeled "Application of Generally Accepted Accounting Principles in the USA." This statement includes the following:

> The calculation of Net income . . . , substantially in accordance with U.S. GAAP, is as follows (in millions of Netherland guilders):

WHAT WOULD
YOU DO?

	1994	1993
Net income as per Consolidated Statements of Income of the PolyGram Group	738	614
Adjustments to reported income:		
a. amortisation of goodwill	(27)	(26)
b. amortisation of intangible assets	(57)	(64)
c. remeasurement of financial statements of entities in hyper-inflated countries	(13)	5
d. other	5	5
Approximate Net income in accordance with U.S. GAAP	646	534

REQUIRED

a. Discuss any unfamiliar terms used by PolyGram in this note.

b. How have the applications of U.S. GAAP affected PolyGram's reported net income? Do these differences seem significant? Why?

c. Reevaluate PolyGram's profitability (see preceding case). Does this new information change your assessment of PolyGram's profitability? How?

d. Why do you think PolyGram reports net income at higher levels in its primary financial statements, and then at lower levels after applying U.S. GAAP?

e. Which of PolyGram's disclosures of net income is more conservative? Which is more comparable to other U.S. companies? Which would you prefer as a manager? As an investor? As a financial analyst? Discuss these differences.

USING FINANCIAL ACCOUNTING ON THE INTERNET

13–63 Access the EDGAR archives (**www.sec.gov/edgarhp.htm**) and locate the 8-K report filed by Disney Enterprises Inc. (formerly Walt Disney Co.) on February 9, 1996. This report was filed on the successful acquisition of a communication corporation. Examine the 8-K report and answer the following questions based on *scenario 1:*

a. Which company did Disney acquire?

b. What were the separate revenue and operating incomes for each company prior to the acquisition (for the year ended September 30, 1995)? Refer to the Pro Forma Combined Condensed Statement of Income and identify the revenue and operating income for the same period had the companies been combined.

c. Separately calculate the operating income percentage and net income percentage (of net sales) for each company and for the combined company. What are your observations?

d. What were the total assets and total liabilities of each company? Compare it to the combined company. What do you observe?

13–66 Kimberly-Clark is a global corporation whose primary product is diapers and tissues. Access the EDGAR archives (**www.gov.sec/edgarhp.htm**) to locate

Kimberly-Clark's 1995 10-K. Answer the following questions based on its Note on Foreign Currency Related Issues.

a. What is the dollar impact of foreign currency transactions included in consolidated net income?
b. How does the company translate the financial statements of foreign operations other than those in hyper-inflationary economies?
c. How does the company translate monetary assets (e.g., accounts receivable and cash) of subsidiaries located in hyper-inflationary economies?
d. Determine the dollar impact on the company of the Mexican peso devaluation in 1995.

13–65 Access the EDGAR archives (**www.sec.gov/edgarhp.htm**) and locate the Schedule 14D1 filing (February 1, 1995) made by Cadbury Schweppes on the successful acquisition of Dr Pepper/Seven-Up Companies Inc. *Hint:* search on "Cadbury" or "Dr Pepper". Examine the section that contains the financial statements of the U.K. corporation and locate the information on differences between U.K. GAAP and U.S. GAAP. In this section, the company has provided a GAAP reconciliation.

REQUIRED

a. What are the primary reasons for the differences in net income and shareholders' equity from U.K. GAAP to U.S. GAAP.
b. Explain the treatments of goodwill and trademarks under U.K. GAAP. How do these differ from U.S. GAAP?
c. Calculate the return on equity under both U.K. and U.S. GAAP. Explain how the different accounting standards have an impact on the computed ratios.

13–66 Access the EDGAR archives (**www.sec.gov/edgarhp.htm**) and locate the Schedule 14D1 filing made by either Amdura Corporation or FKI plc on March 22, 1995 (they are identical). *Hint:* You can search for this filing on the SEC database by inputting the name of either company. It was filed when FKI plc, a U.K. corporation, made a successful tender offer for Amdura Corp., a U.S. corporation. The Schedule 14D1 contains, among other things, the financial statements of FKI plc as per U.K. GAAP and a reconciliation of its net income and shareholders' equity as per U.K. GAAP to the U.S. GAAP equivalent.

REQUIRED

a. Calculate the return on equity of FKI plc as per U.K. GAAP and as per U.S. GAAP. Explain the major reasons for the difference.
b. Calculate the return on assets and operating income percentage of FKI as per U.K. GAAP and U.S. GAAP, and explain the difference.
c. Compare the ratios of FKI plc with the return on equity, return on assets, and operating income percentage of Parker-Hannifin (access EDGAR for the raw data to compute the ratios), a U.S.-based competitor of FKI plc. Should one use the U.S. GAAP-based numbers or the U.K. GAAP-based numbers for FKI plc?

CHAPTER 14

STUDYING THIS CHAPTER
WILL ENABLE YOU TO

1. Interpret the financial statements of firms that have undertaken accounting changes.
2. Analyze information about business segments.
3. Describe annual and interim reports.
4. Identify reports filed with the Securities and Exchange Commission.
5. Explain the efficient market hypothesis and its implications for accounting.
6. Describe the two major roles of financial accounting.

ADDITIONAL DIMENSIONS OF FINANCIAL REPORTING

INTRODUCTION

This chapter deals with several important financial reporting issues that have not been previously discussed. These issues include accounting changes, annual and interim reports, business segment disclosures, reports filed with the Securities and Exchange Commission (SEC), the relationship between accounting information and stock prices, and a synthesis of the major roles that financial accounting information plays in our society. An understanding of these topics will make you a more sophisticated user of accounting information.

ACCOUNTING CHANGES

The term **accounting changes** includes three types of accounting events:

1. a **change in accounting principle,**
2. a **change in accounting estimate,** and
3. a **change in reporting entity.**

Since the accounting for each type of change is different, they are discussed separately.

Change in Accounting Principle

In many situations, corporate managers are free to choose from among several acceptable accounting methods. For example, LIFO or FIFO can be used for inventory valuation, and an accelerated or straight-line method can be used to calculate depreciation expense. Although managers can choose between alternative generally accepted accounting principles (GAAP), once a method is selected, it should be used consistently from period to period. This enhances the interperiod comparability of financial statements. In other words, if a firm consistently uses the same accounting principles from one period to another, changes in the financial statement numbers over time will likely reflect changes in the underlying economics of the firm, rather than the effect of an accounting principle change.

Although the consistent use of accounting principles is desirable, firms do occasionally change from one principle to another. Because financial statement readers do not usually expect such changes, these changes are always highlighted in the auditor's report. Since the existence of an accounting change dramatically alters the interpretation of financial statements, a review of the auditor's report should always be one of the first steps in the analysis of financial statements.

An accounting principle change can be accounted for in several ways. Each approach is used only in clearly defined circumstances.

General Rule. To illustrate the general rule, consider a change in depreciation method for a machine that originally cost $3,700, has an estimated salvage value of $700, and an estimated life of five years. Assume that during the first two years of the machine's life the straight-line method was used. In the third year, the sum-of-the-years'-digits method was adopted.

The general rule requires a **cumulative effect** adjustment. In the year of the change, the account balances are restated to show those amounts that would have appeared if the new method had been used all along. This requires a comparison of depreciation charges under the two methods.

Annual depreciation expense under the straight-line method is $600 [($3,700 − $700)/5], or a total of $1,200 for the first two years. Under the sum-of-the-years'-digits method, total depreciation expense for the first two years would be $1,800:

	Depreciable Base		Fraction		Depreciation
Year 1	($3,700 − $700)	×	5/15	=	$1,000
Year 2	($3,700 − $700)	×	4/15	=	800
					$1,800

If the sum-of-the-years'-digits method had originally been used, depreciation expense for the two years would have been higher by a total of $600. What effect would this have had on the accounting records at the beginning of year three? First, accumulated depreciation would have been higher by $600. Second, since depreciation expense would have been higher, net income and retained earnings would have been lower by $600. The analysis (which for simplicity ignores the tax effect) is as follows:

ASSETS	= LIABILITIES +	SHAREHOLDERS' EQUITY
Accumulated depreciation		Retained earnings
−$600		−$600 (cumulative effect of accounting principle change)

The cumulative effect of $600 appears as the last item on the income statement in the year of the accounting principle change. Future years' depreciation expenses are based on the sum-of-the-years'-digits method.

The general rule for reporting an accounting principle change results in two inconsistencies between the year of the change and prior years:

1. The cumulative effect of adopting the change is included in the adoption year's income. No comparable amount appears in prior or subsequent years' income.

2. Depreciation expense in the year of the change is based on the new method, while in prior years it is based on the old method.

Because of these inconsistencies, GAAP requires footnote disclosure of what net income would have been in the current and prior years had the new method been used. Many accountants refer to these as **pro forma amounts.** Because the pro forma amounts are all based on the new accounting principle, valid comparisons can be drawn between the current and prior years.

Exhibit 14–1 contains a note from the 1991 financial statements of the United States Shoe Corporation (USSC), as well as an income statement summary for three years. In response to a FASB ruling, USSC changed the way in which it accounts for the revenue associated with eyewear maintenance contracts, and it has used the cumulative effect approach to account for the change.

EXHIBIT 14–1
ACCOUNTING PRINCIPLE CHANGE CUMULATIVE EFFECT APPROACH

The United States Shoe Corporation
Consolidated Statement of Earnings (Partial)
(dollars in thousands)

	1991	1990	1989
Earnings (loss) before cumulative effect of accounting change	($27,662)	$49,187	$12,965
Cumulative effect of accounting change related to product maintenance contracts, net of tax effect of $2,343	(3,621)	—	—
Net earnings (loss)	($31,283)	$49,187	$12,965

Note (3) Accounting Change (Adapted)

In December 1990, the Financial Accounting Standards Board issued a technical bulletin on accounting for product maintenance contracts such as those sold by the company's optical retailing group. The bulletin requires the deferral and amortization of revenue from the sales of such contracts on a straight-line basis over the term of the contract (one to two years). Under the accounting method previously followed by the company, a portion of the revenue earned from the sale of eyewear product maintenance contracts was recognized on the date of sale and the remainder was deferred and amortized on a straight-line basis over the term of the contract.

Effective at the beginning of 1991, the company has elected to adopt this new accounting method for all contracts in place. The effect of this change is to increase the net loss in 1991 by $4.3 million, including $3.6 million, which is the cumulative effect of the accounting change.

If this change in accounting method had been in effect during 1990 and 1989, the effects would have been immaterial to net earnings.

The note indicates that the change would have had an immaterial effect on the net earnings of 1990 and 1989. This means that the earnings actually reported in those years closely approximate the earnings that would have been reported under the new accounting method. These numbers, however, cannot be validly compared to the reported loss in 1991; that loss includes the cumulative effect of the change. Proper comparisons, therefore, involve the reported earnings in 1989 and 1990, and the 1991 loss before the cumulative effect, which is $27,662,000. Reality Check 14–1 contains information about an accounting principle charge made by The Kellogg Company.

REALITY CHECK 14–1

CHANGES IN ACCOUNTING PRINCIPLES AND EARNINGS COMPARISONS

The Kellogg Company reported the following financial information ($ in millions):

	1993	1992	1991
Earnings before cumulative effect of accounting change	$680.7	$682.8	$606.0
Cumulative effect of change in method of accounting for postretirement benefits other than pensions (net of tax benefit of $144.6)	—	(251.6)	—
Net earnings	$680.7	$431.2	$606.0

Assume that other than the cumulative effect, earnings for 1992 and 1991 were not materially affected by the change.

REQUIRED

a. Identify the earnings number for each year that would permit valid comparisons.

Exceptions Some accounting principle changes are accounted for **retroactively.** Under this approach, prior years' financial statements are restated to reflect the use of the new method. The obvious advantage of the retroactive approach is that the financial statements of the current and prior years are based on a common set of accounting principles. However, reissuing financial statements with numbers different from those that originally appeared may dilute the public's confidence in financial reporting.

The retroactive approach is only used in the following situations:

1. a change from LIFO to another inventory method,
2. a change in the method of accounting for long-term construction contracts,
3. a change to or from the full-cost method by firms in the extractive industries,
4. a change made by a firm issuing financial statements to the public for the first time, or
5. when required as part of the transition process for a new FASB standard.

The first three changes often result in large cumulative effects that would greatly compromise the interperiod comparability of financial statements. Consequently, these changes are accounted for by retroactive restatement. The fourth situation is one in which the general public has not previously seen the firm's financial statements. Accordingly, it would be best served by a set of financial statements that is comparable across time periods. The fifth exception acknowledges that the FASB uses a variety of transition methods when issuing new standards.

Changes in Accounting Estimates

Many financial statement figures are based on estimates. For example, depreciation expense and the book value of fixed assets are determined by estimates of useful lives and salvage values. As another example, uncollectible accounts expense and the net value of accounts receivable are based on estimates of the number of customers that will not honor their obligations to the firm.

An inherent aspect of estimates is that they do not always prove to be correct. Conceptually, changes in accounting estimates could be accounted for retroactively. That is, when an estimate proves faulty, prior years' financial statements could be restated.

That treatment has been rejected by the accounting profession. For most firms of even modest size, a large number of estimates will miss their mark. The retroactive approach would result in firms continually restating financial statements. This would seriously compromise the credibility and usefulness of financial reporting.

Instead, changes in accounting estimates are accounted for **prospectively** by including them in the year of the change and future years, if appropriate. To illustrate, assume a machine is acquired in 1996 for $14,000. It has a salvage value of $2,000 and an estimated life of five years. Straight-line depreciation is used. The annual depreciation charge is $2,400:

$$\text{Annual depreciation expense} = \frac{(\$14,000 - \$2,000)}{5} = \$2,400$$

Assume that at the beginning of 1998 the machine's total useful life is now estimated to be eight years. Depreciation expense for 1996 and 1997 are not changed. The remaining depreciable base is depreciated over the remaining useful life of six years. Annual depreciation expense for 1998 through 2003 is $1,200:

Cost	$14,000
Less salvage value	(2,000)
Less depreciation to date	(4,800)
Remaining depreciable base	$7,200

$$\text{Annual depreciation expense} = \frac{\text{Remaining depreciable base}}{\text{Remaining life}}$$

$$= \frac{\$7,200}{6}$$

$$= \$1,200$$

The effect of changes in accounting estimates on net income must be disclosed in the notes to the financial statements. As a practical matter, although virtually all firms experience changes in accounting estimates, they are usually too small (immaterial) to require disclosure.

Change in Reporting Entity

A change in reporting entity occurs when a firm changes the specific subsidiaries included in its consolidated financial statements (see Chapter 13). This situation often arises when the parent first acquires the majority share of a subsidiary's voting stock.

The acquisition and consolidation of a new subsidiary essentially result in a different reporting entity. The new subsidiary might substantially change the consolidated group's size, scope and scale of operations, and the nature of the products and services provided. Accordingly, the results of the new consolidated group cannot be validly compared to the results of the old group as previously reported.

A change in reporting entity is accounted for retroactively. Prior years' financial statements are restated to reflect the past results of the new consolidated group. This approach ensures comparability of the financial statements.

SEGMENT REPORTING

Many large corporations operate in a variety of industries and geographic areas. They also serve many customers, both large and small. Financial statements provide figures summed over all such groups. Many analysts feel that they would benefit from more detailed information. They suggest that this information could assist them in making better estimates of a firm's risk and expected return. For example, a firm that generates 10% of its revenue and profit from software development and 90% from manufacturing breakfast cereal will have a different risk and return outlook than one that generates 10% of its revenue and profit from breakfast cereal and 90% from software development.

Accordingly, all publicly held corporations are required to make certain disclosures in financial statement notes. These disclosure requirements are summarized in the following sections.

Industry Segments

An **industry segment** is a component of a firm that provides a product or service, or a group of related products or services, to unaffiliated customers. In identifying industry segments, factors to consider include the underlying nature of the product or service (its purpose), the production process, markets, and the marketing process.

Although already established industry classification schemes exist, such as the Standard Industrial Classification (SIC), firms must examine their products, operations, and internal reporting systems to establish the industry classifications that best suit their circumstances. Thus, industry classifications across firms are not uniform, and interfirm comparisons of segment information should be made with caution.

For each major segment, firms must report:

1. *Revenue:* A segment's revenue includes sales to unaffiliated customers and transfers to other segments. By including intersegment transfers, segment revenue reflects the relative size of each segment. Note, however, that since a transfer from one segment to another segment is not an exchange with an outside party, these amounts are not included in the revenue figure that appears on the income statement. Accordingly, the total revenue of all segments might exceed the revenue figure on the income statement.
2. *Operating profit or loss:* This is calculated by subtracting a segment's operating expenses from its revenue. Operating expenses include those costs incurred by the segment, as well as a segment's share of joint costs incurred with other segments. It does not include an allocation of general corporate expenses (e.g., officer's salaries).
3. *Identifiable assets:* These include assets used exclusively by the segment, and a share of the assets used jointly with other segments. An allocation of general corporate assets (such as the building housing corporate headquarters) is not included.
4. A number of other disclosures including depreciation expense and capital expenditures.

Foreign Operations and Export Sales

A firm's **foreign operations** consist of those revenue-producing activities located outside of the firm's home country. **Domestic operations** are those located within a firm's home country. Disclosure of revenue, operating profit or loss, and identifiable assets must be made for both foreign and domestic operations. If a firm's foreign operations take place in two or more geographic areas, disclosures must be made for each area.

A firm's domestic operations might generate sales to unaffiliated customers both within and outside of the home country. Sales outside the home country are labeled **export sales,** and this amount must be disclosed.

Information about foreign operations and export sales is particularly helpful in assessing a firm's risk. For example, political stability varies considerably from country to country. The safety of a firm's assets in a relatively unstable country, or the continuity of sales in such a country, might be highly uncertain. This is an important consideration in estimating risk.

 Major Customers

Firms are required to disclose if sales to a single **major customer** exceed 10% of revenue. The customer need not be identified, but the customer's industry must be disclosed. This information provides insights into the riskiness of a firm's revenue stream. Greater risk is indicated if a few customers from one industry account for a large portion of revenue. If that industry experiences economic difficulties, the firm's revenue may suffer significantly. Moreover, a customer who accounts for a sizable portion of revenue may be able to demand significant concessions, which could have an unfavorable effect on the firm's future financial performance.

 An Illustration

Exhibit 14–2 contains segment information for Hercules, Inc., which has three industry segments:

1. Chemical Specialties; produces chemicals for use by paper manufacturers and water-soluble polymers that enhance the storage and usage of liquid products.
2. Food and Functional Products; produces products, such as food gums, used in processed meats and baked goods, as well as fat substitutes.
3. Aerospace; provides propulsion systems for virtually all space and military programs.

Based on sales and assets, the segments are generally of comparable size. To assess the relative profitability of the three segments, divide operating profit by assets. This is similar to the return on assets calculation discussed in Chapter 4. The results for 1993 are:

- Chemical Specialties   22.0%
- Food and Functional Products   16.2%
- Aerospace   15.8%

Segment data can also help analysts to assess risks and future trends. For example, the success of Hercules' low-fat products will depend on consumer attitudes regard-

EXHIBIT 14–2   HERCULES, INC., SEGMENT REPORTING DISCLOSURE

OPERATIONS BY INDUSTRY SEGMENT AND GEOGRAPHIC AREA (Dollars in millions)

Industry Segments	Chemical Specialties	Food & Functional Products	Aerospace	Corporate & Other	Total
1993					
Net Sales	$ 976	$ 867	$ 754	$ 176	2,773
Profit (Loss) from Operations	149	113	105	(59)	308
Identifiable Assets	676	699	664	216	2,255
Capital Expenditures	51	68	23	7	149
Depreciation	54	55	44	16	169
1992*					
Net Sales	1,023	865	797	180	2,865
Profit (Loss) from Operations	162	109	52	(79)	244
Identifiable Assets	676	734	835	218	2,463
Capital Expenditures	54	73	17	6	150
Depreciation	51	56	50	15	172
1991*					
Net Sales	1,016	940	795	178	2,929
Profit (Loss) from Operations	117	112	(10)	(32)	187
Identifiable Assets	693	877	845	223	2,638
Capital Expenditures	66	97	35	16	214
Depreciation	49	61	56	14	180

Geographic Areas	United States	Europe	Other	Eliminations	Total
1993					
Net Sales to Unaffiliated Customers	$ 1,994	$ 624	$ 155	$	2,773
Interarea Sales	87	76	16	(179)	–
Total	2,081	700	171	(179)	2,773
Profit from Operations	193	111	4		308
Identifiable Assets	1,627	546	82		2,255
1992					
Net Sales to Unaffiliated Customers	2,023	680	162		2,865
Interarea Sales	93	65	15	(173)	–
Total	2,116	745	177	(173)	2,865
Profit from Operations	135	96	13		244
Identifiable Assets	1,842	532	89		2,463
1991					
Net Sales to Unaffiliated Customers	2,051	692	186		2,929
Interarea Sales	103	67	16	(186)	–
Total	2,154	759	202	(186)	2,929
Profit from Operations	55	120	12		187
Identifiable Assets	1,893	641	104		2,638

* Restated to reflect organizational changes to conform with 1993 presentation.

ing their diets and "eating right." In contrast, the aerospace segment's success will be determined by its ability to adapt to a post–Cold War environment. The trend in the profitability of the aerospace segment is quite favorable. It generated a loss in 1991 and a modest profit in 1992; its profit then doubled in 1993.

Exhibit 14–2 also contains disclosures by geographic area. The majority of Hercules' sales take place in the United States, although about 23% of its sales occur in Europe. Thus, for example, the attitudes of consumers in both the United States and Europe will affect the success of Hercules' low-fat products.

ANNUAL REPORTS

All publicly held corporations, and many closely held ones, issue their financial statements as part of an **annual report** to shareholders. Since these reports are a major means of communicating with shareholders, corporations take great care in their preparation. The reports are usually prepared on glossy paper, contain interesting photographs, and are sometimes quite lengthy. For example, Martin Marietta Corporation's 1993 annual report is 66 pages long. Excerpts from several annual reports appear at the end of this text in Appendixes C through F.

In addition to the financial statements and the related notes, annual reports include the following information:

1. an introductory letter by the chief executive officer highlighting the year's performance and commenting on the prospects for the future,
2. a review of the types of businesses in which the firm is involved,
3. a financial summary (sales, net income, etc.) for each of the 5 or 10 most recent years,
4. management discussion and analysis of the firm's liquidity, capital resources, and operations,
5. the auditor's report expressing an opinion on the fairness of the financial statements,
6. a statement by management acknowledging its responsibility to prepare the financial statements and maintain an adequate system of internal controls,
7. quarterly financial data,
8. quarterly stock price and dividend data, and
9. a listing of officers and directors, along with a limited description of their backgrounds.

Management discussion and analysis (MDA) is one of the newest and most informative sections of the annual report. As noted in item 4, it includes a discussion of liquidity, capital resources, and operations. MDA contains an analysis of past performance and known trends. It also identifies the underlying economic causes of the observed trends.

In addition, forward-looking information is also provided. This information can be of two types. First, management may know of existing circumstances that will have an impact on future operations. For example, the planned sale of a component of the firm will affect both operations and liquidity. Second, management might also comment on anticipated trends and their effect on the firm's future. An illustration of this type of analysis might be a sales forecast based on macroeconomic factors, such as an impending recession or higher interest rates.

Refer to the MDA section in Wendy's annual report (Appendix D). The discussion comments on trends in revenues, expenses, and income, as well as expectations about sales levels in 1994. A discussion of financial condition and liquidity is also provided.

INTERIM REPORTING

Annual financial statements are usually issued between one and three months after a firm's fiscal year-end. Given that firms' transactions occur on an ongoing basis throughout the year, many analysts feel that annual financial statements do not report information in a timely manner. Because of this, all publicly held corporations, and many closely held companies, report financial information on an interim basis throughout the year. Most firms undertaking such **interim reporting** do so quarterly.

Interim financial statements are usually highly abbreviated and contain only limited disclosures in notes. Moreover, they are not audited. Thus, although interim financial statements are more timely, they are not as comprehensive or as reliable as annual financial statements.

In general, interim financial statements are prepared based on the same accounting principles as a firm's annual financial statements. Two exceptions exist. First, interim financial statements frequently require the use of additional estimates. For example, many firms do not undertake a physical count of inventory at the close of each quarter. Instead, the ending inventory amount and cost of goods sold are estimated.

The second exception concerns expense recognition. Some costs that are expensed for annual purposes are not *immediately* expensed for interim reporting if they clearly benefit more than one interim period. Instead, these costs are deferred (treated as an asset) and subsequently allocated as an expense to future interim periods.

The ski industry offers a good example. It would be reasonable for a ski area to have a fiscal year that runs from June 1 to May 31. Since May 31 is a low point in their operations, it is a natural time to tally results. Much of a ski area's repair and maintenance activities, however, take place over the ensuing summer months. In general, we know that repairs and maintenance costs are expensed immediately. However, given that 1) the ski industry earns little revenue in the summer months and 2) the repairs and maintenance costs will clearly benefit operations during the upcoming season, immediately expensing such costs will not result in the most useful interim financial information. Instead, these costs are deferred and allocated as an expense to future interim periods, based on the revenue generated in those periods.

As the ski area example illustrates, the nature of some businesses is quite seasonal. Consequently, care must be exercised in projecting annual results from interim periods. The accounting profession encourages firms to supplement their interim reports with results for the most recent 12-month period.

REPORTS FILED WITH THE SECURITIES AND EXCHANGE COMMISSION

As you know from Chapter 1, the Securities and Exchange Commission (SEC) has legislative authority to regulate financial disclosures of publicly held corporations. Although the SEC requires firms to file a number of different reports, two of these are of the most interest to us: 10-K reports and 10-Q reports.

A firm's **10-K report** includes virtually all of the information contained in its annual report plus some additional disclosures. These disclosures include information about litigation, executive compensation, and shareholdings by officers and directors. Because 10-K reports include such detailed disclosures, they are intended to meet the information needs of rather sophisticated investors. Accordingly, most firms send annual reports to shareholders, and make 10-K reports available on request.

The second SEC report, the **10-Q report,** includes a firm's quarterly financial statements, plus some additional disclosures. These disclosures include information on litigation and defaults on debt securities. Firms usually send quarterly financial statements to shareholders, and send 10-Q reports on request.

Although accounting and finance researchers have now studied the **efficient market hypothesis (EMH)** for several decades, it remains rather controversial. This section describes the EMH and summarizes its implications for accounting.

The Efficient Market Hypothesis

The EMH states that publicly available information is fully reflected in share prices. That is, once a corporation releases information (for example, quarterly net income), that information is quickly and unbiasedly reflected in share prices. This implies that a trading strategy based on publicly available information will not be particularly successful.

Considerable evidence exists indicating that share prices react very quickly to accounting information. Exhibit 14–3 shows the results of a study that examined the number of extreme price changes occurring around the time of the earnings announcements of 96 firms during a two-year period. As can be seen, most of the price changes occurred within a few hours of the announcement. Thus, unless one acts very quickly, no especially large profits are available by trading based on reported earnings announcements.

ACCOUNTING INFORMATION AND THE EFFICIENT MARKET HYPOTHESIS

EXHIBIT 14–3
MARKET REACTION TO EARNINGS ANNOUNCEMENTS

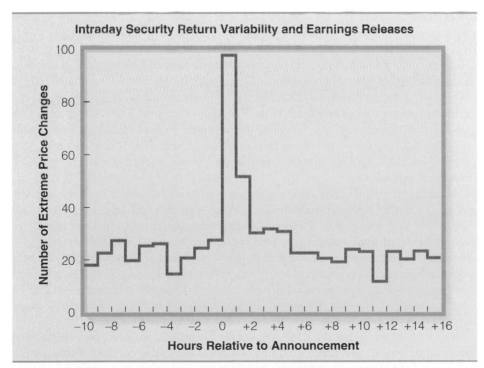

Intraday Security Return Variability and Earnings Releases

SOURCE: J. M. Patell and M. A. Wolfson, "The Intraday Speed of Adjustment of Stock Prices to Earnings and Dividend Announcements," *Journal of Financial Economics,* 1984, p. 240.

Not all research evidence, however, is consistent with the EMH. For example, several studies have shown that while most of the price change associated with an earnings announcement occurs almost immediately, a small portion occurs during the 60 days following the announcement. This suggests that abnormal profits can be made during those 60 days by trading on the publicly available earnings news. However, the price change that occurs during this period is smaller than the transaction costs (brokerage commissions) that most of us would pay. Thus, a net profit could not be made. Because of this, many researchers believe the EMH is a valid description of stock markets.

Overall, the research evidence regarding the EMH is conflicting. As you progress through your business education, pay particular attention to new evidence that pertains to this issue.

Implications of the EMH

The EMH has important messages for corporate managers and individual investors. Acceptance of the EMH should suggest to corporate managers that any attempt to affect share price by using accounting ploys to influence reported earnings is not likely to be successful. For example, inflating earnings by selecting an income-increasing accounting principle will not fool financial statement readers. They will recognize that the increase in income was not due to improvements in the underlying profitability of the firm. Of course, rejection of the EMH results in the opposite inference.

Individual investors who accept the EMH would conclude that they are unable to earn abnormal profits by developing trading strategies based on publicly available information. Accordingly, selecting investments by analyzing annual reports will not prove profitable: The information in those reports is already reflected in share prices by the time the investor is able to obtain the report. These investors would be inclined to diversify their investments, perhaps by choosing mutual funds, which are investment vehicles that own shares in hundreds of corporations. By owning a small part of many companies, an investor's risk is reduced.

Investors who reject the EMH do not feel that share prices necessarily reflect all publicly available information. They feel that a careful analysis of financial statements and other information permits them to identify underpriced securities. Assuming that prices eventually gravitate to their "true values," these stocks represent a favorable investment opportunity.

Accepting the EMH may raise a question about the usefulness of financial statements. If financial statements cannot be used to identify profitable investments, are they of any use? The answer is clearly yes. Even though no individual will be able to earn abnormal profits by trading on the information contained in financial statements, all investors benefit from the disclosure of that information. Financial statements help stock markets identify relatively efficient companies; capital resources can then be allocated to those firms and overall wealth is expanded. Financial statements can also be used in corporate buyouts. By identifying inefficient firms (those firms whose managers are not effectively utilizing its assets), takeover firms can select targets.

Also keep in mind that the EMH applies mostly to large, organized stock markets. Financial statements can be very useful in valuing closely held companies that are not publicly traded. Financial statements can also be used in credit-granting decisions, labor negotiations, and a variety of other situations.

The EMH and Price-to-Earnings Ratios

The price-to-earnings ratio (P/E ratio) was discussed in Chapter 10. It is simply the price of a share of stock divided by earnings per share (EPS):

$$\text{P/E ratio} = \frac{\text{Price}}{\text{EPS}}$$

This ratio usually varies between 10 and 30.

Some analysts view the P/E ratio as a measure of how expensive a stock is. The EPS stream is assumed to continue indefinitely into the future, and the P/E ratio reflects how many dollars investors are willing to pay for a $1 EPS stream. For example, a firm with a share price of $48 and EPS of $4 has a P/E ratio of 12:

$$\text{P/E} = \frac{\$48}{\$4} = 12$$

Investors are willing to pay $12 for every dollar of earnings. This stock would be viewed as less expensive than one with a P/E ratio of 18. In this latter case, investors are paying $18 for every dollar of earnings.

Some critics of the EMH recommend purchasing low P/E stocks. The rationale is that these stocks are cheap, and have a great deal of upside potential. As you might guess, the research evidence regarding the success of this strategy is mixed.

In any event, recognize that P/E ratios vary among firms for several reasons. First, firms use different accounting principles, which systematically affect EPS. Everything else being equal, firms using accelerated depreciation will report relatively low EPS. This will result in a higher P/E ratio than that of firms using straight line depreciation.

Variations in earnings growth are another reason why P/E ratios differ among firms. Recall the assumption that the EPS stream is expected to continue indefinitely. This assumption is not valid for many firms. In particular, firms with a large array of favorable investment prospects are likely to grow at a relatively fast rate. The current EPS number for these growth firms understates the future EPS stream (the stream for which investors are paying), and the P/E ratio is, therefore, overstated for such growth firms.

Relatedly, in any given year, a firm's EPS might contain a transitory component, one that is not expected to persist into the future. For example, a firm will occasionally take a restructuring charge. This is a special charge that reduces net income. Accordingly, the current year's EPS understates the future earnings stream, and the P/E ratio is higher than it otherwise would be.

Interfirm differences in P/E ratios may be questionable guides for investment selection. Instead, differences in P/E ratios might simply reflect differences in accounting methods, earnings growth rates, and transitory earnings components.

An interesting illustration is provided by Warner-Lambert. Based on a 1991 EPS of $0.26, and a December 31, 1991, price of $77.63, Warner-Lambert's 1991 P/E ratio was a lofty 299!

$$\text{P/E} = \frac{\$77.63}{\$.26} = 299$$

However, the 1991 EPS contained two nonrecurring items. First, Warner-Lambert undertook a restructuring of its operations. This entailed a charge of $3.11 per share.

Second, the firm adopted SFAS No. 106, and took a one-time charge of $0.79 per share. Without these charges, EPS would have been $4.16.

EPS as reported	$ .26
Restructuring charge	3.11
Adoption of SFAS 106	.79
Adjusted EPS	$4.16

Adjusted EPS is a better measure of the future earnings stream than actual EPS. Recalculating the P/E ratio based on adjusted EPS yields 18.7, a much more reasonable figure:

$$P/E = \frac{\$77.63}{\$4.16} = 18.7$$

Reality Check 14–2 illustrates the effect accounting changes can have on P/E ratios.

REALITY CHECK 14–2

ACCOUNTING CHANGES AND P/E RATIOS

Reality Check 14–1 contained the following information for the Kellogg Company (in millions, except per share amounts):

	1993	1992	1991
Earnings before cumulative effect of accounting change	$680.7	$682.8	$606.0
Cumulative effect of change in method of accounting for postretirement benefits other than pensions (net of tax benefit of $144.6)	—	(251.6)	—
Net earnings	$680.7	$431.2	$606.0

These figures, stated on a per share basis, are as follows:

	1993	1992	1991
Earnings before cumulative effect of accounting change	$2.94	$2.86	$2.51
Cumulative effect of change in method of accounting for postretirement benefits other than pensions (net of tax benefit of $144.6)	—	(1.05)	—
Net earnings	$2.94	$1.81	$2.51
Price per share	$56¾	$67	$65⅜

REQUIRED

a. Compute the P/E ratio for each year.
b. Why does the 1992 P/E ratio seem unusual?
c. Compute a more meaningful P/E ratio for 1992.

Throughout this text, we have emphasized the two roles that financial accounting plays. One role is to provide information useful for economic decision making. We saw how financial accounting information can be used in a variety of decision contexts, such as credit granting. Financial accounting's second role is to serve as a basis for engaging in contracts. That is, many contracts are based on financial statement numbers. This section summarizes these two purposes.

THE ROLES OF ACCOUNTING

Informational Role

The **informational role** is emphasized by the FASB when it develops GAAP. In fact, the FASB has given considerable thought to the qualities that make information useful. Those qualities are summarized in Exhibit 14–4.

The two primary qualities that contribute to usefulness are relevance and reliability. **Relevance** refers to an item's capacity to make a difference in a decision. For example, few analysts would argue with the assertion that net income is relevant in business valuation. **Reliability** refers to an item's integrity. That is, does it measure what it purports to measure? The cash figure on the balance sheet is usually quite reliable. However, pension obligations are considerably less reliable because of the many estimates involved in their calculation.

Some accountants question the helpfulness of these qualities in selecting accounting principles. In part, this is due to differences among financial statement users. For example, one user may find that expensing research and development (R&D) costs results in the most relevant information, while another user may feel that capitalizing R&D provides the best information. Such differences make it difficult for the FASB to choose the accounting method that is the most useful.

A Basis for Contracting

Serving as a **basis for contracting** is financial accounting's second role. Very frequently, firms enter into contracts that are defined in terms of numbers from the financial statements. For example, the compensation of top executives is often tied to reported net income. As another example, loan agreements require firms to maintain specified levels of various accounting numbers, such as the debt-to-total assets ratio.

Given that contracts are stated in terms of numbers appearing on financial statements, changing the accounting principles used to prepare those statements alters the terms of contracts. Of course, changing contract terms affects the wealth of the contracting parties. Thus, the adoption of a new, income-decreasing accounting principle may, for example, reduce the compensation paid to a firm's executives. This adversely affects their wealth, and since the corporation pays out less cash, the shareholders are benefited.

Because accounting principles can affect the wealth of various parties, some accountants feel that the FASB should consider the economic consequences of their accounting principle choices. They argue that the FASB is a regulatory body that should promote the public interest by maximizing social welfare. They further argue that social welfare can only be maximized by assessing the effects that accounting standards have on all parties.

EXHIBIT 14–4
QUALITIES OF USEFUL
INFORMATION

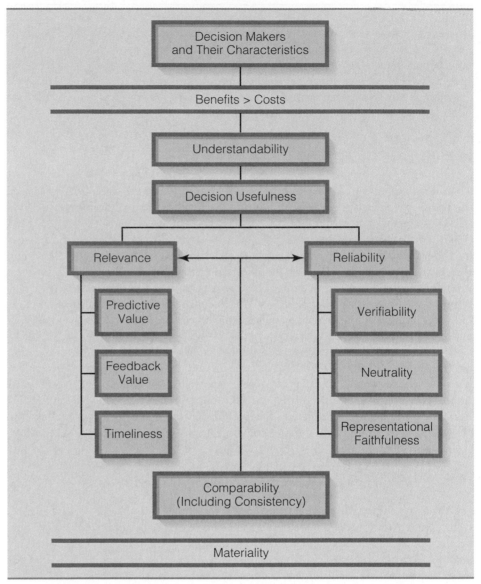

SOURCE: FASB Concepts Statement No. 2, "Qualitative Characteristics of Accounting Information,"
May 1980.

The FASB has consistently rejected this approach. It believes that the effects of accounting principle choices on special interest groups should not influence the FASB's decisions. To do so would compromise the credibility of the financial reporting system. Rather, the FASB seeks "truth in accounting."

Since acceptable alternative accounting principles exist within GAAP, corporate managers also play a role in accounting principle selection. While managers may have some interest in providing information useful for decision making, financial statement readers need to be acutely aware of other managerial motivations. Managers may be motivated to select/change accounting principles and to develop accounting estimates either to enhance their own compensation or to reduce the possibility of violating loan agreements. They may also be motivated to select accounting principles to reduce political costs. Political costs include taxes and other costs imposed on firms by various governmental regulations. Profitable firms are the more likely target for political costs. Therefore, some firms (particularly large, highly visible firms) might be motivated to reduce reported income.

Because some managers may have personal motives related to executive compensation, loan covenants, and political costs, the numbers appearing in financial statements are not necessarily unbiased. Analysts need to look behind the numbers to determine the inferences that should be drawn.

WHAT WOULD YOU DO?

As the chief financial officer for Bullet Enterprises, the chief executive officer (CEO) has asked your advice regarding an accounting principle change she is considering. Many firms in your industry have recently adopted LIFO. These adoptions were motivated by substantial increases in inventory costs. Under such conditions, LIFO can provide significant tax savings. Bullet's inventory costs have also risen, but not as much as your competitor's prices.

However, another issue concerns you. Your compensation package includes a bonus based on reported net income, and the bonus is not activated unless net income exceeds $500,000. Your analysis shows that if LIFO is not adopted, net income will approximate $750,000. If LIFO is adopted, net income will be about $475,000. What would you tell the CEO?

SUMMARY OF LEARNING OBJECTIVES

1. Interpret the financial statements of firms that have undertaken accounting changes.

Given that acceptable alternatives exist within GAAP, firms sometimes change accounting principles. Some changes are accounted for retroactively. That is, prior years' financial statements are restated to reflect the new principle. This ensures that the firm's financial statements are comparable across time periods. Most accounting principle changes, however, are accounted for by the cumulative effect approach. Prior years' statements are not revised. The current year's income statement is based on the new method and it also includes the cumulative effect adjustment. Thus, interperiod comparability is compromised. Changes in accounting estimates are accounted for prospectively. That is, prior years' financial statements are not altered. The effect of the estimate change is reflected in the current and future years' income. Finally, changes in reporting entities are accounted for retroactively.

2. Analyze information about business segments.

Firms are required to make disclosures in financial statements, if they operate in more than one industry or geographic area. This information is intended to help analysts assess the risks and expected returns associated with each business segment.

3. Describe annual and interim reports.

Although this text focuses on financial accounting and the resultant financial statements, the broader context of financial reporting should be considered. Financial reporting includes financial statements, as well as other financial information. Some of this information is contained in annual and interim reports, and includes the president's letter, management discussion and analysis, and the auditor's report.

4. **Identify reports filed with the Securities and Exchange Commission.**

The most common reports filed by firms with the SEC are 10-K and 10-Q reports. These reports contain, respectively, the annual and quarterly financial statements, as well as more detailed disclosures. Relatively sophisticated analysts are the primary users of these reports.

5. **Explain the efficient market hypothesis and its implications for accounting.**

Despite considerable research effort, the validity of the EMH remains unsettled. Proponents believe that managers cannot fool the stock market with accounting gimmicks, and that investors cannot reap abnormal profits by using trading strategies based on publicly available information. Critics of the EMH believe that share prices do not reflect all publicly available information and that profitable strategies can be developed based on that information.

6. **Describe the two major roles of financial accounting.**

First, financial accounting is designed to provide useful information for economic decision making. Second, many contracts are written in terms of accounting numbers. Because different accounting principles result in different accounting numbers, contract terms can be altered simply by changing accounting principles. Thus, corporate managers develop preferences for certain accounting principles. As a result, financial statement numbers are not necessarily unbiased, and they should be interpreted accordingly.

KEY TERMS

Accounting changes	Industry segment
Annual report	Informational role
Basis for contracting	Interim reporting
Change in accounting principle	Major customers
Change in accounting estimate	Pro forma amount
Change in reporting entity	Prospectively
Cumulative effect	Relevance
Domestic operations	Reliability
Efficient market hypothesis (EMH)	Retroactively
Export sales	10-K report
Foreign operations	10-Q report

REALITY CHECK SOLUTIONS

SOLUTION TO REALITY CHECK 14–1

a. Since 1992 was the only year affected by the change, the valid comparisons involve the following:

1993	$680.7
1992	682.8
1991	606.0

SOLUTION TO REALITY CHECK 14–2

a. The P/E ratios for the three years are

1993	1992	1991
$\dfrac{\$56\frac{3}{4}}{\$2.94} = 19.3$	$\dfrac{\$67}{\$1.81} = 37.0$	$\dfrac{\$65\frac{3}{8}}{\$2.51} = 26.0$

b. The P/E ratio in 1992 is considerably higher than in the other two years. This difference results because 1992 earnings includes a rather large transitory element: the cumulative effect of an accounting change.

c. A more meaningful 1992 P/E ratio could be calculated by using an earnings figure that excludes the cumulative effect. This modified P/E ratio is

$$P/E \ = \ \frac{\$67}{\$2.86} \ = \ 23.4$$

QUESTIONS

14–1 Describe three different types of accounting changes.

14–2 Discuss why financial statement users prefer a firm to consistently use the same accounting principles.

14–3 What is the financial statement user's first indication that an accounting change has occurred? Why should this source be examined first when reading a financial statement?

14–4 Discuss the general rule in reporting the effects of an accounting principle change. What is meant by a "cumulative effect" adjustment?

14–5 Under the general rule dealing with accounting principle changes, are the firm's retained earnings changed? Has the firm really gained or lost some of its prior (accumulated) retained earnings? Why?

14–6 Discuss the inconsistencies that are introduced when accounting principle changes occur.

14–7 Are financial statements that include an accounting change more comparable with those of prior years or of subsequent years? Why?

14–8 Under what circumstances are prior years' financial statements retroactively restated? Why do you suppose these exceptions exist?

14–9 Why would a firm that is issuing its first public financial statements have more latitude in using retroactive adjustments for the effects of accounting changes?

14–10 Why does the FASB require that firms make retroactive adjustments when a new reporting standard has been issued?

14–11 When the effects of a change in an accounting estimate are recognized, can prior financial statements be restated retroactively? Why?

14–12 Where are the effects of changes in accounting estimates reported? Why would the financial statement user often not be aware of many of these changes?

14–13 Discuss how the financial statements are changed when two firms merge or engage in some similar restructuring.

14–14 Why do you suppose that a change in reporting entity is shown as a retroactive adjustment, and not a prospective adjustment?

14–15 Identify three types of segment reporting. Where is this information reported? Why do you suppose that these three types of segments have been identified for additional disclosures?

14–16 Describe what is meant by an industry segment and the types of information that must be reported for each segment.

14–17 Why are the identifiable assets for each segment shown as part of segment reporting?

14–18 Why are profits for each segment shown as part of segment reporting?

14–19 Why do you think that domestic and foreign operations are separately disclosed? How would this information be helpful to an investor or creditor?

14–20 Why is information about a firm's major customers reported as part of the notes on the firm's segment? Why not use a threshold higher than 10% as the criterion for determining who is a major customer?

14–21 Describe why a firm with more foreign operations, or more large (greater than 10% of its volume) customers, might be viewed as having higher risk than a domestic company with many small (less than 10%) customers.

14–22 Why does a firm's annual report contain so much information, in such a variety of formats? Would a more condensed format be more useful? Why?

14–23 Why are interim reports less reliable and less useful than annual reports?

14–24 In what major ways do interim reports differ from annual reports?

14–25 Describe the efficient market hypothesis (EMH). Do you believe it is valid? Why?

14–26 Assume a firm changes from FIFO to LIFO during a period of rising prices. Would a proponent of the EMH predict an increase or decrease in the firm's share price as a result of the change in inventory valuations? Why?

14–27 Why do price-to-earnings (P/E) ratios differ between firms?

14–28 Describe financial accounting's two primary roles.

14–29 What are the major criteria that financial accounting must adopt as part of its informational role?

14–30 How do a firm's accounting principles affect contracts that are based on the financial statements?

14–31 Discuss how economic consequences can affect various users of financial statements. How should those who are affected by economic consequences participate in the development of accounting principles?

14–32 Why should financial analysts not be willing to accept all of the information in a firm's financial statements at face value?

EXERCISES

Accounting Principle Change

14–33 Mesple Music, Inc., purchased musical instrument equipment on January 1, 1998, for $25,000. Mesple depreciated it on the straight-line basis, with no salvage value over five years. However, on January 1, 2000, the company realized that the productive capacity of this equipment is declining so it decided to change to the double-declining balance method of depreciation.

REQUIRED

a. Calculate depreciation expense for 1998 and 1999 using the straight-line method.

b. Calculate depreciation expense for 1998 and 1999 using the double-declining balance method. Refer to Chapter 7 for details on double-declining balance depreciation.

c. Show the cumulative effect of the change in the year 2000 in terms of the effects on the balance sheet equation.

Accounting Principle Change

14–34 Central Air Conditioning, Inc., purchased machinery for installing air conditioners. The purchase price of the machine on July 1, 1998, was $35,000. The company chose a seven-year life, sum-of-the-years'-digits (SYD) depreciation, and no salvage value. Unfortunately, the weather during 1998, 1999, and 2000 was extremely mild and the machinery was not used as much as the company had thought. Therefore, it decided that the straight-line method would be more representative of the productive capacity of the machine so it switched to the straight-line method on July 1, 2001.

REQUIRED (ignore income tax)

a. Calculate depreciation expense using SYD (see Chapter 7 for a review of SYD depreciation) for the annual periods ending June 30, 1999, 2000, and 2001.
b. Calculate depreciation expense using the straight-line method for the annual periods ending June 30, 1999, 2000, and 2001.
c. Show the cumulative effect of the change for July 1, 2001, in terms of the balance sheet equation.

Various Accounting Changes

14–35 Match the following terms to the correct description.

a. Change in accounting principle—cumulative effect reported
b. Change in reporting entity
c. Change in accounting estimate
d. Change in principle—retroactive effect reported

___1. Shipley Office Products, Inc., used equipment for three years and depreciated it on the straight-line basis. The original useful life was seven years but after three years the company decided to change the original life to five years.
___2. American Shoe Corporation purchased all of the outstanding stock of Faborini, Inc., in early 1998. American Shoe Corporation is preparing its comparative financial statements for the year-ended December 1998.
___3. Sportscards USA decided to change its inventory costing method from LIFO to FIFO.
___4. The Second Time Through Apparel Shop has been owned by Homer Sampson. He wanted to raise capital to expand, so he decided to "go public" and offer the company stock for sale in the open market. At the same time the company implemented an accounting change for postretirement benefits and calculated the cumulative effect of going from "pay-as-you-go" to estimating retirement benefits and accruing an expense each year.

Various Accounting Changes (continuation of Exercise 14–35)

14–36 Refer to Exercise 14–35. For each situation, describe in words (ignore dollar amounts) what accounting treatments are required.

Ratios: Accounting Change

14–37 Polymer Element Corporation presented the following (partial) income statements ($ in thousands, except EPS):

	December 31		
	1998	1997	1996
Income from continuing operations after tax	$ 207,500	$ 195,400	$ 189,600
Cumulative effect of change in accounting principle	(25,000)	0	(45,000)
Net income	$ 182,500	$ 195,400	$ 144,600
Weighted-average common shares outstanding	146,000	146,000	146,000
Average total shareholders' equity	$3,650,000	$3,908,000	$2,892,000
Market price of stock	$ 20	$ 18	$ 16

REQUIRED

a. Calculate earnings per share (EPS) and calculate the P/E ratio for each year.
b. Calculate return on shareholders' equity for each year.
c. Revise your calculations for parts a and b ignoring the cumulative effect of change in accounting principle.
d. Comment on what impact the preceding differences might have on an investor's preferences or risks.

Role of Accounting

14–38 The Sisters Coffee Emporium has been researching and developing new exotic coffee flavors and innovative coffee equipment. During 1998 it spent over $250,000 on R&D costs. It is now year-end and the company is preparing its balance sheet.

REQUIRED

a. Sisters would like the most relevant information to be reported to investors so the company is considering whether or not to capitalize the R&D costs. Advise Sisters on the concepts of relevance and reliability and how the R&D expenditures should be handled.
b. Discuss the two primary concepts of accounting in the context of Sisters Coffee Emporium.

Interim Reports

14–39 Falcon Entertainment, Inc., chose September 30 as its year-end. Reported below are its quarterly income statements for fiscal 1998 and its annual income statement.

Quarterly	10/1/97 –12/31/97	1/1/98 –3/31/98	4/1/98 –6/30/98	7/1/98 –9/30/98	Annual at 9/30/98
Net sales	$577,441	$571,930	$698,432	$818,034	$2,665,837
Cost of goods	118,563	126,471	134,587	174,259	553,880
Gross profit	458,878	445,459	563,845	643,775	2,111,957

Selling, general & administrative expense	303,755	377,096	393,309	428,588	1,502,748
Depreciation	52,055	51,622	52,651	53,044	209,372
Nonoperating income	(114,062)	(17,251)	(14,845)	(3,315)	(149,473)
Interest expense	28,413	11,515	11,717	9,234	60,879
Income before tax	188,717	22,477	121,013	156,224	488,431
Provision for income tax	51,614	6,412	36,499	44,521	139,046
Net income	$137,103	$ 16,065	$ 84,514	$111,703	$ 349,385

REQUIRED

a. Discuss briefly why Falcon is reporting quarterly information. Is it audited?
b. How does the annual audited information differ from the quarterly data?
c. As an investor, do you see any seasonal trends with this company? Why do you suppose cost of goods sold is higher in the fourth quarter (aside from sales being higher)? *Hint:* Year-end adjustments.

Segment Reporting

14–40 TRW, Inc., is a global company that specializes in producing automotive, spacecraft, and information system products. The following (partial) segment data was reported ($ in millions):

	December 31	
	1994	**1993**
Sales:		
Automotive	$5,679	$4,538
Space and defense	2,812	2,792
Information systems	596	618
Operating Profit:		
Automotive	$ 476	$ 309
Space and defense	175	199
Information systems	96	74
Identifiable Assets:		
Automotive	$3,481	$3,004
Space and defense	1,111	1,253
Information systems	622	752

REQUIRED

a. Calculate return on assets for 1994 for each segment (use operating profit, and ignore interest expense).
b. Calculate for each segment operating income as a percentage of sales.
c. Why is the information by segment and the ratios important for an investor to have?

PROBLEMS

Calculating Depreciation

14–41 Assume that a firm has a computer that originally cost $37,500, has an estimated salvage value of $17,500, and an estimated life of five years. During the first two years, the firm used straight-line (SL) depreciation. In the third year, the sum-of-the-years'-digits (SYD) method was adopted.

REQUIRED

a. Calculate the depreciation expense during the first two years under each method.
b. What would have been the effect, before taxes, on the accounting equation if SYD had been used during the first two years instead of SL?
c. Describe the general principle that must be followed to account for the difference.
d. What is the depreciation expense that will be shown in the third and each subsequent year, using SYD?

Calculating Depreciation

14–42 Assume that a firm has a delivery truck that originally cost $55,000, has an estimated salvage value of $5,000, and an estimated life of 10 years. During the first 2 years, the firm used sum-of-the-years'-digits (SYD) depreciation. At the beginning of the third year, straight-line (SL) depreciation was adopted.

REQUIRED

a. Calculate the depreciation expense during the first two years under each method.
b. What would have been the effect, before taxes, on the accounting equation if SL had been used during the first two years instead of SYD?
c. Describe the general principle that must be followed to account for the difference.
d. What is the depreciation expense that will be shown in the third and each subsequent year, using SL?

Depreciation, Retroactive Adjustments (continuation of Problem 14–42)

14–43 With regard to the prior problem, how would the financial statements be affected if a retroactive adjustment were the appropriate treatment? Does this difference seem important? Why?

Calculating Depreciation Expense

14–44 Assume a copy machine is acquired at the beginning of 1998 for $12,000. It has a salvage value of $2,000 and an estimated life of five years.

REQUIRED

a. Calculate the annual straight-line (SL) depreciation.
b. Assume that at the beginning of the year 2000 the copy machine's total useful life is estimated to be eight years. What is the effect of this change in estimated useful life on net income each year?
c. What is the copy machine's book value at the end of 1998? 1999? 2000?

Calculating Depreciation Expense (continuation of Problem 14-44)

14–45 Use the original data from the previous problem, but assume that you find out at the beginning of 2001 that there will be no salvage value at the end of the fifth year. Assume that the original estimated useful life is still five years.

REQUIRED

a. What is the effect of this change in estimated salvage value on net income in each year?
b. What is the copy machine's book value at the end of the year 1998? 1999? 2000?

Depreciation and Changes in Estimates (continuation of Problems 14–44 and 14–45)

14–46 Refer to the two preceding problems. Assume that both the change in estimated useful life and the change in salvage value both occur as stated.

REQUIRED

a. What is the effect on net income in 2000 and 2001?
b. What is the copy machine's book value at the end of each year?
c. Do these effects seem so important that they would be separately disclosed in the notes? Why?

Calculating Bad Debt Expense

14–47 Dandy's Discount Duds offers credit to all customers. It has estimated that 15% of all such customers will not be able to pay their accounts. Dandy's credit sales in 1998 were $4,000,000. Its estimated bad debt expense was calculated at 15% of annual credit sales.

REQUIRED

a. What is the effect of estimated bad debts on net income in 1998?
b. In early 1999, Dandy discovers that half of its customers have been laid off because a major automaker closed two of its plants. Dandy now estimates that 25% of its customers will not be able to pay their accounts. What impact will this new realization have on Dandy's income for 1999?
c. If you wanted to make a retroactive adjustment to net income in 1998, what else would you need to know that is not shown in this problem, before you could calculate the effect on net income?
d. Why do you think it is appropriate for such adjustments to estimates to be shown on a prospective basis?

Effects of Accounting Changes

14–48 Refer to OshKosh B'Gosh's annual financial statements in Appendix C at the end of this text. Describe any accounting changes that are shown. Do they seem appropriate? Is there sufficient helpful information, about accounting changes, for a potential investor?

Management's Discussion of Accounting Changes

14–49 Refer to OshKosh B'Gosh's annual reports in Appendix C at the end of this text. Read and evaluate management's discussion concerning any accounting changes. Have managers added any appropriate and useful information that clarifies the notes? What else might a potential investor or creditor want to know about these changes?

Calculating P/E Ratios

14–50 Refer to OshKosh B'Gosh's annual financial statements in Appendix C at the end of this text. Calculate the P/E ratio for 1992, 1993, and 1994. Year-end stock prices can be found in the *Wall Street Journal* on the NASDAQ exchange under the names GOSHA and GOSHB for the common stocks class A and class B, respectively. Combine the two stock prices since EPS is shown for class A and class B combined.

Interpreting Financial Statements: Accounting Changes and Restructuring

14–51 Listed below are the income statements for Alco Standard Corporation, the largest distributor of copiers in North America ($ in thousands):

| | September 30 | |
	1994	1993
Revenues:		
Net sales	$7,925,784	$6,387,078
Dividends, interest, and other income	3,537	6,332
Finance subsidiaries	66,731	51,149
	7,996,052	6,444,559
Costs and Expenses:		
Cost of goods sold	5,884,819	4,799,757
Selling and administrative	1,765,483	1,378,814
Interest	43,802	40,189
Finance subsidiaries interest	27,978	23,662
Restructuring costs		175,000
	7,722,082	6,417,422
Loss from unconsolidated affiliate	(117,158)	(2,538)
Income from continuing operations before taxes	156,812	24,599
Taxes on income	86,203	16,984
Income from continuing operations	70,609	7,615
Loss from discontinued operations, net of tax		(7,515)
Net Income	$ 70,609	$ 100

REQUIRED

a. Study Alco Standard's income statement. Identify any unfamiliar or unusual terms.
b. Discuss Alco Standard's different reporting treatment in 1993 for its loss from discontinued operations and its restructuring costs.
c. As an investor, how would you view the two items in part b? What impact do you think they will have on the company's future operations?

Interpreting Financial Statements: Restructuring

14–52 Review Reebok's financial statements in Appendix F.

REQUIRED

a. Read Notes 2 and 12. Identify any unfamiliar or unusual terms.

b. Discuss Reebok's relationship with these firms. What impact did Reebok's actions have on the company's financial statements?

c. Why shouldn't these special charges be reported as retroactive adjustments so that the years are more comparable?

Interpreting Financial Statements: Restructuring

14–53 Review OshKosh B'Gosh's financial statements in Appendix C.

REQUIRED

a. Review the notes and management's discussion. Does the firm disclose any unusual items on its consolidated statement of income? How did these arise?

b. Why shouldn't these unusual items be reported as retroactive adjustments so that the years are more comparable?

Interpreting Financial Statements: Accounting Changes

14–54 Review the Bristol-Myers Squibb financial statements in Appendix E.

REQUIRED

a. Read Note 14 and scan the financial statements. Identify any unfamiliar or unusual terms. What change in financial disclosure did Bristol-Myers' make in 1992?

b. Does the firm disclose any other types of changes, special charges, or restructuring? If so, evaluate the significance of these changes, to the extent possible, using the information in the financial statements.

Interim Reporting

14–55 International Dairy Queen's annual income statement for the year ended November 30, 1994, and its four quarterly income statements are presented below:

	Annual ending 11/30/94	11/30/94	2/24/95	5/26/95	8/25/95
Net sales	$340,833	$76,070	$67,530	$106,150	$115,361
Cost of goods sold	249,985	55,140	47,556	79,220	83,010
Gross profit	90,848	20,930	19,974	26,930	32,351
Selling, general, and administrative	40,495	10,331	12,352	11,136	13,418
Income before depreciation	50,353	10,599	7,622	15,794	18,933
Depreciation	0	0	0	0	0
Nonoperating income	1,578	(56)	498	484	484
Income before tax	51,931	10,543	8,120	16,278	19,417
Provisions for income tax	20,510	4,160	3,210	6,430	7,670
Net income	$ 31,421	$ 6,383	$ 4,910	$ 9,848	$ 11,747

REQUIRED

a. Review the annual income statement for the fiscal year ended 11/30/94 and the quarterly income statements for the four quarters. Discuss the seasonality of this company in terms of its quarterly statements and their choice of November 30 as the fiscal year-end.

Interim Reporting

14–56 GC (General Cinema) Corporation's annual income statement for the year ended October 31, 1994, and its four quarterly income statements are presented below:

	Annual ending 10/31/94	10/31/94	1/31/95	4/30/95	7/31/95
Net sales	$452,563	$107,804	$124,170	$86,876	$136,907
Cost of goods sold	188,616	(61,705)	51,815	31,643	60,809
Gross profit	263,947	169,509	72,355	55,233	76,098
Selling, general, and administrative	227,432	161,778	58,641	52,885	58,624
Income before depreciation	36,515	7,731	13,714	2,348	17,474
Depreciation	19,649	4,702	4,855	5,013	4,789
Nonoperating income	6,828	(1,714)	(2,091)	1,254	1,099
Interest expense	648	167	119	180	171
Income before tax	23,046	1,148	6,649	(1,591)	13,613
Provisions for income tax	9,449	690	2,726	(652)	5,581
Net income	$ 13,597	$ 458	$ 3,923	$ (939)	$ 8,032

REQUIRED

a. Review the annual income statement for the fiscal year ended 10/31/94 and the quarterly income statements for the four quarters. Why do you suppose this company had a negative amount for cost of goods sold for its quarter ended 10/31/94, which also is the last quarter in their fiscal year?

b. Why does GC have a year-end of October 31 and not December 31?

c. Briefly give two reasons why quarterly information is useful to investors. Give one reason why it could be a detriment.

Segment Reporting

14–57 Tyler Corporation reported the following information (partial) in its industry segments footnote ($ in thousands):

	Segment Net Sales			Segment Operating Profits		
	1994	1993	1992	1994	1993	1992
Automotive aftermarket parts	$ 91,849	$ 84,464	$ 78,453	$ 5,006	$7,066	$5,944
Products for fund-raising programs	61,678	—	—	1,820	—	—
Pipe and fittings	204,323	197,939	207,753	(3,273)	1,404	5,637
Segment totals	$357,850	$282,403	$286,206	3,553	8,470	11,581
Interest expense, net				3,820	487	608
Unallocated corporate expense				5,300	5,063	4,868
Income (loss) before income tax (benefit)				$(5,567)	$2,920	$6,105

Identifiable Assets

	1994	1993	1992
Automotive aftermarket parts	$ 43,122	$ 41,288	$ 36,775
Products for fund-raising programs	74,312	—	—
Pipe and fittings	125,612	110,793	122,825
Other	6,018	21,842	14,887
Consolidated	$249,064	$173,923	$174,487

The automotive aftermarket parts segment provides automotive parts and supplies. It specializes in mechanical and electrical parts for customers who do the work themselves. The fund-raising programs segment provides company-supplied products to schools for sale in their fund-raising activities. The pipe and fittings segment manufactures cast iron pipe and fittings for various waste vent and drain applications.

REQUIRED

a. For each segment, calculate the return on assets (use end of year assets and operating profit), and operating income as a percentage of sales for each segment for each year.
b. Evaluate the performance of each segment. What concerns would an investor have after reviewing these results?

Segment Reporting

14–58 The following (partial) information was provided in the industry segment note in American Home Products Corporation's 1994 financial statements ($ in millions):

	Years Ended December 31	
	1994	1993
Net Sales:		
Health care products	$7,885.6	$7,369.1
Food products	997.3	935.8
Agricultural products	83.3	—
Consolidated total	$8,966.2	$8,304.9
Income Before Taxes		
Health care products	$1,839.9	$1,836.7
Food products	155.6	152.4
Agricultural products	16.8	—
Corporate	17.5	3.6
Consolidated total	$2,029.8	$1,992.7
Total Assets at December 31:		
Health care products	$8,118.4	$5,165.3
Food products	558.8	504.4
Agricultural products	1,173.9	—
Corporate	11,823.7	2,017.7
Consolidated total	21,674.8	$7,687.4

Continued on page 618

Net Sales by Geographic Region:

United States	$5,908.0	$5,695.8
Canada and Latin America	1,022.4	897.7
Europe and Africa	1,422.7	1,196.6
Asia and Australia	613.1	514.8
Consolidated total	$8,966.2	$8,304.9

REQUIRED

a. For each segment, calculate the return on assets (use end of year assets and operating profit). Calculate income before tax as a percent of sales.
b. Evaluate the performance of each segment. Regarding the products and services sold by each segment, comment on concerns and outlooks that an investor might have.
c. Comment on the company's sales in the different geographic regions. Could this impact the investor's evaluation of American Home Products' potential future performance?

CASES AND EXTENSIONS

Change in Accounting Principles

14–59 Fitzer, Inc., reported the following data in its 1994 income statement ($ in millions):

Income before cumulative effect of accounting changes	$1,093.5
Cumulative effect of change in accounting for postretirement benefits, net of income taxes	(312.6)
Income taxes	30.0
Net income	$810.9

Fitzer's notes include the following explanations:

In the fourth quarter of 1994, the Company adopted the provisions of SFAS No. 106, Employer's Accounting for Postretirement Benefits Other Than Pensions. This Statement requires the accrual of the projected future cost of providing postretirement benefits during the period that employees render the services necessary to be eligible for such benefits. In prior years, the expenses were recognized when claims were paid.

The Company elected to immediately recognize the accumulated benefit obligation, measured as of January 1, 1994, and recorded a one-time pre-tax charge of $520.5 million ($312.6 million after taxes, or $0.93 per share) as the cumulative effect of this accounting change.

The Company adopted SFAS No. 109. The cumulative effect of the change increased net income by $30.0 million ($0.09 per share) and is reported separately in the 1994 Consolidated Statement of Income.

REQUIRED

a. Describe, in your own words, what changes Fitzer included in 1994's net income.
b. Since these changes were all adopted in fiscal 1994, what is the effect of these changes on prior years?

c. Recalculate the effect on Fitzer's net income, assuming that neither change had been reported in 1994.

d. Why do you suppose Fitzer's managers might have wanted to lump both changes in the same year? Why might they have wanted to recognize the postretirement change in 1994, rather than waiting until 1995?

e. Suppose you also learned that Fitzer had recorded a large charge of $55,000,000 for restructuring the materials group in fiscal 1994. Why would managers want to lump several such changes into net income for the same year?

f. Write a short statement describing your view of management's motivations about recognizing accounting changes. Why is the timing associated with recognizing such changes so important to managers?

Change in Accounting Principles

14–60 Cabot Corporation reported the following data (partial) in its 1994 income statement (dollars in thousands):

	September 30	
	1994	**1993**
Income before cumulative effect of accounting changes	$78,691	$37,410
Cumulative effect of accounting changes	—	(26,109)
Net income	$78,691	$11,301

Cabot's notes included the following:

> Effective October 1, 1992, the Company adopted the provisions of SFAS No. 106, Employers' Accounting for Postretirement Benefits Other Than Pensions. As of October 1, 1992, the cumulative effect of adopting this change was a $43,200,000 after-tax charge.
>
> In the fourth quarter of 1993, the Company adopted SFAS No. 109, Accounting for Income Taxes, retroactive on October 1, 1992. The Company recognized the cumulative effect of adoption in its restated first quarter, resulting in an increase to net income for the year ended September 30, 1993, of approximately $17.1 million.

REQUIRED

a. Describe, in your own words, the changes Cabot included in 1993's net income

b. Since these changes were all adopted in fiscal 1993, what is the effect of these changes on prior years?

c. Recalculate the effect on Cabot's net income, assuming that neither change had been reported in 1993.

d. Why do you suppose Cabot's managers might have wanted to lump both changes in the same year? Why might they have wanted to recognize the postretirement change in 1993, rather than waiting until 1994?

e. What if you also learned that Cabot had recorded a large charge of $47,000,000 for restructuring its Specialty Chemicals and Materials group in fiscal 1993. Why would managers want to lump several such changes into net income for the same year?

f. Write a short statement describing your views of management's motivations about recognizing accounting changes. Why is the timing associated with recognizing such changes so important to managers?

Interpreting Financial Statements: Restructuring

14–61 Bergen Brunswig Corporation reported the following information ($ in thousands) in its 1993 consolidated earnings statement:

Operating earnings from continuing operations	$70,983
Net interest expense	22,723
Earnings from continuing operations before taxes	48,260
Taxes on income from continuing operations	19,653
Earnings from continuing operations	28,607
Extraordinary loss from early extinguishment of debt, net of income tax benefit of	(2,570)
Net earnings	$26,037

REQUIRED

a. Comment on any unusual items in this income statement. Has Bergen Brunswig reported any accounting changes?

b. After looking further in Bergen Brunswig's statements, you find a cost item listed earlier in the income statement, "Restructuring charge, $33,000,000." This item appeared only in the 1993 column, with nothing reported in the prior years. How do you suppose this item related to operations of 1993, and to its continuing operations?

c. After looking further in the notes, you find the following in Note 12, Restructuring and Other Unusual Charges:

> During the fourth quarter of fiscal 1993, the Company approved a restructuring plan which consists of accelerated consolidation of domestic facilities into larger, more efficient regional distribution centers, the merging of duplicate operating systems, the reduction of administrative support in areas not affecting valued services to customers and the discontinuance of services and programs that did not meet the Company's strategic and economic return objective. The estimated pre-tax cost of the restructuring plan is $33.0 million. The restructuring charge represents the costs associated with restructure, primarily abandonment and severance. For those activities or assets where the disposal is expected to result in a gain, no gain will be recognized until realized.

Explain and describe what Bergen Brunswig is accomplishing with this restructuring. What is meant by abandonment and severance? What is meant by accelerated consolidation?

d. Did Bergen Brunswig have a choice on when to recognize the restructuring charge? Where would these costs have been reported if they were not listed in this category of costs?

e. How will the restructuring charges in 1993 affect Bergen Brunswig's future operations? How will these effects be reported in future years?

f. After reading further in the same note, you find another unusual charge:

On June 18, 1993, the Company announced that a joint bid which the Company had made in April 1993 with the French Company, Cooperation Pharmaceutique Francaise, to acquire the largest French pharmaceutical distribution company, Office Commercial Pharmaceutique, had been withdrawn. Accordingly, expenses of $2.5 million, before income tax benefit of $1.0 million associated with the transaction have been recorded in the fourth quarter of fiscal 1993.

These expenses are not listed anywhere, as a separate item, in Bergen Brunswig's income statement. Why? Why must these costs be reported in 1993, and not in 1992, or 1994? Would your conclusions about the reporting of these costs change if you later found that Bergen Brunswig had reported in earlier years a separate section in its income statement called "Discontinued Operations"?

g. Bergen Brunswig's Earnings from continuing operations in 1992 and 1991 were, respectively, $53,012,000 and $58,061,000. How has this trend been affected by the $33,000,000 restructuring charge? If the company had not taken this charge in 1993, what would its earnings from continuing operations have been for 1993, and how would this affect the earlier trend? Why do you suppose that managers might want to take such a charge in 1993?

Effects of Retroactive Adjustment: Percentage Completion Method

14–62 Ace Construction Company has been accounting for all of its long-term contracts on a deferred basis; that is, all revenue and expenses have been deferred until the completion of the contract when all of the costs were known with certainty. While this is a conservative approach, Ace has been having difficulty with its auditors and with the IRS over this approach. It now desires to shift to a percentage-of-completion method. Assume that only one such contract is to be changed at this time. This contract, for $5,000,000 was initiated four years ago, and an equal amount of work was done each year. The contract work cost the firm $4,000,000. To answer this question, you may need to conduct further reading about the percentage of completion method.

REQUIRED

a. Show the effects, on the accounting equation, of the $5,000,000, assuming that it was all reported as income in the final year.
b. Show the effects on the accounting equation of a retroactive adjustment to the firm's financial statements for each of the contract years.
c. Does this set of adjustments seem important to investors or financial analysts? Does it seem to be a useful adjustment that would be viewed as helpful by the readers of the firms' financial statements? Why?

Discussion of Accounting Changes

14–63 Describe a system of reporting accounting changes that does not introduce any inconsistencies in financial reports. Can you design a perfect system?

Discussion of Accounting Changes

14–64 Identify an accounting change (other than a change in depreciation method) that requires a cumulative adjustment. Create a numerical example of this accounting change and show the effects on net income and retained earnings during the year when the change occurs.

Discussion of Accounting Changes

14–65 Why would a change from FIFO, or some other inventory method, to LIFO not require a retroactive adjustment of a firm's financial statements? What would be the cumulative effect of such an adjustment? To answer this question, you will need to refer to other texts or accounting references to learn more about various inventory methods and their effects on net income.

Discussion of Accounting Changes

14–66 Discuss why the effects of a change in an accounting estimate are not reported using the "cumulative effects" rule. Discuss the differences between the "cumulative effects" method and the "prospective" method.

Discussion of How Estimates Are Used in Accounting

14–67 Review the prior chapters in this text, or other accounting texts, to compile a list of at least five areas where estimates are required as part of the accounting measurement process. Determine, through your review, or through interviews with accounting professionals, whether these estimates can generally be made in a reliable manner that requires limited adjustments in later years. In other words, what is the general long-term effect of using these types of estimates?

Evaluation of Disclosure for Two Firms

14–68 Examine notes from the financial statements of two different companies to determine how they report segments of their operations. Rate the level of disclosure, for each firm, in terms of its usefulness.

WHAT WOULD YOU DO?

Possible Violation of Debt/Asset Covenant

14–69 You have just conducted a preliminary analysis of your firm's 1996 financial statements. The firm has not prospered in recent years, and you are particularly concerned about violating a provision of a loan agreement you have with a local bank. Your firm has a $200,000, 9% loan with the bank; the loan is due in 1999. One provision of the loan agreement is that your firm's debt-to-assets ratio not exceed 50%. Your review of the 1996 financial statements indicates a ratio of 58%.

You are very confident that violation would result in a renegotiated interest rate of about 10.5%. Your firm would find meeting this higher interest charge to be quite difficult.

The only alternative to violating this provision that you can think of is to change depreciation methods. Currently, your firm uses double-declining balance. You have calculated that changing to the straight-line method would reduce your debt-to-total assets ratio to 49%.

REQUIRED

a. How much additional interest expense would be incurred if the loan agreement is violated?

b. What are the ethical implications of this decision?

14–70 Locate the most recent 10-K filing by Banc One and Time Warner from the EDGAR archives **(www.sec.gov/edgarhp.htm).** Refer to the note on Significant Accounting Policies in the Notes to the Financial Statements to identify changes in accounting policies. Identify any changes the companies might have made in their methods of accounting. How have changes in accounting principles impacted their consolidated income statements?

14–71 Locate the most recent 10-K filing by Gillette Corporation from the EDGAR archives **(www.sec.gov/edgarhp.htm).** The Notes to the Financial Statements contain detailed segment information.

REQUIRED

a. Identify the major business (industry) segments in which Gillette is involved.

b. What is the percentage contribution of each segment to the company's net sales and profit from operations? Which is the most important business segment?

c. For which geographic areas does Gillette have a material presence? Which is the most profitable geographic area?

d. In your opinion, is Gillette a U.S. company or a global company?

14–72 Access the SEC archives at **http://www.sec.gov/edgarhp.htm.** Use the search routine to locate the SEC disclosures for the corporate filings listed below.

REQUIRED

Based on these filings, answer the questions.

a. 10-K for Centurion Mines Corp (February 7, 1996)

- The report was for which accounting year?
- What industry is Centurion in and what is its Standard Industrial Classification number?
- How many shares of stock were outstanding as of January 1, 1996?
- When did Centurion's predecessor organization begin operations? (from Section 1)
- What was the amount of net operating revenues?
- Who audited Centurion's financial statements? (from Section F2)

b. 10-Q for SCI Systems Inc. (February 7, 1996)

- The report is for which quarter of the fiscal year?
- How many shares of stock were outstanding on January 23, 1996?
- What was the amount of net sales for the three months ended 12-24-95?

c. S-8 for Campbell Soup Co. (February 6, 1996)

- What securities were registered (be specific)?
- What amount of securities were registered?
- What was the proposed maximum offering price per share?
- What was the amount of the registration fee?

d. DEF 14A for ADAC Laboratories (February 7, 1996)

- What items of business were to be conducted at the 1996 annual meeting of shareowners (be brief)?

e. 8-K for Hawaiian Airlines Inc/HI (February 7, 1996)

- Who was the new chairman of the board of directors?

STUDYING THIS APPENDIX
WILL ENABLE YOU TO

1. Prepare and post journal entries.
2. Calculate account balances.
3. Prepare and post adjusting entries.
4. Prepare and post closing entries.
5. Generate balance sheets and income statements
from general ledger accounts.

ACCOUNTING PROCEDURES

INTRODUCTION

This book focused on conceptual accounting issues and the uses of accounting information. In contrast, this appendix summarizes the detailed procedures used by accountants to generate financial statements. Although, in theory, the basic accounting equation can be used to prepare financial statements, virtually all firms would find that approach to be extremely cumbersome. Far more efficient processes are needed by firms that have hundreds of different assets and liabilities and make thousands of transactions.

THE GENERAL LEDGER

Recall from Chapter 2 that the core of financial accounting is the analysis of transactions in terms of the basic accounting equation:

$$\text{ASSETS} \ = \ \text{LIABILITIES} \ + \ \text{SHAREHOLDERS' EQUITY}$$

The purpose of this analysis is to summarize the effects of different types of transactions on the equation's elements. In real business settings, this summarization is done in the **general ledger.** Although most account systems are computerized, at this stage we will illustrate a manual system. In such a system, the general ledger often takes the form of a loose-leaf notebook. Each page is assigned to a particular equation item (such as cash, inventory, accounts payable, or invested capital) and is referred to as an account.

Debits and Credits

To show increases and decreases in account amounts, plus (+) and minus (−) signs could be used. For several reasons, however, the accounting profession has discarded this alternative. Instead, each account is divided into a left-hand side, and a right-hand side; increases are recorded on one side and decreases are recorded on the other.

For *all* accounts, the left-hand side is the **debit** side and the right-hand side is the **credit** side. For accountants, debit and credit have no meanings other than left and right, respectively. This can be a source of confusion. Many nonaccountants associate the term credit with something good. The accountant does not.

In actual business practice, general ledger accounts can take many forms. For simplicity, they are illustrated here using T-accounts. T-accounts for cash and accounts payable are shown:

Cash		Accounts Payable	
Dr	Cr	Dr	Cr

The side of an account in which increases and decreases are recorded depends on the nature of the account. Increases in assets are recorded by debits, and decreases are recorded by credits. The rules for liabilities and shareholders' equity are the reverse: Increases are recorded as credits, and decreases are recorded as debits. These rules are summarized in Exhibit A–1.

EXHIBIT A–1
DEBIT AND CREDIT RULES

ASSETS		=	LIABILITIES		+	SHAREHOLDERS' EQUITY	
Dr	Cr		Dr	Cr		Dr	Cr
+	−		−	+		−	+

The debit and credit rules are largely arbitrary. Accordingly, with one exception, do not look for any special logic in them. One aspect of the rules does make sense. Because assets appear on the opposite side of the basic accounting equation from liabilities and shareholders' equity, the debit and credit rules for assets are the opposite of the rules for liabilities and shareholders' equity. The reasoning for this is discussed later in the appendix.

An Example

Consider two illustrative transactions. First, shareholders invest $10,000 in a firm. In terms of the basic equation, this transaction increases cash and increases shareholders' equity (invested capital):

ASSETS	=	LIABILITIES	+	SHAREHOLDERS' EQUITY
Cash				Invested capital
+$10,000				+$10,000

In the general ledger, an increase in cash is recorded as a debit, and an increase in shareholders' equity is recorded as a credit. After the analysis, the amounts would appear as follows:

Cash		Invested Capital	
$10,000			$10,000

The second transaction involves a purchase of inventory for $2,000. This transaction increases inventory and decreases cash:

ASSETS		=	LIABILITIES	+	SHAREHOLDERS' EQUITY
Cash	Inventory				
−$2,000	+$2,000				

The decrease in cash is recorded as a credit, and the increase in inventory is recorded as a debit, as shown in these T-accounts:

Cash		Inventory	
$10,000	$2,000	$2,000	

As previously mentioned, the rules for assets (which appear on the left side of the equation) are the opposite of the rules for liabilities and shareholders' equity (which appear on the right side of the equation). This is no coincidence. By reversing the rules, the equality of debits and credits for each transaction (and in total) is assured. For example, when inventory was purchased for cash, inventory was debited and cash was credited by $2,000 each. The equality of debits and credits helps accountants identify and eliminate errors from the accounting process.

Balancing Accounts

To determine the net amount of cash, inventory, etc., at the end of an accounting period, the accounts must be **balanced.** This is done by totaling the debits and credits in each account and taking their difference. This difference is shown on the side of the account that has the larger amount. These balances are the basis for the financial statements. The balanced cash account shows an $8,000 debit balance:

Cash	
10,000	2,000
Bal 8,000	

Chart of Accounts

Firms have a great deal of discretion in choosing their account titles and the number of accounts they employ. Accordingly, most firms develop a **chart of accounts.** A chart of accounts is essentially an index to the general ledger. It lists accounts titles and account numbers. Account numbers are often employed because they provide a firm's personnel with an efficient and unambiguous way to communicate. Exhibit A–2 illustrates a chart of accounts.

THE GENERAL JOURNAL

In the general ledger, the information about a given transaction is spread across two or more accounts. This makes it difficult for auditors and others to review all the information about a given transaction. The **general journal** is another major accounting record. It provides a chronological listing of all transactions and events. This enables the auditor to easily see all the accounts affected by a single transaction. As with the general ledger, the general journal in a manual system consists of a loose-leaf notebook.

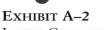

EXHIBIT A–2
JACOBS GOLF AND TENNIS
CHART OF ACCOUNTS

Account	Account Number
Cash	110
Accounts Receivable	120
Prepaid Rent	130
Inventory	140
Equipment	150
Accumulated Depreciation	160
Accounts Payable	210
Unearned Revenue	220
Utilities Payable	230
Interest Payable	240
Notes Payable	250
Invested Capital	310
Retained Earnings	320

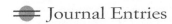 Journal Entries

General journal entries are actually the first step in the *formal* financial accounting process. This step occurs after the accountant has conceptually analyzed the transaction, ascertained which accounts have increased or decreased, and translated the increases and decreases into debits and credits. A transaction's **journal entry** consists of

1. the date,
2. the account(s) to be debited,
3. the account(s) to be credited,
4. the amounts, and
5. an explanation.

For example, if shareholders invest $10,000 in a firm on January 1, cash is increased and shareholders' equity is increased. Translated into debits and credits, cash is debited and invested capital is credited. In journal entries, the debits are shown first, and the credits are indented and shown after the debits. The journal entry for the $10,000 investment would be:

January 1   Cash 10,000
                        Invested Capital 10,000
                   To record shareholders' investment

Notice that the journal contains two dollar columns. The one to the left is for debits and the one to the right is for credits.

Posting

To determine account balances, the amounts in the journal entries need to be placed in the general ledger. Transcribing the amounts from journal entries into the general ledger is called **posting.** From a procedural standpoint, transactions, events, etc., are never initially entered into the general ledger. General journal entries are always prepared first and then posted to the general ledger.

Summary

The accounting process, to the extent we have examined it, includes the following steps:

1. Identify transactions and events.
2. Analyze transactions and events in terms of the basic accounting equation.
3. Translate the equation analysis into debits and credits.
4. Prepare journal entries and post to the general ledger.

These steps, along with others we have yet to cover, are summarized in Exhibit A–3.

Chapter 2 provided a comprehensive example involving Jacobs Golf and Tennis (JG&T). JG&T began operations in January 1998 and engaged in a number of transactions. That example is used here to demonstrate the accounting procedures just discussed. The only difference between Chapter 2 and the treatment here is that we now assume JG&T is organized as a corporation.

AN ILLUSTRATION OF ACCOUNTING PROCEDURES

EXHIBIT A–3
THE ACCOUNTING PROCESS

1. Identify transactions and events.
2. Analyze transactions and events in terms of the basic accounting equation.
3. Translate the transaction analysis into debits and credits.
4. Prepare journal entries and post to the general ledger.
5. Prepare and post adjusting entries.
6. Prepare the income statement.
7. Prepare and post closing entries.
8. Prepare the balance sheet.

Transaction 1: Shareholders invest $50,000.
Analysis: Increase cash; increase invested capital.
Debits and credits: Increase cash (an asset) by a debit; increase invested capital (an equity account) by a credit.

Journal entry:
January 1

Cash 50,000	
Invested Capital 50,000	

To record investment by shareholders

Transaction 2: Borrowed $20,000 from a bank.
Analysis: Increase cash; increase notes payable.
Debits and credits: Increase cash by a debit; increase notes payable by a credit.
Journal entry:
January 1

Cash 20,000
               Notes Payable 20,000

To record note payable

Transaction 3: Paid in advance one year's rent of $12,000.
Analysis: Increase prepaid rent; decrease cash.
Debits and credits: Increase prepaid rent by a debit; decrease cash by a credit.
Journal entry:
January 1

Prepaid Rent 12,000
               Cash 12,000

To record prepayment of one year's rent

Transaction 4: Purchased inventory on account, $30,000.
Analysis: Increase inventory; increase accounts payable.
Debits and credits: Increase inventory by a debit; increase accounts payable by a credit.
Journal entry:
January 1

Inventory 30,000
               Accounts Payable 30,000

To record the purchase of inventory on account

Transaction 5: Purchased Equipment for $25,000.
Analysis: Increase equipment; decrease cash.
Debits and credits: Increase equipment by a debit; decrease cash by a credit.
Journal entry:
January 1

Equipment 25,000
               Cash 25,000

To record purchase of equipment for cash

At this point, journal entries have been prepared for all of JG&T's preliminary transactions. The next step is to post these entries to general ledger accounts. Exhibit A-4 contains general ledger accounts that reflect these postings.

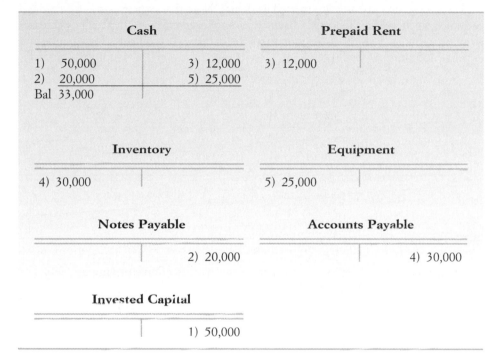

REVENUE AND EXPENSE ACCOUNTS

Revenue and expense transactions affect the retained earnings component of shareholders' equity. For example, if a firm renders services in the amount of $100 to clients, on account, accounts receivable increases and retained earnings increases:

ASSETS	=	LIABILITIES	+	SHAREHOLDERS' EQUITY
Accounts receivable				Retained earnings
+$100				+$100 (sales)

As you know from Chapter 2, the income statement summarizes the many types of revenue and expense transactions that affect retained earnings during a period. If all revenue and expense transactions were commingled in that one account, ascertaining the detailed amounts for each line item on the income statement would be quite difficult.

Consequently, general ledger accounts are established for each revenue and expense item desired on the income statement. Instead of initially debiting or crediting retained earnings for revenue and expense transactions, the revenue and expense accounts are used. These accounts are best viewed as temporary accounts, which are really components of retained earnings. Increases in revenues are shown as credits, while increases in expenses are treated as debits. Note that expenses reduce retained earnings; so increasing the debit balance in an expense account actually decreases retained earnings. Exhibit A–5 summarizes the debit and credit rules for revenue and expense accounts.

EXHIBIT A–5
DEBIT AND CREDIT RULES
FOR REVENUE AND EXPENSE
ACCOUNTS

Revenue		Expense	
Dr	Cr	Dr	Cr
−	+	+	−

Illustrative Entries

This section analyzes JG&T's revenue and expense transactions for January 1998. For convenience, assume that all transactions occur on January 15.

Transaction 6: Rendered services to customers for $200 plus a promised future payment of $400.

Analysis: Increase cash; increase accounts receivable; increase service revenue.

Debits and credits: Debit cash by $200; debit accounts receivable by $400; credit service revenue by $600.

Journal Entry:
January 15   Cash 200
                    Accounts Receivable .... .400
                         Service Revenue 600
                    To record service revenue

The preceding entry is referred to as a **compound journal entry.** Its distinguishing characteristic is that more than one account is either debited or credited (or both). As with all journal entries, the total dollar amount of debits equals the total dollar amount of credits.

Transaction 7: Received $100 from customers for services to be performed at a later date.

Analysis: Increase cash; increase unearned revenue (remember that unearned revenue is a liability).

Debits and credits: Debit cash; credit unearned revenue.

Journal entry:
January 15   Cash 100
                    Unearned revenue 100
                    To record customers' prepayment of revenue

Transaction 8:   Paid workers' salaries of $700.
Analysis: Decrease cash; decrease retained earnings via salary expense.
Debits and credits: Credit cash; debit salary expense.
Journal entry:
     January 15   Salary Expense 700
                    Cash 700
             To record payment of salary expense

Transaction 9:   Received a $120 utility bill for services already used. Payment was not immediately made.
Analysis: Utilities expense increases; utilities payable increases.
Debits and Credits: Debit utilities expense; credit utilities payable.
Journal entry:
     January 15   Utilities Expense 120
                    Utilities Payable 120
             To record January utilities expense

Transaction 10:   Sold, for $4,000 on account, inventory costing $2,200.
Analysis: Accounts receivable increases; sales increases; inventory decreases; cost of goods sold (CGS) increases.
Debits and credits: Debit accounts receivable; credit sales; credit inventory; debit CGS.
Journal entry:
     January 15   Accounts Receivable 4,000
                    Sales 4,000
             To record a credit sale on account

             CGS 2,200
                    Inventory 2,200
             To record CGS on credit sale

Exhibit A–6 contains ledger accounts reflecting the posting of these entries.

ADJUSTING ENTRIES

As you know from Chapter 2 adjustments to the accounting records are typically needed before financial statements are prepared. The adjustments are needed to ensure that the account balances are correct and up to date. These adjustments result from interest accruals, depreciation and a variety of other matters. Adjustments to the account balances are accomplished by journal entries. We now analyze JG&T's adjustments.

Transaction 11:   Incurred, but did not pay, interest expense of $133.
Analysis: Increase interest expense; increase interest payable.
Debits and credits: Debit interest expense; credit interest payable.
Journal entry:
     January 31   Interest Expense 133
                    Interest Payable 133
             To record January interest expense

EXHIBIT A–6
JACOBS GOLF AND TENNIS
GENERAL LEDGER

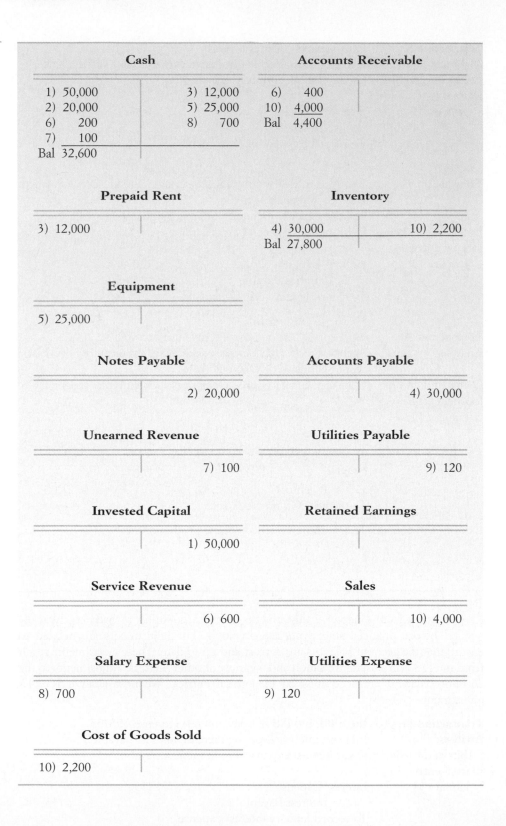

Cash

1)	50,000	3)	12,000
2)	20,000	5)	25,000
6)	200	8)	700
7)	100		
Bal	32,600		

Accounts Receivable

6)	400	
10)	4,000	
Bal	4,400	

Prepaid Rent

3) 12,000	

Inventory

4) 30,000	10) 2,200
Bal 27,800	

Equipment

5) 25,000	

Notes Payable

	2) 20,000

Accounts Payable

	4) 30,000

Unearned Revenue

	7) 100

Utilities Payable

	9) 120

Invested Capital

	1) 50,000

Retained Earnings

Service Revenue

	6) 600

Sales

	10) 4,000

Salary Expense

8) 700	

Utilities Expense

9) 120	

Cost of Goods Sold

10) 2,200	

Transaction 12:   Used $1,000 of prepaid rent.

Analysis: Increase rent expense; decrease prepaid rent.

Debits and credits: Debit rent expense; credit prepaid rent.

Journal entry:

    January 31   Rent Expense 1,000

                       Prepaid Rent 1,000

                 To record January rent expense

Transaction 13:   Depreciation on equipment amounted to $208.

Analysis: Increase depreciation expense; decrease equipment by increasing the balance in the contra-asset account, accumulated depreciation.

Debits and credits: Debit depreciation expense; credit accumulated depreciation.

Journal entry:

    January 31   Depreciation Expense 208

                       Accumulated Depreciation 208

                 To record January depreciation expense

Transaction 14:   Earned $50 of the $100 advance payment previously made by customers.

Analysis: Decrease unearned revenue; increase service revenue.

Debits and credits: Debit unearned revenue; credit service revenue.

Journal entry:

    January 31   Unearned Revenue 50

                       Service Revenue 50

                 To record revenue earned

General ledger accounts with these postings appear in Exhibit A–7. The balances in the revenue and expense accounts are now correct and the income statement, contained in Exhibit A–8, can be prepared based on the revenue and expense accounts.

CLOSING ENTRIES

At this point, a problem exists in preparing JG&T's balance sheet. Since the revenue and expense transactions, which really affect retained earnings, were not recorded in that account, the balance sheet will not balance. Therefore, the amounts in the revenue and expense accounts must be transferred to retained earnings. This is done via closing entries.

JG&T's closing entries at the end of January appear in Exhibit A–9. Viewed in isolation, closing entries do not make a great deal of sense. However, keep in mind their purpose: to transfer balances from revenue and expense accounts to retained earnings. General ledger accounts that reflect the posting of these entries appear in Exhibit A–10. The balance now in retained earnings is that which would have been there if all the revenue and expense transactions were initially recorded in that account.

Note that after posting the closing entries the balance in each revenue and expense account is zero. This is why they are called **temporary** (or **nominal**) **accounts.** Moreover, since the balances are zero, next month they will only reflect the revenue and expense amounts for February, and not a cumulative amount beginning with January. This will enable the easy preparation of an income statement for the month of February.

Cash

1)	50,000	3)	12,000
2)	20,000	5)	25,000
6)	200	8)	700
7)	100		
Bal	32,600		

Accounts Receivable

6)	400		
10)	4,000		
Bal	4,400		

Prepaid Rent

3)	12,000	12)	1,000
Bal	11,000		

Inventory

4)	30,000	10)	2,200
Bal	27,800		

Equipment

5)	25,000

Accumulated Depreciation

13)	208

Notes Payable

2)	20,000

Accounts Payable

4)	30,000

Unearned Revenue

14)	50	7)	100
Bal			50

Utilities Payable

9)	120

Interest Payable

11)	133

Invested Capital

1)	50,000

Retained Earnings

Service Revenue

		6)	600
		14)	50
Bal			650

Sales

10)	4,000

Salary Expense

8)	700

Utilities Expense

9)	120

Cost of Goods Sold

10)	2,200

Interest Expense

11)	133

Rent Expense

12)	1,000

Depreciation Expense

13)	208

Jacobs Golf and Tennis
Income Statement
For the month ended January 31, 1998

Revenue
Sales	$4,000	
Services	650	
Total revenue		$4,650

Expenses
Cost of goods sold	2,200	
Rent	1,000	
Salary	700	
Depreciation	208	
Interest	133	
Utilities	120	
Total expenses		4,361
Net income		$ 289

EXHIBIT A–8
INCOME STATEMENT

Jacobs Golf & Tennis
General Journal

January 31

15) Retained earnings	4,361	
Salary expense		700
Utilities expense		120
Cost of goods sold		2,200
Interest expense		133
Rent expense		1,000
Depreciation expense		208
To close expense accounts		
16) Service revenue	650	
Sales	4,000	
Retained earnings		4,650
To close revenue accounts		

EXHIBIT A–9
CLOSING ENTRIES

JG&T engaged in one more transaction in January. It declared and paid a $100 dividend to the shareholders. The analysis is as follows:

Transaction 17: Paid dividends of $100.
Analysis: Cash decreases; retained earnings decreases.
Debits and credits: Debit retained earnings; credit cash.
Journal entry:
January 31	Retained earnings 100	
	Cash 100	
	To record dividends	

DIVIDENDS

EXHIBIT A–10
JACOBS GOLF & TENNIS
GENERAL LEDGER

Balance Sheet Accounts

Cash			Accounts Receivable		
1) 50,000		3) 12,000	6) 400		
2) 20,000		5) 25,000	10) 4,000		
6) 200		8) 700	Bal 4,400		
7) 100		17) 100			
Bal 32,500					

Prepaid Rent			Inventory		
3) 12,000		12) 1,000	4) 30,000		10) 2,200
Bal 11,000			Bal 27,800		

Equipment		Accumulated Depreciation	
5) 25,000			13) 208

Notes Payable		Accounts Payable	
	2) 20,000		4) 30,000

Unearned Revenue		Utilities Payable	
14) 50	7) 100		9) 120
Bal	50		

Interest Payable	
	11) 133

Invested Capital		Retained Earnings	
	1) 50,000	15) 4,361	16) 4,650
		17) 100	
		Bal	189

Income Statement Accounts

Service Revenue			Sales		
		6) 600	16) 4,000		10) 4,000
16) 650		14) 50			Bal 0
		Bal 0			

Salary Expense			Utilities Expense	
8) 700	15) 700		9) 120	15) 120
Bal 0			Bal 0	

Cost of Goods Sold	
10) 2,200	15) 2,200
Bal 0	

Interest Expense			Depreciation Expense	
11) 133	15) 133		13) 208	15) 208
Bal 0			Bal 0	

Rent Expense	
12) 1,000	15) 1,000
Bal 0	

The posting of this entry is also reflected in the general ledger accounts appearing in Exhibit A–10.

At this point, all transactions have been journalized and posted, and the revenue and expense accounts have been closed to retained earnings. A balance sheet based on the account balances in Exhibit A–10 can be prepared. It appears in Exhibit A–11.

Jacobs Golf and Tennis
Balance Sheet
January 31, 1998

Assets			Liabilities and Shareholders' Equity	
Cash		$ 32,500	Liabilities	
Accounts receivable		4,400	Accounts payable	$ 30,000
Prepaid rent		11,000	Utilities payable	120
Inventory		27,800	Interest payable	133
Equipment	$25,000		Unearned revenue	50
Less: Accumulated			Notes payable	20,000
depreciation	(208)	24,792		
				50,303
			Shareholders' equity	
			Invested capital	50,000
			Retained earnings	189
				50,189
			Total liabilities and	
Total assets		$100,492	shareholders' equity	$100,492

OTHER PROCEDURAL MATTERS

One chapter cannot cover all of accounting's detailed procedures. However, a few additional items deserve attention.

Trial Balances and Worksheets

The equality of debits and credits implies that the total of all accounts with debit balances should equal the total of all accounts with credit balances. As a check on this, accountants prepare **trial balances** at various points in the accounting process.

A trial balance is simply a listing of general ledger accounts and their amounts. Two columns are used: one for accounts with debit balances and one for accounts with credit balances. Exhibit A–12 contains an illustration of a trial balance based on the account balances in Exhibit A–10. Note that the totals in the two columns balance.

An extended form of the trial balance is the **worksheet.** The worksheet serves two purposes. First, it includes a trial balance so, accordingly, it provides a check on certain errors. Second, it serves as a testing ground for adjusting and closing entries. That is, prior to inserting the adjusting and closing entries into the general journal and ledger, many accountants test these entries in the worksheet, which is not a formal part of the accounting records. By doing this, errors in these entries can, hopefully, be eliminated before they are entered in the formal books of account. Worksheets are highly mechanical, so they are not considered further in this text.

EXHIBIT A–12
TRIAL BALANCE

Jacobs Golf & Tennis Trial Balance January 31, 1998	Debit	Credit
Cash	32,500	
Accounts receivable	4,400	
Prepaid rent	11,000	
Inventory	27,800	
Equipment	25,000	
Accumulated depreciation		208
Notes payable		20,000
Accounts payable		30,000
Unearned revenue		50
Utilities payable		120
Interest payable		133
Invested capital		50,000
Retained earnings		189
	100,700	100,700

Subsidiary Ledgers

This chapter has discussed only two formal accounting records: the general ledger and general journal. In actual practice, there are many more. One type of record is a **subsidiary ledger.** The purpose of a subsidiary ledger is to provide detailed information regarding a particular general ledger account.

Consider, for example, accounts receivable. This account indicates the total amount due from customers. Of course, firms also need to know the amount owed by each individual customer. Unfortunately, the accounts receivable account does not easily provide this information. The accounts receivable subsidiary ledger is designed to do this. Envision the subsidiary ledger as a separate loose-leaf notebook with a page (account) assigned to each customer.

To illustrate, assume that the Pine Company is owed a total of $700 from its three customers. Customer A owes $400, Customer B owes $200, and Customer C owes $100. As shown in Exhibit A–13, Pine's accounts receivable general ledger account shows a balance of $700. The subsidiary ledger, appearing in the lower half of the exhibit, shows the detail of each customer's indebtedness. Notice that the total of the subsidiary ledger accounts is $700, which agrees with the accounts receivable general ledger account.

Several other general ledger accounts, such as accounts payable and equipment, have subsidiary ledgers.

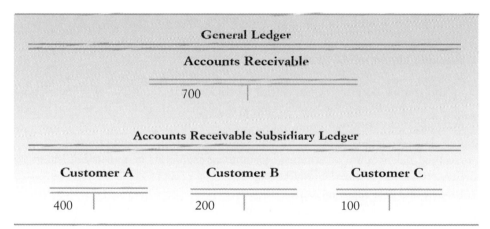

EXHIBIT A–13
PINE COMPANY
GENERAL AND SUBSIDIARY
LEDGERS

Special Journals

Preparing general journal entries for each transaction is a laborious, time-consuming process: Account titles must be written and often the same amount must be written twice in the same entry. Because of this, accountants have devised streamlined journalizing procedures that make use of **special journals.** Special journals are constructed to achieve great efficiencies in journalizing transactions. Examples of special journals include sales journals, cash receipts journals, and cash payment journals.

Computerization

This appendix emphasized manual (pen-and-ink) accounting systems. These systems are simple and straightforward. Accordingly, they help you envision the flow of information.

However, the vast majority of actual accounting systems are computerized. Computerized accounting systems have several advantages. First, they are able to process large numbers of transactions more quickly than manual systems. Consequently, they provide financial statements and other reports in a more timely manner. Second, they achieve a greater degree of accuracy than manual systems. Finally, they permit a greater amount of information (different reports) to be generated.

Computerized accounting systems require both hardware and software. Hardware consists of a computer's physical components such as storage disks, monitors, keyboards, and central processing units. Computers range in size from laptop models to mainframe computers that can occupy an entire floor.

Software refers to coded instructions given to the computer. The instructions tell the computer how to process information. A set of instructions concerning one or more related tasks is called a program. Some firms develop their own programs for accounting tasks. Other firms rely on programs developed by software specialists. Many programs currently exist that enable small- and medium-sized firms to computerize their accounting functions quickly and inexpensively.

SUMMARY OF LEARNING OBJECTIVES

1. **Prepare and post journal entries.**
   Journal entries translate a transaction's basic accounting equation analysis into debits and credits. Because journal entries do not summarize the effects of transactions on the various financial statement elements, journal entries must be posted to general ledger accounts.

2. **Calculate account balances.**
   Account balances are determined by summing the debits in an account, summing the credits, and taking the difference.

3. **Prepare and post adjusting entries.**
   Adjusting entries are prepared at the end of a time period (usually a month, quarter, or year). Adjusting entries are needed because certain events might not have been reflected in the account balances. Typical examples include interest expense and depreciation expense. Adjusting entries update the account balances so that correct financial statements can be prepared.

4. **Prepare and post closing entries.**
   Revenue and expense transactions are initially recorded in revenue and expense accounts. This permits the preparation of a detailed income statement. Because these transactions ultimately affect retained earnings, closing entries are needed to transfer the balances in revenue and expense accounts to retained earnings.

5. **Generate balance sheets and income statements from general ledger accounts.**
   Financial statements can be prepared by simply transcribing the balances from the relevant general ledger accounts onto the appropriate financial statement.

Balanced
Chart of accounts
Compound journal entry
Credit
Debit
General journal
General ledger

Journal entry
Posting
Special journals
Subsidiary ledger
Temporary (nominal) accounts
Trial balance
Worksheet

KEY TERMS

QUESTIONS

A–1 Define the terms *debit* and *credit*.

A–2 Draw a diagram reflecting the parts of the accounting cycle, showing how journals, ledgers, etc., are used to record transactions.

A–3 Define the term *posting.*

A–4 Discuss why a firm might use subsidiary ledgers.

A–5 Why are adjusting entries used?

A–6 Would a cash-based system have a need for adjusting entries? Why?

A–7 Why are closing entries used?

A–8 If a firm never prepared periodic financial statements, would it need to prepare adjusting or closing entries? Why?

A–9 What are some of the conditions that might cause a trial balance not to be "in balance"?

PROBLEMS

A–10 (Similar to Exercise 2–12) John Hasty opened his bakery on March 1, 1998. The following transactions took place in early March:

1. Deposited $10,000 into a checking account in the name of the Hasty Bakery.
2. Leased a small kitchen for one year at $500 per month. One month's rent was paid at this time.
3. Purchased kitchen equipment for $3,000.
4. Purchased baking ingredients for $6,000 on account.
5. Obtained a $2,000, 9%, one-year loan.
6. Rented a delivery truck for three years. The monthly payment of $200 is due at the end of each month. Nothing was paid in March.
7. Obtained a one-year insurance policy on the kitchen equipment. Paid the entire premium of $500.

REQUIRED

a. Prepare the journal entries necessary to record these transactions.
b. Prepare any necessary adjusting entries (e.g., interest expense).
c. Post all journal entries to T-accounts.
d. Prepare a trial balance.
e. Prepare a balance sheet for the Hasty Bakery, as of March 31, 1998.

A–11 (Similar to Problem 2–20) The following account balances are shown on November 30, 1998, for the Clever Bookstore.

Cash	$ 8,000	Accounts payable	$ 4,000
Accounts receivable	9,000	Salaries payable	2,000
Inventory	60,000	Notes payable	35,000
Supplies	3,000	J. Clever, capital	39,000
Total	$80,000	Total	$80,000

The following transactions occurred during December.

1. Paid workers the $2,000 owed them on November 30.
2. Made sales totaling $40,000. One-half of the sales were for cash. The other half were on account. The cost of goods sold was $25,000.
3. Purchased inventory on account, $15,000.
4. Collected in cash $22,000 of receivables.
5. Used supplies totaling $800.
6. Paid accounts payable of $12,000.
7. Paid December's interest on the note payable in the amount of $300.

REQUIRED

a. Prepare the journal entries necessary to record these transactions.
b. Prepare any necessary adjusting entries.
c. Post all journal entries to T-accounts.
d. Prepare a trial balance.
e. Prepare a balance sheet for Clever Bookstore, as of December 31, 1998.

A–12 (Similar to Exercise 2–16) The following transactions all occurred on January 2 of the current year.

1. A company paid a $2,000 bill for a fire insurance policy that covers the current year and next year.
2. A company purchased for $200 a trash compactor that has an expected life of five years.
3. Two attorneys, associated in a (limited liability) corporation, decide that a ski chalet at Vail is necessary to entertain current and prospective clients. At the same time, they are considering the addition of a third attorney. This new attorney has a ski chalet that she purchased five years ago for $120,000. Its market value was $200,000 when she transferred it to the corporation.

REQUIRED

a. Prepare the journal entries necessary to record these transactions.
b. Prepare any necessary adjusting entries for the company's December 31 year-end (e.g., depreciation expense).
c. Post all journal entries to T-accounts.

A–13 (Similar to Exercise 2–17) On June 1 you formed a sole proprietorship to sell and service personal computers. During the first six months the following transactions occurred:

1. On June 1 you invested $50,000 in the business.
2. On July 1 you purchased a four-wheel-drive pickup truck for $22,000 (on account) that will be used in the business.

3. On September 1 you paid fuel and repairs costs of $1,750 for the truck.
4. On December 31, the truck proves to be a "lemon" and it is sold to a used car dealer for $1,000.

REQUIRED

a. Prepare the journal entries necessary to record these transactions.
b. Prepare any necessary adjusting entries for the company's December 31 year-end (e.g., depreciation expense).
c. Post the journal entries and accruals to T-accounts.
d. Prepare a trial balance.
e. Prepare a balance sheet for the December 31 year-end.

A–14 (Similar to Exercise 2–19) Seaver & Co., CPAs, prepare their own financial statements with a December 31 year-end.

1. As of December 31, 1998, Seaver & Co. have rendered $2,500 worth of services to clients for which they have not yet billed the client, and for which they have not made any accounting entry.
2. Seaver & Co. owns equipment (computers, etc.) having an original cost of $12,000. The equipment has an expected life of six years.
3. On January 1, 1998, Seaver borrowed $15,000. Both principal and interest are due on January 1, 1999. The interest rate is 11%.
4. On January 1, 1998, Seaver rented storage space for three years. The entire three-year charge of $1,500 was paid at this time. Seaver correctly created a prepaid rent account in the amount of $1,500.
5. As of December 31, workers have earned $1,200 worth of wages that are unpaid and unrecorded.

REQUIRED

a. Calculate any adjusting entries necessary to prepare the financial statements (e.g., depreciation expense).
b. Post the journal entries to T-accounts.

A–15 (Similar to Problem 2–21) Susan's Sweets opened a candy shop on January 1.

1. Susan invested $100,000 in cash on January 1, 1998 (sole proprietorship).
2. Susan paid $20,000 for a six-month lease. The lease is renewable for another six months on July 1.
3. Susan purchased candy and other "sweetments" at a cost of $10,000 in cash.
4. Susan purchased store fixtures at a cost of $15,000, paying $5,000 in cash. These store fixtures have a useful life of five years, with no expected salvage value.
5. During the first month of operations, Susan's sales totaled $32,000. At the end of the first month, her outstanding accounts receivable were only $1,500. Her cost of sales was $9,500.
6. During the first month, her other operating expenses were $37,300 on account. She also paid herself a "salary" of $10,000, which was really a withdrawal.
7. Susan recorded depreciation for the first year.

REQUIRED

a. Prepare the journal entries necessary to record these transactions.
b. Prepare any necessary adjusting entries (e.g., rent expense).
c. Post the entries to T-accounts.
d. Prepare a trial balance.
e. Prepare an income statement and balance sheet for Susan's Sweets to "tell the story" of the first month's operations.

A–16 (Similar to Problem 2–22) Susan's Shoe Shop opened on January 1. The following transactions took place during the first month:

1. Deposited $30,000 in the firm's checking account.
2. Purchased shoes, boots, socks, and other inventory for $45,000 on account.
3. Purchased display shelving, chairs, and other fixtures for $10,000 cash and $40,000 on account. Assume a useful life of five years.
4. Obtained a three-year $20,000 bank loan at 8% annual interest.
5. Paid $10,000 to two different creditors.
6. Signed an application for a one-year insurance policy and paid the year's premium of $2,400.
7. Paid three employees a monthly salary of $2,000 each.
8. Collected $35,000 from customers.

REQUIRED

a. Prepare the journal entries necessary to record these transactions.
b. Prepare any necessary adjusting entries (e.g., rent expense).
c. Post all journal entries to T-accounts.
d. Prepare a trial balance.
e. Prepare an income statement and balance sheet dated January 31 for Susan's Shoe Shop.

A–17 (Similar to Problem 2–29) Matt's Ski Shop is in the process of acquiring a vehicle for the business. The following transactions took place in December 1998.

1. Verbally agreed to purchase a used car from Slee-Z-Auto for $3,500.
2. Paid $300 for a warranty on the used car.
3. Took the car on a test drive, found it faulty, and told the salesperson you wanted a different car.
4. The sales manager kindly transferred the warranty to the second vehicle.
5. Paid $6,500 for the vehicle, which has a useful life of five years, and no salvage value.
6. Paid license and taxes of $275.
7. Bought new tires for $450.
8. On a cold winter morning, the car failed to start.
9. Purchased a new battery for $65.
10. Filed a warranty claim for the new battery.
11. Received $45 payment under the warranty.

REQUIRED

a. Prepare the journal entries necessary to record these transactions.
b. Prepare any necessary adjusting entries (e.g., depreciation expense).

c. Post all journal entries to T-accounts.

A–18 (Similar to Problem 2–30) Matt, the sole proprietor of Matt's Ski Shop, traveled to Switzerland to attend the Alpine Equipment Exposition. The following transactions occurred:

1. Paid $2,000 for airline tickets, hotel accommodations, and tour guidance from Hugo's U-Go Travel.
2. Changed the airline reservation.
3. Paid a $35 fee to change the reservation.
4. Arrived at the hotel and checked in.
5. Found his room to be next to the hotel laundry, and facing the noisy loading zone. Furthermore, the room only had two cheap radios, no television!
6. Asked the hotel manager for a more suitable room.
7. Tipped the bellhop $5 after his luggage was moved.
8. Upon checking out of the hotel at the end of the week, found a $50 per day upgrade charge on his hotel bill.
9. Paid $257 for meals and phone charges on his hotel bill, but denied liability and responsibility for the upgrade charges.
10. The hotel manager insisted that the upgrade charges were his responsibility, and would be added to his credit card balance.
11. Filed a complaint with Hugo's U-Go Travel and with the credit card issuer.
12. Received a refund of $200 from Hugo.
13. Received a credit for the upgrade charges form the credit card issuer.
14. Took films from the exposition to a photo shop for developing. Charges for developing and printing these films were expected to be $45.
15. Paid the $45 two weeks later.

REQUIRED

a. Prepare the journal entries for these related transactions.

A–19 Alternate Problems (A) or (B)

Problem (A)
(Similar to Problem 2–34) John's Anti-Mediation League (JAML) engaged in the following transactions in 1998:

1. On January 1, JAML borrowed $100,000 at 6% per year with interest due quarterly.
2. JAML paid a $1,000 kickback to a good friend who helped obtain the loan.
3. JAML had not yet paid any interest after the loan had been in effect for three months.
4. On June 30, JAML paid the interest due.
5. On July 1, JAML renegotiated the terms of the loan, which increased the interest rates to 9% per year.
6. At the end of September, John paid the interest on the loan from his personal account.
7. At the end of December, JAML accrued the interest due.
8. On January 1, 1999, JAML paid the interest due to the lender and to John's personal account.

REQUIRED

a. Prepare the journal entries necessary to record these transactions.

b. Post all journal entries to T-accounts.

Problem (B)

(Similar to Problem 2–34) Sue's Mediation League (SML) engaged in the following transactions in 1998:

1. On January 1, SML borrowed $250,000 at 9% per year with interest due quarterly.
2. SML paid $1,000 to a good friend who helped obtain the loan.
3. SML had not yet paid any interest after the loan had been in effect for three months.
4. On June 30, SML paid the interest due.
5. On July 1, SML renegotiated the terms of the loan, which decreased the interest rate to 6% per year.
6. At the end of September, Sue paid the interest on the loan from her personal account.
7. At the end of December, SML accrued the interest due.
8. On January 1, 1999, SML paid the interest due to the lender and to Sue's personal account.

REQUIRED

a. Prepare the journal entries necessary to record these transactions.

b. Post all journal entries to T-accounts.

A–20 Alternate Problems (A) or (B)

Problem (A)

(Similar to Problem 2–35) Sharon's Affairs and Parties (SAAP) engaged in the following transactions in 1998:

1. SAAP borrowed $150,000 at 10% per year to begin operations.
2. SAAP accrued the first month's interest on the loan.
3. SAAP accrued the second month's interest.
4. SAAP paid the interest due at the end of the second month.
5. Sharon loaned SAAP $10,000 at 24% interest per year.
6. SAAP accrued interest for the next month, on both loans.
7. SAAP paid accrued interest at the end of the third month.
8. SAAP repaid Sharon's loan, along with a loan cancellation fee of $2,500.
9. SAAP accrued interest for the next month.
10. SAAP repaid the original loan, along with nine months accrued interest at the end of 1998.

REQUIRED

a. Prepare the journal entries necessary to record these transactions.

b. Post all journal entries to T-accounts.

Problem (B)

(Similar to Problem 2–35) Hilger's Intimate Promises (HIP) engaged in the following transactions in 1998:

1. HIP borrowed $50,000 at 8% per year to begin operations.
2. HIP accrued the first month's interest on the loan.
3. HIP accrued the second month's interest.
4. HIP paid the interest due at the end of the second month.
5. Hilger loaned HIP $10,000 at 24% interest per year.
6. HIP accrued interest for the next month, on both loans.
7. HIP paid accrued interest at the end of the third month.
8. HIP repaid Hilger's loan, along with a loan cancellation fee of $1,500.
9. HIP accrued interest for the next month.
10. HIP repaid the original loan, along with nine months accrued interest at the end of 1996.

REQUIRED

a. Prepare the journal entries necessary to record these transactions.
b. Post all journal entries to T-accounts.

CAREERS IN ACCOUNTING

INTRODUCTION

The field of accounting offers a variety of interesting and challenging career opportunities. *Money* magazine's 1994 evaluation of 100 occupations ranked accounting as the twenty-third most popular. Accounting was rated high in short-term outlook, job security, and prestige. It was rated low in stress and strain. (Try telling that to a tax accountant on April 14!) This appendix describes possible accounting career choices.

Many individuals who begin their careers as accountants remain accountants throughout their work lives. Others use accounting as a stepping stone. For example, some members of congress are accountants, and at least one TV star (Bob Newhart) is a former accountant. Moreover, many chief executive officers have accounting backgrounds.

The American Institute of CPAs (AICPA) has compiled a summary of the placement results of recent college graduates. It shows the following:

	Bachelor's	Master's
Public accounting	29%	47%
Business/industry	27	24
Government	6	3
Other areas	3	3
Graduate school	7	2
Unknown	28	21
Total	100%	100%

Although this text concentrates on financial accounting, a wide array of employment possibilities are discussed here.

PUBLIC ACCOUNTING

CPA firms are the most visible employer of accountants. This visibility, in part, stems from the auditing relationship that CPA firms have with the very largest corporations. The financial statements of all publicly held companies are accompanied by an auditor's report, thereby providing CPA firms with significant publicity. Additionally, CPA firms have recently undertaken advertising campaigns costing millions of dollars. These firms regularly place advertisements in business publications such as *The Wall Street Journal* and *Fortune.* They also utilize television commercials. One firm has even aired a commercial during the Super Bowl.

CPA firms provide three primary services: auditing, tax preparation and planning, and management consulting. These services and the associated career opportunities are discussed in the following sections.

Auditing

As you know, a major role of CPA firms is to audit financial statements. The purpose of an audit is to ascertain if the statements comply with generally accepted accounting principles. In essence, audits enhance the reliability of financial statements.

CPA firms generally have four hierarchical levels:

1. partners,
2. managers,
3. senior accountants, and
4. staff accountants.

Most CPA firms hire recent college graduates as staff accountants. These individuals have excellent educational backgrounds, but usually little or no practical experience. Accordingly, firms provide both formal and on-the-job training.

Staff accountants perform the "pick and shovel" work on an audit. Typical tasks include conducting test counts of inventory, sending letters to the client's customers to confirm accounts receivable, preparing and reviewing bank reconciliations, and verifying payroll withholdings. Computer-based tests and analyses are beginning to replace some of the drudgery associated with these tasks.

After two or three years of experience, many staff accountants are promoted to senior accountant. Senior accountants' responsibilities are much more interesting than those of staff accountants. Seniors play a major role in planning the audit. This entails specifying the audit tests necessary for a particular client. Seniors also supervise the fieldwork. That is, they oversee the staff accountants who perform the audit tests at the client's place of business.

After a total of five or six years of experience, some candidates are promoted to manager. Managers, along with senior accountants, participate in planning the audit. They supervise senior accountants, and review the work of both senior and staff accountants. Managers also have significant interactions with the client's upper-level management. Many decisions, such as the timing of fieldwork, must be made jointly by the auditor and the client.

After a total of about 12 years of employment in large firms, successful candidates are promoted to partner. Less time is usually needed in smaller firms. Partners have ultimate responsibility for the quality of an audit. Partners confer with the manager and senior accountant regarding difficult or sensitive problems. They are also the primary liaison with the client's top executives. In addition, a major part of their job entails practice development, such as getting new clients and retaining current clients. CPA firms are, after all, businesses that need clients in order to generate revenue and profit.

Tax

A major function of CPA firms is to assist clients with their taxes. Both individuals and business organizations, such as corporations, need this help. In general, CPAs provide two types of tax services. One is tax compliance. This entails completing tax returns at year-end. The other service is tax planning. This involves structuring transactions so as to minimize their tax effects.

Staff accountants and senior accountants are highly involved in tax compliance. Managers and partners review the work of staff and seniors and also provide clients with tax planning advice.

As increasingly important area is international tax. The globalization of business is prompting many corporations to conduct their affairs in more than one country. This requires knowledge of the tax laws of those countries, and the tax treaties among those countries.

Management Consulting

Members of CPA firms are widely recognized, not only for their expertise in accounting, auditing, and taxes, but also for their overall business knowledge. Because of this, CPA firms offer a wide variety of consulting services to their clients. Perhaps the most prominent service is the installation of computerized information systems. Other services include employee benefits, mergers and acquisitions, and health care consulting.

CPA firms have been extremely successful in their consulting endeavors. For example, a recent survey by the AICPA showed that small businesses were three times more likely to seek advice from their CPA than from any other source.

Characteristics of CPA Firms

CPA firms can be described based on several characteristics. This section summarizes many important aspects of CPA firms.

Organizational Form. CPA firms have traditionally been organized as sole proprietorships or partnerships. Recall that the owners of these organizations have unlimited legal liability. That is, their personal assets are available to meet all obligations of the business.

The individual states, which regulate the accounting profession, have been reluctant to permit accounting firms to organize as corporations. Many regulators feel that professionals (doctors, lawyers, accountants) should be fully responsible for their actions, and should not enjoy the shield of limited liability provided by corporations.

An excellent counterargument exists, however. Consider a national CPA firm with offices in many cities. Let's assume that one of the firm's owners in the Boston office conducts a faulty audit and that the firm is sued. Should the personal assets of the firm's owners who work in, say, the Seattle office be available to satisfy any claims that may arise? These owners had nothing to do with the faulty audit, and might have only a passing acquaintance with the owner from the Boston office.

The accounting profession is currently seeking ways to limit the exposure of CPAs for damages arising from the actions of others. In many states, several organizational forms have recently become available to CPAs. Two of these are professional corporations and limited liability partnerships. Both of these organizational forms place limits on the liability of owners for acts committed by other owners. Owners are still fully responsible for the consequences of their own acts. Professional corporations are typically used by accounting firms that conduct business in only one state. Limited liability partnerships are used by firms that operate in two or more states.

Size. CPA firms vary dramatically in size. Many CPA firms consist of only an owner and maybe a few employees. In contrast, a number of CPA firms are extremely large, international organizations. Exhibit B–1 contains a listing of the ten largest public accounting firms in the United States. The largest six firms are often referred to as the "Big Six." To gain an appreciation for their size, examine the columns labeled "Number of Professional Staff" and "Number of Offices." You can see that they are considerably larger than the other firms listed.

Of course, many medium-sized CPA firms exist. Without doubt, the public's best interest is served by a wide array of firm sizes. For example, small individual taxpayers (like us) might appreciate the personal attention (and relatively low fees) of a small or midsized firm. In contrast, a large international corporation will need the services of a large CPA firm that has multiple offices and specializes in international and domestic taxes and auditing.

The last three columns of Exhibit B–1 show the services emphasized by each firm. Most firms focus on accounting and auditing. Only one firm, Arthur Andersen & Co., earns the largest percentage of its revenue from management consulting services.

EXHIBIT B–1   TEN LARGEST U.S PUBLIC ACCOUNTING FIRMS

Rank by Revenue	Firm/HQ Location	Revenue			No. of Partners	No. of Professional Staff	No. of Offices	No. of SEC Clients	Revenue Split (%)			
		FYE	U.S. Net Revenue ($ mil)	% Change versus Previous Year					A&A	Tax	MCS	Other
1	Arthur Andersen & Co., SC/Chicago, Ill.	Aug	2680.1	8.8	1,365	18,879	89	1,808	35	20	45	0
2	Ernst & Young/New York, N.Y.	Sep	2281.0	1.6	1,836	12,815	106	2,469	51	23	26	0
3	Deloitte & Touche/Wilton, Conn.	Jun	1955.0	0.2	1,472	10,128	116	2,028	54	23	23	0
4	KPMG Peat Marwick/New York, N.Y.	Jun	1800.0	-0.7	1,494	11,997	135	2,212	53	27	20	0
5	Coopers & Lybrand/New York, N.Y.	Sep	1557.0	5.9	1,251	11,255	126	1,435	58	18	24	0
6	Price Waterhouse/New York, N.Y.	Jun	1370.0	7.0	933	8,191	109	1,948	45	27	28	0
7	Grant Thornton/Chicago, Ill.	Jul	222.0	7.8	280	1,600	29	220	54	32	14	0
8	McGladrey & Pullen/Minneapolis, Minn.	Apr	196.6	4.3	369	1,196	69	165	36	35	16	13
9	Kenneth Leventhal & Co./Los Angeles, Calif.	Sep	188.2	3.4	76	802	14	32	52	13	35	0
10	BDO Seidman/New York, N.Y.	Jun	182.3	0.7	235	1,068	39	164	59	33	8	0

SOURCE: *Public Accounting Report.* Copyright 1993 by Strafford Publications, Inc., 590 Dutch Valley Rd., N.E., Atlanta, GA 30324-5330. 404/881-1141.

Compensation. Exhibit B–2 summarizes salary information for several U.S. cities and the nation as a whole. Salaries vary considerably, based on location. This variation reflects both cost of living differences, and supply and demand factors.

Based on level within the firm, the biggest jump in compensation occurs between manager and partner. This makes sense, given that a manager is simply an employee of the firm, whereas a partner is an owner.

Exhibit B–2 contains averages for firms of all sizes. Compensation is usually higher in the larger firms. For example, according to *Bowman's Accounting Report* the average Big Six partner earned $269,600 in 1992.

	New York	Detroit	Denver	Nationwide
Entry level	$ 33,100	$ 27,600	$24,100	$26,000
Staff (1–2 years)	38,900	33,200	30,800	30,000
Senior (3–5 years)	47,800	40,100	36,800	35,000
Manager (6–9 years)	67,800	56,000	52,600	54,000
Partner (first year)	122,000	107,900	89,000	90,000

SOURCE: *Accounting & Finance Salary Survey,* 1994, by Source Finance.

EXHIBIT B–2
PUBLIC ACCOUNTING SALARIES

Overtime. Employees of CPA firms have very demanding work schedules, largely due to the needs of their clients. All individual taxpayers must file their returns by April 15. Calendar year-end corporations must file their returns by March 15, and publicly held corporations with a calendar year-end must submit their audited financial statements by March 31.

Clearly, January through April are busy months for CPA firms. Employees of CPA firms work substantial overtime during this period. Average workweeks of 60 hours (or more) are common.

Fortunately, there is a silver lining to the overtime cloud. Many firms provide a leisure bank. Overtime hours worked during busy season enable employees to take additional vacation days during slow season. Most firms also provide the option of monetary compensation for overtime hours.

Travel. Large CPA firms have large clients, who have a number of physical locations. Many employees of large CPA firms undertake some out-of-town travel. The auditing and management consulting staffs do most of the travel. Although generalizations are difficult, two or three weeks of travel each year is a reasonable average. The tax staff usually travels considerably less.

Accountants who work in corporate settings perform a wide array of functions. The following sections describe general accounting, internal auditing, taxes, cost accounting, and budgeting.

CORPORATE (INDUSTRY) ACCOUNTING

General Accounting

Corporations are, of course, responsible for the preparation of their financial statements. This is a significant task, particularly for large corporations. Because of this, corporations employ many accountants to generate the information needed for financial statements.

Corporations are also subjected to other reporting requirements. For example, lenders will sometimes ask for more detailed information than that found in financial statements. As another example, corporations must prepare SEC registration statements when they sell securities to the public. These and other requirements increase the need for general accounting personnel.

Internal Auditing

Virtually all large corporations, and many midsized ones, have internal audit staffs. A primary objective of an internal audit is the same as that of an external audit performed by public accountants: to help ensure the reliability of financial statements.

However, the role of internal auditing is somewhat broader. It also includes operational auditing, which assesses the effectiveness and efficiency of the corporation's operations. In part, this entails determining if internal policies are being followed. For example, many firms have a policy of paying quickly for purchases so that favorable discounts can be taken. Internal audits periodically assess if this policy is actually followed. Internal audits may also deal with much more complex issues, such as compliance with environmental laws and regulations.

Taxes

Tax accountants who work for corporations participate in the two primary tax-related activities of compliance and planning. Compliance can be quite complex for large corporations that operate in a number of jurisdictions. Federal tax returns must be completed, as well as multiple state returns. If the corporation operates in other nations, foreign returns must be compiled. Tax accountants are also responsible for returns related to payroll taxes, sales taxes, real estate taxes, and personal property taxes.

Tax planning is also a major responsibility for corporate tax accountants. The area of mergers and acquisitions is an increasingly important one for tax planning. It involves important issues such as these:

1. Should the target corporation's stock or the underlying assets be acquired?
2. Should the acquisition be funded by issuing stock, using available cash, or incurring new debt?

Careful attention to these questions can have a large impact on the amount of taxes paid.

Cost Accounting

It is crucially important for corporations to know the cost of the products and services that they produce. Without such knowledge, the profitability of different products and customers cannot be measured. This could result in unwise business decisions.

Calculating product costs in single-product firms is relatively straightforward. All manufacturing costs are related to that one product and are included in its cost. The task becomes much more difficult in multiproduct firms. In these firms, the same manufacturing facility is frequently used to produce several (perhaps many) products. Because of this, the cost of the facility must be allocated to the various products. The basis for such allocations is frequently not obvious, and cost accountants must decide how the costs are to be assigned to each product.

Cost accountants also accumulate information to help in controlling costs. For example, an important cost in many organizations is inventory handling costs, which include receiving, shipping, and storage costs. Knowing the amount spent on these activities is an essential ingredient to controlling the costs.

Budgeting

To be successful, corporations must identify goals and develop plans to achieve those goals. Budgets are quantitative expressions of corporate plans. They reflect a corporation's expectations regarding future results. Realistic budgets help identify profitable opportunities. Moreover, the departure of actual results from budget targets will suggest areas in need of corrective action.

Accountants play a major role in budgeting. In conjunction with operating personnel, they develop forecasts of future operations. Accountants then trace through the effects of these forecasted operations on various financial statement items. For example, forecasts of sales and costs are a prerequisite for cash flow planning. That is, accountants will assess the impact and timing of forecasted sales and costs on cash to ascertain if future borrowings will be needed or if excess cash will be generated.

Personnel Policies

Corporations differ considerably regarding overtime, travel, training, etc. Every situation is different, and job candidates should be careful to ask the necessary questions.

Compensation also varies, but surveys have been done that provide average salary figures. Exhibit B–3 contains entry-level averages for several types of corporate accounting positions. There is little variation across position categories, although there are considerable geographic differences. The exhibit also contains average salaries for controllers, the chief accounting officers in firms.

	New York	Detroit	Denver	Nationwide
Entry level				
General accounting	$28,100	$23,900	$20,000	24,000
Internal auditor	30,200	26,200	22,500	26,000
Tax accounting	31,900	27,500	23,200	25,000
Cost accounting	29,200	26,000	22,800	27,000
Controller	88,700	58,400	54,300	64,000

SOURCE: *Accounting & Finance Salary Survey,* 1994, by Source Finance.

EXHIBIT B–3
CORPORATE ACCOUNTING SALARIES

OTHER OPPORTUNITIES

Accountants are employed by many different organizations. Virtually all governmental units (federal, state, and local) rely on accountants to monitor their flow of funds. The Internal Revenue Service (IRS) employs a large number of tax accountants to interpret tax laws, provide assistance to taxpayers, and audit returns. Not-for-profit organizations, such as hospitals and charitable organizations, also need the services of accountants. Accountants in these organizations perform many of the same tasks as those undertaken in corporations.

CERTIFICATION

Potential employers and the public at large have an interest in identifying competent accountants. To assist in this process, several professional organizations have established certification programs. For example, the Institute of Management Accountants operates the Certified Management Accountant (CMA) program. Other certification programs include Certified Internal Auditor (CIA) and Certified Fraud Examiner (CFE). Some certificate programs outside of the accounting field (Certified Financial Analyst) also require a knowledge of accounting.

To become certified, accountants submit their credentials for evaluation against standardized criteria established by the sponsoring organization. Most certificate programs require candidates to have a specified educational background, pass a rigorous exam, and have a certain amount of work experience. The following sections describe the two most well-known certificates: CPA and CMA.

Certified Public Accountant

The most widely known and widely held certificate is the CPA. In fact, becoming a CPA involves more than receiving the blessing of a private organization. CPAs, like doctors and lawyers, are licensed by the individual states. Each state has its own specific licensing requirements. This section provides a general overview of these requirements.

Education. Most states require at least a baccalaureate degree and a specified array of accounting and related business courses. Many states require 21 to 27 semester hours of accounting. Courses might include intermediate financial accounting, intermediate managerial accounting, auditing, and taxes. Approximately 24 semester hours in other business courses, such as management, economics, finance, business law, and information systems, are also required.

There is a strong movement among the states to require 150 semester hours, rather than 120, for licensing. The rationale for this change is that both business in general, and accounting in particular, are becoming so complex that an adequate introduction to these topics requires 150 hours. The AICPA recommends the following allocation of semester hours:

General education	60–80
Education in business administration	35–50
Accounting education	25–40

The 150-hour requirement has been implemented or is being phased in by more than half of the states. The AICPA's goal is to have all states adopt this requirement by the year 2000. Of course, all those CPAs who have 120 semester hours and are licensed prior to adoption of the 150-hour provision retain their licenses.

The CPA Exam. All states require candidates to pass the Uniform CPA Exam, developed by the AICPA. The exam is given twice a year, on the first Wednesday and Thursday in May and November. It is an exhausting experience, taking 7½ hours on Wednesday and 8 hours on Thursday.

The exam has four parts.

1. Financial Accounting and Reporting
2. Accounting and Reporting—Taxation, Managerial, Governmental and Not-for-Profit Organizations
3. Auditing
4. Business Law and Professional Responsibilities

The most difficult aspect of the exam is its breadth. It is equivalent to taking a comprehensive final exam on approximately 12 courses during a two-day period. Obviously, candidates must spend a great deal of time preparing for this exam. Only about 20% of first-time candidates pass all parts. However, many candidates ultimately prove to be successful by retaking the parts they initially fail.

Work Experience. Most states require one to three years of public accounting experience as a condition of licensing. Some states permit alternative work experiences, such as internal auditing. A few states have no experience requirement.

Other Requirements. Many states require CPA candidates to pass an ethics exam. Most candidates complete a self-study course to prepare for this exam. Some states also have residency or employment requirements.

Nearly all states also require that their certificate holders engage in ongoing continuing professional education. This requirement usually involves 40 hours of training per year that is designed to enhance the competence of CPAs.

Career Implications. Individuals are precluded from practicing *public* accounting without being a CPA. Thus, a CPA certificate is public accounting's entry requirement. (Keep in mind that you can work for a CPA firm without being a CPA.) However, more broadly, in evaluating job candidates, many employers use easily implemented screening criteria, of which a CPA license is one. As a result, many CPAs are employed by corporations, governmental units, and other organizations.

Certified Management Accountant

The CMA program has four objectives:

1. to establish management accounting as a recognized profession by identifying the role of the management accountant and financial manager, the underlying body of knowledge, and a course of study by which such knowledge is acquired;

2. to encourage higher educational standards in the management accounting field;
3. to establish an objective measure of an individual's knowledge and competence in the field of management accounting; and
4. to encourage continued professional development by management accountants.

Education. To become a CMA, a candidate must hold a bachelor's degree or a CPA certificate. Although the CMA program does not designate specific course work, the CMA exam, as a practical matter, effectively requires candidates to take a certain array of courses.

The CMA Exam. The CMA exam is a four-part exam intended to measure candidates' knowledge of management accounting and financial management. In addition, the exam assesses candidates' ability to analyze information and to communicate the results of that analysis. Ethical responsibilities are also addressed throughout the exam. The CMA exam's four parts are:

1. Economics, Finance, and Management
2. Financial Accounting and Reporting
3. Management Reporting, Analysis, and Behavioral Issues
4. Decision Analysis and Information Systems

Candidates who have passed the CPA exam are given credit for part 2, Financial Accounting and Reporting.

Candidates may register for any number of parts and take the parts in any order. However, the entire exam must be passed within three years. Each part takes four hours and the entire exam is given over a two-day period in mid-June and mid-December.

Other Requirements. CMA candidates must have two continuous years of management accounting experience or three years of auditing experience in public accounting. Holders of CMA certificates must meet a continuing professional education requirement that consists of 30 hours per year. Qualifying subjects include management accounting, corporate taxation, finance, computer science, systems analysis, statistics, management skills, insurance, marketing, business law, or other subjects relevant to the CMA's career development or employer needs.

THE FUTURE

As with many fields of endeavor, accounting faces continual change. Robert Half International, a leading employment agency specializing in accounting, has identified several factors that will affect accounting as we approach the twenty-first century. The following sections discuss these factors.

Computers

Computers are a fact of life for nearly every accountant. Even very small organizations have computerized their accounting functions. The widespread use of computers is due to (1) the rapidly declining cost of computers, (2) the increased power of such computers, and (3) the availability of low-cost accounting software.

Accountants must be familiar with both hardware and software. College courses and continuing professional education classes address these issues. Since many computers operate in a similar fashion, most courses focus on software. Fortunately for accountants, many software packages are user-friendly. They require no knowledge of computer programming languages. Software packages usually include readable instruction manuals, as well as on-screen tutorials and help functions.

Although employers often provide training, they also look quite favorably on job candidates who already have some computer expertise. In fact, some employers pay a 5 to 10% premium to candidates who have experience with certain software packages.

Globalization

Businesses are now looking at the entire world as their marketplace. Both corporations and public accounting firms are expanding their international operations. This trend creates the need for accountants with a global view. Accountants need to know the business practices, accounting procedures, language, and social customs of the countries in which their firms operate. Much of this knowledge is gained through experience. Some of it, including language training, can be obtained through formal classes.

Demographics and Personnel Policies

Perhaps the most noteworthy demographic trend in accounting is the increasing number of female accountants. More than half of recent accounting graduates were women. This suggests an increase in two-career couples. Managing two demanding work schedules and a family life is quite difficult. Because of this, organizations are becoming more flexible in their terms of employment. Part-time employment and job-sharing are more commonplace. Some public accounting firms have a partnership track that entails less than full-time work.

Although women comprise a majority of recent accounting graduates, men still dominate the upper levels in most firms (the "glass ceiling" effect). A study done by the AICPA showed that in large public accounting firms only 6% of the partners are female. Because of this, many firms have established formal mentoring programs to ensure that their female staff do not feel alienated and are given proper career guidance.

SUMMARY AND REVIEW

Accounting offers a variety of career opportunities, many of which are rather lucrative. Accountants are employed by public accounting firms, corporations, governmental units, and not-for-profit organizations. Accounting professionals engage in a variety of functions, such as financial accounting, taxes, cost accounting, and budgeting.

Certification is an important step in an accountant's career path. It is an indication of a candidate's qualifications. The most recognized certificate is the CPA. The CMA is, perhaps, the second most recognized certification.

The future job outlook for accountants is good. Demand for accountants is expected to be strong, and accountants continue to be respected by the business community. Accounting is also a road to the top of business organizations; many chief executive officers began their careers as accountants.

OSHKOSH B'GOSH

▼▼▼▼▼▼▼▼▼▼▼▼▼▼▼▼▼▼▼▼▼▼▼

Financial Section

1994

▲▲▲▲▲▲▲▲▲▲▲▲▲▲▲▲▲▲▲▲▲▲

quarterly financial data (unaudited)

OshKosh B'Gosh, Inc. and Subsidiaries

(Dollars in thousands, except share and per share amounts)

	Net Sales	Gross Profit	Net Income (Loss)	Net Income (Loss) Per Share
1994 Quarter Ended:				
March	$ 87,394	$22,407	$ 895	$ 0.06
June	66,158	19,438	(742)	(0.05)
September	118,397	35,034	5,272	0.38
December	91,414	27,068	1,614	0.12
1993 Quarter Ended:				
March	$ 93,234	$25,695	$ 3,937	$ 0.27
June	63,306	17,931	1,347	0.09
September	103,114	29,497	5,394	0.37
December	80,532	22,137	(6,155)*	(0.42)*

*Restructuring costs reduced net income by $7,100 or $.49 per share in the fourth quarter.
See Note 2 to consolidated financial statements.

quarterly common stock data

	1994			1993		
	Stock Price High / Low		Dividends Per Share	Stock Price High / Low		Dividends Per Share
Class A Common Stock						
1st	21-3/4	14-1/2	$0.1025	22-1/2	14-1/2	$0.1025
2nd	15	12-1/4	0.1025	19	14-1/2	0.1025
3rd	15-1/2	13-1/2	0.1025	18-1/4	13-1/2	0.1025
4th	15-1/4	13	0.07	20-1/2	16-1/4	0.205
Class B Common Stock						
1st	22	16-3/4	$0.09	18	12	$0.09
2nd	17	13-3/4	0.09	18-1/4	15-1/4	0.09
3rd	15-1/2	14	0.09	18	13-3/4	0.09
4th	15-1/4	13-1/2	0.06	20-3/4	17	0.18

The Company's Class A common stock and Class B common stock trade on the Over-The-Counter market and is quoted on NASDAQ under the symbols GOSHA and GOSHB, respectively. The table reflects the "last" price quotation on the NASDAQ National Market System and does not reflect mark-ups, mark-downs, or commissions and may not represent actual transactions.

As of February 17, 1995, there were 1,963 Class A common stock shareholders of record and 196 Class B common stock shareholders of record.

management's discussion and analysis of results of operations and financial condition

Results of Operations

Year Ended December 31, 1994
Compared to Year Ended December 31, 1993

Net sales in 1994 were $363.4 million, an increase of $23.2 million (6.8%) over 1993 sales of $340.2 million. The Company's 1994 domestic wholesale business of approximately $234 million was 9% less than 1993 sales of approximately $257 million, with a corresponding decline in unit shipments of approximately 6.7%. The decrease in domestic wholesale unit shipments related primarily to the effects of the competitive environment in the children's wear business combined with the effects of prior years' poor shipping performance and perceived weakness in product design. The Company's Spring, 1995 children's fashion offering has been well received. Company initiatives undertaken during 1994 resulted in significantly improved shipping performance to customers. In addition, improved product design contributed to better "sell-thrus" and margins for a majority of our wholesale customers. The Company currently anticipates that unit shipments of its Spring, 1995 wholesale product offering will exceed Spring, 1994 by over 10%. Early indications of acceptance of the Company's Fall, 1995 children's fashion offering have also been promising.

Company retail sales at its OshKosh B'Gosh branded outlet stores and Genuine Kids stores were approximately $99.4 million for 1994, a 52.6% increase over 1993 retail sales of approximately $65.2 million. This retail sales increase was primarily driven by the opening of an additional 46 retail stores during 1994. In addition, the Company's comparable store sales for 1994 were up approximately 3.6%. At year end the Company operated 61 OshKosh B'Gosh branded stores and 77 Genuine Kids stores. The Company anticipates continued expansion of its retail business through the opening of approximately 35 additional retail stores during 1995.

The Company's gross profit margin as a percent of sales improved to 28.6% in 1994, compared with 28.0% in 1993. This gross profit margin improvement was due primarily to the impact of the Company's increased retail sales at higher gross margins relative to its domestic wholesale business. The favorable impact of the Company's retail gross margins was offset in part by the domestic wholesale gross margin, which was down in 1994 primarily as a result of the adverse

impact of reduced unit volume on our manufacturing operations and slightly lower pricing to wholesale customers. As a result of capacity reduction initiatives implemented during 1994 and early 1995, along with increased utilization of contracted manufacturing resources outside of the United States, the Company anticipates further improvement in its gross profit margins during 1995.

Selling, general and administrative expenses for 1994 increased $16.5 million over 1993. As a percent of net sales, selling, general and administrative expenses were 26.1% in 1994, up from 23.1% in 1993. The primary reason for the increased selling, general and administrative expenses is the Company's aggressive expansion of its retail business. In addition, the Company's increasing focus on its international operations resulted in an increase in 1994's selling, general and administrative expenses of approximately $2.7 million. Also, the Company's catalog division, initiated in the second half of 1993, added approximately $1.6 million to selling, general and administrative expenses in 1994. Continued expansion of the Company's retail business, along with further development of its foreign business and catalog division, will result in higher selling, general and administrative expenses in relation to its net sales in 1995.

During the fourth quarter of 1993, the Company recorded a pretax restructuring charge of $10.8 million. Restructuring costs (net of income tax benefit) reduced net income by $7.1 million ($.49 per share) in 1993. The restructuring charge included approximately $3.3 million for facility closings, write-down of the related assets and severance costs pertaining to work force reductions. The restructuring charge also reflected the Company's decision to market its Trader Kids line of children's apparel under the new name Genuine Kids and the resulting costs of the Company's decision not to renew its Boston Trader license arrangement beyond 1994, as well as expenses to consolidate its retail operations. Accordingly, the restructuring charge also included approximately $7.5 million for write-off of unamortized trademark rights and expenses relating to consolidating the Company's retail operations.

▼▼▼▼▼▼▼▼▼▼▼▼▼▼▼▼

management's discussion and analysis of results of operations and financial condition

During 1994, the Company implemented its restructuring plan. The Company closed its McKenzie, Tennessee facility and announced plans to close its Dover, Tennessee facility, which was completed in early 1995. Closing of the Dover facility in 1995 will reduce the Company's work force by approximately 270 employees. The Company was able to sell both operating facilities, and reached satisfactory agreements with all affected employees concerning severance arrangements. The Company began to market a portion of its children's wear line under the Genuine Kids label, discontinuing the Trader Kids line of children's apparel. The Company also consolidated the operations of its retail business into its Oshkosh office. As of December 31, 1994, the Company estimates that remaining restructuring costs are sufficiently provided for in the residual restructuring liability. Remaining costs include charges for facility closings, including disposal of the real estate and severance costs pertaining to work force reductions. This plan should be substantially completed during 1995.

The Company's effective tax rate for 1994 was 45.7% compared to 51.3% in 1993. The relatively high effective tax rates for both years result primarily from the Company's foreign operating losses, which provide no tax benefit. In addition, the high 1993 effective tax rate was the result of substantially lower income before income taxes in 1993 (which resulted in part from the restructuring charge). Company management believes that the $11.5 million deferred tax asset at December 31, 1994 can be fully realized through reversals of existing taxable temporary differences and the Company's history of substantial taxable income which allows the opportunity for carrybacks of current or future losses.

In November of 1992, the Financial Accounting Standards Board issued its Statement No. 112 entitled "Employers' Accounting for Post Employment Benefits." This standard had no significant impact on the Company's 1994 financial statements.

Year Ended December 31, 1993 Compared to Year Ended December 31, 1992

Net sales in 1993 were $340.2 million, down 1.7% from 1992 sales of $346.2 million. The Company's domestic wholesale business of approximately $257 million in 1993 was 9.3% less than 1992 sales, due primarily to a decline in unit shipments of approximately 10% in 1993 from 1992.

The decrease in domestic wholesale unit shipments related primarily to the effects of the competitive pricing environment in the children's wear business, the Company's difficulty in meeting the delivery requirements of its wholesale customers as well as perceived weakness in its product design.

Company retail sales at its OshKosh B'Gosh branded outlet stores and its Trader Kids stores (now marketed under the Genuine Kids name) expanded to approximately $65.2 million in 1993, a 49.9% increase over 1992 retail sales of approximately $43.5 million. Retail sales increases resulted primarily from the opening of an additional 38 retail stores during 1993.

Gross profit margin as a percent of sales improved to 28.0% in 1993, compared with 25.1% in 1992. During 1993, the Company experienced a slight improvement in its domestic wholesale gross margins. Increased retail store sales, at higher gross profit margins, had a significant impact on improved overall gross-margin performance. Gross margins for 1992 were unfavorably impacted by manufacturing inefficiencies resulting from the restructuring of production lines and increasing workers' compensation insurance and employee health care costs.

Selling, general and administrative expenses increased $12.1 million in 1993 from 1992. As a percent of net sales, selling, general and administrative expenses were 23.1% in 1993, up from 19.2% in 1992. The primary reason for the increased selling, general and administrative expenses was the Company's increased focus on its retail business. In addition, the Company initiated a catalog division in the second half of 1993 which added approximately $1.2 million to its selling, general and administrative expenses. Increased emphasis on foreign sales opportunities, including the start-up cost associated with the opening of sales offices, also added to the Company's selling, general and administrative expenses during 1993.

During the fourth quarter of 1993, the Company recorded a pretax restructuring charge of $10.8 million. Restructuring costs (net of income tax benefit) reduced net income by $7.1 million ($.49 per share) in 1993.

During 1992, the Company reduced its estimate of the Absorba line restructuring costs originally recorded in 1991 by $2.8 million, due to the efficient and orderly wind down of operations and favorable settlement of lease obligations. This adjustment to restructuring costs (net of income taxes) increased 1992 net income by $1.8 million ($.12 per share).

▲▲▲▲▲▲▲▲▲▲▲▲▲▲▲▲

▼▼▼▼▼▼▼▼▼▼▼▼▼▼▼▼▼▼

management's discussion and analysis of results of operations and financial condition

Royalty income, net of expenses, was $3.4 million in 1993, as compared to $2.6 million in 1992. The increase in net royalty income resulted primarily from additional foreign license agreements.

The effective tax rate for 1993 was 51.3% compared to 39.8% in 1992. The higher 1993 effective tax rate resulted from the Company's foreign operating losses, which provide no tax benefit, combined with the Company's substantially lower income before income taxes in 1993 (which resulted in part from the restructuring charge). The Company's early adoption of Statement of Financial Accounting Standards No. 109, "Accounting for Income Taxes," in 1992 had no material impact on 1992's results of operations.

The Company elected early adoption of the Statement of Financial Accounting Standards No. 106, "Employers' Accounting for Post Retirement Benefits Other Than Pensions," in 1992. The Company elected to record the entire transition obligation in 1992, which resulted in a net $.6 million after tax ($.04 per share) reduction in net income.

Seasonality

The Company's business is increasingly seasonal, with highest sales and income in the third quarter which is the Company's peak retail selling season at its retail outlet stores. The Company's second quarter sales and income are the lowest both because of relatively low domestic wholesale unit shipments and relatively modest retail outlet store sales during this period. The Company anticipates this seasonality trend to continue to impact 1995 quarterly sales and income.

Financial Position, Capital Resources and Liquidity

The Company's financial position remained strong throughout 1994. At December 31, 1994, the Company's cash and cash equivalents were $10.5 million, compared to $17.9 million at the end of 1993 and $21.1 million at the end of 1992. Net working capital at the end of 1994 was $102.5 million, compared to $111.8 million at 1993 year end and $111.1 million at 1992 year end. Cash provided by operations was approximately $22.1 million in 1994; compared to $21.6 million in 1993 and $22.9 million in 1992.

Accounts receivable at December 31, 1994 were $23.9 million compared to $19.5 million at December 31, 1993. Inventories at the end of 1994 were $93.9 million, down $6.1 million from 1993. Management believes that year end 1994 inventory levels are generally appropriate for anticipated 1995 business activity.

Capital expenditures were approximately $9.9 million in 1994 and $9 million in 1993. Capital expenditures for 1995 are currently budgeted at approximately $12 million.

On June 14, 1994, the Company announced a stock repurchase program for up to 1,500,000 shares of its Class A common stock in open market transactions at prevailing prices. Through December 31, 1994, the Company has repurchased approximately 1,084,000 shares of its Class A common stock for approximately $15 million.

In June 1994, the Company finalized a credit agreement with participating banks. This arrangement provides a $60 million, three year revolving credit facility and a $40 million revocable demand line of credit for cash borrowings, issuance of commercial paper and letters of credit. The agreement expires in June 1997. The Company believes that these credit facilities, along with cash generated from operations, will be sufficient to finance the Company's stock repurchase program as well as its capital expenditure, seasonal working capital, remaining restructuring and business development needs.

Dividends on the Company's Class A and Class B common stock totaled $.3775 per share and $.33 per share, respectively, in 1994, compared to $.5125 per share and $.45 per share on the Company's Class A and Class B common stock, respectively, in 1993. The dividend payout rate was 75% of net income in 1994 and 163% in 1993. The Company's lower earnings from operations in 1993 combined with the fourth quarter 1993 restructuring charge resulted in the unusually high 1993 payout rate.

Inflation

The effects of inflation on the Company's operating results and financial condition were not significant.

▲▲▲▲▲▲▲▲▲▲▲▲▲▲▲▲▲▲

consolidated balance sheets

OshKosh B'Gosh, Inc. and Subsidiaries

(Dollars in thousands, except share and per share amounts)

| | December 31, | |
	1994	1993
Assets		
Current assets		
Cash and cash equivalents	$ 10,514	$ 17,853
Accounts receivable, less allowances of $3,700 in 1994 and $3,310 in 1993	23,857	19,477
Inventories	93,916	99,999
Prepaid expenses and other current assets	2,510	3,810
Deferred income taxes	11,510	10,716
Total current assets	142,307	151,855
Property, plant and equipment, net	69,829	71,755
Other assets	5,075	5,521
Total assets	$217,211	$229,131
Liabilities and Shareholders' Equity		
Current liabilities		
Current maturities of long-term debt	$ 240	$ 536
Accounts payable	9,436	9,720
Accrued liabilities	30,168	29,805
Total current liabilities	39,844	40,061
Long-term debt	517	757
Deferred income taxes	2,869	3,040
Employee benefit plan liabilities	15,167	13,275
Commitments	—	—
Shareholders' equity		
Preferred stock, par value $.01 per share:		
Authorized — 1,000,000 shares;		
Issued and outstanding — None	—	—
Common stock, par value $.01 per share:		
Class A, authorized — 30,000,000 shares;		
Issued and outstanding — 12,233,787 shares in 1994		
— 13,280,572 shares in 1993	122	133
Class B, authorized — 3,750,000 shares;		
Issued and outstanding — 1,267,713 shares in 1994		
— 1,305,228 shares in 1993	13	13
Additional paid-in capital	—	2,971
Retained earnings	158,933	169,182
Cumulative foreign currency translation adjustments	(254)	(301)
Total shareholders' equity	158,814	171,998
Total liabilities and shareholders' equity	$217,211	$229,131

See notes to consolidated financial statements.

consolidated statements of income
OshKosh B'Gosh, Inc. and Subsidiaries
(Dollars and shares in thousands, except per share amounts)

| | Year Ended December 31, | | |
	1994	1993	1992
Net sales	$363,363	$340,186	$346,206
Cost of products sold	259,416	244,926	259,344
Gross profit	103,947	95,260	86,862
Selling, general and administrative expenses	94,988	78,492	66,414
Restructuring	—	10,836	(2,800)
Operating income	8,959	5,932	23,248
Other income (expense):			
Interest expense	(1,034)	(626)	(797)
Interest income	1,048	1,114	1,022
Royalty income, net of expenses	3,442	3,417	2,562
Miscellaneous	543	(545)	91
Other income — net	3,999	3,360	2,878
Income before income taxes and cumulative effect of accounting change	12,958	9,292	26,126
Income taxes	5,919	4,769	10,390
Income before cumulative effect of accounting change	7,039	4,523	15,736
Cumulative effect of change in accounting for nonpension postretirement benefits	—	—	(601)
Net income	$ 7,039	$ 4,523	$ 15,135
Weighted average common shares outstanding	14,144	14,586	14,586
Income per share before cumulative effect of accounting change	$ .50	$ .31	$ 1.08
Change in accounting for nonpension postretirement benefits	—	—	(.04)
Net income per common share	$ .50	$ .31	$ 1.04

See notes to consolidated financial statements.

consolidated statements of changes in shareholders' equity

OshKosh B'Gosh, Inc. and Subsidiaries

(Dollars and shares in thousands, except per share amounts)

| | Common Stock | | | | Additional Paid-In Capital | Retained Earnings | Cumulative Foreign Currency Translation Adjustments |
| | Class A | | Class B | | | | |
	Shares	Amount	Shares	Amount			
Balance — December 31, 1991	12,777	$128	1,809	$18	$2,971	$164,263	$ —
Net income	—	—	—	—	—	15,135	—
Dividends—Class A ($.5125 per share)	—	—	—	—	—	(6,548)	—
—Class B ($.45 per share)	—	—	—	—	—	(814)	—
Balance — December 31, 1992	12,777	128	1,809	18	2,971	172,036	—
Net income	—	—	—	—	—	4,523	—
Dividends—Class A ($.5125 per share)	—	—	—	—	—	(6,667)	—
—Class B ($.45 per share)	—	—	—	—	—	(710)	—
Foreign currency translation adjustments	—	—	—	—	—	—	(301)
Conversions of common shares	504	5	(504)	(5)	—	—	—
Balance — December 31, 1993	13,281	133	1,305	13	2,971	169,182	(301)
Net income	—	—	—	—	—	7,039	—
Dividends—Class A ($.3775 per share)	—	—	—	—	—	(4,886)	—
—Class B ($.33 per share)	—	—	—	—	—	(425)	—
Foreign currency translation adjustments	—	—	—	—	—	—	47
Conversions of common shares	37	—	(37)	—	—	—	—
Repurchase of common shares	(1,084)	(11)	—	—	(2,971)	(11,977)	—
Balance — December 31, 1994	**12,234**	**$122**	**1,268**	**$13**	**$ —**	**$158,933**	**$(254)**

See notes to consolidated financial statements.

consolidated statements of cash flows

OshKosh B'Gosh, Inc. and Subsidiaries

(Dollars in thousands)

	Year ended December 31,		
	1994	1993	1992
Cash flows from operating activities			
Net income	$ 7,039	$ 4,523	$15,135
Adjustments to reconcile net income to net cash provided by operating activities:			
Depreciation and amortization	10,692	9,233	8,375
(Gain) loss on disposal of assets	(185)	63	85
Minority interest in loss of consolidated subsidiary	—	—	(108)
Provision for deferred income taxes	(965)	(5,537)	35
Pension expense, net of contributions	979	1,852	1,753
Cumulative effect of accounting change	—	—	1,001
Restructuring	—	10,836	(2,800)
Changes in operating assets and liabilities:			
Accounts receivable	(4,380)	4,948	(643)
Inventories	6,083	(7,247)	1,478
Prepaid expenses and other current assets	1,300	(1,624)	(252)
Accounts payable	(284)	(1,376)	(2,522)
Accrued liabilities	1,863	5,940	1,313
Net cash provided by operating activities	22,142	21,611	22,850
Cash flows from investing activities			
Additions to property, plant and equipment	(9,914)	(8,990)	(12,563)
Proceeds from disposal of assets	1,425	1,159	625
Investments in subsidiaries	—	—	(900)
Additions to other assets	(186)	(1,783)	(1,602)
Net cash used in investing activities	(8,675)	(9,614)	(14,440)
Cash flows from financing activities			
Proceeds from long-term borrowings	—	—	7,000
Payments of long-term debt	(536)	(7,896)	(1,270)
Dividends paid	(5,311)	(7,377)	(7,362)
Repurchase of common stock	(14,959)	—	—
Net cash used in financing activities	(20,806)	(15,273)	(1,632)
Net increase (decrease) in cash and cash equivalents	(7,339)	(3,276)	6,778
Cash and cash equivalents at beginning of year	17,853	21,129	14,351
Cash and cash equivalents at end of year	$10,514	$ 17,853	$21,129
Supplementary disclosures			
Cash paid for interest	$ 638	$ 1,030	$ 823
Cash paid for income taxes	$ 3,937	$ 12,194	$ 9,877

See notes to consolidated financial statements.

29

▼▼▼▼▼▼▼▼▼▼▼▼▼▼▼▼▼▼▼

notes to consolidated financial statements
OshKosh B'Gosh, Inc. and Subsidiaries
(Dollars in thousands, except share and per share amounts)

Note 1. Significant accounting policies

Business—OshKosh B'Gosh, Inc. and its wholly-owned subsidiaries (the Company) are engaged primarily in the design, manufacture and marketing of apparel to wholesale customers and through Company owned retail stores.

Principles of consolidation—The consolidated financial statements include the accounts of all wholly-owned subsidiaries. All significant intercompany accounts and transactions have been eliminated in consolidation.

Cash equivalents—Cash equivalents consist of highly liquid debt instruments such as money market accounts and commercial paper with original maturities of three months or less. The Company's policy is to invest cash in conservative instruments as part of its cash management program and to evaluate the credit exposure of any investment. Cash and cash equivalents are stated at cost, which approximates market value.

Inventories—Inventories are stated at the lower of cost or market. Inventories stated on the last-in, first-out (LIFO) basis represent 95.7% of total 1994 and 90.6% of total 1993 inventories. Remaining inventories are valued using the first-in, first-out (FIFO) method.

Property, plant and equipment—Property, plant and equipment are carried at cost. Depreciation and amortization for financial reporting purposes is calculated using the straight line method based on the following useful lives:

	Years
Land improvements	10 to 15
Buildings	10 to 40
Leasehold improvements	5 to 10
Machinery and equipment	5 to 10

Income taxes—Effective January 1, 1992, the Company accounts for income taxes under the provisions of Statement of Financial Accounting Standards (SFAS) No. 109, "Accounting for Income Taxes." This Statement requires recognition of deferred tax assets and liabilities for all temporary differences between the financial reporting and income tax basis of the Company's assets and liabilities. The effect of this accounting change at January 1, 1992 was not material.

Foreign currency translation—The functional currency for certain foreign subsidiaries is the local currency. Accordingly, assets and liabilities are translated at year end exchange rates, and income statement items are translated at average exchange rates prevailing during the year. Such translation adjustments are recorded as a separate component of shareholders' equity.

Revenue recognition—Revenue within wholesale operations is recognized at the time merchandise is shipped to customers. Retail store revenues are recognized at the time of sale.

Income per common share—Income per common share amounts are computed by dividing income by the weighted average number of shares of common stock outstanding. There are no common stock equivalents.

Advertising—Advertising costs are expensed as incurred and totaled $9,858, $11,209, and $10,180 in 1994, 1993, and 1992, respectively.

Note 2. Restructuring

During 1993, the Company recorded a pretax restructuring charge of $10,836. The restructuring charge included approximately $3,300 for facility closings, write-down of the related assets and severance costs pertaining to work force reductions. The restructuring charge also reflected the Company's decision to market its Trader Kids line of children's apparel under the new name Genuine Kids and the resulting costs of the Company's decision not to renew its Boston Trader license arrangement beyond 1994, as well as expenses to consolidate its retail operations. Accordingly, the restructuring charge included approximately $7,500 for write-off of unamortized trademark rights and expenses related to consolidating the Company's retail operations. Restructuring costs (net of income tax benefit) reduced net income by $7,100 ($.49 per share) in 1993.

During 1994, the Company implemented its restructuring plan. The Company closed its McKenzie, Tennessee facility, and announced plans to close its Dover, Tennessee facility, which was completed in early 1995. The Company was able to sell both operating facilities, and reached satisfactory agreements with all affected work force concerning severance arrangements. The Company also began to market a portion of its children's wear line under the Genuine Kids label, discontinuing the Trader Kids line of children's apparel. The Company also successfully consolidated the operations of its retail business into its Oshkosh office. As of December 31, 1994, the Company estimates that remaining restructuring costs are sufficiently provided for in the residual restructuring liability. Remaining costs include charges for facility closings, including disposal of the real estate and severance costs pertaining to work force reductions. This plan should be substantially completed in early 1995.

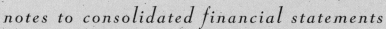

notes to consolidated financial statements

OshKosh B'Gosh, Inc. and Subsidiaries

(Dollars in thousands, except share and per share amounts)

During 1992, the Company reduced its estimate of the Absorba line restructuring costs originally recorded in 1991 by $2,800, due to the efficient and orderly wind down of operations and favorable settlement of lease obligations. This adjustment to restructuring costs (net of income taxes) increased 1992 net income by $1,800 ($.12 per share).

Note 3. Inventories

A summary of inventories follows:

	December 31, 1994	1993
Finished goods	$75,187	$82,737
Work in process	7,410	5,008
Raw materials	11,319	12,254
Total	$93,916	$99,999

The replacement cost of inventory exceeds the above LIFO costs by $16,122 and $14,716 at December 31, 1994 and 1993, respectively.

Note 4. Property, plant and equipment

A summary of property, plant and equipment follows:

	December 31, 1994	1993
Land and improvements	$ 4,139	$ 4,172
Buildings	37,442	37,640
Leasehold improvements	7,862	5,268
Machinery and equipment	70,498	67,026
Construction in progress	9	291
Total	119,950	114,397
Less: accumulated depreciation and amortization	50,121	42,642
Property, plant and equipment, net	$ 69,829	$ 71,755

Depreciation and amortization expense on property, plant and equipment for the years ended December 31, 1994, 1993, and 1992 amounted to approximately $9,972, $8,425, and $7,909, respectively.

Note 5. Lines of credit

In June 1994, the Company entered into a credit agreement with a number of banks which provides a $60,000 three year revolving credit facility and a $40,000 revocable demand line of credit for cash borrowings, issuance of commercial paper, and letters of credit. The agreement expires in June 1997.

Under the terms of the agreement, interest rates are determined at the time of borrowing and are based on London Interbank Offered Rates plus .625% or the prime rate. Commitment fees of .125% are required on the $100,000 credit facilities. The Company is required to maintain certain financial ratios in connection with this agreement.

The Company also has a $12,500 unsecured credit facility available at December 31, 1994 for issuance of letters of credit.

There were no outstanding borrowings against these credit arrangements at December 31, 1994. Letters of credit of approximately $26,150 were outstanding at December 31, 1994, with $23,774 of the unused revocable demand line of credit available for borrowing.

Note 6. Accrued liabilities

A summary of accrued liabilities follows:

	December 31, 1994	1993
Compensation	$ 8,491	$ 4,701
Group health insurance	—	1,700
Worker's compensation	10,800	8,600
Income taxes	1,729	640
Restructuring costs	2,381	8,186
Other	6,767	5,978
Total	$30,168	$29,805

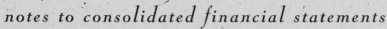

notes to consolidated financial statements
OshKosh B'Gosh, Inc. and Subsidiaries

(Dollars in thousands, except share and per share amounts)

Note 7. Long-term debt

The Company's long-term debt is summarized as follows:

	December 31, 1994	1993
Obligation under industrial development revenue bonds	$200	$ 666
Other mortgage notes and loans with interest at varying rates	557	627
Total	757	1,293
Less current maturities	240	536
Total long-term debt	$517	$ 757

The final payment on the industrial development revenue bond is due October 1, 1995. The interest rate on the bond is approximately 80% of prime rate (prime rate was 8.5% at December 31, 1994).

Annual total maturities of principal on long-term debt are as follows:

Year ending December 31,	
1995	$240
1996	42
1997	43
1998	45
1999	47
Thereafter	340
Total	$757

Note 8. Leases

The Company leases certain property and equipment including retail sales facilities and regional sales offices under operating leases. Certain leases provide the Company with renewal options. Leases for retail sales facilities provide for minimum rentals plus contingent rentals based on sales volume.

Minimum future rental payments under noncancellable operating leases are as follows:

Year ending December 31,	
1995	$10,202
1996	9,148
1997	8,452
1998	7,608
1999	6,151
Thereafter	17,034
Total minimum lease payments	$58,595

Total rent expense charged to operations for all operating leases is as follows:

	Year Ended December 31, 1994	1993	1992
Minimum rentals	$11,139	$7,718	$5,921
Contingent rentals	196	167	179
Total rent expense	$11,335	$7,885	$6,100

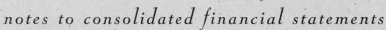

notes to consolidated financial statements

OshKosh B'Gosh, Inc. and Subsidiaries

(Dollars in thousands, except share and per share amounts)

Note 9. Income taxes

Income tax expense (credit) is comprised of the following:

| | Year Ended December 31, | | |
	1994	1993	1992
Current:			
Federal	$ 5,653	$ 8,571	$ 8,155
State and local	1,231	1,735	1,800
	6,884	10,306	9,955
Deferred	(965)	(5,537)	435
Total	$ 5,919	$ 4,769	$10,390

The components of the Company's deferred tax asset and deferred tax liability include:

| | December 31, | |
| | 1994 | 1993 |
	[Assets (Liabilities)]	
Current deferred taxes		
Accounts receivable allowances	$ 1,402	$ 1,272
Inventory valuation	2,835	2,129
Accrued liabilities	5,994	3,714
Restructuring costs	834	3,204
Other	445	397
Total net current deferred tax asset	$11,510	$10,716
Non-current deferred taxes		
Depreciation	$(8,497)	$(8,266)
Deferred employee benefits	5,234	4,419
Trademark	394	807
Foreign loss carryforwards	2,418	1,807
Valuation allowance	(2,418)	(1,807)
Total net long-term deferred tax liability	$(2,869)	$(3,040)

For financial reporting purposes, income before income taxes and cumulative effect of accounting change includes the following components:

| | Year Ended December 31, | | |
	1994	1993	1992
Pretax income (loss):			
United States	$14,319	$11,704	$27,574
Foreign	(1,361)	(2,412)	(1,448)
Total	$12,958	$ 9,292	$26,126

A reconciliation of the federal statutory income tax rate to the effective tax rates reflected in the consolidated statements of income follows:

| | Year Ended December 31, | | |
	1994	1993	1992
Federal statutory tax rate	35.0%	35.0%	34.0%
Differences resulting from:			
State and local income taxes, net of federal income tax benefit	4.5	4.1	4.2
Foreign losses with no tax benefit	3.7	9.1	1.9
Other	2.5	3.1	(.3)
Total	45.7%	51.3%	39.8%

Note 10. Retirement plans

The Company has defined contribution and defined benefit pension plans covering substantially all employees. Charges to operations by the Company for these pension plans totaled $4,309, $4,621, and $4,477 for 1994, 1993 and 1992, respectively.

▼▼▼▼▼▼▼▼▼▼▼▼▼▼▼▼

notes to consolidated financial statements

OshKosh B'Gosh, Inc. and Subsidiaries

(Dollars in thousands, except share and per share amounts)

Defined benefit pension plans—The Company sponsors several qualified defined benefit pension plans covering certain hourly and salaried employees. In addition, the Company maintains a supplemental unfunded salaried pension plan to provide those benefits otherwise due employees under the salaried plan's benefit formulas, but which are in excess of benefits permitted by the Internal Revenue Service.

The benefits provided are based primarily on years of service and average compensation. The pension plans' assets are comprised primarily of listed securities, bonds, treasury securities, commingled equity and fixed income investment funds and cash equivalents. Plan assets included 7,000 shares of OshKosh B'Gosh, Inc. Class A common stock at December 31, 1993 and 9,500 and 5,000 shares of OshKosh B'Gosh, Inc. Class B common stock at December 31, 1994 and 1993, respectively, with a total market value of approximately $128 and $236 at December 31, 1994 and 1993, respectively.

The Company's funding policy for qualified plans is to contribute amounts which are actuarially determined to provide the plans with sufficient assets to meet future benefit payment requirements consistent with the funding requirements of federal laws and regulations.

The actuarial computations utilized the following assumptions:

	December 31,		
	1994	1993	1992
Discount rate	7.5%	7.0%	7.0-7.5%
Expected long-term rate of return on assets	8.0%	7.0%	7.5-8.0%
Rates of increase in compensation levels	0-4.5%	0-4.5%	0-5.5%

Net periodic pension cost was comprised of:

	December 31,		
	1994	1993	1992
Service cost — benefits earned during the period	$2,212	$2,318	$2,309
Interest cost on projected benefit obligations	1,888	1,808	1,601
Actual return on plan assets	(1,118)	(1,708)	(1,037)
Net amortization and deferral	552	1,259	636
Net periodic pension cost	$3,534	$3,677	$3,509

The following table sets forth the funded status of the Company's defined benefit plans and the amount recognized in the Company's consolidated balance sheets. The funded status of plans with assets exceeding the accumulated benefit obligation (ABO) is segregated by column from that of plans with the ABO exceeding assets.

	December 31,			
	1994		1993	
	Assets Exceed ABO	ABO Exceeds Assets	Assets Exceed ABO	ABO Exceeds Assets
Actuarial present value of benefit obligations:				
Vested benefits	$ 9,365	$ 6,599	$ 9,051	$ 6,308
Nonvested benefits	916	313	1,604	449
Total accumulated benefit obligation	$10,281	$ 6,912	$10,655	$ 6,757
Projected benefit obligation	$19,334	$ 7,244	$22,299	$ 6,835
Plan net assets at fair value	12,451	2,980	12,070	2,777
Projected benefit obligation in excess of plan net assets	(6,883)	(4,264)	(10,229)	(4,058)
Unamortized transition asset	(1,382)	(20)	(1,535)	(23)
Unrecognized prior service cost	2,586	3,022	2,821	2,867
Unrecognized net (gain) loss	(604)	(679)	3,546	(592)
Adjustment to recognize minimum liability	—	(2,000)	—	(2,200)
Accrued pension liability at December 31	$ (6,283)	$(3,941)	$ (5,397)	$(4,006)

Defined contribution plan—The Company maintains a defined contribution retirement plan covering certain salaried employees. Annual contributions are discretionary and are determined by the Company's Executive Committee. Charges to operations by the Company for contributions under this plan totaled $531, $565 and $658 for 1994, 1993 and 1992, respectively.

The Company also has a supplemental retirement program for designated employees. Annual provisions to this unfunded plan are discretionary and are determined by the Company's Executive Committee. Charges to operations by the Company for additions to this plan totaled $244, $379 and $310 for 1994, 1993 and 1992, respectively.

Deferred employee benefit plans—The Company has deferred compensation and supplemental retirement arrangements with certain key officers.

34

▲▲▲▲▲▲▲▲▲▲▲▲▲▲▲▲

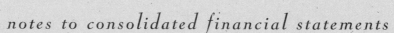

notes to consolidated financial statements
OshKosh B'Gosh, Inc. and Subsidiaries

(Dollars in thousands, except share and per share amounts)

Postretirement health and life insurance plan — The Company sponsors an unfunded defined benefit postretirement health insurance plan that covers eligible salaried employees. Life insurance benefits are provided under the plan to qualifying retired employees. The postretirement health insurance plan is offered, on a shared cost basis, only to employees electing early retirement. This coverage ceases when the employee reaches age 65 and becomes eligible for Medicare. Retiree contributions are adjusted periodically.

In 1992, the Company adopted the provisions of SFAS No. 106, "Employers' Accounting for Postretirement Benefits Other Than Pensions." In applying this pronouncement, the Company elected to immediately recognize the accumulated postretirement benefit obligation as of the beginning of 1992 of approximately $1 million in the first quarter of 1992 as a change in accounting principle. The charge, net of an income tax benefit of $400, was $601 or $.04 per share.

The following table sets forth the funded status of the plan and the postretirement benefit cost recognized in the Company's consolidated balance sheets:

	December 31,	
	1994	1993
Accumulated postretirement benefit obligation:		
Retirees	$ 159	$ 119
Fully eligible active plan participants	169	216
Other active plan participants	523	670
	851	1,005
Plan assets	—	—
Unrecognized net gain	497	281
Accrued postretirement benefit cost	$1,348	$1,286

Net periodic postretirement benefit cost was comprised of:

	Year Ended December 31,		
	1994	1993	1992
Service cost-benefits attributed to employee service during the year	$ 67	$ 98	$119
Interest cost on accumulated postretirement benefit obligation	53	61	75
Net amortization and deferral	(38)	(18)	—
Net periodic postretirement benefit cost	$ 82	$141	$194

The discount rate used in determining the accumulated postretirement benefit obligation was 7% in 1994 and 1993. The assumed health care cost trend rate used in measuring the accumulated postretirement benefit obligation was 12%, declining gradually to 6% by 2012 and then declining further to an ultimate rate of 4% by 2022.

The health care cost trend rate assumption has a significant impact on the amounts reported. Increasing the assumed health care cost trend rate by one percentage point would increase the accumulated postretirement benefit obligation at December 31, 1994 by approximately $108 and the aggregate of the service and interest cost components of net periodic postretirement benefit cost for 1994 by approximately $13.

Note 11. Common stock

In May 1993, shareholders of the Company approved a stock conversion plan whereby shares of Class B common stock may be converted to an equal number of Class A common shares.

The Company's common stock authorization provides that dividends be paid on both the Class A common stock and Class B common stock at any time that dividends are paid on either. Whenever dividends (other than dividends of Company stock) are paid on the common stock, each share of Class A common stock is entitled to receive 115% of the dividend paid on each share of Class B common stock.

The Class A common stock shareholders are entitled to receive a liquidation preference of $7.50 per share before any payment or distribution to holders of the Class B common stock. Thereafter, holders of the Class B common stock are entitled to receive $7.50 per share before any further payment or distribution to holders of the Class A common stock. Thereafter, holders of the Class A common stock and Class B common stock share on a pro-rata basis in all payments or distributions upon liquidation, dissolution or winding up of the Company.

Note 12. Business and credit concentrations

The Company provides credit, in the normal course of business, to department and specialty stores. The Company performs ongoing credit evaluations of its customers and maintains allowances for potential credit losses.

The Company's customers are not concentrated in any specific geographic region. In 1993, sales to a customer, as a percentage of total sales, amounted to approximately 10%. In 1992, sales to two customers, as a percentage of total sales, amounted to approximately 12% each.

report of Ernst & Young LLP, independent auditors
OshKosh B'Gosh, Inc. and Subsidiaries

The Board of Directors
OshKosh B'Gosh, Inc. and Subsidiaries

We have audited the accompanying consolidated balance sheets of OshKosh B'Gosh, Inc. and subsidiaries (the Company) as of December 31, 1994 and 1993, and the related consolidated statements of income, changes in shareholders' equity and cash flows for the years then ended. These financial statements are the responsibility of the Company's management. Our responsibility is to express an opinion on these financial statements based on our audits. The financial statements of the Company for the year ended December 31, 1992 were audited by other auditors whose report, dated February 15, 1993, expressed an unqualified opinion on those statements.

We conducted our audits in accordance with generally accepted auditing standards. Those standards require that we plan and perform the audit to obtain reasonable assurance about whether the financial statements are free of material misstatement. An audit includes examining, on a test basis, evidence supporting the amounts and disclosures in the financial statements. An audit also includes assessing the accounting principles used and significant estimates made by management, as well as evaluating the overall financial statement presentation. We believe that our audits provide a reasonable basis for our opinion.

In our opinion, the 1994 and 1993 financial statements referred to above present fairly, in all material respects, the consolidated financial position of the Company at December 31, 1994 and 1993, and the consolidated results of its operations and its cash flows for the years then ended in conformity with generally accepted accounting principles.

As discussed in Notes 1 and 10 to the consolidated financial statements, effective January 1, 1992, the Company changed its method of accounting for income taxes and nonpension postretirement benefits.

Ernst & Young LLP

Milwaukee, Wisconsin
February 6, 1995

shareholder information

Form 10K

Certain parts of the information in this report along with additional data concerning the Company is included in OshKosh B'Gosh, Inc.'s Annual Report on Form 10K which is filed with the Securities and Exchange Commission. A copy of this report may be obtained upon written request to the VP-Finance/Treasurer & CFO, OshKosh B'Gosh, Inc., P.O. Box 300, Oshkosh, Wisconsin 54902.

Auditors
Ernst & Young LLP
111 East Kilbourn Avenue
Milwaukee, Wisconsin 53202

General Counsel
Quarles & Brady
411 East Wisconsin Avenue
Milwaukee, Wisconsin 53202

Transfer Agent and Registrar
Harris Trust and Savings Bank
111 West Monroe
P.O. Box 755
Chicago, Illinois 60690

Annual Meeting
10:00 a.m., May 5, 1995
Pioneer Inn
1000 Pioneer Drive
Oshkosh, Wisconsin 54901

Common Stock
Listed on the NASDAQ
National Market System
Symbol GOSHA and GOSHB

Regional Sales Offices
Empire State Building
New York, New York

The Apparel Mart
Dallas, Texas

California Apparel Mart
Los Angeles, California

Corporate Offices
112 Otter Avenue
Oshkosh, Wisconsin 54901
Telephone: (414) 231-8800

WENDY'S INTERNATIONAL, INC.

AT TWENTY-FIVE, WE'RE A

HIGHLY VALUED BRAND,

WENDY'S INTERNATIONAL, INC.

FINANCIALLY STRONG,

1994 SHAREHOLDER REPORT

WITH ENORMOUS

GROWTH POTENTIAL!

Wendy's can be found on the Internet at http:\\www.wendys.com

Glossary of Terms

AVERAGE CHECK: The average spent per transaction at a Wendy's restaurant (might be for more than one person). The average check in 1994 was about $4.10.

BRAND DEVELOPMENT INDEX (BDI): Measure of a chain's market penetration relative to its average U.S. penetration. Indices above 100 indicate above average market penetration. Indices below 100 indicate below average penetration. Indices equal to 100 indicate parity between market and average U.S. penetration levels.

BRAND EQUITY: Brand equity is the value attributed to a specific name or brand (i.e. Wendy's) that embodies that which the brand has come to symbolize: quality, fresh, made-to-order, etc.

DAYPART: The business day is divided into primarily four dayparts: lunch (11 a.m.-2 p.m.), afternoon snack (2 p.m.-4 p.m.), dinner (4 p.m.-8 p.m.) and p.m. snack (8 p.m.-close). Breakfast is served in only about 200 Wendy's restaurants.

MARKET PENETRATION: Measure of the number of Wendy's in a market versus the population of a market.

MENU PRICING: The actual retail price of products as listed on the menu board in a restaurant.

OFF-PREMISES, ON-PREMISES: Product ordered and eaten inside the restaurant is termed on-premises. Off-premises is both pick-up window and carry-out orders which are eaten off the restaurant property.

PRODUCT MIX: The relative measure of different products sold at any one time to the total products sold.

QUICK-SERVICE RESTAURANT BUSINESS: The U.S. quick-service restaurant industry totaled $93.2 billion in 1994. The major chain restaurants in the industry are Wendy's, McDonald's, Burger King, Hardee's and PepsiCo's group: Pizza Hut, Taco Bell and KFC.

REMODEL: Updating and upgrading primarily the appearance of the restaurant, but may also include equipment changes, kitchen configuration, etc.

RETAIL SALES: Primarily the sales from the company owned and operated restaurants, but also includes bun sales from Wendy's bakery to 1,136 franchised restaurants.

RESTAURANT OPERATING PROFIT MARGIN: Retail sales less cost of sales (COS) and company restaurant operating costs (CROC) divided by retail sales.

RETROFIT: An extensive restaurant enhancement package that includes the addition of a register, a second drive-thru window and the new outdoor menu board order digital readout.

RETURN ON AVERAGE ASSETS: ROA is calculated by dividing income before income taxes and interest charges by the quarterly average of the assets.

RETURN ON AVERAGE EQUITY: ROE is calculated by dividing net income by the quarterly average equity.

ROYALTY: The fee a franchisee agrees to pay Wendy's on an ongoing basis. The current royalty fee is generally 4% of gross sales.

SUPER VALUE MENU: This permanent menu offering encompasses nine items each priced at 99 cents. In most cases this is the Junior Bacon Cheeseburger, Garden Salad, baked potato, chili, Biggie Fry, Biggie Drink, Frosty, Junior Cheeseburger Deluxe, Caesar Salad.

SYSTEMWIDE SALES: The total of all sales of both company-operated and franchised restaurants. In 1994 systemwide sales were $4.2 billion.

TECHNICAL ASSISTANCE FEE: The one-time fee paid by a franchisee upon opening a restaurant (currently $25,000).

TURNOVER: A measure of the stability of the workforce. The number of people hired for a restaurant per year divided by the number of people currently employed per store.

WeShare: WeShare is Wendy's broad stock option program encompassing all full-time employees. WeShare was established to bring a shareholder's perspective to all employees.

WENDY'S NATIONAL ADVERTISING PROGRAM (WNAP): WNAP was established to collect and administer funds contributed by the company and franchisees for national advertising. These contributions currently total 2.5% of net sales. (Another 1.5% is spent on local advertising.)

MANAGEMENT'S REVIEW AND OUTLOOK

RESULTS OF OPERATIONS

1994 Overview

Fully diluted earnings per share increased 20% to a record $.91 for the year ending January 1, 1995, from $.76 in 1993. The company also reported record net income of $97.2 million for 1994, a 23% increase over the $79.3 million recorded for 1993.

Systemwide restaurant sales, or sales from all company and franchised restaurants, reached $4.2 billion in 1994, the company's highest level ever. Company and franchised restaurants both attained record average net sales per restaurant. Average net sales per domestic company-operated restaurant increased to $1,001,000 in 1994, the first time the company achieved million dollar average sales per restaurant.

Wendy's restaurant operating margin continued to show improvement, reaching 15.4% for 1994 versus 14.5% for 1993 and 13.8% for 1992. The margin has increased each year since 1989. This reflects the continuing emphasis on control of restaurant operating costs, expanding average sales per restaurant and, in 1994, favorable purchase prices of key food items.

New restaurants opened systemwide totaled 298 in 1994, an increase of 47 more restaurants than the number opened in 1993, and the most restaurants opened in the last eight years. There were also 65 restaurants under construction at year-end. The company typically experiences higher average net sales in newly opened restaurants.

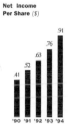

Net Income Per Share ($)

'90 '91 '92 '93 '94
.41 .52 .63 .76 .91

Retail Sales

Total company retail sales were $1.3 billion in 1994 compared with $1.2 billion in 1993, a 4.8% increase. This increase reflected a 2.4% increase in average domestic net restaurant sales and an additional 26 average domestic restaurants open.

The improvement in average domestic net sales was a result of solid restaurant operations, effective marketing campaigns featuring both existing and new products, and a value menu strategy combined with the quality and variety of offerings. This improvement was tempered by the intense competition in the quick-service restaurant industry, and to a lesser extent adverse weather conditions at the start of the year. The average number of transactions increased approximately 1.2% in 1994 compared with a 4.2% increase in 1993. Domestic selling prices for the company remained unchanged for 1994 compared with a decrease of approximately .4% in 1993. Selling prices for 1994 remain below 1990 levels as the company continued to emphasize its value strategy.

The following chart reflects average net sales per domestic restaurant for the last three years:

	1994	1993	1992
Company	$1,001,000	$978,000	$924,000
Franchise	$ 982,000	$960,000	$907,000
Total domestic	$ 988,000	$966,000	$912,000

Average net sales per domestic company restaurant for 1994 increased 2.4% over 1993 and 8.3% over 1992. As 1992 was a 53-week fiscal year, these amounts have been adjusted to a comparable 52-week year basis.

Restaurant Operating Costs and Expenses

Cost of sales declined to 58.3% of retail sales in 1994 from 58.9% in 1993. Domestic food costs as a percent of domestic retail sales decreased to 29.3% in 1994 from 30.2% in 1993. This reflects favorable purchase prices for key products such as beef, chicken, and produce.

Domestic restaurant labor costs as a percent of domestic retail sales were 24.8% in 1994 compared with 24.5% in 1993. The higher percentage in 1994 reflects restaurant labor wage rate increases of approximately 4% partially offset by the 2.4% increase in average domestic net sales. In addition, selected markets increased restaurant management staffing levels to provide better customer service. The company controls labor hours by adherence to its labor guidelines.

Total company restaurant operating costs were $330.5 million in 1994 versus $319.4 million in 1993, or 26.3% and 26.6% of retail sales in 1994 and 1993, respectively. Improvement as a percent of retail sales was seen in advertising, utilities, and insurance expenses.

COMPANY RESTAURANT OPERATING PROFIT MARGIN

(Dollars in millions)	1994 $	1994 % of Sales	1993 $	1993 % of Sales	1992 $	1992 % of Sales
Retail sales	$1,256.2	100.0%	$1,198.8	100.0%	$1,123.9	100.0%
Cost of sales	731.7	58.3	705.7	58.9	662.9	59.0
Company restaurant operating costs	330.5	26.3	319.4	26.6	306.4	27.2
	1,062.2	84.6	1,025.1	85.5	969.3	86.2
Company restaurant operating profit margin	$ 194.0	15.4%	$ 173.7	14.5%	$ 154.6	13.8%

Royalties

Royalty income, before reserves, was $116.4 million for the year 1994 versus $106.3 million for 1993, a 9.4% increase. Reserves against royalties for the current year amounted to $2.8 million compared with $1.7 million for 1993.

Average net sales per domestic franchise restaurant increased to $982,000 in 1994 from $960,000 in 1993, an increase of 2.3%. Royalties also increased from domestic and international franchise restaurant openings.

Management reviews reserves on a regular basis and believes the company has adequate levels for royalty and other franchise-related receivables and contingencies. When the outlook changes for reserve levels established in prior years, they are modified accordingly and the impact is reflected in general and administrative expenses, as discussed below.

Other Revenues

Pretax gains on restaurants sold to franchisees amounted to $11.6 million for 1994 compared with $8.1 million in 1993. The company sold 49 restaurants to franchisees during 1994 versus 86 restaurants in 1993. Certain dispositions have resulted in land and buildings being retained by the company and leased to franchisees. This source of rental income to the company increased $1.4 million over 1993 for a total of $11.6 million in rental income for 1994. In both years, franchisees exercised options to purchase real estate originally retained by the company and leased to the franchisee. In 1994, 32 properties were sold pursuant to options exercised by franchisees for a $2.4 million gain and in the prior year 17 properties were sold for a $780,000 gain.

The company also has various write-offs and retirements of assets each year which reduce other revenues. These result from the continuing program of remodeling restaurants, monitoring restaurant performance for potential relocations or closings, and disposing of unnecessary assets. Such write-offs totaled $4.5 million in 1994 and $3.2 million in 1993, partly offsetting gains from franchising restaurants. Also, a reserve of $2.8 million was provided in 1993 for 12 underperforming restaurants which were closed in January 1994. This reflected amounts for lease buy outs, the write down of assets to realizable value, and other related expenses.

General and Administrative Expenses

General and administrative expenses were $108.3 million or 7.7% of revenues for the year 1994 compared with $102.2 million or 7.7% for 1993. Salaries and related benefits, the largest component of general and administrative expenses, increased $6.2 million, primarily reflecting annual merit-based employee compensation increases and minimal administrative staff additions to support new restaurant development. Insurance expense declined $3.1 million in 1994 as the prior year included an additional $4.0 million accrual to reflect trends in year-end 1993's workers' compensation and general liability claims.

As a result of continuing improvement in the financial strength of the franchise community, net reserve reversals reduced expenses by $2.1 million in 1994 and $2.2 million in 1993.

Interest

Net interest expense decreased in 1994 primarily as a result of lower interest expense of $18.7 million in 1994 compared with $21.6 million in 1993. This was due to the early retirement of $30 million of debt in late 1993. Interest income was lower at $8.8 million for 1994 versus $9.8 million for 1993 due to reduced earnings on short-term investments.

Income Taxes

The effective income tax rate for 1994 was 35% compared with 31.4% in 1993. In 1993, the company generated a Canadian tax benefit of $6.0 million. This was a result of regionalizing Canadian operations which produced overall administrative and operational efficiencies and more closely aligned the organization to domestic operations.

Comparison of 1993 to 1992

Net income for the year ended January 2, 1994, was $79.3 million, a 23% increase over the $64.7 million reported for 1992. Fully diluted earnings per share was $.76 in 1993 compared with $.63 for 1992.

Total company retail sales increased 6.7% in 1993 to $1.2 billion compared with $1.1 billion in 1992. This increase reflected a 5.8% increase in average domestic net restaurant sales and an additional 32 average domestic restaurants open. Total retail sales for 1993 reflected one week's fewer sales as 1992 was a 53-week fiscal year.

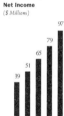

Net Income
($ Millions)

97
79
65
51
39

'90 '91 '92 '93 '94

The improvement in average domestic net sales was a result of the company's emphasis on restaurant operations, highly effective marketing campaigns of both existing and new products, and the value menu strategy, such as Super Value Menu, Combo Meals, and Kids' Meals. The average number of transactions increased approximately 4.2% in 1993. Domestic selling prices for the company were down approximately .4% in 1993 following a 1.9% decrease in 1992.

Total company cost of sales as a percent of retail sales decreased slightly to 58.9% in 1993 from 59.0% in 1992. Domestic food costs as a percent of domestic retail sales increased to 30.2% in 1993 from 29.7% in 1992. This reflected increases primarily in beef, chicken, and lettuce prices coinciding with reductions in selling prices.

Domestic labor costs as a percent of domestic retail sales were 24.5% in 1993 compared with 24.9% in 1992.

This improvement reflected efforts to adhere to the company's labor guidelines along with the impact from higher average domestic net restaurant sales offset by restaurant labor wage rate increases of approximately 2% in 1993.

Total company restaurant operating costs were $319.4 million or 26.6% of retail sales for 1993. This compared with costs in 1992 of $306.4 million or 27.2% of retail sales. A significant portion of this percentage improvement resulted from the relatively fixed nature of some of the cost components, while average sales levels increased. In addition, group insurance and coupon expenses declined as a percent of sales.

Royalty income, before reserves, was $106.3 million for the year ended January 2, 1994, and $97.6 million for the year ended January 3, 1993, or a 9.0% increase. Royalty reserves amounted to $1.7 million in 1993 compared with $1.2 million in 1992. Average net sales per domestic franchise restaurant increased to $960,000 in 1993 from $907,000 in 1992, an increase of 5.9% on a comparable 52-week year basis. The remainder of the increase reflected royalties from additional domestic and international franchise restaurants.

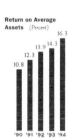

Return on Average Assets (Percent)

'90 10.8
'91 12.3
'92 13.9
'93 14.3
'94 16.3

Pretax gains on restaurant dispositions for 1993 amounted to $8.1 million compared with $7.7 million in 1992. There were 86 company restaurants sold to franchisees in 1993 versus 44 restaurants in 1992. Certain dispositions resulted in land and buildings being retained by the company and leased to franchisees. This provided a source of rental income to the company which increased $1.8 million over 1992 to $10.1 million.

A reserve of $2.8 million was provided in the fourth quarter of 1993 to reflect lease buy outs, the write down of assets to realizable value, and other related expenses to close certain underperforming restaurants. Also, $30 million of debt was retired early resulting in $672,000 of redemption expenses.

General and administrative expenses were approximately the same percent of revenues in both 1993 and 1992. In recognition of continuing improvement in the financial strength of the franchise community, net reserve reversals were $2.2 million in 1993 and 1992 reversals were $1.7 million. Insurance accruals were increased $4.0 million in 1993 to reflect trends in workers' compensation and general liability claims. Salaries and related benefits rose $7.9 million over 1992, primarily reflecting annual employee merit increases and minimal administrative staff additions to support new restaurant development.

Net interest expense decreased in 1993 primarily reflecting lower interest expense. Interest income was $9.8 million in 1993 versus $10.1 million in 1992. Interest expense was $21.6 million in 1993 compared with $22.5

million in 1992. This primarily reflected a 52-week fiscal year in 1993 versus a 53-week fiscal year in 1992, and a reduction of expense on capitalized leases.

The effective income tax rate for 1993 decreased to 31.4% from 36% in 1992. In 1993, the company regionalized its Canadian operations. This was intended to produce overall administrative and operational efficiencies and closely align the organization to domestic operations. In connection with this restructuring the company was able to generate Canadian tax benefits of $6.0 million.

FINANCIAL POSITION

Overview

Total assets increased $89.6 million or 9.0% over 1993 primarily due to additions to property and equipment for restaurant development. Cost in excess of net assets acquired, net increased $6.5 million as a result of the acquisition of a franchise. Total cash and short-term investments amounted to $134.9 million at year-end 1994 compared with $112.3 million at year-end 1993. Return on average assets was 16.3% in 1994 compared with 14.3% in 1993, the fifth consecutive year this ratio increased.

Long-term debt was reduced in 1994 as $50 million was reclassed to current portion debt for the 12⅛% Notes which are due in April of 1995. This caused the long-term debt to equity ratio to drop to 21% for year-end 1994, compared with 33% at year-end 1993, and 44% at year-end 1992.

Shareholders' equity per share reached $6.70 at January 1, 1995, an increase of 12.4%. At year-end 1994, shareholders' equity was equal to 63% of total assets. The company's return on average equity was 15.2% in 1994 compared with 14.2% in 1993. This is the eighth consecutive year return on average equity has increased.

The following chart shows year-end reserve balances related to royalty receivables and other franchise-related receivables and contingencies by balance sheet category:

(In millions)	JANUARY 1, 1995	JANUARY 2, 1994
Accounts receivable, net	$4.0	$5.2
Notes receivable, net	.8	.4
Other assets	2.3	1.9
Accrued expenses, other	.6	.8
	$7.7	$8.3

Cash Flow

Cash provided by operating activities was $165.7 million in 1994, $146.7 million in 1993, and $120.5 million in 1992. Cash from operations exceeded capital expenditures by $24.2 million in 1994 and $30.1 million in 1993. Additionally in 1994, cash provided by operations exceeded the total of long-term obligations.

Over the last three years, cash provided by operating activities was primarily used for capital expenditures, dividend payments, debt repayments, and acquisitions of franchised restaurants. During this time, the company acquired 88 restaurants and retired early over $31 million of higher rate debt and $33 million in convertible subordinated debentures. In April of 1995, the company will retire $50 million of 12⅛% Notes.

Cash proceeds of $21.1 million were realized in 1994 from the sale of company restaurants to franchisees, while $17.2 million was provided in 1993 and $12.9 million in 1992.

The company invests excess cash in various short-term investments. Instruments with maturities exceeding three months are classified as short-term investments on the balance sheet. The company liquidated these investments in January 1995 in anticipation of the $50 million debt retirement and other potential cash requirements needed in early 1995. The company also invests a portion of excess cash in more liquid investments, included as cash equivalents on the balance sheet. These include state and municipal securities, Euro Time Deposits, and other securities, a portion of which are tax-exempt.

During 1994, capital expenditures amounted to $142 million. New restaurant expenditures amounted to $74 million; $38 million was spent for improvements to existing restaurants; and $30 million was spent for other additions. Current plans are to open or have under construction about 400 new Wendy's restaurants in 1995, of which approximately 120 will be company-operated. Capital expenditures could total as much as $170 million in 1995. Cash provided by operating activities, cash and investments on hand, existing revolving credit agreements, and possible asset dispositions should enable the company to meet its financial requirements through 1995. If additional cash is needed for capital expenditures, future acquisitions of restaurants from franchisees, or for other corporate purposes, the company believes it would be able to obtain additional cash through existing revolving credit agreements, new revolving credit agreements which the company believes it could execute, or through the issuance of debt securities. In December 1994, the company filed a registration statement with the United States Securities and Exchange Commission for $200 million of debt securities which could be issued for the next two years if needed.

INFLATION

Financial statements determined on a historical cost basis may not accurately reflect all the effects of changing prices on an enterprise. Several factors tend to reduce the impact of inflation for the company. Inventories approximate current market prices, there is some ability to adjust prices, and liabilities are repaid with dollars of reduced purchasing power.

INTERNATIONAL

During 1994, the company focused on assessing and strengthening current international operations. Also, a strategic plan was developed to achieve future growth. For 1995 and beyond, the company will implement these strategies for profitable and rapid expansion. Wendy's intends to open or have under construction at least 100 international restaurants in 1995, and anticipates higher levels in succeeding years. Although international growth will come primarily through franchising, the company may enter into joint venture agreements and possibly open company-operated restaurants outside of Canada. On January 1, 1995, there were 413 Wendy's restaurants operating outside the United States and in 33 countries and territories. Of these, 177 were in Canada, with 96 being operated by the company.

Canada is our largest international market, and like domestic markets, the restaurant industry is extremely competitive. The environment includes a difficult economy, adverse tax laws, and minimum wage increases. Nevertheless, 1994 was a very productive year as average net sales of company-operated restaurants increased 5.9% in local currency, following a 7.8% increase a year ago. Restaurant level profitability likewise improved once again. The regionalization of Canadian operations initiated at the end of 1993 was beneficial to the company both operationally and administratively in 1994. Combination units of Wendy's and Tim Hortons, a Canadian chain of bakery and coffee shops, has proved very successful and several more units are planned to be added in 1995.

Cash Flows – Operations and Capital Expenditures
($ Millions)

79 113 120 147 166

'90 '91 '92 '93 '94

■ CASH FLOWS – OPERATIONS
■ CAPITAL EXPENDITURES

MANAGEMENT'S OUTLOOK

The quick-service restaurant industry remains extremely competitive. The company will continue to adhere to the strategies developed in the past few years. The strategies of restaurant expansion and improvement of retail sales and restaurant profitability are key components to improved future performance. Statistics indicate that Wendy's is an underpenetrated concept relative to total market potential.

Therefore, responsible system growth will accelerate in 1995, focusing on the markets with the best potential for sales and return on investment. Each proposed site must undergo an extensive operational and financial review before being approved. The company plans on opening or having under construction 120 new company-operated restaurants and 280 new franchised restaurants in 1995. The company's expansion will be accomplished by use of cash and investments on hand, cash provided by 1995 operations, existing revolving credit agreements, new revolving credit agreements which the company believes it could execute, possible asset dispositions, and possible borrowings.

Retail sales increases along with improved restaurant profitability in existing restaurants are essential components to future growth. The company will continue to focus on restaurant cost control by use of company guidelines for food, labor, and other expenses. Continued emphasis on operational execution, new promotional and permanent menu items, local and national marketing to increase customer awareness, and restaurant remodels are all strategies aimed at growing system sales. Selling prices did not change in 1994, and any potential change in 1995 should be very modest.

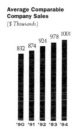

Average Comparable Company Sales
($ Thousands)

832 874 924 978 1001
'90 '91 '92 '93 '94

In cooperation with vendors, Wendy's closely monitors purchase prices while maintaining exacting quality standards for all products in each restaurant. To protect the customer, the company is committed to a program of ongoing food safety which includes quality suppliers, state-of-the-art testing, proper equipment, rigid adherence to operational procedures, and emphasis on sanitation and personal hygiene.

Cost control of administrative overhead is monitored through the use of budgets for each corporate and field department. Actual expenses are monitored by comparison to the budget and to historical results. All additions to staffing must be justified based on the contribution to the company or franchise operations support, or to restaurant development.

Wendy's will continue its strategy of acquiring restaurants from and selling restaurants to franchisees where prudent. Acquired restaurants, which may be underperforming, can be improved and then operated profitably by the company or sold to a qualified franchisee. Other restaurants may be acquired due to geographic or operational benefits to existing company-operated markets. Selling restaurants generates cash which is used for new development, acquisitions, and remodeling programs. During the last three years, the company purchased 88 franchised restaurants and sold 179 company-operated restaurants to franchisees. Underperforming restaurants, whether company or franchise operated, are monitored carefully and revitalized where economically possible or closed if necessary for the financial health of the system.

The strength and vitality of the franchise community is an essential part of the continued success of the Wendy's system. Various strategies have been developed to assist individual franchisees and the overall franchise system. The aim of these strategies is to encourage responsible new restaurant development, increase franchisees' financial health, increase royalty income, and improve royalty receivable collection rates. The company will continue to maintain appropriate reserves against franchise receivables.

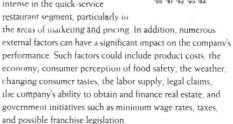

Company Restaurant Operating Profit Margin
(Percent)

12.5 13.0 13.8 14.5 15.4
'90 '91 '92 '93 '94

Competition is extremely intense in the quick-service restaurant segment, particularly in the areas of marketing and pricing. In addition, numerous external factors can have a significant impact on the company's performance. Such factors could include product costs, the economy, consumer perception of food safety, the weather, changing consumer tastes, the labor supply, legal claims, the company's ability to obtain and finance real estate, and government initiatives such as minimum wage rates, taxes, and possible franchise legislation.

DOMESTIC AND INTERNATIONAL RESTAURANTS

	SYSTEMWIDE			COMPANY			FRANCHISE		
	1994	1993	1992	1994	1993	1992	1994	1993	1992
Open at beginning of year	4,168	3,962	3,804	1,224	1,208	1,162	2,944	2,754	2,642
Opened	298	251	235	76	79	74	222	172	161
Closed	(55)	(45)	(77)	(20)	(10)	(6)	(35)	(35)	(71)
Acquisitions within the system	82	119	66	33	33	22	49	86	44
Dispositions within the system	(82)	(119)	(66)	(49)	(86)	(44)	(33)	(33)	(22)
Open at end of year	4,411	4,168	3,962	1,264	1,224	1,208	3,147	2,944	2,754

CONSOLIDATED STATEMENT OF INCOME

Fifty-two weeks ended January 1, 1995, and January 2, 1994, and fifty-three weeks ended January 3, 1993

(In thousands, except per share data)	1994	1993	1992
Revenues			
Retail sales	$1,256,192	$1,198,777	$1,123,868
Royalties	113,558	104,663	96,403
Other	28,107	16,655	18,235
	1,397,857	1,320,095	1,238,506
Costs and expenses			
Cost of sales	731,691	705,671	662,892
Company restaurant operating costs	330,480	319,367	306,356
General and administrative expenses	108,254	102,161	94,068
Depreciation and amortization of property and equipment	68,070	65,655	61,686
Interest, net	9,891	11,706	12,414
	1,248,386	1,204,560	1,137,416
Income before income taxes	149,471	115,535	101,090
Income taxes	52,315	36,268	36,392
Net income	$ 97,156	$ 79,267	$ 64,698
Primary earnings per share	$.93	$.77	$.64
Fully diluted earnings per share	$.91	$.76	$.63
Dividends per share	$.24	$.24	$.24
Primary shares	104,238	102,897	101,414
Fully diluted shares	112,368	111,245	109,650

CONSOLIDATED BALANCE SHEET

January 1, 1995, and January 2, 1994
(Dollars in thousands)

	1994	1993
Assets		
Current assets		
Cash and cash equivalents	$ 119,639	$ 71,698
Short-term investments, at market	15,292	40,647
Accounts receivable, net	28,015	27,381
Notes receivable, net	7,446	5,259
Deferred income taxes	13,067	12,244
Inventories and other	19,702	21,478
	203,161	178,707
Property and equipment, at cost		
Land	222,671	203,651
Buildings	359,503	329,023
Leasehold improvements	189,243	182,519
Restaurant equipment	335,474	289,242
Other equipment	53,265	65,197
Capital leases	63,531	64,148
	1,223,687	1,133,780
Accumulated depreciation and amortization	(457,368)	(426,496)
	766,319	707,284
Cost in excess of net assets acquired, net	30,780	24,314
Deferred income taxes	16,142	15,250
Other assets	69,690	70,931
	$1,086,092	$ 996,486
Liabilities and Shareholders' Equity		
Current liabilities		
Accounts and drafts payable	$ 69,845	$ 68,735
Accrued expenses		
Salaries and wages	22,173	16,288
Taxes	15,248	14,935
Insurance	26,037	21,345
Other	11,409	11,160
Income taxes	1,683	2,896
Deferred income taxes	3,108	2,299
Current portion of long-term obligations	57,674	5,611
	207,177	143,269
Long-term obligations		
Term debt	104,842	156,741
Capital leases	40,018	43,892
	144,860	200,633
Deferred income taxes	39,799	40,859
Other long-term liabilities	12,758	10,930
Commitments and contingencies		
Shareholders' equity		
Preferred stock, authorized: 250,000 shares		
Common stock, $.10 stated value, authorized: 200,000,000 shares		
Issued: 101,787,000 and 100,823,000 shares, respectively	10,179	10,082
Capital in excess of stated value	171,004	161,238
Retained earnings	503,712	430,866
Translation adjustments	(19)	1,347
Pension liability adjustment	(3,212)	(2,572)
	681,664	600,961
Treasury stock at cost: 29,000 shares	(166)	(166)
	681,498	600,795
	$1,086,092	$ 996,486

CONSOLIDATED STATEMENT OF CASH FLOWS

Fifty-two weeks ended January 1, 1995, and January 2, 1994, and fifty-three weeks ended January 3, 1993

(In thousands)	1994	1993	1992
Cash flows from operating activities			
Net income	$ 97,156	$ 79,267	$ 64,698
Adjustments to reconcile net income to net cash provided by operating activities			
Depreciation and amortization	73,726	68,978	63,374
Deferred income taxes	(1,910)	(6,370)	(28)
Net gain from restaurant dispositions	(11,588)	(8,140)	(7,681)
Net loss on other asset dispositions	2,123	6,466	4,424
Net reserves for receivables and other contingencies	667	(747)	(545)
Loss on early extinguishment of debt		672	23
Changes in operating assets and liabilities net of effects of acquisitions and dispositions of restaurants			
Accounts and notes receivable	(7,266)	(386)	(9,104)
Inventories and other	1,648	(4,478)	(1,801)
Accounts and drafts payable and accrued expenses	6,434	8,580	(1,458)
(Increase) decrease in other assets	(67)	(305)	2,463
Income taxes	(1,214)	(4,356)	1,700
Other changes, net	6,002	7,495	4,412
Net cash provided by operating activities	165,711	146,676	120,477
Cash flows from investing activities			
Proceeds from restaurant dispositions	21,065	17,155	12,943
Proceeds from other asset dispositions	14,302	9,710	2,018
Capital expenditures	(141,507)	(116,573)	(119,567)
Acquisition of franchises	(12,761)	(8,685)	(7,602)
Proceeds from (investment in) marketable securities	25,355	(6,387)	(19,002)
Other investing activities	(1,414)	(2,107)	(3,242)
Net cash used in investing activities	(94,960)	(106,887)	(134,452)
Cash flows from financing activities			
Proceeds from issuance of common stock	7,360	12,890	9,381
Principal payments on long-term obligations	(5,581)	(34,463)	(13,738)
Dividends paid	(24,310)	(23,826)	(23,523)
Net cash used in financing activities	(22,531)	(45,399)	(27,880)
Effect of exchange rate changes on cash	(279)	(104)	(210)
Increase (decrease) in cash and cash equivalents	47,941	(5,714)	(42,065)
Cash and cash equivalents at beginning of period	71,698	77,412	119,477
Cash and cash equivalents at end of period	$119,639	$ 71,698	$ 77,412
Supplemental disclosures of cash flow information			
Interest paid	$ 19,236	$ 21,874	$ 22,478
Interest received	8,335	8,832	10,106
Income taxes paid	52,937	41,517	32,092
Debt converted to common stock		1,510	
Capital lease obligations incurred			1,541
Acquisition of franchises			
Fair value of assets acquired, net	$ 15,859	$ 13,170	$ 7,818
Cash paid	12,761	8,685	7,602
Liabilities assumed	$ 3,098	$ 4,485	$ 216

CONSOLIDATED STATEMENT
OF SHAREHOLDERS' EQUITY

Fifty-two weeks ended January 1, 1995, and January 2, 1994, and fifty-three weeks ended January 3, 1993

(In thousands)	1994	1993	1992
Common stock at stated value			
Balance at beginning of period	$ 10,082	$ 9,885	$ 9,741
Exercise of options	97	188	144
Conversion of subordinated debentures		9	
Balance at end of period	10,179	10,082	9,885
Capital in excess of stated value			
Balance at beginning of period	161,238	141,558	130,473
Exercise of options, including tax benefits	9,766	18,179	11,085
Conversion of subordinated debentures		1,501	
Balance at end of period	171,004	161,238	141,558
Retained earnings			
Balance at beginning of period	430,866	375,425	334,250
Net income	97,156	79,267	64,698
Dividends paid	(24,310)	(23,826)	(23,523)
Balance at end of period	503,712	430,866	375,425
Translation adjustments	(19)	1,347	2,072
Pension liability adjustment	(3,212)	(2,572)	(119)
Treasury stock at cost	(166)	(166)	(166)
Shareholders' equity	$681,498	$600,795	$528,655
Common shares			
Balance issued at beginning of period	100,823	98,855	97,410
Exercise of options	964	1,882	1,445
Conversion of subordinated debentures		86	
Balance issued at end of period	101,787	100,823	98,855
Treasury shares	(29)	(29)	(29)
Common shares issued and outstanding	101,758	100,794	98,826

NOTES TO THE
CONSOLIDATED FINANCIAL STATEMENTS

NOTE 1 **Summary of Significant Accounting Policies**

Description of business

The company's principal business is the operation of quick-service restaurants serving high-quality food. At year-end 1994 the company and its franchise owners operated 4,411 of these restaurants under the name "Wendy's" in 50 states and in 33 other countries and territories.

Fiscal year

The company's fiscal year ends on the Sunday nearest to December 31. The 1994 and 1993 fiscal years consisted of 52 weeks and the 1992 fiscal year consisted of 53 weeks.

Basis of presentation

The Consolidated Financial Statements include the accounts of the company and its subsidiaries. All significant intercompany accounts and transactions have been eliminated in consolidation.

For purposes of the Consolidated Statement of Cash Flows, the company considers short-term investments with original maturities of three months or less as cash equivalents. A substantial portion of these investments are tax-exempt instruments.

Inventories

Inventories are stated at the lower of cost (first-in, first-out) or market, and consist primarily of restaurant food items and paper supplies.

Property and equipment

Depreciation and amortization are recognized on the straight-line method in amounts adequate to amortize costs over the following estimated useful lives: buildings, up to 25 years; leasehold improvements, up to 25 years; restaurant equipment, up to 15 years; other equipment, up to ten years; and property under capital leases, the primary lease term. Interest cost associated with the construction of new restaurants is capitalized, while certain other costs, such as ground rentals and real estate taxes, are expensed as incurred.

Cost in excess of net assets acquired

The cost in excess of net assets acquired is amortized on the straight-line method over periods ranging from ten to 40 years which, for leased restaurants, include the original lease period plus renewal options, if applicable. The company periodically reviews goodwill and, based upon undiscounted cash flows, impairments will be recognized when a permanent decline in value has occurred. Accumulated amortization of cost in excess of net assets acquired was $14.8 million and $13.2 million at January 1, 1995, and January 2, 1994, respectively.

Pre-opening costs

The company capitalizes certain operating costs which are incurred prior to the opening of a new restaurant. These costs are amortized over a one-year period.

Capitalized software development costs

The company capitalizes internally developed software costs which are amortized over a seven-year period.

Franchise operations

The company grants franchises to independent operators who in turn pay technical assistance fees, royalties, and in some cases, rents for each restaurant opened. A technical assistance fee is recorded as income when each restaurant commences operations. Royalties, four percent of monthly net sales, are recognized as income on the accrual basis. The company has established reserves related to the collection of franchise royalties and other franchise-related receivables and commitments (see Note 8). Included in other assets is the long-term portion of notes receivable amounting to $31.0 million and $29.7 million at January 1, 1995, and January 2, 1994, respectively. The carrying amount of notes receivable currently approximates fair value.

Franchise owners receive assistance in such areas as real estate site selection, construction consulting, purchasing, and marketing from company personnel who also furnish these services to company-operated restaurants. Franchise expenses are included in general and administrative expenses.

Foreign operations

At January 1, 1995, the company and its franchise owners operated 177 restaurants in Canada. Additionally, 236 restaurants were operated by franchise owners in other foreign countries and territories.

Net income per share

Primary earnings per share is computed by dividing net income by the weighted average number of common shares outstanding and dilutive common share equivalents during each period. Fully diluted computations assume full conversion of the subordinated debentures into common shares, when dilutive, and the elimination of related expenses, net of income taxes.

NOTE 2 Term Debt

Term debt at each year-end consisted of the following:

(In thousands)	1994	1993
Notes, unsecured, and Mortgages Payable with a weighted average interest rate of 8.6%, due in installments through 2004	$ 5,465	$ 5,639
Industrial Development Revenue Bonds, with a weighted average interest rate of 8.7%, due in installments through 2002	1,624	1,980
12¼% Notes, due April 1, 1995	49,995	49,977
7% Convertible Subordinated Debentures, due April 1, 2006	100,000	100,000
	157,084	157,596
Current portion	(52,242)	(855)
	$104,842	$156,741

The industrial development revenue bonds were issued to provide funds for the acquisition, construction, and improvement of various restaurants.

The 12¼% notes may not be redeemed prior to maturity.

The 7% convertible debentures are subordinated as to principal, premium, if any, and interest to all senior indebtedness as defined in the indenture. The conversion price is $12.30 per common share, subject to adjustment in certain events. The debentures are redeemable, with limited exceptions, at the option of the company on or after April 5, 1996.

The company purchased $28.6 million and $8.3 million of debt in 1993 and 1992, respectively. These purchases resulted in losses of $672,000 and $23,000 in 1993 and 1992, respectively.

Based on quoted market prices for the convertible subordinated debentures and future cash flows for all other term debt, the fair value of total term debt was approximately $185 million at January 1, 1995, and $214 million at January 2, 1994.

The combined aggregate amounts of future maturities for all term debt are as follows:

(In thousands)	
1995	$ 52,242
1996	541
1997	422
1998	282
1999	228
Later years	103,369
	$157,084

Subsequent to year-end, the company expanded its contractual lines of credit and currently has approximately $100 million from various financial institutions, generally at their respective prime rates.

Net interest expense for each year consisted of the following:

(In thousands)	1994	1993	1992
Total interest charges	$18,720	$21,554	$ 22,511
Interest income	(8,829)	(9,848)	(10,097)
	$ 9,891	$11,706	$ 12,414

NOTE 3 Leases

The company occupies land and buildings and uses equipment under terms of numerous lease agreements expiring on various dates through 2027. Terms of land only and land and building leases are generally for 20 to 25 years. Many of these leases provide for future rent escalations and renewal options. Certain leases require contingent rent, determined as a percentage of sales, when annual sales exceed specified levels. Most leases also obligate the company to pay the costs of maintenance, insurance, and property taxes.

At each year-end capital leases consisted of the following:

(In thousands)	1994	1993
Buildings	$ 63,531	$ 64,148
Accumulated amortization	(31,764)	(29,972)
	$ 31,767	$ 34,176

At January 1, 1995, future minimum lease payments for all leases, and the present value of the net minimum lease payments for capital leases, were as follows:

(In thousands)	Capital Leases	Operating Leases
1995	$ 9,965	$ 24,670
1996	9,858	23,744
1997	9,442	22,510
1998	8,553	21,333
1999	6,809	18,437
Later years	25,280	88,801
Total minimum lease payments	69,907	$199,495
Amount representing interest	(24,457)	
Present value of net minimum lease payments	45,450	
Current portion	(5,432)	
	$ 40,018	

Total minimum lease payments have not been reduced by minimum sublease rentals of $1.1 million under capital leases, and $23.9 million under operating leases due in the future under noncancelable subleases.

Rent expense for each year is included in company restaurant operating costs and amounted to:

(In thousands)	1994	1993	1992
Minimum rents	$28,510	$28,425	$28,346
Contingent rents	7,035	7,238	6,544
Sublease rents	(3,224)	(3,256)	(3,283)
	$32,321	$32,407	$31,607

In connection with the franchising of certain restaurants, the company has leased land, buildings, and equipment to the related franchise owners.

Most leases provide for monthly rentals based on a percentage of sales, while others provide for fixed payments with contingent rent when sales exceed certain levels. Lease terms are approximately ten to 20 years with one or more five-year renewal options. The franchise owners bear the cost of maintenance, insurance, and property taxes.

The company generally accounts for the building and equipment portions of the fixed payment leases as direct financing leases. The land portion of leases and leases with rents based on a percentage of sales are accounted for as operating leases.

At each year-end the net investment in financing leases receivable, included in other assets, consisted of the following:

(In thousands)	1994	1993
Total minimum lease receipts	$ 36,315	$ 45,548
Estimated residual value	4,542	4,662
Amount representing unearned interest	(19,659)	(25,806)
Current portion, included in accounts receivable	(927)	(911)
	$ 20,271	$ 23,493

At each year-end assets leased under operating leases consisted of the following:

(In thousands)	1994	1993
Land	$ 54,230	$ 52,063
Building	83,130	81,060
Equipment	15,911	16,288
	153,271	149,411
Accumulated amortization	(43,685)	(41,090)
	$109,586	$108,321

At January 1, 1995, future minimum lease receipts were as follows:

(In thousands)	Financing Leases	Operating Leases
1995	$ 3,008	$ 2,934
1996	2,984	2,948
1997	3,003	2,656
1998	2,990	2,602
1999	2,866	2,398
Later years	21,464	13,697
	$36,315	$27,235

Net rental income for each year is included in other revenues and amounted to:

(In thousands)	1994	1993	1992
Minimum rents	$ 1,868	$ 1,860	$1,182
Contingent rents	9,685	8,255	7,180
	$11,553	$10,115	$8,362

NOTE 4 Income Taxes

The provision for income taxes for each year consisted of the following:

(In thousands)	1994	1993	1992
Current			
Federal	$49,802	$39,512	$32,239
State and local	4,403	3,126	4,181
Foreign	20		
	54,225	42,638	36,420
Deferred			
Federal	(1,418)	(243)	(24)
State and local	(213)	(127)	(4)
Foreign	(279)	(6,000)	
	(1,910)	(6,370)	(28)
	$52,315	$36,268	$36,392

In the first quarter of 1993, the company adopted Financial Accounting Standard Number 109 (SFAS 109) – "Accounting for Income Taxes". Under SFAS No. 109, like Financial Accounting Standard Number 96 (SFAS 96) – "Accounting for Income Taxes" which the company adopted in 1989, deferred income taxes are recognized by employing the liability method. The company elected not to restate prior years' financial statements under the provisions of SFAS No. 109 and has determined that the cumulative effect of the implementation was not significant.

The temporary differences which give rise to deferred tax assets and liabilities at each year-end consisted of the following:

(In thousands)	1994	1993
Deferred tax assets		
Lease transactions	$ 4,285	$ 4,410
Reserves not currently deductible	12,468	12,116
Foreign operations	12,946	14,040
All other	6,654	4,951
	36,353	35,517
Valuation allowance	(7,144)	(8,023)
	$29,209	$27,494
Deferred tax liabilities		
Lease transactions	$ 8,128	$ 9,345
Depreciation	29,356	27,904
All other	5,423	5,909
	$42,907	$43,158

A deferred tax asset for foreign operations was established, upon the adoption of SFAS 109, for excess capital allowances and net operating loss carryovers which are related to a Canadian subsidiary. This deferred tax asset was largely offset by a valuation allowance. As a result of the regionalization and legal entity restructuring of Canadian operations, the company reduced the valuation allowance by $279,000 and $6.0 million in 1994 and 1993, respectively, primarily due to the realization of Canadian tax benefits.

A reconciliation of the statutory U.S. Federal income tax rate of 35% in 1994 and 1993 and 34% in 1992 to the company's effective tax rate for each year is shown below:

(In thousands)	1994	1993	1992
Income taxes at statutory rate	$52,315	$40,437	$34,371
Effect of foreign operations	(1,112)	720	1,305
State and local taxes, net of federal benefit	2,737	1,949	2,757
Canadian restructuring benefit	(279)	(6,000)	
Jobs and other tax credits	(722)	(456)	(1,785)
Tax-exempt interest	(616)	(537)	(756)
Goodwill amortization	407	526	388
Other	(415)	(371)	112
Income taxes at effective rate	$52,315	$36,268	$36,392

NOTE 5 Stock Option and Shareholder Rights Plans

The company has various stock option plans which provide options for certain employees and outside directors to purchase common shares of the company. Grants of options to employees and the periods during which such options can be exercised are at the discretion of the Board of Directors. Grants of options to outside directors and the periods during which such options can be exercised are specified in the plan applicable to directors and do not involve discretionary authority of the Board. All options expire at the end of the exercise period. Options are granted at the fair market value of the company's common shares on the date of grant and no amounts applicable thereto are reflected in net income. The company makes no recognition of the options in the financial statements until they are exercised.

On August 2, 1990, the Board of Directors adopted the WeShare Stock Option Plan (WeShare Plan), a non-qualified stock option plan to provide for grants of options equal to ten percent of each eligible employee's earnings, with a minimum of 20 options to be made to each eligible employee annually. An aggregate of 4.0 million common shares of the company have been reserved pursuant to the WeShare Plan.

The options have a term of ten years from the grant date and become exercisable in installments of 25 percent on each of the first four anniversaries of the grant date. On August 9, 1994, August 5, 1993, and July 30, 1992, approximately 865,000 options, 860,000 options, and 950,000 options were granted to eligible employees at an exercise price of $15.38 per share, $14.38 per share, and $11.69 per share, respectively.

In addition, the Board of Directors also adopted the 1990 Stock Option Plan (1990 Plan) on August 2, 1990, and amended the 1990 Plan on August 1, 1991, and February 23, 1994. An aggregate of 12.5 million common shares of the company have been reserved for issuance to key employees and outside directors under the 1990 Plan, as amended. On August 9, 1994, August 5, 1993, and July 30, 1992, approximately 1.3 million options, 1.1 million options, and 1.0 million options were granted to key employees at an exercise price of $15.38 per share, $14.38 per share, and $11.69 per share, respectively.

The following is a summary of stock option activity for the last three years:

(Shares in thousands)	Shares Under Option	Option Price Per Share
Balance at December 29, 1991	8,797	$ 4.06-$10.44
Granted	2,038	11.69- 13.69
Exercised	(1,445)	5.13- 9.87
Cancelled	(498)	
Balance at January 3, 1993	8,892	4.06- 13.69
Granted	2,091	12.56- 16.44
Exercised	(1,882)	4.13- 12.56
Cancelled	(560)	
Balance at January 2, 1994	8,541	4.06- 16.44
Granted	2,500	14.38- 18.06
Exercised	(964)	4.06- 14.38
Cancelled	(423)	
Balance at January 1, 1995	9,654	$ 5.13-$18.06

Options exercisable to purchase common shares totaled 4.6 million, 3.1 million, and 2.7 million at January 1, 1995, January 2, 1994, and January 3, 1993, respectively. Shares reserved under the plans at each year-end were 14.1 million in 1994, 10.5 million in 1993, and 12.4 million in 1992.

The company has a Shareholder Rights Plan which provides for the distribution of one preferred stock purchase right (Right), as a dividend for each outstanding common share. Each Right entitles a shareholder to buy one ten-thousandth of a share of a new series of preferred stock for $25 upon the occurrence of certain events. Rights would be exercisable once a person or group acquires 20 percent or more of the company's common shares, or ten days after a tender offer for 20 percent or more of the common shares is announced. No certificates will be issued unless the Rights Plan is activated.

Under certain circumstances, all Rights holders, except the person or company holding 20 percent or more of the company's common shares, will be entitled to purchase common shares at about half the price that such shares traded for prior to the announcement of the acquisition. Alternatively, if the company is acquired after the Rights plan is activated, the Rights will entitle the holder to buy the acquiring company's shares at a similar discount. The company can redeem the Rights for one cent per Right under certain circumstances. If not redeemed, the Rights will expire on August 10, 1998.

NOTE 6 Acquisitions

During 1994, the company acquired 29 restaurants in the Kansas City market for cash of $10.5 million and the assumption of certain liabilities. The company acquired four other domestic restaurants from franchisees for $2.3 million during 1994.

In 1993 and 1992, the company acquired 33 domestic restaurants and 13 domestic and nine Canadian restaurants for a total of $8.7 million and $7.6 million, respectively.

NOTE 7 Dispositions

In 1994, the company franchised 49 domestic restaurants. The company franchised 86 domestic restaurants and 42 domestic and two Canadian restaurants in 1993 and 1992, respectively. These transactions resulted in pretax gains of approximately $11.6 million, $8.1 million, and $7.7 million in 1994, 1993, and 1992, respectively, and are included in other revenues.

Notes receivable related to dispositions were $25.9 million at January 1, 1995, and $23.0 million at January 2, 1994, and are included in notes receivable and other assets.

NOTE 8 Commitments and Contingencies

At January 1, 1995, and January 2, 1994, the company's reserves established for doubtful royalty receivables were $4.2 million and $5.3 million, respectively. Reserves related to possible losses on notes receivable, real estate, guarantees, claims, and contingencies involving franchisees totaled $3.5 million at January 1, 1995, and $3.0 million at January 2, 1994. These reserves are included in accounts receivable, notes receivable, other assets, and other accrued expenses.

The company has guaranteed certain leases and debt payments of franchise owners with average annual obligations of $9.2 million over the next five years. In the event of default by a franchise owner, the company generally retains the right to acquire possession of the related restaurants.

The company is self-insured for most workers' compensation, general liability, and automotive liability losses subject to per occurrence and aggregate annual liability limitations. The company is also self-insured for health care claims for eligible participating employees subject to certain deductibles and limitations. The company determines its liability for claims incurred but not reported on an actuarial basis.

The company has entered into long-term purchase agreements with some of its suppliers. The range of prices and volume of purchases under the agreements may vary according to the company's demand for the products and fluctuations in market rates.

The company and its subsidiaries are parties to various legal actions and complaints arising in the ordinary course of business; many of these are covered by insurance. It is the opinion of the company that such matters will not materially affect the company's financial condition or earnings.

NOTE 9 Retirement Plans

The company's retirement program covers substantially all full-time employees qualified as to age and service. The program includes a contributory defined benefit pension plan and a defined contribution plan for management and administrative employees. The defined benefit pension plan allows for employee contributions and provides a matching benefit from the company in addition to a basic benefit which is independent of employee contributions. The pension plan also provides for a guaranteed rate of return on employee account balances. The defined contribution plan provides for an annual discretionary contribution which is determined each year by the Board of Directors. In addition, the retirement program includes a noncontributory defined benefit pension plan for all eligible crew employees and shift managers of the company.

The company also has supplemental retirement plans for certain key employees to replace benefits otherwise not available from the pension and profit sharing plans due to the limitations imposed under the Internal Revenue Code and to assure that projected benefit levels were not decreased by the changes to the retirement program which were implemented January 1, 1989.

The funded status of the pension plans for each year-end consisted of the following:

(In thousands)	1994	1993
Accumulated benefit obligation:		
Vested	$(27,537)	$(26,387)
Nonvested	$(2,978)	$(3,408)
Projected benefit obligation	$(32,700)	$(32,731)
Fair value of plan assets	29,822	28,097
Unrecognized net transition asset	(384)	(576)
Unrecognized net loss	8,047	7,677
Unrecognized prior service costs	189	708
Minimum pension adjustment	(5,390)	(4,873)
Pension liability	$ (416)	$ (1,698)

In determining the present value of benefit obligations, discount rates of 8.0% and 7.0% were used in 1994 and 1993, respectively. The net effect of changes in actuarial assumptions resulted in a $1.0 million reduction of pension expense for 1992. The expected long-term rate of return on assets used was 8.5% in 1994 and 1993. The assumed rate of increase in compensation levels was 8.0% for 1994 and 1993. Plan assets as of January 1, 1995, consisted of debt and equity instruments and cash and cash equivalents.

Net periodic pension cost for each year consisted of the following:

(In thousands)	1994	1993	1992
Service cost	$ 3,761	$ 3,326	$2,935
Interest cost on projected benefit obligation	2,432	2,165	1,672
Return on plan assets	564	(1,607)	(939)
Net amortization	(3,139)	(142)	(442)
	$ 3,618	$ 3,742	$3,226

The company provided for profit sharing and supplemental retirement benefits of $2.8 million, $2.3 million, and $1.9 million for 1994, 1993, and 1992, respectively.

A minimum pension liability equal to the excess of the accumulated benefit obligation over the fair value of plan assets and liabilities already accrued is reflected in the balance sheet by recording an intangible asset and reducing shareholders' equity.

The company has an agreement with the Chairman of the Board which provides for severance pay and commencement of retirement benefits if he terminates employment for any reason. Upon termination the agreement requires the executive to be available for consultation and prohibits him from competing against the company for a two-year period. The agreement also provides that the company may require him to return to active employment for up to 12 months under certain circumstances. Retirement by the executive in 1995 would result in an expense charge of approximately $3.1 million.

NOTE 10 Wendy's National Advertising Program

The Wendy's National Advertising Program, Inc. (WNAP) is a not-for-profit corporation which was established to collect and administer funds contributed by the company and all domestic franchise owners. These contributions total 2% of net sales and are used for advertising programs designed to increase sales and enhance the reputation of the company and its franchise owners. For 1995, 1994, and 1993, the domestic system agreed to increase national advertising spending from 2% to 2.5% of net sales. During 1994, 1993, and 1992, the company contributed $29.0 million, $27.7 million, and $20.7 million, respectively, to WNAP. These contributions were recognized in company restaurant operating costs. At January 1, 1995, and January 2, 1994, the company's payable to WNAP amounted to $2.2 million and $2.1 million, respectively.

NOTE 11 Quarterly Financial Data (unaudited)

The following is a summary of selected quarterly financial data:

Quarter	First		Second		Third		Fourth	
(In thousands except per share data)	1994	1993	1994	1993	1994	1993	1994	1993
Revenues	$319,790	$310,371	$367,204	$345,160	$359,350	$338,890	$351,513	$325,674
Company restaurant operating profit	37,968	35,840	54,698	47,156	52,366	46,169	48,989	44,574
Net income	12,486	9,839	33,348	27,352	29,764	24,484	21,558	17,592
Primary earnings per share	.12	.10	.32	.27	.29	.24	.21	.17
Fully diluted earnings per share	.12	.10	.31	.26	.28	.23	.20	.17

MANAGEMENT'S STATEMENT OF RESPONSIBILITY FOR FINANCIAL STATEMENTS

TO OUR SHAREHOLDERS Management is responsible for the preparation of the financial statements and other related financial information included in this Annual Report. The financial statements have been prepared in conformity with generally accepted accounting principles, incorporating management's reasonable estimates and judgments, where applicable.

The company maintains a system of internal accounting controls designed to provide reasonable assurance that assets are safeguarded, that transactions are executed as authorized, and that transactions are recorded and reported properly. The control system is supported by written policies and procedures, appropriate divisions of responsibility and authority and an effective internal audit function.

The company engages Coopers & Lybrand L.L.P. as independent public accountants to perform an independent audit of the financial statements. Their report, which appears herein, is based on obtaining an understanding of the company's accounting systems and procedures and testing them as they deem necessary.

The Board of Directors has an Audit Committee composed entirely of outside directors. The Audit Committee meets periodically with representatives of internal audit and Coopers & Lybrand L.L.P., and both have unrestricted access to the Audit Committee.

James W. Near
Chairman of the Board

John K. Casey
Vice Chairman and Chief Financial Officer

Lawrence A. Laudick
Vice President. General Controller

REPORT OF INDEPENDENT ACCOUNTANTS

TO THE SHAREHOLDERS OF WENDY'S INTERNATIONAL, INC.

We have audited the accompanying consolidated balance sheet of Wendy's International, Inc. and Subsidiaries as of January 1, 1995, and January 2, 1994, and the related consolidated statements of income, shareholders' equity, and cash flows for the years ended January 1, 1995, January 2, 1994, and January 3, 1993. These financial statements are the responsibility of the company's management. Our responsibility is to express an opinion on these financial statements based on our audits.

We conducted our audits in accordance with generally accepted auditing standards. Those standards require that we plan and perform the audit to obtain reasonable assurance about whether the financial statements are free of material misstatement. An audit includes examining, on a test basis, evidence supporting the amounts and disclosures in the financial statements. An audit also includes assessing the accounting principles used and significant estimates made by management, as well as evaluating the overall financial statement presentation. We believe that our audits provide a reasonable basis for our opinion.

In our opinion, the financial statements referred to above present fairly, in all material respects, the consolidated financial position of Wendy's International, Inc. and Subsidiaries at January 1, 1995, and January 2, 1994, and the consolidated results of their operations and their cash flows for the years ended January 1, 1995, January 2, 1994, and January 3, 1993, in conformity with generally accepted accounting principles.

Coopers & Lybrand L.L.P.

Columbus, Ohio
February 23, 1995

APPENDIX E

BRISTOL-MYERS SQUIBB COMPANY (BMS)

Bristol-Myers Squibb can be found on the Internet at
http:\\www.bms.com

CONSOLIDATED STATEMENTS OF EARNINGS AND RETAINED EARNINGS

Bristol-Myers Squibb Company

DOLLARS IN MILLIONS, EXCEPT PER SHARE AMOUNTS	YEAR ENDED DECEMBER 31,		
	1994	1993	1992
EARNINGS			
Net Sales	$11,984	$11,413	$11,156
Expenses:			
Cost of products sold	3,122	3,029	2,857
Marketing, selling and administrative	3,166	3,098	3,075
Advertising and product promotion	1,367	1,255	1,291
Research and development	1,108	1,128	1,083
Special charge	750	500	—
Provision for restructuring	—	—	890
Other	(84)	(168)	(27)
	9,429	8,842	9,169
Earnings from Continuing Operations Before Income Taxes	2,555	2,571	1,987
Provision for income taxes	713	612	449
Earnings from Continuing Operations	1,842	1,959	1,538
Discontinued Operations, net	—	—	670
Earnings Before Cumulative Effect of Accounting Change	1,842	1,959	2,208
Cumulative Effect of Accounting Change (net of income tax benefit of $144)	—	—	(246)
Net Earnings	$ 1,842	$ 1,959	$ 1,962
Per Common Share:			
Earnings from continuing operations	$3.62	$3.80	$2.97
Discontinued operations	—	—	1.29
Earnings before cumulative effect of accounting change	3.62	3.80	4.26
Cumulative effect of accounting change	—	—	(.47)
Net earnings	$3.62	$3.80	$3.79
Average Common Shares Outstanding (in millions)	509	515	518
RETAINED EARNINGS			
Retained Earnings, January 1	$7,243	$6,769	$6,235
Net earnings	1,842	1,959	1,962
	9,085	8,728	8,197
Less dividends	1,485	1,485	1,428
Retained Earnings, December 31	$7,600	$7,243	$6,769

The accompanying notes are an integral part of these financial statements.

CONSOLIDATED BALANCE SHEET

Bristol-Myers Squibb Company

	DECEMBER 31,		
DOLLARS IN MILLIONS	**1994**	1993	1992
ASSETS			
Current Assets:			
Cash and cash equivalents	$ 1,642	$ 2,421	$ 2,137
Time deposits and marketable securities	781	308	248
Receivables, net of allowances	2,043	1,859	1,984
Inventories	1,397	1,322	1,490
Prepaid expenses	847	660	762
Total Current Assets	6,710	6,570	6,621
Property, Plant and Equipment	3,666	3,374	3,141
Insurance Recoverable	968	1,000	—
Excess of cost over net tangible assets received in business acquisitions	939	191	153
Other Assets	627	966	889
	$12,910	$12,101	$10,804
LIABILITIES			
Current Liabilities:			
Short-term borrowings	$ 725	$ 177	$ 375
Accounts payable	693	649	562
Accrued expenses	2,116	1,550	1,422
U.S. and foreign income taxes payable	740	689	941
Total Current Liabilities	4,274	3,065	3,300
Product Liability	1,201	1,370	63
Other Liabilities	1,087	1,138	1,245
Long-Term Debt	644	588	176
Total Liabilities	7,206	6,161	4,784
STOCKHOLDERS' EQUITY			
Preferred stock, $2 convertible series: Authorized 10 million shares; issued and outstanding 21,857 in 1994, 25,798 in 1993 and 28,517 in 1992, liquidation value of $50 per share	—	—	—
Common stock, par value of $.10 per share: Authorized 1.5 billion shares; issued 540,173,669 in 1994, 532,688,458 in 1993 and 532,673,413 in 1992	54	53	53
Capital in excess of par value of stock	397	353	435
Cumulative translation adjustments	(301)	(332)	(208)
Retained earnings	7,600	7,243	6,769
	7,750	7,317	7,049
Less cost of treasury stock—32,887,848 common shares in 1994, 20,782,281 in 1993 and 14,689,052 in 1992	2,046	1,377	1,029
Total Stockholders' Equity	5,704	5,940	6,020
	$12,910	$12,101	$10,804

The accompanying notes are an integral part of these financial statements.

CONSOLIDATED STATEMENT OF CASH FLOWS

Bristol-Myers Squibb Company

	YEAR ENDED DECEMBER 31,		
DOLLARS IN MILLIONS	**1994**	1993	1992
Cash Flows From Operating Activities:			
Earnings from continuing operations	$1,842	$1,959	$1,538
Depreciation and amortization	328	308	295
Special charge	750	500	—
Provision for restructuring	—	—	890
Other operating items	18	49	50
Receivables	(63)	41	(125)
Inventories	(36)	129	(163)
Prepaid expenses	27	63	14
Accounts payable	(20)	134	75
Accrued expenses	(73)	(77)	(268)
Income taxes	(8)	(197)	(213)
Product liability	(384)	(93)	(2)
Other liabilities	(80)	(236)	(63)
Net Cash Provided by Operating Activities	2,301	2,580	2,028
Cash Flows From Investing Activities:			
Proceeds from sales of time deposits and marketable securities	35	993	169
Purchases of time deposits and marketable securities	(482)	(1,049)	(269)
Additions to fixed assets	(573)	(570)	(647)
Proceeds from sales of businesses	285	98	1,150
Purchases of businesses and other investments	(667)	(63)	(4)
Other, net	(22)	(6)	31
Net Cash (Used in) Provided by Investing Activities	(1,424)	(597)	430
Cash Flows From Financing Activities:			
Short-term borrowings	496	(228)	(169)
Long-term debt	27	394	40
Issuances of common stock under stock plans	24	38	37
Purchases of treasury stock	(701)	(419)	(228)
Dividends paid	(1,485)	(1,485)	(1,428)
Net Cash Used in Financing Activities	(1,639)	(1,700)	(1,748)
Effect of Exchange Rates on Cash	(17)	1	(8)
(Decrease)Increase in Cash and Cash Equivalents	(779)	284	702
Cash and Cash Equivalents at Beginning of Year	2,421	2,137	1,435
Cash and Cash Equivalents at End of Year	$1,642	$2,421	$2,137

The accompanying notes are an integral part of these financial statements.

NOTES TO CONSOLIDATED FINANCIAL STATEMENTS

NOTE 1 ACCOUNTING POLICIES
Basis of Consolidation
The consolidated financial statements include the accounts of Bristol-Myers Squibb Company and all of its subsidiaries.

Cash and Cash Equivalents
Cash and cash equivalents primarily include securities with a maturity of three months or less at the time of purchase, recorded at cost, which approximates market.

Time Deposits and Marketable Securities
Time deposits and marketable securities are available for sale and are recorded at fair value, which approximates cost.

Inventory Valuation
Inventories are generally stated at average cost, not in excess of market.

Property and Depreciation
Expenditures for additions, renewals and betterments are capitalized at cost. Depreciation is generally computed by the straight-line method based on the estimated useful lives of the related assets.

Excess of Cost over Net Tangible Assets
The excess of cost over net tangible assets received in business acquisitions subsequent to October 31, 1970 is being amortized on a straight-line basis over periods not exceeding 40 years.

Earnings Per Share
Earnings per common share are computed using the weighted average number of shares outstanding during the year. The effect of shares issuable under stock plans is not significant.

NOTE 2 SPECIAL CHARGE
As described in Note 18, the company is party to a settlement concerning pending and future breast implant product liability claims (related to a previously discontinued business of a subsidiary) brought against it, its Medical Engineering Corporation subsidiary, and certain other subsidiaries. In the fourth quarter of 1993, the company recorded a special charge of $500 million before taxes, $310 million after taxes, or $.60 per share. The charge consisted of $1.5 billion in anticipation of its share of the pending settlement and costs of the litigation ($1.4 billion recorded as a long-term liability in Product Liability and $100 million recorded as a current liability in Accrued Expenses), offset by $1 billion of expected insurance proceeds (recorded as Insurance Recoverable). Although the company is currently engaged in coverage litigation with certain of its insurers, expected insurance proceeds represent the amount of insurance which the company considers appropriate to record as recoverable at this time. The company believes that ultimately it will obtain substantial additional amounts of insurance proceeds.

Various events occurred in 1994, including a number of claimants opting out of the settlement. Based upon preliminary analyses of the number of such opt outs and of other issues, in the fourth quarter of 1994 the company recorded a special charge to earnings of $750 million before taxes, $488 million after taxes, or $.96 per share ($320 million of which was recorded as a current liability in Accrued Expenses).

NOTE 3 ACQUISITIONS AND DIVESTITURES
In August 1994, the company acquired Matrix Essentials, Inc., the leading manufacturer in North America of professional hair care and beauty products sold exclusively in beauty salons. In connection with the acquisition, the company issued 7,452,818 shares of common stock.

In September 1994, the company completed the acquisition of the remaining ownership interest in the UPSA Group, which develops and markets a wide range of nonprescription health and pharmaceutical products, including analgesics and cardiovascular and gastrointestinal specialties. The company held a minority stake in UPSA since 1990.

In January 1995, the company completed the acquisition of Calgon Vestal Laboratories, a skin care and infection control products business.

In April 1994, the company completed the sale of Xomed-Treace, Inc., a manufacturer of specialty surgical products, to Merocel Corporation.

In July 1994, the company sold Squibb Diagnostics, its diagnostic contrast media and radiopharmaceuticals businesses, to Bracco S.p.A. The company will continue manufacturing certain diagnostic products, including ProHance and Isovue, and nuclear medicine products. The company also will act as Bracco's distributor in Canada.

In 1993, the company sold certain assets of Edward Weck Incorporated and completed the sale of the beauty appliance division of Clairol.

In 1992, the company completed the sale of The Drackett Company, its household products business, to S.C. Johnson & Son, Inc., for $1.15 billion in cash. The sale resulted in a gain of $952 million before taxes, or $605 million after taxes. Drackett has been reported as a discontinued operation in 1992 and prior years.

NOTE 4 PROVISION FOR RESTRUCTURING
In the fourth quarter of 1992, a charge of $890 million before taxes was recorded in connection with various restructuring actions taken by the company to strengthen its four core businesses in recognition of changing worldwide health care trends. This charge primarily covered the costs of reducing employment levels, including a voluntary retirement program for the company's U.S. employees, and streamlining worldwide production and distribution operations. The after-tax effect of the charge was $570 million.

Note 5   Foreign Currency Translation

Cumulative translation adjustments, which represent the effect of translating assets and liabilities of the company's non-U.S. entities, except those in highly inflationary economies, were:

Dollars in Millions	1994	1993	1992
Balance, January 1	$332	$208	$ 90
Effect of balance sheet translations:			
Amount	(43)	141	151
Tax effect	12	(17)	(33)
Balance, December 31	$301	$332	$208

Included in net earnings were (losses) gains resulting from foreign currency transactions and translation adjustments related to non-U.S. entities operating in highly inflationary economies of $(44) million, $21 million and $(63) million in 1994, 1993 and 1992, respectively.

Note 6   Other Income and Expenses

	YEAR ENDED DECEMBER 31,		
Dollars in Millions	1994	1993	1992
Interest income	$124	$ 96	$ 78
Interest expense	(68)	(57)	(49)
Other—net	28	129	(2)
	$ 84	$168	$ 27

Interest expense was reduced by $15 million in 1994, $14 million in 1993 and $13 million in 1992 due to interest capitalized on major property, plant and equipment projects. Cash payments for interest, net of amounts capitalized, were $62 million, $51 million and $46 million in 1994, 1993 and 1992, respectively.

Note 7   Provision for Income Taxes

The components of earnings before income taxes were:

	YEAR ENDED DECEMBER 31,		
Dollars in Millions	1994	1993	1992
U.S.	$1,328	$1,561	$1,248
Non-U.S.	1,227	1,010	739
	$2,555	$2,571	$1,987

The provision for income taxes consisted of:

	YEAR ENDED DECEMBER 31,		
Dollars in Millions	1994	1993	1992
Current:			
U.S. Federal	$369	$257	$341
Non-U.S.	377	307	310
State and local	54	42	60
	800	606	711
Deferred:			
U.S.	(92)	(35)	(178)
Non-U.S.	5	41	(84)
	(87)	6	(262)*
	$713	$612	$449

* Primarily resulted from the provision for restructuring.

Income taxes paid during the year were $718 million, $783 million and $606 million in 1994, 1993 and 1992, respectively.

The company's provision for income taxes in 1994, 1993 and 1992 was different from the amount computed by applying the statutory United States Federal income tax rate to earnings before income taxes, as a result of the following:

	% OF EARNINGS BEFORE INCOME TAXES		
	1994	1993	1992
U.S. statutory rate	35.0%	35.0%	34.0%
Tax exemptions of operations in Puerto Rico	(7.3)	(10.1)	(8.7)
State and local taxes	1.4	1.1	.2
Non-U.S. operations	(1.9)	(.2)	(1.8)
Other	.7	(2.0)	(1.1)
	27.9%	23.8%	22.6%

Prepaid taxes at December 31, 1994, 1993 and 1992 were $591 million, $377 million and $405 million, respectively. The deferred income tax asset, included in Other Assets, at December 31, 1994, 1993 and 1992 was $65 million, $230 million and $160 million, respectively.

The components of prepaid and deferred income taxes consisted of:

	DECEMBER 31,		
Dollars in Millions	1994	1993	1992
Product liability	$ 304	$ 183	$ 30
Postretirement and pension benefits	247	275	144
Restructuring and integrating businesses	38	149	356
Depreciation	(205)	(198)	(166)
Other	272	198	201
	$ 656	$ 607	$ 565

The company has settled its United States Federal income tax returns through 1989 with the Internal Revenue Service.

United States Federal income taxes have not been provided on substantially all of the unremitted earnings of non-U.S. subsidiaries, since it is management's practice and intent to reinvest such earnings in the operations of these subsidiaries. The total amount of the net unremitted earnings of non-U.S. subsidiaries was approximately $2,004 million at December 31, 1994.

NOTE 8 INVENTORIES

| | DECEMBER 31, | | |
DOLLARS IN MILLIONS	**1994**	1993	1992
Finished goods	$ 781	$ 741	$ 846
Work in process	233	239	272
Raw and packaging materials	383	342	372
	$1,397	$1,322	$1,490

NOTE 9 PROPERTY, PLANT AND EQUIPMENT

| | DECEMBER 31, | | |
DOLLARS IN MILLIONS	**1994**	1993	1992
Land	$ 159	$ 148	$ 145
Buildings	2,103	1,814	1,741
Machinery, equipment and fixtures	3,061	2,779	2,763
Construction in progress	513	495	383
	5,836	5,236	5,032
Less accumulated depreciation	2,170	1,862	1,891
	$3,666	$3,374	$3,141

NOTE 10 ACCRUED EXPENSES AND OTHER LIABILITIES

The components of accrued expenses were:

| | DECEMBER 31, | | |
DOLLARS IN MILLIONS	**1994**	1993	1992
Product liability	$ 635	$ 100	$ —
Medicaid and other rebates	207	173	98
Restructuring and integrating businesses	92	288	326
Other	1,182	989	998
	$2,116	$1,550	$1,422

The components of other liabilities were:

| | DECEMBER 31, | | |
DOLLARS IN MILLIONS	**1994**	1993	1992
Postretirement benefits	$ 465	$ 452	$ 402
Pension benefits	148	305	73
Restructuring and integrating businesses	—	82	460
Other	474	299	310
	$1,087	$1,138	$1,245

NOTE 11 SHORT-TERM BORROWINGS AND LONG-TERM DEBT

At December 31, 1994, short-term borrowings included amounts due to banks of $438 million, current installments of long-term debt of $21 million and a deferred payment of $266 million. At December 31, 1993 and 1992, short-term borrowings included amounts due to banks of $163 million and $314 million, respectively, and current installments of long-term debt of $14 million and $61 million, respectively. The increase in amounts due to banks and the deferred payment of $266 million at December 31, 1994 primarily resulted from the acquisition of the remaining ownership interest in UPSA.

The company has short-term lines of credit with domestic and foreign banks. At December 31, 1994, the unused portions of these lines of credit were approximately $200 million and $686 million, respectively.

The components of long-term debt were:

| | DECEMBER 31, | | |
DOLLARS IN MILLIONS	**1994**	1993	1992
7.15% Debentures, due in 2023	$343	$343	$ —
5.0% Term Loan, due in 2000	71	64	—
6.18% Term Loan, due in 1997	65	60	53
5.3% Term Loan, due in 1996	60	55	49
5.75% Industrial Revenue Bonds, due in 2024	34	—	—
6 3/8% and 6 1/2% Notes, due annually from 1995 to 2004	27	30	30
Other, due in varying amounts through 2008	44	36	44
	$644	$588	$176

Long-term debt at December 31, 1994 was payable:

YEARS ENDING DECEMBER 31,

DOLLARS IN MILLIONS

1996	$ 75
1997	79
1998	9
1999	7
2000	76
2001 and later	398
	$644

NOTE 12 FINANCIAL INSTRUMENTS

The company enters into foreign exchange option and forward contracts to manage its exposure to currency fluctuations.

The company has exposures to net foreign currency denominated assets and liabilities, which approximated $1,117 million, $1,210 million and $1,081 million at December 31, 1994, 1993 and 1992, respectively, primarily in Deutsche marks, French francs, Italian lira and Japanese yen. The company mitigates the effect of these exposures through third party borrowings and foreign exchange forward contracts.

Foreign exchange option contracts, which typically expire within one year, are used to hedge intercompany shipments expected to occur during the next year. Gains on these contracts are deferred and are recognized in the same period as the hedged transactions. Certain foreign exchange forward contracts are used to minimize exposure of foreign currency transactions and firm commitments to fluctuating exchange rates. Gains or losses on these contracts are recognized in the basis of the transaction being hedged. The notional amounts of the company's foreign exchange option and forward contracts at December 31, 1994, 1993 and 1992 were $1,200 million, $790 million and $1,454 million, respectively.

The company does not anticipate any material adverse effect on its financial position resulting from its involvement in these instruments, nor does it anticipate non-performance by any of its counterparties.

At December 31, 1994, 1993 and 1992, the carrying value of all financial instruments, both short and long-term, approximated their fair values.

NOTE 13 RETIREMENT BENEFIT PLANS

The company and certain of its subsidiaries have defined benefit pension plans for regular full-time employees. The principal pension plan is the Bristol-Myers Squibb Retirement Income Plan. The company's funding policy is to contribute amounts to provide for current service and to fund past service liability.

Cost for the company's defined benefit plans included the following components:

YEAR ENDED DECEMBER 31,

DOLLARS IN MILLIONS	1994	1993	1992
Service cost—benefits earned during the year	$ 114	$ 104	$ 94
Interest cost on projected benefit obligation	166	152	144
Actual losses(earnings) on plan assets	11	(232)	(119)
Net amortization and deferral	(158)	54	(73)
Net pension expense	$ 133	$ 78	$ 46

The weighted average actuarial assumptions for the company's pension plans were as follows:

DECEMBER 31,

	1994	1993	1992
Discount rate	8.8%	7.0%	8.2%
Compensation increase	5.3%	4.5%	5.0%
Long-term rate of return	10.0%	11.0%	12.0%

The funded status of the plans was as follows:

DECEMBER 31,

DOLLARS IN MILLIONS	1994	1993	1992
Actuarial present value of accumulated benefit obligation:			
Vested	$(1,624)	$(1,758)	$(1,354)
Non-vested	(178)	(201)	(155)
	$(1,802)	$(1,959)	$(1,509)
Total projected benefit obligation	$(2,138)	$(2,339)	$(1,892)
Plan assets at fair value	1,836	1,702	1,681
Plan assets less than projected benefit obligation	(302)	(637)	(211)
Unamortized net assets at adoption	(90)	(103)	(129)
Unrecognized prior service cost	89	96	105
Unrecognized net losses	309	510	313
Adjustment required to recognize minimum pension liability	(23)	(171)	—
(Accrued) Prepaid pension expense	$ (17)	$ (305)	$ 78

In 1994, the decrease in plan assets less than projected benefit obligation and the adjustment required to recognize minimum pension liability was primarily due to a higher discount rate.

In 1993, the increase in the actuarial present value of accumulated benefit obligation and in plan assets less than projected benefit obligation was primarily due to a lower discount rate and the effect of the voluntary retirement program offered to the company's U.S. employees.

In 1994, the adjustment required to recognize minimum pension liability was recorded in Other Assets. In 1993, $112 million of the adjustment required to recognize minimum pension liability was recorded in Other Assets and $59 million was recorded as a reduction in Stockholders' Equity.

Plan assets less than projected benefit obligation included $120 million, $113 million and $73 million in an unfunded benefit equalization plan at December 31, 1994, 1993 and 1992, respectively.

Plan benefits are primarily based on years of credited service and on participant's compensation. Plan assets principally consist of equity securities and fixed income securities.

NOTE 14 POSTRETIREMENT BENEFIT PLANS OTHER THAN PENSIONS

The company provides comprehensive medical and group life benefits to substantially all U.S. retirees who elect to participate in the company's comprehensive medical and group life plans. The medical plan is contributory. Contributions are adjusted periodically and vary by date of retirement and the original retiring company. The life insurance plan is non-contributory.

Effective January 1, 1992, the company adopted the provisions of Statement of Financial Accounting Standards No. 106, Employers' Accounting for Postretirement Benefits Other Than Pensions. This statement requires that the costs of postretirement benefits, primarily health care benefits, be accrued during an employee's active working career. In prior years, these costs were expensed as paid. The company recorded the discounted value of expected future benefits attributed to employees' service rendered prior to 1992 as a cumulative effect of an accounting change. This one-time non-cash accounting change was $390 million before taxes, $246 million after taxes, or $.47 per share.

Cost for the company's postretirement benefit plans included the following components:

DOLLARS IN MILLIONS	YEAR ENDED DECEMBER 31,		
	1994	1993	1992
Service cost—benefits earned during the year	$ 9	$ 8	$ 8
Interest cost on accumulated post-retirement benefit obligation	37	32	30
Actual earnings on plan assets	—	(2)	—
Net amortization and deferral	(2)	—	—
Net postretirement benefit expense	$44	$38	$38

The status of the plans was as follows:

DOLLARS IN MILLIONS	DECEMBER 31,		
	1994	1993	1992
Accumulated postretirement benefit obligation:			
Retirees	$(386)	$(380)	$(251)
Fully eligible active plan participants	(13)	(17)	(27)
Other active plan participants	(118)	(124)	(131)
	(517)	(521)	(409)
Plan assets at fair value	41	28	7
Accumulated postretirement benefit obligation in excess of plan assets	(476)	(493)	(402)
Unrecognized prior service cost	1	(1)	—
Unrecognized net losses	10	42	—
Accrued postretirement benefit expense	$(465)	$(452)	$(402)

In 1993, the increase in the accumulated postretirement benefit obligation was primarily due to a lower discount rate and the effect of the voluntary retirement program offered to the company's U.S. employees.

For measurement purposes, an annual rate of increase in the per capita cost of covered health care benefits of 9.8% for participants under age 65 and 8.4% for participants age 65 and over was assumed for 1995; the rate was assumed to decrease gradually to 6.0% in 2007 and to remain at that level thereafter. Increasing the assumed medical care cost trend rates by 1 percentage point in each year would increase the accumulated postretirement benefit obligation as of December 31, 1994 by $29 million and the aggregate of the service and interest cost components of net postretirement benefit expense for the year then ended by $2 million. The weighted-average discount rate used in determining the accumulated postretirement benefit obligation was 8.8% in 1994, 7.0% in 1993 and 8.2% in 1992.

Plan assets principally consist of equity securities and fixed income securities. The expected long-term rate of return on plan assets was 10.0% in 1994, 11.0% in 1993 and 12.0% in 1992.

Bristol-Myers Squibb Company

NOTE 15 STOCKHOLDERS' EQUITY

Changes in capital shares and capital in excess of par value of stock were:

	SHARES OF COMMON STOCK		CAPITAL IN EXCESS OF PAR VALUE OF STOCK (DOLLARS IN MILLIONS)
	ISSUED	TREASURY	
Balance, December 31, 1991	532,659,944	13,142,575	$485
Issued pursuant to stock plans, options, rights and warrants	3,052	(1,464,223)	(50)
Conversions of preferred stock	10,417	—	—
Purchases	—	3,010,700	—
Balance, December 31, 1992	532,673,413	14,689,052	435
Issued pursuant to stock plans, options, rights and warrants	3,530	(1,183,365)	(23)
Conversions of preferred stock	11,515	—	—
Purchases	—	7,276,594	—
Other	—	—	(59)
Balance, December 31, 1993	532,688,458	20,782,281	353
Issued pursuant to stock plans, options, rights and warrants	15,747	(518,733)	(15)
Conversions of preferred stock	16,646	—	—
Purchases	—	12,624,300	—
Other	7,452,818	—	59
Balance, December 31, 1994	540,173,669	32,887,848	$397

Each share of the company's preferred stock is convertible into 4.24 shares of common stock and is callable at the company's option. The reductions in the number of issued shares of preferred stock in 1994, 1993 and 1992 were due to conversions into common stock.

Dividends per common share were $2.92 in 1994, $2.88 in 1993 and $2.76 in 1992.

Under the company's stock option plans, officers, directors and key employees may be granted options to purchase the company's common stock at 100% of the market price on the day the option is granted. Additionally, the plans provide for the granting of stock appreciation rights whereby the grantee may surrender exercisable options and receive common stock and/or cash measured by the excess of the market price of the common stock over the option exercise price.

On May 4, 1993, the stockholders approved amendments to the 1983 Stock Option Plan extending its term for 10 years, authorizing additional shares in the amount of 0.9% of the outstanding shares per year for each of the additional 10 years, incorporating the company's existing long-term performance award plan and providing for the payment of long-term performance awards in shares of common stock valued at 100% of the market price on the date of payment.

The company's restricted stock award plan provides for the granting of up to 3,000,000 shares of common stock to key employees, subject to restrictions as to continuous employment except in the case of death or normal retirement. Restrictions generally expire over a five-year period from date of grant. At December 31, 1994, a total of 565,668 shares were outstanding under the plan.

Stock option and long-term performance award transactions were:

	SHARES OF COMMON STOCK	
	AVAILABLE FOR OPTION/AWARD	UNDER PLAN
Balance, December 31, 1991	7,385,732	14,102,731
Granted	(3,593,775)	3,593,775
Exercised	—	(2,258,396)
Surrendered		(7,243)
Lapsed	467,773	(475,107)
Balance, December 31, 1992	4,259,730	14,955,760
Authorized	4,661,859	—
Granted	(5,464,022)	5,464,022
Exercised	—	(1,264,638)
Lapsed	787,946	(790,981)
Balance, December 31, 1993	4,245,513	18,364,163
Authorized	4,607,156	—
Granted	(5,296,982)	5,296,982
Exercised	—	(686,507)
Lapsed	1,012,237	(1,027,651)
Balance, December 31, 1994	4,567,924	21,946,987

At December 31, 1994, there were exercisable options outstanding to purchase 12,450,900 shares of common stock at prices ranging from $16.45 to $87.31 per share. Shares of common stock under option were exercised at prices ranging from $10.94 to $56.56 in 1994, from $9.44 to $56.13 in 1993 and from $9.34 to $76.38 in 1992.

At December 31, 1994, 33,428,296 shares of common stock were reserved for issuance pursuant to stock plans, options and conversions of preferred stock.

Attached to each outstanding share of the company's common stock is one Right. The Rights will be exercisable if a person or group acquires beneficial interest of 15% or more of the company's outstanding common stock, or commences a tender or exchange offer for 15% or more of the company's outstanding common stock. Each Right will entitle stockholders to buy one one-thousandth of a share of a new series of participating preferred stock of the company at an exercise price of $200. The Rights will expire on December 18, 1997. In the event of certain merger, sale of assets or self-dealing transactions, each Right will then entitle its holder to acquire shares having a value of twice the Right's exercise price. The company may redeem the Rights at $.01 per Right at any time until the 15th day following public announcement that a 15% position has been acquired.

NOTE 16 LEASES
Minimum rental commitments under all noncancelable operating leases, primarily real estate, in effect at December 31, 1994 were:

YEARS ENDING DECEMBER 31,

DOLLARS IN MILLIONS

1995	$122
1996	98
1997	76
1998	63
1999	50
Later years	299
Total minimum payments	708
Less total minimum sublease rentals	198
Net minimum rental commitments	$510

Operating lease rental expense (net of sublease rental income of $23 million in 1994, $21 million in 1993 and $20 million in 1992) was $136 million in 1994, $142 million in 1993 and $141 million in 1992.

NOTE 17 SEGMENT INFORMATION
The company's products are reported in four industry segments as follows:

Pharmaceutical Products—includes prescription medicines, mainly cardiovascular, anti-infective and anti-cancer drugs, which comprise about 40%, 25% and 20%, respectively, of the segment's sales, central nervous system drugs and other pharmaceutical products.

Medical Devices—includes orthopaedic implants, which comprise about 40% of the segment's sales, ostomy and wound care products, surgical instruments and other medical devices.

Nonprescription Health Products—includes infant formulas and other nutritional products, which comprise about 65% of the segment's sales, analgesics, cough/cold remedies and skin care products.

Toiletries and Beauty Aids—includes haircoloring and hair care preparations, which comprise about 75% of the segment's sales in 1994 and 65% in both 1993 and 1992, and deodorants, anti-perspirants and other toiletries and beauty aids.

Unallocated expenses principally consist of general administrative expenses and net interest income, and in 1992 include a portion of the charge for restructuring. Other assets are principally cash and cash equivalents, time deposits and marketable securities. Inter-area sales by geographic area for the years ended December 31, 1994, 1993 and 1992, respectively, were: United States—$867 million, $859 million and $915 million; Europe, Mid-East and Africa—$428 million, $504 million and $382 million; Other Western Hemisphere—$37 million, $41 million and $36 million; and Pacific—$28 million, $43 million and $26 million. These sales are usually billed at or above manufacturing costs.

Net assets relating to operations outside the United States amounted to $2,286 million, $1,511 million and $1,369 million at December 31, 1994, 1993 and 1992, respectively.

Bristol-Myers Squibb Company

INDUSTRY SEGMENTS	NET SALES			PROFIT			YEAR-END ASSETS		
DOLLARS IN MILLIONS	**1994**	1993	1992	**1994**[a]	1993[a]	1992[b]	**1994**	1993	1992
Pharmaceutical Products	$ 6,970	$ 6,524	$ 6,313	$2,270	$2,133	$1,584	$5,180	$4,628	$4,622
Medical Devices	1,685	1,693	1,665	(253)	(24)	305	2,001	2,030	1,063
Nonprescription Health Products	2,043	1,964	1,959	456	463	268	1,635	872	839
Toiletries and Beauty Aids	1,286	1,232	1,219	168	163	10	663	548	547
Net sales, operating profit and assets	$11,984	$11,413	$11,156	$2,641	$2,735	$2,167	$9,479	$8,078	$7,071

GEOGRAPHIC AREAS	NET SALES			PROFIT			YEAR-END ASSETS		
DOLLARS IN MILLIONS	**1994**	1993	1992	**1994**[a]	1993[a]	1992[c]	**1994**	1993	1992
United States	$ 7,846	$ 7,586	$ 7,362	$1,610	$1,777	$1,467	$ 5,637	$ 5,591	$ 4,587
Europe, Mid-East and Africa	3,139	3,062	3,163	675	591	534	2,894	1,708	1,813
Other Western Hemisphere	1,039	987	939	213	197	138	416	443	426
Pacific	1,320	1,225	1,051	179	194	86	949	829	717
Inter-area eliminations	(1,360)	(1,447)	(1,359)	(36)	(24)	(58)	(417)	(493)	(472)
Net sales, operating profit and assets	$11,984	$11,413	$11,156	2,641	2,735	2,167	9,479	8,078	7,071
Unallocated expenses and other assets				(86)	(164)	(180)	3,431	4,023	3,733
Earnings before income taxes and total assets				$2,555	$2,571	$1,987	$12,910	$12,101	$10,804

INDUSTRY SEGMENTS	CAPITAL EXPENDITURES			DEPRECIATION		
DOLLARS IN MILLIONS	**1994**	1993	1992	**1994**	1993	1992
Pharmaceutical Products	$379	$379	$426	$205	$194	$186
Medical Devices	37	55	84	38	35	34
Nonprescription Health Products	112	81	70	38	34	28
Toiletries and Beauty Aids	26	23	34	23	24	28
Identifiable industry totals	554	538	614	304	287	276
Other	23	42	40	24	21	19
Consolidated totals	$577	$580	$654	$328	$308	$295

[a] The operating profit of the Medical Devices segment and of the United States included a special charge for pending and future product liability claims of $750 million in 1994 and $500 million in 1993.

[b] The 1992 operating profit of the company's industry segments included the charge for restructuring as follows: Pharmaceutical Products—$371 million; Medical Devices—$155 million; Nonprescription Health Products—$150 million; and Toiletries and Beauty Aids—$150 million.

[c] The 1992 earnings before income taxes included the charge for restructuring as follows: United States—$595 million; Europe, Mid-East and Africa—$134 million; Other Western Hemisphere—$51 million; Pacific—$46 million; and unallocated expenses—$64 million.

NOTE 18 CONTINGENCIES

Various lawsuits, claims and proceedings of a nature considered normal to its businesses are pending against the company and certain of its subsidiaries. The most significant of these are described below.

Breast Implant Litigation

As of December 31, 1994, approximately 20,000 plaintiffs have filed suit against the company, its subsidiary, Medical Engineering Corporation (MEC), and certain other subsidiaries, in federal and state courts and in certain Canadian provincial courts, alleging damages for personal injuries of various types resulting from polyurethane covered breast implants and smooth walled breast implants. Most of these plaintiffs are participants in a class action settlement approved by the federal District Court in Birmingham, Alabama, and that settlement is now subject to appeals. Of those who have chosen to opt out of the settlement, the company estimates that approximately 3,000 United States claimants may assert claims based upon MEC implants. Under the settlement, the company would make payments totaling $1.154 billion over a period of 30 years. Note 2 sets forth the special charges recorded in connection with this litigation. If the value of approved current disease claims under the settlement exceeds certain limits, payments to claimants would be reduced and claimants would have another opportunity to opt out of the settlement. If this were to occur, the company and other defendants could renegotiate the terms of the settlement or withdraw. The company is unable to predict when these events may occur but, based on information available at this time, it does not seem likely before late 1995. Dependent on these and other future developments, the company would record such additional charge as may be required. The amount of such a charge, if any, cannot be estimated.

Other Actions

The company is a defendant in a number of actions brought against it and other pharmaceutical companies in federal and state courts by the children or grandchildren of women who ingested diethylstilbestrol (DES), a product which had been, but is no longer, manufactured or sold by an affiliate of the company.

The company is a defendant in several state antitrust actions (some of which have been removed to federal court) filed on behalf of purported classes of individual purchasers of infant formula products, and by three state Attorneys General, alleging a conspiracy regarding pricing of infant formula products and other violations of state antitrust or deceptive trade practice laws and seeking treble damages, statutory and civil penalties

and injunctive relief. Five other state Attorneys General have commenced civil investigations of pricing practices and marketing activities in the infant formula industry. The Canadian Bureau of Competition Policy has commenced a civil and criminal investigation of the Canadian infant formula market. The company is also a defendant in one federal court action filed by the State of Louisiana on behalf of indirect purchasers of infant formula alleging a conspiracy regarding pricing of infant formula products and seeking treble damages, civil penalties and injunctive relief.

As of December 31, 1994, the company is a defendant in over 60 separate actions commenced against the company and other pharmaceutical manufacturers, wholesalers and others in various federal district courts on behalf of certain chain pharmacies, supermarket chains and independent drug stores. Plaintiffs' actions have been brought by drug retailers either on an individual basis or as representatives of nationwide classes of retail pharmacies. These cases all seek treble damages in an as yet unspecified amount and injunctive relief on account of alleged antitrust violations in the pricing and marketing of brand-name prescription drugs. A class of retail pharmacists has been certified in the multi-district litigation and the individual claims have been coordinated for purposes of pretrial proceedings. State court cases brought under state law and alleging similar grounds are proceeding in California, Alabama and Wisconsin, but generally these actions are less advanced than the coordinated federal cases.

The company has entered into a settlement of a class action filed in the United States District Court for the Southern District of New York alleging violations of federal securities laws and regulations in connection with, among other things, earnings projections. The settlement is subject to approval by the Court.

The company, together with others, is a party to, or otherwise involved in, a number of proceedings brought by the Environmental Protection Agency or comparable state agencies under the Comprehensive Environmental Response, Compensation and Liability Act (CERCLA or Superfund) or comparable state laws directed at the cleanup of hazardous waste sites.

While it is not possible to predict with certainty the outcome of these cases, it is the opinion of management that these lawsuits, claims and proceedings which are pending against the company are without merit or will not have a material adverse effect on the company's operating results, liquidity or consolidated financial position.

REPORT OF MANAGEMENT

Management is responsible for the accompanying consolidated financial statements, which are prepared in accordance with generally accepted accounting principles. In management's opinion, the consolidated financial statements present fairly the company's financial position, results of operations and cash flows. In addition, information and representations included in the company's Annual Report are consistent with the financial statements.

The company maintains a system of internal accounting policies, procedures and controls intended to provide reasonable assurance, given the inherent limitations of all internal control systems, at appropriate costs, that transactions are executed in accordance with company authorization, are properly recorded and reported in the financial statements, and that assets are adequately safeguarded. The company's internal auditors continually evaluate the adequacy and effectiveness of this system of internal accounting policies, procedures and controls, and actions are taken to correct deficiencies as they are identified.

The Audit Committee of the Board of Directors is comprised solely of non-employee directors and is responsible for overseeing and monitoring the quality of the company's accounting and auditing practices. The Audit Committee meets several times during the year with management, the internal auditors and the independent accountants to discuss audit activities, internal controls and financial reporting matters. The internal auditors and the independent accountants have full and free access to the Audit Committee.

The appointment of Price Waterhouse LLP as the company's independent accountants by the Board of Directors was ratified by the stockholders. Price Waterhouse LLP's Report to the Board of Directors and Stockholders of Bristol-Myers Squibb Company appears on this page.

Richard L. Gelb
Chairman of the Board

Charles A. Heimbold, Jr.
President and
Chief Executive Officer

Michael F. Mee
Senior Vice President and
Chief Financial Officer

REPORT OF INDEPENDENT ACCOUNTANTS

To the Board of Directors
and Stockholders of
Bristol-Myers Squibb Company

In our opinion, the accompanying consolidated balance sheet and the related consolidated statements of earnings and retained earnings and of cash flows present fairly, in all material respects, the financial position of Bristol-Myers Squibb Company and its subsidiaries at December 31, 1994, 1993 and 1992, and the results of their operations and their cash flows for the years then ended in conformity with generally accepted accounting principles. These financial statements are the responsibility of the company's management; our responsibility is to express an opinion on these financial statements based on our audits. We conducted our audits of these statements in accordance with generally accepted auditing standards which require that we plan and perform the audit to obtain reasonable assurance about whether the financial statements are free of material misstatement. An audit includes examining, on a test basis, evidence supporting the amounts and disclosures in the financial statements, assessing the accounting principles used and significant estimates made by management, and evaluating the overall financial statement presentation. We believe that our audits provide a reasonable basis for the opinion expressed above.

As discussed in Note 14 to the financial statements, effective January 1, 1992, the company adopted Statement of Financial Accounting Standards No. 106, Employers' Accounting for Postretirement Benefits Other Than Pensions.

Price Waterhouse LLP

1177 Avenue of the Americas
New York, New York 10036
January 19, 1995

TEN-YEAR FINANCIAL SUMMARY

DOLLARS IN MILLIONS, EXCEPT PER SHARE AMOUNTS	1994	1993	1992
OPERATING RESULTS			
Net Sales	$11,984	$11,413	$11,156
Expenses:			
Cost of products sold	3,122	3,029	2,857
Marketing, selling and administrative	3,166	3,098	3,075
Advertising and product promotion	1,367	1,255	1,291
Research and development	1,108	1,128	1,083
Other *	666	332	863
	9,429	8,842	9,169
Earnings from Continuing Operations Before Income Taxes	2,555	2,571	1,987
Provision for income taxes	713	612	449
Earnings from Continuing Operations	$ 1,842	$ 1,959	$ 1,538
Dividends paid on common and preferred stock	$ 1,485	$ 1,485	$ 1,428
Earnings from continuing operations per common share *	3.62	3.80	2.97
Dividends per common share	2.92	2.88	2.76
FINANCIAL POSITION AT DECEMBER 31			
Current assets	$ 6,710	$ 6,570	$ 6,621
Property, plant and equipment	3,666	3,374	3,141
Total assets	12,910	12,101	10,804
Current liabilities	4,274	3,065	3,300
Long-term debt	644	588	176
Total liabilities	7,206	6,161	4,784
Stockholders' equity	5,704	5,940	6,020
Average common shares outstanding (in millions)	509	515	518
Book value per common share	$ 11.25	$ 11.61	$ 11.62

* Includes a special charge for pending and future product liability claims of $750 million before taxes, $488 million after taxes, or $.96 per share, in 1994 and $500 million before taxes, $310 million after taxes, or $.60 per share, in 1993. In 1992, includes a provision for restructuring of $890 million before taxes, $570 million after taxes, or $1.10 per share. In 1989, includes a provision for integrating businesses of $855 million before taxes, $693 million after taxes, or $1.32 per share.

Bristol-Myers Squibb Company

	1991	1990	1989	1988	1987	1986	1985
	$10,571	$9,741	$8,578	$7,986	$7,044	$6,163	$5,393
	2,717	2,665	2,418	2,255	2,096	1,905	1,769
	2,946	2,717	2,461	2,310	2,023	1,725	1,494
	1,263	1,189	1,073	1,055	979	851	760
	983	873	781	680	556	467	405
	(122)	(136)	661	(119)	(165)	44	(137)
	7,787	7,308	7,394	6,181	5,489	4,992	4,291
	2,784	2,433	1,184	1,805	1,555	1,171	1,102
	793	742	496	603	533	420	404
	$ 1,991	$1,691	$ 688	$1,202	$1,022	$ 751	$ 698
	$ 1,249	$1,116	$ 722	$ 641	$ 526	$ 404	$ 342
	3.82	3.22	1.32	2.29	1.90	1.38	1.29
	2.40	2.12	2.00	1.68	1.40	1.06	.90 1/2
	$ 5,567	$5,670	$5,552	$5,422	$5,006	$4,264	$3,641
	2,936	2,631	2,350	2,188	1,927	1,716	1,534
	9,416	9,215	8,497	8,273	7,514	6,592	6,046
	2,752	2,821	2,659	2,613	2,129	1,766	1,541
	135	231	237	284	279	327	299
	3,621	3,797	3,413	3,325	2,759	2,398	2,093
	5,795	5,418	5,084	4,948	4,755	4,194	3,953
	521	525	523	525	538	543	542
	$ 11.16	$10.34	$ 9.67	$ 9.49	$ 8.88	$ 7.84	$ 7.30

REEBOK INTERNATIONAL LTD.

Reebok International Ltd.

1994 Annual Report

Reebok can be found on the Internet at
http:\\www.planetreebok.com

Consolidated Balance Sheets

Reebok International Ltd.

Amounts in thousands, except share data

December 31	1994	1993
Assets		
Current assets:		
Cash and cash equivalents	$ 83,936	$ 79,347
Accounts receivable, net of allowance for doubtful accounts		
(1994, $44,862; 1993, $46,455)	532,475	457,399
Inventory	624,625	514,027
Deferred income taxes	66,456	54,784
Prepaid expenses	29,952	21,558
Total current assets	1,337,444	1,127,115
Property and equipment, net	164,848	130,607
Non-current assets:		
Intangibles, net of amortization	96,196	94,262
Deferred income taxes	2,910	1,250
Other	48,063	38,477
	147,169	133,989
	$1,649,461	$1,391,711
Liabilities and Stockholders' Equity		
Current liabilities:		
Notes payable to banks	$ 63,837	$ 23,852
Current portion of long-term debt	5,190	3,009
Accounts payable	170,622	138,188
Accrued expenses	157,479	143,784
Income taxes payable	102,392	81,240
Dividends payable	6,068	6,285
Total current liabilities	505,588	396,358
Long-term debt, net of current portion	131,799	134,207
Minority interest	21,569	14,529
Commitments and contingencies		
Stockholders' equity:		
Common stock, par value $.01; authorized 250,000,000 shares;		
issued 117,155,611 shares in 1994, 119,902,298 shares in 1993	1,172	1,199
Additional paid-in capital	167,953	266,890
Retained earnings	1,428,058	1,198,190
Less 36,210,902 shares in treasury at cost	(603,241)	(603,241)
Unearned compensation	(2,598)	(3,276)
Foreign currency translation adjustment	(839)	(13,145)
	990,505	846,617
	$1,649,461	$1,391,711

The accompanying notes are an integral part of the consolidated financial statements.

Consolidated Statements of Income

Reebok International Ltd.

Amounts in thousands, except per share data

Year ended December 31	1994	1993	1992
Net sales	$3,280,418	$2,893,900	$3,022,627
Other income	7,165	33	39,719
	3,287,583	2,893,933	3,062,346
Costs and expenses:			
Cost of sales	1,966,138	1,719,869	1,809,304
Selling, general and administrative expenses	889,590	769,744	807,078
Special charges	—	8,449	155,000
Amortization of intangibles	4,345	10,052	16,587
Minority interest	8,896	8,261	1,787
Interest expense	16,515	25,021	20,080
Interest income	(6,373)	(10,710)	(5,454)
	2,879,111	2,530,686	2,804,382
Income before income taxes	408,472	363,247	257,964
Income taxes	153,994	139,832	143,146
Net income	$ 254,478	$ 223,415	$ 114,818
Net income per common share	$ 3.02	$ 2.53	$ 1.24
Dividends per common share	$ 0.30	$ 0.30	$ 0.30
Weighted average common and common equivalent shares outstanding	84,311	88,348	92,697

The accompanying notes are an integral part of the consolidated financial statements.

Consolidated Statements of Stockholders' Equity

Reebok International Ltd.

Dollar amounts in thousands

	Common Stock		Additional Paid-in Capital	Retained Earnings	Treasury Stock	Unearned Compen-sation	Foreign Currency Translation Adjustment
	Shares	Par Value					
Balance, December 31, 1991	127,184,410	$ 1,272	$502,962	$ 913,002	$ (603,241)	$ (74)	$ 9,616
Net income				114,818			
Adjustment for foreign currency translation							(17,035)
Issuance of shares to certain employees	33,058	1	1,020			(1,021)	
Amortization of unearned compensation						484	
Shares repurchased and retired	(2,337,100)	(23)	(70,179)				
Shares issued under employee stock purchase plans	152,310	1	3,164				
Shares issued upon exercise of stock options	541,613	5	7,724				
Income tax reductions relating to exercise of stock options			3,365				
Dividends declared				(27,205)			
Balance, December 31, 1992	125,574,291	1,256	448,056	1,000,615	(603,241)	(611)	(7,419)
Net income				223,415			
Adjustment for foreign currency translation							(5,726)
Issuance of shares to certain employees	102,400	1	2,956			(2,957)	
Amortization of unearned compensation						292	
Shares repurchased and retired	(6,235,100)	(62)	(193,959)				
Shares issued under employee stock purchase plans	149,977	1	3,493				
Shares issued upon exercise of stock options	310,730	3	4,648				
Income tax reductions relating to exercise of stock options			1,696				
Dividends declared				(25,840)			
Balance, December 31, 1993	119,902,298	1,199	266,890	1,198,190	(603,241)	(3,276)	(13,145)
Net income				254,478			
Adjustment for foreign currency translation							12,306
Issuance of shares to certain employees	19,293		611			(611)	
Amortization of unearned compensation						827	
Shares repurchased and retired	(3,261,200)	(33)	(112,105)				
Shares retired	(16,000)		(462)			462	
Shares issued under employee stock purchase plans	158,965	2	4,082				
Shares issued upon exercise of stock options	352,255	4	6,172				
Income tax reductions relating to exercise of stock options			2,765				
Dividends declared				(24,610)			
Balance, December 31, 1994	**117,155,611**	**$ 1,172**	**$167,953**	**$ 1,428,058**	**$ (603,241)**	**$(2,598)**	**$ (839)**

The accompanying notes are an integral part of the consolidated financial statements.

Consolidated Statements of Cash Flows

Reebok International Ltd.

Amounts in thousands

Year ended December 31	1994	1993	1992
Cash flows from operating activities:			
Net income	$254,478	$223,415	$114,818
Adjustments to reconcile net income to net cash provided by operating activities:			
Depreciation and amortization	32,228	25,209	27,214
Amortization of intangibles	4,345	10,052	16,587
Minority interest	8,896	8,261	1,787
Amortization of unearned compensation	827	292	484
Deferred income taxes	(13,332)	17,470	(38,190)
Special charges	—	8,449	155,000
Gain on sale of CML common stock	—	—	(29,648)
Changes in operating assets and liabilities, exclusive of those arising from business acquisitions:			
Accounts receivable	(64,786)	(44,682)	(27,598)
Inventory	(81,948)	(84,020)	(39,135)
Prepaid expenses	(7,752)	2,023	7,945
Other	(15,789)	(23,012)	10,402
Accounts payable and accrued expenses	35,211	6,035	(33,068)
Income taxes payable	20,236	(6,959)	21,006
Total adjustments	(81,864)	(80,882)	72,786
Net cash provided by operating activities	172,614	142,533	187,604
Cash flows from investing activities:			
Payments to acquire property and equipment	(61,839)	(26,628)	(36,513)
Proceeds from sale of CML common stock	—	—	31,648
Payments for business acquisitions, net of cash acquired	(4,297)	(10,321)	(3,958)
Proceeds from sale of businesses held for sale	—	36,500	—
Net cash used for investing activities	(66,136)	(449)	(8,823)
Cash flows from financing activities:			
Net borrowings (repayments) of notes payable to banks	37,148	19,961	(5,930)
Proceeds from issuance of common stock to employees	13,025	9,841	14,259
Dividends paid	(24,827)	(26,276)	(27,300)
Repayments of long-term debt	(2,585)	(4,351)	(78,748)
Proceeds from long-term debt	—	20,000	—
Repurchases of common stock	(112,138)	(194,021)	(70,202)
Net cash used for financing activities	(89,377)	(174,846)	(167,921)
Effect of exchange rate changes on cash	(12,512)	6,723	9,809
Net increase (decrease) in cash and cash equivalents	4,589	(26,039)	20,669
Cash and cash equivalents at beginning of year	79,347	105,386	84,717
Cash and cash equivalents at end of year	$ 83,936	$ 79,347	$105,386
Supplemental disclosures of cash flow information:			
Interest paid	$ 19,135	$ 24,348	$ 20,900
Income taxes paid	135,060	132,456	148,783

The accompanying notes are an integral part of the consolidated financial statements.

Notes to Consolidated Financial Statements

Dollar amounts in thousands, except per share data

Reebok International Ltd.

1. Summary of Significant Accounting Policies

Business activity

The Company and its subsidiaries design and market sports and fitness products, including footwear and apparel, as well as footwear and apparel for non-athletic "casual" use, under various trademarks, including REEBOK, WEEBOK, THE PUMP, INSTAPUMP, Boks, the GREG NORMAN Logo, AVIA, ROCKPORT, and TINLEY.

Principles of consolidation

The consolidated financial statements include the accounts of the Company and its subsidiaries. All significant intercompany transactions and accounts are eliminated in consolidation.

Recognition of revenues

Sales are recognized upon shipment of products.

Advertising

Advertising production costs are expensed the first time the advertisement is run. Media (TV and print) placement costs are expensed in the month the advertising appears. Advertising expense (excluding cooperative advertising) amounted to $133,004, $125,027 and $158,980 for the years ended December 31, 1994, 1993 and 1992, respectively.

Cash equivalents

Cash equivalents are defined as highly liquid investments with maturities of three months or less at date of purchase.

Inventory valuation

Inventory, substantially all finished goods, is recorded at the lower of cost (first-in, first-out method) or market.

Property and equipment and depreciation

Property and equipment are stated at cost. Depreciation is computed principally on the straight line method over the assets' estimated useful lives. Leasehold improvements are amortized over the shorter of the lease term or the estimated useful lives of the assets.

Intangibles

Excess purchase price over the fair value of assets acquired is amortized using the straight line method over periods ranging from 5 to 40 years. Other intangibles are amortized using the straight line method over periods ranging from 3 to 40 years.

Foreign currency translation

Assets and liabilities of most of the Company's foreign subsidiaries are translated at current exchange rates. Revenues, costs and expenses are translated at the average exchange rates for the period. Translation adjustments resulting from changes in exchange rates are reported as a separate component of stockholders' equity. Other foreign currency transaction gains and losses are included in the determination of net income.

For those foreign subsidiaries operating in a highly inflationary economy or having the U.S. dollar as their functional currency, net nonmonetary assets are translated at historical rates and net monetary assets are translated at current rates. Translation adjustments are included in the determination of net income.

Income taxes

The Company accounts for income taxes in accordance with FASB Statement No. 109 "Accounting for Income Taxes" ("Statement 109"). Tax provisions and credits are recorded at statutory rates for taxable items included in the consolidated statements of income regardless of the period for which such items are reported for tax purposes. Deferred income taxes are recognized for temporary differences between financial statement and income tax bases of assets and liabilities for which income tax benefits will be realized in future years.

Net income per common share

Net income per common share is computed based on the weighted average number of common and common equivalent shares outstanding for the period.

Reclassification

Certain amounts in prior years have been reclassified to conform to the 1994 presentation.

Notes to Consolidated Financial Statements

Dollar amounts in thousands, except per share data

2. Special Charges

In December 1992, the Company's Board of Directors approved a plan which included offering for sale the Company's Boston Whaler, Inc. ("Boston Whaler") and Ellesse U.S.A., Inc. ("Ellesse") subsidiaries, a write-down of the carrying value of its Avia subsidiary, the planned consolidation and relocation of its performance apparel operation and certain other office relocations. In connection therewith, the Company recorded a $155,000 pre-tax special charge in 1992 for estimated costs and losses to be incurred. The sale of Boston Whaler was completed on July 30, 1993 and the sale of Ellesse was completed on September 28, 1993. In connection with the sales, the Company recorded an additional pre-tax special charge in 1993 of $8,449.

3. Property and Equipment

Property and equipment consist of the following:

December 31	1994	1993
Land	$ 32,243	$ 27,994
Buildings	60,440	41,709
Machinery and equipment	156,046	124,568
Leasehold improvements	34,506	25,355
	283,235	219,626
Less accumulated depreciation and amortization	118,387	89,019
	$164,848	$130,607

4. Intangibles

Intangibles consist of the following:

December 31	1994	1993
Excess of purchase price over fair value of assets acquired (net of accumulated amortization of $128,545 in 1994 and $126,316 in 1993)	$49,811	$45,808
Other intangible assets:		
Purchased technology	52,827	52,827
Company tradename and trademarks	50,104	50,019
Other	13,693	13,731
	116,624	116,577
Less accumulated amortization	70,239	68,123
	46,385	48,454
	$96,196	$94,262

5. Short-Term Borrowings

The Company has various arrangements with numerous banks which provide an aggregate of approximately $762,000 of uncommitted facilities, substantially all of which are available to the Company's foreign subsidiaries. Of this amount, $211,000 is available for short-term borrowings and bank overdrafts, with the remainder available for letters of credit for inventory purchases. In addition to amounts reported as notes payable to banks, approximately $331,000 was outstanding for open letters of credit for inventory purchases at December 31, 1994.

On November 1, 1994, the Company replaced its existing $175,000 credit agreement with a $200,000 credit agreement which expires on October 31, 1995 and a $100,000 loan agreement which expires on October 31, 1999. These agreements, to the extent available, support the Company's commercial paper program under which it can issue up to $125,000.

The weighted average interest rate on notes payable to banks was 4.9% and 5.6% at December 31, 1994 and 1993, respectively.

6. Leasing Arrangements

The Company leases various offices, warehouses, retail store facilities and certain of its data processing and warehouse equipment under lease arrangements expiring between 1995 and 2008. Minimum annual rentals for the five years subsequent to December 31, 1994 and in the aggregate are as follows:

1995	$ 29,049
1996	20,966
1997	15,073
1998	12,803
1999	10,154
2000 and thereafter	21,302
Total minimum lease obligations	$109,347

Total rent expense for all operating leases amounted to $29,167, $23,868 and $20,496 for the years ended December 31, 1994, 1993 and 1992, respectively.

7. Long-Term Debt

Long-term debt consists of the following:

December 31	1994	1993
9.75% debentures due September 15, 1998, with interest payable semiannually on March 15 and September 15	$ 99,645	$ 99,549
Medium-term notes, bearing interest at rates approximating 6%, due February 11, 1998, with interest payable semiannually on February 15 and August 15	20,000	20,000
Bank and other notes payable	17,344	17,667
	136,989	137,216
Less current portion	5,190	3,009
	$131,799	$134,207

Maturities of long-term debt during the five-year period ending December 31, 1999 are $5,190 in 1995, $4,316 in 1996, $3,758 in 1997, $123,313 in 1998, and $88 in 1999.

Land and buildings, having a net book value of $24,168 at December 31, 1994, are pledged as collateral for certain bank notes payable.

8. Employee Benefit Plans

The Company sponsors defined contribution retirement plans covering substantially all of its domestic employees and certain employees of its foreign subsidiaries. Contributions are determined at the discretion of the Board of Directors. Aggregate contributions made by the Company to the plans and charged to operations in 1994, 1993 and 1992 were $13,660, $11,833 and $8,536, respectively.

9. Stock Plans

The Company has various stock option plans which provide for the grant of options to purchase shares of the Company's common stock to key employees, other persons or entities who make significant contributions to the success of the Company, and eligible members of the Company's Board of Directors. The Board of Directors approved the 1994 Equity Incentive Plan on December 15, 1993 which replaced three of the Company's existing stock option and stock bonus plans. Under this new Equity Incentive Plan, options may be incentive stock options or "non-qualified options" under applicable provisions of the Internal Revenue Code. The exercise price of any stock option granted may not be less than fair market value at the date of grant except in certain limited circumstances. The exercise period cannot exceed ten years from the date of grant. The vesting schedule for options granted under the 1994 Equity Incentive Plan is determined by the Compensation Committee of the Board of Directors. With respect to the Plan for Directors, grants vest in equal annual installments over three years.

Notes to Consolidated Financial Statements

Dollar amounts in thousands, except per share data

The following schedule summarizes the changes in stock options during the three years ended December 31, 1994:

	Number of Shares Under Option		
	Incentive Stock Options	Non-Qualified Stock Options	Option Price Per Share
Outstanding at December 31, 1991	3,516	5,848,755	1.42-30.63
Granted	—	544,000	21.38-39.77
Exercised	(3,516)	(538,097)	1.42-20.46
Cancelled	—	(343,520)	10.63-31.25
Outstanding at December 31, 1992	—	5,511,138	8.75-39.77
Granted	—	1,605,800	11.38-41.74
Exercised	—	(310,730)	8.75-27.63
Cancelled	—	(399,240)	11.38-33.25
Outstanding at December 31, 1993	—	6,406,968	8.75-41.74
Granted	—	**212,797**	**28.88-38.88**
Exercised	—	**(352,255)**	**8.75-33.25**
Cancelled	—	**(387,935)**	**11.38-41.74**
Outstanding at December 31, 1994	—	**5,879,575**	**8.75-39.77**

At December 31, 1994 and 1993, options to purchase 3,241,684 and 2,485,340 shares of common stock were exercisable, and 4,351,514 and 5,785,355 options, respectively, were available for future grants under the Company's stock option plans.

The 1994 Equity Incentive Plan also provides for the Company to grant restricted stock to key employees, and other persons or entities who make significant contributions to the success of the Company. The vesting schedule for restricted stock granted under this Plan is determined by the Compensation Committee of the Board of Directors.

The Company has two employee stock purchase plans. Under the 1987 Employee Stock Purchase Plan eligible employees are granted options to purchase shares of the Company's common stock through voluntary payroll deductions during two option periods, running from January 1 to June 30 and from July 1 to December 31, at the lower of 85% of market value at the beginning or end of each period. The number of options granted to each employee under this plan is limited to a fair market value of $12.5 during each option period. Under the 1992 Employee Stock Purchase Plan, for certain foreign based employees, eligible employees are granted options to purchase shares of the Company's common stock during two option periods, running from January 1 to June 30 and from July 1 to December 31, at the market price at the beginning of the period. The option becomes exercisable 90 days following the date of grant and expires on the last day of the option period. During 1994, 1993 and 1992, respectively, 158,965, 149,977, and 152,310 shares were issued pursuant to these plans.

In June 1990, the Company adopted a shareholders' rights plan and declared a dividend distribution of one common stock purchase right ("Right") for each share of common stock outstanding. Each Right entitles the holder to purchase one share of the Company's common stock at a price of $60 per share, subject to adjustment. The Rights will be exercisable only if a person or group of affiliated or associated persons acquires beneficial ownership of 10% or more of the outstanding shares of the Company's common stock or commences a tender or exchange offer that would result in a person or group owning 10% or more of the outstanding common stock, or in the event that the Company is subsequently acquired in a merger or other business combination. When the Rights become exercisable, each holder would have the right to purchase, at the then-current exercise price, common stock of the surviving company having a market value of two times the exercise price of the Right. The Company can redeem the Rights at $.01 per Right at any time prior to expiration on June 14, 2000.

At December 31, 1994, 11,176,621 shares of common stock were reserved for issuance under the Company's various stock plans and 92,121,330 shares were reserved for issuance under the shareholders' rights plan.

10. Acquisition of Common Stock

On October 4, 1994, the Board of Directors authorized the repurchase of up to an additional $200,000 in Reebok common stock in open market or privately-negotiated transactions. This authorization was in addition to the $200,000 share repurchase programs adopted by the Company in July 1992 and July 1993. As of December 31, 1994, the Company had approximately $223,600 available for future repurchases of common stock under these programs.

11. Financial Instruments

The following methods and assumptions were used by the Company to estimate the fair value of its financial instruments:

Cash and cash equivalents and notes payable to banks: the carrying amounts reported in the balance sheet approximate fair value. Long term-debt: the fair value of the Company's corporate bonds is estimated based on quoted market prices. The fair value of other long-term debt is estimated using discounted cash flow analyses, based on the Company's incremental borrowing rates for similar types of borrowing arrangements. Unrealized gains or losses on foreign currency exchange contracts: the fair value of the Company's foreign currency exchange contracts is estimated based on current foreign exchange rates.

The carrying amounts and fair value of the Company's financial instruments are as follows:

December 31	Carrying Amount 1994	1993	Fair Value 1994	1993
Long-term debt	$136,989	$137,216	$139,842	$146,504
Unrealized gains (losses) on foreign currency exchange contracts	(2,152)	1,662	(179)	4,516

The Company enters into forward currency exchange contracts to hedge its exposure for merchandise purchased in U.S. dollars that will be sold to customers in other currencies. Realized and unrealized gains and losses on these contracts are included in net income except that gains and losses on contracts which hedge specific foreign currency commitments are deferred and accounted for as a part of the transaction.

The Company also uses forward currency exchange contracts to hedge significant intercompany assets and liabilities denominated in other than the functional currency. Contracts used to hedge intercompany balances are marked to market and the resulting transaction gain or loss is included in the determination of net income. Foreign currency gains or losses included in net income for the years ended December 31, 1994, 1993 and 1992 were not significant.

At December 31, 1994, the Company had forward currency exchange contracts, all having maturities of less than one year, with a notional amount aggregating $306 million. Deferred gains on these contracts at December 31, 1994 and 1993, approximated $2 million and $2.9 million, respectively.

12. Other Income

Other income in 1992 included a gain of $29,648 resulting from the sale of 1,161,403 shares of common stock of CML acquired upon the exercise of a warrant obtained as part of the October 1989 purchase of Boston Whaler.

13. Income Taxes

The components of income before income taxes are as follows:

	1994	1993	1992
Domestic	$171,166	$141,428	$ 22,453
Foreign	237,306	221,819	235,511
	$408,472	$363,247	$257,964

Notes to Consolidated Financial Statements

Dollar amounts in thousands, except per share data

The provision for income taxes consists of the following:

	1994	1993	1992
Current:			
Federal	$ 66,879	$ 39,725	$ 68,456
State	16,607	14,082	15,588
Foreign	83,840	68,555	97,292
	167,326	122,362	181,336
Deferred:			
Federal	(3,038)	16,244	(23,868)
State	(303)	(310)	(1,100)
Foreign	(9,991)	1,536	(13,222)
	(13,332)	17,470	(38,190)
	$153,994	$139,832	$143,146

In 1992, deferred tax credits attributable to special charges approximated $16,200.

Undistributed earnings of the Company's foreign subsidiaries amounted to approximately $316,099, $215,559 and $161,421 at December 31, 1994, 1993 and 1992, respectively. Those earnings are considered to be indefinitely reinvested and, accordingly, no provision for U.S. federal and state income taxes has been provided thereon. Upon distribution of those earnings in the form of dividends or otherwise, the Company would be subject to both U.S. income taxes and foreign withholding taxes, less an adjustment for applicable foreign tax credits. Determination of the amount of U.S. income tax liability that would be incurred is not practicable because of the complexities associated with its hypothetical calculation; however, unrecognized foreign tax credits would be available to reduce some portion of any U.S. income tax liability.

Income taxes computed at the federal statutory rate differ from amounts provided as follows:

	1994	1993	1992
Tax at statutory rate	35.0%	35.0%	34.0%
State taxes, less federal tax effect	2.6	2.5	3.7
Effect of tax rates of foreign subsidiaries and joint ventures	(1.3)	(.8)	2.1
Amortization of intangibles	.5	.6	.8
Special charges	—	—	13.9
Other, net	.9	1.2	1.0
Provision for income taxes	37.7%	38.5%	55.5%

Effective January 1, 1993, the Company adopted Statement 109. Under Statement 109, the liability method is used in accounting for income taxes. Under this method, deferred tax assets and liabilities are determined based on differences between financial reporting and tax bases of assets and liabilities and are measured using the enacted tax rates and laws that will be in effect when the differences are expected to reverse. Prior to the adoption of Statement 109, income tax expense was based on items of income and expense that were reported in different years in the financial statements and tax returns and were measured at the tax rate in effect in the year the difference originated.

As permitted by Statement 109, the Company did not restate the financial statements of any prior years. The effect of the change on net income for 1993 was not material.

Deferred income taxes reflect the net tax effects of temporary differences between the carrying amount of assets and liabilities for financial reporting purposes and the amounts used for income tax purposes.

Reebok International Ltd.

Deferred taxes are attributable to the following temporary differences at December 31:

	1994	1993
Inventory	$34,757	$27,595
Accounts receivable	27,825	26,252
Other — net	6,784	2,187
	$69,366	$56,034

14. Operations by Geographic Area

Sales to unaffiliated customers, net income and identifiable assets by geographic area are summarized below:

	1994	1993	1992
Sales:			
United States	$1,974,904	$1,775,496	$1,982,153
United Kingdom	506,658	434,249	414,745
Europe	502,029	465,770	425,451
Other countries	296,827	218,385	200,278
	$3,280,418	$2,893,900	$3,022,627
Net income:			
United States	$ 126,916	$ 98,692	$ (852)
United Kingdom	62,949	65,734	75,112
Europe	28,290	34,575	24,964
Other countries	36,323	24,414	15,594
	$ 254,478	$ 223,415	$ 114,818
Identifiable assets:			
United States	$ 963,462	$ 916,962	$ 929,495
United Kingdom	282,795	152,206	172,012
Europe	221,771	146,541	95,384
Other countries	181,433	176,002	148,455
	$1,649,461	$1,391,711	$1,345,346

There are various differences between income before income taxes for domestic and foreign operations as shown in Note 13 and net income shown above.

Notes to Consolidated Financial Statements

Dollar amounts in thousands, except per share data

15.   Contingencies

On February 5, 1993, a lawsuit was filed against the Company and its then wholly owned subsidiary Ellesse U.S.A., Inc., in the United States District Court for the District of Massachusetts. A second related lawsuit was filed on August 10, 1993 in the United States District Court for the District of Massachusetts. These two cases have been consolidated. Both complaints allege, among other things, that the Company breached an agreement with the plaintiff and misappropriated trade secrets in connection with the development of the Company's THE PUMP inflatable technology and its procurement of its patent for the basic THE PUMP technology. The complaint requests a declaratory judgment stating that the plaintiff is the owner/inventor of the Company's THE PUMP patent, an assignment of the Company's patent, recovery of the Company's profits and other substantial damages from the Company.

On July 1, 1993, a lawsuit was filed against the Company in the Central District of Los Angeles County Superior Court and subsequently moved to the United States District Court for the District of California. The complaint alleges, among other things, fraud, misappropriation and conversion, unfair competition, tortuous interference with prospective economic advantage in connection with the development of the Company's THE PUMP technology and patent infringement. The complaint requests compensatory damages, punitive damages, costs and attorneys' fees.

On February 7, 1994, a lawsuit was filed against the Company in California Superior Court challenging the Company's resale pricing practices in California under California state law and seeking unspecified damages, including treble damages, injunctive relief and costs.

The Company intends to vigorously defend these lawsuits and believes that these lawsuits are without merit, and further believes that it is unlikely any subsequent outcome would have a material adverse effect on the financial condition of the Company.

Report of Ernst & Young LLP, Independent Auditors

Reebok International Ltd.

Board of Directors and Stockholders
Reebok International Ltd.
Stoughton, Massachusetts

We have audited the consolidated balance sheets of Reebok International Ltd. and subsidiaries as of December 31, 1994 and 1993, and the related consolidated statements of income, stockholders' equity, and cash flows for each of the three years in the period ended December 31, 1994. These financial statements are the responsibility of the Company's management. Our responsibility is to express an opinion on these financial statements based on our audits.

We conducted our audits in accordance with generally accepted auditing standards. Those standards require that we plan and perform the audit to obtain reasonable assurance about whether the financial statements are free of material misstatement. An audit includes examining, on a test basis, evidence supporting the amounts and disclosures in the financial statements. An audit also includes assessing the accounting principles used and significant estimates made by management, as well as evaluating the overall financial statement presentation. We believe that our audits provide a reasonable basis for our opinion.

In our opinion, the consolidated financial statements referred to above present fairly, in all material respects, the consolidated financial position of Reebok International Ltd. and subsidiaries at December 31, 1994 and 1993, and the consolidated results of their operations and their cash flows for each of the three years in the period ended December 31, 1994 in conformity with generally accepted accounting principles.

Ernst & Young LLP

Boston, Massachusetts
January 31, 1995

Quarterly Results of Operations

Amounts in thousands, except per share data

	First Quarter	Second Quarter	Third Quarter	Fourth Quarter
Year ended December 31, 1994				
Net sales	$857,366	$776,753	$937,148	$709,151
Gross profit	337,522	307,774	375,330	293,654
Net income	65,789	51,008	84,655	53,026
Net income per common share	.77	.60	1.01	.64
Cash dividends per common share	.075	.075	.075	.075
Year ended December 31, 1993				
Net sales	$825,220	$657,613	$808,493	$602,574
Gross profit	335,381	267,282	322,644	248,724
Net income	67,769	41,028	63,933	50,685
Net income per common share	.74	.46	.74	.59
Cash dividends per common share	.075	.075	.075	.075

Net income for the third quarter of 1993 includes an after-tax special charge of $7,037 ($.08 per share).

Report of Management

Financial Statements

The management of Reebok International Ltd. and its subsidiaries has prepared the accompanying financial statements and is responsible for their integrity and fair presentation. The statements, which include amounts that are based on management's best estimates and judgments, have been prepared in conformity with generally accepted accounting principles and are free of material misstatement. Management has also prepared other information in the annual report and is responsible for its accuracy and consistency with the financial statements.

Internal Control System

Reebok International Ltd. and its subsidiaries maintain a system of internal control over financial reporting, which is designed to provide reasonable assurance to the Company's management and Board of Directors as to the integrity and fair presentation of the financial statements. Management continually monitors the system of internal control for compliance, and actions are taken to correct deficiencies as they are identified. Even an effective internal control system, no matter how well designed, has inherent limitations—including the possibility of the circumvention or overriding of controls—and therefore can provide only reasonable assurance with respect to financial statement preparation. Further, because of changes in conditions, internal control system effectiveness may vary over time.

The Company maintains an internal auditing program that monitors and assesses the effectiveness of the internal controls system and recommends possible improvements thereto. The Company's accompanying financial statements have been audited by Ernst & Young LLP, independent auditors, whose audit was made in accordance with generally accepted auditing standards and included a review of the system of internal accounting controls to the extent necessary to determine the audit procedures required to support their opinion on the consolidated financial statements. Management believes that, as of December 31, 1994, the Company's system of internal control is adequate to accomplish the objectives discussed herein.

Reebok International Ltd.,

Paul Fireman
Chairman
President and Chief Executive Officer

Paul R. Duncan
Executive Vice President and Chief Financial Officer

STUDYING THIS APPENDIX
WILL ENABLE YOU TO

1. Recognize the various applications of the Internet and the World Wide Web.
2. Access and view a page on the WWW using Netscape.
3. Locate pages using directories and search programs.
4. Locate financial accounting information on the World Wide Web.

INTRODUCTION TO THE INTERNET AND THE WORLD WIDE WEB

INTRODUCTION

The **Internet** is the vast group of interconnected computers and local area networks that use a standardized protocol (TCP/IP) to transfer data files from one location to another. The Internet is connected via high-speed, wide-bandwidth digital telephone lines. Users can send files to another computer or receive files from another computer. For as long as the Internet and its predecessors have existed, the most popular application has been **e-mail,** which allows messages to be sent by one user to another. Another popular application has been for users in government and university settings to send data files to other locations for processing.

The Internet now stretches around the world. Although 60% of all Internet users (numbered in the tens of millions) live in the United States, even remote locations of the world are now going online.

The **World Wide Web (WWW)** is a hot new use of the Internet that has captured the notice and imagination of people around the world. The WWW permits one user (a provider) to place a file on a computer system for recall upon demand by another user from anywhere on the Internet. What makes the WWW so appealing is that these files contain up-to-date information of general interest and can be enhanced with graphics, audio, and video. Some people describe the WWW as a new publication channel, with file displays resembling glossy magazines or pamphlets. The WWW is expected to overtake e-mail as the most popular use of the Internet.

Appendix G written by W. David Albrecht and Niranjan Chipalkatti

HISTORY OF THE INTERNET AND THE WWW

The Internet is a recent phenomenon, but it has deep roots. In the context of the Cold War, the Advanced Research Projects Agency (ARPA) within the U.S. Department of Defense was charged with the responsibility of finding the best way to connect computer sites to preserve the ability to transfer research and military information in case of nuclear attack. The ARPANET was created in 1970, connecting computers from four Western universities. The ARPANET was supplanted as other networks were created in the late 1970s and early 1980s, and as other universities wished to gain the benefits of e-mail and file transfers. BITNET, a well-known network established in 1983, was one such network that was used extensively by several major universities in the United States.

The Internet was born when the National Science Foundation network (NSFnet) was established in the late 1980s to create a high-speed network of research computers. All institutions that wanted to be on the network had to be sponsored by a U.S. government agency. When this requirement was dropped in 1990, the Internet began to experience explosive growth. Today, the NSFnet is dead, but the Internet connects thousands of networks, millions of computers, and tens of millions of users.

As networks developed, different applications became popular. Adoption of the first **FTP** (File Transfer Protocol) in 1971 made it possible for a user to retrieve a file from another site. For example, an individual at one site might place a file in disk storage for retrieval by a group of end users at different sites. To avoid passing the provider's password around so that other users could gain access, the provider would designate his or her disk storage as an **anonymous FTP** site, whereby no password would be necessary for *anyone* to retrieve the file. Anonymous FTP is a fundamental tool of the WWW.

Then came **Archie,** which was software for finding files on anonymous FTP sites. Archie was difficult to use because the search required the exact name (or a substring) of the desired file. In other words, it was not possible to travel to the anonymous FTP site to see what was available. It was first necessary to know precisely what was wanted before the search was begun.

Gopher, the next development, quickly became widely successful because it provided a means for end users to look at menus of available materials before they retrieved the files over the Internet. Gopher uses server and client software. A **server program** is used on the computer system where the files reside, and automatically handles the process of serving up files to people requesting it via anonymous FTP. Computers storing these programs have come to be known as **servers.** A **client application** is software on the end user's computer that is necessary in order to call up data from another server. With Gopher software, it is possible to travel to other sites without first knowing what is available. Users started viewing the Internet as an incredible electronic encyclopedia because of all of the information that was made available. Gopher's principal shortcoming is that it only provides access to text files in ASCII format.

As client computers became more powerful, and the Internet backbone of digital phone lines increased in capacity, the stage was set for the creation of the WWW. Gopher is still used today, but the WWW has almost done away with it. The WWW also uses a server–client style of software, but its **HTML** (Hyper Text Markup Language) protocol permits information providers to use various graphical styles in presenting the text. In addition, graphic images and audio or video clips may be used to enhance the end user's application of the information.

HTML has evolved since its creation. At the time of this writing, information providers are formatting files for WWW applications using HTML level 3. As new levels are adopted, information providers are given additional flexibility in graphical layout.

The files that end users retrieve are called **pages.** As noted earlier, the WWW has made possible an environment whereby information providers publish on the WWW. The graphic, audio, and video enhancements permit the information to be displayed in a format similar to magazine and pamphlet layouts, hence the term *page.*

HOW TO USE THE WWW

To use the WWW, you will first need to gain access to a **browser** program. In 1995, Netscape Navigator® became overwhelmingly popular because of its options for graphics layout and design, and its fast retrieval of files. Other browsers, such as Lynx® and Mosaic®, are still used but have lost much of their earlier popularity because of graphics and speed limitations.

To retrieve a file from a browser, you will need to know the file's Internet address, which is called an URL (Uniform Resource Locator, pronounced "Earl"). The low-speed home page for West Publishing Corporation is at **http://www.westpub. com/lsphome.htm.** The URL has three parts. The *http://* designates the file transfer as WWW instead of FTP or Gopher. The *www.wespub.com* is called the domain, or the address, of the server on which the files are stored. Domain names usually contain a code for the type of site. For example, *com* designates a commercial site, *edu* designates an educational site, *gov* designates a government site, and *org* is used by organizations. If the server is within the United States, it usually contains no geographic code (*us* is occasionally used). Common geographic codes are *au,* Australia; *jp,* Japan; *gb,* Great Britain; and *fr,* France. The *lsphome.htm* is the file name. Note that URLs are case sensitive.

When you first turn on a computer and open the Netscape program, a "home," or starting, page opens by default. If you are in a university computer lab, the home page default is typically set to the university's home page. At the top of the screen, you will notice buttons for the operation of Netscape. The most important part is the location box. This location box contains the URL of the page you are viewing.

You have three primary choices whenever you view a page. First, you can read it. Second, you can choose to travel to another page by clicking on a link included on the current page. This link is generally underlined and in a different color from the base text of the current page. Point the cursor to the link and click the left mouse button. Third, you can choose to travel to another page using a known address and typing it into the location box.

So how do you find the URL of a WWW file? If you wanted to locate a phone number, you would either look in a telephone directory or you would call directory assistance. URLs are located in the same manner. There are general-purpose directories and narrow focus directories. The most popular general-purpose directory is called Yahoo!® **(http://www.yahoo.com/).** Yahoo was first created in late 1994 by two Stanford students who spent a great deal of time browsing for files on the WWW. Their personal directory became very popular because of the shortage of other general-purpose directories. Their directory grew so large and popular (more than one million uses per day) that they have left school and gone commercial.

The most popular directory database is Lycos® **(http://www.lycos.com/).** Lycos has a program that locates pages stored on servers connected to the Internet. Lycos claims to have cataloged 90% of all WWW pages into a database searchable by key-words. Lycos usually adds a newly created page to its directory within two or three weeks of its creation.

WWW SOURCES OF FINANCIAL ACCOUNTING INFORMATION

The information necessary for financial statement analysis comes from the financial statements for particular companies and from industry statistics. Financial ratios for industries are not yet available on the WWW. However, the accounting information from financial statements is available from many sources.

The premier financial accounting database is provided by the Securities and Exchange Commission (SEC). Publicly traded corporations must file many types of disclosures, such as the 10-K, 10-Q, and 8-K forms and the proxy statement. For several years, the SEC has asked corporations to voluntarily submit this information electronically. This database of electronically filed statements is called EDGAR. Since 1994, the SEC has permitted public access to EDGAR through the Internet **(http://www.sec.gov/edgarhp.htm)**.

A second source of financial information is the WWW displays of the companies themselves. Tens of thousands of companies maintain Web pages. The largest companies have sections for shareholder relations, many of which include an HTML-formatted set of financial statements.

Another source of financial information on the WWW is to go to companies that sell information. Quote.Com **(http://www.quote.com/)** is one such company that has a site through which it sells financial accounting information.

EDGAR ASSIGNMENT

The primary purpose of this assignment is to gain familiarity with the EDGAR archives. A secondary purpose of this assignment is to gain familiarity with specific SEC disclosure forms (10-K, 10-Q, S-8, proxy statement, 8-K).

Access the SEC archives at **http://www.sec.gov/edgarhp.htm.** Use the search routine to locate the SEC disclosures for the AAR Corporation and the Atlas Corporation (or other companies of your instructor's choosing).

The following reports are available on EDGAR for the AAR Corp.:

- 10-K   8-11-95
- 10-Q   4-14-95
- S-8   2-17-94
- DEF 14A   8-24-94

The following reports are available on EDGAR for the Atlas Corp.:

- 8-K   8-24-95

Locate and read the preceding forms, then answer the following questions.

10-K AAR Corp. (8-11-95)

1. What is AAR Corp.'s Standard Industrial Classification number?
2. How many shares of stock were outstanding as of 7-31-95?
3. When did AAR's predecessor organization begin operations?
4. What were net sales for the year ended 5-31-95?
5. How many people did AAR employ as of 5-31-95?

10-Q AAR Corp. (4-14-95)

1. What is the conformed period of this report?
2. What were net sales for the three months ended 2-28-95?
3. What was net income for the three months ended 2-28-95?

S-8 AAR Corp. (2-17-95)

1. What securities are being registered (be specific)?
2. What amount of securities are being registered?
3. What is the proposed maximum offering price per share?
4. What is the proposed maximum aggregate offering price?
5. What is the amount of the registration fee?

DEF 14A AAR Corp. (8-24-95)

1. What two items of business will be conducted at the 1995 annual meeting of AAR Corp. shareowners?

8-K Atlas Corp. (8-24-95)

1. What items (and their numbers) are disclosed in this filing?
2. What did Atlas Corp. purchase?
3. Who is the new president of Atlas Corp.?
4. Who signed this filing?

GLOSSARY

A

accelerated depreciation Depreciation method that recognizes greater depreciation in an asset's earlier years and results in less income. Accelerated depreciation is widely used for federal tax purposes.

account A category created in order to group like transactions for the purpose of recording activity and providing information.

accounting The systematic process of measuring the economic activity of an entity to provide useful information to those who make business and economic decisions.

accounting changes Includes a change in accounting principle, a change in estimate, and a change in reporting entity.

accounting information system The processes and procedures required to generate accounting information.

Accounting Principles Board (APB) Predecessor to the FASB.

accounts payable Unwritten obligations arising in the normal course of business. Accounts payable typically result from the purchase of inventory, supplies, and services.

accounts receivable Credit sales that have not yet been collected. The relevant amount is the estimated cash to be generated from collections of the accounts. See *allowance for uncollectible accounts* and *net realizable value* for related terms.

accounts receivable as a percent of sales A liquidity ratio used to assess a company's collection procedures and working capital management. Calculated as gross accounts receivable divided by sales.

accrual basis of accounting Records revenues when goods or services have been earned, regardless of when cash is received. Records expenses when incurred, regardless of when cash is distributed.

accrued expenses (liabilities) A current liability that represents services already consumed, but no cash has been paid.

accumulated benefit obligation The amount of pension benefits, calculated under actuarial and present value assumptions, that employees have earned to date, based on current salary levels.

accumulated depreciation The total amount of depreciation that has been recognized to date on a long-lived asset. Presented as a "contra-asset" account that is subtracted from the asset's cost to determine its net book value.

accumulated postretirement benefit obligation The actuarial present value of the future postretirement benefits that employees and retirees have earned to date.

acid-test ratio See *quick ratio*.

acquisition A business combination in which a buyer firm acquires more than 50% of the voting stock of an investee firm, and thereby controls the investee.

actuarial assumptions Assumptions about future events based on historic data such as employee turnover, service lives, and longevity that are used to estimate future costs such as pension benefits.

adjusting entries Journal entries entered into the accounting records typically before financial statements are prepared. Adjusting entries are needed to ensure that the account balances are correct and up to date.

adjustment A change in the accounting equation to record accruals, deferrals, and other estimates so that the equation reflects changes in assets, liabilities, and equities. Could also refer to an *adjusting entry*.

administrative expenses Support function expenses consisting of senior managers' salaries, accounting and auditing costs, insurance, depreciation of administrative offices, etc.

advances from customers See *unearned revenue*.

aging method Refers to classifying accounts receivable by the number of days they are past due; for example, 0 to 30 days, 31 to 60 days, 61 to 90 days, more than 90 days, etc.

allowance for uncollectible accounts An overall estimate of the amount of accounts receivable that will not be collected. Presented as a "contra-asset" account that is subtracted from accounts receivable.

amortization The periodic recognition of the consumption (expense) of an intangible asset.

annual report The annual report includes financial statements as well as notes to the statements, management discussion, and the independent auditor's report.

annuity Equal cash flows over uniform time intervals.

APB See *Accounting Principles Board.*

arms-length transaction Transactions that are conducted by independent parties, each acting in their own self-interest.

asset management ratios Show the composition of the firm's assets, as well as changes in the composition of assets over time.

assets Valuable resources that an entity owns or controls. They represent probable future economic benefits and arise as a result of past transactions or events.

associating cause and effect An application of the matching principle where a clear and direct relationship or link exists between an expense and its associated revenue. See *matching principle.*

audit An evaluation of the credibility of a firm's financial statements by independent CPAs. The audit opinion is the product of the audit and reflects the auditor's professional judgment regarding whether the financial statements are presented fairly in accordance with generally accepted accounting principles.

audit opinion An auditor's report expressing an opinion as to whether the financial statements were prepared according to generally accepted accounting principles. See *audit.*

authorized shares Shares of stock that the firm is permitted to issue according to its corporate charter.

available-for-sale securities An investment for which unrealized gains and losses are not included in net income.

average cost method A method for determining the per unit cost of inventories by summing the beginning inventory cost plus all purchases and dividing by the number of units available for sale. Contrast with FIFO or LIFO method.

average exchange rate Refers to converting financial amounts expressed in terms of one country's currency into a different monetary unit. The average exchange rate over a month or a year can be used to make the foreign currency translation, as compared to using the *current exchange rate.*

B

balance sheet A financial statement that shows, at a specified time, a firm's financial condition, which is determined by its assets, liabilities, and owners' equity. Also referred to as *statement of financial position.*

basic accounting equation A simple three-element equation that corresponds to the balance sheet. The equation is Assets = Liabilities + Owners' Equity, where Owners' Equity is synonymous with Shareholders' Equity.

basis of comparison Assessing a firm's economic condition by establishing a reference or benchmark for the firm's financial information. Benchmarks include the firm's prior performance, industry averages, and that of other firms.

big bath When a firm reports large accounting losses in a single year that do not truly reflect the performance or profitability of the firm. The losses are created by accounting treatments that are motivated by reasons such as favorable bonuses for management in a subsequent year.

bond or bonds payable Liability in the form of a note, issued to investors.

book value An asset's cost less its accumulated depreciation.

bottom line See *net income.*

budgets Quantitative expressions of corporate plans and expectations of future results.

buildings See *plant.*

business combination The general term for the activity in which one firm takes over or assumes control over another firm. Forms of business combinations include mergers, consolidations, and acquisitions.

C

capital Conventional terminology for sole proprietorships that denotes the owners' interest in the assets of the business.

capital acquisition ratio Capital structure analysis that indicates the proportion of cash flows from operating activities that are used to finance expansion. Calculated as cash flows from operating activities divided by net cash outflows from investing activities.

capital gains (or losses) Result from increases (or decreases) in the market price of stocks over the period they are held by investors.

capital lease A lease agreement that is treated like an installment purchase (sale) of an asset. Capital leases increase the amounts of reported long-term assets and long-term debt for the lessee. The lessor records a receivable and eliminates the leased asset from its accounting records.

capital structure Analysis of a firm's strategy for financing its assets with relative amounts of debt and equity.

capitalize Record expenditures related to an asset's acquisition, installation, or refurbishment as part of the cost of the asset. The carrying (book) value of the asset is increased by these costs.

carrying value The historical cost of an asset less its accumulated depreciation.

cash and cash equivalents Includes currency, bank deposits, and various marketable securities that can be turned into cash on short notice. These amounts are available to meet the firm's cash payment requirements.

cash basis of accounting Records revenue when cash is received and records expenses when cash is distributed.

cash flows from financing activities Cash flow transactions to obtain or repay owners' investment, bonds, and long-term loans. Reported on the *statement of cash flows.*

cash flows from investing activities Cash flow transactions for acquiring or disposing of long-term assets and long-term investments. Reported on the *statement of cash flows.*

cash flows from operating activities (CFOA) The net cash increase (decrease) resulting from the firm's operating activities. Reported on the *statement of cash flows.*

cash interest coverage ratio Shows the relationship between all cash available to pay interest and the interest actually paid. Calculated as CFOA plus interest and taxes paid divided by interest paid.

cash return on assets Ratio to analyze a firm's profitability and financial returns. Calculated as (cash flow from operating activities plus interest paid) divided by average total assets.

cash return on shareholders' equity Ratio to analyze a firm's profitability and financial returns. Calculated as cash flow from operating activities divided by average shareholders' equity.

cash-to-debt coverage ratio Capital structure analysis that indicates the proportion of cash flow from operating activities (CFOA) relative to debt. Calculated as CFOA divided by total debt.

change funds Cash funds to enable cashiers to make change for their customers. Included in cash on the balance sheet. See *petty cash.*

change in accounting estimate Refers to a change in an estimate that underlies financial statement amounts. Includes changes in useful lives and salvage values of fixed assets.

change in accounting principle A change by a reporting entity in the accounting principles used to prepare its financial statements.

change in reporting entity A change in the subsidiaries that comprise a consolidated group.

chart of accounts Lists account titles and account numbers that serve as an index to the general ledger.

charter Formal registration document filed with the state of incorporation that includes the corporation's business purpose, and authorizes the firm to issue one or more types of ownership shares. Referred to as "corporate charter."

closing entries Transfer the amounts in the revenue and expense (nominal) accounts to retained earnings.

CMA (Certified Management Accountant) Professional certification program administered by The Institute of Management Accountants.

collateral Specific assets pledged for security as part of a loan agreement. The creditor may have the right to seize the collateral in the event of loan default by the borrower.

collection period The average length of time it takes to collect a receivable. Calculated by dividing accounts receivable by average sales per day.

commitments Agreements with suppliers, customers, employers, or other entities that relate to "not yet completed" transactions and consequently have not been recognized in the accounts. When significant, they should be disclosed in the notes to the financial statements.

common size income statements Vertical analysis that measures and reports all the components on the income statement as a percentage of net sales. This technique allows comparability across periods and firms.

common stock Basic type of stock ownership that typically entitles the stockholder to vote on corporate matters and share in profits. Common shareholders are the true residual owners of the corporation.

common stock equivalent Securities and stock options that can be converted to common stock.

compensating balances Deposits or funds that a firm agrees to keep in accounts with a lender that pay little or no interest. The lender usually earns interest on such funds, which is not paid to the borrower.

composition analysis The starting point for any analysis of capital structure. It provides a description of the relative amounts of capital obtained from each major source of financing. See *asset management ratios* or *capital structure..*

compound interest The process of earning interest on interest from previous periods.

conservatism principle When doubt exists about the accounting treatment for a given transaction, the alternative that reports lower asset values and lower net income is usually selected.

consolidated financial statements Reports that combine financial position, cash flows, and operating results for all firms that are under the parent company's control.

consolidation A business combination in which a new corporation is created to acquire the stock or the net assets of two or more existing companies. The original companies then cease to exist as separate corporations.

contingencies Conditions which may result in gains and losses, and which will be resolved by the occurrence of future events.

contra account Account that is used solely to record and accumulate reductions in the balance of its related account. A contra account balance is subtracted from the balance of the related account.

contra-equity account A "negative" equity account; a deduction from another shareholders' equity account. For example, *treasury stock* is always shown as a deduction from shareholders' equity. See *contra account.*

contributed capital The portion of shareholders' equity that arises from direct contributions (investments) from the owners.

convertible bonds Bonds that entitle the bondholder to exchange the bonds for a specified number of shares of stock at a specified future time.

convertible preferred stock Preferred shares that may be exchanged for common shares at a specified future time.

copyright Granted by the federal government to convey the exclusive right to use artistic or literary works for a period of 75 years.

corporation A separate accounting and legal entity, apart from its owners (shareholders), granted the right to exist under its charter by individual states.

cost accounting Determines product costs and other relevant information used for managerial decision making.

cost method of accounting The parent company recognizes income on its financial statements from the subsidiary only when the subsidiary declares a dividend.

cost of goods sold The direct cost of acquiring or manufacturing a product that has been sold.

cost of goods sold percentage Cost of goods sold divided by net sales.

coupon rate The stated interest rate in a bond contract. Also referred to as the *nominal, stated,* or *face* rate.

CPA (Certified Public Accountant) CPAs are licensed by individual states. The CPA exam is administered by the American Institute of Certified Public Accountants.

CPA firms Provide the three primary services that comprise public accounting: auditing, tax preparation, and management consulting.

credit The right-hand side of an entry in the double-entry accounting system.

cumulative effect The usual approach for implementing a change in accounting principle. The cumulative effect is included in the current year's net income.

cumulative preferred stock Shares that accumulate dividends when dividends are not declared by the firm. Accumulated dividends must be paid before any dividends can be paid to common shareholders.

currency forward market Market in which foreign currencies are bought and sold for future delivery.

current assets Includes cash and other assets that will typically be converted to cash or be consumed in one year or one operating cycle (if greater than one year).

current exchange rate Refers to converting financial amounts expressed in terms of one country's currency into a different monetary unit. The current exchange rate at the end of a month or a year can be used to make the foreign currency translation, as compared to using the *average exchange rate.*

current liabilities Includes trade accounts payable and other short-term obligations that will be due in one year or one operating cycle, if greater than one year. Also includes the *current maturities of long-term debt.*

current maturities of long-term debt The portion of long-term debt due within the upcoming period.

current ratio The most popular liquidity ratio, calculated by dividing all current assets by all current liabilities.

D

date of declaration Date the firm has obligated itself to make a dividend payment. On that date, owners' equity (retained earnings) is decreased and liabilities (dividends payable) is increased.

date of payment Date the actual dividend payment is made. Cash and dividends payable (liability) are reduced.

date of record Date that determines who will receive the dividend. The investor that holds the stock on that day will be paid the dividend.

debit The left-hand side of an entry into the double-entry accounting system.

debt management ratios Analysis of the balance sheet that focuses on the composition of a firm's debt including long-term notes, bonds, and lines of credit.

debt securities Investments in debt instruments such as commercial paper or bonds. These instruments provide evidence of indebtedness and can be negotiated (sold).

debt-to-assets ratio A primary indicator of a firm's debt management and leverage position that employs percentage composition analysis. Calculated as total debt divided by total assets.

declining-balance methods (DB) Accelerated depreciation method where depreciation expense is calculated by multiplying an asset's book value at the beginning of the year by a percentage equal to a multiple of the straight-line method rate.

deferred tax liability A liability for income taxes due in future periods.

defined benefit plan A pension plan specifying the benefits that employees will receive at retirement.

defined contribution plan A pension plan that specifies the periodic amount, usually a percentage of an employee's current salary, that the firm agrees to contribute to a pension fund.

denominated Refers to the conversion of financial amounts expressed in one country's currency into a different monetary unit. For example, yen might be denominated, or stated, in U.S. dollars.

deontology The consequences of the act do not solely dictate its correctness; the nature of the act itself influences its correctness.

depletion The allocation of the cost (using up) of natural resources, which is systematically expensed over time.

deposits-in-transit Bank deposits delayed by processing. These cash receipts have been recorded in the firm's accounting records.

depreciable basis Cost of an asset less its estimated salvage value.

depreciation The decline, over time, of the service potential of long-lived tangible assets, most notably plant and equipment. Since this service potential is consumed, a periodic expense is recorded.

depreciation expense Recognize depreciation as an expense that is reported gradually and systematically over the asset's useful life or until its disposal. Depreciating an asset is an attempt to allocate the original cost as an expense to the periods that benefit from the asset's use.

dilutive The effect on earnings per share (EPS) when common stock equivalents are used in the EPS calculation.

direct approach A method for preparing and displaying the cash flow statement where cash from operating activities is calculated on the basis of all cash flows with customers, suppliers, employees, and other operating activities. Contrast with *indirect approach.*

direct rates Used to indicate the rate at which U.S. dollars are translated into foreign currencies. Direct rates specify the number of units of U.S. dollars that are equivalent to one unit of the foreign currency. See *indirect rates.*

discontinued operations A segment of a company that has been sold, abandoned, or disposed that represents a distinct major line of business. Such a segment is reported apart from operating income as discontinued operations on the income statement.

discount on bonds A bond is issued below its *face* amount, indicating that the coupon rate is lower than the market rate for similar bonds (e.g., risk, maturity). See *par value* and *premium on bonds.*

discount rate An interest rate used in calculating the present value of money. This rate is often not explicit and is derived by taking into account the risk of the investment and prevailing market rates.

discounted note A noninterest-bearing note where the interest charge has been deducted from the principal in advance.

discounts taken Savings in the form of a percentage deducted from the purchase price of goods and services offered by the seller to induce early payment.

dividends Distributions of assets, usually cash, that the corporation elects to make periodically to its stockholders.

double-declining-balance method A declining-balance method using a multiple of 200% of the straight-line rate.

double-entry accounting Transactions are recorded in the accounting records by entering equal amounts in the left-hand (debit) side and right-hand (credit) side.

double taxation Income taxes are paid by corporations on their earnings. These earnings are again taxed when shareholders pay taxes on dividends they receive from corporations.

earnings See *net income.*

earnings per share (EPS) Indicates the net income earned by each share of outstanding common stock.

earnings quality The sustainability of currently reported earnings in future periods. Also relates to the *conservatism principle.*

economic assumptions Related to pension accounting, including the assumed interest rate used to discount future pension benefits, and the anticipated rate of return on pension plan assets.

economic value The market value of a company's stock.

efficient market hypothesis Proposes that all publicly available information is reflected in security prices.

entity assumption Accounting records are kept for the business entity as distinct from the entity's owners. This allows the owner to assess the status and performance of the business on a stand-alone basis.

equipment Includes office desks and chairs, tools, drill presses, robots, computers, x-ray and other scanners, podiums, etc. Equipment and *plant* are major resources of many organizations.

equity capital Represents ownership interests in the corporation in the form of stock bought by investors. Equity capital is not a liability to be repaid at a future date.

equity method of accounting The parent company recognizes its share of the subsidiary's reported income (or loss) on its financial statements and adjusts the basis of the investment (asset) in the subsidiary.

equity securities Represent ownership interests in the form of stocks issued by corporations. This interest would be reported on the balance sheet as an asset (investments).

ex dividend stock Subsequent purchasers will not be entitled to receive the previously declared dividend. Investors on the date of record will receive the dividend.

executory contracts Contracts formed merely by an exchange of promises. No substantive exchange of cash or services has occurred to meet the "past transaction" criterion for the contract to be recognized for financial accounting purposes.

expected return Increase in the investor's wealth, in the form of increased market value of the investment and dividends, that is anticipated over a set amount of time.

expenses The consumption of resources as a result of conducting business for the purpose of generating revenues and profits.

export sales Sales of domestically manufactured products to buyers in foreign countries.

external expansion Occurs as firms take over, or merge with, other existing firms.

externally acquired goodwill The amount that a firm pays in excess of the net assets of another business that the firm acquires. The excess is recorded as *goodwill,* an asset on the balance sheet.

extraordinary items Events and transactions that are unusual in nature (not typical of the firm's operations) and infrequent in occurrence (not expected to recur in the foreseeable future). These items are reported apart from operating income on the income statement.

factor Selling accounts receivable for cash.

factor receivables Obtaining funds from a factor or lender by pledging or transferring accounts receivable to the factor.

FASB See *Financial Accounting Standards Board.*

FIFO (first in, first out) A method for valuing inventory that assumes the goods "first in" are those "first out" as they are sold or used in a production process.

financial accounting Provides financial statements, prepared following GAAP, to decision makers external to the business.

Financial Accounting Standards Board (FASB) Private organization that issues Statements of Financial Accounting Standards (SFAS) that currently are the most authoritative source of GAAP. The FASB is empowered by the SEC to set GAAP.

financial leverage ratio See *debt-to-assets ratio.*

financing activities Describes a firm's sources of cash through borrowing or equity transactions. A category shown on the cash flow statement.

finished goods Completed inventory items that are awaiting sale.

fiscal year A financial reporting period that may be different from the calendar year. A firm uses a fiscal year because it is conventional to their industry and more convenient to their production or sales activity.

fixed asset turnover A ratio that analyzes how effectively a firm is utilizing its productive capacity (fixed assets). Calculated by dividing sales by the average book value of property, plant, and equipment.

fixed assets Tangible, long-lived assets, primarily property, plant, and equipment.

foreign currency transactions Transactions that are settled with a nondomestic currency.

foreign exchange rage Specifies the number of U.S. dollars (from a U.S. perspective) that are needed to obtain one unit of a specific foreign currency.

foreign operations Operational activities that take place in a foreign country.

forward rate The rate of exchange for future delivery of foreign currencies.

franchise Rights to market a particular product or service, typically within a geographic area. These rights have economic value.

free cash flow Cash flow from operating activities less cash needed to replace productive resources.

full cost method Capitalizes, as an asset, the exploration costs of both successful and unsuccessful natural resource sites. Used in accounting for mining and oil and gas exploration.

functional currency The currency a company uses to conduct its business.

future value The concept that money earns interest over time and the value of money will be greater in the future as interest accumulates with the principal amount.

future value factor Using multiplication, converts the initial deposit to its future value.

GAAP See *generally accepted accounting principles.*

GAAS See *generally accepted auditing standards.*

gains Profits realized from activities that are incidental to a firm's primary operating activities.

general journal The entry point of transactions to the accounting records. Provides a chronological listing of all transactions and events recorded.

general ledger Contains accounts and balances that summarize a firm's transactions.

general purpose Meets the common information needs of a variety of financial statement users.

generally accepted accounting principles (GAAP) Most widely used accounting treatments for financial reporting. The FASB, with SEC support, sets GAAP.

generally accepted auditing standards (GAAS) Developed by the accounting profession to provide guidance in the performance of an audit.

going concern concept Assumption underlying accounting and auditing that a firm will continue doing business in the future.

goodwill The amount paid in excess of the fair market value of an acquired firm's identifiable net assets. Goodwill should not be confused with *internally generated goodwill* that results from reputation, location, and client lists.

gross margin Revenues less cost of goods sold. Important to any retailer or manufacturer as a source of operating profit. See *gross profit (margin) percentage.*

gross profit See *gross margin.*

gross profit (margin) percentage A profitability measure calculated as gross profit (margin) divided by revenues.

hedge Entering into a contract to buy or sell foreign currencies in the forward market in order to protect against the risks of foreign exchange rate fluctuations.

hedging contract A contract to buy or sell foreign currencies in the forward market to protect against the risks of foreign exchange rate fluctuations. Also referred to as a *hedge.*

historical cost Exchange price on the date of acquisition of the asset, usually indicated by the amount of cash that changed hands.

horizontal analysis Trend analysis where components of the current year's financial statements are compared to components of a prior year's statements.

hybrid securities A security that is neither clearly debt nor clearly equity. Instead, it combines certain features of both types of securities. See *convertible bonds.*

immediate recognition An expenditure is expensed immediately because it has no discernible future benefit.

income statement A financial statement that summarizes the firm's earnings during a specified period of time. It contains at least two major sections: revenues and expenses. Also referred to as *statement of earnings.*

income taxes Expenses based on the firm's earnings imposed by the federal, state, and local governments and by foreign jurisdictions.

indentures Provisions and restrictions attached to a bond that make the bond more attractive for investors.

indirect approach A method for preparing and displaying the cash flow statement where the cash from operating activities is calculated indirectly by adding or subtracting various noncash adjustments to the reported net income. Contrast with *direct approach.*

indirect rates Used to indicate the rate at which foreign currencies are translated into U.S. dollars. Indirect rates specify the number of units of the foreign currency that are equivalent to one U.S. dollar. See *direct rates.*

industry segment A component of an organization providing a product or related products (or services) to outside parties.

informational role The objective of accounting designed to provide information useful for decision making.

intangible asset Noncurrent assets that lack physical substance. Intangible assets often consist of legal rights including patents and copyrights. Intangibles are important resources controlled by the organization and in some cases may be the most important resource.

intangibles Type of long-term asset representing nonmaterial rights or contractual privileges, such as patents, copyrights, etc.

intercompany receivables and payables Receivables and payables among a parent company and its subsidiary(s). They are eliminated in consolidation reporting.

intercompany sales Sales among a parent company and its subsidiary(s). They are eliminated in consolidation reporting.

interest-bearing note A debt instrument(note) that pays interest at a stated rate for a stated period.

interest cost As related to pension accounting, it is the interest on the projected benefit obligation. As related to accounting for postretirement benefit obligations other than pensions, it is the beginning of the year accumulated benefit obligation multiplied by the discount rate.

interest expense The firm's cost of borrowing money from creditors. Often simply referred to as *interest.*

interim reporting (interim reports) Reporting financial results more frequently than once a year.

internal auditing Performed within the firm to ensure the reliability of financial statements. Internal audit also assesses the effectiveness and efficiency of the corporation's operations.

internal expansion Occurs as firms invest in new plant and equipment, research, and other productive assets in order to serve growing markets or to extend the scope of their operations into new products and markets.

internally generated goodwill The unrecognized, unreported costs incurred that enhance the value of the organization. Examples of value include good reputation and customer base, successful relationships with suppliers, skilled labor force, talented management, etc.

inventory Items that have been purchased or manufactured for resale to customers.

invested capital Amounts received by a corporation upon sale of its stock to investors. Includes par value and paid-in capital.

investing activities Describes a firm's uses of cash to acquire other assets. A category shown on the cash flow statement.

investor ratios Indicates a firm's performance with regard to its shares' market value. Primarily of interest to owners or investors.

issued shares Shares of stock that have been issued to investors.

Journal entry An entry that appears in the general journal and consists of the date, the account(s) to be debited, the account(s) to be credited, the amounts, and an explanation.

lease An agreement where the *lessor* conveys to the *lessee* the right to use property, plant, and equipment for a designated future period.

lessee The user or renter of property in a lease agreement.

lessor The owner of property in a lease agreement.

leverage Financing a large proportion of asset acquisitions with long-term debt, as opposed to equity, that results in leveraged returns (profits) to the common equity shareholders.

liabilities Obligations of the entity to convey something of value in the future. They are probable future sacrifices of economic benefit that arise as a result of past transactions or events.

license Rights to engage in a particular activity.

LIFO (last in, first out) A method for valuing inventory that assumes "last in" purchases of inventory are those first sold or first used in the production process.

liquidate Refers to how quickly the firm's inventory and other assets in order to raise cash as demanded by creditors and owners.

liquidity Refers to how quickly the firm's current assets can be converted to cash.

liquidity ratios Group of ratios used to evaluate the firm's short-term solvency and how effectively it manages its working capital.

losses Losses realized from activities that are incidental to a firm's primary operating activities.

lower of cost or market (LCM) Required method of valuing inventory under generally accepted accounting principles where market is defined as current replacement cost.

major customers A customer from which an organization generates 10% or more of its revenue.

managerial accounting Provides information that is custom-tailored, detailed, and proprietary for a firm's managers to make operating decisions.

market rate The "cost of money" (i.e., interest), as determined by the monetary market forces (supply and demand).

market-to-book value ratio Indicates the relationship between the market's valuation of the firm and the book values shown in the firm's financial statements. Calculated as the quoted price per share on a stock exchange divided by the firm's asset value per share.

market value The replacement cost of an asset. Also, the market price of a marketable security.

marketable securities A debt or equity security that is readily marketable on a securities exchange registered with the SEC, some foreign exchanges, or if its price is available through the National Association of Securities Dealers Automated Quotations Systems (NASDAQ) or the National Quotation Bureau.

matching principle A principle underlying expense recognition indicating that all resources consumed in generating revenue should be recorded in the same time period as the revenue. This accrual basis approach provides a better portrayal of a firm's performance as reflected on the income statement.

materiality principle States that separate disclosure is not required if an item is so small that knowledge of it would not affect the decision of a reasonable financial statement reader. A guideline used by auditors and accountants to determine whether a particular item or cost will have a potential significant effect on a decision.

maturity date Date on which the principal of a note becomes due.

merger A business combination in which the buyer firm acquires either the stock, or the assets and liabilities, of an investee firm. The investee is then dissolved, and no longer exists as a separate corporation.

minority interest in consolidated subsidiaries The book value of the outstanding shares of stock of a subsidiary that are not under the control of the parent.

mortgage payable A loan agreement where the title to real property is secured by the lender to manage the risk of loan default by the borrower. The payable is a liability for the borrower.

multiple-step income statement Calculates certain subtotals for the reader such as gross profit and operating income.

natural resources Assets such as mines containing gold, silver, copper, or other minerals, wells containing oil or gas, and timberlands. Natural resources are also called "wasting assets."

net assets The excess (residual) amount of assets over liabilities measured by an entity's accounting. Net assets are equivalent to owners' equity as shown by rearranging the basic accounting equation: Owners' Equity = Assets − Liabilities. Also referred to as *net worth*.

net book value The initial (recorded) cost of an asset less the accumulated depreciation. Also referred to as the *carrying value* of an asset.

net income Amount by which total revenues exceed total expenses. The *bottom line* on the income statement.

net income percentage A profitability ratio that indicates the proportion of net income earned on every sales dollar. Calculated as net income divided by sales.

net loss Amount by which expenses exceed revenues.

net of tax Indicates that expected tax effects have already been considered as part of a particular calculation or figure. Indicates that taxes have been deducted from a particular financial component.

net profit See *net income*.

net realizable value The estimated cash to be collected from an asset.

net sales Gross sales revenue less any allowances or discounts.

net worth See *net assets*.

nominal account Revenue and expense accounts that are initialized to zero when the amounts are transferred to retained earnings at the end of the reporting period. Also referred to as a *temporary* account.

nonbusiness organizations Any organization that does not have a profit objective or motivation. May refer to a *nonprofit* or *not-for-profit organization*.

noncash investing and financing activities A category of investing and financing activities that does not involve cash flows.

noncurrent assets Long-term assets that are used in the conduct of the business. The replacement cycle for a noncurrent asset is greater than one year.

noncurrent liabilities Liabilities that represent obligations, typically from long-term borrowing that generally require payment over periods longer than a year.

noninterest-bearing note A debt instrument (note) that does not explicitly pay interest but is usually bought at a discount.

note A written promise to pay signed by the debtor. The obligation to pay has arisen from past borrowing transactions.

note payable A formal written agreement with a fixed repayment date(s) that the debtor signs in order to borrow funds from banks or other lenders. Note payable may be either interest bearing or noninterest bearing and can usually be further negotiated by the owner.

notes to the financial statements Information that clarifies and extends the material presented in the financial statements with narrative and detail.

number of days sales in accounts receivable A liquidity ratio that indicates how quickly the firm is "turning" or "cycling" its accounts receivable. A high number indicates poor management of accounts receivable. Calculated as ending accounts receivable divided by sales per day.

number of days sales in ending inventory (NDS) A liquidity ratio used to measure inventory levels. A low number indicates efficient inventory levels. Calculated as ending inventory divided by cost of goods sold per day.

obligations for warranties Liabilities resulting from offering assurances of repairs, replacements, and/or refunds in the event of product failures or customer dissatisfaction.

on account Purchases or sales on credit.

operating activities Activities involved with completing the ordinary day-to-day transactions needed to carry on business.

operating capacity The ability of a firm to produce goods or services that can be assessed by analyzing the firm's tangible and intangible noncurrent assets.

operating cycle The time needed to purchase raw materials, manufacture inventory, sell the inventory, and collect cash from the customer.

operating income Gross margin or gross profit less all other operating expenses.

operating income percentage A profitability ratio calculated by dividing operating income by sales revenues. Also called operating income ratio.

operating lease A lease agreement treated as an ordinary rental, where the asset is merely used by the lessee and rental payments are reported as expense.

opportunity cost A cost that exists as a result of lost profits due to more profitable alternative investments being precluded by less profitable investments currently undertaken.

other items (net) A component of pension expense that includes amortization of the transition amount, prior service cost, and gains and losses.

outstanding checks Checks that are included in the accounting records but not shown on the bank statement.

outstanding shares Issued shares that are not held in treasury by the issuing firm. Only outstanding shares are eligible for dividends.

overhead Manufacturing costs other than direct labor and materials.

owners' equity Represents the owners' interest in the assets of the business. It is the residual amount that equals assets minus liabilities. See *basic accounting equation*.

P

paid-in capital Term used to describe a component of shareholders' equity. Represents the difference between amounts invested by shareholders and the par value of their investment.

par value (bonds) The amount due on the bond's maturity date.

par value (stock) Stated amount per share for legal purposes. Usually the amount is minor and represents a fraction of the market value, or issued amount, of the stock.

parent The term applied to the buyer company in a business combination.

partnership An unincorporated business owned by more than one owner and operated under a legal contract (partnership agreement) among the partners. Partnerships are not separate legal entities apart from their owners, but they are separate accounting entities.

patents Granted by the federal government to convey the exclusive right to use a product or process for a period of 17 years.

pay-as-you-go The method used prior to 1993 for accounting of nonpension postretirement benefits, where expenses were reported on the cash basis, and no obligations were recognized for future payments.

pension Benefits (compensation) provided by firms to their retired employees.

percentage composition (analysis) Refers to a ratio analysis of financial statement data based on the relative proportions of column totals. See *vertical analysis*. Contrast with *horizontal analysis*.

percentage-of-completion Recognizes a portion of the revenue, cost, and profit each year according to the percentage of the job completed.

petty cash (fund) Small quantity of funds kept on hand for incidental expenditures requiring quick cash. These funds are included in the cash amount on the balance sheet.

plant Includes office, retail or factory buildings, warehouses or supply depots, or hospitals and health clinics. Along with equipment, plant is a primary productive resource of any organization.

political costs Costs that are imposed on firms by the political process. Examples include taxes and costs to implement regulations.

pooling of interests The accounting treatment used in a business combination when firms combine by an exchange of voting stock. These combinations are interpreted as a "uniting of ownership interests" rather than a purchase of one firm by another.

posting Transcribing the amounts from journal entries into the general ledger.

preferred stock Equity capital shares that have priority over common shares with regard to dividends and distributions of assets in the event of firm liquidation.

premium on bonds The amount by which a bond is bought and sold above its *face* amount. See *par value* and *discount on bonds*.

prepaid expenses Unexpired assets that have been paid for in advance and represent the rights to future benefits. Prepaid expenses are classified as current assets.

prepaid rent A prepaid expense representing the right to occupy property.

present value The value today of an amount to be received or paid in the future.

present value factor Using multiplication, converts a future value to its present value.

price-to-earnings (P/E) ratio Widely used investor ratio that indicates the relationship between market prices and earnings. Calculated as the stock's market price per share divided by its earnings per share.

principal The original or base amount of a loan or investment.

privatization The selling to private investors of government-owned or -controlled enterprises.

pro forma amount Hypothetical or projected amount. Synonymous with "what if" analyses. Pro forma statements indicate what would have happened under specified circumstances.

profit See *net income*.

profitability ratios Group of ratios that analyze the return on investment to the owners and the level of gross and net profit margins being generated by revenues.

projected benefit obligation The amount of pension benefits that employees have earned to date, based on the expected future salary levels.

property Usually represents land on which the firm's offices, factories, and other facilities are located. May also be used generically to refer to factories, warehouses, etc.

prospectively The method of accounting for changes in estimates whereby past financial statements are not affected. The change impacts only future periods.

Q

quality of income ratio A cash ratio calculated by dividing cash from operating activities by net income.

quality of sales ratio A liquidity ratio that indicates the proportion of sales revenue that has generated cash in the current year. Cash sales are considered high-quality sales while credit sales are low-quality sales. Calculated as cash received from customers divided by sales.

quick ratio A liquidity ratio that only considers those current assets that may be available quickly. Calculated as cash plus cash equivalents plus net receivables divided by current liabilities. Also referred to as the *acid-test ratio*.

R

raw materials Materials, components, or ingredients that have not yet entered the manufacturing process. They are shown as inventory on the balance sheet.

realize Recognizing a gain or loss in the financial statements.

recognition Recording a transaction in the accounting records.

relevant Information that makes a difference in the decision making process.

reliable Information that is free from error and bias.

research and development costs Costs incurred to generate new knowledge or to translate knowledge into a new product or process. According to GAAP, these costs should be expensed immediately.

residual interest See *net assets*.

residual owners Refers to constituents who have a secondary or "final" ownership interest in an organization. Often refers to shareholders who take a secondary position relative to bondholders or preferred shareholders.

residual value See *salvage value*.

restrictive covenants Limitations imposed by a creditor on a debtor's actions. Covenants are often based on accounting measurements of assets, liabilities, and/or income.

restructure The term used to describe corporate downsizing and refocus of operations. The total estimated costs of restructuring should be expensed in the current year.

retained earnings The portion of shareholders' equity that reflects the increase (or decrease) in the shareholders' interest from revenue and expense transactions.

retroactively The method of accounting for accounting principle changes whereby past years' financial statement are restated to reflect the use of the new method.

return on assets (ROA) ratio A profitability ratio that indicates the rate of return on the firm's assets. It is used to compare the firm's rate of return with alternative investments that could be undertaken. Calculated as net income plus interest expense times one minus the tax rate, all divided by average total assets.

return on equity (ROE) ratio A profitability ratio used to relate net income to shareholders' equity.

return on plan assets As related to pension accounting, it is a reduction in pension expense because of the return that is expected on the plan's assets. The reduction is based on anticipated, not actual, return.

return on shareholders' equity ratio Ratio that links the income statement and the balance sheet by dividing net income by average shareholders' equity.

revenue Inflows of assets (or reductions in liabilities) in exchange for providing goods and services to customers (e.g., sales) or inflows from collecting interest, rent, royalties, etc.

revenue recognition principle States that revenue should be recognized in the accounting records when the earnings process is substantially complete and the amount to be collected is reasonably determinable.

risk The uncertainty surrounding estimates of future cash flows.

S

sale Delivery of goods or services in exchange for cash or other consideration.

sales return Items returned by customers for credit or other adjustment. Usually defective or unacceptable merchandise.

salvage value The estimated amount a firm expects to receive when an asset is sold at the end of its useful life. Also referred to as *residual value*.

Securities Exchange Commission (SEC) Created by the Securities Exchange Act of 1934, the SEC has the power to set accounting principles and financial disclosure requirements for firms with securities traded on public exchanges.

security As related to debt, it is synonymous with collateral. As related to investments, it is synonymous with publicly traded stocks and bonds (securities).

selling expenses A category of expenses shown on the income statement related to marketing and other selling activities.

service cost As related to pension accounting, service cost (normal cost) is the present value of future pension benefits that employees earned during the current year. As related to accounting for postretirement benefit obligations other than pensions, it is the amount of the accumulated benefit obligation that was earned by employees during the current year.

service lives Working years of employees prior to retirement, as used in accounting for postretirement benefit obligations.

SFAS See *Statements of Financial Accounting Standards*.

shareholders' equity Represents the shareholders' interest in the assets of the firm. It is the residual amount that equals assets minus liabilities. See *basic accounting equation*.

single-step format Refers to an income statement format where all revenues are shown in one category, and all expenses are shown in another category, without calculating intermediate subtotals. Contrast with *multiple-step income statement*.

single-step income statement Summarizes all revenues in one section and all expenses in another.

sinking fund A fund that is designated for a special purpose, such as the retirement of outstanding debt or the replacement of operating assets.

sole proprietorship A business owned and usually operated by the same individual. The owner and business are not separate legal entities but are separate accounting entities.

specific identification method A method for determining the cost of inventory by maintaining the identity and cost of each item, usually by serial number or other code, such that each item or unit can be tracked throughout the holding and selling process.

spot rate The rate of exchange for immediate delivery of foreign currencies.

statement of cash flows A financial statement that reports the sources and uses of cash by a firm during a specified period. Three major activities of the firm are reported: operating, investing, and financing. This statement is intended to provide information about a firm's ability to generate cash.

statement of earnings A financial statement that summarizes the firm's earnings during a specified period of time. It contains at least two major sections: revenues and expenses. Also referred to as the *income statement*.

statement of financial position A financial statement that shows, at a specified time, a firm's financial condition, which is determined by its assets, liabilities, and owners' equity. Also referred to as the *balance sheet*.

statement of owners' equity A financial statement that summarizes the changes that took place in owners' equity over a period of time.

statement of shareholders' equity A financial statement that summarizes the changes that took place in shareholders' equity over a period of time.

Statements of Financial Accounting Standards (SFAS) The primary sources of GAAP. The statements provide explicit accounting treatment for financial transactions. Currently they are created by the FASB.

stock dividend Additional shares of stock are received by investors in the form of a dividend. Retained earnings is reduced and invested capital is increased.

stock option Rights to purchase a firm's stock at a specific price over some designated future period.

stock split An exchange of shares of a firm's stock for existing outstanding shares that usually results in more shares issued.

straight-line method (SL) A depreciation method that allocates an equal amount of expense to each year in an asset's life.

subsidiary The term applied to the investee firm in a business

combination when the firm continues to exist.

subsidiary ledger Provides detailed information regarding a particular general ledger account.

successful efforts method Immediately expenses the cost of unsuccessful oil and gas sites. Only the costs directly associated with locating and developing successful sites are capitalized.

sum-of-the-years'-digits method (SYD) An accelerated depreciation method where the numerator is the number of useful remaining years and the denominator is the sum of the years' digits in the asset's useful life. The denominator is calculated as $[N \times (N + 1)]/2$, where N is the number of years in the asset's life.

sustainability Describes the ability of an organization to continue its operations and achieve its objectives. May relate to *going concern concept*.

systematic and rational allocation Method used to implement the matching principle where costs that cannot be directly linked to specific revenue transactions are recognized as an expense in the years it helps generate revenue.

 T

T-account A form of ledger page used to record (or illustrate) the entry of debits and credits into ledger accounts.

tax accounting Encompasses the two functions of tax compliance and tax planning. Tax compliance involves the process of completing tax forms and the calculation of a firm's tax liability. Tax planning entails providing advice about the effects that business transactions will have on the firm's tax liability.

tax benefit A reduction in taxes, or a tax credit or refund, due to a particular action or expense incurred by a taxable entity.

tax compliance Entails completing tax returns at period end or year-end.

tax planning Involves structuring transactions so as to minimize their tax effects.

taxes payable Represents unpaid taxes that are owed to a governmental unit and will be paid within a year.

temporary differences Cases where book accounting and tax accounting measurements differ and will be offset by opposite deviations in later periods.

time value of money The concept that funds (money) earn interest over time. This implies that a dollar to be received a year from now is worth less than a dollar received today.

times interest earned ratio An indicator of relative risk of bankruptcy or other default. Times interest earned indicates the "cushion" or margin of safety that the firm enjoys in meeting its interest expenses. Calculated as earnings before interest and taxes divided by interest expense.

trade receivables See *accounts receivable.*

trademarks Words, symbols or other distinctive elements used to identify a particular firm's products.

trading securities Securities held by firms for brief periods of time that are intended to generate profits from short-term differences in price.

transactions The exchange of resources between the firm and other parties.

translation adjustment The process of converting monetary units stated in terms of one country's currency into a different monetary unit. See *foreign currency transactions* and *foreign exchange rate.*

treasury stock Repurchased outstanding shares of a firm's own stock.

trend analysis Comparing financial numbers across periods of time.

trial balance A listing of all general ledger accounts and their balances for the purpose of verifying that total debits equal total credits.

10-K report Mandatory report filed by a company on an annual basis with the Securities and Exchange Commission.

10-Q report Mandatory report filed by a company on a quarterly basis with the Securities and Exchange Commission.

unearned revenue Advance payments from customers for the right to receive goods or services in the future. The advance payment is recorded as a liability until the goods are delivered or the services are rendered to the customer.

unrealized gain (loss) on marketable securities The difference between a security's historical cost and its market value.

unrealized inventory profits Inventory that has been transferred among a parent company and its subsidiary(s). Profits related to these inventories that have not been sold to outside entities are removed from the consolidated financial statements.

users of financial statements Interested parties with an economic interest in the firm that need financial information. Typical users include the firm's owners, creditors, managers, employees, customers, and suppliers. Some users obtain information directly from the firm, others rely on quarterly and annual reports.

utilitarianism Judges the moral correctness of an act based solely on its consequences. The act that maximizes overall favorable consequences should be taken.

vertical analysis Examines the composition of elements on the income statement (balance sheet) as a percentage of net revenues (total assets).

vertical percentage analysis Refers to a ratio analysis of financial statement data. Is based on relationships between a target figure (like total revenues or total assets) and other figures shown on the same report. Often used to examine capital structure or other financing relationships. See *percentage composition analysis.*

vested benefit obligation Indicates amounts to which employees have irrevocable rights, even if they leave the firm prior to retirement.

warranty obligations Represent the firm's estimated future costs to fulfill its obligations for repair or refund guarantees of products sold or services provided prior to the balance sheet date.

weighted average Each level of outstanding shares of common stock is weighted by the fraction of a year that it stayed constant.

working capital Current assets minus current liabilities.

work-in-process Consists of manufactured or assembled items that are partially completed at the balance sheet date.

worksheet An extended form of the trial balance.

INDEX